CREATING AMERICA

Reading and Writing Arguments

SECOND EDITION

JOYCE MOSER *and*
ANN WATTERS
Stanford University

PRENTICE HALL
Upper Saddle River, New Jersey 07458

FOR TOM, TOM JR., AND FREDRIKA MOSER

FOR TOM, ANDREW, AND MIKE WATTERS

Library of Congress Cataloging-in-Publication Data

Creating America : reading and writing arguments / [edited by] Ann
    Watters and Joyce Moser.—2nd ed.
        p.   cm.
    Includes indexes.
    ISBN 0-13-081421-0
    1. Readers—United States.   2. United States—Civilization—
Problems, exercises, etc.   3. Report writing—Problems, exercises,
etc.   4. English language—Rhetoric.   5. Persuasion (Rhetoric)
6. College readers.   I. Watters, Ann.   II. Moser, Joyce, 1946–   .
PE1127.H5C74   1999
808'.0427—dc21   98-39877
                                                            CIP

Editorial Director: Charlyce Jones Owen
Executive Editor: Leah Jewell
Editorial Assistant: Patricia Castiglione
AVP, Director of Production and Manufacturing: Barbara Kittle
Senior Managing Editor: Bonnie Biller
Editorial/Production Supervisor: Mary Rottino
Production Editor: Julie Sullivan
Manufacturing Buyer: Mary Ann Gloriande
Director, Image Resource Center: Lori Morris-Nantz
Photo Researcher: Elsa Peterson
Cover Designer: Anthony Gemmellaro
Cover Image: Courtesy of the Library of Congress

Acknowledgments for copyrighted material may be found beginning
on p. 547, which constitutes an extension of the copyright page.

Printed in the United States of America
10 9 8 7 6 5 4 3 2 1

ISBN 0-13-081421-0

Prentice-Hall International (UK) Limited, *London*
Prentice-Hall of Australia Pty. Limited, *Sydney*
Prentice-Hall Canada, Inc., *Toronto*
Prentice-Hall Hispanoamericana, S.A., *Mexico*
Prentice-Hall of India Private Limited, *New Delhi*
Prentice-Hall of Japan, Inc., *Tokyo*
Simon & Schuster Asia Pte. Ltd., *Singapore*
Editoria Prentice-Hall do Brazil, Ltda., *Rio de Janeiro*

Contents

"The truth is that the last decade has seen a powerful counter assault on women's rights, a backlash, an attempt to retract the handful of small and hard-won victories that the feminist movement did manage to win for women."

"The legacies that parents and church and teachers left to my generation of Black children were priceless but not material: a living faith reflected in daily service, the discipline of hard work and stick-to-it-ness, and a capacity to struggle in the face of adversity."

A psychologist examines reasons why young women's voices become silenced.

"The model minority myth precludes the possibility that some Asian Americans may not be upwardly mobile and successful. Yet our parents expect us to become upwardly mobile and successful. Our parents' expectations personalize the society's model minority expectations for us."

A story of three generations of a Mexican American family in Southern California.

Chapter 6: Work and Play   295

"As I knew, or thought I knew, what was right and wrong, I did not see why I might not always do the one and avoid the other. But I soon found I had undertaken a Task of more Difficulty than I had imagined. While my Care was employ'd in guarding against one Fault, I was often surpriz'd by another."

"Each woman born, re-humanized by the current of race activity carried on by her father and re-womanized by her traditional position, has had to live over again in her own person the same process of restriction, repression, denial; the smothering 'no' which crushed down all her human desires to create, to discover, to learn, to express, to advance."

"I didn't really have much time to worry about right and wrong back then, because during these mass-cals we'd be up for 36 hours at a stretch. Nobody wanted to quit until the last surgery case was stabilized. By that time, we were emotionally and physically numb. You couldn't see clearly; you couldn't react."

Preface

∞

Creating America is a reader-rhetoric focusing on argument and persuasion in American cultures. Spanning centuries, traditions, and genres, the selections demonstrate the core debates and discussions that have always interested and engaged Americans. The chapter selections—eighteenth-century woodcuts, nineteenth-century essays and political cartoons, and twentieth-century speeches, as well as narratives, photographs, advertisements, and legal cases—all help students learn to analyze and criticize the arguments they encounter in academic discourse and in contemporary culture.

We developed the second edition of *Creating America* to continue to provide a book that focuses on arguments in the context of American history and tradition: a book that brings together materials revolving around issues that have always concerned Americans. This edition maintains the first edition's focus on argumentation in context, and it broadens one chapter theme and integrates new material in several chapters. The chapter on "Work and Success" has evolved into "Work and Play" in order to integrate that key element of American cultures, sports, and to link it to the marketing of sports. Compelling visual and textual arguments have been added in all chapters. A key change in this edition is that all rhetorical material formerly distributed throughout the book has been consolidated in Part I, "Contexts for Reading and Writing Arguments," for ease of use and coherence in discussing rhetorical issues. Those wishing to use the rhetorical material on analyzing and writing arguments will find it all in Chapters 1 and 2. In addition, a sample student analytical essay is now included in Chapter 2 to demonstrate how one might approach writing a paper analyzing a visual argument, a task unfamiliar to some teachers and students. Additional student analytical essays, Chris Countryman's analysis of a Langston Hughes poem (Chapter 4) and Peter Douglas's essay analyzing a propaganda poster included in the book (both in Chapter 8) provide additional models.

Teachers integrating the rhetorical material with readings, as well as teachers wishing to use the readings alone and teach with a different model of argument, such as the Toulmin model, will find a rich range of materials in Part II, "Argument in the American Tradition." Part II offers textual and visual arguments for analysis and discussion. Chapter 3, "Identities," includes a range of materials from early discussions of what is uniquely American to contemporary struggles of building community yet maintaining cultural identity. Chapter 4, "American Dreams," includes selections on both political and material dreams and success. Chapter 5, "Images of Gender and Family," offers different perspectives on what makes a family and what constitutes the particular roles and rights of men, women, and children; Chapter 6, "Work and Play," looks at the business of America—business; and at the business of play, or contemporary American sports. Chapter 7, "Justice and Civil Liberties," brings together core readings and images of American freedoms and the struggles that precede and accompany them. Chapter 8, "War and the Enemy," offers visual and textual arguments about how we lionize our friends and demonize our enemies. Chapter 9, "Frontiers," analyzes both the idea and the reality of the frontier and the West.

Each chapter includes an introduction to the core theme or issue. Selections follow, with headnotes for context and background information; journal prompts to guide reflective writing; and questions for discussion and writing, with a focus on analysis and argumentation. In each chapter we include a recommended film that should be available as a video rental in most colleges or communities. Most chapters also include at least one student essay, generally written in response to a chapter writing suggestion; inclusion of these essays is based on the premise that student writing is an appropriate focus for analysis and discussion.

Creating America, second edition, is designed for use in a first-year course in composition, particularly one emphasizing argumentative writing. The underlying pedagogy is based on an Aristotelian model, but it is informed by the theories of Kenneth Burke, Carl Rogers, and feminist critics. Our premise is that people use, to quote Aristotle, "all of the available means of persuasion" to argue a point; therefore, we do not treat argument and persuasion separately. Rather, we focus on the appeals to ethos, pathos, and logos, introducing induction and deduction under logos as the basic principles by which to evaluate and through which to develop arguments. The selections represent a range of arguments, from rather combative debate to more dialogic, narrative explorations of difficult questions and complex issues.

Acknowledgments

We gratefully acknowledge the assistance of Dr. Elena Danielson, Director of the Hoover Institution Archives, and her staff; the Bishop Museum of Honolulu; and Rose Adams and Dr. Kathy Kerns of Stanford University Libraries; as well as fellow instructors including Susan Wyle and Robert Chodat, for providing helpful resources, suggestions, insights, or research assistance. We also thank Barbara Charlesworth Gelpi, Albert Gelpi, Joan L'Heureux, John L'Heureux, Linda Jo Bartholomew, George Dekker, Sue Koppett, Len Koppett, Maclin Bocock Guerard, Albert Guerard, Ron Rebholz, John Swensson, and Diana Maltz for their support, suggestions, encouragement, and priceless friendship. Andrew and Mike Watters provided valuable assistance in manuscript preparation, and Dr. Ginny Bassi, the San Mateo coffee group, the Tahoe group, and the Sunset intern group, especially Heidi Davis, offered their confidence, feedback, and moral support throughout the process. We are grateful to Leah Jewell and Patricia Castiglione at Prentice Hall, and we particularly wish to thank Julie Sullivan for her ongoing help and professionalism in getting the second edition through the production process. We also appreciate the excellent critiques and feedback provided by our reviewers: Paul Almonte, Salt Lake Community College; Scott Ash, Nassau Community College; Alison Fernley, Salt Lake Community College; Daniel Halpern, University of Texas at Austin; Cathy Metcalf, California State University, Fullerton; Michael Moran, University of Georgia; Troy Nordman, Butler County Community College; Kalu Ogbaa, Southern Connecticut State University; Bryan Polk, Abington College of the Pennsylvania State University; Katherine Rodier, Marshall University; Emily Thiroux, California State University, Bakersfield; and Timothy Twohill, Lee College.

Finally, we thank our students for their responses to and suggestions for the second edition, and we offer a special note of appreciation to our families.

1

*Reading and
Analyzing Arguments*

When the founding fathers were about to publish the Declaration of Independence and set themselves on a course that would put them in direct conflict with the British government, Benjamin Franklin is reported to have said, "Gentlemen, we must all hang together, or assuredly we shall all hang separately."

In a sense, this book takes Franklin's observation and applies it more generally to thinking and writing about the nation Franklin and his co-Revolutionists were in the process of establishing. The pieces of American life—people who come from many countries, cultures, and religions; states that differ from one another in topography, industry, and demographics; huge variations in urban and suburban lifestyles, in income and interests—are so heterogeneous that they could have hardly been expected to coexist as they have for more than two hundred years, but they have. *Creating America* offers a way of examining and writing about what it is that has caused them to hang together.

Reading American Cultures

The selections assembled in this book are not limited to any one time period; there are eighteenth-century cartoons, nineteenth- and twentieth-century advertisements, and contemporary films; great political speeches from the 1770s to the present; essays on relations between men and women and between parents and children; paintings of the pre–Civil War South and photographs of Yosemite in the 1870s; propaganda posters from World War I, and Henry David Thoreau on civil disobedience; Frederick Douglass on the horrors of slavery, Jacqueline Navarra Rhoads on the horrors of war, and Gloria Steinem on the pleasure and pain of a good day's work.

Our central premise is that certain ideas run back to the earliest days of America as a political and social entity and continue to do so today, and those threads can be read across centuries and across genres. Every generation of Americans reinterprets and reargues these ideas in the light of its own experience. This book provides a wide array of materials that vary in kind and across time—fiction, essays, cartoons, posters, journals, paintings, poetry, legal proceedings, advertisements, movies—and thus form a core sample of American culture.

The ability to analyze these materials can work both ways. An eighteenth-century etching about what constitutes appropriate behavior for a young woman instructs us about earlier norms and helps us to understand more recent conflicts about feminism, freedom, and self-expression. And a contemporary advertisement that sells sex in order to sell clothing also helps us understand the limits against which earlier generations of women defined themselves.

In the same way, F. Scott Fitzgerald's article "Early Success," from *The Crack-Up*, is highly informative about the American association of romance and money, which Fitzgerald understood so well; but so is advertising music on MTV. Reading Susan B. Anthony on the First Amendment and freedom of speech may give you insight into the argument about whether the Internet should be censored, and reading Martin Luther King, Jr., on nonviolent resistance may help you understand why his intellectual ancestor, Thoreau, refused to pay taxes and insisted, with some relish, on going to jail to protest a war he could not support.

Persuasion

As you study the selections in this book, you will find that most of the authors are engaged in arguments of one kind or another about a particular political stance, a contemporary ethical problem, or the status quo. Frequently the fight is not so much about an individual opponent as about an idea or a belief. However varied the subject matter or the historical events surrounding it, this kind of argument is characteristically a manifestation of disagreement in a democracy. It is argument that encourages rather than stifles disagreement and allows the expression of different, even completely opposing points of view, and it protects the right of individual Americans to say and express ideas that other Americans find highly offensive. It is argument designed not to bludgeon opposition into submission but rather to persuade.

The target of such persuasive argument is often the American public at large or a particular group of citizens within a larger political unit. Americans take for granted their right to argue publicly and privately and to criticize their government, their elected officials, their school boards, their neighbors. This chapter provides suggestions for analyzing and using persuasion as a basis for your own experiments in reading and writing critically about American materials.

Persuasion is a process in which a *rhetor*—a speaker, writer, or artist—tries to elicit a desired response from an *audience* by identifying commonalities in the interests of both parties. It is a process that deals not in certainties but in probabilities—in arguing from evidence or reasons and assumptions to a conclusion. This textbook is designed to enable you to develop your ability to understand and analyze the strategies of persuasion in what you read and to develop your own ability to write persuasively. Studying persuasive texts can help you to become a more critical reader and listener and to communicate more clearly and effectively. By focusing on diverse kinds of arguments in American culture, by looking at context and purpose, by looking beneath the surface at strategies and appeals, you will see persuasion all around you in daily life—not only in books you read, but also in advertising, flyers, posters, news magazines, newspapers, and so forth. A persuasive text is one that asserts a point of view and seeks a desired response; it attempts to induce the readers to agree with whatever is being expounded on. A description of orderly governance in an American Indian tribe, for example, implicitly argues for respect for that culture. Sometimes the desired response is self-sacrifice; a poster advertising war bonds appeals to the interests of the audience—whether self-interest or desire to belong—to garner financial support for the war effort. Ultimately, persuasion can change beliefs, behavior, or even government policy; in *Brown* v. *Board of Education,* a legal argument citing inequities in segregated education changed the law of the land and the future of millions of Americans.

Persuasion and American Cultures

American cultures have common threads that are woven in tremendous diversity. Persuasive appeals in public discourse must take this into account in order to succeed, tapping into the assumptions and common values and beliefs while acknowledging divergent views. More so than the speakers and writers in more homogeneous cultures, Americans wishing to persuade their fellow Americans must understand something about their audience: who they are, what they believe and assume, how they communicate, and what they value. Some assumptions and values remain constant over time, but each age brings with it a different view anchored in that particular time and culture. Examining persuasive texts from different time periods in American history and from different cultural perspectives may help us to understand our own age and culture better while considering them in a larger historical context.

As the preceding discussion suggests, the themes in this text represent some of the core debates in American history. Who are Americans? What are their dreams? What makes an American family? What are

Americans' values about work and success? What are their concepts of justice and liberty? Why do they construct an "other" or enemy, and how do they take action against the other? What is their image of the frontier, and how, having reached the geographical limits of the continent, do they search for new frontiers? Each type of question or problem lends itself to a particular aspect of argumentation.

Rhetor and Audience

Understanding the arts of persuasion entails understanding how others persuade you and how you can persuade others through your own arguments. Although some scholars have argued that argument relies on logic and persuasion on emotion, Aristotelian rhetoric makes no such clear-cut distinction. Aristotle's *Rhetoric* suggests that reason, beliefs and values, and emotion—*logos, ethos,* and *pathos*—work together to engage the whole person and guide him or her toward appropriate judgment of the issue at hand. A traditional view suggests that argument entails an adversarial relationship between two sides—generally writer or speaker and audience. In debate, for example, the two opposing sides each offer arguments that the other side then refutes; in propaganda, the audience is inundated with generally one-sided, unsupported assertions. Such persuasion is rhetoric "to gain advantage, of one sort or another," as critic Kenneth Burke notes, and to some degree, it reflects Aristotle's primary definition of rhetoric as "understanding all of the available means of persuasion."

Recently some scholars have argued for different approaches to argumentation. Drawing on the work of psychologists such as Carl Rogers, they outline a model that suggests that both rhetor, or communicator, and audience are participants in the argument and should work together, much like a client and therapist, to pursue knowledge and truth. Some feminist critics suggest that our traditional views of argumentation are male-centered, adversarial, and combative; they emphasize a more collaborative approach to argumentation, with negotiation rather than debate as the dominant mode. In such an approach, both sides identify their common interests and attempt to close the distance between their respective positions.

Another view suggests rereading Aristotle to understand the connection between rhetor and audience. (The term *rhetor* will in this textbook refer to an individual attempting to persuade orally or in written text or image.) In this view, the rhetor and audience work together to pursue and develop a solution to a problem, a difference of opinion, or an issue. Audience and rhetor are dynamically involved in argument, and no argument can begin from scratch; the rhetor relies on and presumes a certain background on the part of the audience, including certain assumptions, beliefs, values, and reservoir of knowledge.

Audiences and Cultures

Scholars of rhetoric have shown that persuasion in homogeneous cultures tends to leave many reasons and assumptions unexpressed; a shared heritage tends to include a fair number of shared assumptions and values. In a heterogeneous society such as the United States, arguments rely on some common ground, but they tend to be more forcefully and clearly articulated, with premises and steps in the logic more often stated than assumed. The argumentative style and organization tend to be more indirect in countries where a direct approach could be considered offensive and where the rhetor might instead broach a subject, move away from it, then return to supporting points later. The point, again, is to analyze audiences carefully, to visualize them and consider their beliefs, values, attitudes, and style of interaction, rather than concentrating only on one's own point of view. Understanding audience assumptions and expectations is crucial in developing persuasive argumentative strategies

Audiences from Other Times

Analyzing arguments written for readers from other time periods brings with it its own complexity. Although the basic strategies of argument remain much the same through the ages, the role of public debate and the particular concerns and issues vary with each age and culture. The early America of European colonial culture was largely agricultural, with people living on farms and in towns isolated from each other; it took days for information to reach New York City from Philadelphia. Today Americans and the rest of the world are connected by a global media. Colonial culture was more homogeneous, but space and time separated its communications; American society today is more diverse, but most Americans are exposed to the same news and popular culture. Superficially, then, we have more in common, but the increased variety in cultures means that we come to the discussion with different cultural perspectives. People who seek to persuade others in American cultures and media cannot count on the kinds of shared assumptions held by the audiences of Benjamin Franklin or Thomas Jefferson. Understanding persuasive texts from other times, then, will require not only analyzing the texts themselves but also considering the assumptions, values, beliefs, and needs of the audiences for whom they were intended.

Audience and Appeals: Ethos, Pathos, and Logos

In order to induce others to identify with them or their point of view, rhetors use a number of strategies. Aristotle outlined three modes of persuasion that relate to the connection between writer and audience: appeals to ethos, pathos, and logos.

Appeals to Ethos   Rhetors commonly attempt to establish credibility, authority, and a common identity with the audience by using appeals to ethos, which invoke the values and beliefs that the rhetor and audience have in common in order to establish credibility and authority. According to Aristotle, ethos appeals establish the "personal character of the speaker." A politician who presents himself as the product of an economically poor background is appealing to common beliefs about success as a product of hard work and drive. John F. Kennedy appealed to an ethos of service to others in his "Inaugural Address." Franklin Delano Roosevelt appealed to Americans' beliefs and values about fair play when he vilified the Japanese during World War II. Martin Luther King, Jr., appealed to values of fairness in arguing for civil rights on behalf of all Americans. Academic writers appeal to the ethos of rigorous inquiry and well-supported assertions by presenting themselves as being reasonable and well-informed, using credible sources, and paying attention to the conventions of academia and of various disciplines. Writers who include unsupported assertions, use inflammatory or biased language, or fail to consider opposing views violate an ethos of reasoned discourse expected in academic writing; they also undermine their credibility as scholars and writers.

Let's look at an example of appeals to ethos. Consider the following argument:

This stenciled statement-plus-images can be found painted near drains in many cities and towns. Such appeals target local concerns; in some areas, *bay* would be replaced with *river* or *ocean*, and sometimes the images would be different—fish rather than birds, for example. The argument includes an assertion (do not dump waste here), a reason (because it will flow to the bay), and implied consequences (and damage the waterways and wildlife).

Although the argument ostensibly rests primarily on reason, appeals to values and beliefs pervade this argument. The rhetor assumes that the audience values the environment, represented in the water symbol and the small animal outline, and that viewers will accept some responsibility for protecting natural resources.

Consider alternative messages for this argument: for example, instead of "flows to bay," the rhetor could have stated, "$500 fine." Why might the rhetor appeal to ethos rather than threaten violators with a fine? What are the advantages, and disadvantages, of appealing to values and beliefs in this rhetorical situation?

Appeals to Pathos The good rhetorician, said Aristotle, seeks to understand the emotions and then to put the audience in the right frame of mind to hear an argument. Appeals to pathos, like appeals to ethos, relate to identification. If one can empathize, one can identify with another, put oneself in the other's position, and understand the other's feelings and point of view. Critics have argued that emotional appeals are less appropriate than logos or ethos appeals, perhaps over concern about manipulating audience emotions or relying on emotional appeals to cover up a lack of logic and evidence. Yet persuasion engages the whole individual, and pathos appeals can create a more balanced argument or a more ethical decision. Cost-benefit analyses may argue against any intervention in postcommunist Eastern Europe, but showing the human costs and suffering, in text or images, may provide a kind of evidence that eludes the rigorous economical and political analyses. By the same token, logically staking out the political benefits of uninterrupted oil shipments to the United States may not present the whole picture unless one includes the human costs, on both sides, of a war in the Middle East.

In the "no dumping" argument cited above, the rhetor didn't select images of snakes and rats, for example, but rather more appealing animals that evoke a desire to protect, such as a baby bird. Further, most of these arguments are painted in blue and white, which mirror colors found in nature and suggest pristine natural surroundings, rather than mudslides or other unappealing natural phenomena. Are there any disadvantages to using emotional appeals in this rhetorical situation? Do these appeals go far enough in persuading the reader? How might physical location, culture and local customs, economic status, or other elements of the rhetorical situation affect the selection of appeals?

The rhetor cannot generally invoke emotions directly by asking the readers to feel a certain way or to empathize with someone. He or she must use language, examples, and details that clearly convey situations with which the audiences can identify. Appeals to pathos are frequently made through specific detail or connotative language—language that evokes feelings or emotional responses. In the Prologue to *Invisible*

Man, for example, Ralph Ellison invites the reader to identify with a man who is invisible in his society; Ellison persuades readers to see another point of view by invoking their empathy for the narrator's situation.

Appeals to Logos   Appeals to logos refer to the logic and shape of the argument. Nearly every argument at least pretends to possess some logic in the form of reasons why the audience should change their views. Aristotle cites two basic methods of developing logos appeals: induction, arguing from evidence; and deduction, arguing from general principles.

In *induction,* the rhetor generalizes from a number of observations, specific cases, or examples and draws inferences or conclusions based on data. Induction deals not with certainties but with probabilities; the rhetor cannot test every single case or provide an infinite number of examples, so he or she uses examples and evidence to draw conclusions about another case or a larger population.

When the rhetor reasons from examples to a conclusion, she asks the audience to make an inductive leap—a leap of faith from the known and verifiable specific cases presented in the argument, across an unknown and unknowable stretch, to a probable conclusion. The relevance, breadth, and number of examples reduce the leap audiences must make and therefore strengthen the credibility of the argument. Since rhetors have a limited amount of time and space to devote to their examples, they must select those most persuasive and most suited to the audience and purpose. When Martin Luther King, Jr., describes driving all night because he can't find a motel that will accept his business, or having to explain to his child why she can't play in a playground that is for whites only, or seeing that his people's wives, mothers, and sisters are denied the respected title of "Mrs." and that grown men are called "boy," his vivid, specific examples make a strong case for the conclusion that Americans of African descent endure relentless and pervasive racism. In academic writing as well, each author must include relevant, sufficient, and representative examples to build a persuasive case for the conclusion. Scientists carefully record data about sampling, methods, and observations to substantiate credibly the conclusions they draw from their data.

Inductive arguments can go wrong in one of two ways: either the evidence is inadequate for the conclusion drawn, or the reasoning from evidence to conclusion is faulty. Readers of academic prose as well as other kinds of arguments must be critical of the kinds of examples offered and mindful of biased or inadequate sampling. They should also examine critically the "leap" they are asked to make from evidence to conclusion.

Say, for example, a friend of yours works in a hospital transcribing medical notes written by physicians. On his first day of work, he sees six patient charts, and all six contain doctors' notes in handwriting that is almost illegible. He might conclude that doctors have terrible handwriting. If he tells you, "All doctors have terrible handwriting," he would be guilty of overgeneralizing. In fact, he hasn't seen all doctors' handwriting. If he said, "All of the doctors whose handwriting I have seen write illegibly," he would be making a statement that is accurate (assuming others share his standards) but is limited to the sample he describes. Induction, like other forms of argumentation, is open to question; if it weren't, there would be no reason for debate. But reasonable people will be likely to accept the conclusions one draws if they are based on sufficient evidence and if the conclusion logically follows from the evidence. What we most want induction to do is to enable us to generalize from a sample to larger populations and other cases; we want to be able to say, with some degree of certainty, that the conclusion is true based on our evidence.

Deduction, the other primary method of organizing arguments, takes a general principle (also called a premise or an assumption) and draws a conclusion or makes an assertion based on it. The *syllogism* is a classic outline of deduction used to test the logic of the argument. It entails a statement of a general premise, a specific case, and a conclusion derived from the general premise and specific case. For example, consider the following statements:

> All physicians have terrible handwriting.
> Dr. Weller is a physician.
> Therefore, Dr. Weller has terrible handwriting.

Clearly the generalization forming the conclusion of the argument is highly questionable. Sketching out an argument in this form frequently enables readers to examine both the premises being made and the conclusions being drawn. Generally, though, arguments don't occur in this explicit form. More often, writers persuade through collapsed arguments, with generalizations and assumptions left out or buried within the argument.

Such a compact deductive argument, known as an *enthymeme*, unites the author's statement and conclusion with a part of the argument that is understood or assumed by the audience. The syllogism generally spells out the general principle, the specific case, and the conclusion. The enthymeme leaves out one of the premises, often the generalization or underlying assumption. Drawing from the example, the argument would appear something like this:

> Dr. Weller, being a physician, has terrible handwriting.

or

> Of course Dr. Weller has terrible handwriting—she's a physician.

Both statements have buried within them the outlined argument in the syllogism, but rather than sketching out all the steps, the rhetor relies on assumptions shared with the audience. The rhetor's task is to analyze the audience and to know how much background information to supply, what definitions to include or exclude, what the audience already accepts or believes, what points must be argued and supported with evidence. In the compact argument of the enthymeme, the rhetor assumes that the audience will supply certain links in the chain of argument.

A number of selections in this book provide examples of deductive arguments. The Declaration of Independence (Chapter 7) argues extensively from principle, explicitly stating premises and assumptions, testing those premises against a specific case (the British government of the colonies), and then drawing the conclusion that the break with Britain is justified. If one accepts the premises—governments derive their authority from the consent of the governed; governments exist to protect the rights of life, liberty, and the pursuit of happiness—then one must accept the validity of the conclusion—that governments that do not protect these rights no longer deserve their authority and should be abolished.

Often one can identify enthymemes by examining assertions connected to subordinate clauses beginning with conjunctions such as *since* and *because*. In the selection from *Backlash* included in Chapter 5, Susan Faludi identifies and then questions the logic in an enthymeme commonly cited by detractors of feminism: women are unhappy because of their newfound equality. Faludi refutes the argument by questioning the assumption that women are equal and by claiming that women are unhappy, in fact, because they are blocked from full equality.

Errors in Logic

Arguments can go wrong in a number of ways. Critical readers and careful writers need to question the arguments in what they read and take care with the evidence, assumptions, and reasons they offer and the conclusions they draw. In a deductive argument, a critical reader can argue with the reasons and assumptions, sometimes called premises, on which the conclusion is based or question the reasoning process from premises to conclusions. In inductive reasoning, one can question the evidence offered or the conclusion drawn about that evidence. Both methods can lead to a number of errors in logical argumentation, or fallacies. Below are some of the most common fallacies.

1. *Hasty generalization.* Leaping in logic from a very few cases to a broad conclusion can be considered hasty generalization. If, for example, we find that two senators have financial assets worth millions of dollars and we conclude that all public officials are wealthy, we have made a leap that is unsupported by the evidence. We have leaped too hastily from examples to a conclusion.

2. *Inadequate or biased sampling.* This fallacy is related to hasty generalization. If a writer's conclusions are based on too few samples or a skewed or biased collection of samples, the conclusions are not necessarily generalizable to the larger issue or population. If we sampled only the senators included in a list of the fifty wealthiest Americans to draw conclusions about all senators, we would be using a biased sample. We need to cast our net wider and draw from a more representative sampling. Drawing at random a sample of ten or twenty from the list of one hundred senators and examining their financial statements would give us more representative and complete data and enable us to make generalizations about the larger population of senators.

3. *Straw man.* A straw man in argumentation is a false target: the writer sets up a misstatement of the opponent's view and then attacks that misstatement instead of the real argument. An argument attacking someone who does not support specific pro-choice legislation might suggest that the opponent wants "all women barefoot and pregnant" instead of discussing the specific legislation in question.

4. *Ad hominem.* In the ad hominem argument, literally meaning "against the man," the writer attacks an individual holding the position rather than the position. If a writer says, "Governor Jones is in favor of nationalized health insurance, so it must be a bad idea," that writer is attacking the governor but not addressing the merits of his specific arguments.

5. *False analogy.* Argument by analogy is one of the weakest strategies and highly vulnerable to attack. A false analogy entails erroneously suggesting that two people, situations, or issues are analogous or comparable in certain ways. In recent years, any number of potential military conflicts have been argued against because they might represent "another Vietnam," whether or not there are, in fact, any similarities between the two situations.

6. *Post hoc ergo propter hoc.* Literally, this expression translates into "after this, therefore because of this." The mistake in logic lies in suggesting that because A happened before B, A caused B. The watchword in statistics and many social sciences, however, is that correlation does not equal causation. Because the divorce rate increased after the advent of widespread television viewing, there is no reason to conclude that television viewing causes divorce.

7. *False dilemma.* A false dilemma is an either-or situation in which the writer implies that we have only two choices: "Either we get rid of television once and for all, or we resign ourselves to being a nation with the leading divorce rate in the civilized world."

8. *Slippery slope.* In this lapse in logic, the writer argues that one first step will inevitably lead to disastrous consequences. For example, someone opposed to genetic engineering might argue, "Once we allow scientists to map human chromosomes, we will see people murdering their children because they don't have blond hair and blue eyes."

9. *Begging the question.* Begging the question is essentially assuming something as a given that has not been proved. A related strategy, circular reasoning, restates the proposition as a conclusion: "Students who have bad grades and don't study should not be allowed to watch television because viewing might be detrimental to their schoolwork."

10. *Non sequitur.* Literally, this term means, "It does not follow." Advertisements are full of fallacious reasoning but make something of a specialty of non sequiturs: "Crock Cola tastes great: America's fastest-growing cola company!" Taste and relative corporate growth are juxtaposed as if one leads to the other; such, regrettably for consumers, is not necessarily the case. Sometimes the term *non sequitur* is used more generally to indicate any lapse in logic.

Understanding Persuasion in Practice

In addition to evaluating the appeals to ethos, pathos, and logos in an argument, taking arguments apart on a structural, sentence-by-sentence level to see how they work can be instructive. Understanding both general principles of persuasion and specific, sentence-level strategies enables us to evaluate the arguments that confront us daily, in college studies and in our communities.

Examples of persuasion surround us in academic texts, mass media, personal conversations—even as we walk down the street. Let's examine a specific piece of persuasion encountered on a college campus recently. A flyer posted on the wall of a campus building has the following message spray-painted on it, in red letters on a white background, as if through a stencil:

> Oil in Kuwait
> Oil in Panama
> No Oil in Bosnia
> Get it?

Unpacking the argument takes a bit of thought and involves reader response and input to make the argument work. First, we observe that this is not an impromptu message, since it was created through a stencil, which presumes multiple applications of the message in various locations. The somewhat diffuse red spray-paint draws attention to the message and suggests blood; the rhetor, through the parallel structure of the phrases, argues that the situations are analogous: that the United States intervened militarily in other countries when doing so was in its own best interests; that it has not intervened in Bosnia because there is no economic motive to do so. In a rather taunting manner, the rhetorical question of the last line invites audience engagement in the discussion.

As it happens, some audience members—people of the academic community who passed by the notice—did engage in the argument. Written in ballpoint pen ink between lines two and three are, "No oil in Vietnam" and "No oil in Grenada," a reference to other U.S. military involvement without apparent economic benefit.

Except for the rhetorical question, each of the other elements in the argument is a phrase, which the audience has to fill in to complete a statement. Those statements might look something like this:

> The United States intervenes militarily in other countries only to protect its interests, such as access to suppliers of oil.
> Bosnia is not a supplier of oil.
> Therefore the United States will not intervene militarily to protect its interests in Bosnia.

For the conclusion to be true, the premises leading to the conclusion must be true. If they are not, the argument breaks down. When critiquing an argument, the audience can question the premises or the reasoning process that leads to the conclusion or claim. The scrawled messages in ballpoint pen refute the argument by attacking the premise that the United States intervenes militarily only when oil is at stake.

Examining the style of the message, we see that the rhetor made use of an excellent stylistic tactic, parallelism. The grammatical structures of the first three lines are equivalent: noun, preposition, noun, with a negative added to the last line. Parallel structures can help to clarify and emphasize connections and equivalence between ideas, as the rhetor was trying to suggest.

Let's examine another use of helpful grammatical structure, a balanced sentence:

> When guns are outlawed, only outlaws will have guns.

What is your immediate reaction to this slogan? Imagine you saw it on a bumper sticker of a car. Does it seem sensible or logical? Now read it aloud and take it apart:

> When guns are outlawed
> Only outlaws will have guns.

First, examine the rhythm. Which words are stressed? How do the stresses contribute to the rhythm? What words are then destressed and deemphasized? How does the sense of balance, of equivalence, contribute to the sense of logic or make it seem that the slogan "makes sense"?

Now look critically at the diction, or word choice. First look at the ambiguous term, *guns.* Does it refer to handguns? Shotguns? Rifles? Semiautomatics? Uzis? What does *outlawed* mean? Does it mean people must register for a gun? That they must wait ten days before purchasing one so that the seller can check for a criminal record? Does it mean children can't buy guns? Then examine that unstressed word, *only.* Is it true that only outlaws or criminals will have guns? What about police officers? Forest rangers? Brinks guards? The assumptions and assertions of the slogan do not bear up under close examination. In a fleeting statement as on a bumper sticker or in a cartoon, such arguments can sometimes make an impression or erode the position of the opposition just a bit.

Though you need to avoid falling into fallacious arguments, or those in which the logic breaks down, as in the example of the bumper sticker, you can use structures such as parallelism and balance to show viable relationships between things and ideas. You can choose whether to use *denotative* language, which is explicit language that attempts to convey objectivity, or *connotative* language, which is emotion-laden language that attempts to evoke an image or idea. By the same token, you can understand when you are being hornswoggled or fooled by eloquent language disguising a weak argument.

Let's look at the way another rhetorical strategy, antithesis, which is a balanced structure with opposing elements, can reinforce the effects of language:

> We observe today
> not a victory of party
> but a celebration of freedom.

These opening lines to John F. Kennedy's "Inaugural Address" stress the orderly changing of administrations, emphasizing not the rancorous 1960 presidential race against and defeat of Richard Nixon, not the onset of Democratic rule, but the sense that the inauguration itself is a link of history, part of the ritual of democratic government. A few lines later, Kennedy makes use of highly connotative language to evoke a sense of tradition, grandeur, and solemnity:

> For I have sworn before you and Almighty God the same, solemn oath our forebears prescribed nearly a century and three quarters ago.

Why would a modern president—one who used the relatively new medium of television to his advantage, one who represented youth and change, one who frightened some citizens simply by virtue of being Catholic—speak in archaic, formal diction? How do you think you would have reacted to such a speech? What tone, approach, and mood does this rhetor evoke? And how do these strategies support his goals?

Sometimes simple repetition of a key phrase can drive a point home forcefully and eloquently. You may have been told in the past to avoid being repetitious; now is a good time to examine the difference between needless, annoying repetition that occurs when you have not taken care with your essay or paragraph organization, and repetition that reinforces points and ideas, suggests connections between ideas, clarifies meaning, and delivers pleasing balance and rhythm to the audience. As we saw with the bumper sticker, rhythm and balance are no substitute for logic and evidence; nevertheless, well-crafted prose is itself more persuasive than plodding, hard-to-follow prose. And unless you are deliberately trying to obfuscate or muddy up the issues, clarity too is a virtue. Let's look at an eloquent example of *anaphora*, or a repeated sentence opener, from Martin Luther King, Jr.'s "I Have A Dream" speech:

> So let freedom ring from the prodigious hilltops of New Hampshire.
> Let freedom ring from the mighty mountains of New York.
> Let freedom ring from the heightening Alleghenies of Pennsylvania!
> Let freedom ring from the snowcapped Rockies of Colorado!
> Let freedom ring from the curvaceous peaks of California!
> But not only that;
> Let freedom ring from Stone Mountain of Georgia!
> Let freedom ring from Lookout Mountain of Tennessee!
> Let freedom ring from every hill and molehill of Mississippi.
> From every mountainside, let freedom ring!

This section follows King's recitation of the lyrics to "America" and picks up the thread of the last line of that song in the repeated "let freedom ring," and the image of "from every mountainside" in the second to last line of the song. Examine the progression of King's lines. What geographical regions are included? Then examine the break, midway, and the change in direction. In what ways does this repetition, attached to the diverse regions, reinforce a theme?

You can read the full text of this speech in Chapter 4. As you review this and other selections, remember to analyze not only themes and overall structure but also patterns of sentences, words, and images; all contribute to and underscore the persuasive message of the rhetor.

Persuasion works on many levels: to engage the audience, to get them to identify with the point of view of the rhetor, and, if possible, to move them in belief or in action to the position suggested by the rhetor. Since argument relies on moving beyond the supporting materials to draw conclusions, whether that support is based on examples or derived from a general proposition, the strength and effectiveness of appeals to ethos, pathos, and logos are crucial in persuading audiences. Such appeals operate at the level of the main point of a text, the supporting points, and the words and sentences themselves that convey those points. In Chapter 2 we focus the discussion of appeals and logical arrangement on the writing process; in every chapter that follows, we urge you to analyze texts critically, and when you write, to reason carefully and to provide solid support for your arguments.

Analyzing Persuasion

In previous English classes you may have been asked to analyze a poem or a short story and to write up your impressions in an expository essay. You may also have analyzed persuasive texts, such as arguments, essays, or speeches, using techniques like those we have just illustrated. In analyzing an argument, you break apart and examine the different elements that make it persuasive. In a persuasive written text, most of the points are clearly articulated, although they may rest on unwritten and even unsupported premises.

Analyzing an image can be more challenging because the argument tends to be less explicit. Although visual advertising can be direct, it too relies on associations, interpretations, and connotations, and of course on many unsupported premises. The discussion of genres later in this chapter will provide a brief review of the specific demands of different types of visual persuasion, but it may also be useful to look at how one student took on the challenge of analyzing a visual argument.

Student writer Kris Andeen had such an assignment for his expository writing class: find a visual argument and analyze it. He browsed some books containing World War I and II era posters at the school library and selected "Hasten the Homecoming—Buy Victory Bonds" by Norman Rockwell. He made a color photocopy of the poster to attach to the submitted essay. Then he brainstormed a list of his first impressions of the poster, jotting them all down as they came to him.

Next, he reviewed what he had learned about Aristotle's appeals—to ethos, pathos, and logos—and examined the poster with those elements in mind, generating more material on the poster. The outline that follows organized these impressions:

"Hasten the Homecoming—Buy Victory Bonds," USA, 1939–1945. Norman Rockwell painting, originally for *Saturday Evening Post*

I. First Impressions
   A. First thing which draws the eye is red line: "Buy Victory Bonds."
      1. This makes sense since it is most important part of the poster.
   B. After one's eyes have seen red "Buy Victory Bonds," the eyes are next taken to the red sweater of the mother who is reaching out to her son.
      1. Her eyes point towards her son, which is next place viewer's eyes look.
   C. After viewer has seen son, he/she begins to see the rest of the picture, but by this point, a central association has been made in the viewer's mind: "Buy victory bonds, and the men will come home."

1. Rest of picture reveals 16 faces witnessing the soldier's return—17, if you count the dog!!
2. All faces are smiling (with exception of one), which associates happiness with the return of the soldier.
3. Obviously, this is not a mansion, but a lower-class, more common American home. Therefore, the ad will appeal to a large percentage of the American population.

    4. It appears as though some previous problems with the roof are being repaired.

    5. There also appears to be light shining down on the scene from the upper right-hand corner of the picture as if it is just coming out of the clouds.

II. Appeals

  A. Appeals to Ethos

    1. The family portrayed in the poster represents the common American family of the time.

      a. excited, motherly figure

      b. Pops is smoking a pipe

      c. lots of kids (neighborhood too)

      d. Sparky, the dog

    2. The scene represents the common American neighborhood.

      a. After depression ('30s), people still living in lower-class homes.

      b. Clothes dried on clothesline.

      c. The classic American sweetheart is waiting for soldier-boy just around the corner.

    3. The headlines for the poster, "Hasten the Homecoming—Buy Victory Bonds," are printed in red and blue against a white background→red, white, and blue→patriotism, nationalism.

  B. Appeals to Pathos

    1. If you did not have any children/family members in the war, this poster still might make you feel sorry for those with loved ones at war, so you might be convinced to buy victory bonds to bring your neighbor's son home. Neighbors *are* shown in the picture, with smiles on their faces.

    2. If you were a wealthy American, you might feel sorry for lower-class citizens upon seeing this poster, and thus be convinced to buy victory bonds.

  C. Appeals to Logos

    1. As earlier stated, this poster seems to suggest that if one were to buy victory bonds, then the men of the war could come home faster, thus bringing happy smiles, repairs, and bright sunshine.

III. Audience

I believe this poster can be aimed at three types of people: families with relatives fighting in the war, neighbors of people fighting in the war and their families, and wealthy citizens who feel sorry for lower-class families with relatives in the war.

After putting the project aside for a day or two, Kris tried to compose a draft based on his working outline. He considered and reconsidered his dominant impression or thesis—the main assertion or inference he would make based on his material—so that he would be able to focus the essay and make sure it stayed on track. Kris identified this as his dominant point: "the poster's strength lay in its ability to identify with the common American."

After reviewing the biographical notes on Rockwell in the book of posters and in a reference book on American biographies, Kris drafted some background information for the introduction to provide context and help prepare the reader to listen to his analysis. The introduction led smoothly into the thesis for this draft. For the draft, Kris didn't use all the material he had generated; the assignment was to write a two- to three-page analysis of a visual argument, and he had generated enough material for a longer paper. Once he developed his thesis around the notion of identifying with the common person, he was able to determine what to keep and what to let go. The first body paragraph focuses on Rockwell's use of the family in the poster; he then expands his point to involve the neighborhood; he then shifts to broader American attitudes, values, and desire for an end to the war. All paragraphs stay focused on the theme of appeals to the common American.

Kris Andeen
English 1D5
10/1/97
Draft

The Common American

Norman Rockwell's work represents a hallmark of the American *great*
background
dream. His paintings during the early half of this century are known for

You ordinarily
portraying the common American. The U.S. government recognized this, *need a noun*
after "this"
and used one of his cover paintings for *The Saturday Evening Post* in a *to avoid*
reference errors.
poster encouraging financial support for World War II. Although Rock-

well probably wasn't commissioned by the U.S. government to paint this

picture, it served the government's purposes quite well. The poster's
the poster's? Or the other way works because Americans can identify w/ the
the
esis can
placed
strength lies in its ability to identify with the common American. Indeed, *scene portrayed?*
t end of
ntro to
Rockwell was so skilled at depicting the people of the time, that his
lead into
move to
essay.
painting could have been used for any of a number of causes and still *end of*
essay?
have been successful.

check w.c.

The first way which this poster appeals to the common American is

dominant?   *rephrase?*

through the family, the most dominating figure of which (in this painting)

is the mother. Thanks to her bright red sweater, Mom stands out as the

first figure that catches the viewer's eye. Traditionally, she represents the

passionate, caring head of the family, just as she is portrayed here with

her arms outstretched. She is also shown as a white person (as is the

whole neighborhood) as white people represented the largest racial per-

centage of the nation's population. Also seen on the front porch is Dad,

who appears to have just gotten out of his recliner, pipe still in hand.

Again, this fits the classic image we have of the fatherly figure who rests

after a day at work in his recliner with his pipe and slippers. And of

course, the American family is not a small one—indeed, there are plenty

whom

of children about, some of which may be assumed are siblings. But

Rockwell doesn't stop at human figures—Sparky, the dog, plays a crucial

role in the classic American family, and he too can be seen running anx-

iously towards) the returning soldier

     Another way in which Rockwell is able to identify with the people

vague   of the time is to associate with the neighborhood. In this painting, the

neighborhood plays an even larger role than the family. So what did the

common American neighborhood look like from 1939 to 1945? One

must remember that during this time, not only was the U.S. at war, but it

Usually capitalized

was still recovering from the great depression. A very large percentage of

Andeen 3

unclear sentence

the population lived in the city, and inner-city housing wasn't any more

beautiful then than it is now. The brick house, the clotheslines, the

garbage-ridden street, the sweetheart around the corner, the hordes of

frolicking children (they weren't inside playing Nintendo or surfing the

Web back then), the repairman on the roof, and even the faded paint on

the porch all contribute in providing an archetypal image of the urban

Needed?

American neighborhood. (Once again,) Rockwell has identified with the

American population by meticulously allegorizing the American home.

One last key theme in identifying with America is happiness and an

Check w.c. —needed? most precise?

odium for war. The American people don't like to be active in wars.

There are many reasons for this; increased stress on the household, pos-

sible increase on the price of imports, and the threat of attack. But most

of all, Americans are troubled by the absence of loved ones who may or

may not return after the war. With the return of the soldier in Rockwell's

painting we see a number of happy connotations. For one, there are

Write out numbers up to 99 (a convention).

16 smiling faces in the picture, and that's if you don't count Sparky. We

also see (consciously or unconsciously) green leaves emerging from the

tree which otherwise appears not to have any foliage. This suggests Spring-

time and a new happiness. Another suggestion of such happiness is that

while most of the scene appears to be very dark, with the exception of

Mom's clothesline, there appears to be a bright light shining down from

the upper right-hand corner of the picture. This implies the sun breaking

[margin notes:]
lso
g with
s.)
ory Bonds
not just for
wealthy,
c.

could use,
such as . . . or a
colon. But the
semicolon
won't work
here.

void
shifts to
2nd person
point of
view

great
details

through the clouds of wartime, another concept which America most

Transition? Needed?

certainly welcomes. So once again, Rockwell has identified with the

Ref?

American through its desire for an end to the war and the return of

happy times.

    Happy times are just what the American public wanted. Norman

Rockwell was aware of this, and by incorporating such values into his

painting he was able to identify with the nation. His abilities in relating

Resource? (See if you want the connotatic

to the nation's people made him a valuable tool for the U.S. government.   *that "tool*

provides.

The power of such identification in art could just as well have been used

to rouse the country in a cultural diversity campaign. If Mom were

for example,

stretching her arms out to a newly arrived Japanese family, then the same

concepts of identification would work in promoting the acceptance of

the Japanese culture. Indeed, Rockwell's work, with its nationalistic   *Good*

analysis

morals and commonplace subjects, provides an excellent example of

the power of ethos appeals.

    To revise this essay, Kris chose to keep the focus that he developed in this draft, so his work was primarily geared toward crafting smoother transitions and effective prose. He had already incorporated evidence from the "text," or image, to support his assertions; indeed, in an inductive process he had generated his evidence and then used inferences from that evidence to make a point. In the essay, the inferences are structured as topic sentences, which are then, in turn, supported by the evidence, examples, and images from the poster.

    Kris's draft went through two reviews before final submission, including one peer review. Since this essay was written early in the term, peers were not yet well skilled in providing substantial feedback, so much of the peer's suggestions focused on word choice or mechanics. The instructor's suggestions targeted focus and placement of the thesis (end of introduction or end of essay), selection of evidence to support topic ideas, and some matters of style that needed attention (inappropriate transitions, word choice). Kris also chose to change his title from "The Common American" to "End of the Tunnel," because the artist's strategy of identification with the common man or woman was, in fact, a means to a larger end—expressing the persuasive message that the end of the war is near and that the troops will be home even sooner if we all do our part and buy Victory Bonds. The title ties in well with the conclusion, where Kris amplifies this point.

Kris's final essay, while not perfect, is an excellent example of how a writer analyzes, selects, focuses, and organizes material to develop a coherent expository essay on a visual argument. Kris made particular choices and used a particular approach in doing the analysis and writing the essay. You could take the same image and come up with a very different essay, because your own ideas, creativity, ability to analyze, interests, and skill would determine the outcome.

Kris Andeen
English 1D5
Revision

End of the Tunnel

Norman Rockwell's art represents a hallmark of the American dream. His paintings in the early half of this century are known for portraying the common American and his/her struggles and joys in this society. The U.S. government recognized Rockwell's talent, and in 1939 they used one of his cover paintings for *The Saturday Evening Post* in a poster encouraging financial support for World War II. Although Rockwell wasn't commissioned by the U.S. government to paint this picture, it served the government's purposes quite well. The poster's persuasive strength lay in the ease with which the common American could identify with the scene portrayed.

The first way in which this poster appealed to the common American was through the family. The most dominant figure of the family, in this painting, is the mother. Thanks to her brilliant red sweater, Mom

stands out as the first figure who catches the viewer's eye. Traditionally,

she represents the passionate, caring head of the family, just as she is

portrayed here with her arms outstretched. She is also shown as a white

person (as is the whole neighborhood) since white people represented

the largest racial percentage of the nation's population. Also seen on the

front porch is Dad, who appears to have just gotten out of his recliner,

pipe still in hand. Rockwell's painting fits the classic image we have of

the fatherly figure who rests after a day at work in his recliner with his

pipe and slippers. And of course, the American family is not a small

one—indeed, there are plenty of children about, some of whom may be

assumed are siblings. But Rockwell doesn't stop at human figures—

Sparky, the dog, plays a crucial role in the classic American family, and

he too can be seen running anxiously toward the returning soldier.

Another way in which Rockwell was able to identify with the peo-

ple of the time was to associate his painting with the American neigh-

borhood. In this painting, the neighborhood plays an even larger role

than the family. So what did the common American neighborhood look

like from 1939 to 1945? One must remember that during this time the

U.S. was not only at war, but it was still recovering from the Great De-

pression. A large percentage of the population lived in the city, and inner-

city housing wasn't any more beautiful then than it is now. The brick apartment building, the clotheslines, the garbage-ridden street, the sweetheart around the corner, the hordes of frolicking children (they weren't inside playing Nintendo or surfing the Web), the repairman on the roof, and even the faded paint on the porch all contribute in providing an archetypal image of the urban American neighborhood. In a sense, Rockwell has painted his audience's neighborhood, providing a mirror in which they may see themselves.

One last key theme in identifying with America is happiness and a repugnance for war. The American people don't like to be active in wars. There are many reasons for this isolationist mindset, such as increased stress on the household, possible increase on the price of imports, and the threat of attack. But most of all, Americans are troubled by the absence of loved ones who may or may not return after the war. With the return of the soldier in Rockwell's painting we see a number of happy connotations. For one, there are *sixteen* smiling faces in the picture, and that's if you don't count Sparky. We also see (consciously or subconsciously) green leaves emerging from the tree which otherwise appears barren. This emerging foliage suggests Springtime and a new happiness. Another suggestion of such happiness is that while the lighting in most of the scene is very dark (with the exception of Mom's clothesline), there appears to be a bright light shining down from the upper right-hand corner of the picture. Such illumination implies the sun breaking through the clouds of wartime, another concept which America most certainly welcomes. Subconsciously, these hints of joy suggest a light at the end of the tunnel, a tunnel of war and depression which all Americans were anxious to exit.

An end to the tunnel is just what the American public wanted. Norman Rockwell was aware of this desire and by incorporating such values into his painting he was able to identify with the nation. The power of such identification in Rockwell's art is so strong that it could have been used successfully to support any number of causes. For example, if Mom were stretching her arms out to a newly arrived Japanese family, then the same concepts of identification would work in promoting the acceptance of the Japanese culture. Indeed, Rockwell's work, with its nationalistic morals and commonplace subjects, provides an excellent example of the power of ethos appeals.

Kris wrote the following reflection on how he went about completing his essay assignment:

> Our assignment was to choose an advertisement and write about the different ways in which it appealed to its audience. We weren't restricted to war ads, but I was familiar with war ads since we had been analyzing them in class. So I went to the library and looked up books about war advertising. There were quite a few books, each filled with full-color war ads. I checked out a few of the books and chose three possible posters to write about. Then I wrote possible hypotheses for each and reasoned that the Rockwell poster had the strongest, most supportable thesis.
>
> Since my thesis focused on Rockwell's remarkable appeals to ethos, I wrote down every aspect of the scene that was common to the American family. My list was long, and with such a list of supporting images, writing the essay itself wasn't very difficult. My outline was basic. The

first paragraph would be my lead-in, with some background on Rockwell and the thesis. Each paragraph of the body would cite different aspects of the poster and their relation to the common American. The closing paragraph would wrap up my argument, restating the thesis.

As far as revision went, I read back through my essay to check for fluency in tone and clear progression of thought. Transitions were important and I was careful to use varied transitions where necessary. My professor also read through the rough draft and made some suggestions. For example, she cited my continual use (near the end of each paragraph) of the phrase "once again," or "again we see . . ." I had been using these types of phrases to wrap up each paragraph and tie the paragraphs back to the thesis. However, the use of "again" was repetitive and unoriginal, and I was overrelying on these words to make connections between my points. We were able to rephrase each of these instances, creating a more diverse paragraph structure.

Finally, after making all of my own revisions and those that my professor suggested in our conference, I subjected my prose to my class peers. My peers and their reactions were valuable since they provided me with different, fresh feedback. Then I revised my paper for style and mechanics one more time and submitted the essay.

Kris Andeen is a college student from Beaverton, Oregon, who attends a California university.

Elements of Persuasion

Assumptions

In everyday life we make countless assumptions: that the water will flow out of the tap when we turn it on, that the bus will come more or less on time to take us to school or work. That sometimes the water main breaks or the bus is quite late does not change the fact that we take these things for granted. When we arrive at school, we assume that a paper we turn in will be read and evaluated; we assume that the data we obtain from reliable sources—books, reputable journals, people we trust—are reported accurately. Sometimes we explicitly state the assumptions on which we are operating; for example, we might say, "With inflation holding steady for the rest of the quarter, we predict stable interest rates."

Assumptions are the unseen glue in an argument, providing the connection between the evidence or proof and the conclusions drawn from that proof. They are underlying principles on which we base our claims and part of the shared values or wisdom of a community, whether a society, culture, workplace, or academic discipline. We might conclude, for example, that a family might be dysfunctional based on our own criteria for functional families. Or we might assume that nuclear families have always been the norm, until we reflect on other community structures such as clans, tribes, and the like, or research alternative families in American history.

There is nothing inherently bad about assumptions; life would be extremely difficult if we had to start from scratch every day. But critical readers and careful writers do need to recognize assumptions in arguments, particularly those that are unstated. Careful readers question assumptions in the arguments they read, interrogating the text (or image) and writing notes in the margins or a notebook: "Who says? Why do you say that? Do you have any proof? Why did you draw that conclusion?" They will check for missing links between evidence and claim, or a jump from reason to conclusion that does not seem warranted by the reason itself. In addition to asking questions, one can diagram a selection by blocking out on paper the conclusion and the specific reasons that support it, and then examine them for underlying assumptions.

Analyzing Assumptions in Arguments   The American family is a subject that taps into our emotions, values, beliefs, and principles. Ongoing arguments about the form and role of families, marriage, and children, about relations within and between families, nearly always rest on assumptions with which we were raised in our own families, whether the core issue is power, or control of sexuality, or the treatment of children as property and potential labor, or the transmission of property and family names.

Within Chapter 5, for example, the arguments, both verbal and visual, depend on assumptions as their taking-off point. Sometimes writers or illustrators assume that an assumption is so deep-seated in the society that most readers or viewers will concur with an argument based on that assumption. *Keep Within Compass* is aimed at defining proper behavior for women; the author depends on assumptions about the image of women that women—and men—would find appealing: the woman industriously doing needlework as she walks on the grounds of a pleasant estate. Contrasted with this assumption about how women *should* behave are fairly lurid portrayals of what the Fates have in store for unvirtuous women. The Charles Atlas advertisement assumes that men want muscular bodies and that women prefer such men; its creators also hoped that readers would assume that the Atlas system would work, as it apparently did for Atlas. Bruce Fein assumes that readers share his assumptions that two-parent, two-gender nuclear families are best for children. Marian Wright Edelman writes movingly of the assumptions of her childhood family and community and the ways in which those assumptions, or shared values and beliefs, have guided her life and her life's work.

Often, arguments about families in America have focused on challenging or refuting assumptions. Keenan Peck, for example, challenges readers' assumptions about what makes a family a family—questioning the very definition of the word "family" and developing a new definition based on different assumptions. Susan Faludi spends considerable effort and evidence challenging two core assumptions—that women are unhappy and that they are "equal"—in order to question the conclusion drawn by critics of feminism that "all that equality" must be making women unhappy.

Assertions

Assertions are the conclusions one draws based on some combination of reasons and assumptions. The main assertion in an essay is often referred to as a *thesis statement*. Reasons are the support the writer offers—the evidence on which she or he has based those assertions. Assumptions are the often unstated beliefs, values, and principles we hold that interplay with other assumptions and reasons. Some writers refer to assumptions and reasons as premises; the term *premise* is prominent in discussions of formal logic and the syllogism, or deductive argument in outline form. For the sake of clarity, we will use *assertions* consistently throughout this text but will note synonyms that other writers sometimes use.

Analyzing Assertions in Arguments   Assertions vary in tone and in language because of differences in the assumptions that underlie them and because of differences in temperament, background, and purpose. Some assertions are factual; some are statements of values; some are drawn from research; and some are meant as calls to action, to suggest changes in policy or procedure.

Although visual and textual arguments in every chapter of this text rely on assertions, Chapter 6, "Work and Play," includes particularly good examples of two very different but effective ways of using assertions for argumentative purposes. Had he chosen to, Benjamin Franklin could have made assertions about anything he wanted; his genius gave him more latitude, but his good sense gave him restraint. So even his most definite assertions are couched in modest terms and phrased in such a way as to be useful to other people without drumming in the fact that he was smarter than anyone he might have been talking to. For example, in explaining how he taught himself to stop overpowering other people in conversation, he says mildly that he has learned how *not* to assert himself: "I made it a rule to forbear all direct contradiction to the sentiments of others, and all positive assertion of my own. . . . When another asserted something that I thought an error, I denied myself the pleasure of contradicting him abruptly." Franklin's security and self-knowledge are clear; he can assert without trying to dominate, and in doing so he is more forceful than if he had been argumentative.

But Charlotte Perkins Gilman, writing out of a feeling of powerlessness and frustration, makes her assertions sharply and with a point:

"All that [a woman] may wish to have, all that she may wish to do, must come through a single channel and a single choice. Wealth, power, social distinction, fame . . . ease and pleasure, her bread and butter—all must come to her through a small gold ring. This is a heavy pressure." Gilman's values—those of a woman who wants an active and atypical role in pursuit of financial and personal independence—are at variance with the role for which she was trained, and the conflict she feels is clear in her list of dependencies, combined with the short, angry assertion at the end: "This [marriage] is a heavy pressure."

When the purpose of an assertion is to question policies or propose new ones, it tends to be direct because the author wants to be sure that the point comes across. For example, when Gloria Steinem attacks the idea that women still pretend to work only because they need the money for their families and not because they like it, she says: "A job as a human right is a principle that applies to men as well as women. But women have more cause to fight for it." There are no metaphors or figures of speech here—only the bare assertion, said clearly and distinctly.

In argumentative papers based largely on research, the same directness may inform assertions about the subject, because they will be drawn partly from authorities and partly from the writer's understanding of the material and purpose in choosing it. In his paper on the rise of prejudice against Mexican Americans during the Great Depression, Jorge Flores uses both outside sources and his own opinion in making his assertions: "there was a great demand for Mexicans to fill up menial . . . jobs such as working in steel mills, mines, meat packing plants, brickyards, canneries, but most importantly in agriculture (Hoffman 4). Mexican labor was in high demand . . . because Mexicans were cheap and reliable workers." The point of such an approach is to use outside authorities as validation for the writer's ideas, not as a substitution for the writer's ability to sort through and identify relevant information.

Finally, some assertions are intended not to convey research, to affect policy, or to express personal opinions so much as to affect the decision making of the reader or viewer. This is usually the case with advertisements, which may appeal to the reader's value system directly or indirectly but only with the intention of getting him or her to buy something. The Edsel advertisement in Chapter 5, for example, spreads its primary assertion across the top of the page: "They'll know you've *arrived* when you drive up in an Edsel." Here the assertion is clearly an appeal to the prospective buyer's vanity, to the desire not just to keep up with the Joneses but to take a big step ahead of them. The advertisement will succeed only if its author has gauged the reader's value system correctly, which is what makes assertions in advertising such a delicate business.

Examples

Technically, an example is a single part chosen to show the nature or character of a whole, or a sample of a larger unit, or a typical sample of something; George Washington is an example of an American president, and Chris Rock is an example of a comedian.

Practically, though, examples fulfill two crucial functions in writing. First, they enable an audience to identify emotionally and/or intellectually with the writer or the writer's subject. This is especially important if the writer wants to move the audience to action, or knows that the audience is hostile or indifferent or just unfamiliar with the material. For instance, in the speech "I Have a Dream," Martin Luther King, Jr., included examples of how prejudice affected the lives of African Americans doing ordinary things—like trying to book a hotel room or get a seat on a bus—to explain the effects of racial segregation to an audience, many of whose members had no personal experience of segregation. These common and easily understandable examples help persuade through *identification*—identification between King and his audience, between the people he is talking about and the people he is talking to.

The second role that example fills is to support persuasion through *evidence*; examples can act as proof for general statements or assertions. Just as abstractions without examples are emotionally uninvolving, assertions without examples are unconvincing. Examples are as essential to a persuasive argument as results are to an experiment.

The following two paragraphs show the difference between a paragraph without clear examples and the same paragraph rewritten by the author to include examples. The argument concerns whether dropping the atomic bomb on Japan hastened the end of World War II. The writer, Paul Fussell, is criticizing John Kenneth Galbraith, the economist, who thought that the atomic bomb made no difference.

Without Examples

On the other hand, John Kenneth Galbraith is persuaded that the Japanese would have surrendered by November without an invasion. He thinks the atomic bombs were not decisive in bringing about the surrender and he implies that their use was unjustified. What did he do in the war? He was in the Office of Price Administration in Washington, and then he was director of the United States Strategic Bombing Survey. He was thirty-seven in 1945, and I don't demand that he experience having his ass shot off. I just note that he didn't. In saying this I'm aware of its offensive implications ad hominem. But here I think that approach justified. What's at stake in an infantry assault is so entirely unthinkable to those without any experience of one, even if they possess very wide-ranging imaginations and sympathies, that experience is crucial in this case.

With Examples

On the other hand, John Kenneth Galbraith is persuaded that the Japanese would have surrendered surely by November without an invasion. He thinks the A-bombs were unnecessary and unjustified because the war was ending anyway. The A-bombs meant, he says, "a difference, at most, of two or three weeks." But at the time, with no indication that surrender was on the way, the kamikazes were sinking American vessels, the *Indianapolis* was sunk (880 men killed), and Allied casualties were running to over 7,000 per week. "Two or three weeks," says Galbraith. Two weeks more means 14,000 more killed and wounded, three weeks more, 21,000. Those weeks mean the world if you're one of those thousands or related to one of them. During the time between the dropping of the Nagasaki bomb on August 9 and the actual surrender on the 15th, the war pursued its accustomed course: on the 12th of August eight captured American fliers were executed (heads chopped off); the fifty-first United States submarine, *Bonefish,* was sunk (all aboard drowned); the destroyer *Callaghan* went down, the seventieth to be sunk, and the Destroyer Escort *Underhill* was lost. That's a bit of what happened in six days of the two or three weeks posited by Galbraith. What did he do in the war? He worked in the Office of Price Administration in Washington. I don't demand that he experience having his ass shot off. I merely note that he didn't.

The first paragraph gives no evidence to support or refute Galbraith's contention that the use of the bombs was unnecessary. The second, with its example upon example of the numbers and types of casualties that occurred in the last days of the war, certainly puts the writer in a stronger position to persuade the reader that Galbraith was wrong.

Analyzing Examples in Arguments   The most effective examples are both genuine expressions of an author's temperament and suited to his or her audience and purpose. Any successful piece of persuasive writing, whether framed as a narrative, an exposition, or an argument, comes from a writer who knows his or her audience at least well enough to strike a chord of recognition; it reaches for some common emotional bond, shared beliefs, shared hopes. But a writer seeking common ground will be effective only if there is something else as well—a powerful sense of his or her individuality. One of the great paradoxes of writing, art, film, or good conversation is that the only way to have a general effect is to be particular. Abstractions don't move people and don't convince them. If you want to communicate powerfully, you must find a way to connect to your audience directly, and that's what good, specific examples do.

In choosing and presenting examples, bear in mind the types of experiences an audience is likely to sympathize with and understand; examples far removed from the experience of most people generally do not work well.

Examples are not difficult for the reader to recognize in a text or for a viewer to recognize in a picture (see the examples of wealth in the *California, Cornucopia of the World* poster in Chapter 4). As the writer or speaker, your purpose is to find examples that are comfortable to you, are appropriate to your material, and create the best emotional connections between you, your material, and your audience.

If the examples are well chosen, however, they can be not only rhetorically effective but politically powerful. For example, the central section of the most famous persuasive document in American history, the Declaration of Independence (Chapter 7) relies almost entirely on examples. The list is long: George III has quartered troops in Americans' homes; he has ignored the people's rights; he has refused to assent to laws for the people's good; he has made judges dependent on his will; he has plundered seas, ravaged coastline, burnt towns, etc. It is not that Jefferson believes that George III has done any of that personally, or that he means these examples as an even-handed account of relations between the colonists and the British crown. On the contrary, he uses examples argumentatively—to convince readers, including Englishmen and other Europeans who might be sympathetic to the Revolution, that independence is the logically inevitable and thoughtful result of external pressures not of the colonists' choosing.

Frederick Douglass, an escaped slave, author of a great autobiography, and a man whose intellectual brilliance made him the most powerful spokesman for the abolition of slavery, faced a different audience but a problem not completely unrelated to Jefferson's when he was asked to deliver a Fourth of July speech in Rochester, New York in 1852—eight years before the Civil War. His audience was composed largely of white Americans who lived in the North, where there was no slavery, but who were not emotionally involved in the struggle to free slaves from the South. His job was to educate them about how little Independence Day meant to slaves, and how hypocritical they were in expecting Douglass to celebrate their generosity to him.

Douglass sprinkled his speech with language that echoed the Declaration—liberty, freedom, justice, independence, glorious anniversary, Fourth of July, declarations of the past—but his examples were far more concrete. With slavery as his subject and his audience's insensitivity to the humanity of slaves as his object, he listed some of the many occupations in which free blacks participated: clerks, merchants, secretaries, doctors, ministers, poets, authors, editors, orators, teachers, prospectors for gold, whalers, ranchers, farmers. Since these examples could have equally been a list of activities pursued by whites, they form the basis of argument for the self-evident nature of racial equality.

The point is that both Jefferson and Douglass, thinkers and actors whose objective was the broadening of collective and individual freedom, knew how to use examples as rhetorical and moral weapons. They understood that specificity is crucial, and they knew that a combination of elegant and thrilling abstraction and concrete language was better than reliance on one mode to the exclusion of the other. Jefferson speaks of life, liberty, and the pursuit of happiness, but he also enumerates acts of George III's government against the colonists which interfere with their rights as British citizens; Douglass speaks biblically of jubilation, grief, and memory, and he also enumerates many peaceful occupations open to free Americans, but closed to slaves. The result in both cases is persuasive language at the very highest level.

Definition

Definition entails explaining or clarifying a word or expression. Defining terms accurately is crucial in argument; if writers and readers are to debate an issue, they must first understand each other and the basic terms of the discussion. If they do not establish a mutual understanding of the terms of debate, they are like two people talking to each other in different languages, conveying little except confusion. Agreeing on terms establishes common ground from which to launch a discussion.

Sometimes we can agree on common terms and proceed. When we cannot, the definitions themselves may become the argument. *American culture,* for example, has different meanings to Alexis de Tocqueville and Luther Standing Bear (see Chapter 3), not only because of the times in which they lived but also because of their different cultural perspectives. Explaining what they mean requires more than a sentence or two and more than one strategy of definition.

Defining terms effectively and appropriately requires a good sense of audience awareness. If writers define terms with which their audiences are already familiar, they waste time and space and try their readers' patience; they may also inadvertently insult readers' intelligence, which will undercut efforts to persuade. But writers should not assume that the audience knows specialized terms or understands a particular interpretation of an abstract term. Analyzing intended audiences—their education, experience, familiarity with the subject of discussion—must guide writers in determining how much they need to define.

When proposing a definition is the central purpose in a piece of persuasive writing, the writer must provide supporting evidence. In "What the Indian Means to America," Luther Standing Bear defines the Native American as "of the soil, whether it be the region of forests, plains, pueblos, or mesas." He supports that statement with subsequent passages about Indian physique, crafts, love of nature, and principles of brotherhood. All of these examples suit his emphasis on differences between Indian and white cultural patterns. The author has used the kind of evidence he thought would be most effective for the expected audience and purpose of the writing. When you read extended definitions supported by examples, facts, narratives, case histories, and so on, consider whether the evidence is strong enough to support the proposed definition.

Analyzing Definitions in Arguments   Because definitions are fundamental building blocks in argument, an essential step in analyzing persuasive writing is to identify and understand the definitions the writer has used. Because any discussion of American identities must include a definition of what is meant by *American*, the writers and visual artists in Chapter 3 have all used definitions. The type of definition used depends on the occasion, the audience, the purpose, and the subject matter.

Student writer Martha Serrano explicitly addresses definition in her essay "Chicana," and argues passionately that being defined by others as Hispanic, or even as Mexican American, fails to capture both the core and the nuances of her identity. She cites historical and linguistic evidence to support her argument that these terms are inadequate and inappropriate. But writers do not always call attention to the ways in which they are defining terms. Often the most important definitions are implicit. For example, Ralph Ellison, in the Prologue to *Invisible Man*, is apparently examining the phenomenon of cultural invisibility and its consequences for Americans of African descent. However, he is also providing an implicit definition of *American:* in this term, Ellison would argue, we must include all those who live in and contribute to American society, whether they are powerful and white or excluded and black. Others are very explicit in defining key terms. The cartoonist who created *U.S. Hotel* quite clearly considered bomb throwing, incendiary talk, and communism—and all those who embrace these practices—to be un-American. Be alert to both implicit and explicit definitions.

Refutation

Refutation is proof that an argument or statement is wrong. It comes into existence only when there is an opponent or another side. Refutation means that someone else has gone first; it is the answer to an assumption, or a point of view, or a statement with which one disagrees.

In one sense, then, refutation is not a completely independent rhetorical strategy; it needs to bounce off and argue against something else. The emphasis in refutation is less on stating one's own principles than on taking the material presented by an opponent and dismantling it.

In another sense, refutation is based on instinct, on the impulse to react negatively when we hear an idea that infuriates us or strikes us as stupid or unethical or unjust. But refutation is more disciplined than that. An artful, well-prepared writer or speaker uses refutation to overturn an opponent's argument or to take his or her ideas and reverse them to advantage.

It is possible to refute an argument logically without necessarily having a deep intellectual belief in the view expressed by the refutation. For example, an excellent logician could refute the argument of someone he or she agrees with by pointing up inconsistencies; a member of a debating team could be randomly assigned either side of an argument and would be expected to find ways to damage the other side's approach. And criminal attorneys are routinely expected to fulfill their duty of defending people whom they dislike, distrust, or even believe to be guilty, mostly by refuting the prosecution's evidence and raising doubt in the mind of a jury or judge.

The higher forms of refutation, however, are neither mechanical nor uncommitted. They come from one's involvement with an issue or a principle, and they do more than decimate the opposing viewpoint; they can change the way people think and move them to action.

In extraordinary cases—like those expressed in Chapter 7 by Henry David Thoreau, Frederick Douglass, and Martin Luther King, Jr.—refutation can acquire a significant symbolic authority, which resonates over time to larger and more distant audiences. It can even move and inspire otherwise ordinary people to risk their own security and freedom in the name of an idea. Thoreau, for example, argued so powerfully for the effectiveness of nonviolent resistance over the use of force that both Mahatma Gandhi and Martin Luther King, Jr. were able to apply his approach to two of the most powerful civil rights movements of the twentieth century.

Analyzing Refutation in Arguments   A number of writers represented in Chapter 7 spent their lives challenging accepted beliefs in the public arena; the ability to use refutation successfully was a professional requirement for them. As a rule, they were less likely to spend their time refuting individual opponents than in arguing against established beliefs and ideas. For example, when Douglass argued in his Fourth of July speech that Independence Day was an insult to slaves who had never had any independence, he was not debating a particular person but disproving an assumption: that the Fourth of July holds the same meaning for all Americans.

In the same way, when Susan B. Anthony argued for women's right to vote, she was arguing against a whole set of established stereotypes about women's weakness, their need to be told what to do by their husbands, their inability to function outside the home, and so on. To refute those beliefs, she used the one body of evidence that was valid to both her and her opponents: the Declaration of Independence, the Constitution, and the Fourteenth and Fifteenth Amendments. But while her opponents used that evidence to prove that women were not entitled to equal protection under the law, Anthony used it to demonstrate that excluding women from the vote was both philosophically illogical and silly. She was so effective that her career functioned as a sort of living refutation to the idea that women were too weak and helpless to use the vote intelligently.

In *Brown* v. *Board of Education*, however, Chief Justice Earl Warren wanted to refute not only a previous Supreme Court ruling on the separate but equal doctrine that had survived for fifty years but, by implication, the whole structure of segregation that it supported. He needed more ammunition than he could get from a refutation based purely on logic. His solution was to broaden the kinds of evidence on which the refutation could be based. He accepted testimony from sociologists and psychologists on the damage segregation did to the self-esteem of young black children in the South and used it to show that, in fact, separate schooling could never be equal. In effect, since the doctrine he wanted to refute was immovable if taken on its own terms, he succeeded in refuting it by changing the terms of the debate.

Finally, in "Letter from Birmingham Jail," Martin Luther King, Jr. used a broad base of evidence to refute the criticism of black clergy who were frightened by civil rights activism. His evidence was of a very different kind from Justice Warren's; as a minister arguing with other ministers, he used biblical analogies, theological references, and philosophical teachings, as well as the Declaration of Independence and the Constitution, contemporary history, and his own forceful presentation. But his problem was similar: how to refute a theory of political nonintervention that masks a deep-seated reluctance to change.

The Language of Persuasion

Reading and writing arguments entail an understanding of the role of language in persuasion. The words we read or write, the ways in which we, or the writers we read, put those words into phrases, clauses, and sentences, contribute to the persuasive power of an argument in ways both apparent and hidden. Through language, the writer conveys voice, tone, and stance. Logical structures, clear connections between points, parallelism, balance, coordination and subordination, active verbs, and concrete nouns all work to produce persuasive arguments. Through language, appeals to ethos engage beliefs and values and invoke credibility and authority; through language, appeals to logos engage the mind, and appeals to pathos engage the heart and emotions.

Analyzing Persuasive Language in Arguments   To understand how we persuade through language—for example, in Chapter 8, the ways we create an "other," or enemy—we need to understand the ways in which language can evoke associations and emotional responses, the ways in which language unites the rhetor, or communicator, and audience to make meaning. Studying the persuasive texts of this chapter and other readings in this book can help you sharpen your ability to analyze persuasive language.

Style, or language and structure, reflects a rhetor's purpose in communicating and the rhetor's relationship with the audience. Through their language and the structure of their persuasive messages, combined with careful attention to the targeted audience, the authors in Chapter 8 argue about war and develop images of us versus them, the good versus the evil. Thomas Paine wanted to sound an alarm and move people to action, and his lively, barn-burning style supported this end. Abraham Lincoln, in "The Gettysburg Address," strove not to divide a people or to evoke feelings of animosity, but to unify North and South, and "take increased devotion to that cause." Lincoln linked the themes of life and death, of endings and beginnings. His language is somber and appropriate to the event, and his syntax utilizes balance and antithesis to reflect the division and unity of his rhetorical situation.

Mark Twain's "The War Prayer" relies on an ironic stance, in which the words convey meaning other than their ostensible, literal meaning, while Franklin D. Roosevelt's "Pearl Harbor Address" relies on forceful, clear, but highly connotative diction ("dastardly," "treachery") that is reinforced by the repetition and parallelism of the sentence structure.

A different kind of persuasive "language" is that of visual images. That "language" offers students the opportunity to examine the truism "a picture is worth a thousand words," and to compare the currencies of words and images in analyzing effective strategies of persuasion. Images for this exercise include posters, advertising, and photographs as well as argumentative texts and the narrative of Vietnam nurse Jacqueline Navarra Rhoads. For example, the advertisement *"We Smash 'Em HARD"* is obvious on some levels—in attacking the evil "Huns"—and subtle on others—in its suggestions about manliness and virility. In contemporary cultures, words and images frequently keep company in persuasive texts; examining both types of persuasion, singly and in tandem, can sharpen skills in looking critically at persuasion in print, video, and audio media.

Persuasion in Diverse Genres

There are any number of genres in which a writer or artist can be persuasive; some of them are obviously argumentative, like a pro-and-con debate, a legal case, or a series of political cartoons; some of them less obviously so, like fiction, poetry, or film. But all of them can be enormously successful at conveying a point of view and swaying an audience. In this book we include a variety of genres with strong persuasive elements. The brief explanations that follow are designed to help you read these materials, regardless of medium, for ideas, themes, and argumentative and persuasive content, as well as for the pleasure of encountering American writers and artists on their home ground.

Essays

Essays are generally reflective, expository, or argumentative. The reflective essay was invented by the Renaissance writer Michel de Montaigne. He used it as a way of getting to know himself better. Informal, ironic, funny, full of anecdotes and charm, Montaigne's essays started as quotations on which he made comments and ended as an exploration of his psychological makeup and view of the world. He tested out his thoughts, pains, prejudices, and pleasures against the measure of his own intelligence. Great reflective essays demand a high level of honesty from the writer, but they also provide a kind of immediacy and intimacy, a one-on-one exchange between reader and writer that is very satisfying. The essay persuades through a form of verbal seduction— by enabling the reader to look with the writer's eyes and the writer's own viewpoint. Reflective essays also present the personality of the writer distinctively; when you get to know a great essayist, invariably you will recognize his or her voice.

In an expository essay, the writer gives information in order to explain a point of view on a topic. This kind of essay presents you, as the writer, with an opportunity to work out your ideas in a broad context— on the environment, for example, or privacy, or relations between men and women. Your research, reflections, and interpretations all contribute to the assertions you make and how you make them, but the goal of an expository essay is to express or explain your ideas clearly and to persuade the reader to accept the merit of your thesis or main point, rather than to change the reader's opinion or behavior.

An argumentative essay argues a point of view or presupposes an opposing point of view, and it is geared directly to anticipating and refuting that point of view. Like the expository essay, it clearly puts ideas in the public arena, but with the goal of stimulating debate, eliciting criticism, or persuading readers to change the way they think or what they do or to persuade them to take action in a particular direction. The best argumentative essays, however, are not divorced from the writer; they engage readers most thoroughly when the author is passionate about the subject matter.

Occasionally an author is able to write an essay that is simultaneously reflective and expository or argumentative, for example, the excerpt from Thoreau's *Civil Disobedience* in Chapter 7. Thoreau tells us about himself—his political beliefs, how he expresses them, why he believes civil disobedience to unjust laws is the most accurate expression of his individuality and personality. He is so eloquent on the importance of the lone conscience in a democracy, the trouble with Congress, and the moral obligation to stand up and be counted at any cost that his personal creed also becomes a persuasive argument for nonviolent resistance as a general political tool. Few essayists can manage to combine both forms of the essay in one, but Thoreau will give you some idea of how many forms of self-expression and powerful persuasion a good essay can present.

Fiction and Poetry

Students don't usually think of fiction or poetry as persuasive writing because the arguments they make are more subtly stated, enveloped in character and language and plot. They are *about* someone or something. In fact, a great story or poem can move people profoundly and change their ideas, or enlighten them, in ways that more direct forms of address cannot. For example, Ralph Ellison's *Invisible Man* is a novel about an African American man who finds himself both literally and figuratively invisible in white America. Nowhere in the text does Ellison deliver a lecture on prejudice, or the corrupting influence of racism, or the tragic denial of ordinary freedoms. (See Chapter 3 for the Prologue of this novel.) But his characters, the voice of the narrator, and the story are so lucid and so affecting that the theme argues more profoundly than any explicit statement could.

Poetry is characterized by a kind of compression that makes its point through concentrated images and language. In her poem "Dear John Wayne," Louise Erdrich makes a forceful argument against the treatment Native Americans have received in the media, in popular culture, and in the way other Americans perceive them (see Chapter 9). Rather than assemble statistics about life on the reservation, she sets out an illustration whose point is vividly clear: the experience of Indian teenagers at a drive-in movie, watching John Wayne, the all-American hero, shoot apparently endless numbers of their ancestors in a movie battle. The oversimplification of the movie's portrait of good guys and bad guys, combined with the ordinariness of watching a movie at a drive-in, urge us to rethink our perspective and reevaluate our ideas—the goal of every well-written argument.

Legal Cases

Legal cases are a good way to clarify the elements of persuasive argument because that's exactly what they are about: two opponents in a court of law, arguing against each other in order to persuade a judge or jury to decide in their favor, knowing that only one side can win, and using every psychological and intellectual strategy they can think of to get the decision to go their way.

Trials are adversarial by definition; there have to be two sides and a neutral third party—a judge or a jury guided by a judge. Once the verdict has been reached, based on the evidence—once the third party has been persuaded by one side or the other—the trial is over. If the losing side is dissatisfied with the verdict, it can write an appeal, a piece of purely persuasive writing that goes to a panel of judges who then decide if they want to overrule the trial court decision or have the case tried again.

The U.S. Supreme Court is the court of last resort for appeals, but certain threshold conditions must be met for an appeal to be submitted to it; for example, the Court can decide to rule on a case involving the interpretation or application of the Constitution of the United States to a particular situation. Two of the cases in this book are Supreme Court cases. As you read the decisions the Court made in *Plessy* v. *Ferguson* and *Brown* v. *Board of Education,* keep four points in mind.

First, the Court often relies on the accumulated body of law already decided in related cases—called *precedent*—to explain why it is not overturning the verdict in the case before it. Occasionally—and *Brown* is the most famous example in American law—the Court rejects all precedent and makes a new law or takes the law, and the country, in a new direction.

Second, every year the Court receives many requests to hear cases on appeal and accepts only a fraction—usually those involving issues of substantial national importance. When it refuses a case, whatever the previous state or federal court decided remains unchanged.

Third, once the Supreme Court makes a decision, it is the law, until or unless Congress passes a different one. There is no higher court of appeal. It is a remarkable feature of our political life that Americans accept the Court's authority, though many of them may disagree with individual decisions.

Finally, Supreme Court decisions are rarely unanimous. With nine justices, the vote on a given case can be anything from 9-to-0 to 5-to-4. When you turn to *Plessy,* you will first read the majority decision, which prevailed. Then you will see Justice John Harlan's minority dissent—an opinion written by a justice who disagrees with the majority or is not persuaded by its reasoning and wants to set the reasons down clearly. *Brown,* in contrast, was decided unanimously.

Sometimes a dissenting opinion in one case forms the basis for a majority decision in another case years later. That is what happened between the *Plessy* decision and the *Brown* case almost fifty years afterward; Justice Harlan's argument against racial segregation was rejected in his lifetime, but in 1954 the Supreme Court found his language persuasive and used it in reversing the *Plessy* decision.

Images and Pictures

Every chapter in this book contains images or pictures—paintings, advertisements, posters, cartoons, or etchings. Images are persuasive. Advertisements, for example, convince us to buy certain food, drink, or clothing or to cultivate a certain appearance; movie and television images attract us by creating heroes, reinforcing our ideas, or catering to our fantasies and our need to escape. Posters and cartoons communicate social and political ideas to vast audiences.

Your experience as a viewer will serve you well in analyzing how the persuasiveness of images works, even when the images are previously unfamiliar to you. For example, you've seen automobile advertisements all your life; you don't have to have lived in the 1950s to get the point of an advertisement for a 1958 car complete with enormous fins and a huge front grill. And when you see an eighteenth-century etching showing a woman confined within the outlines of a compass, you will probably have little difficulty in figuring out that it illustrates the limits of what women were allowed to do. Although pictures from different times are directed to different audiences and your own reaction to those from the past may be different from those of the original viewers, keep in mind that the skill involved in "reading" images is one you practice every time you look at the advertisements in a magazine, a television show, or a movie.

Following is a brief rundown of some of the varieties of visual images in this book, as well as some strategies for analyzing and enjoying them.

Photographs, Paintings, and Cartoons Photographs punctuate news coverage. Whether still photos in a newspaper or "live-action video" on a television news program, photographs bring the story to life and capture the event in ways that complement the textual material and sometimes supplant it entirely. They appear to be objective records, yet the photographer "edits" by choosing to leave certain things out of the picture. Photographs are taken from a certain perspective, from a specific point of view; they record, but they also select; they capture the event, but at the same time they leave out part of the picture, often the larger context. Photos taken to report the news can move viewers to change their point of view and, in some cases, to change policy; the Pulitzer Prize–winning photographs in Chapter 8 are examples of the persuasive power of photography.

Perhaps it is less common to think of paintings, like fiction or poetry, as persuasive, even when they capture specific events or appear to be recording a simple moment in time. Students don't often think of paintings as being persuasive. Alfred Bierstadt's *Giant Redwood Trees of California* in Chapter 9 may seem to be simply an impressive landscape. But the interpolation of tiny figures—and Native American figures at that—is what articulates the scale of the trees. And at the same time, because the viewers of the painting would typically be white, those Native American figures help to explain what the wilderness used to be like and how it is changing.

Editorial cartoons make no pretense of objectivity. Often visual images with brief text, they must capture attention and make a point in only a second or two. Benjamin Franklin's woodcut and the *U.S. Hotel* cartoon, both in Chapter 3, and most of the editorial cartoons in contemporary newspapers tap into cultural references common to rhetor and audience as a kind of shorthand for longer arguments. In a sense, they are visual enthymemes, since the audience supplies the missing links in the argument in order to get the point.

Broadsides and Posters   Broadsides and posters are records of events and issues of their times. A broadside, a single sheet printed on one side and meant to be circulated publicly, can inform people about current events, argue a point, comment on an issue, or entertain with humorous verse. For example, in the eighteenth century, the hangings of convicted criminals were carried out in public and attracted large audiences. These events were frequently accompanied by broadsides with melodramatic or lurid descriptions of the crime and were sold at the scene of the execution. Their tone was not altogether dissimilar from that of some of the tabloid newspapers that are so successful today.

Posters developed out of nineteenth-century technology and the need to communicate with a larger audience. They advertised performances and goods, appealed for labor and military recruits, and in time of war and national distress sought to maintain morale and denounce the enemy. Posters were a dominant communication device from the late nineteenth century until the rise of newsreel, radio, and later television. They were still useful, as a quickly and cheaply produced mass medium, but their impact declined as the other media appeared. For posters to persuade (and that was generally their purpose), they had to be able to attract attention and to inform. The audience generally would have been passers-by, so, rather like political cartoons, they had to make their point quickly. Effective posters generally convey a strong impression in a matter of seconds, and a single strong element and strategic use of color, such as a single bold color accent on a muted background, can draw the eye to the core issue or theme immediately. Other elements can be more subtle; in one poster in the Hoover Archives collection, for example, a German poster stressing soldiers' efforts to save women and children of the fatherland includes a small cross hanging around a woman's neck, tapping into the "Christian" identity of the woman and, presumably, her soldier-savior.

In evaluating posters as persuasive discourse, we look to some of the same criteria we use in judging other works of art. While we can't always know the artist's personal beliefs or the extent to which the poster represents mass opinion, we can examine the rhetorical strategies employed by the artist and the themes implicit in the poster. We can assume that the posters were meant to inform or persuade and that the appeals employed by the artist were designed to evoke audience response. We can then make inferences about the intended audience, remembering that we are generalizing from the data the posters provide. We can look to color, placement of objects in the poster, designs, motifs, and themes to analyze their effectiveness.

Advertisements   Like posters, advertisements reveal much about the cultures in which they appear, or at least the dominant culture of the society. Often shortchanging logic in favor of associations and emotional appeals, ads can appear in print or on video, radio, or film; they can be made up of text or image or both; and their arguments can be expected and explicit or unexpected and implicit. Purveyors of products go to great effort to have their products featured in films. Ads have also moved to a more explicit form in home videos. And an enormous battle has been waged as schools and school boards have debated whether to accept offers of free television equipment in exchange for including a certain amount of advertising in the television "curriculum." Even a historically advertising-free medium, public television, is offering longer and longer "thanks" to corporate sponsors of its programs.

As in writing about art, posters, and texts, writing about advertisements entails evaluating purpose, appeals, and aesthetics. The purpose is generally evident: the purchase of a product. Much fruitful analysis of advertising focuses on the assumptions, the flaws in logic, and the ethos, pathos, and logos appeals in the ads. Many of the points made earlier about these appeals pertain to advertising. Logical fallacies are rampant. Emotional appeals are often evident but are also often hidden beneath ostensibly logical claims. For example, an advertisement for soup might claim that soups will warm a child up before she runs outside on a cold day; such an ad relies on emotional appeals (warmth, nurturing, home and hearth) more than physiological fact.

Critically assessing the layout, color, and image of advertisements can yield rich information about its persuasive tactics. Often products are strategically placed on the page, or near certain parts of the anatomy of a model; other times, a product (lipstick, beverage) is deliberately presented in a sexually suggestive position. Sometimes the advertiser wants part of the ad to recede into the background. For example, look at some magazine advertisements for cigarettes and try to find the surgeon general's warning. A good way to see where the eye falls in magazine ads is to flip through a magazine and notice which part of the page you see first; then assess what key feature of the product is made prominent and which pushed to the side.

The language of advertising is highly connotative, associative, and image-laden; writers have to convey maximum impact in the fewest words possible. Student writers could indeed learn a lot about conciseness by examining well-written advertisements. The structure of textual arguments in advertising, though, is something to avoid in academic arguments; it is commonly designed to shortchange logic and to get consumers to draw a particular inference (they should buy a certain product) from the limited "data" presented.

There is no getting away from advertising in mainstream American culture. There are different ways of approaching the issue—from economic, sociological, psychological, political, and aesthetic pespectives, to name a few. You may wish to investigate some of these perspectives as you develop longer, documented essays for college courses. Professor Jean Kilbourne, for example, examines damaging attitudes toward and treatment of women in advertisements in the lecture/film *Still Killing Us Softly* that may be available through your college library. For the purposes of this text, we focus on the rhetorical strategies used to persuade audiences.

Films

We have included a film selection in each chapter. Film critic Robin Wood says that movies express not only the dreams of the people who make them but the dreams of the audience watching them. No other art form is more wholly or characteristically American. Hollywood became known long ago as the "Dream Factory," and there is no aspect of American life that is not refracted sooner or later through the lens of a camera. Sometimes the result is realistic; sometimes it is more an expression of wish fulfillment or escapism. Sometimes it is insulting; minorities watched movies for generations, looking for images of themselves and seeing nothing or seeing themselves portrayed in stereotypical or debased characterizations. But it would be impossible to imagine American culture in the twentieth century without movies. And every theme in this book has provided and continues to provide material for the vast film audience. Movies are so embedded in our lives that many of the most profound notions Americans have about themselves are as much a result of what they see on the screen as of what they read or learn from experience.

We can look for common themes shared by the posters, political cartoons, films, fiction, essays, and arguments to find the common denominators in the way different media treat particular themes. You can pursue research by looking up particular themes or issues (women in the workforce, support on the home front, vilification of the enemy) that interest you and then analyzing treatment of them in the different media. Maybe your library has access to back issues of *Life* magazine, for example. One student researched issues of *Time* magazine from the 1940s, found an article entitled "How to Tell Your Friends from the Japs," and was able to trace racial stereotypes from posters and cartoons as well as the popular general interest magazines of the times. Other sources for this kind of research include Sam Keen's book *Faces of the Enemy* and the film of the same name, a thoughtful look at the ways in which we create an enemy through various media, including posters and cartoons. Another excellent source for propaganda and war-era posters is *Persuasive Images,* by Peter Paret et al.

Critical Reading and Persuasive Writing

We hope that these suggestions for analyzing persuasive strategies, audiences, cultures, and genres will help you to learn to read diverse arguments critically and to become better thinkers, learners, and writers. While this chapter focuses on critical and analytical skills for reading arguments, Chapter 2 offers suggestions for developing written essays and for integrating research into your arguments. In order to integrate critical reading and persuasive writing, the chapters in Part II, "Argument in the American Tradition," combine critical readings with suggestions for analytical and persuasive writing. Each chapter develops a core thematic issue and links that issue to important aspects of argumentation through an introduction, diverse persuasive materials, an end-of-chapter discussion, and assignments that develop your ability to construct your own effective arguments. We hope that the arguments you find included in this book, as well as the suggestions for good writing, will stimulate your imagination, your critical thinking, and your understanding of persuasion in what you read and what you write. Debate in American culture rages on, and we hope you will jump in and become part of our ongoing discussion and debate—part of the American tradition.

2

∞

Writing and Research

Developing Essays

Writing an essay is a recursive process: you start with an idea or something you've wondered about, or you get an idea, maybe from reading or discussion. You read, review, discuss, perhaps take notes—and in the process integrate what you are learning with what you already know. Writing is a way of learning; we write to elicit what we already know and to develop and clarify thoughts and ideas. Writing essays and other prose forces us to develop, organize, and transmit clearly our ideas, evidence, and interpretations. Writing is also a way to record information and demonstrate knowledge. It remains the primary means of disseminating knowledge and information in the academic world, and despite the pervasiveness of visual and audio media, it remains a crucial means of communication in the rest of society as well.

There are several different kinds of persuasive writing: reports, exposition, and argumentation. The writing situation—the audience, purpose, and subject—dictates the form that is needed. This book focuses on argumentation, but we suggest considering persuasion in communication not as a discrete, separate genre but as a continuum with varying degrees of argumentative edge.

Along the continuum of persuasion in written discourse, *reports* tend to be the least overtly persuasive. A report writer presents information accurately in a relatively unbiased manner; indeed, the writer's thoroughness and accuracy may in themselves be persuasive of a certain conclusion, but the report itself does not necessarily suggest that conclusion. A lab report is an example of the kind of report writing commonly used in college. In business, people other than the report writer often make decisions based on the report, although some reports also include recommendations.

An *expository essay* is more persuasive; it asserts a point of view and is persuasive insofar as the writer wants to convince readers of the merits of his or her case. The expository or analytical essays most college students write often work in conjunction with other texts and materials; that is, the writer is responding to a text, an idea, a concept, or a situation. Such essays often entail developing a point of view or an assertion about a subject and then supporting that point of view with evidence from personal observation, a literary text, or a prominent theory in the field. Essays analyzing a literary work or a historical event are good examples of the kinds of expository writing commonly practiced in college courses.

An *argumentative essay* clearly attempts to persuade its readers to identify with the writer, to change their minds, to change their behavior, to adopt or abandon a policy or course of action. The argument rests on assumptions, reasoning, and assertions that one infers or derives from the evidence.

All three kinds of essays can integrate research. We suggest that you consider research a process you undertake whenever the response to a question or the testing of a hypothesis requires that you look beyond your own knowledge and experience for supporting evidence. John Wu, for example, whose essay "Making and Unmaking the 'Model Minority'" appears in Chapter 5, could have written a piece based solely on his own experience. It might have persuaded the reader of the truth of Wu's experience but wouldn't necessarily suggest that it is pervasive in American society. Instead, drawing from outside experts and evidence, Wu presents a far more convincing case. In the sections that follow, we first discuss developing essays that may not require outside research and then outline suggestions for integrating research.

Techniques for Developing Essays

All forms of writing involve a process of prewriting, writing, and revising. During this process, it may be helpful to use some of the following prompts and questions to help you think about, focus, structure, and develop your paper.

1. *Freewrite.* Start with a focused freewrite, that is, writing without attention to grammar, style, or spelling. Keep pen to page, or fingers to keyboard, and write for five or ten minutes to get started. Do you have some general topic area to think about? Jot down everything you can think of about your topic. Then review your notes and try again with a more focused view of some aspect of the topic that came up in the freewrite. If you don't have an assignment or a specific topic in mind, freewriting can help you figure out what you might find interesting to write about.

2. *Brainstorm.* Write down ideas, images, possible directions—anything that comes to mind about your potential topic—in a list down the page, rather than in the continuous flow of the freewrite. Review your list and try again, focusing on something interesting that came up in the brainstorming.

3. *Do invisible writing.* If you have access to a computer, this exercise may be useful. Turn off the monitor or screen brightness and write continuously without viewing what you are writing. This technique is useful for people who tend to get writer's block or censor their writing and ideas even before they can get the words out.

4. *Review what you have written.* Do you see possibilities to focus on? Do you see connections or angles you didn't think of before? If so, select one of the exercises above—freewriting, brainstorming, or invisible writing—that seemed the most productive for you, and do another session of writing on the focused area you discovered in the exercises. Review the topic and see if it looks promising for further development.

5. *Consider your own biases.* After you have developed a tentative focus, the next couple of exercises may be useful. First, write out all of your biases or preconceived notions about the topic. This is particularly important if you are developing an argumentative researched essay. It is crucial that you conduct your research in an open-minded manner, one that enables you to seek out material and data on both sides of the question. An argument implies an opposition, so take care to look at both sides in your research as well as in your structuring of your argument.

6. *Construct a dialogue between the two sides.* Personify each side of the argument and have the two sides debate the issue. That is, assign a position or a personality to each side, and let them argue for a while, with you writing the script.

7. *Refine your topic and focus.* In a sentence, try to write what the focus and approach of your paper will be. If you can't write it now, at least narrow your topic to something that seems manageable for the length and depth of the paper assigned.

8. *Try the journalistic method.* After generating some material about your topic, it might be useful to adopt a systematic approach based on the journalistic method, which asks and responds to the following questions: what, who, when, where, why, and how.

- *What* is happening, or what has happened, in terms of your topic?
- *Who* (or perhaps *what*) was or is involved in your topic? Who or what does something, or to whom or to what does something happen?
- *When* did it happen?
- *Where* did it happen? What is the background of the situation?
- *Why* did it happen? Why did the agent (*who*) cause it to happen? What are the implications of this purpose?
- *How* was the action or event brought about? What were the means, methods, resources involved?

9. *Break your topic into parts.* After generating yet more information, through prewriting and through research and note taking, think about how you might break down or analyze the parts of your topic. Draft out the major divisions or aspects of your topic on paper or on screen. Don't worry about the form of the outline; just get the major divisions on paper so you can see where your project is going and so that you have a sense of the magnitude and direction of the topic at this stage.

10. *Go back to the question of focus.* Have you determined a tentative, working thesis statement? If not, review your notes, your preliminary thoughts and ideas, and the materials you have developed. Try to understand where they are taking you. What connections can you make? What inferences can you make from your findings? Draft several thesis statements; one or two probably will come close to representing the direction in which your research is taking you. Also, review the guidelines in item 14 on thesis statement.

11. *Consider coherence.* Having listed the major divisions of your subject area, consider whether all of the parts you have set forth still belong in your paper. Are all parts closely related to the key question of your preliminary focus? If not, will you adapt your thesis or throw out the irrelevant material?

12. *Review your main topic divisions.* Does an order suggest itself? Does there seem to be a best way to present your points to the reader?

13. *Pay attention to contradictions and opposing views.* At what point do they suggest themselves? If you are writing a persuasive essay, opposing views may come up at any time in the process; if they don't come to mind, you'll need to seek them out. Ask yourself questions. Why isn't what I propose already in place? Why wouldn't people want what I am advocating? If you don't consider and deal with opposing views, the reader will certainly be thinking of them, and you will undercut your credibility if you don't concede to or refute opposing arguments.

14. *Focus your thesis statement.* Try to write a more focused thesis statement to state the argument or point you want to make (review notes on thesis statements in the introduction).

15. *Write out a plan.* If at this point you see the overall pattern of your paper emerging, take the time now to write a prospectus—a plan that summarizes the purpose, organization, and main points of your paper. If you are not yet ready to do so, answer some of the following questions:

- Why is the subject important to you or to potential readers? Why have you chosen to write about it, and what do you plan to transmit to others?

- How much additional reading will you need to do, and where will you go to find the information you need?

- How much background information do your readers need to understand the significance of your topic or the issues involved?
- What points will you be making about your topic, and what kinds of evidence will you include?

16. *Consider methods and sources of research.* For researched essays, review the rest of the chapter for advice about taking notes, integrating sources, and documenting sources.

Using Assumptions in Arguments

Your own argumentation will likely involve one of the noted strategies: relying on assumptions to make your argument and to support your reasoning from the evidence to the conclusion; and challenging assumptions made by others in their arguments. Be careful in relying on assumptions. Your most basic step will be analyzing your audience. If you and they share assumptions, beliefs, and values, your efforts to persuade can focus on establishing that common ground, in the same way that you establish common definitions of terms as the basis for argument. Perhaps you will need to remind the audience of those shared values. In doing so, you will increase your audience's identification with you and encourage them to listen to you and to your argument. As you proceed, gauge when to offer additional support of your view and when to assume that the audience shares your view and needs no further convincing.

In academic writing, you should be alert to appropriate and inappropriate assumptions about knowledge and procedure. If, for example, you are writing a researched essay about string theory or dark matter for your writing course, you should not assume that your instructor has more than a generalist's familiarity with the concepts of physics; nor should you assume that your physics instructor would understand an analogy to the theory of archetypes in literary criticism. Each discipline has its own set of assumptions and beliefs, and familiarizing yourself with those beliefs is part of your training as a scholar.

If you are writing for an audience whose assumptions and values you are unfamiliar with or if you are communicating to an audience with diverse values, you need to spend more time supporting the claims you make, never assuming that your audience agrees with you and always checking to see if you are offering enough evidence and reasons to support your view. For example, if you want to persuade your classmates that money from your residence hall or living group discretionary or social funds should not be used to pay for alcohol for dorm events, you need to figure out what your fellow students' assumptions are. Do they believe that social funds should pay for social events, and that social events for college students must necessarily offer alcoholic beverages? Do they assume that fees collected from everyone should support the drinking habits of some residents, in the manner that everyone pays taxes even if they don't support government policy? Do they assume that laws governing consumption of alcohol by minors should be suspended for college social functions?

When you are writing to refute assumptions, you need to be particularly careful to inform yourself fully about what you are trying to disprove. Why do people hold on to this or that particular belief? What in their experiences might account for their assumptions? How fixed are the assumptions? Are they movable or unmovable? Do you need to do research to arm yourself with data to counter what you believe are frequently held but generally unexamined assumptions?

Usually you will need to be direct when writing to refute assumptions. Lay out your argument within the first couple of paragraphs, including a clear summary of the idea you are trying to disprove and a powerful statement of your own thesis. Support each point you make— *for* your argument, *against* the assumption under discussion—with reasons backed by evidence, logical as well as emotional. Look carefully at your argument and that of your opposition to make sure that no assumptions go unstated. Spell out your own points, and, if necessary, make a list of all the assumptions, both explicitly stated and implicit, in the opposing argument. You probably do not need to present every item on that list in your own argument, but having made it will ensure that you do not overlook important nuances of the structure and substance of the opposing argument.

Using Assertions in Arguments

In college writing as well as in personal writing and writing on the job, you will generally be asserting a position or a point of view. Assertions are derived from some interplay of assumptions and evidence; sometimes you argue a point based on long-standing belief or values; at other times you generalize from observation, experience, or other types of evidence such as statistics or results of surveys. When you argue *inductively,* you are drawing your assertion from the evidence; when you argue *deductively,* you are taking a general principle or belief or assumption (sometimes called a premise) and applying it to a particular situation. In either case, in your writing you will most often introduce your topic, state your general assertion, and then support that assertion with evidence. In other words, you assert your conclusion or finding first, and then present the evidence that led to that conclusion.

Assertions About Facts   Assertions about facts are generally supported by evidence rather than by other types of reasons and assumptions. Assertions about facts, less prominent in many arguments than other types of assertions, state that a thing does or does not exist, that something is or is not true. Since they are supported by factual evidence, factual assertions can generally be proved or disproved by reliable outside sources. A social scientist making claims about the makeup of contemporary U.S. households can find verification (or refutation) in the U.S. census and other demographic sources. Sometimes, however, assertions about facts, particularly in research and scientific arenas, are disputed or revised. A scientist asserting that HIV does not cause AIDS is stating a "fact" that many others currently dispute and will need convincing research data to support such an assertion.

Assertions About Values Sometimes assertions are intended to evaluate or offer a judgment about things, ideas, or people. The painting *American Gothic,* one might assert, is aesthetically pleasing (or appallingly ugly). *Moby-Dick* is a fine piece of literature (or a long, plodding yarn). Richard Nixon was an outstanding president (or an embarrassment). Blue-collar values are admirable (or not), you might argue, based on reading Alfred Lubrano's "Bricklayer's Boy" (Chapter 5). Corporate life is punishing for both men and women, so the workplace itself needs to change. Nevertheless, corporate life ought to be more accessible to women, you might respond.

Value is the core of the term *evaluating,* or measuring the worth of something by comparing it to some predetermined criteria, principles, or ideas about what is good. To argue successfully about the painting, the book, or the president, we need to operate from a set of standards that either we argue for or can agree on with the audience. Frequently, an argument about value will have to set forth criteria, either early on in the essay or as each point is made.

Once you have set forth your criteria, you still have the task of persuading your reader that your judgment is correct; that is, the object in question does or does not meet the criteria set forth. For example, some graffiti in the women's rest room at one college stated, "Fur is murder." The writer's argument contains the assumption about values that killing an animal is the equivalent of willfully killing a human being, an act most of us would call murder. The writer also relies on audience agreement about certain facts: that fur is from animals, that taking the fur requires the death of the animal. The writer, in effect, states that for humans to wear fur is not merely extravagant but morally reprehensible. For some in the audience, her criteria for judging an act to be murder are highly arguable.

Assertions That Propose Action Assertions intended to move people to action, to change a situation, or to argue about policy are often called proposals. One could argue, for example, that corporations should change the way they treat people—or that people should avoid working for corporations. People should or should not work if they don't have to. There should be no minimum wage, and employers should be able to pay workers whatever the market will bear. There should be protection against piecework garment labor. Any such proposal would require a careful consideration of various options: Why hasn't the proposal in question been tried before? What are the objections? What are the pros and cons of each side? How will this particular proposal or plan be different? Audience awareness will guide not only the arguments selected but also the order in which supporting evidence is presented. If multiple projects have been tried and have failed, or if considerable controversy surrounds your idea, you may need to acknowledge the facts or deal with objections up front, before making your proposal. If you believe your proposal will get a fair hearing and that your readers mainly need to hear the specifics of how you will carry out your plan, then you can introduce your proposal and support it with evidence, dealing with any lingering concerns later in the essay. A helpful pattern for writing proposals is to explain the problem, clarify why action is needed, and detail how such action will resolve the issue, dealing with objections to the plan and supporting your proposal with evidence at the most feasible points in the essay for doing so.

A core premise of argumentation is the expression "He who asserts must prove." Whether you are making an assertion about facts, about values, or about a course of action, you need to support your view with evidence, standards by which to judge merit, or specific proposals for action. Any assertion will also need to rely on shared assumptions about acceptable evidence or criteria for judgment. The writing assignments in Chapters 3 through 9 encourage you to practice developing and asserting a point of view and then supporting that view with evidence appropriate to the topic, the assertion being made, and the context of argument.

Using Examples in Arguments

How you select examples is determined by your audience, your purpose, and the medium in which you are working—all of which together form your rhetorical framework. Suppose you want to tell your closest friend about a fight you had with your father. You might say, "My father and I had a disagreement." That might be accurate but is completely uncommunicative and not very interesting. Besides, you want your friend to know exactly how you felt—why you thought you were right and your father wrong—and exactly what you said and what your father said, what you did and what he did. You must give examples. No matter what you are writing about, when you want your audience to know exactly what you mean and to believe you, specific examples are the best and easiest way of helping you to make a direct connection. This is true whether your audience is personally sympathetic and known to you or indifferent or even hostile. It is also true whether your subject is your personal experience, a research topic, or an argument in your dormitory about the house rules.

The following categories give some of the most useful sources of examples.

Personal Experience and Observation   Your first source of examples is you: your own experience, your relationships with your family and friends, your own conflicts, your own education, and your own temperament. If you are writing about yourself, those elements are relevant as examples and will form a natural part of your subject matter. Suppose you are writing a paper on the dreams of people trying to immigrate to America today, and you or your immediate family are first-generation immigrants. You will probably write some general statements about political freedom, or opportunity, or equality. But if you really want to explain dreams of coming to America, you need specific examples, drawn from you and your family's own experience—what you thought your new home would look like, whether the smells and the foods were different, how tired your parents looked, what the furniture in your first American house was like, what frightened you, what you thought about and said. The use of such examples requires that you have the courage to look at yourself honestly, but the attention you pay to accuracy and to details pays off in vivid writing that both pleases and persuades your readers.

Field Research   Your ability to draw examples from your own experience extends to observations of people who are strangers to you and to situations in which you participate by getting information from sources other than yourself. Suppose you are writing a research paper on contemporary immigration, and as part of your research you attend a hearing of the Immigration and Naturalization Service to listen to the testimony of a man asking for asylum because he is afraid of persecution and torture in his home country. You would take notes on the testimony, including quotations from the dialogue and conversation. But you would also pay attention to tones of voice, the body language of the applicant, the temperature in the hearing room, the number of spectators, their manner of dress, and other details.

As an alternative, you might interview a new arrival in this country and ask questions about why the person came, how hard it was, what she misses about home, and so on. In your paper, you would want to draw some conclusions about reasons for coming to America, but you would support them with some of the dialogue between you and your subject. In fact, the formulation of your general statements could be heavily influenced by the observations you have already made in the course of the interview; they may change the direction of your research and the conclusions you draw.

Library Research   Library materials are primarily drawn from the experiences and observations of other people, so in a sense the examples you find through library research are drawn from the work someone else has already done. But it's up to you to determine which elements to choose, how to order and connect them, and what ideas of yours they can support. Evaluating library materials is like considering evidence in a trial; it has to be sifted and weighed, so you can separate out pertinent examples from a much larger body of information.

Suppose that in your research project about immigration you need to learn about the background of the U.S. Immigration and Naturalization Service (INS). You can look in the government documents section for INS regulations; and you can look in a law school library or the local courthouse library for examples of immigration cases. Consult the *Congressional Record* for the legislative history of immigration laws and examples of how attitudes toward immigration policy have changed over the years. In your college library or main city library branch, check the microfiche index for old newspaper articles about immigration that give examples of immigrants' personal experience; read the first-person accounts of recent immigrants or the autobiographies of earlier ones; find old photographs and read diaries that immigrants or their families kept; and use newspapers, magazines, and movies to see how different ethnic groups are portrayed in the time period you are researching.

Sometimes students early in their college writing careers have an unfortunate tendency to think that if they use big words and grandiose sentences and, especially, if they make broad and inclusive generalizations about enormous subjects, the results will sound more impressive. Actually, the opposite is true. If you write about a subject you know well because it is close to you, or if you write about an unfamiliar area you have gotten to know because you researched it, and you support either subject with specific and honest examples, you will produce something of quality.

There is no formula to follow here. Whatever examples you choose will emerge from your subject, your ideas, your experience, and your willingness to stay aware of what you want your audience to take away. The more you learn to be observant and the more energy you are willing to invest in looking for examples, the better your writing will be. Good, specific examples prove that you can express yourself in understandable terms, that your writing has substance, that you have evaluated the evidence, and that you respect the intelligence of your audience.

Using Definitions in Arguments

When writing your own arguments, be careful to provide clear, effective definitions whenever they are needed. To decide whether a definition is needed, consider whether your readers are likely to know the term and whether they will be confused or misled if a definition is not provided.

Following are some common strategies used for defining terms.

When you need to define terms only as the basis for an argument, one or two of these strategies should do. When you are arguing for the definition of a complex or abstract term—and when that term is controversial—you may find it useful to combine several strategies to persuade your reader that your definition and interpretation of the term are appropriate.

Essential Definition   An essential definition assigns the thing defined to a general class and then identifies the characteristics that distinguish it from every other member of this class: "An American is a person born in America." In this definition, the term defined is "an American," the general class is "person," and the distinguishing characteristic is "born in America." A person born in France would not be an American by this definition. A good essential definition is like a mathematical formula with the verb *is* acting as an equals sign; you should be able to turn it around and still have a true, logical statement: "A person born in America is an American."

Dictionary definitions are often essential definitions, and a good dictionary, such as *Webster's Third New International Dictionary* or the *Oxford English Dictionary*, may provide you with precisely the definition you need. Sometimes definitions from specialized dictionaries—a dictionary of music or philosophy, for example—will help you use and define particular technical terms. Using a dictionary definition is most useful when your readers are likely to agree with your definition or will accept the authority of the source.

Definition by Comparison   Comparison is a useful way to define a term, if you can relate it to something with which the reader is already familiar. Some comparisons are explicit and literal. Luther Standing Bear, for example, defines elements of his American Indian culture by comparing and contrasting it with the dominant European American culture. Explicit comparisons are most useful when you expect readers to agree with your definition. If you think readers will disagree, you will be forced to provide enough evidence to support the validity of the comparison, which will distract you from the points you wanted to draw from the comparison.

Other comparisons used as definitions are implicit, often communicated through metaphors. For example, Ralph Ellison uses the metaphor of invisibility to define the experience of being a black American: being a black person in America is like being invisible (see Chapter 3). Implicit comparisons are useful when the reader is likely to be familiar with the concept or image you select for your metaphor and when other means of definition seem inadequate; it would be difficult for Ellison to convey literally the day-in and day-out inequities of being black in mid–twentieth-century America without inducing guilt or alienation on the part of his white readers. Metaphors and other implied comparisons allow you to present a potentially objectionable or problematic definition subtly and gradually; you must eventually provide evidence that the definition is a sound one, but readers will probably grant you more leeway.

Definition by Example Examples are often used to define abstract or complex terms. When Arturo Islas sought to define the nature of his ambivalence about his Mexican American heritage, he used a series of anecdotes from his personal life. When Alexis de Tocqueville wanted to define the American character, he used examples drawn from legal and political history. (See Chapter 3 for these selections.). Narratives and other examples can be effective in clarifying and explaining a complex term, but be sure that your readers will accept the examples you select. If they view the examples as atypical, irrelevant, or simply unclear, your definition will not be successful.

Stipulative Definition A stipulative definition differentiates a specialized or temporary use of a term from its conventional or common usage. For example, the term *racism* is defined in the dictionary as the belief that race is the primary determinant of human traits and capacities. Many people, however, believe that the term cannot be applied to nonwhites because racism can be perpetuated only by those in power, and in America nonwhites lack the power to enforce racism institutionally. Such a writer would need to clarify that, in his or her writing *racism* is the term that will apply to biased white people and *prejudiced* is the term that will apply to biased nonwhite people. A stipulative definition can help ensure that you and your reader understand each other when you use a term likely to have more than one meaning.

Negative Definition Most definitions are stated in positive terms: "*x* is *y*." However, sometimes the most effective way to convey what something *is* is to define what it *is not*. The cartoonist who created *The U.S. Hotel* defined good Americans by identifying the traits they should *not* have: a penchant for bomb throwing, incendiarism, communism, and so on.

Often a negative definition can be used in conjunction with a positive definition, as when President Kennedy declared that his election was "not a victory of party but a celebration of freedom." Martha Serrano used this strategy as well when she first established that she is not a Hispanic, not a Latina, and not a Mexican American; she is a Chicana. Such an approach is helpful when the reader is likely to have preconceived definitions of a term in mind and the writer needs to deal with those misconceptions before moving on to state what the term *does* mean. (See Chapter 3 for these selections.)

Using Persuasive Language in Arguments

First, let us look at the basic unit of language: words. Words can be connotative as well as denotative. *Denotation* refers to the explicit, "dictionary" meaning of a word. *Connotation* refers to the associations or evocations of a word or expression. Compare *house* and *home,* for example. Which word would you select if you were a real estate agent? Which word conveys more positive associations to a reader or potential buyer? In the sentences below, what connotations do the different versions of the same event convey?

The besieged governor, looking exhausted yet thoughtful, rode away in a government vehicle.

The indicted politician, unshaven and frowning, sped away in his taxpayer-supported limousine.

As a writer, you need to pay attention to your word choice and to your readers' associations with and reactions to words. Not only the adjectives and adverbs but also the nouns and verbs you choose will convey your stance, position, and biases toward the subject. In the above sentences, for example, *politician, sped,* and *limousine* are a noun, a verb, and a noun, respectively, but they convey quite different associations from the words they replaced.

Another element of style that serves argumentative goals is syntax, or sentence structure. The syntax used can reinforce and underscore the themes and associations you are trying to convey. When you use parallel structure, or grammatically equivalent elements in a sentence, you are drawing parallels between the ideas represented in that parallel form, as Abraham Lincoln does in his parallel prepositional phrases: "government *of* the people, *by* the people, *for* the people." When you set up an antithesis, or state what something is not and then what it is, you are drawing a sharp contrast, as Thomas Paine does when he writes, "I call not upon a few but upon all." When you craft coordinate phrases or clauses (A *or* B, C *and* D, E *yet* F, *neither* G *nor* H), you suggest equivalence; when you use subordinate or dependent phrases and clauses, you also suggest a relationship between parts in the sentence.

Political speeches often rely heavily on parallelism because speech, except on recorded media such as video, cannot be reread, reviewed, underlined, or annotated in the way written texts can. Parallelism and coordination, combined with transitional words and phrases such as *first, second, next,* and the like, help the audiences keep track of points and help the speaker keep the audience tuned into his or her argument. Such strategies also underscore and stress points that the speaker wants to drive home. Franklin Delano Roosevelt, for example, uses a repeated parallel structure—or series—to outline the extent of the Japanese attack on Pearl Harbor and to reinforce the premeditated nature of the attack—a significant point in Roosevelt's argument:

Last night, Japanese forces attacked Hong Kong. Last night, Japanese forces attacked Guam. Last night, Japanese forces attacked the Philippine Islands. Last night, Japanese forces attacked Wake Island.

Subordinate, or dependent, clauses can deemphasize certain points that must be included but that the speaker wants to move to the background. For example, Roosevelt says,

> No matter how long it may take us to overcome this premeditated invasion, the American people in their righteous might will win through to absolute victory.

Subordinating "No matter how long it may take" effectively sets up the statement as an assumption or foregone conclusion. A rallying cry such as this one must acknowledge the effort war will involve, but the smart rhetor will, as does Roosevelt, emphasize the positive—"American people," "righteous might," "absolute victory." (See Chapter 8 for the selections cited in this section.)

In persuasion, language is an important means of inducing cooperation, identification, and agreement. But where is the line between reader awareness and audience manipulation? How do you persuade your reader to see things from your point of view, to identify with your concerns and interests? Does presenting your own evidence in a positive light constitute unethical conduct? Does delaying the bad news in a letter until the second paragraph indicate a lack of fairness? How do we determine when something is argument and when it is propaganda?

As you review your writing, consider some of the following questions: Are you using emotionally charged words to evoke a sentiment you don't want to elicit outright? Are you appealing to hatred, bigotry, or stereotypes? Are you substituting loaded terms for evidence and logical reasoning? Are you being deliberately ambiguous or euphemistic to hide your true purposes? Are you dishonestly selecting the material you include as evidence and misrepresenting the evidence or the position of someone you are quoting? Are you arguing to pursue truth or to obscure it? Your own ethics, your values and beliefs, will need to guide you as you develop your ability to persuade with evidence, with sound reasoning, and with language that fairly represents both your position and that of opposing views.

Your academic essays will need to attend to language as well. You may, in certain disciplines, need to use language that deemphasizes the writer and reports results or events in as neutral a language and tone as possible. But in striving for passive voice, writing that emphasizes the action and not the actor, take care that you don't end up with convoluted prose that links up series of prepositional phrases and abstract nouns. The efficient, precise use of language in a comprehensible style is appreciated by nearly any audience, but certainly by your instructors. Much of your college writing, though, and certainly argumentative writing, not only allows for, but calls for a point of view, a sense of a real person behind the prose with beliefs, values, opinions, intellect. You will generally be expected to convey a point of view, whether it is your interpretation of a literary text or your assessment of recent elections in Mexico and the economic ramifications for the United States.

Using Refutation in Arguments

Since argument occurs because more than one point of view exists and since refutation takes place in response to a previously articulated difference of opinion, most of the essays you have written and perhaps most of the informal conversations you have had with your peers have elements of one, or the other, or both. But crafting a successful refutation in an argument about principles is especially challenging and requires a combination of discipline and creativity. The following strategies will help you formulate your refutation.

1. *Familiarize yourself with the ideas of the opposing side, concentrating on its strongest argumentative elements.* The natural tendency is to state your own position and ignore anyone else's, but recognizing and respecting the strengths of your opponent's ideas is the best basis for successful refutation. This can be a difficult strategy to practice if your opponent's views are so unpleasant or so infuriating that you would rather not make a detailed study of them. But it is when you have the strongest emotional reaction to another viewpoint that you have to pay the most attention to it. Frederick Douglass must have found it difficult, as a former slave, to have to refute pro-slavery propositions one at a time when the immorality of slavery was so obvious to him. And Susan B. Anthony was frustrated at having to review ad infinitum all the arguments against women's capabilities (see Chapter 7). But even if the point of view you are opposing seems easy to criticize, you still need to identify what its difficulties are, and, unless you have a photographic memory, take notes.

2. *Know what you believe and what principles you are supporting.* This strategy may seem obvious, but it is crucial. No matter how many holes you can poke in someone else's argument, your refutation will be successful only in direct proportion to how much it reflects your own ideas and reinforces your own argument.

3. *Have factual material that you can use as evidence for the points you want to make.* The ability to refute someone else's argument depends on your being well prepared yourself, with whatever kinds of information the situation demands, such as statistics, analogies, and historical and contemporary references. If you were disagreeing about how much trade the United States does with China, you would recognize that your opponent was understating the financial value of this trade only if you knew what the value was yourself. Lacking evidence, you may find yourself with the vague feeling that somewhere there is a good point you could have made, and you will leave

the impression that your opponent's argument is much stronger than it actually is.

4. *Look for factual mistakes in the opposing argument*—not only statistical errors but the deeper errors that come from relying too heavily on a narrow band of information and ignoring other relevant material. For example, keep in mind the difference between the very narrow grounds on which *Plessy* was decided and the much broader grounds that the Warren Court in *Brown* used to refute it (see Chapter 7).

5. *Look for sweeping, glittering generalities in the opposing argument.* These are the easiest and most substantive kinds of mistakes to refute. Sentences that begin with overboard classifications—all children are impossible; all parents are inconsistent—are often good candidates for refutation; so are general statements about particular groups or about historical events or eras.

6. *Look for logical inconsistencies or lapses.* These usually take the form of changes in the pattern of an argument. For example, the reasons an opposing argument proposes to use in justifying a conclusion may disappear somewhere in the course of argument and never be heard from again, or two previously unconnected ideas may be suddenly yoked together.

7. *Be specific about what points in the opposing argument you want to refute.* Quote them if possible; go through the points one at a time so that everyone understands what is being refuted and why. That way you will simultaneously organize your counterargument and weaken your opponent's case.

8. *Conclude with your own views.* Once you have refuted as much as you can of the opposing argument, remember that the animating force behind good refutation is a struggle over principle. No matter what anyone else's argument is, you must understand and put forth what you really believe in.

Successful refutation requires that you pay close attention to the position or the ideas you want to attack. But you have leeway. You are not required to take each opposing point in the order in which it was given, and you do not have to accept all the terms of someone else's argument. The way you order your points, the consistency and tightness of your logic, your ability to vary your tone, and, above all, your power to argue more persuasively than someone who has not thought the issue through—all draw heavily on your imagination, your spirit, and your creativity.

Using Revision in Arguments

Revision entails work on many levels. You can begin by reviewing the thesis—the core claim or idea—in light of what you have read, discussed, understood, or thought about your initial working thesis or hypothesis. What surprised you? What didn't you expect to find? What challenges your previous views or understanding? And how can or will you incorporate this new information into what you already know?

Keeping an open mind is at the heart of scholarly endeavor. To generate and transmit new knowledge and learning, scholars have to be willing to consider new views, alternative hypotheses, adjusted thesis statements and claims. At the heart of scientific inquiry is *hypothesis testing*: advancing a hypothesis and proving it or not (always being ready to acknowledge that an experiment showed the opposite of what was expected).

Throughout life, you will often be asked to reconsider your views, or you will find that new evidence encourages you to modify your beliefs or position on an issue. Revising conceptually entails a kind of synthesis, or merging of what you knew with what you learn, to create new knowledge and understanding. Following are some ideas you can use to revise the texts you write.

1. *Start early.* It's impossible to revise a paper at 3:00 A.M. of the day it's due. If you are writing a research paper, you will have more time to work on it than on a short expository paper, but there is so much material to gather and evaluate that it's still risky to procrastinate on the actual writing.

2. *After you write the first draft, put the paper aside for a day or longer, and then look at it again.* You will have left it long enough so that it will have lost its absolute familiarity. When you reread it, you will be seeing it freshly, and the act of revision will begin automatically as you look it over.

3. *Note rough spots as you read.* In the process of looking at your paper again, you will notice sentences or ideas that aren't synchronized with the rest of the text, or paragraphs that don't lead in to one another. Mark them, or take notes on them, as you are reading; later you won't remember exactly what corrections you wanted to make and will be happy to have made a list.

4. *Look for your topic ideas and thesis statement.* Start by identifying the thesis statement and the most important sentence in every paragraph, and underline them. When you have one sentence in each paragraph underlined, read all of them over. They should make sense, and it should be possible to tell where your paper is headed. If not, you will at least be able to tell where the paper started to go off track. You can take your revision another step by trying to rephrase the underlined sentences, and then rebuilding their paragraphs around them.

This strategy serves another purpose as well: if you *cannot* find a topic sentence in every paragraph, you will have identified the precise area in your paper that is most in need of revision. Try to fill in that missing sentence by writing down, even in completely colloquial language, what it is that you wanted to say. You can refine it later. Alternatively, read the paragraph out loud: that will also give you a sense of what is missing.

5. *Show your paper to a peer whose reading and writing skills you trust*—a friend or a tutor, for example. Ask that person to read your paper over, partly to get an overall sense of it and partly to look for the topic sentences you were trying to find yourself. A second reader is invaluable. You are more likely to pay attention to an evaluation when it comes from someone else; another person may notice points you have missed; and he or she will be seeing the paper from another perspective and without preconceived notions.

If the second reader brings up a problem—a lack of clarity, or a fuzzy thesis—that you had suspected yourself, the second opinion is good confirmation that you were on the right track. But the reader will also see where your strengths are: for example, ideas could be expanded or paragraphs could be moved to give your argument greater vitality.

6. *Trade papers with someone else in your class.* To focus your mutual reviews, you might make up a short list of questions for both of you to keep in mind when reading each other's drafts. What is this paper about? Is it interesting? Why or why not? What is the thesis? Is it clearly organized? How could it be improved? What are its strongest points?

Reading someone else's paper is good for the person who wrote it, but it's also useful for the person who does the reading. From reviewing someone else's work, you can get ideas about how to solve problems in your own paper, and that will make you see your own writing more clearly. It is easier to be objective about someone else's work, but that objectivity carries over at least as far as helping you to recognize problems similar to your partner's in your own work.

7. *Look at your title.* Make sure that it fits your paper. If it doesn't—say, if you chose it because you liked the way it sounded—it may not have much to do with the point of your paper. On the other hand, if the title is the one part of the paper you have confidence in, then it can act as a pointer when you are checking on how consistently you have made your point. In any case, the title is the first indication of where your paper is headed, and it can be an additional check on your work as well as a guide to the direction in which you really want your writing to go.

Developing a Core Assertion: The Thesis Statement

Critical readers learn to detect and analyze the main idea in a text. Persuasive writers develop a thesis statement to focus and guide the development of their essays. By *thesis statement*, we mean the core assertion, the main point being argued for and supported. In an expository or informative essay, the thesis statement indicates your limited topic and your approach to that topic; it still asserts a point of view or perspective, but it tends not to have an argumentative edge to it. A thesis statement in a persuasive piece of discourse seeks to argue for a certain position or point of view, not merely informing but pushing for some change in viewpoint or attitude on the part of the audience. An expository thesis statement does not necessarily provoke a response or an argument; a persuasive thesis statement generally does. While readers of informative or explanatory information will want to see the evidence or support that led to the thesis statement, the persuasive essay will also need to respond to counterarguments; the thesis itself will generally be a stronger assertion of a position than the expository thesis statement. Clearly there is overlap between expository and argumentative thesis statements, but the edge of an opinion, statement of belief, or more forceful assertion generally signals to the reader that an argument follows. For example, an essay might include one of the following core assertions.

- "Martin Luther King, Jr.'s 'I Have a Dream' speech was the turning point of the March on Washington."

- "Martin Luther King, Jr.'s 'I Have a Dream' speech confronted white America with its own sorry record on civil rights for black Americans."

- "If America is to support the ideals for which Martin Luther King, Jr., fought, it must do more than pay lip service to civil rights rulings—it must enforce them."

The first statement could serve as the thesis for an expository essay; it selects and limits a topic and conveys an approach and an attitude toward that topic. The writer may try to convince the reader as to the merits of his case but does not invite counterarguments or try to change attitudes. The second statement also focuses the topic and indicates an approach; in addition, it addresses beliefs and values and engages the reader through value-laden terms (*confronted, sorry*), though it could soften them (i.e., *poor record*) and still argue a point. This sentence invites debate, if not dialogue. The third sentence doesn't argue a point of view or value judgment, like the second sentence, but it proposes a course of action: enforcing civil rights legislation. Buried within the third statement is the assumption or principle that all Americans should support the values for which King fought.

Many expository thesis statements look something like the first sentence; some arguments about values, beliefs, and principles look like the second; proposals or attempts to move the reader to a specific course of action often look like the third. There are many different variations and types of sentences, and we will examine them throughout this book. Essentially, though, a thesis is an assertion that focuses the topic; it indicates an approach to be followed in the essay or other discourse, and in the case of persuasive and argumentative works, it argues for a position, a belief or value, or a course of action.

A thesis is not a statement of acknowledged fact; if it were, there would be little point in discussion. It is not an effusion of emotion or a matter of taste; those too defy reasoned debate. It is an element that reflects and guides the essay. An essay exists to amplify or prove the thesis; the thesis is an encapsulation of the essay. The two must echo and reinforce each other if the essay is to be coherent, to be linked throughout.

Not all pieces of writing explicitly state a thesis. Some use implication, meaning the audience has to infer, or figure out, from the essay what the point or assertion is. Generally, argumentative essays clearly state a position, but pieces that are less explicitly persuasive often do not. The etching *Keep Within Compass* in Chapter 5 states its point, though the values and beliefs supporting that point are implied through other text and the artwork.

As you practice writing, you will generally need to develop a clear statement of purpose, focus, approach, or proposal. Not every piece of writing you will ever do will need a clear, explicit thesis statement, but generally college writing (and much out-of-college writing) will require you to state your position or point clearly and then support it with appropriate evidence. When do you devise a thesis statement? That depends. If you have an idea of what you want to assert, even if it is not fully formed or is tentative, write it down, perhaps trying several variations. Often freewriting a bit after you have jotted down several possibilities will help you to discern what it is you are trying to say. If you are exploring a topic—say, an analysis of an argumentative piece— read, discuss, and take notes until you feel ready to develop a working thesis statement. Some students find that a simple outline for a thesis statement can help them focus it. While writing down a topic or a phrase is a good start, it is more difficult to get off the fence and state an assertion or proposal. Two outlines that students have found useful are the following:

1. I shall argue that _____.

This reminds you that you need to assert something, not just throw out a topic, even a narrowed topic, although that is a useful stage in the process before you develop a thesis.

2. Although _____ , I believe/I shall argue that _____
   because _____.

This outline can guide you by making sure you are looking at potential objections to your argument, that you assert something, and that you have lined up some evidence to support your view.

These are working outlines and need not appear in your essay. In fact, the second outline could produce an exceedingly cumbersome thesis, or at least an inelegant one. But you will be able to decide how explicit to make your thesis statement as you revise, and you will be able to refine the language in revision as well. The Hofstadter selection in Chapter 9 is a superb example of an explicitly stated thesis.

Structuring Arguments

In Chapter 1 we discussed the basic logical approaches of induction and deduction. Reasoning from evidence to conclusion, from examples or specific cases to a conclusion based on those examples, is called *induction* (or, sometimes, *scientific method*). Many of your processes of research and writing entail induction; you generally begin with a question or hypothesis and then investigate it, through reading or other research methods, to confirm or refute it. But in presenting your findings, you will often find it useful to reverse this order, stating your conclusion or thesis and *then* presenting the evidence that led you to draw that conclusion.

Handling Opposing Views   In argumentative essays, you need to deal with your readers' assumptions, views, and expectations. Argument implies the existence of another view. Do you meet such alternative or opposing views early on in an argument, to refute them or concede to them? Or do you develop your own case, offering evidence to support your view, before responding to objections and counterarguments? The answer depends on your audience, purpose, and topic. Will your readers want to have certain immediate objections cleared away before they will listen to your case? Or is it more important to establish your main point and supporting arguments first? Will certain alternative views or objections surface only after the readers have considered some of your views or proposals? Will your argument be clearer and more convincing if you end on several strong points?

This last question brings us to the topic of conclusions. In traditional argumentation, the conclusion is the place for a ringing reiteration of your core point or argument—sometimes as a summary, sometimes with an example or a look to the future, sometimes with a reference to the theme or tone established in the introduction. Recent critics have suggested a more collaborative, cooperative approach to argumentation. Its goal is not simply a hammering away at the opposing position, but a search for common ground and a joint pursuit of knowledge. Such an approach calls for a conclusion that reflects and recognizes the audience's position, reiterates common ground agreed upon or established in the essay, and perhaps acknowledges issues that remain to be resolved.

Choosing a Pattern   A direct pattern calls for the writer to assert and then support. It is often a preferred pattern in academic essays and in writing in the workplace. You assert and then prove your point, and your reader knows the destination and makes the trip with you. An indirect pattern entails setting out evidence and reasoning first and then deriving a thesis, presented later in the essay, from that evidence. An indirect organization can be preferable when dealing with controversial topics; you want your readers to listen to your evidence and reasons before you assert your main point; if they know where you are headed, they may hop off the train at the next stop. Within these overall patterns there are a number of ways to arrange the materials in the body of the essay. Several possible methods are sketched out here:

1. *Chronological order.* This pattern refers to presenting material over time, in a linear manner. It is more common in expository writing, especially in narratives and case histories, than in argumentation, but sometimes within a persuasive essay, such an organization is useful—for example, in presenting a series of events that preceded a current condition or proposal.

2. *Spatial order.* This method uses a physical description—organizing details according to the physical layout of a place—in supporting and working with other argumentative strategies. A reformer's description of a tenement, for example, could persuade others to deal with the problems of slums. With such methods of development, the reader must decide whether to lead with such information, or to assert a point and then support it with the information.

3. *Increasing order of importance.* This method starts with less-strong assertions and builds up to the strongest ones in order to establish a sense of momentum and emphasize the most important points.

4. *Cause and effect.* This strategy begins with an issue or entity and points to potential effects in the future. The writer needs to take care not to overstate potential effects in order to avoid fallacious reasoning.

5. *Effect and underlying causes.* The writer starts by describing an event or effect and examines underlying causes—why things happened, for example, or what caused particular effects. As with a cause-and-effect strategy, the writer must take care to avoid post hoc fallacies (after this, therefore because of this) and not to confuse correlation (two things being associated with each other) with causation (one thing causing the other).

6. *Proposal.* In a proposal the writer outlines a problem and proposes a solution. The writer can cite a problem; mention a number of previously proposed solutions, showing why each will not work; and then propose one that, the writer argues, will work. The writer can also outline a proposed course of action, argue why it will work, then sketch out alternative methods that won't work and reiterate the original plan. Other proposals can argue for a specific course of action, arguing why action is needed and then outlining the steps to be taken in chronological order. Objections can be responded to at each stage as they are likely to come up in the reader's mind, or they can be answered all at once after the proposal is sketched out.

Using Organization for Effective Style

Effective organization at the paragraph and sentence level can add to the persuasiveness of your writing. Whether you are dealing with essays, paragraphs, or sentences, first and last elements get the most attention. Thesis statements tend to appear early on or near the end in an essay; bad news in business memos tends to get delayed to the middle paragraph. Topic ideas tend to be stated early on or near the end of paragraphs; the subjects of clauses tend to appear near the beginning of clauses, with important nouns or verbs ending sentences more often than prepositions, articles, or other less important parts of the sentence. Emphasis deals not with correctness but with style; it is not a grammatical rule that writers avoid ending sentences with prepositions but a stylistic one—why waste that important end-of-sentence emphasis on a word that serves to connect rather than denote an object or an action?

Most of the authors in this book make excellent use of the organization and placement of words, sentences, and ideas to emphasize their messages. As you craft your essays in response to the writing suggestions, consider what you have learned from writers whose style you admire, and practice placing sentences and words within sentences to achieve the emphasis you desire.

Integrating Research into Writing

College is a community of scholars. The academic community develops and transmits scholarly opinion, research findings, and reports in papers, books, lectures, and, in some cases, computer programs. Being part of that community entails pursuing the ongoing and exciting enterprise known as research. As you begin to research, you take part in worldwide conversations and construction of knowledge. As you see how to integrate research into your writing and writing into your research, you learn to set other ideas and evidence next to your own and to draw connections between them.

A writer who invites other voices into the text must strive to represent their views fairly, to credit them appropriately, and to manage these multiple voices in such a way that she remains the author of this particular paper and the dominant voice in it. The experts can support her, but she must make the core proposal and maintain control of the flow of conversation. She must also take responsibility for everything in the paper and must stand behind her core assertion, her key supporting points, and the evidence she includes.

Researched essays sometimes get a poor reputation for being long, dry exercises in library treasure hunts or fussy documentation styles. To maintain this view is to miss one of the most exciting aspects of the academic community: learning to think, read, write, and contribute as a scholar. As you learn to conduct and carry out research, to use the library, to communicate with other scholars, you claim membership in the community and also equip yourself to become a thoughtful, contributing member of society.

Research activities are complex and recursive processes. As in writing an essay, you start with an idea—maybe from reading or discussion. You discuss, read, review, perhaps take notes, and in the process integrate what you are learning with what you already know. You determine what you know enough about and what you need to learn more about—and that "learning more about" is one of the main reasons you do research. During the process of research, it may be useful to employ some of the prompts and questions included the earlier section on techniques for developing essays to help you think about, focus, structure, and develop your paper. Generally your process of writing researched essays will entail the steps of prewriting, close reading, note taking, organizing ideas, drafting, and revising.

Before proceeding, it may be useful to look at the role of research in expository and argumentative essays. Remember that they are different parts of a continuum, with exposition developing an assertion that is not highly controversial and argument developing an assertion with an argumentative edge.

Expository essays can be based on your own experience, observations, reflections, interpretations of readings, and the like. They are used to explain, and although they convey a point of view and develop an assertion, their goal is not necessarily to change beliefs or behavior. Sometimes you will research a subject to add credibility to the assertions you make in your expository essay; you will analyze a development, a historical process, the causes of a situation, the potential effects of some event. You might research the history of jazz or different drafts of a novel, or convey the history or the background of some event or issue. Expository essays in the humanities might include materials from the text to support an interpretation; essays in the sciences and social sciences generally incorporate evidence acceptable in their disciplines to support their assertions, whether that evidence is statistics or observations. The point of the evidence is generally to suggest how the assertion or conclusion was obtained and to support the writer's interpretations.

In an *argumentative essay*, you need to be concerned with the skeptical reader who asks, "Who says so?" and "Why should I believe it?" To answer the first question, you bring in reinforcements in the form of expert opinion and testimony to back up any claims. While your voice needs to remain dominant in the essay, the authority of the experts you quote adds support to your argument. To answer the second question, you turn to evidence—examples, observations, statistics, or whatever other data are respected in the discipline.

An argumentative essay that integrates outside research is still similar to one that does not in that its goal is to persuade people to change their minds—about the ramifications of European settlement of the American continent, or the behavior of an ethnic group toward other Americans, or support of educational or public policy. For example, Susan Faludi's essay in Chapter 5 offers substantial evidence to support her argumentative thesis that there is a backlash against the modest gains American women have made. In deciding the landmark case *Brown* v. *Board of Education* (Chapter 7), the Supreme Court used a sociologist's report to help decide the case.

Research has an important place in both expository and argumentative essays, but special caution must be exercised in argumentative essay research. As you browse through potential sources, it may be tempting to fall prey to "selective attention," a situation in which you look for evidence that supports your view and avoid materials that contradict it. Remember that you must consider opposing views; similarly, in researching controversial or argumentative topics, you need to consider material that contradicts your hypothesis or your belief. Such open-mindedness will help you develop sound scholarly research methods and ultimately will strengthen your paper by demonstrating that you have researched alternatives to your belief or proposal. Dealing with contradictory evidence in your essay will appeal to ethos by ensuring readers that you have a broad background in the topic, that you are not trying to slant the evidence in your favor, and that your argument is strong and well supported enough to withstand contrary evidence. In any case, your readers will already be considering opposing views; your willingness to acknowledge them will only strengthen your case.

Beginning the Process

Begin by selecting the topic and developing a research question. If you have been assigned a topic, determine some aspect of it that interests you and that you can develop fully in the time and space allowed. If you choose your own topic, be guided by your interests but also by the limits of time and paper length; having the freedom to choose a topic often entails a more careful assessment of what you can manage. Additional concerns about topic selection for a documented essay include selecting a subject about which you can find enough materials with the resources available to you; also, since you will likely spend considerable time with your topic, you should find a subject that genuinely engages your interest. Finally, remember your role as a contributing member of the academic community; don't bother researching something that is obvious or a foregone conclusion. And consider researching subjects about which you can truly contribute: legislative research that serves the public interest, for example, or environmental research that can help your community or school make informed decisions about policy.

An underappreciated aspect of research papers, especially in first-year courses, is developing a research question. When you identify a question to which you truly want to find some answers, you are more likely to be interested in your topic and to keep an open mind as you research. For example, "Was the Civil War truly about economic issues?" or "What stereotypes have remained constant through different stages in American history?" are both much more likely to help you focus and develop a topic than if you say to yourself, "Maybe I can write about the Civil War or about prejudice." A research question can guide your research, help you to develop a working thesis, and prevent you from floundering around in a sea of readings, papers, notes, and miscellaneous unfocused ideas.

The next step is to set the schedule. Determine the due dates for your paper and any intermediate due dates for parts of the paper during the research process. Often instructors establish checkpoints by which time you will have established a research question, tentative thesis, preliminary research, a working bibliography, an annotated bibliography, a working outline and revised thesis statement, a draft, peer reviews, a revision. If you have not received such guidelines, make your own, and stick to the schedule. It is too easy to let big projects slide in the face of daily competing demands for your time and interest. The results of waiting too long to start include finding that most of the best sources have been checked out, that you don't have time to do careful research, and that you are fresh out of ideas late in the night before the draft is due.

Finally, consider the audience. With any piece of writing, understanding the audience is crucial in making decisions about the subject and focus of the researched essay. If you are writing about literature in a composition class, you are in the position of being a generalist writing to an expert in the field. Your audience knows more about the topic than you do, but you bring with you new insights on the topic and unique responses to the texts you are interpreting. You may also uncover unique connections between sources and new insights in recent critical interpretations. In that same composition class, when you research particular topics of interest that are not literary topics, you will probably become the expert on the topic at hand. You will then have to be particularly aware of your readers' backgrounds and assumptions about your topic.

When you write as an expert to other experts, as you do when you are advancing in your chosen major or discipline, you have the advantage of a common language and a common understanding of the core concepts of the discipline. If you are writing papers for your courses, you will still be writing to specialists who know more than you do in the discipline, but you will have less explaining of terminology to do and can draw on shared assumptions and background knowledge.

Let us say that you are interested in physics or astronomy—in string theory or dark matter in the universe or nanotechnology. Your interest in the topic may carry you through the extensive technical research that will be needed, but if you are writing the essay in response to an open assignment in your writing class, the additional task remains of translating concepts and technical jargon for an audience of writing class peers and instructor. Such a writing situation is not restricted to writing courses; scientists and scholars frequently must translate the concepts of their work either to publish in general periodicals or to write grant proposals to outside funding sources who may be highly educated but unfamiliar with the particulars of the scientist's work.

Gathering Information

In addition to thinking about the functions of research and researched essays in college, you should consider expanding your sense of sources. Probably in high school, you used books and articles as main sources for papers, and these remain excellent choices, but in the academic community other sources now become necessary and helpful. For example, your college faculty includes experts in various fields and disciplines; plan to visit these faculty to obtain their expert opinion on issues related to your research. Faculty are away from time to time, so plan ahead; call the department and find out who in the field is knowledgeable about the issue in question. Then ask for that professor's office hours and call to schedule an appointment. Try to read this person's articles or books before your visit, so that you can ask informed questions and can use the time to best advantage. Experts in business, schools, and industry are other people you can interview for information about topics you might be researching. Other members of the community can help as well. If you are doing oral histories, for example, as Studs Terkel does (Chapter 6), you will be interviewing people to find out their stories or their attitudes about some part of their lives.

To assemble background information about your topic, ask yourself some questions about what you know. Where did you first learn about the topic? Do you have class materials or notes? Do you know people who can serve as resources? And finally, how will you start your library search strategy?

The first part of your search for information should help you to develop a brief overview of the topic: important names, dates, and terminology associated with the topic; related subjects and terms to use for searching for articles; and a list of potential sources for information. After collecting a basic list of core terms and key words, you are ready to search.

Library Sources   Library sources, both print and other media, will probably serve as your core materials for research, so it is important to get to know your library system. You have probably already used reference materials and library books to find information you needed; you may be less familiar with alternatives—electronic media, for example, including on-line, or networked, researching capabilities and CD-ROMs, which store large amounts of information and are updated frequently. Familiarize yourself with such data-gathering resources as soon as possible, because they will become more and more prominent in the future. Ask your instructor or a librarian for class or individual instruction on using them. Some public libraries now have such sources to search for magazine articles; generally, they are "user friendly" and entail only punching a few clearly marked buttons.

Materials in the library fall into three categories. *Primary sources* are original materials, such as interviews, survey data, oral histories, photographs, posters, advertisements, paintings, and literary works. What constitutes a primary resource depends on the field and context, but generally they are the raw data about which others may write or which they may interpret. Examples of primary sources in this book are *Keep Within Compass* and the writings of Frederick Douglass. Student writer John Wu used statistical evidence as a primary source in his research paper (Chapter 5).

Secondary sources are materials written *about* the primary sources: authors describe, interpret, or otherwise integrate primary sources into their writings. Langston Hughes's poem "Let America Be America Again" (Chapter 4) is an example of a primary source. Chris Countryman's essay analyzing the poem is a secondary source. A student analyzing propaganda materials could use both primary materials, such as posters, and secondary materials to develop an analytical or argumentative essay about techniques of propaganda.

Tertiary sources are third-level materials, such as bibliographies, which list collections of both primary and secondary sources. *The Mexican American: A Selected and Annotated Bibliography* is a tertiary source.

Finding Sources   The sources you need will vary depending on the research stage. Initially, general sources, such as general or specialized encyclopedias, can provide an overview of the topic and identify the core concepts and issues. Encyclopedias range from the general, such as *Encyclopaedia Britannica*, to the specialized, such as encyclopedias of music, religion, social science, and the like. Encyclopedias and specialized dictionaries are shelved in the reference sections of the library, and they generally are listed in on-line catalogs as well. While you are doing basic general information gathering, look up your topic's key words in the Library of Congress Subject Headings reference guide, which should be available in the reference room as well. As on-line searches for materials become more and more important in conducting research, it is essential that you have a good working list of key words with which to conduct your searches. For example, people researching Latino studies may need to use key words such as *ethnic identity, Cuban Americans,* or *Puerto Rico—U.S.*

Once you have general background information, you can start digging for additional, more focused materials. Compile a list of selections in books, academic journals, and general interest magazines to help you find more detailed information.

To find books on your topic, consult either the card catalog or whatever on-line computer catalog your institution or local library uses. Start with the list of key words and browse for titles that look interesting. Consider both general and more specific levels of your topic, and pay special attention to any bibliographies or books that indicate that they include bibliographies.

To find articles, search periodical indexes in both print and media forms. You are probably familiar with the *Reader's Guide to Periodical Literature*, but you may not yet have used specialized indexes. Some important ones are the *Humanities Index, Social Science Index, General Science Index, Alternative Press Index, Index to Black Periodicals, Women's Studies Abstracts, Historical Abstracts, MLA Bibliography, PAIS International, Psych Abstracts,* and, for general information, a newspaper index such as *The New York Times Index.*

The electronic media include both general and specific magazine and journal indexes as well as reference sources. Lexis-Nexis, as one example, provides full texts of articles in business, general news, and law. Specialized sources you may have access to include *Bibliography of Native North Americans, EconLit, Psychlit, Art Index,* and the on-line *Oxford English Dictionary,* as well as duplication of print versions of *MLA Bibliography* and *Historical Abstracts.*

In addition to the general reference and research sources already outlined, your library may have some specialized sources for research on American themes. Following are some of the possible categories of specialized references and some examples of the kinds of material you may be able to find to help you investigate your subject.

General Sources for American Themes

American Writers Before 1800

American Writers

American Drama Criticism: Interpretations, 1890–1977

MLA International Bibliography

American Humanities Index

The Democracy Reader: Classic and Modern Speeches, Essays, Poems, Declarations, and Documents on Freedom and Human Rights

The Bill of Rights: A Documentary History

Encyclopedia of the American Constitution

Documentary History of the Modern Civil Rights Movement

Slavery in the Courtroom: Annotated Bibliography of Cases

Black Slavery in the Americas

The American Civil Liberties Union: An Annotated Bibliography

Social Reform and Reaction in America: An Annotated Bibliography

Women's Rights Movement in the United States

Encyclopedia of the American Constitution

Index on Censorship

The Anthropology of War: A Bibliography

Encyclopedia of Military History

Peace Research Abstracts Journal

American Public Opinion Index

American Public Opinion Data

Public Opinion, 1935–1946

The Gallup Poll: Public Opinion (annual)

An American Profile: Opinions and Behavior, 1972–1989

Public Opinion Polls and Survey Research: Selective Annotated Bibliography of U.S. Guides and Studies from the 1980s

Statistical Abstracts of the United States (from the U.S. Census Bureau)

Historical Statistics of the United States: Colonial Times to 1970

Social Indicators III: Selected Data and Social Conditions and Trends in the United States

American Statistics Index

The Official Washington Post *Index*

Immigration and Ethnicity: A Guide to Information Sources

Statistical Abstracts of the United States

We the People: An Atlas of America's Ethnic Diversity

America: History and Life

Film Studies

The American Film Industry: A Historical Dictionary

The Film Encyclopedia

Blacks in American Films and Television

The Hispanic Image on the Silver Screen: An Interpretive Filmography from Silents

Contemporary Theatre, Film and Television

Who's Who in American Film

Film Study: An Analytical Bibliography

The New Film Index: A Bibliography of Magazine Articles in English, 1930–1970

Ethnic and Racial Images in American Film and Television: Historical Essays and Bibliography

Blacks in Film and Television: A Pan-African Bibliography of Films, Filmmakers, and Performers

Film Literature Index

New York Times *Film Reviews*

Film Review Index

Index to Critical Reviews

African American Studies

Some key words for searching: Afro-Americans—Race-Identity; Afro-American Press; Afro-Americans—History; Black Power—United States; Civil Rights—United States; School Integration—United States.

The African American Encyclopedia

Dictionary of Afro-American Slavery

Encyclopedia of Black America

Encyclopedia of Southern Culture

Notable Black American Women

Black Women in America

The Harlem Renaissance: A Historical Dictionary

The Negro Almanac: A Reference Work on the Afro-American into Sound, 1898–1935

Women of Color and Southern Women: A Bibliography of Social Science Research

Afro-American Folk Culture

Afro-American History

Afro-American Reference: An Annotated Bibliography of Selected Resources

Black Adolescence: Current Issues and Annotated Bibliography

Black American Writers: Bibliographical Essays

The Black Family in the United States

Black Rhetoric: A Guide to Afro-American Communication

Index to Black Periodicals

Latino Studies

Some key words for searching: Mexican Americans—Ethnic Identity; Hispanic Americans—Ethnic Identity; Cuban Americans; Mexican American Women; Migrant Agricultural Laborers; Puerto Ricans—U.S.

Chicano Literature: A Reference Guide

Dictionary of Mexican American History

Bibliografía Chicana: A Guide to Information Sources

A Bibliography of Criticism of Contemporary Chicano Literature

Bibliography of Mexican American History

Chicano Anthology Index: A Comprehensive Author, Title, and Subject Index to Chicano Anthologies, 1965–1987

The Chicana Studies Index: Twenty Years of Gender Research, 1972–1991

Latinos in the United States: A Historical Bibliography

The Mexican American: A Selected and Annotated Bibliography

Mexican American Biographies: A Historical Dictionary

Statistical Handbook on U.S. Hispanics

The Chicano Index

Latin American Studies

Native American Studies

The Library of Congress term for the aboriginal peoples of the Western Hemisphere, including the Inuit, is *Indians.* The Western Hemisphere is divided into regions: North America, Mexico, Central America, West Indies, and South America. Works on Indians of a particular region are listed as, for example, *Indians of North America.* Individual tribal names are used as appropriate, such as *Navaho Indians* or *Choctaw Indians.* Other key words include: Western Algonquin Indians; Athapascan Indians; Caddoan Indians; Eskimos; Mound-builders; Ojibwa Indians; Piegan Indians; Shoshoni Indians; Tinne Indians; United States—Civilization—Indian influences.

Atlas of Ancient America

Atlas of the North American Indian

A Concise Dictionary of Indian Tribes of North America

Dictionary of Daily Life of Indians of the Americas

Dictionary of the American Indian

Encyclopedia of Native American Religions: An Introduction

Encyclopedia of Native American Tribes

Handbook of the American Frontier: Four Centuries of Indian-White Relationships

Handbook of North American Indians

Native American Almanac: A Portrait of Native America Today

American Indian Women: A Guide to Research

Native American Folklore, 1879–1979: An Annotated Bibliography

Native North Americans: Crime, Conflict, and Criminal Justice: A Research Bibliography

Southwest Native American Arts and Material Culture: A Guide to Research

Bibliography of Native North Americans on Disc (on CD-ROM)

Who Was Who in Native American History: Indians and Non-Indians from Early Contacts Through 1900

Native Women: A Statistical Overview

Reports of the American Indian Family History Project

Statistical Record of Native North Americans

Nations Within a Nation: Historical Statistics of American Indians

Asian American Studies

The Library of Congress uses *Asian American*, but other headings include the following: American Literature—Asian American Authors, Chinese Americans, East Indians, Filipino Americans, Filipinos in the United States, Hawaiians, Japanese Americans, Korean Americans, Oceanian Americans, Pacific Islander Americans, Vietnamese Americans.

Asian-Americans Information Directory

The Chinese-American Heritage

The Chinese in America, 1920–1973

The Filipinos in America, 1898–1974

The Koreans in America, 1882–1974

Dictionary of Asian American History

Japanese American History: An A to Z Reference from 1868 to the Present

Harvard Encyclopedia of American Ethnic Groups

Refugees in the United States

Asian American Literature: An Annotated Bibliography

The Asian American Media Reference Guide, 2d ed.

Asian American Studies: An Annotated Bibliography and Research Guide

A Comprehensive Bibliography for the Study of American Minorities

Images of Color: A Guide to Media from and for Asian, Black, Latino and Native American Communities

Immigrant Women in the United States: A Selectively Annotated Multidisciplinary Bibliography

Pacific/Asian American Research

A Selected Bibliography on the Asians in America

South Asians in North America: An Annotated and Selected Bibliography (covers 1900–1986)

Biographical Sources

Chinese American Portraits: Personal Histories, 1828–1988

Who's Who Among Asian Americans

Statistical Record of Asian Americans

A number of sources already listed can also be good sources for information on Asian Americans.

Focusing the Search

Once you have found a general overview of your subject and a list of potential sources, deepen your search for materials. Many of the general and bibliographical sources are in the reference area of your library; your next step will probably be to collect some important books and periodical articles in the field.

In some fields, books will be your most important sources; a scholarly book has the advantage of being an in-depth examination of some issue or element in the field. A periodical, on the other hand, by virtue of the recurrent issuing of the material, offers less in-depth but more current information.

Books are generally spread out through the library storage system in what are commonly called *stacks*. Sometimes the stacks are closed, and you need to request books you want from the circulation desk. If stacks at your library are open, you can browse the shelves in your subject area. If the book you tracked down in a bibliography isn't available, perhaps another interesting book is. Or perhaps other nearby books on the shelves look helpful. You should plan on taking some time in the stacks and perusing tables of contents, introductory chapters, and bibliographies of books in the area of your topic.

Working with Sources

As you assemble general, preliminary, and increasingly specialized sources, you will need to keep track of your materials, both the original sources and your notes on them. Few experiences in academia are more frustrating than finding an excellent piece of information or an idea and then losing track of where you located it. Different writers approach notes and note taking in different ways.

First, you have to determine what you are looking for when you read sources. In addition to keeping in mind the general advice offered in Chapter 1 for reading critically, pay special attention to the following questions when critiquing sources:

1. What is the theme? What is the author's purpose in writing? Who are the intended audiences? What are the author's assumptions? Do you share those assumptions? Do the author's assumptions or emphasis indicate bias?

2. What is the overall idea the author develops? What is the primary organizing plan (cause-effect, problem-solution, definition, process)?

3. Is the evidence presented clearly? Is it persuasive? Do the author's conclusions logically follow from the evidence?

4. How does the selection connect with other readings? Does it provide information on other sources? Does it provide an example of a point made in another source? Does it contradict another source? Are there points of comparison or contrast with another source? What common threads run through the sources?

Taking Notes As a fellow scholar in the academic community, you are expected not to take your sources at face value but to challenge and question them, to assess the merit of their arguments and the logic of their conclusions critically.

Be an active, assertive reader. Question information as you read it; argue with the text. If you own the book or you are using photocopies, make extensive marginal notes. Otherwise, use note cards, computer "note cards" (such as HyperCard files on a Macintosh), or notepaper to keep track of your information. Try to use a medium for taking notes that allows you to sort the notes by topic as you collect more information.

As you take notes, write down not only the information itself but key words, phrases, reactions to points the author makes, critical arguments and comments, and reactions you may have. *But take great care to keep track of exactly what information comes from the sources and which comments are your own reflections on the source.* When information or ideas appear in a number of sources (usually three or more), most writers will consider it common knowledge in the field and will not document the source. Until you have researched enough to know what will need citing, however, you should keep track of the sources in your notes.

There are three different types of notes we generally use to record our research of sources: summaries, paraphrase, and direct quotation. *Summaries* of information from the source help you to make sure you have digested the material and help you to translate the information into your own words. They pull out the key ideas of a source. *Paraphrases* are a kind of running commentary or translation of the original source; they capture essentially all of the material in the original. Paraphrase is a frequent suspect in plagiarism, the unacknowledged use of the ideas or phrases of others. The difference between summary and paraphrase can be seen in the following example, based on an excerpt from "The Gettysburg Address."

Original

Four score and seven years ago our fathers brought forth on this continent, a new nation, conceived in Liberty, and dedicated to the proposition that all men are created equal.

Now we are engaged in a great civil war, testing whether that nation, or any nation so conceived and so dedicated, can long endure. We are met on a great battlefield of that war. We have come to dedicate a portion of that field as a final resting-place for those who here gave their lives that that nation might live. It is altogether fitting and proper that we should do this.

Summary

Eighty-seven years ago a country was founded on the principles of freedom and equality. We are now involved in a war that will test whether the nation and those principles will survive. Appropriately, we gather on a battlefield of that war to dedicate a cemetery for those who died here fighting for the nation's survival.

Paraphrase

Eighty-seven years ago the founding fathers created on the American continent a new country, born in freedom and committed to the ideal that everyone is created equal.

We are now involved in a large-scale civil war that will determine if a nation with such ideals and such a purpose can last. We meet at the site of one of the great battles of that war and we are here to dedicate part of the battlefield as a cemetery for those who died here to save the nation. It is appropriate that we do so.

Direct quotations *must* be taken down exactly as written and put inside quotation marks. They should be saved for those occasions when the quotation so perfectly captures a concept, idea, or image that it would require a great deal more time and space to say the same thing that would have much less impact. They, too, need to be carefully documented. Sometimes you can summarize an author's point and then put key or specialized words into quotations. If you use only parts of a quotation by an author, be sure to use ellipses—three spaced dots—to indicate that you have left material out; be careful not to change the author's intended meaning. For a quotation within a quotation, use single quotation marks; if the author quotes someone else you want to quote directly, your citation would say, for example, "(Pritchard, qtd. in Garcia 32)." Keep careful track of who says what in your sources so that you can quote accurately.

Avoiding Plagiarism   Plagiarism is the unacknowledged use of the ideas or words of others. Whether accidental or intentional, plagiarism is a serious offense. To avoid plagiarism, you should follow these general guidelines.

Cite your sources in the following cases: an original idea from a source, whether you summarize it, paraphrase it, or quote it directly; factual information that is not common knowledge; any exact wording or unique phrasing taken from a source.

There is no need to cite when material is considered common knowledge; that is, it appears in a number of sources or can be verified by agreed-on measurement or criteria. How many sources must it appear in? Some scholars suggest a minimum of three sources; others say five. We have found that if the material is general background information and occurs in three sources or more, it can safely be considered common knowledge. But if you are writing about some scientific findings and it is relevant that a number of scientists duplicated certain results, then you would be better off citing even a large number of studies, since the confirmation of some findings by others is crucial to the information's credibility. Again, you need to develop judgment about audience, purpose, and subject as you make such decisions. Too many citations can interrupt the flow of your paper or give the impression that the sources' voices are taking over your paper, but when in doubt, it is better to cite rather than not.

Plagiarism is essentially the passing off of the ideas or words of others as your own. Keep in mind the spirit of the law and you will be guided by it as you make specific decisions about particular pieces of information in your essay.

Using On-Line Resources in Research: The Web

Remember that libraries are not simply about books—they are about information. Libraries are in a sense a storage and retrieval system that manages information. Because we are accustomed to books and periodicals as the means of transmitting knowledge, we sometimes think that on-line resources represent a different type of information and require entirely different research strategies. Remember the common denominator: storage and retrieval of information. It's not surprising, then, that libraries have invested heavily in technical equipment and access to on-line resources, and now most college libraries are able to provide access to information beyond their own physical bound-aries. A key difference between on-line and more traditional "hard copy" resources, however, is the speed of transmission of information.

When you search the World Wide Web, for example, you can start a search, refine it, click on a topic area, click on the title of a linked page, and generally zip around all kinds of resources in a matter of minutes. Links between related topics are often already in place, and you can ex-plore several closely related areas, explore your own topic in depth, save your places with "bookmarks," print out materials, get bibliogra-phies—accomplish what would have been a painstaking, time-intensive process in a matter of moments.

A second key feature of Web-based research, mentioned above, is the linking of information. Find the Purdue Writing Center site, for example, and in moments you have access to all kinds of related sites, including the Library of Congress and the different rooms and the dis-plays currently featured. Any number of sites related to writing and re-search are accessible from the initial page, and often different sites will lead you to other interesting, related ones. And many sites have infor-mation not easily available in most libraries. If you wanted to investi-gate traditional music of an American Indian tribe, for example, you could likely find a site with a sample recording and background information.

Access to a wide range of information, however, does not guaran-tee accuracy or even a truly representative sampling of knowledge on a given topic. Although a selection of library books may be limited—librarians can't buy every book printed—researching on-line creates the opposite problem. Your desktop can be overloaded with all kinds of on-line information, some of which may be authoritative and the rest questionable. The time you save in physically going from place to place in the library, the reference room, the bookshelves, back to the catalog for another search, and the like, should be devoted to evaluating on-line sources. Nearly anyone can create a Web page and post informa-tion. You have to use your scholarly skills, as well as common sense, in determining the credibility of such sources. The Library of Congress Web site, for example, has tremendous authority behind it, whereas Joe Zook's Cool Disco Revival may not (then again, it may have recordings of popular disco tunes or a top-ten list of disco hits, and if you are re-searching popular culture, you went to the right place after all). But if you are just starting to inform yourself on a topic, you can start brows-ing and learn what the principal divisions or elements of your topic are and follow your interest and the available links.

Linking on the Web is not an exact science, however, and it's im-portant not to overrely on the links; they are someone else's idea of how topics should be connected. Use links to interesting Web pages to inform yourself in a general area of knowledge, but only as part of a larger, thoughtful research strategy. And when you have ten thousand "hits" for your search, it's time to reconsider your focus.

When you begin a search on the Web, take advantage of the search engines or browsers. The makeup of the Web is changing too fast to set forth specific guidelines here, but Yahoo and AltaVista are two examples (as of this writing) of search engines that will enable you to research particular categories or topics. Such tools can help you gradually refine your topic.

Finally, a caution: ownership of text can get especially murky on the Web. Text is easily uploaded, downloaded, modified, integrated, and otherwise manipulated and shaped. You still bear the responsibility of ethical scholarship: when you quote, quote exactly and give credit. When you summarize or integrate information, particularly if it is unique in content or phrasing, credit the source. If you are ever tempted to do the unthinkable and to lift a paper or part of a paper off the Web, or to overrely on a source for an assignment, remember: your instructor and classmates have access to the Web just like you do. A sobering lesson at our institution occurred when two students both plagiarized the same paper off the Web. But these reminders should be beside the point: as a scholar and a thinker, you need to do your own original thinking and writing. Sources will help you think through and then build your own arguments—not argue in your place while you tag along for the ride.

Keep in mind, then, good sense, critical thinking skills, and traditional research techniques and let them guide you through the maze of networked information.

Writing Drafts

As you collect information, review notes, and sift through ideas and evidence, connections should begin to form in your mind, and responses to your initial research question begin to suggest themselves. You can foster this process by reviewing notes as you collect new information, determining where the new sources fit with the material you already know. Take time at regular intervals to freewrite about your topic, either in a journal or in scheduled bursts of freewriting at the computer after a research session.

Some writers find it helpful to take notes from different sources and then begin to sort them by subtopic; or go back to their research question and divide the question into smaller questions; or review the working hypothesis, refine it, and divide it into categories. For example, a paper on the myth of the model minority could focus on the family ethos of work, the glass ceiling in corporations, the different patterns of immigration from Asia, the relative economic and educational status of each group, and so on. Sometimes a diagram or flowchart helps, with lines and circles connecting various parts of the material. Whatever your method, try to begin lining up the general elements of the material.

Consider the kinds of supporting assertions you can make based on your evidence; review your tentative thesis or hypothesis and refine it, if needed, based on your findings. Review your supporting assertions in light of your refined thesis. Those supporting assertions can become your topic ideas. Line up those supporting assertions in the order in which your reader needs to hear them and in an order that links up one point to the next. Then draft a working outline based on the assertions you have identified, work through the material to find the support for your assertions, and write a rough draft. At this stage, you are primarily interested in getting the basic structure down. While you should keep track of where your information is coming from, don't worry too much about the specifics of documentation or style: "(Smith 21)" or "(Smith teaching article p. 21)" in some form is sufficient at this stage, but try to keep track of article and page number. Checking spelling and worrying about specifics of grammar are tasks for a later stage of writing. Just get your core argument down. Save your file often if you are working on the computer! If you are writing out or typing your draft, photocopy it as you write large parts of it to guard against losing your work.

Revising the Draft

After you get the basic structure of the rough draft down, review the logic of your assertions. Determine whether they still support the thesis and whether the thesis still allows you to engage the parts of your topic that you want to cover. Thesis and support must remain connected and mutually reinforcing. Review your draft and determine if you need more evidence or if you should cut out parts that don't seem relevant. Peer feedback at this stage can be useful. Exchange drafts with a classmate and try to give each other "big picture" feedback on the thesis, basic structure, and supporting evidence. Then revise your essay as needed to attend to criticism from your peer. Remember, though, that as the author, you have the final decision over changes you make. Accept feedback, but use your own judgment in deciding how much and what kind of advice to take.

You should certainly spell-check your paper if you are using a computer to write it, but such tools do not find all the errors and lapses in good style that your draft may have. Peer feedback is also helpful for detecting errors that you may not find, since at this point in the draft your eyes may see what they expect to see (or want to see) rather than what is on the page. You and a peer should both go over your paper in fine detail, attending to issues of style, appropriateness of language, level of diction, proper syntax, and correct documentation style.

Documentation

When you converse in the academic community, you generally need to use the conventions of the various disciplines to communicate ideas and research findings. As you begin to think of yourself as a part of the scholarly community, you will see how citation forms work as a kind of shorthand that permits scholars to share their findings with others in the national and international academic communities and helps those scholars follow up on each other's work. The cooperative nature of research may help explain the very specific formats used in different disciplines. In the social sciences, for example, the date of a research study is crucial, so the American Psychological Association (APA) format puts the date right after the author's name. In humanities fields, on the other hand, where the date of the findings is less important, the Modern Language Association (MLA) format for in-text citations contains a name or book title and page number. In the "Works Cited" list as well, the date comes last.

You may have been instructed to use a particular documentation style. Your instructor may provide guidance, or you can use a style book. Both MLA and APA have style books. Some examples of style manuals in other disciplines include *Council of Biology Editors Style Manual: A Guide for Authors, Editors, and Publishers; A Manual for Authors of Mathematical Papers;* and *Style Manual for Guidance in the Preparation of Papers.*

Most composition courses suggest following either the MLA or APA style. If you have a choice and you know you are interested in humanities or social science, you may want to start using the format you are likely to use in future classes and to buy the appropriate manual. Following are the general guidelines for documenting your essays and citing your sources.

How to Document Sources   Most disciplines are moving toward parenthetical within-text citation, and that is the style we will use here. In APA style, supply the last name of the author(s) and the year of publication: (Garcia & Collins, 1988). In MLA style, if you are referring to a work by an author, cite the author's name and a page number: (Garcia 38). Note that in MLA style you don't need a comma or "p." to indicate page number. If Garcia's name or book or article title is implied in the context, you can simply use the page number (38) as the reference. If you are citing two works by Garcia, you can use a brief title of the work (Messages 28) to indicate to the reader which work this particular quotation comes from. Look at the documented student essays in this book for samples; John Wu (Chapter 5) documented his essay in correct MLA style. If you have substantive notes or "asides" to the reader, you can include those as footnotes or endnotes. If you use endnotes, place them at the end of the paper, but before your list of references.

References/Works Cited   Within the general guidelines for documentation, there are specific forms that should be followed for different types of sources. A "Works Cited" list is now commonly used with MLA style; it contains only the references actually cited in the paper. The APA style uses a "References" list with all relevant readings that may have influenced the paper.

Sample Documentation   The following lists provide samples of common works that you will use. Note that underlining may be substituted for italics if you are writing by hand or on a typewriter.

A book by one author

> *MLA:*   Sowell, Thomas. *Ethnic America.* New York: Basic Books, 1981.
>
> *APA:*   Sowell, T. (1981). *Ethnic America.* New York: Basic Books.

A book by two authors

> *MLA:*   Neesom, Lisa, and George Madera. *Early American Art.* Englewood Cliffs: Prentice-Hall, 1955.
>
> *APA:*   Neesom, M., & Madera, G. (1955). *Early American art.* Englewood Cliffs, NJ: Prentice-Hall.

A book by three authors

> *MLA:*   Lewis, Peter, A. J. McGee, and Martin Washington. *American Folk Art.* 3rd ed. New York: McGraw-Hill, 1993.
>
> *APA:*   Lewis, P., McGee, A. J., & Washington, M. (1993). *American folk art* (3rd ed.). New York: McGraw-Hill.

A book with more than three authors

> *MLA:*   Isselbacher, Kurt J., et al. *Harrison's Principles of Internal Medicine.* 9th ed. New York: McGraw-Hill, 1980.
>
> *APA:*   Isselbacher, K. J., Adams, D. A., Braunwald, E., Petersdorf, R. G., Wilson, J. D. (1980). *Harrison's principles of internal medicine* (9th ed.). New York: McGraw-Hill.

The edited work of an author

> *MLA:*   Hawthorne, Nathaniel. *The Portable Hawthorne.* Ed. Malcolm Cowley. New York: Viking, 1969.

APA: Hawthorne, N. (1969). *The portable Hawthorne.* (M. Cowley, Ed.). New York: Viking Press.

A work in an anthology

MLA: Hawthorne, Nathaniel. "Young Goodman Brown." *Heritage of American Literature.* Ed. James E. Miller, Jr., with Kathleen Farley. Vol. 1. New York: Harcourt Brace, 1991. 1413–21.

APA: Hawthorne, N. (1991). Young Goodman Brown. In J. E. Miller, Jr. (Ed.), *Heritage of American literature: Vol. 1* (pp. 1413–1421). New York: Harcourt Brace.

A work in translation

MLA: Pushkin, Aleksander. *Eugene Onegin.* Trans. Vladimir Nabokov. 4 vols. New York: Bollingen Foundation, 1964.

APA: Pushkin, A. (1964). *Eugene Onegin* (Vols. 1–4). (V. Nabokov, Trans.). New York: Bollingen Foundation.

An article in a journal with separate pagination for each issue

MLA: Budd, Matthew A. "Human Suffering: Road to Illness or Gateway to Learning?" *Advances: The Journal of Mind-Body Health* 3 (Summer 1993): 28–35.

APA: Budd, M. A. (1993, Summer). Human suffering: Road to illness or gateway to learning? *Advances: The Journal of Mind-Body Health, 3,* 28–35.

An article in a journal with continuous pagination

MLA: Frey, Olivia. "Beyond Literary Darwinism: Women's Voices and Critical Discourse." *College English* 52 (1990): 507–26.

APA: Frey, O. (1990). Beyond literary Darwinism: Women's voices and critical discourse. *College English, 52,* 507–526.

An unsigned newspaper article or editorial

MLA: "Small Companies Earn Big Honors." *San Francisco Examiner* 20 May 1994: B1.

APA: Small companies earn big honors. (1994, May 20). *San Francisco Examiner,* p. B1.

A signed newspaper article or editorial

MLA: Ulrich, Allan. "Variations on a Gould-en Theme." *San Francisco Examiner* 20 May 1994: C1.

APA: Ulrich, A. (1994, May 20). Variations on a Gould-en theme. *San Francisco Examiner,* p. C1.

A public document

MLA: United States Department of Health and Human Services, Administration for Children, Youth and Families, Children's Bureau. *Child Welfare Strategies in the Coming Years.* Washington: Office of Human Development Services, 1978.

APA: U.S. Department of Health and Human Services, Administration for Children, Youth and Families, Children's Bureau. (1978). *Child welfare strategies in the coming years.* Washington: Office of Human Development Services.

A film

MLA: *Judgment at Nuremberg.* Stanley Kramer, dir. United Artists, 1961.

APA: Kramer, S. (Director). (1961). *Judgment at Nuremberg* [Film]. United Artists.

A lecture

MLA: Rebholz, Ronald. "Shakespeare and the Power of an Idea." Centennial Lecture Series. Stanford U. 23 Sept. 1991.

APA: Rebholz, Ronald. (1991, September 23). *Shakespeare and the power of an idea.* Lecture presented at the Centennial Lecture Series, Stanford University.

An interview

MLA: Garcia, Juana. Personal interview. 3 Dec. 1993.
APA: Garcia, J. (1993, December 3). [Interview].

A computer program

MLA: Watters, Ann. *The Art of Persuasion.* Vers. 1.0. Computer software, CD-ROM. Focus Interactive, 1995.

APA: Watters, A. (1995). The art of persuasion [Computer software]. Menlo Park, CA: Focus Interactive.

Legal cases

Plessy v. Ferguson, 163 U.S. 537 (1896).

(Note: Both the MLA and APA follow the style set forth in *A Uniform System of Citation,* 15th edition, published by the Harvard Law Review Association in 1991.)

3

∞

Identities

Whom do you visualize when you hear the term *American*? Do you identify a specific gender, race, occupation, or age that you consider typical? Do you see a white male banker? A Native American high school student? A family of migrant farmers? A Chinese American factory worker? All of these people can be American citizens, of course, but is there one that seems *more* American to you than the others?

America is a confluence of cultures: American Indians who have lived here for millennia; European and Asian immigrants who came here in search of a better life; people of African descent brought by force. Over time, these cultures have mingled and evolved into something new and recognizably American. How do all of these disparate identities come together to form an American identity?

In understanding American identities, we need to come to terms with unity and division, with separateness and common ground. The question, What do we mean by American? encompasses a host of related questions: Is there a distinctly American identity? Is there one overriding, generalized American culture? Or are there only disparate subcultures that form strategic alliances for survival? Should we retain the old metaphor of the melting pot, into which various cultures are tossed, melted down, and pulled out as generic Americans? If so, what are the characteristics of that generic American? If we reject the metaphor of the melting pot, what should we use as a more fitting metaphor: A mosaic? A puzzle?

Identity has always been a difficult question nagging the collective American mind. We wonder how much we have in common besides living in the same country. We argue about a common culture, a shared set of values—whether there is one, whether we should try to cobble one together, whether we should try to revise one that has been thrust upon us or simply evolved. We debate whether it is more important for Americans of a particular ethnic, racial, or cultural heritage to celebrate that history or to feel part of mainstream America—or whether both can coexist.

The question of who or what is an American is clearly important on a personal level as each of us comes to terms with who we are. But it is also a pressing political issue because citizenship, government entitlements, voting rights, job protection, civil liberties, and every other advantage or opportunity that America offers depend ultimately on whether a person is considered a true American.

American Identities Through History

As long as there has been an America, Americans have wondered and argued about who they were. The dominant issues and topics have shifted over time, but the same concerns have surfaced time and time again. All of the authors in this chapter have taken part in the debate about Americans and American identities, about individuality and cohesion, on both personal and political levels.

One of the first issues was whether there was—or could be—a unified American identity at all. Before the American Revolution, European settlers typically thought of themselves as residents of their own colonies and subjects of European monarchs, not as part of a unified new nation. In the 1750s, however, with the French and Indian War looming, Benjamin Franklin and others began calling for a union of the colonies for mutual protection. Franklin's lithograph *Join, or Die* is a graphic representation of the advantages of such unity: self-preservation rather than destruction.

After the Revolution, when political unity had been established, observers began offering assessments of the American character and culture, based almost exclusively on the Anglo Americans of the northeast and eastern seaboard. Alexis de Tocqueville attempts to define the American character by describing the political and social history of its most dominant group, and he identifies that group as English settlers, especially in New England. The approach that he takes—seeing the English character as the origin of true American culture—is one that almost all succeeding writers have had to address.

Although Tocqueville and other historians at the time focused on the British ancestry of mainstream America, many other cultures were contributing to the American identity. Over the course of the nineteenth century, the American population became more and more diverse: Irish fleeing famine; Jews and Catholics fleeing religious persecution; Italians, Swedes, Chinese, Russians, and others seeking jobs and opportunities. How were all these people—whose looks, languages, and actions were generally quite different from the dominant Anglo culture—to be incorporated into the American identity?

These immigrants generally favored assimilation. After arriving in America, each group found itself faced with further hardship and discrimination because they were so easily identified as "foreign." Their desire to succeed became a desire to escape the unwanted attention of other groups, to merge with mainstream American culture. The dominant ideal became that of the melting pot, with foreign differences melted away and identical Americans rolling off the assembly line.

At one time or another, every foreign element or influence associated with new immigrants was considered suspect. The artist who created *The U.S. Hotel* cartoon clearly wanted to preserve America for Americans—that is, for the people who were already here and the few newcomers who would completely accept those established cultural values. At other times, especially when America was faced with an outside enemy, all Americans were considered acceptable, regardless of their heritage. The divisiveness of *The U.S. Hotel* is completely absent from the propagandistic posters from World War I like *Victory Liberty Loan*, which proudly presented a diverse but united America.

One name often missing even from a picture of multicultural America is a recognizable Native American. European immigrant groups were not, of course, writing their history on a blank page. For countless generations, Native Americans had identified themselves with the American land. Luther Standing Bear articulates the argument that the true American is the Indian, identified with the essence of the American continent. Another group struggling in the early twentieth century to be recognized as full-fledged Americans were African Americans. Because the American identity had always been defined in terms of whites, African Americans were, as Ralph Ellison pointed out, invisible. In the Prologue to *Invisible Man,* Ellison uses the metaphor of invisibility to explore how the prevailing definition of *American* has kept some groups dominant and others excluded.

By the mid–twentieth century, the melting pot ideal was falling into disfavor. Clearly, not all Americans had been accounted for, and those who had been were beginning to challenge the value of assimilation. Critic Kenneth Burke suggests, "If men were not apart from one another, there would be no need for the rhetorician to proclaim their unity." John F. Kennedy, elected president in 1960, sought to unite the divided nation by proclaiming its unity. In his inaugural address, he defines a new American identity based on the nation's role in the international scene and its presumed unity of purpose.

In recent decades, many writers have focused on forging a coherent personal identity as Americans living within—and sometimes living as examples of—a cultural mosaic. Novelist Arturo Islas wrote of a bicultural American family celebrating that most American of holidays in "Thanksgiving Border Crossing," a chapter from his novel *Migrant Souls*. But some commentators, such as historian and educator Arthur Schlesinger, Jr., suggest that recognition of America's ethnic subcultures has gone too far. In his essay "The Cult of Ethnicity," he argues that the traditional American values of integration and assimilation have been rejected to the detriment of society. Issues of race and gender are sensitive and politically charged topics that can easily move from discussion to angry monologues, but some authors find ways to handle such sensitive issues that are less confrontational, more openly communicative, and therefore persuasive. In "Aunt Jeannette's Arm: On a Lesson of Being Jewish," Daniel Taube reflects on his own heritage and concerns about belonging while at the same time acknowledging the privilege accorded him through skin color. And Jeanne Wakatsuki Houston's speech, "A Tapestry of Hope," makes a strong case, without insult or accusation, for the strength to be found in America's diversity. In "Chicana," the chapter's student essay, student writer Martha Serrano argues for her right to define her own identity, choosing a label that accurately reflects her heritage. The film for this chapter, *The Joy Luck Club*, highlights the forging of several young Chinese American women's identities within and across cultures.

As you read and reflect on the selections that follow, consider not only your own personal identity and cultural origins but also the social and political implications of your identity and that of others as you begin to take part in the obligations and privileges of citizenship: open debate, difference of opinion, and the need to take a stand on important issues. Ask yourself the questions that the readings pose: Who is an American? Who is entitled to what America has to offer? What are our common bonds, our goals, our ethics and beliefs as a society?

∞ *Join, or Die* (1754)

BENJAMIN FRANKLIN

Benjamin Franklin (1706–1790), American statesman, author, printer, inventor, was apprenticed at age twelve to his brother, a printer, and in 1723 went to Philadelphia, where he eventually set up his own paper and published Poor Richard's Almanack. *Franklin was active throughout the American Revolution and was a signer of the Declaration of Independence. "Join, or Die," considered the first American cartoon, was Franklin's contribution to the debate about unity among the colonies as the French and Indian War approached. Franklin was the delegate from Pennsylvania as seven colonies sent representatives to negotiate with the Iroquois Nation, but his argument for a union of colonies with "one general government" for common defense would serve in other crises as well. To make his point, Franklin draws upon a myth that is familiar to his audience: a cut-up snake that is reassembled before sundown will come back to life.*

For Journals

Some created images, such as the American flag or the Statue of Liberty, evoke a sense of America for many people. What images from nature, whether plant or animal, embody your sense of America?

For Discussion

1. What is the primary argument of the cartoon? What does Franklin want the audience to do? Why?

2. Woodcuts with a moral or lesson in text below a visual image date back centuries. What are some advantages of making an argument in both text and image? What audiences can an author hope to reach in this way?

3. What are some of the advantages of visual argument over text, especially a simple design, as in this cartoon? Consider your own responses to other visual images, such as cartoons and advertisements, as well as the response you would expect of Franklin's contemporaries.

4. Mid-twentieth-century audiences may find the image of a snake threatening or disturbing, but what of the largely agrarian American population of the mid–eighteenth century? Do you suspect they had a similar response? Why might Franklin have wanted to identify the united colonies as a dangerous creature? Consider the use of other, similar slogans in early U.S. history, such as "don't tread on me," frequently accompanying an image of a coiled snake.

5. If a separated snake can unite its parts before sundown and survive, to what symbolic, political sundown is Franklin drawing an analogy?

6. What identity does Franklin foresee for the colonies? In what ways is this identity a precursor to other identities for America?

For Writing

1. Look through some newspapers, especially in the editorial pages, and select a political cartoon dealing with some aspect of American identity (foreign policy or immigration, for example). Analyze the allusions or references in the cartoon that readers need to know in order to understand the point of it. Will audiences fifty, one hundred, or two hundred years from now understand the cartoon you have selected? Explain your answer.

2. Research some aspect of American history or politics at the beginning of the twentieth century by looking at cartoons from the era—during an election, for example. You could review old newspapers or look at a cartoon collection at the library. Alternatively, browse through old newspapers or magazines and see what you can infer about the social or political debates of the times. To what extent do you understand the allusions or jokes? Why do you think this is so? Write up your findings in an analytical essay; if possible, include photocopies of the cartoons you analyze.

∽ *Origin of the Anglo-Americans* (1839)

ALEXIS DE TOCQUEVILLE

Count Alexis [Charles Henri Maurice Clerel] de Tocqueville (1805–1859), magistrate and political observer, held a number of positions in the French government. His observations of and writings on the workings of democracy in the United States, based on an extended visit to America, comprise the well-known work Democracy in America (De la démocratie en Amérique), *from which the following selection is excerpted. Written between 1835 and 1839, this work is considered a landmark study of American institutions and is often quoted to this day. It is valuable in studying both historical and contemporary aspects of American cultures.*

After the birth of a human being, his early years are obscurely spent in the toils or pleasures of childhood. As he grows up, the world receives him, when his manhood begins, and he enters into contact with his fellows. He is then studied for the first time, and it is imagined that the germ of the vices and the virtues of his maturer years is then formed. This, if I am not mistaken, is a great error. We must begin higher up; we must watch the infant in his mother's arms; we must see the first images which the external world casts upon the dark mirror of his mind, the first occurrences which he witnesses; we must hear the first words which awaken the sleeping powers of thought, and stand by his earliest efforts,—if we would understand the prejudices, the habits, and the passions which will rule his life. The entire man is, so to speak, to be seen in the cradle of the child.

The growth of nations presents something analogous to this; they all bear some marks of their origin. The circumstances which accompanied their birth and contributed to their development affect the whole term of their being. If we were able to go back to the elements of states, and to examine the oldest monuments of their history, I doubt not that we should discover in them the primal cause of the prejudices, the habits, the ruling passions, and, in short, of all that constitutes what is called the national character. We should there find the explanation of certain customs which now seem at variance with the prevailing manners; of such laws as conflict with established principles; and of such incoherent opinions as are here and there to be met with in society, like those fragments of broken chains which we sometimes see hanging from the vaults of an old edifice, and supporting nothing. This might explain the destinies of certain nations which seem borne on by an unknown force to ends of which they themselves are ignorant. But hitherto facts have been wanting to researches of this kind: the spirit of inquiry has only come upon communities in their latter days; and when they at length contemplated their origin, time had already obscured it, or ignorance and pride adorned it with truth-concealing fables.

America is the only country in which it has been possible to witness the natural and tranquil growth of society, and where the influence exercised on the future condition of states by their origin is clearly distinguishable. . . . America, consequently, exhibits in the broad light of day the phenomena which the ignorance or rudeness of earlier ages conceals from our researches. Near enough to the time when the states of America were founded, to be accurately acquainted with their elements, and sufficiently removed from that period to judge of some of their results, the men of our own day seem destined to see further than their predecessors into the series of human events. Providence has given us a torch which our forefathers did not possess, and has allowed us to discern fundamental causes in the history of the world which the obscurity of the past concealed from them. If we carefully examine the social and political state of America, after having studied its history, we shall remain perfectly convinced that not an opinion, not a custom, not a law, I may even say not an event, is upon record which the origin of that people will not explain. The readers of this book will find in the present chapter the germ of all that is to follow, and the key to almost the whole work.

The emigrants who came at different periods to occupy the territory now covered by the American Union differed from each other in many respects; their aim was not the same, and they governed themselves on different principles. These men had, however, certain features in common, and they were all placed in an analogous situation. The tie of language is, perhaps, the strongest and the most durable that can unite mankind. All the emigrants spoke the same tongue; they were all offsets from the same people. Born in a country which had been agitated for centuries by the struggles of faction, and in which all parties had been obliged in their turn to place themselves under the protection of the laws, their political education had been perfected in this rude school; and they were more conversant with the notions of right, and the principles of true freedom, than the greater part of their European contemporaries. At the period of the first emigrations, the township system, that fruitful germ of free institutions, was deeply rooted in the habits of the English; and with it the doctrine of the sovereignty of the people had been introduced into the bosom of the monarchy of the house of Tudor. . . .

5   Another remark, to which we shall hereafter have occasion to recur, is applicable not only to the English, but to . . . all the Europeans who successively established themselves in the New World. All these European colonies contained the elements, if not the development, of a complete democracy. Two causes led to this result. It may be said generally, that on leaving the mother country the emigrants had, in general, no notion of superiority one over another. The happy and the powerful do not go into exile, and there are no surer guaranties of equality among men than poverty and misfortune. It happened, however, on several occasions, that persons of rank were driven to America by political and religious quarrels. Laws were made to establish a gradation of ranks; but it was soon found that the soil of America was opposed to a territorial aristocracy. To bring that refractory land into cultivation, the constant and interested exertions of the owner himself were necessary; and when the ground was prepared, its produce was found to be insufficient to enrich a proprietor and a farmer at the same time. This land was then naturally broken up into small portions, which the proprietor cultivated for himself. Land is the basis of an aristocracy, which clings to the soil that supports it; for it is not by privileges alone, nor by birth, but by landed property handed down from generation to generation, that an aristocracy is constituted. A nation may present immense fortunes and extreme wretchedness; but unless those fortunes are territorial, there is no true aristocracy, but simply the class of the rich and that of the poor.

All the British colonies had then a great degree of family likeness at the epoch of their settlement. All of them, from their beginning, seemed destined to witness the growth, not of the aristocratic liberty of their mother country, but of that freedom of the middle and lower orders of which the history of the world had as yet furnished no complete example. In this general uniformity, however, several striking differences were discernible, which it is necessary to point out. Two branches may be distinguished in the great Anglo-American family, which have hitherto grown up without entirely commingling; the one in the South, the other in the North.

Virginia received the first English colony; the emigrants took possession of it in 1607. The idea that mines of gold and silver are the sources of national wealth was at that time singularly prevalent in Europe; a fatal delusion, which has done more to impoverish the European nations who adopted it, and has cost more lives in America, than the united influence of war and bad laws. The men sent to Virginia were seekers of gold, adventurers without resources and without character, whose turbulent and restless spirit endangered the infant colony, and rendered its progress uncertain. Artisans and agriculturists arrived afterwards; and, although they were a more moral and orderly race of men, they were hardly in any respect above the level of the inferior classes in England. No lofty views, no spiritual conception, presided over the foundation of these new settlements. The colony was scarcely established when slavery was introduced; this was the capital fact which was to exercise an immense influence on the character, the laws and the whole future of the South. Slavery . . . dishonors labor; it introduces idleness into society, and with idleness, ignorance and pride, luxury and distress. It enervates the powers of the mind, and benumbs the activity of man. The influence of slavery, united to the English character, explains the manners and the social condition of the Southern States.

In the North, the same English character . . . received totally different colors. Here . . . the two or three main ideas which now constitute the basis of the social theory of the United States were first combined. . . . They now extend their influence . . . over the whole American world. The civilization of New England has been like a beacon lit upon a hill, which, after it has diffused its warmth immediately around it, also tinges the distant horizon with its glow. . . .

The settlers who established themselves on the shores of New England all belonged to the more independent classes of their native country. Their union on the soil of America at once presented the singular phenomenon of a society containing neither lords nor common people, and we may almost say, neither rich nor poor. These men possessed, in proportion to their number, a greater mass of intelligence than is to be found in any European nation of our own time. All, perhaps without a single exception, had received a good education, and many of them were known in Europe for their talents and their acquirements. The other colonies had been founded by adventurers without families; the emigrants of New England brought with them the best elements of order and morality; they landed on the desert coast accompanied by their wives and children. But what especially distinguished them from all others was the aim of their undertaking. They had not been obliged by necessity to leave their country; the social position they abandoned was one to be regretted, and their means of subsistence were certain. . . . In facing the inevitable sufferings of exile, their object was the triumph of an idea.

10   The emigrants, or, as they deservedly styled themselves, the Pilgrims, belonged to that English sect the austerity of whose principles had acquired for them the name of Puritans. Puritanism was not merely a religious doctrine, but it corresponded in many points with the most absolute democratic and republican theories. It was this tendency which had aroused its most dangerous adversaries. Persecuted by the government of the mother country, and disgusted by the habits of a society which the rigor of their own principles condemned, the Puritans went forth to seek some rude and unfrequented part of the world, where they could live according to their own opinions, and worship God in freedom. . . . Puritanism . . . was scarcely less a political than a religious doctrine. No sooner had the emigrants landed on the barren coast . . . than it was their first care to constitute a society, by subscribing the [Mayflower Compact]:

"In the name of God. Amen. We, whose names are underwritten, the loyal subjects of our dread Sovereign Lord King James, &s, &c., Having undertaken for the glory of God, and advancement of the Christian Faith, and the honour of our King and country, a voyage to plant the first colony in the northern parts of Virginia; Do by these presents solemnly and mutually, in the presence of God and one another, covenant and combine ourselves together into a civil body politick, for our better ordering and preservation, and furtherance of the ends aforesaid: and by virtue hereof do enact, constitute, and frame such just and equal laws, ordinances, acts, constitutions, and offices, from time to time, as shall be thought most meet and convenient for the general good of the Colony: unto which we promise all due submission and obedience. . . ."

This happened in 1620, and from that time forwards the emigration went on. The religious and political passions which ravaged the British empire during the whole reign of Charles I drove fresh crowds of sectarians every year to the shores of America. In England, the stronghold of Puritanism continued to be in the middle classes; and it was from the middle classes that most of the emigrants came. The population of New England increased rapidly; and whilst the hierarchy of rank despotically classed the inhabitants of the mother country, the colony approximated more and more the novel spectacle of a community homogeneous in all its parts. A democracy, more perfect than antiquity had dared to dream of, started in full size and panoply from the midst of an ancient feudal society.

For Journals

Whom do you think of as the first Americans?

For Discussion

1. Why do you think Tocqueville frames his study of America and Americans using the analogy of studying the child to know the man? How does this image illuminate and clarify his purpose?

2. To what in the Anglo Americans' history does Tocqueville attribute their knowledge of the principles of freedom? Are you persuaded by his conclusion? Do you think his contemporaries would have been?

3. How does Tocqueville characterize New England and the Puritans? Pay special attention to the passages he cites to illuminate "the spirit of these pious adventurers." What conclusions does he draw from his evidence? Do you think his contemporary audience would have been convinced? Are you convinced of the Puritans' character based on the passage he cites?

4. According to Tocqueville, what effects does slavery have on a society in general? What do you infer from his remark, "The influence of slavery, united to the English character, explains the manners and the social condition of the Southern states"?

5. Tocqueville writes in paragraph 4, "The tie of language is, perhaps, the strongest and the most durable that can unite mankind." What assumption is he making about language and culture? How does this approach to culture define "American"? Do you agree with his assumption and with this definition? How do you think his contemporaries would have reacted to his assertion?

For Writing

1. Drawing from your discussions in response to discussion items 3 and 4 above, write an essay in which you compare and contrast Tocqueville's treatment of North and South and the American identities that developed in each region. Which identity do you find more clearly articulated? Which assertions are more persuasive? Do you find his generalizations merited, based on the evidence he offers? How is your assessment of his argument biased by your own cultural or geographical identity?

2. Tocqueville's discussion of a common language has had strong reverberations in recent debates over "English only" in schools and over policies establishing English as the official language of the United

States. Research one of these issues, checking recent journal, newspaper, and magazine indexes for both educational journals and popular magazines, as well as books, so that you have up-to-date information. Develop a thesis about the topic and support it with well-reasoned arguments based on evidence from your research.

⇨ *The U.S. Hotel Badly Needs a Bouncer* (ca. 1890)

JOSEPH KEPPLER

The following cartoon was published in Puck, *the first successful American weekly humor magazine.* Puck *was started in 1876 by Joseph Keppler, one of the well-known color cartoonists of the great age of political cartooning, which flourished from approximately 1870 to 1900. While other American magazines printed perhaps one cartoon per issue, Keppler published three a week in* Puck, *perhaps accounting in part for the magazine's popularity. Color cartoons at that time were larger than those we are used to today.* Puck, *for example, included full-page cartoons on the front and back covers and a two-page spread. This golden age of cartooning and the production of* Puck, *which was published until 1918, coincided with a huge influx of European immigrants in America—some 14 million between 1869 and 1900. It is not surprising that issues of immigration, and American identity, appeared as the subject matter for such cartoons.*

For Journals

Do you think there are certain people who should be encouraged to come to America or discouraged from coming?

For Discussion

1. Study the cartoon, noting the figures and their appearance, their arrangement, the relationships between them, and their identities. What sorts of people are represented by which types of figures? Which are the "good" identities or qualities? Which are the undesirable traits?

2. Discuss the overall point of the cartoon. From what evidence, or examples, did you infer that point? What assumptions about America, Americans, and immigrants are implied? State the cartoon's argument in your own words.

3. Why do you believe the artist chose the metaphor of the hotel? What effect does this metaphor have on the argument? Do you believe America should be a hotel rather than a home? Should bouncers be able to evict people?

4. How might the artist's contemporaries have reacted to the cartoon? Judging from the artist's persuasive strategies, what can you infer from

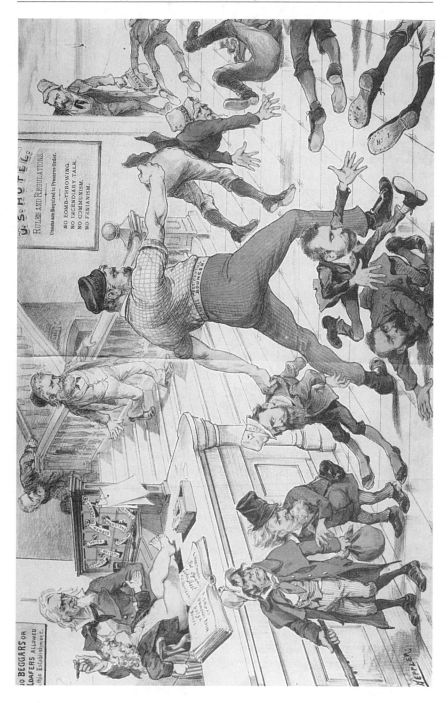

the cartoon about immigration issues of the times? About the cartoon's audiences and their beliefs and values? Does the message seem more directed at getting people to behave well or encouraging them to regulate the behavior of others?

For Writing

1.   Compare the argument and assumptions in *The U.S. Hotel* with other selections in this chapter, such as Ralph Ellison's Prologue to *Invisible Man*. Alternatively, compare the persuasiveness of this cartoon with the posters in Chapter 8, "War and the Enemy." What common strategies or themes do you find?

2.   Select a recent social or political cartoon—from the editorial pages of a newspaper, for example—on an issue related to American identities, such as immigration. Compare and contrast the cartoon you choose with *The U.S. Hotel*, focusing on strategies of persuasion and the artists' implicit assumptions about their audiences.

3.   How do you think audiences have changed since this cartoon was published? In what ways have they remained the same? How have strategies or techniques of persuasion changed or remained the same?

∽ *Victory Liberty Loan* (1919)

HOWARD CHANDLER CHRISTY

World War I began in Europe in 1914, and the United States entered the war in 1917. In the year and a half following the U.S. declaration of war, civilian efforts to support the war included some $18 billion in war-bond purchases. War bonds, or funds through which consumers lent money to the government at a modest interest rate, helped finance war matériel without harsh increases in federal income taxes; to some extent, bonds were said to help deal with currency inflation that can ensue when there are few consumer goods to buy. More important, though, Americans were also persuaded to "buy into" the war through purchasing bonds. William Gibbs McAdoo, who was then secretary of the Treasury, wrote: "We went directly to the people, and that means to everybody—to business men, workmen, farmers, bankers, millionaires, school-teachers, laborers. We capitalized on the profound impulse called patriotism. It is the quality of coherence that holds a nation together; it is one of the deepest and most powerful of human motives." Artists such as Christy were commissioned to create posters to advertise the bonds, while film stars and others appeared at rallies to urge people to buy bonds—and to support the war. This particular design was quite successful both during and for some time after the war.

For Journals

What visual symbols remind you of America? What kinds of symbols appeal to your sense of patriotism?

AMERICANS ALL!
HONOR ROLL
Du Bois
Smith
O'Brien
Cejka
Haucke
Pappandrikopolous
Andrassi
Villotto
Levy
Turovich
Kowalski
Chriczanevicz
Knutson
Gonzales
Victory Liberty Loan

For Discussion

1. What draws your eye when you first look at the poster? What are the poster's most prominent features? What did the artist want the viewer to see and feel first? Why?

2. Is the clothing of the female figure in the poster what you expect for its era? How would you account for her style of dress?

3. What do the wreath, the gold star, and the honor roll symbolize? (In what other contexts have you seen these symbols?) The woman is literally draping herself in the American flag. What do her posture and gestures suggest?

4. Read the list of names under the heading "Honor Roll" carefully. What do you notice? What point is the artist trying to make?

5. Who do you think was the intended audience for this poster? Explain your answer.

For Writing

1. Compare and contrast the assumptions about the American identity evident in this poster and in the cartoon *The U.S. Hotel.* Are the assumptions similar or different? Explain your assessment.

2. Select a modern advertisement that tries to appeal to Americans with a variety of ethnic heritages. Write an essay analyzing the choice of persuasive strategies in the ad and their effectiveness.

3. If you were asked to provide a poster or flyer to appeal to patriotism, what design choices would you make? Try to design such a poster or flyer (you may want to take an existing one and give it a patriotic edge), writing out the text and sketching the images you would use. Write an essay explaining your choices.

∞ *What the Indian Means to America* (1933)

LUTHER STANDING BEAR

Luther Standing Bear (1868–1947), a member of a Teton Sioux tribe, attended the government Indian school at Carlyle, Pennsylvania, and later worked in jobs ranging from storekeeper to minister to performer in Buffalo Bill's Wild West Show. Having lived during and observed firsthand the forcible removal of Native Americans to reservations during the rapid expansion of the West, Standing Bear found the government practices untenable. His views are set out in My People the Sioux *(1928),* My

Indian Boyhood (1931), Stories of the Sioux *(1934), and* Land of the Spotted Eagle *(1933), from which the following selection is excerpted. In this essay, Standing Bear identifies the American Indian as the one who truly understands the American lands.*

The feathered and blanketed figure of the American Indian has come to symbolize the American continent. He is the man who through centuries has been moulded and sculpted by the same hand that shaped its mountains, forests, and plains, and marked the course of its rivers.

The American Indian is of the soil, whether it be the region of forests, plains, pueblos, or mesas. He fits into the landscape, for the hand that fashioned the continent also fashioned the man for his surroundings. He once grew as naturally as the wild sunflowers; he belongs just as the buffalo belonged.

With a physique that fitted, the man developed fitting skills—crafts which today are called American. And the body had a soul, also formed and moulded by the same master hand of harmony. Out of the Indian approach to existence there came a great freedom—an intense and absorbing love for nature; a respect for life; enriching faith in a Supreme Power; and principles of truth, honesty, generosity, equity, and brotherhood as a guide to mundane relations. . . .

The white man does not understand the Indian for the reason that he does not understand America. He is too far removed from its formative processes. The roots of the tree of his life have not yet grasped the rock and soil. The white man is still troubled with primitive fears; he still has in his consciousness the perils of this frontier continent, some of its fastnesses not yet having yielded to his questing footsteps and inquiring eyes. He shudders still with the memory of the loss of his forefathers upon its scorching deserts and forbidding mountaintops. The man from Europe is still a foreigner and an alien. And he still hates the man who questioned his path across the continent.

But in the Indian the spirit of the land is still vested; it will be until 5 other men are able to divine and meet its rhythm. Men must be born and reborn to belong. Their bodies must be formed of the dust of their forefathers' bones.

The attempted transformation of the Indian by the white man and the chaos that has resulted are but the fruits of the white man's disobedience of a fundamental and spiritual law. The pressure that has been brought to bear upon the native people, since the cessation of armed conflict, in the attempt to force conformity of custom and habit has caused a reaction more destructive than war, and the injury has not only affected the Indian, but has extended to the white population as well. Tyranny, stupidity, and lack of vision have brought about the situation now alluded to as the "Indian Problem."

There is, I insist, no Indian problem as created by the Indian himself. Every problem that exists today in regard to the native population is due to the white man's cast of mind, which is unable, at least reluctant, to seek understanding and achieve adjustment in a new and a significant environment into which it has so recently come.

The white man excused his presence here by saying that he has been guided by the will of his God; and in so saying absolved himself of all responsibility for his appearance in a land occupied by other men.

Then, too, his law was a written law; his divine decalogue reposed in a book. And what better proof that his advent into this country and his subsequent acts were the result of divine will! He brought the Word! There ensued a blind worship of written history, of books, of the written word, that has denuded the spoken word of its power and sacredness. The written word became established as a criterion of the superior man—a symbol of emotional fineness. The man who could write his name on a piece of paper, whether or not he possessed the spiritual fineness to honor those words in speech, was by some miraculous formula a more highly developed and sensitized person than the one who had never had a pen in hand, but whose spoken word was inviolable and whose sense of honor and truth was paramount. With false reasoning was the quality of human character measured by man's ability to make with an implement a mark upon paper. But granting this mode of reasoning be correct and just, then where are to be placed the thousands of illiterate whites who are unable to read and write? Are they, too, "savages"? Is not humanness a matter of heart and mind, and is it not evident in the form of relationship with men? Is not kindness more powerful than arrogance; and truth more powerful than the sword?

10   True, the white man brought great change. But the varied fruits of his civilization, though highly colored and inviting, are sickening and deadening. And if it be the part of civilization to maim, rob, and thwart, then what is progress? . . .

After subjugation, after dispossession, there was cast the last abuse upon the people who so entirely resented their wrongs and punishments, and that was the stamping and labeling of them as savages. To make this label stick has been the task of the white race and the greatest salve that it has been able to apply to its sore and troubled conscience now hardened through the habitual practice of injustice.

But all the years of calling the Indian a savage has never made him one; all the denial of his virtues has never taken them from him; and the very resistance he has made to save the things inalienably his has been his saving strength—that which will stand him in need when justice does make its belated appearance and he undertakes rehabilitation.

All sorts of feeble excuses are heard for the continued subjection of the Indian. One of the most common is that he is not yet ready to accept the society of the white man—that he is not yet ready to mingle as a social entity.

This, I maintain, is beside the question. The matter is not one of making over the external Indian into the likeness of the white race—a process detrimental to both races. Who can say that the white man's way is better for the Indian? Where resides the human judgment with the competence to weigh and value Indian ideals and spiritual concepts; or substitute for them other values?

Then, has the white man's social order been so harmonious and ideal as to merit the respect of the Indian, and for that matter the thinking class of the white race? Is it wise to urge upon the Indian a foreign social form? Let none but the Indian answer!

Rather, let the white brother face about and cast his mental eye upon a new angle of vision. Let him look upon the Indian world as a human world; then let him see to it that human rights be accorded to the Indians. And this for the purpose of retaining for his own order of society a measure of humanity. . . .

The spiritual health and existence of the Indian was maintained by song, magic, ritual, dance, symbolism, oratory (or council), design, handicraft, and folk-story.

Manifestly, to check or thwart this expression is to bring about spiritual decline. And it is in this condition of decline that the Indian people are today. There is but a feeble effort among the Sioux to keep alive their traditional songs and dances, while among other tribes there is but a half-hearted attempt to offset the influence of the Government school and at the same time recover from the crushing and stifling regime of the Indian Bureau.

One has but to speak of Indian verse to receive uncomprehending and unbelieving glances. Yet the Indian loved verse and into this mode of expression went his deepest feelings. Only a few ardent and advanced students seem interested; nevertheless, they have given in book form enough Indian translations to set forth the character and quality of Indian verse.

Oratory receives a little better understanding on the part of the white public, owing to the fact that oratorical complications include those of Indian orators.

Hard as it seemingly is for the white man's ear to sense the differences, Indian songs are as varied as the many emotions which inspire them, for no two of them are alike. For instance, the Song of Victory is spirited and the notes high and remindful of an unrestrained hunter or warrior riding exultantly over the prairies. On the other hand, the song of the *Cano unye* is solemn and full of urge, for it is meant to inspire the young men to deeds of valor. Then there are the songs of death and the spiritual songs which are connected with the ceremony of initiation. These are full of the spirit of praise and worship, and so strong are some of these invocations that the very air seems as if surcharged with the presence of the Big Holy.

The Indian loved to worship. From birth to death he revered his surroundings. He considered himself born in the luxurious lap of Mother Earth and no place was to him humble. There was nothing between him and the Big Holy. The contact was immediate and personal, and the blessings of Wakan Tanka flowed over the Indian like rain showered from the sky. Wakan Tanka was not aloof, apart, and ever seeking to quell evil forces. He did not punish the animals and the birds, and likewise He did not punish man. He was not a punishing God. For there was never a question as to the supremacy of an evil power over and above the power of Good. There was but one ruling power, and that was *Good.*

Of course, none but an adoring one could dance for days with his face to the sacred sun, and that time is all but done. We cannot have back the days of the buffalo and the beaver; we cannot win back our clean blood-stream and superb health, and we can never again expect the beautiful *rapport* we once had with Nature. The springs and lakes have dried and the mountains are bare of forests. The plow has changed the face of the world. Wi-wila is dead! No more may we heal our sick and comfort our dying with a strength founded on faith, for even the animals now fear us, and fear supplants faith.

And the Indian wants to dance! It is his way of expressing devotion, of communing with unseen power, and in keeping his tribal identity. When the Lakota heart was filled with high emotion, he danced. When he felt the benediction of the warming rays of the sun, he danced. When his blood ran hot with success of the hunt or chase, he danced. When his heart was filled with pity for the orphan, the lonely father, or bereaved mother, he danced. All the joys and exaltations of life, all his gratefulness and thankfulness, all his acknowledgments of the mysterious power that guided life, and all his aspirations for a better life, culminated in one great dance—the Sun Dance.

25   When the Indian has forgotten the music of his forefathers, when the sound of the tomtom is no more, when noisy jazz has drowned the melody of the flute, he will be a dead Indian. When the memory of his heroes are no longer told in story, and he forsakes the beautiful white buckskin for factory shoddy, he will be dead. When from him has been taken all that is his, all that he has visioned in nature, all that has come to him from infinite sources, he then, truly, will be a dead Indian. His spirit will be gone, and though he walk crowded streets, he will, in truth, be—*dead!*

But all this must not perish; it must live, to the end that America shall be educated no longer to regard native production of whatever tribe—folk-story, basketry, pottery, dance, song, poetry—as curios, and native artists as curiosities. For who but the man indigenous to the soil could produce its song, story, and folk-tale; who but the man who loved the dust beneath his feet could shape it and put it into undying, ceramic form; who but he who loved the reeds that grew beside still waters, and the damp roots of shrub and tree, could save it from seasonal death, and with almost superhuman patience weave it into enduring objects of beauty—into timeless art!

Regarding the "civilization" that has been thrust upon me since the days of reservation, it has not added one whit to my sense of justice; to my reverence for the rights of life; to my love for truth, honesty, and generosity; nor to my faith in Wakan Tanka—God of the Lakotas. For after all the great religions have been preached and expounded, or have been revealed by brilliant scholars, or have been written in books and embellished in fine language with finer covers, man—all man—is still confronted with the Great Mystery.

So if today I had a young mind to direct, to start on the journey of life, and I was faced with the duty of choosing between the natural way of my forefathers and that of the white man's present way of civilization, I would, for its welfare, unhesitatingly set that child's feet in the path of my forefathers. I would raise him to be an Indian!

For Journals

What do you know about the relationship between American Indians and the land?

For Discussion

1. How does Standing Bear establish the argument that the American Indian is not only the true symbol but also the essence of the American continent? In what ways do the American Indian and the land share an identity?

2. Standing Bear contrasts the American Indians and the whites in terms of their relationship with the land. What does he mean when he asserts that "in the Indian the spirit of the land is still vested"? How can others inherit that spirit?

3. According to Standing Bear, in what ways are whites foreigners in America? What kind of assimilation do white people need to undergo so as not to be aliens? How is this process similar to and different from other kinds of assimilation you have heard of?

4. How have the pressure and "conformity of custom" injured both American Indians and whites?

5. How do whites justify their presence in America and their subjugation of Indians? How does the author refute these arguments? Standing Bear published this selection in 1933 as part of a larger work. How do you think his audiences responded to the initial arguments of whites and to Standing Bear's refutation? How do you respond?

For Writing

1.   Write an essay summarizing Standing Bear's definition of a true American and then either offer support for or refute his position.

2.   Research the Trail of Tears, the establishing of the reservation system, or some other specific issue in the history of Indian-white relations in America, and write a documented essay explaining the issue or event. Alternatively, investigate the current status of the relationship between one or more of the Native American nations and the U.S. government, focusing on the degree to which Indian-white relations have, or have not, changed since the publication of Standing Bear's books in the late 1920s and early 1930s.

∞ *Prologue to* Invisible Man (1947)

RALPH ELLISON

Born in Oklahoma in 1914 and educated at the Tuskegee Institute in Alabama, Ralph Ellison established his considerable reputation with his first and only novel, Invisible Man, *first published in 1947 and reprinted numerous times since, most recently in 1990. This selection from the Prologue is typical of Ellison's lyrical and unflinching portrayal of black identity in American society, an identity the novelist has fleshed out more fully in collections of essays such as* Shadow and Act *(1964) and* Going to the Territory *(1986). Ellison lectured at Yale, Columbia, and New York Universities, and remains a dominant figure on the American literary landscape even after his death in 1994.*

I am an invisible man. No, I am not a spook like those who haunted Edgar Allan Poe; nor am I one of your Hollywood-movie ectoplasms. I am a man of substance, of flesh and bone, fiber and liquids—and I might even be said to possess a mind. I am invisible, understand, simply because people refuse to see me. Like the bodiless heads you see sometimes in circus sideshows, it is as though I have been surrounded by mirrors of hard, distorting glass. When they approach me they see only my surroundings, themselves, or figments of their imagination—indeed, everything and anything except me.

Nor is my invisibility exactly a matter of a biochemical accident to my epidermis. That invisibility to which I refer occurs because of a peculiar disposition of the eyes of those with whom I come in contact. A matter of the construction of their *inner* eyes, those eyes with which they look through their physical eyes upon reality. I am not complaining, nor am I protesting either. It is sometimes advantageous to be unseen, although it is most often rather wearing on the nerves. Then too, you're constantly being bumped against by those of poor vision. Or again, you often doubt if you really exist. You wonder whether you aren't simply a phantom in other people's minds. Say, a figure in a nightmare which the sleeper tries with all his strength to destroy. It's when you feel like this that, out of resentment, you begin to bump people back. And, let me confess, you feel that way most of the time. You ache with the need to convince yourself that you do exist in the real world, that you're a part of all the sound and anguish, and you strike out with your fists, you curse and you swear to make them recognize you. And, alas, it's seldom successful.

One night I accidentally bumped into a man, and perhaps because of the near darkness he saw me and called me an insulting name. I sprang at him, seized his coat lapels and demanded that he apologize. He was a tall blond man, and as my face came close to his he looked insolently out of his blue eyes and cursed me, his breath hot in my face as he struggled. I pulled his chin down sharp upon the crown of my head, butting him as I had seen the West Indians do, and I felt his flesh tear and the blood gush out, and I yelled, "Apologize! Apologize!" But he continued to curse and struggle, and I butted him again and again until he went down heavily, on his knees, profusely bleeding. I kicked him repeatedly, in a frenzy because he still uttered insults though his lips were frothy with blood. Oh yes, I kicked him! And in my outrage I got out my knife and prepared to slit his throat, right there beneath the lamplight in the deserted street, holding him in the collar with one hand, and opening the knife with my teeth—when it occurred to me that the man had not *seen* me, actually; that he, as far as he knew, was in the midst of a walking nightmare! And I stopped the blade, slicing the air as I pushed him away, letting him fall back to the street. I stared at him hard as the lights of a car stabbed through the darkness. He lay there, moaning on the asphalt; a man almost killed by a phantom. It unnerved me. I was both disgusted and ashamed. I was like a drunken man myself, wavering about on weakened legs. Then I was amused: Something in this man's thick head had sprung out and beaten him within an inch of his life. I began to laugh at this crazy discovery. Would he have awakened at the point of death? Would Death himself have freed him for wakeful living? But I didn't linger. I ran away into the dark, laughing so hard I feared I might rupture myself. The next day I saw his picture in the *Daily News,* beneath a caption stating that he had been "mugged." Poor fool, poor blind fool, I thought with sincere compassion, mugged by an invisible man!

Most of the time (although I do not choose as I once did to deny the violence of my days by ignoring it) I am not so overtly violent. I remember that I am invisible and walk softly so as not to awaken the sleeping ones. Sometimes it is best not to awaken them; there are few things in the world as dangerous as sleepwalkers. I learned in time though that it is possible to carry on a fight against them without their realizing it. For instance, I have been carrying on a fight with Monopolated Light & Power for some time now. I use their service and pay them nothing at all, and they don't know it. Oh, they suspect that power is being drained off, but they don't know where. All they know is that according to the master meter back there in their power station a hell of a lot of free current is disappearing somewhere into the jungle of Harlem. The joke, of course, is that I don't live in Harlem but in a border area. Several years ago (before I discovered the advantages of being invisible) I went through the routine process of buying service and paying their outrageous rates. But no more. I gave up all that, along with my apartment, and my old way of life: That way based upon the fallacious assumption that I, like other men, was visible. Now, aware of my invisibility, I live rent-free in a building rented strictly to whites, in a section of the basement that was shut off and forgotten during the nineteenth century, which I discovered when I was trying to escape in the night from Ras the Destroyer. But that's getting too far ahead of the story, almost to the end, although the end is in the beginning and lies far ahead.

5   The point now is that I found a home—or a hole in the ground, as you will. Now don't jump to any conclusion that because I call my home a "hole" it is damp and cold like a grave; there are cold holes and warm holes. Mine is a warm hole. And remember, a bear retires to his hole for the winter and lives until spring; then he comes strolling out like the Easter chick breaking from its shell. I say all this to assure you that it is incorrect to assume that, because I'm invisible and live in a hole, I am dead. I am neither dead nor in a state of suspended animation. Call me Jack-the-Bear, for I am in a state of hibernation.

My hole is warm and full of light. Yes, *full* of light. I doubt if there is a brighter spot in all New York than this hole of mine, and I do not exclude Broadway. Or the Empire State Building on a photographer's dream night. But that is taking advantage of you. Those two spots are among the darkest of our whole civilization—pardon me, our whole *culture* (an important distinction, I've heard)—which might sound like a hoax, or a contradiction, but that (by contradiction, I mean) is how the world moves: Not like an arrow, but a boomerang. (Beware of those who speak of the *spiral* of history; they are preparing a boomerang. Keep a steel helmet handy.) I know; I have been boomeranged across my head so much that I now can see the darkness of lightness. And I love light. Perhaps you'll think it strange that an invisible man should need light, desire light, love light. But maybe it is exactly because I *am* invisible. Light confirms my reality, gives birth to my form. A beautiful girl once told me of a recurring nightmare in which she lay in the center of a large dark room and felt her face expand until it filled the whole room, becoming a formless mass while her eyes ran in bilious jelly up the chimney. And so it is with me. Without light I am not only invisible, but formless as well; and to be unaware of one's form is to live a death. I myself, after existing some twenty years, did not become alive until I discovered my invisibility.

For Journals

Are there groups of people in your community—ethnic minorities, older people, disabled people—whom you rarely notice?

For Discussion

1. How is the notion of invisibility developed in this selection? Why do you think Ellison uses the idea of invisibility? What associations does it have? What could a person do—or not do—if invisible?

2. The speaker notes that he found a home, a "hole in the ground," literally in a basement of a building restricted to whites. What is significant about his living in such a place? What is special, literally and metaphorically, about the light and the power company?

3. In what sense is the invisible man's identity related to and developed by how others see him? Consider his growing awareness of being invisible, the incident with the blond stranger, and his relationship with the power company.

4. In an introduction to *Invisible Man* that accompanied an edition printed in 1981, Ellison writes, "My task was one of revealing the human universals hidden within the plight of one who was both black and an American." What do you infer from this selection about the plight of those who live with this double identity?

For Writing

1. Write an essay discussing the effects of others' perceptions on developing one's own identity, whether in terms of ethnicity, race, culture, nationality, or age. You could develop this assignment as a personal essay; alternatively, you could investigate and incorporate recent research on the subject, found in psychology or sociology books and journals.

2. Ellison wrote that his task in *Invisible Man* was to deal with "the sheer rhetorical challenge involved in communicating across our barriers of race and religion, class, color, and region—barriers which consist of the many strategies of division that were designed, and still function, to prevent what would otherwise have been a more or less natural recognition of the reality of blackness." How does he cope with

the rhetorical challenges—obstacles to persuasion—he mentions here? In what ways do his metaphor of invisibility and the voice and tone of the speaker serve to meet those challenges?

∞ *Inaugural Address* (1961)

JOHN F. KENNEDY

John Fitzgerald Kennedy (1917–1963) was born in Brookline, Massachusetts, and graduated from Harvard University. He served as a torpedo boat commander in the Pacific during World War II and received both the Navy Medal and the Purple Heart for his service. For his book Profiles in Courage *(1956) Kennedy won the Pulitzer Prize, and after a career in Congress he became the youngest elected and first Roman Catholic president. His administration was cut tragically short when rifle fire from an assassin in Dallas, Texas, ended his life in 1963. Kennedy's famous inaugural address exemplifies the youth, vitality, and vision of a generation and remains a classic of American rhetoric.*

We observe today not a victory of party but a celebration of freedom—symbolizing an end as well as a beginning, signifying renewal as well as change. For I have sworn before you and Almighty God the same solemn oath our forebears prescribed nearly a century and three-quarters ago.

The world is very different now. For man holds in his mortal hands the power to abolish all forms of human poverty and all forms of human life. And yet the same revolutionary beliefs for which our forebears fought are still at issue around the globe: the belief that the rights of man come not from the generosity of the state but from the hand of God.

We dare not forget today that we are the heirs of that first revolution. Let the word go forth from this time and place, to friend and foe alike, that the torch has been passed to a new generation of Americans—born in this century, tempered by war, disciplined by a hard and bitter peace, proud of our ancient heritage—and unwilling to witness or permit the slow undoing of those human rights to which this nation has always been committed, and to which we are committed today at home and around the world.

Let every nation know, whether it wishes us well or ill, that we shall pay any price, bear any burden, meet any hardship, support any friend, oppose any foe to assure the survival and the success of liberty.

5   This much we pledge—and more.

To those old allies whose cultural and spiritual origins we share, we pledge the loyalty of faithful friends. United, there is little we cannot do in a host of cooperative ventures. Divided, there is little we can do—for we dare not meet a powerful challenge at odds and split asunder.

To those new states whom we welcome to the ranks of the free, we pledge our word that one form of colonial control shall not have passed away merely to be replaced by a far more iron tyranny. We shall not always expect to find them supporting our view. But we shall always hope to find them strongly supporting their own freedom—and to remember that, in the past, those who foolishly sought power by riding the back of the tiger ended up inside.

To those people in the huts and villages of half the globe struggling to break the bonds of mass misery, we pledge our best efforts to help them help themselves, for whatever period is required—not because the Communists may be doing it, not because we seek their votes, but because it is right. If a free society cannot help the many who are poor, it cannot save the few who are rich.

To our sister republics south of the border, we offer a special pledge: to convert our good words into good deeds—in a new alliance for progress—to assist free men and free governments in casting off the chains of poverty. But this peaceful revolution of hope cannot become the prey of hostile powers. Let all our neighbors know that we shall join with them to oppose aggression or subversion anywhere in the Americas. And let every other power know that this hemisphere intends to remain the master of its own house.

To that world assembly of sovereign states, the United Nations, our 10 last best hope in an age where the instruments of war have far outpaced the instruments of peace, we renew our pledge of support—to prevent it from becoming merely a forum for invective, to strengthen its shield of the new and the weak, and to enlarge the area in which its writ may run.

Finally, to those nations who would make themselves our adversary, we offer not a pledge but a request: that both sides begin anew the quest for peace, before the dark powers of destruction unleashed by science engulf all humanity in planned or accidental self-destruction.

We dare not tempt them with weakness. For only when our arms are sufficient beyond doubt can we be certain beyond doubt that they will never be employed.

But neither can two great and powerful groups of nations take comfort from our present course—both sides overburdened by the cost of modern weapons, both rightly alarmed by the steady spread of the deadly atom, yet both racing to alter that uncertain balance of terror that stays the hand of mankind's final war.

So let us begin anew, remembering on both sides that civility is not a sign of weakness, and sincerity is always subject to proof. Let us never negotiate out of fear. But let us never fear to negotiate.

Let both sides explore what problems unite us instead of belabor- 15 ing those problems which divide us.

Let both sides, for the first time, formulate serious and precise proposals for the inspection and control of arms—and bring the absolute power to destroy other nations under the absolute control of all nations.

Let both sides seek to invoke the wonders of science instead of its terrors. Together let us explore the stars, conquer the deserts, eradicate disease, tap the ocean depths, and encourage the arts and commerce.

Let both sides unite to heed in all corners of the earth the command of Isaiah—to "undo the heavy burdens . . . [and] let the oppressed go free."

And if a beachhead of cooperation may push back the jungle of suspicion, let both sides join in creating a new endeavor, not a new balance of power, but a new world of law, where the strong are just and the weak secure and the peace preserved.

20   All this will not be finished in the first one hundred days. Nor will it be finished in the first one thousand days, nor in the life of this administration, nor even perhaps in our lifetime on this planet. But let us begin.

In your hands, my fellow citizens, more than mine, will rest the final success or failure of our course. Since this country was founded, each generation of Americans has been summoned to give testimony to its national loyalty. The graves of young Americans who answered the call to service surround the globe.

Now the trumpet summons us again—not as a call to bear arms, though arms we need; not as a call to battle, though embattled we are—but a call to bear the burden of a long twilight struggle, year in and year out, "rejoicing in hope, patient in tribulation," a struggle against the common enemies of man: tyranny, poverty, disease, and war itself.

Can we forge against these enemies a grand and global alliance, north and south, east and west, that can assure a more fruitful life for all mankind? Will you join in that historic effort?

In the long history of the world, only a few generations have been granted the role of defending freedom in its hour of maximum danger. I do not shrink from this responsibility—I welcome it. I do not believe that any of us would exchange places with any other people or any other generation. The energy, the faith, the devotion which we bring to this endeavor will light our country and all who serve it—and the glow from that fire can truly light the world.

25   And so, my fellow Americans: Ask not what your country can do for you—ask what you can do for your country.

My fellow citizens of the world: Ask not what America will do for you, but what together we can do for the freedom of man.

Finally, whether you are citizens of America or citizens of the world, ask of us here the same high standards of strength and sacrifice which we ask of you. With a good conscience our only sure reward, with history the final judge of our deeds, let us go forth to lead the land we love, asking His blessing and His help, but knowing that here on earth God's work must truly be our own.

For Journals

What have you learned, from people older than you or in the media, about the Kennedy administration? What images, expressions, and values come to mind?

For Discussion

1. Identify the audience for and purpose of an inaugural address. What special demands do they place on the speaker? Kennedy was not only the youngest and first-ever Catholic president elected; he also won by an exceedingly narrow margin. What additional demands did he need to meet? What strategies did he use to meet these demands? Was he successful?

2. How does Kennedy define his generation? How does he link these definitions to the goals of his administration?

3. What rhetorical strategies does Kennedy use to unite his audience and evoke a sense of shared purpose? Focus specifically on word choice and on literary or biblical allusions in the speech. How do you think most people in Kennedy's audiences reacted, either consciously or unconsciously, to his words? Do you think such a speech would be suitable for an audience of your contemporaries? Why or why not?

4. Study the themes of the address. What do you infer about how Americans at that time defined their role in international affairs? In what ways does their identity rest on a contrast with the Soviet Union?

5. Kennedy draws a particular portrait of America and Americans. Write out or discuss in your own words the visions, goals, and ideas either suggested by or articulated in the speech.

For Writing

1. Choose a topic from one of the burning issues of the early 1960s—civil rights, space exploration, communism, youth culture, rock music, free speech, or something else—to explore. Develop a research question; then collect information by reading books and essays on the topic and also by finding and evaluating magazines, newspapers, television shows, radio broadcasts, and music lyrics or albums of the time that were written on the topic. Try to interview people who were young adults at the time. Develop your findings into a presentation to share with your peers.

2. Communicating clearly through a speech is different from communicating through writing. Good public speakers must take advantage of word choice, strong organization, parallelism, rhythm, and other elements of style to make their points. In other words, they take many features of good prose and accentuate them. Write an essay analyzing the use of one or more of these stylistic features in Kennedy's address. Try to show how the president used stylistic devices to emphasize his themes.

∞ *Thanksgiving Border Crossing* (1990)

ARTURO ISLAS

Arturo Islas (1938–1991), novelist and educator, was from the border town of El Paso, Texas. He wrote the novels The Rain God *(1984) and* Migrant Souls *(1990), from which this selection is excerpted. His third novel,* La Mollie and the King of Tears, *edited by Paul Skenazy, was published posthumously in 1994. Islas was a professor of English at Stanford University.*

For Thanksgiving in 1947, Eduviges, in a fit of guilt, decided to bake a turkey with all the trimmings. She had memorized the recipes in the glossy American magazines while waiting her turn at the Safeway checkout counter.

Because the girls were in public school and learning about North American holidays and customs, Eduviges thought her plan would please them. It did and even Josie allowed her mother to embrace her in that quick, embarrassed way she had of touching them. As usual, Sancho had no idea why she was going to such lengths preparing for a ritual that meant nothing to him.

"I don't see why we can't have the enchiladas you always make," he said. "I don't even like turkey. Why don't you let me bring you a nice, fat pheasant from the Chihuahua mountains? At least it'll taste like something. Eating turkey is going to turn my girls into little *gringas*. Is that what you want?"

"Oh, Daddy, please! Everybody else is going to have turkey." The girls, wearing colored paper headdresses they had made in art class, were acting out the Pocahontas story and reciting from "Hiawatha" in a hodgepodge of Indian sentiment that forced Sancho to agree in order to keep them quiet.

5   "All right, all right," he said. "Just stop all the racket, please. And Serena, *querida*, don't wear that stuff outside the house or they'll pick

you up and send you to a reservation. That would be okay with me, but your mother wouldn't like it."

Serena and Josie gave each other knowing glances. "They" were the *migra*, who drove around in their green vans, sneaked up on innocent dark-skinned people, and deported them. Their neighbor down the block—Benito Cruz, who was lighter-skinned than Serena and did not look at all like an Indian—had been picked up three times already, detained at the border for hours, and then released with the warning that he was to carry his identification papers at all times. That he was an American citizen did not seem to matter to the immigration officers.

The Angel children were brought up on as many deportation stories as fairy tales and family legends. The latest border incident had been the discovery of twenty-one young Mexican males who had been left to asphyxiate in an airtight boxcar on their way to pick cotton in the lower Rio Grande Valley.

When they read the newspaper articles about how the men died, both Josie and Serena thought of the fluttering noises made by the pigeons their mother first strangled and then put under a heavy cardboard box for minutes that seemed eternal to the girls. They covered their ears to protect their souls from the thumping and scratching noises of the doomed birds.

Even their mother had shown sympathy for the Mexican youths, especially when it was learned that they were not from the poorest class. "I feel very bad for their families," she said. "Their mothers must be in agony."

What about their fathers? Josie felt like asking but did not. Because 10 of the horror she imagined they went through, Josie did not want to turn her own feelings for the young men into yet another argument with her mother about "wetbacks" or about who did and did not "deserve" to be in the United States.

In the first semester of seventh grade, Josie had begun to wonder why being make-believe North American Indians seemed to be all right with their mother. "Maybe it was because those Indians spoke English," Josie said to Serena. Mexican Indians were too close to home and the truth, and the way Eduviges looked at Serena in her art class getup convinced Josie she was on the right track.

That year on the Saturday before Thanksgiving, their mother and father took them across the river in search of the perfect turkey. Sancho borrowed his friend Tacho Morales' pickup and they drove down the valley to the Zaragoza crossing. It was closer to the ranch where Eduviges had been told the turkeys were raised and sold for practically nothing. Josie and Serena sat in the front seat of the pickup with their father. Eduviges and Ofelia followed them in the Chevy in case anything went wrong.

Sancho was a slower, more patient driver than their mother, who turned into a speed demon with a sharp tongue behind the wheel. More refined than her younger sisters, Ofelia was scandalized by every phrase that came out of Eduviges' mouth when some sorry driver from Chihuahua or New Mexico got in her way.

"Why don't they teach those imbecilic cretins how to drive?" she said loudly in Spanish, window down and honking. Or, "May all your teeth fall out but one and may that ache until the day you die" to the man who pulled out in front of her without a signal.

15   Grateful that her mother was being good for once and following slowly and at a safe distance behind the pickup, Ofelia dozed, barely aware of the clear day so warm for November. Only the bright yellow leaves of the cottonwood trees reminded her that it was autumn. They clung to the branches and vibrated in the breeze, which smelled of burning mesquite and Mexican alders. As they followed her father away from the mountains and into the valley, Ofelia began to dream they were inside one of Mama Chona's Mexican blue clay bowls, suspended in midair while the sky revolved around them.

To Josie and Serena, it seemed their father was taking forever to get to where they were going. "Are we there yet?" they asked him until he told them that if they asked again, he would leave them in the middle of nowhere and not let their mother rescue them. The threat only made them laugh more and they started asking him where the middle of nowhere was until he, too, laughed with them.

"The middle of nowhere, smart alecks, is at the bottom of the sea and so deep not even the fish go there," Sancho said, getting serious about it.

"No, no," Serena said. "It's in the space between two stars and no planets around."

"I already said the middle of nowhere is in Del Sapo, Texas," Josie said, not wanting to get serious.

20   "I know, I know. It's in the Sahara Desert where not even the tumbleweeds will grow," their father said.

"No, Daddy. It's at the top of Mount Everest." Serena was proud of the B she had gotten for her report on the highest mountain in the world. They fell silent and waited for Josie to take her turn.

"It's here," Josie said quietly and pointed to her heart.

"Oh, for heaven's sake, Josie, don't be so dramatic. You don't even know what you are saying," Serena said. Their father changed the subject.

When they arrived at the ranch, he told Eduviges and the girls that the worst that could happen on their return was that the turkey would be taken away from them. But the girls, especially, must do and say exactly as he instructed them.

25   Their mother was not satisfied with Sancho's simple directions and once again told them about the humiliating body search her friend from

New Mexico, *la señora* Moulton, had been subjected to at the Santa Fe Street bridge. She had just treated her daughter Ethel and her granddaughters, Amy and Mary Ann, to lunch at the old Central Cafe in Juarez. When *la señora* had been asked her citizenship, she had replied in a jovial way, "Well, what do I look like, sir?"

They made her get out of the car, led her to a special examining cell, ordered her to undress, and made her suffer unspeakable mortifications while her relatives waited at least four hours in terror, wondering if they would ever see her again or be allowed to return to the country of their birth. Then, right on cue, Josie and Serena said along with Eduviges, "And they were Anglos and blond!"

While their parents were bargaining for the bird, the girls looked with awe upon the hundreds of adult turkeys kept inside four large corrals. As they walked by each enclosure, one of the birds gobbled and the rest echoed its call until the racket was unbearable. Serena was struck by an attack of giggles.

"They sure are stupid," Josie said in Spanish to their Mexican guide.

"They really are," he said with a smile. "When it rains, we have to cover the coops of the younger ones so they won't drown." He was a dark red color and very shy. Josie liked him instantly.

"How can they drown?" Serena asked him. "The river is nowhere 30 near here. Does it flood?"

"No," the young man said, looking away from them. "Not from the Rio Bravo. From the rain itself. They stretch their necks, open their beaks wide, and let it pour in until they drown. They keel over all bloated. That's how stupid they are." He bent his head back and showed them as they walked by an enclosure. "Gobble, gobble," the guide called and the turkeys answered hysterically.

Josie and Serena laughed all the way back to the pickup. Ofelia had not been allowed to join them because of the way their mother thought the guide was looking at her. She was dreaming away in the backseat of the Chevy while their father struggled to get the newly bought and nervous turkey into a slatted crate. Eduviges was criticizing every move he made. At last, the creature was in the box and eerily silent.

"Now remember, girls," Sancho said, wiping his face, "I'll do all the talking at the bridge. You just say 'American' when the time comes. Not another word, you hear? Think about Mrs. Moulton, Josie." He gave her a wink.

The turkey remained frozen inside the crate. Sancho lifted it onto the pickup, covered it with a yellow plastic tablecloth they used on picnics, and told Serena to sit on top of it with her back against the rear window.

"Serena," he said, "I'd hate to lose you because of this stupid bird, 35 but if you open your mouth except to say 'American,' I won't be responsible for what happens. Okay?" He kissed her on the cheek as if in farewell forever, Josie thought, looking at them from the front seat. She

was beginning to wish they had not begged so successfully for a traditional North American ceremony. Nothing would happen to Ofelia, of
course. She was protected in their mother's car and nowhere near the
turkey. Josie felt that Serena was in great peril and made up her mind to
do anything to keep her from harm.

On the way to the bridge, Josie made the mistake of asking her father if they were aliens. Sancho put his foot on the brake so hard that
Eduviges almost rear-ended the truck. He looked at Josie very hard and
said, "I do not ever want to hear you use that word in my presence
again. About anybody. We are not aliens. We are American citizens of
Mexican heritage. We are proud of both countries and have never and
will never be that word you just said to me."

"Well," Josie said. Sancho knew she was not afraid of him. He
pulled the truck away from the shoulder and signaled for his wife to
continue following them. "That's what they call Mexican people in all
the newspapers. And Kathy Jarvis at school told me real snotty at recess
yesterday that we were nothing but a bunch of resident aliens."

After making sure Eduviges was right behind them, Sancho said in
a calmer, serious tone, "Josie, I'm warning you. I do not want to hear
those words again. Do you understand me?"

"I'm only telling you what Kathy told me. What did she mean? Is
she right?"

40   "Kathy Jarvis is an ignorant little brat. The next time she tells you
that, you tell her that Mexican and Indian people were in this part of the
country long before any *gringos,* Europeans (he said 'Yurrupbeans') or
anyone else decided it was theirs. That should shut her up. If it doesn't,
tell her those words are used by people who think Mexicans are not human beings. That goes for the newspapers, too. They don't think anyone is human." She watched him look straight ahead, then in the
rearview mirror, then at her as he spoke.

"Don't you see, Josie. When people call Mexicans those words, it
makes it easier for them to deport or kill them. Aliens come from outer
space." He paused. "Sort of like your mother's family, the blessed Angels, who think they come from heaven. Don't tell her I said that."

Before he made that last comment, Josie was impressed by her father's tone. Sancho seldom became that passionate in their presence
about any issue. He laughed at the serious and the pompous and especially at religious fanatics.

During their aunt Jesus Maria's visits, the girls and their cousins
were sent out of the house in the summer or to the farthest room away
from the kitchen in the winter so that they would not be able to hear her
and Sancho arguing about God and the Church. Unnoticed, the children sneaked around the house and crouched in the honeysuckle under
the kitchen window, wide open to the heat of July. In horror and amusement, they listened to Jesus Maria tell Sancho that he would burn in hell

for all eternity because he did not believe in an afterlife and dared to criticize the infallibility of the Pope.

"It's because they're afraid of dying that people make up an afterlife to believe in," Sancho said.

"That's not true. God created Heaven, Hell, and Purgatory before 45 He created man. And you are going to end up in Hell if you don't start believing what the Church teaches us." Jesus Maria was in her glory defending the teachings of Roman Catholicism purged by the fires of the Spanish Inquisition.

"Oh, Jessie—" he began.

"Don't call me that. My name is Jesus Maria and I am proud of it." She knew the children were listening.

"Excuse me, Jesus Maria," he said with a flourish. "I just want to point out to you that it's hotter here in Del Sapo right now than in hell." He saw her bristle but went on anyway. "Haven't you figured it out yet? This is hell and heaven and purgatory right here. How much worse, better, or boring can the afterlife be?" Sancho was laughing at his own insight.

"If you are going to start joking about life-and-death matters, I simply won't talk about anything serious with you again," their aunt said. They knew she meant it. "I, like the Pope, am fighting for your everlasting soul, Sancho. If I did not love you because you are my sister's husband, I would not be telling you these things."

"Thank you, Jessie. I appreciate your efforts and love. But the pope 50 is only a man. He is not Christ. Don't you read history? All most popes have cared about is money and keeping the poor in rags so that they can mince about in gold lamé dresses."

"Apostate!" their aunt cried.

"What's that?" Serena whispered to Josie.

"I don't know but it sounds terrible. We'll look it up in the dictionary as soon as they stop." They knew the arguing was almost over when their aunt began calling their father names. Overwhelmed by the smell of the honeysuckle, the children ran off to play kick the can. Later, when Josie looked up the word "apostate," she kept its meaning to herself because she knew that Serena believed in an afterlife and would be afraid for her father.

That one word affected her father more than another was a mystery to Josie. She loved words and believed them to be more real than whatever they described. In her mind, she, too, suspected that she was an apostate but, like her father, she did not want to be an alien.

"All right, Daddy. I promise I won't say that word again. And I 55 won't tell Mother what you said about the Angels."

They were now driving through the main streets of Juarez, and Sancho was fighting to stay in his lane. "God, these Mexicans drive like your mother," he said with affection.

At every intersection, young Indian women with babies at their breast stretched out their hands. Josie was filled with dread and pity. One of the women knocked on her window while they waited for the light to change. She held up her baby and said, *"Señorita, por favor. Dinero para el niño."* Her hair was black and shiny and her eyes as dark as Josie's. The words came through the glass in a muted, dreamlike way. Silent and unblinking, the infant stared at Josie. She had a quarter in her pocket.

"Don't roll down the window or your mother will have a fit," Sancho said. He turned the corner and headed toward the river. The woman and child disappeared. Behind them, Eduviges kept honking almost all the way to the bridge.

"I think it was blind," Josie said. Her father did not answer and looked straight ahead.

60   The traffic leading to the declaration points was backed up several blocks, and the stop-and-go movement as they inched their way to the American side was more than Josie could bear. She kept looking back at Serena, who sat like a *Virgen de Guadalupe* statue on her yellow plastic-covered throne.

Knowing her sister, Josie was certain that Serena was going to free the turkey, jump out of the truck with it, gather up the beggarly women and children, and disappear forever into the sidestreets and alleys of Juarez. They drove past an old Indian woman, her long braids silver gray in the sun, begging in front of Curley's Club. And that is how Josie imagined Serena years from that day—an ancient and withered creature, bare feet crusted with clay, too old to recognize her little sister. The vision made her believe that the middle of nowhere was exactly where she felt it was. She covered her chest with her arms.

"What's the matter? Don't tell me you're going to be sick," her father said.

"No. I'm fine. Can't you hurry?"

Seeing the fear in her face, Sancho told her gently that he had not yet figured out how to drive through cars without banging them up. Josie smiled and kept her hands over her heart.

65   When they approached the border patrolman's station, the turkey began gobbling away. "Oh, no," Josie cried and shut her eyes in terror for her sister.

"Oh, shit," her father said. "I hate this goddamned bridge." At that moment, the officer stuck his head into the pickup and asked for their citizenship.

"American," said Sancho.

"American," said Josie.

"Anything to declare? Any liquor or food?" he asked in an accusing way. While Sancho was assuring him that there was nothing to declare, the turkey gobbled again in a long stream of high-pitched gurgles that sent shivers up and down Josie's spine. She vowed to go into the cell with Serena when the search was ordered.

"What's that noise?" the patrolman wanted to know. Sancho 70 shrugged and gave Josie and then the officer a look filled with the ignorance of the world.

Behind them, Serena began gobbling along with the bird and it was hard for them to tell one gobble from another. Their mother pressed down on the horn of the Chevy and made it stick. Eduviges was ready to jump out of the car and save her daughter from a fate worse than death. In the middle of the racket, the officer's frown was turning into anger and he started yelling at Serena.

"American!" she yelled back and gobbled.

"What have you got there?" The officer pointed to the plastic-covered crate.

"It's a turkey," Serena shouted. "It's American, too." She kept gobbling along with the noise of the horn. Other drivers had begun honking with impatience.

The patrolman looked at her and yelled, "Sure it is! Don't move," 75 he shouted toward Sancho.

Eduviges had opened the hood and was pretending not to know what to do. Rushing toward the officer, she grabbed him by the sleeve and pulled him away from the pickup. Confused by the din, he made gestures that Sancho took as permission to drive away. "Relax, *señora*. Please let go of my arm."

In the truck, Sancho was laughing like a maniac and wiping the tears and his nose on his sleeve. "Look at that, Josie. The guy is twice as big as your mother."

She was too scared to laugh and did not want to look. Several blocks into South Del Sapo, she was still trembling. Serena kept on gobbling in case they were being followed by the *migra* in unmarked cars.

Fifteen minutes later, Eduviges and Ofelia caught up with them on Alameda Street. Sancho signaled his wife to follow him into the vacant lot next to Don Luis Leal's Famous Tex-Mex Diner. They left the turkey unattended and silent once more.

"Dumb bird," Sancho said. With great ceremony, he treated them to 80 *menudo* and *gorditas* washed down with as much Coca-Cola as they could drink.

For Journals

Describe a time when your family changed some element of a holiday celebration. Or write about one particular, consistent family ritual. What did that change or ritual mean to you?

For Discussion

1.   Explore the role of "deportation stories" in the children's lives.

2.   What is the meaning of the word *alien* as you understand it generally? What is the significance of *alien* in this story?

3.   Examine the parallels between the idea of a border crossing, the complementary and contradictory holiday celebrations, and the notion of a bi-cultural identity. What is significant about the border crossing occurring on what is likely the most universally celebrated and cross-cultural American holiday?

For Writing

1.   Argument and persuasion in fiction are implicit rather than explicit. What do you believe is the implied point of this story? Write an essay arguing for your point of view, drawing evidence from the text to support it.

2.   Research the history and origins of a holiday celebration in America. You could focus on specific cultural holidays, such as Kwanzaa, or on particular ways of celebrating, such as exchanging gifts or preparing certain foods. You could consider holidays that are religious in purpose rather than specifically American, such as Ramadan, and explore the meaning of the holiday and the manner of celebration as a cultural connection and an expression of personal identity.

∞ *The Cult of Ethnicity* (1991)

ARTHUR M. SCHLESINGER, JR.

Arthur M. Schlesinger, Jr. (1917–), educator and historian, is well known for his service during the Kennedy and Johnson administrations. His books, which have earned him awards such as the Pulitzer Prize and National Book Award, include The Age of Jackson *(1945),* The Age of Roosevelt *(1957, 1959, 1960),* A Thousand Days: John F. Kennedy in the White House *(1965),* Robert Kennedy and His Times *(1978), and, more recently,* The Disuniting of America *(1992). The following essay appeared in* Time *magazine.*

The history of the world has been in great part the history of the mixing of peoples. Modern communication and transport accelerate mass migrations from one continent to another. Ethnic and racial diversity is more than ever a salient fact of the age.

But what happens when people of different origins, speaking different languages and professing different religions, inhabit the same locality and live under the same political sovereignty? Ethnic and racial conflict—far more than ideological conflict—is the explosive problem of our times.

On every side today ethnicity is breaking up nations. The Soviet Union, India, Yugoslavia, Ethiopia, are all in crisis. Ethnic tensions disturb and divide Sri Lanka, Burma, Indonesia, Iraq, Cyprus, Nigeria, Angola, Lebanon, Guyana, Trinidad—you name it. Even nations as stable and civilized as Britain and France, Belgium and Spain, face growing ethnic troubles. Is there any large multiethnic state that can be made to work?

The answer to that question has been, until recently, the United States. "No other nation," Margaret Thatcher has said, "has so successfully combined people of different races and nations within a single culture." How have Americans succeeded in pulling off this almost unprecedented trick?

We have always been a multiethnic country. Hector St. John de 5 Crèvecoeur, who came from France in the 18th century, marveled at the astonishing diversity of the settlers—"a mixture of English, Scotch, Irish, French, Dutch, Germans and Swedes . . . this promiscuous breed." He propounded a famous question: "What then is the American, this new man?" And he gave a famous answer: "Here individuals of all nations are melted into a new race of men." *E pluribus unum.*

The U.S. escaped the divisiveness of a multiethnic society by a brilliant solution: the creation of a brand-new national identity. The point of America was not to preserve old cultures but to forge a new, American culture. "By an intermixture with our people," President George Washington told Vice President John Adams, immigrants will "get assimilated to our customs, measures and laws: in a word, soon become one people." This was the ideal that a century later Israel Zangwill crystallized in the title of his popular 1908 play *The Melting Pot.* And no institution was more potent in molding Crèvecoeur's "promiscuous breed" into Washington's "one people" than the American public school.

The new American nationality was inescapably English in language, ideas and institutions. The pot did not melt everybody, not even all the white immigrants; deeply bred racism put black Americans, yellow Americans, red Americans and brown Americans well outside the pale. Still, the infusion of other stocks, even of nonwhite stocks, and the experience of the New World reconfigured the British legacy and made the U.S., as we all know, a very different country from Britain.

In the 20th century, new immigration laws altered the composition of the American people, and a cult of ethnicity erupted both among non-Anglo whites and among nonwhite minorities. This had many healthy consequences. The American culture at last began to give shamefully overdue recognition to the achievements of groups subordinated and spurned during the high noon of Anglo dominance, and it began to acknowledge the great swirling world beyond Europe. Americans acquired a more complex and invigorating sense of their world—and of themselves.

But, pressed too far, the cult of ethnicity has unhealthy consequences. It gives rise, for example, to the conception of the U.S. as a nation composed not of individuals making their own choices but of inviolable ethnic and racial groups. It rejects the historic American goals of assimilation and integration.

10   And, in an excess of zeal, well-intentioned people seek to transform our system of education from a means of creating "one people" into a means of promoting, celebrating and perpetuating separate ethnic origins and identities. The balance is shifting from *unum* to *pluribus.*

That is the issue that lies behind the hullabaloo over "multiculturalism" and "political correctness," the attack on the "Eurocentric" curriculum and the rise of the notion that history and literature should be taught not as disciplines but as therapies whose function is to raise minority self-esteem. Group separatism crystallizes the differences, magnifies tensions, intensifies hostilities. Europe—the unique source of the liberating ideas of democracy, civil liberties and human rights—is portrayed as the root of all evil, and non-European cultures, their own many crimes deleted, are presented as the means of redemption.

I don't want to sound apocalyptic about these developments. Education is always in ferment, and a good thing too. The situation in our universities, I am confident, will soon right itself. But the impact of separatist pressures on our public schools is more troubling. If a Kleagle of the Ku Klux Klan wanted to use the schools to disable and handicap black Americans, he could hardly come up with anything more effective than the "Afrocentric" curriculum. And if separatist tendencies go unchecked, the result can only be the fragmentation, resegregation and tribalization of American life.

I remain optimistic. My impression is that the historic forces driving toward "one people" have not lost their power. The eruption of ethnicity is, I believe, a rather superficial enthusiasm stirred by romantic ideologues on the one hand and by unscrupulous con men on the other: self-appointed spokesmen whose claim to represent their minority groups is carelessly accepted by the media. Most American-born members of minority groups, white or nonwhite, see themselves primarily as Americans rather than primarily as members of one or another ethnic group. A notable indicator today is the rate of intermarriage across ethnic lines, across religious lines, even (increasingly) across racial lines. "We Americans," said Theodore Roosevelt, "are children of the crucible."

The growing diversity of the American population makes the quest for unifying ideals and a common culture all the more urgent. In a world savagely rent by ethnic and racial antagonisms, the U.S. must continue as an example of how a highly differentiated society holds itself together.

For Journals

What are your beliefs about what makes someone "American"?

For Discussion

1. What does Schlesinger mean by "the cult of ethnicity"? Do you agree with his definition? What is his assertion about it? What evidence does he offer for support? What counterpoints does he neglect?

2. The author suggests that a focus on ethnicity, if "pressed too far," results in rejecting assimilation and integration. Do you agree that rejecting these historic goals is unhealthy? How do you think the author defines "too far"? How should a society determine when the focus on ethnicity, at the expense of assimilation, has gone too far?

3. Set up a debate in your whole class, with half the class taking the "assimilation" perspective and half the class arguing for recognizing ethnic diversity. Have someone keep track of the main points made by each side, on the board or overhead projector. Then, evaluate the merit and persuasiveness of arguments made on each side. (This activity could also be carried out in small groups.)

4. Do you agree with the author's assertion that "most American-born members of minority groups, white or nonwhite, see themselves primarily as American rather than primarily as members of one or another ethnic group"? Discuss, providing evidence to support your view.

For Writing

1. Using material developed in discussion item 3, write a response to Schlesinger arguing in favor of maintaining unique ethnic cultural traditions and groups in American society. Be sure to respond to his main points as you shape your own argument.

2. If you agree with Schlesinger, write an argument that takes the same stand and responds to Schlesinger's likely critics, again using material generated in discussion item 3 as a starting point.

3. How would one of the other authors in this chapter respond to Schlesinger? Create an imaginary dialogue between Schlesinger and Taube, Serrano, or Islas, debating one or more of the key points raised in this essay.

✒ *Aunt Jeannette's Arm*
On a Lesson of Being Jewish (1993)

DANIEL O. TAUBE

Daniel O. Taube (1953–) was born in Stamford, Connecticut and grew up in nearby Norwalk, Connecticut. He received his J.D. (1985) and his Ph.D. (1987) from the Hahnemann/Villanova Psychology and Law Graduate Program and is currently an associate professor in the Family/Child Emphasis Area at the California School of Professional Psychology at Alameda. He has published articles on professional ethics and legal issues, ethics in psychological research, drug addiction, and psychotherapy. Dr. Taube's areas of interest include ethical and legal issues in professional practice, and policy for, prevention of, and intervention into child maltreatment. This essay was presented to a psychology graduate class on intercultural issues. It was composed in response to the request of the instructor following a series of class sessions in which the students had become polarized with respect to issues of race, religion, and comparative levels of discrimination.

My first recollection of what it meant to be Jewish was when I was about three—the first time I clearly remember seeing my Aunt Jeannette (I learned later that she was actually a great aunt). I remember the sunlight in her small kitchen in Far Rockaway, New York. It was a warm Spring afternoon, fragrant with blossoms.

Aunt Jeannette had this aura of warmth—giving us European chocolate when we visited, hovering, speaking softly in her strange accent. A gentle hand tousling hair. Being so kind. It was then, sometime in my third year, for the first time, that I saw her tattoo. A faded, but distinct number on her left arm. Blurred, blue ink numerals. I had no idea what it was, but when I asked my mother, she explained, her voice unnaturally strained. Far away, in another country, Aunt Jeannette had been in a place called Auschwitz, a horrible place where Jews had been sent to be killed. I don't remember what I said. I just felt odd, numb, sad. This woman was so warm. What could she have done to be in such a horrible place? Years later, I heard other pieces of the story. She had lost her two sons and her husband in that place. And she felt that it was—it had to be—some divine retribution for some terrible, unknown deed she had done. It did not make sense to her that her suffering was undergone by virtue of being Jewish.

My next clearest recollection was in kindergarten or first grade. I was on the playground and an older child called me a dirty Jew. I did not understand the content, though I knew that I had been insulted. So we fought. When I got home I asked my mother what it meant. I saw her distress; I saw my father's rage.

Months later I recall visiting friends of my parents in a nearby town, and as my parents drove, hearing them talking about the fact that Jews and Negroes were not allowed to live in that town. And I remember driving to the beach in my hometown, for years, and passing the country club that I knew didn't allow Jews or Negroes.

I remember stories told in hushed tones among adults, when they 5 assumed we didn't hear, or couldn't understand what was being said: my father's Zeda (grandfather) whose fingers were permanently crippled because of a Cossack's sword blow to his hands as he held himself aloft on a gallows for hours; a great-aunt being raped; yet another hiding in a hay wagon to cross the border out of Russia, whose infant was killed when border guards bayonetted the stack of hay to make sure Jews did not leave the country.

And interspersed regularly throughout my upbringing were heated dinnertime debates: "You can like friends—we are all people, everyone is equal, of course—but you can only trust family. Only family will protect you, will do all they can." "Yes, so and so is a good friend, a good person, but would her family protect you from the ovens?" "We have always been uneasy settlers—not accepted, always having to leave, at best, to wander on." "Non-Jews may seem good, may be good, but you always have to be careful. You never know until the hatred breaks out again, and by then it will be too late."

So over many years, I developed this sense of being Jewish in America. Not the images of being smart, or having money (we didn't)—but the bone-deep experience of not belonging, of being on the outside, of trying to belong, but never really succeeding. And straining, trying to trust, but having the nagging sense that *it* could happen. Knowing, in the way that we know things our ancestors knew, that at any moment, no matter how comfortable or at ease or accepted I felt, it could all change. Horror could reign as it has so many times over more than twenty centuries and in so many other places where my ancestors fled.

So, this faint dread has been a constant companion. And many American Jewish people I know feel it too. It is usually not spoken about directly. But it is ever present. And also ever present with this faint dread is the need to go back and touch it—like a wound, like a worry bead, like a touchstone that reminds you who you are when you forget. This dread highlights any statements made by non-Jewish others about Jews—with a tinge of fear, a heightened perception of the cast of a statement. Is it anti-Semitic? Will they support us when it happens? Is it happening again? Is it time to go, before we are killed? Before they kill our children? My child?

So this is the low-level fear I and many of my people live with—at least here in America. And for many of us, it pushes us to try to blend in—to "pass." We change our names. We assimilate. We never go to synagogue. And when clear slurs are made, we steel ourselves against them, and may remain quiet. Or pretend not to hear. Or, if we do not try to pass,

out of the same dread I think, we must talk about Jewishness at every opportunity—making the points over again about the Holocaust, about our
suffering—another talisman, another way of touching the wound to
ward it off, pushing off the seemingly archetypal, inevitable events.

10   What is surprising is that this low-level dread has not killed compassion. Indeed, Jewish people historically seem to have a remarkable
social consciousness, a remarkable ability to keep a flame of humanity
alive. But this dread can take its toll. Sadly, I have seen it cause some of
my people to become blind to the suffering of others. To feel the heat
and worry about what will happen to us, but fail to see what is happening to others around us—to other people who live with us, day to
day, but whose oppression is made invisible, as the camps were made
invisible. I don't think this loss of compassion is uncommon, nor particularly Jewish in nature. I think it is a reaction born of fear.

But what am I if I cannot move beyond my own fear? What am I if
I cannot open myself to understanding my own experience and history,
as well as the current suffering and oppression of others, here and now?
What am I if I cannot hold the reality that we have suffered greatly, and
at the same time hold the reality that others are suffering deeply, because of their history, because of their skin color or other status-based
factor, and in ways that are similar to the suffering of my people, but in
many ways, vastly different? What have I learned from all this suffering and hatred? What worth are my sweat-filled nightmares of smokestacks and human ashes, what worth my memories of my sweet Aunt
Jeannette's tattoo?

Little, I think. Little, unless I can appreciate and respect the differ-
ences between the suffering of Jews, and the suffering of other people.
These differences come from many sources; but one of the primary dif-
ferences in suffering, at least in this country, comes from skin color.
Whether I like it or not, mine is white. And in this country, the fact that
I have lightly complected skin provides me with privilege.

It is not a privilege that I asked for—having light skin. I inherited it.
Despite my status as a Jewish person, I am white. And even though
I may abhor and decry the history and present suffering of African
Americans, Latinos, Native Americans, and others, I have benefited
and continue to benefit from that oppression. Indeed, even while I live
with the faint dread, I do not suffer the daily indignities, the daily hu-
miliations that other minorities suffer. I do not suffer the extensive, obscene laundry list that Peggy McIntosh (a feminist who has chronicled
many of the ways in which being white in America provides privilege)
has just begun to make. Doors open because of my skin color—doors
that I do not even think about, and may not even want to have opened.
People respond to me because of my skin color, in ways subtly and yet
dramatically different than they respond to others. I have come to see
this. I have come to see that I do not have the same experience as my
African American, or Asian or Latino or Native American colleagues.

This is, I believe, in part because I can pass. Even if I choose not to. And it is because I can and do benefit from having a light skin.

I have also come to see that I violate the memories, the sacredness of my ancestors' suffering, indeed, my integrity, when I fail to understand the fact of this benefit. Because to deny it is to let a great injustice continue. To deny it is to let work the very oppression that has caused so much pain to my own people for so many centuries. To deny that I am a benefactor, that I have grown up in a time and place where racist and other oppressive beliefs abound, to deny that I have absorbed and held such beliefs, is to cut off any ability I have to challenge those beliefs, to examine them, to see how the more subtle, nondramatic forms of racism and oppression work; to understand the ways in which whites (I) have unwittingly learned to be comfortable at the expense of others. We have accepted our place at the center of the racial world (if not the religious or gender or ability world). To deny these beliefs removes any possibility of acting responsibly toward them, of changing them.

But these subtle realities are easy to deny. We with light skin—Jewish and non-Jewish—will argue that we have many friends of color, that we strongly believe in equality, that our own suffering has been so great that it exempts us from holding racist beliefs. But I have come to believe, more and more, that all of us with light skin in the United States, and in many other countries, have inherited privilege, to a greater or lesser degree. And along with it, the subtle and sometimes overt racist beliefs that enforce that privilege. There are few if any exceptions, whether one is Jewish, or gay, or disabled.

But to get frozen in guilt or fear is not the point. For me, as a Jewish man, the purpose of my people's suffering is to kindle not only compassion, but responsibility. I did not choose my ethnic/religious heritage. I did not choose the unearned advantage that I am granted by virtue of my skin color, not to mention by virtue of my gender. Indeed, that is my—and I believe all of our—paradoxical lot in life. But I can choose to be responsible for all of these accidents of birth. Ultimately, that is the lesson of my Jewishness. That is the lesson my Aunt Jeannette taught me.

For Journals

A song from the popular 1950s musical *South Pacific* argues that "you've got to be taught" to be afraid of others who are different from you and your family. Write a journal entry reflecting on this statement in view of your own upbringing.

For Discussion

1. Although the author's essay is an argument, its thesis and premises are not as explicitly stated as they often are in argumentative writing.

Identify the thesis, key supporting points, and types of evidence used in this essay.

2.   Taube uses an inductive/indirect organization rather than a direct/deductive plan. How might this approach have enhanced his persuasiveness? Explain your answer, taking into consideration the piece's audience and purpose. How might a more confrontational style have undercut the persuasiveness of his essay?

3.   The essay concludes with the charge to "be responsible" for accidents of birth. Discuss ways in which people can claim and practice such responsibility in their daily lives.

For Writing

1.   Write an essay reflecting on your own identity or on myths and stereotypes in your family about other cultures or groups. What do you think are the sources of your beliefs and attitudes? When did you first become aware of a sense of "otherness" or distinctiveness from other cultures or groups? What did that difference mean to you?

2.   Write a response to Taube. Begin with your own personal anecdote if you wish, but be sure to address the main points of his argument.

3.   Research the history of relations between African Americans and Jewish Americans. You can research areas rife with stereotypes, such as the slave trade, or more recent conflicts, such as racial strife in Brooklyn or charges of racism or anti-Semitism in the speeches of political leaders. Consider multiple points of view, and be sure to use documented evidence to support your inferences.

4.   Taube's essay calls for change in beliefs or attitudes. Using material developed in discussion item 3, write an essay outlining ways you might put this call for change into practice.

∞ *A Tapestry of Hope*
America's Strength Was, Is, and Will Be Its Diversity   (1994)

JEANNE WAKATSUKI HOUSTON

Jeanne Wakatsuki Houston (1934–) was born in Los Angeles and lived in Santa Monica with her family until the Japanese attack on Pearl Harbor on December 7, 1941; her father was a fisherman. After the attack, President Roosevelt signed an order (see Chapter 8, "War and the Enemy") that led to the internment of many thousands of Japanese Americans in camps on the grounds that they might prove disloyal. They did not, but they lost their homes and livelihoods; the Wakatsukis were forced to

spend three and a half years in a camp called Manzanar, in the Owens Valley in Cali-
fornia. In 1973, Wakatsuki Houston and her husband, writer James Houston, wrote
what became the most famous Japanese American memoir of the internment camps,
Farewell to Manzanar. *The following speech was delivered by Wakatsuki Houston*
at the graduation ceremonies at De Anza College in California in June 1994.

Many years ago—43 to be exact—when I stood on the ground where De Anza College now stands, I looked out onto lush orchards, fragrant with blossoms in springtime and ladened with plump fruit in summer. I viewed acres of foliage carpeting the earth with green— patches of beans, tomatoes, and squash, and long furrows of strawber- ries, glistening red under their leafy canopies. In those days I knew this area well, for I had spent several summers picking those berries at a large strawberry ranch called Esperanza, located not far from here. Es- peranza, the Spanish word for "hope," was farmed by Japanese fami- lies in partnership with the Driscoll brothers. They were sharecroppers. My father sharecropped with the Driscolls at another ranch in South County from 1951 to 1955.

In 1945 when our family re-entered society after three and a half years of incarceration at Manzanar, a concentration camp for Japanese- Americans during World War II, my father's fishing license was re- voked. It forced him to seek a livelihood outside a successful pre-war fishing occupation.

Starting at economic zero, at age 59 he seized the opportunity to be- gin again and brought his family to San Jose from Southern California to farm strawberries. Although my father had been in this country for more than 35 years, and his family, including my mother, had been born here, we arrived at this luscious valley like new immigrants, refugees from another world.

Why do I tell you this? I tell you this because when I picked those berries I never dreamed I would be speaking at a college that someday would rise up within view of where I knelt in the dirt. It was beyond my imagination. But here I am sharing with you some thoughts and in- sights I have accrued since those days in the strawberry fields more than 40 years ago.

As Santa Clara Valley's landscape has changed, so has its con- 5 sciousness. I'm not going to lecture about how tough it was then to be Asian, to be poor, and to be a woman. But I would like to say a few words to remind us how we have changed, how things are different— especially in attitudes toward ethnic diversity.

When I was growing up in the '50s, being "American" and accept- able into mainstream society meant one had to assimilate, melt into one great pot where the broth was predominantly Anglo-European flavored.

No one talked about the concept of cultural diversity as a mosaic or as a tapestry of multi-colored threads that when woven together cre- ated a vibrantly rich and textured fabric. "Real Americans" were white.

People of color had to think and act "white" to prove their "American-ness." And while I was growing up after the war, muted by the intern-ment experience, it never occurred to me to question this attitude.

Not even when I was told I should not continue with a journalism major at San Jose State because I was "Oriental" and a female. There were no jobs in the field. So I changed my major to social welfare. And when I was told again by the head of Juvenile Probation Services that they could not hire me as a probation officer because the community was not "ready" for "Orientals," I did not protest—although I had been educated enough by then to know it was wrong. But that was the '50s.

Equal opportunity laws were non-existent. I remained silent, return-ing to the safety zone of invisibility and "don't make waves" mentality.

Rediscovering Our Histories

10   Then in the '60s, the Black Power movement changed forever the way racial and ethnic minorities thought of themselves. Black leaders led us to rediscover our cultural backgrounds and our histories. We re-discovered our participation in and our contributions to the develop-ment of this country, and with this recognition came a sense of pride and identity.

For the first time in U.S. history, an awareness of values inherent in America's sub-cultures rose into public consciousness. We began to see that when individuals have a strong sense of identity, of pride in one's heritage, this sense of self-worth strengthens the larger society. Not only were attitudes changing in the dominant culture, but also sub-groups themselves began to recognize that America is a land of immi-grants, and that all immigrants had a hand in developing it.

Thirty years ago, the word "immigrant" seemed reserved for peo-ple of color, individuals from the Third World. Today, this still seems to be the prevailing myth. I hear so often the comment, "America is be-coming—so multi-cultural with all this immigration from Asia and south of the border." Some people are surprised or mystified or threat-ened by this idea that the country is becoming so diverse, when in fact, it always has been.

From the moment Portuguese and Italian sailors landed in the New World to mingle with indigenous peoples in what we now call the West Indies, America began its cross-cultural heritage. And up North, more than 500 indigenous tribes, speaking as many different languages, for centuries had lived on this vast and fertile continent.

Ethnicity is not the exclusive property of people of color. We all have ethnicity. We are descendants of individuals from China, Ireland, Ethiopia, Vietnam, El Salvador, Canada—to name a few. Ideally, Amer-icans should not have a problem with identity; we must realize there is no need to "wanna-be ethnic"—because, in fact, we all are.

"The World Is Watching"

I would like to share an experience I had two years ago when I was   15
in Japan. I met a Japanese man, a visionary who founded a grass-roots
movement called "the Sweet Potato Movement." It was a calling back
to the land from the cities, the dense urban areas he referred to as the
"fourth world."

He surprised me with this comment, "The world is watching
America deal with its diversity. For the Japanese, America is the role
model for democracy. We may be strong economically, but we need
your country to lead us in human rights and values. You must succeed
if democracy is to succeed around the world."

He was one of many Japanese I met who saw multi-culturalism as
a pivotal test for America's democratic ideals.

I like to view our diversity as a metaphor, a microcosm of the
macrocosm of a world of nations. I like to see America as a great experiment, a laboratory for testing ideals—the big test today being tolerance
and cooperation. If we can't get along in our own communities because
of our cultural differences, how can we expect nations around the
world to co-exist peacefully?

One of our greatest challenges is to embrace our differences while
seeking out the common bonds that hold us together. What are those
bonds? What are those threads, the warp in the loom that sets the pattern for who we are as Americans? For me, those threads are the ideals
of freedom, equality, opportunity, justice. I also include the human
qualities of gratitude, generosity, curiosity and love. Those threads together provide the strength and foundation around which our individual cultural differences weave, making each and every one of us unique
and interesting Americans.

As I noted earlier, there was a major shift in perception to reach the   20
point of agreement that we are, indeed, a multi-cultural society, that we
began with diversity. But there is a difference between cultural diversity and cross-cultural understanding. They are not synonymous. The
great opportunity now is to seek out ways to enhance cross-cultural understanding and not fall back on separatism and attitudes of "our tribe
against theirs."

The Search for Scapegoats

Today, in a time of economic crisis, there are those in our political
leadership who are all too ready to find scapegoats.

More and more, it seems, those scapegoats are immigrants. The
voices of fear echo daily on the front pages of newspapers, in our television broadcasts: "They are different from us. They have no idea of

democracy and freedom. They won't speak our language and they keep to themselves."

Those are the words used today to describe the newest Americans. How many of us who lived through the racism and internment of Japanese-Americans during World War II remember what it was like to have those words directed against one innocent group?

In 1942, we had no one to speak up for us. But after the war, empowered by the Civil Rights movement of the '60s, Japanese-Americans began a 10-year drive for redress from our government. It culminated with the passage of the Civil Liberties Act of 1988, which officially apologized for the internment.

25 Japanese-Americans were vindicated in the eyes of history. But this victory was not for Japanese-Americans alone. It was a great victory for all Americans, for it proved our Constitution is not just a piece of parchment under glass in the National Archives. It is a living, vital contract that binds us all together as Americans.

And if that contract is broken—as it was in 1942—it is not just the rights of individuals that are threatened, but the very fabric of this nation. And we know that the fabric is woven from threads representing many different groups. If one of those threads is cut, stretched out of proportion, or bleached of color, the design becomes listless and in danger of unraveling.

I began this talk with a memory, a powerful memory, which should underline one of the ironic possibilities of living in America. Who knows what the future holds for any of us? But whatever measure of success we have achieved is because we own a certain capacity. That capacity is hope.

When I was a teenager picking strawberries on that ranch, so appropriately named "Esperanza," I did not have vision. I could not envision the future I have today. Yet, I did have an unexplainable pull to fulfill some possibility, some unknown challenge. I now know that urge to fulfill was hope, a submerged belief in my own power, in the possibility I could accomplish "something."

Today I salute the accomplishments of all people and their faith— their faith in themselves and thus, in a future for this country.

For Journals

Do you believe there is strength in cultural diversity? Why or why not?

For Discussion

1. Graduation speeches tend to exhort the graduates to action, but they have a reputation for being rather long and dry. Imagine yourself in the audience listening to this speech. How do you think you would have reacted, and why? What strategies does Houston use in this speech to keep her audience's attention and to enable them to follow her points? Consider language, paragraphing, and other rhetorical strategies you have studied.

2. Like Daniel Taube in the preceding selection, Houston begins her speech with a memory, an anecdote, to lead into her argument. How effective do you find this strategy? What other introductions might Houston have used? Do you think they would be more, or less, effective than the speech as given?

3. What strategies does the author use to identify with her audience? To what beliefs and values does she appeal? To what emotions?

For Writing

1. Using material developed in response to the discussion questions as a starting point, write an essay analyzing the persuasive strategies in this speech.

2. Houston writes, "Ethnicity is not the exclusive property of people of color. We all have ethnicity." Write an essay exploring your own ethnic identity. Draw upon memories, stories, family history, oral histories, or outside research to develop and support your dominant theme.

∞ *Chicana* (1994)

MARTHA SERRANO

Martha Serrano grew up in Los Angeles. In her adolescent years she was a member of a gang, but she dropped out of it to concentrate on high school studies. A recent college graduate, she plans to attend law school and work on behalf of her people. As part of a first-year writing course, Serrano wrote the essay that follows in response to writing assignment 1 at the end of this chapter.

Don't call me Hispanic. Don't call me Latina. Don't call me Mexican. Don't call me Mexican American. I want to be called Chicana. I am *mestiza*—indigenous and Spanish. My heritage is struggle and strength. I join my strength and struggle to that of my *hermanas*, my sisters. I am a woman of *Aztlan*, the southwestern United States. I don't want to be called Hispanic because I don't want people to tell me who I am and where I come from.

Most, if not all, of the people who call me Hispanic do not know that "Hispanic" is a term imposed on Americans of Latin descent by federal regulators, unprepared educators, and merchants who want our money but not us. In the mid 1970s, the U.S. Census Bureau first admitted that its 1970 census had seriously undercounted persons of Latin American descent in the United States. Under pressure from Latino activists to avoid a repetition of that mistake in the 1980 head count, the bureau searched for an all-encompassing word to describe the diverse assortment of Latin Americans living in this country: Mexican Americans and Mexican citizens, Puerto Ricans and Cuban Americans, and "other Hispanics" was the Census Bureau's solution.

The term "Hispanic" denies my cultural heritage. However, a Chicana is both Hispanic and Indian. For the Chicana, her world has been shaped by historical forces beyond the barrio and this country. My ancestors are the *conquistadores* and the conquered indigenous people of 1492. Our vanquished heritage has always haunted us and has been ignored by American historians.

The term "Chicana" is linked to my indigenous past. The roots of the word date back to the conquest of *El Valle de México.* Back then, Mexico was pronounced "meshico." The Spaniards had no letter or sound in their alphabet for the Nahuatl "sh" or hard "j" so they put an "x" in its place. In Meshico, "Mejico" became "Mexico" and "Tejas," "Texas." Mexico's Catholicism (which came from the encounter between Spaniards and Native Americans), and its food, art, and customs manifest Indian presence. Moreover, the Mexican dialect of Spanish, used to create world-famous prose and poetry, is influenced by Aztec words.

5   The first *mestizos* were born of Spanish soldiers and indigenous maidens. This scorned underclass was called Meshicanos and evolved to shicanos, Chicanos. Culturally, in the past, the word "Chicano" was a pejorative, class-bound adjective. Latinos used to associate the word "Chicano" with violent gangsters who had nothing better to do but hang out in the street and cause trouble. Now, however, it is the root idea of a new cultural identity for my people. It reveals a growing solidarity and the development of a common social praxis. Today, the widespread use of the word signals a rebirth of pride and confidence. It embodies an ancient truth: "Man is never closer to his true self as when he is close to his community."

All Chicanos agree that being Chicano/a is more than being an American of Mexican descent; it is a way of thinking. It means being politically and culturally aware. It means knowing who you are and where you came from. It means being proud of your ethnic background and history. Most important of all, it means resisting assimilation into American mainstream society. Chicanos fight for self-determination and tackle issues facing the Chicano community. Chicanos struggle for the betterment of *La Raza,* the people.

Chicanos are *mestizos*, or the blending of two races and cultures. No matter what our differences may be, all Chicanos believe that education, especially higher education, leads to progress and the development of our community. We believe that once our people get educated, we can go to our own lawyers, doctors, architects, engineers, and others to help build a stronger and united Chicano community. However, we believe that education must contribute to the formation of a complete man or woman who truly values life and freedom. I am Chicana!

For Journals

Are there particular ways in which people categorize you that you dislike? What do you know about the origins of these labels?

For Discussion

1. Do your intellect and emotion respond in the same way to Serrano's argument? If not, how do your reactions conflict? Do you find her introduction effective? Explain your answer.

2. What connections is Serrano making between the term "Chicana" and cultural identity? What is the connection between the individual, the community, and culture in forming identity?

3. Serrano describes the history of the terms "Chicana" and "Hispanic" to support her view that the former is the better term for her identity and her people. Are you persuaded by the information she provides? Could she offer other arguments to support her view?

4. Serrano rejects the term "Hispanic" as one imposed by others. Should people be able to name and define their own ethnicity and culture as they wish?

5. Serrano writes of resisting assimilation; some of the other readings in this chapter, however, assume that assimilation is good. Working in groups or pairs in class, argue that being American does or does not entail assimilation into mainstream American society. In the process, try to come up with a working definition of assimilation for contemporary Americans.

For Writing

1. Compare and contrast Serrano's idea of cultural identity with Daniel Taube's. Alternatively, construct a dialogue between Serrano and Jeanne Wakatsuki Houston on claiming a cultural identity.

2. Analyze the ways in which exposure to others of your ethnic group or national origin has, or has not, helped you form an identity.

∾ Film: The Joy Luck Club (1994)

This film follows the story of four lifelong friends, including both their joys and tragedies, and shows how their experiences have not only shaped their own lives, but have also affected their hopes and dreams for their children. It is based on the novel, of the same name, by Amy Tan. (139 minutes)

For Journals

This film contains both tragic and comic elements. Write a journal entry reflecting on your emotional response to the film and to its central characters.

For Discussion

1.   Comment on the technique of narrative, or storytelling, in the film, exploring, for example, the ways in which it weaves together past and present. How does such a technique contribute to your understanding of the characters and their cultures?

2.   Which story line was most compelling to you? Why? Cite material from the film to support your view.

3.   In what ways does the interplay of ethnic heritage and American identity become apparent? Cite specific examples or incidents from the film to support your view.

For Writing

1.   Take a specific example or scene from the film, such as the scene in which the young white man, Rick, comes to dinner, and analyze the film's handling of cross-cultural differences. How does the scene implicitly convey a point about cultures and customs? What does the scene later in the film, with the same characters, suggest to you about cultural differences?

2.   Write a review of the film for your school paper, your class, or a friend. Would you recommend it? Why or why not? In your review, remember to introduce the topic, develop a dominant impression or core assertion, and then briefly summarize the plot before analyzing the film's strengths and weaknesses.

Writing Assignments

1. Write a memoir, narrative, or autobiography that conveys a sense of your personal identity as an American and what the term "American" means to you. Review the readings by Ellison, Taube, and Serrano to find ways in which these authors developed their self-definition or search for identity. Make sure to determine a specific focus or claim about your identity rather than string together examples or anecdotes without a persuasive intent.

2. Investigate past or contemporary issues in immigration policy. Examine how people are defined as American citizens, who is a citizen automatically and who must apply, what kinds of restrictions are in place, whether different categories of immigrants are able to enter in higher numbers, and why. Some research questions you might consider include the following: What kinds of immigrants does American policy favor? How can definitions be used to favor particular groups? In what ways have policies changed over the years? Present your thesis and findings in an essay that documents this research.

3. Imagine that you are an advertising copywriter who has been asked to create a public relations campaign for a political candidate that defines the best that America and Americans have to offer. The audience is a group of U.S. citizens. Sketch out your strategy, propose it to your client, and argue that your strategy will be effective.

Alternatively, design a campaign for a U.S. tourism organization that will target an overseas audience from a country or region you designate. It might be interesting, for example, to devise a campaign encouraging citizens of countries of the former Soviet Union to visit the United States.

4. Currently, scholars, activists, and students are discussing the notion of "identity politics"—or the belief that people from nondominant cultures should define themselves rather than have identities imposed on them by others. Martha Serrano's essay is an example of the kinds of debate revolving around conflicts between how people identify themselves and how others define them. Research this concept in recent periodicals, and write an essay explaining the concept to your classmates or other peer group. Alternatively, argue for a redefinition of an ethnic group or culture with which you identify.

4

American Dreams

The selections in this chapter revolve around the most familiar but elusive expression of the American national character, the American dream. It is an expression that turns up everywhere in our culture; open any newspaper or watch any news program, and you will probably find more samples like these:

- An African American banker helps provide mortgages to minority applicants. The headline of the newspaper story is "The American Dream"; the subtitle is "Doing Well by Doing Good."

- Three promising navy officers, a woman and two men, are killed in a double murder and suicide. The news story focuses on the poignancy of the loss by pointing out that all three officers were on the way to achieving the American dream.

- A teenage television actor becomes wealthy and famous; a television magazine program reporting on his newfound stardom calls it an example of the American dream.

As these examples show, the American dream is so well established—both as an expression and as an idea—that no one feels the need to define it; however, no one seems to agree on exactly what it means. Perhaps the closest we can come is to say that the American dream represents both what Americans believe themselves entitled to and what they believe themselves capable of. In other words, it is the promise inherent in the idea of America itself.

The idea of America actually began with a mistake; Renaissance Europeans in search of a route to the East Indies stumbled on it. As the famous naval historian Samuel Eliot Morison remarked, they spent the next fifty years trying to get around or through it. Actually finding such a continent, even by accident, had exciting and unsettling impact on the European imagination. As a result, early European dreams about America reflected a curious combination of fantasy and science fiction. Writers who had never been to America described Native Americans with feathers sprouting from their feet, precious stones growing out of their chests, heads that grew from below their shoulders, no government, no private property, a taste for cannibalism, and a life span of 150 years.

Of course the reality was very different, and dreams changed, from the discovery of golden cities to the acquisition of land for farming. But two early elements were fixed—that America represented the possibility of prosperity and that whoever came here could make a new start.

From the beginning, then, the American dream has existed as a series of evolving promises and discrepancies, of continuous conflicts and renewed possibilities for achievement, of the tension between faith in a glorious promise and the more difficult task of making that promise come true under less-than-ideal conditions. These contradictions are elements in a three-hundred-year debate that continues to this day, because, while most Americans believe in the American dream, there is much disagreement on its particulars. We argue about what the dream consists of—money, social equality, power, success, democratic ideals; we argue about the means to achieve it—hard work, luck, aggressiveness, drive, or the will to succeed at any cost; we argue about who is entitled to it—long-term residents, new immigrants, everyone, or just the lucky few. And finally, we argue over how much each person is entitled to—the complete fulfillment of his or her dream, or just the right to compete?

American Dreams Through History

The selections in this chapter reflect reality and myth, coexisting contradictions, disappointing experience, and renewed optimism in pursuing the American dream. William Bradford, one of the first great writers of the colonial period, wrote the *History of Plymouth Plantation*, the first major document of English settlement in the New World. He was party to the Mayflower Compact, a statement of religious belief and secular English law constituting the first American document to posit the idea of the common good as the basis for a civil government. And he was so completely trusted by his quarrelsome contemporaries that they elected him governor of the Plymouth Plantation no less than thirty times.

The Europeans' fascination with America, or their dream of it, encouraged the production of images and writings that were less factual than fictional, not to mention exotic. Although an early tradition of accurate and beautiful drawings of animals, plants, and birds, culminating in John J. Audubon's great folios in the nineteenth century, faithfully portrayed the continent, Europeans who had never been to America would have had difficulty separating relatively scientific drawings from the purely fanciful, even bizarre versions that competed for their attention.

One of the most popular allegorical representations depicted America as a woman, sometimes beautiful and sexual, sometimes armed and dangerous, sometimes both simultaneously. Often she carried a bow and arrow, like an Amazon warrior or Diana, goddess of the hunt. In this chapter we see a nineteenth-century variation from *Union Magazine of Literature & Art*: a female figure of Liberty, dressed in classical garb, offers the European arts of music, literature, and science to a half-naked female America, whose sensual richness has little in common with the political and religious experience Bradford records.

For most immigrants, however, the untold wealth of America remained as remote and insubstantial as a picture (see *California, the Cornucopia of the World*). Instead, life in America involved a continual, often painful effort to learn English, find a community, and make what living they could. Chinese Americans, for example, had the extra burden of struggling not only against the usual traumas of immigration, but also against the especially harsh anti-Chinese laws to which they were subject. Sui Sin Far, in "In the Land of the Free," examines the results of miscommunication and differing cultural values in an encounter between a young Chinese immigrant mother and the well-meaning but uncomprehending American woman who disrupts her life, and that of her child, with tragic consequences.

The dream remained equally elusive for some of the people who had lived in America the longest. Langston Hughes, the African American poet, writer, and leader in the great cultural explosion of the Harlem Renaissance in the 1920s, repeatedly questioned why the dream of success and equality that was so clear in theory remained so inaccessible in practice to so many. Both angry and hopeful, he wrote a series of poems, including "Let America Be America Again," in which he underlined the contradictions between the dream of opportunity and fulfillment and a much grimmer reality, between what America held out as a promise and what it delivered.

A decade later, America was in the midst of the Great Depression, an economic disaster so enormous that it made an indelible impression on those who lived through it. Fifteen million people were out of work. The poor got poorer, and, more than at any other time in our history, the middle class, the primary carriers of belief in the rewards of work and the inevitability of success, found themselves unemployed. The savings of a lifetime disappeared when banks failed; frugality and honesty were not rewarded; and confidence in one's ability to mold the future was destroyed.

Margaret Bourke-White, a famous photographer for *Life* and *Time* magazines, took many pictures of Americans coping with the terrors of the Depression; one of her best photos, the ironically titled "There's No Way like the American Way," captures an image of poor people juxtaposed with an image of a rich, secure America that seems utterly distant from their experience. For F. Scott Fitzgerald, the Depression had psychological as well as financial aspects. Probably no writer had understood better the enormous energy behind the American love of success, and he experienced it himself when he became a best-selling author at the age of twenty-three with his college novel, *This Side of Paradise*. His later novel, *The Great Gatsby*, had a hero who could never have been anything but American in his ambition, his drive, and his naive if ruthless faith in the connections between love and money. But by 1937, Fitzgerald was forgotten, drinking too much and writing about disintegration—his own and the country's—in a series of essays called *The Crack-Up*. The selection here, "Early Success," is his own remarkably objective look at what it means to succeed when you're too young to understand either success or failure.

America didn't fully recover from the Great Depression until the beginning of World War II, when the need for war matériel put factories on overtime and created an immense need for laborers. Another side effect of the war was that millions of women who had never expected to work outside the home suddenly found themselves recruited for well-paying jobs vacated by the men who had joined the armed forces. For the first time, many found themselves in business, earning money and feeling successful in ways that had traditionally been reserved for men.

As soon as the war ended and the men returned, though, women were rerouted back into domestic life with a vengeance. Magazines like *Woman's Day* emphasized not their lost earning power but their ability to make a good tuna casserole. Men, on the other hand, were expected to provide more and more material proof of their own success at the office: the split-level ranch house in the suburbs, the healthy 2.3 children, and an ever-changing model of American-made car.

The sweepstakes advertisement in this chapter illustrates the cheerful materialism and the need for concrete proof of success for an American family. At the same time, with its childless couple sitting on the lawn, surrounded by masses of furniture they won rather than paid for, this advertisement reinforces the idea that the American dream has alternative paths, and that having possessions is more important than the way you get them.

But the more idealistic sense of fulfillment that Langston Hughes had articulated in his poetry was still a factor in the American agenda. In 1963, thirty years after Hughes made his plea for a renewed commitment to the American dream, Martin Luther King, Jr., the leader of the modern civil rights movement, made the most famous American speech of the twentieth century: the largely extemporaneous address at the Lincoln Memorial, "I Have a Dream." At the time, most southern blacks could not share a water fountain, a beach, a bus seat, a school room, or a voting booth with southern whites. King, a believer in the power of nonviolent resistance, had already led a successful bus boycott in Montgomery, Alabama, and a long series of marches, demonstrations, and sit-ins at ordinary places like lunch counters; he had been arrested by southern sheriffs and was the frequent recipient of death threats. But a huge civil rights march in Washington, D.C., gave him the opportunity to address a larger American audience and to locate civil rights at the political center of the American dream, to make one the expression of the other.

These two strains of the American dream—the ideals of opportunity and achievement based on character, perseverance, and fairness, versus the charms of getting rich quick, winning or borrowing money, and keeping ahead of, rather than even with, the Joneses—continue to dominate contemporary American life. Jacob Weisberg, the editor of an on-line magazine, explores in "United Shareholders of America" the debilitating effects of stock market madness on middle-class Americans. He sees the current passion for betting one's future on rising stock prices as yet another instance of how short Americans' memories are; not only have they forgotten the causes of the Great Depression, but they still think they can circumvent the less glamorous paths to the dream, like saving money, by engaging in what is effectively a different kind of sweepstakes.

On a somewhat more hopeful note, urban studies expert Witold Rybczynski visits a new community, Celebration, which attempts to reinvigorate the American sense of community while accommodating it to the computer age, in effect seeking the best of the past and the present. The fact that "Tomorrowland," as he calls it, was built by the Disney Corporation raises interesting issues about how much the American dream owes both to nostalgia and self-perpetuated mythology. Chris Countryman returns to Langston Hughes and his plea to "Let America Be America Again"; he proves how eloquent the voice of a poet, shaping lines and stanzas, can be in arguing that the best way for the American dream to be realized is for America to return to its first, best promise.

Finally, in the film *Avalon,* we see a classic example of the dream at work in three generations of one family, beginning with brothers who immigrate to America early in the twentieth century and encompassing their children and grandchildren, with unexpected results.

All selections in this chapter, separated as they are by time and distance, speak to us in distinct and recognizable American voices. In Chapter 3, you read about Americans trying to establish their identities by defining, for themselves as much as for anyone else, who an American is. This chapter's selections continue that process by trying to express what Americans want and what they feel are their unique opportunities; the selections appeal to a common sense of possibility that both shapes our ambitions and survives our experience.

∽ FROM *History of Plymouth Plantation* (1645)

WILLIAM BRADFORD

William Bradford (1590–1657), the leader of the Plymouth Colony and one of the greatest early colonials, was born in Yorkshire, England, and joined a separatist Protestant sect when he was twelve. Mostly self-educated, he became a serious student of the Bible and was able to read some Hebrew, Dutch, French, and Greek. He and his group went to Holland to avoid religious persecution; by the time they moved to America, he was already a recognized leader and remained so all his life. Trusted and respected by his fellow religionists, he was reelected governor of the Plymouth Colony over thirty times, after the death of the first governor, John Carver. Bradford was also the author of History of Plymouth Plantation, *from which this excerpt is taken.*

from *Chapter XI: The Remainder of Anno 1620*

The Mayflower Compact

I shall a little return back, and begin with a combination[1] made by them before they came ashore; being the first foundation of their government in this place. Occasioned partly by the discontented and mutinous speeches that some of the strangers[2] amongst them had let fall from them in the ship: That when they came ashore they would use their own liberty, for none had power to command them, the patent they had being for Virginia and not for New England, which belonged to another government, with which the Virginia Company had nothing to do. And partly that such an act by them done, this their condition considered, might be as firm as any patent, and in some respects more sure.

The form was as followeth:

In the Name of God, Amen.

We whose names are underwritten, the loyal subjects of our dread Sovereign Lord King James, by the Grace of God of Great Britain, France, and Ireland King, Defender of the Faith, etc.

Having undertaken, for the Glory of God and advancement of the Christian Faith and Honour of our King and Country, a Voyage to plant the First Colony in the Northern Parts of Virginia,[3] do by these presents solemnly and mutually in the presence of god and one of another, Covenant and Combine ourselves together into a Civil Body Politic, for our better ordering and preservation and furtherance of the

---

[1] Agreement.
[2] People on the *Mayflower* who belonged to churches other than Winthrop's.
[3] New England.

ends aforesaid; and by virtue hereof to enact, constitute and frame such just and equal Laws, Ordinances, Acts, Constitutions and Offices, from time to time, as shall be thought most meet and convenient for the general good of the Colony, unto which we promise all due submission and obedience. In witness whereof we have hereunder subscribed our names at Cape Cod, the 11th of November, in the year of the reign of our Sovereign Lord King James, of England, France and Ireland the eighteenth, and of Scotland the fifty-fourth. Anno Domini 1620.

After this they chose, or rather confirmed, Mr. John Carver[4] (a man godly and well approved amongst them) their Governor for that year. And after they had provided a place for their goods, or common store (which were long in unlading for want of boats, foulness of the winter weather and sickness of divers) and begun some small cottages for their habitation; as time would admit, they met and consulted of laws and orders, both for their civil and military government as the necessity of their condition did require, still adding thereunto as urgent occasion in several times, and as cases did require.

In these hard and difficult beginnings they found some discontents and murmurings arise amongst some, and mutinous speeches and carriages in other; but they were soon quelled and overcome by the wisdom, patience, and just and equal carriage of things, by the Governor and better part, which clave[5] faithfully together in the main.

The Starving Time

But that which was most sad and lamentable was, that in two or 5
three months' time half of their company died, especially in January and February, being the depth of winter, and wanting houses and other comforts; being infected with the scurvy and other diseases which this long voyage and their inaccommodate condition had brought upon them. So as there died some times two or three of a day in the foresaid time, that of 100 and odd persons, scarce fifty remained. And of these, in the time of most distress, there was but six or seven sound persons who to their great commendations, be it spoken, spared no pains night nor day, but with abundance of toil and hazard of their own health, fetched them wood, made them fires, dressed them meat, made their beds, washed their loathsome clothes, clothed and unclothed them. In a word, did all the homely and necessary offices for them which dainty and queasy stomachs cannot endure to hear named; and all this willingly and cheerfully, without any grudging in the least, showing herein

---

[4] John Carver was the first governor of the Pilgrim colony.
[5] Stuck to, adhered.

their true love unto their friends and brethren; a rare example and worthy to be remembered. Two of these seven were Mr. William Brewster, their reverend Elder, and Myles Standish, their Captain and military commander, unto whom myself and many others were much beholden in our low and sick condition. And yet the Lord so upheld these persons as in this general calamity they were not at all infected either with sickness or lameness. And what I have said of these I may say of many others who died in this general visitation, and others yet living; that whilst they had health, yea, or any strength continuing, they were not wanting to any that had need of them. And I doubt not but their recompense is with the Lord.

But I may not here pass by another remarkable passage not to be forgotten. As this calamity fell among the passengers that were to be left here to plant, and were hasted ashore and made to drink water that the seamen might have the more beer, and one[6] in his sickness desiring but a small can of beer, it was answered that if he were their own father he should have none. The disease began to fall amongst them[7] also, so as almost half of their company died before they went away, and many of their officers and lustiest men, as the boatswain, gunner, three quartermasters, the cook and others. At which the Master was something strucken and sent to the sick ashore and told the Governor he should send for beer for them that had need of it, though he drunk water homeward bound.

But now amongst his company there was far another kind of carriage in this misery than amongst the passengers. For they that before had been boon companions in drinking and jollity in the time of their health and welfare, began now to desert one another in this calamity, saying they would not hazard their lives for them, they should be infected by coming to help them in their cabins; and so, after they came to lie by it, would do little or nothing for them but, "if they died, let them die." But such of the passengers as were yet aboard showed them what mercy they could, which made some of their hearts relent, as the boatswain (and some others) who was a proud young man and would often curse and scoff at the passengers. But when he grew weak, they had compassion on him and helped him; then he confessed he did not deserve it at their hands, he had abused them in word and deed. "Oh!" (saith he) "you, I now see, show your love like Christians indeed one to another, but we let one another lie and die like dogs." Another lay cursing his wife, saying if it had not been for her he had never come this unlucky voyage, and anon cursing his fellows, saying he had done this and that for some of them; he had spent so much and so much amongst them, and they were now weary of him and did not help him, having

---

[6] That was Bradford himself.
[7] The crew.

need. Another gave his companion all he had, if he died, to help him in his weakness; he went and got a little spice and made him a mess of meat once or twice. And because he died not so soon as he expected, he went amongst his fellows and swore the rogue would cozen[8] him, he would see him choked before he made him any more meat; and yet the poor fellow died before morning.

Indian Relations

All this while the Indians came skulking about them, and would sometimes show themselves aloof off, but when any approached near them, they would run away; and once they stole away their tools where they had been at work and were gone to dinner. But about the 16th of March, a certain Indian came boldly amongst them and spoke to them in broken English, which they could well understand but marveled at it. At length they understood by discourse with him, that he was not of these parts, but belonged to the eastern parts where some English ships came to fish, with whom he was acquainted and could name sundry of them by their names, amongst whom he had got his language. He became profitable to them in acquainting them with many things concerning the state of the country in the east parts where he lived, which was afterwards profitable unto them; as also of the people here, of their names, number and strength, of their situation and distance from this place, and who was chief amongst them. His name was Samoset. He told them also of another Indian whose name was Squanto, a native of this place, who had been in England and could speak better English than himself.

Being, after some time of entertainment and gifts dismissed, a while after he came again, and five more with him, and they brought again all the tools that were stolen away before, and made way for the coming of their great Sachem, called Massasoit. Who, about four or five days after, came with the chief of his friends and other attendance, with the aforesaid Squanto. With whom, after friendly entertainment and some gifts given him, they made a peace with him (which hath now continued this 24 years)[9] in these terms:

1. That neither he nor any of his should injure or do hurt to any of their people.

2. That if any of his did hurt any of theirs, he should send the offender, that they might punish him.

---

[8] Cheat.

[9] This was the first Indian treaty and it lasted almost twenty-five years, until Massasoit's son attacked the English in 1675–76 in a futile attempt to get them to leave.

3. That if anything were taken away from any of theirs, he should cause it to be restored; and they should do the like to his.

4. If any did unjustly war against him, they would aid him; if any did war against them, he should aid them.

5. He should send to his neighbours confederates to certify them of this, that they might not wrong them, but might be likewise comprised in the conditions of peace.

6. That when their men came to them, they should leave their bows and arrows behind them.

10   After these things he returned to his place called Sowams, some 40 miles from this place, but Squanto continued with them and was their interpreter and was a special instrument sent of God for their good beyond their expectation. He directed them how to set their corn, where to take fish, and to procure other commodities, and was also their pilot to bring them to unknown places for their profit, and never left them till he died. He was a native of this place, and scarce any left alive besides himself. He was carried away with divers others by one Hunt, a master of a ship, who thought to sell them for slaves in Spain. But he got away for England and was entertained by a merchant in London, and employed to Newfoundland and other parts, and lastly brought hither into these parts by one Mr. Dermer, a gentleman employed by Sir Ferdinando Gorges and others for discovery and other designs in these parts.

But to return. The spring now approaching, it pleased God the mortality began to cease amongst them, and the sick and lame recovered apace, which put as [it] were new life into them, though they had borne their sad affliction with much patience and contentedness as I think any people could do. But it was the Lord which upheld them, and had beforehand prepared them; many having long borne the yoke, yea from their youth. Many other smaller matters I omit, sundry of them having been already published in a journal made by one of the company, and some other passages of journeys and relations already published, to which I refer those that are willing to know them more particularly.

And being now come to the 25th of March, I shall begin the year 1621.

from *Chapter XII: Anno 1621*

Indian Diplomacy

Having in some sort ordered their business at home, it was thought meet to send some abroad to see their new friend Massasoit, and to bestow upon him some gratuity to bind him the faster unto them; as also that hereby they might view the country and see in what manner he lived, what strength he had about him, and how the ways were to his place, if at any time they should have occasion. So the second of July they sent Mr. Edward Winslow and Mr. Hopkins, with the foresaid Squanto for their guide; who gave him a suit of clothes and a horseman's coat, with some other small things, which were kindly accepted; but they found but short commons[10] and came both weary and hungry home. For the Indians used then to have nothing so much corn as they have since the English have stored them with their hoes, and seen their industry in breaking up new grounds therewith.

They found his place to be forty miles from hence, the soil good and the people not many, being dead and abundantly wasted in the late great mortality, which fell in all these parts about three years before the coming of the English, wherein thousands of them died. They not being able to bury one another, their skulls and bones were found in many places lying still above the ground where their houses and dwellings had been, a very sad spectacle to behold. But they brought word that the Narragansetts[11] lived but on the other side of that great bay, and were a strong people and many in number, living compact together, and had not been at all touched with this wasting plague.

About the latter end of this month, one John Billington lost himself in the woods, and wandered up and down some five days, living on berries and what he could find. At length he light on an Indian plantation twenty miles south of this place, called Manomet; they conveyed him further off, to Nauset among those people that had before set upon the English when they were coasting whilst the ship lay at the Cape, as is before noted. But the Governor caused him to be inquired for among the Indians, and at length Massasoit sent word where he was, and the Governor sent a shallop for him and had him delivered. Those people also came and made their peace; and they gave full satisfaction to those whose corn they had found and taken when they were at Cape Cod.

Thus their peace and acquaintance was pretty well established with the natives about them. And there was another Indian called Hobomok come to live amongst them, a proper lusty man, and a man of account for his valour and parts amongst the Indians, and continued very faithful and constant to the English till he died. He and Squanto being gone upon business among the Indians, at their return (whether it was out of envy to them or malice to the English) there was a sachem called Corbitant, allied to Massasoit but never any good friend to the English to this day, met with them at an Indian town called Namasket, fourteen miles to the west of this place, and began to quarrel with them and offered to stab Hobomok. But being a lusty man, he cleared himself of him and came running away all sweating, and told the Governor what had befallen him. And he feared they had killed Squanto, for they

---

[10] Supplies.
[11] Very powerful Indian tribe which spoke the Algonquin language.

threatened them both; and for no other cause but because they were friends to the English and serviceable unto them. Upon this the Governor taking counsel, it was conceived not fit to be borne; for if they should suffer their friends and messengers thus to be wronged, they should have none would cleave to them, or give them any intelligence, or do them service afterwards, but next they would fall upon themselves. Whereupon it was resolved to send the Captain and fourteen men well armed, and to go and fall upon them in the night. And if they found that Squanto was killed, to cut off Corbitant's head, but not to hurt any but those that had a hand in it.

Hobomok was asked if he would go and be their guide and bring them there before day. He said he would, and bring them to the house where the man lay, and show them which was he. So they set forth the 14th of August, and beset the house round. The Captain, giving charge to let none pass out, entered the house to search for him. But he was gone away that day, so they missed him, but understood that Squanto was alive, and that he had only threatened to kill him and made an offer to stab him but did not. So they withheld and did no more hurt, and the people came trembling and brought them the best provisions they had, after they were acquainted by Hobomok what was only intended. There was three sore wounded which broke out of the house and assayed to pass through the guard. These they brought home with them, and they had their wounds dressed and cured, and sent home. After this they had many gratulations from divers sachems, and much firmer peace; yea, those of the Isles of Capawack sent to make friendship; and this Corbitant himself used the mediation of Massasoit to make his peace, but was shy to come near them a long while after.

After this, the 18th of September they sent out their shallop to the Massachusetts, with ten men and Squanto for their guide and interpreter, to discover and view that Bay and trade with the natives. The which they performed, and found kind entertainment. The people were much afraid of the Tarentines, a people to the eastward which used to come in harvest time and take away their corn, and many times kill their persons. They returned in safety and brought home a good quantity of beaver, and made report of the place, wishing they had been there seated. But it seems the Lord, who assigns to all men the bounds of their habitations, had appointed it for another use. And thus they found the Lord to be with them in all their ways, and to bless their outgoings and incomings, for which let His holy name have the praise forever, to all posterity.

First Thanksgiving

They began now to gather in the small harvest they had, and to fit up their houses and dwellings against winter, being all well recovered in health and strength and had all things in good plenty. For as some were thus employed in affairs abroad, others were exercised in fishing, about cod and bass and other fish, of which they took good store, of which every family had their portion. All the summer there was no want; and now began to come in store of fowl, as winter approached, of which this place did abound when they came first (but afterward decreased by degrees). And besides waterfowl there was great store of wild turkeys, of which they took many, besides venison, etc. Besides they had about a peck a meal a week to a person, or now since harvest, Indian corn to that proportion. Which made many afterwards write so largely of their plenty here to their friends in England, which were not feigned but true reports.

For Journals

When you hear expressions such as "the Pilgrims" or "Plymouth Rock" or "the First Thanksgiving," what images come to mind? How do you imagine the Pilgrims?

For Discussion

1.   What political principles are suggested or stated in the language of the Mayflower Compact? Which ones have become such essential parts of American political tradition that we take them for granted? The Compact is an agreement—who agrees to do what, and why?

2.   Like relations between white settlers and Plains Indians in the nineteenth-century West, relations between the Plymouth settlers and Indians were much more complicated than later movie simplifications would suggest. How would you characterize the settlers' attitude toward the Indians here, and vice versa? Look for specific language or incidents in Bradford's narration to support your contentions.

3.   Europeans thought of America in many, often conflicting ways: as a new Garden of Eden, an exotic paradise, a threatening and dangerous environment, a source of riches, a land waiting to be conquered, and so on. Which of these perceptions, if any, do you find in Bradford's account? Which image of America seems to predominate? Find quotations from Bradford to use as supporting evidence.

For Writing

1.   There are two agreements in this reading: the Mayflower Compact among the settlers, and the peace treaty between the settlers and the Indians. Write an essay in which you compare and contrast these two, and consider the following questions: How do the attitudes the settlers have toward one another differ from the attitudes they have toward the Indians? What values are most important in each? How is the fact that the Indians and the settlers do not quite trust each other revealed in the agreement? Who, if anyone, got the advantage in the second agreement?

2. It is often said that history is written by the victors. Rewrite the meeting between the colonists and the Indians from the Indians' point of view.

∞ *Liberty Introducing the Arts to America* (1849)

SARTAIN'S *UNION MAGAZINE OF LITERATURE & ART*

> *As early as the 1500s, European artists began portraying America as an exotically clothed Indian girl, often shown sitting on an alligator throne, accompanied by a parrot, or holding a cornucopia. In later American versions like this 1849 image, America is still exotic in her skirt and headdress, but she faces another popular icon— Liberty, a white woman in classical clothing.*

For Journals

What souvenirs, toys, or memorabilia have you ever owned that you think of as being distinctly American symbols?

For Discussion

1. Look closely at the standing female figure, who represents Liberty and is analogous to Minerva, the Roman goddess of wisdom. What objects is she showing America, and what are the cherubs playing with? What point do you think the artist was making about what Europe had to offer America? What does wisdom have to do with liberty and what does liberty have to do with arts?

2. What would you have expected to see as an early representation of America? If you were creating a modern image of America, what would it look like? A man? A woman? How would the person be dressed? What would this person be doing?

3. In what ways is the picture of America a welcoming image? A threatening one? Judging from the way it looks, what kinds of fantasies do you think Europeans had about America? What kinds of fears?

For Writing

1. Returning to discussion item 2, write an essay describing your idea of an image you would call America—not an actual historical person, but a figure whose appearance you determine in accordance with your own imagination. Use the same pose as the one in the illustration—seat

the figure, and have him or her holding or being surrounded by what you think of as characteristically American paraphernalia.

2.   Alternately, do a library search or an Internet search, or both, for other American icons of the past, like kewpie dolls, Teddy bears, or cigar-store Indians. Research the history of the older icon and write a paper in which you examine at least three of the following: When did it come into use? Where did it get its name? Where and for what purposes was it used? Is it still popular or has it faded? Was it used in advertisements? Was it a toy? And particularly, what was its appeal, and what contemporary toy, image, or figure do you see as the current equivalent of that older icon?

∞ *Wealth* (1889)

ANDREW CARNEGIE

Andrew Carnegie (1835–1919) emigrated from Scotland to the United States. He began his career as a weaver like his father, but then he became a telegraph messenger

*boy and eventually a telegraph operator and superintendent. He made his fortune
in railroads, communications, and steel; he sold his interest to J. P. Morgan in 1901
for $250 million. When he retired from public life, he dedicated much of his fortune to
establishing institutions for the public good, including Carnegie Tech (later Carnegie-
Mellon University), Carnegie Hall, the Carnegie Foundation, the Carnegie Endow-
ment for Peace, and libraries in many towns and cities in the United States and
Britain. Most of his writings concern the importance of preserving and maintaining world peace, but he also wrote about business and money.*

The problem of our age is the proper administration of wealth, so
that the ties of brotherhood may still bind together the rich and poor in
harmonious relationship. The conditions of human life have not only
been changed, but revolutionized, within the past few hundred years.
In former days there was little difference between the dwelling, dress,
food, and environment of the chief and those of his retainers. The Indians are to-day where civilized man then was. When visiting the Sioux,
I was led to the wigwam of the chief. It was just like the others in external appearance, and even within the difference was trifling between it
and those of the poorest of his braves. The contrast between the palace
of the millionaire and the cottage of the laborer with us to-day measures the change which has come with civilization.

This change, however, is not to be deplored, but welcomed as
highly beneficial. It is well, nay, essential for the progress of the race, that
the houses of some should be homes for all that is highest and best in literature and the arts, and for all the refinements of civilization, rather
than that none should be so. Much better this great irregularity than
universal squalor. Without wealth there can be no Maecenas.[1] The
"good old times" were not good old times. Neither master nor servant
was as well situated than as to-day. A relapse to old conditions would
be disastrous to both—not the least so to him who serves—and would
sweep away civilization with it. But whether the change be for good or
ill, it is upon us, beyond our power to alter, and therefore to be accepted
and made the best of. It is a waste of time to criticise the inevitable.

It is easy to see how the change has come. One illustration will serve
for almost every phase of the cause. In the manufacture of products we
have the whole story. It applies to all combinations of human industry,
as stimulated and enlarged by the inventions of this scientific age. Formerly articles were manufactured at the domestic hearth or in small
shops which formed part of the household. The master and his apprentices worked side by side, the latter living with the master, and therefore
subject to the same conditions. When these apprentices rose to be masters, there was little or no change in their mode of life, and they, in turn,
educated in the same routine succeeding apprentices. There was, sub-

---

[1] Maecenas (70?–8 B.C.) was a Roman statesman and patron whose name has become synonymous with generosity to artists and writers.

stantially, social equality, and even political equality, for those engaged in industrial pursuits had then little or no political voice in the State.

But the inevitable result of such a mode of manufacture was crude articles at high prices. To-day the world obtains commodities of excellent quality at prices which even the generation preceding this would have deemed incredible. In the commercial world similar causes have produced similar results, and the race is benefited thereby. The poor enjoy what the rich could not before afford. What were the luxuries have become the necessaries of life. The laborer has now more comforts than the farmer had a few generations ago. The farmer has more luxuries than the landlord had, and is more richly clad and better housed. The landlord has books and pictures rarer, and appointments more artistic, than the King could then obtain.

The price we pay for this salutary change is, no doubt, great. We as- 5 semble thousands of operatives in the factory, in the mine, and in the counting-house, of whom the employer can know little or nothing, and to whom the employer is little better than a myth. All intercourse between them is at an end. Rigid Castes are formed, and, as usual, mutual ignorance breeds mutual distrust. Each Caste is without sympathy for the other, and ready to credit anything disparaging in regard to it. Under the law of competition, the employer of thousands is forced into the strictest economies, among which the rates paid to labor figure prominently, and often there is friction between the employer and the employed, between capital and labor, between rich and poor. Human society loses homogeneity.

The price which society pays for the law of competition, like the price it pays for cheap comforts and luxuries, is also great; but the advantages of this law are also greater still, for it is to this law that we owe our wonderful material development, which brings improved conditions in its train. But, whether the law be benign or not, we must say of it, as we say of the change in the conditions of men to which we have referred: It is here; we cannot evade it; no substitutes for it have been found; and while the law may be sometimes hard for the individual, it is best for the race, because it insures the survival of the fittest in every department. We accept and welcome, therefore, as conditions to which we must accommodate ourselves, great inequality of environment, the concentration of business, industrial and commercial, in the hands of a few, and the law of competition between these, as being not only beneficial, but essential for the future progress of the race. Having accepted these, it follows that there must be great scope for the exercise of special ability in the merchant and in the manufacturer who has to conduct affairs upon a great scale. That this talent for organization and management is rare among men is proved by the fact that it invariably secures for its possessor enormous rewards, no matter where or under what laws or conditions. . . .

We start, then, with a condition of affairs under which the best interests of the race are promoted, but which inevitably gives wealth to the few. Thus far, accepting conditions as they exist, the situation can be surveyed and pronounced good. The question then arises,—and, if the foregoing be correct, it is the only question with which we have to deal,—What is the proper mode of administering wealth after the laws upon which civilization is founded have thrown it into the hands of the few? And it is of this great question that I believe I offer the true solution. It will be understood that *fortunes* are here spoken of, not moderate sums saved by many years of effort, the returns from which are required for the comfortable maintenance and education of families. This is not *wealth*, but only *competence*, which it should be the aim of all to acquire.

There are but three modes in which surplus wealth can be disposed of. It can be left to the families of the decedents; or it can be bequeathed for public purposes; or, finally, it can be administered during their lives by its possessors. Under the first and second modes most of the wealth of the world that has reached the few has hitherto been applied. Let us in turn consider each of these modes. The first is the most injudicious. In monarchical countries, the estates and the greatest portion of the wealth are left to the first son, that the vanity of the parent may be gratified by the thought that his name and title are to descend to succeeding generations unimpaired. The condition of this class in Europe to-day teaches the futility of such hopes or ambitions. The successors have become impoverished through their follies or from the fall in the value of land. Even in Great Britain the strict law of entail has been found inadequate to maintain the status of an hereditary class. Its soil is rapidly passing into the hands of the stranger. Under republican institutions the division of property among the children is much fairer, but the question which forces itself upon thoughtful men in all lands is: Why should men leave great fortunes to their children? If this is done from affection, is it not misguided affection? Observation teaches that, generally speaking, it is not well for the children that they should be so burdened. Neither is it well for the state. Beyond providing for the wife and daughters moderate sources of income, and very moderate allowances indeed, if any, for the sons, men may well hesitate, for it is no longer questionable that great sums bequeathed oftener work more for the injury than for the good of the recipients. Wise men will soon conclude that, for the best interests of the members of their families and of the state, such bequests are an improper use of their means. . . .

As to the second mode, that of leaving wealth at death for public uses, it may be said that this is only a means for the disposal of wealth, provided a man is content to wait until he is dead before it becomes of much good in the world. . . .

10   It is well to remember that it requires the exercise of not less ability than that which acquired the wealth to use it so as to be really beneficial

to the community. Besides this, it may fairly be said that no man is to be extolled for doing what he cannot help doing, nor is he to be thanked by the community to which he only leaves wealth at death. Men who leave vast sums in this way may fairly be thought men who would not have left it at all, had they been able to take it with them. The memories of such cannot be held in grateful remembrance, for there is no grace in their gifts. It is not to be wondered at that such bequests seem so generally to lack the blessing.

The growing disposition to tax more and more heavily large estates left at death is a cheering indication of the growth of a salutary change in public opinion. The State of Pennsylvania now takes—subject to some exceptions—one-tenth of the property left by its citizens. The budget presented in the British Parliament the other day proposes to increase the death-duties; and, most significant of all, the new tax is to be a graduated one. Of all forms of taxation, this seems the wisest. Men who continue hoarding great sums all their lives, the proper use of which for public ends would work good to the community, should be made to feel that the community, in the form of the state, cannot thus be deprived of its proper share. By taxing estates heavily at death the state marks its condemnation of the selfish millionaire's unworthy life. . . .

This policy would work powerfully to induce the rich man to attend to the administration of wealth during his life, which is the end that society should always have in view, as being that by far most fruitful for the people. Nor need it be feared that this policy would sap the root of enterprise and render men less anxious to accumulate, for to the class whose ambition it is to leave great fortunes and be talked about after their death, it will attract even more attention, and, indeed, be a somewhat nobler ambition to have enormous sums paid over to the state from their fortunes.

There remains, then, only one mode of using great fortunes; but in this we have the true antidote for the temporary unequal distribution of wealth, the reconciliation of the rich and the poor—a reign of harmony—another ideal, differing, indeed, from that of the Communist in requiring only the further evolution of existing conditions, not the total overthrow of our civilization. It is founded upon the present most intense individualism, and the race is prepared to put it in practice by degrees whenever it pleases. Under its sway we shall have an ideal state, in which the surplus wealth of the few will become, in the best sense, the property of the many, because administered for the common good, and this wealth, passing through the hands of the few, can be made a much more potent force for the elevation of our race than if it had been distributed in small sums to the people themselves. Even the poorest can be made to see this, and to agree that great sums gathered by some of their fellow-citizens and spent for public purposes, from which the masses reap the principal benefit, are more valuable to them than if scattered among them through the course of many years in trifling amounts.

If we consider what results flow from the Cooper Institute,[2] for instance, to the best portion of the race in New York not possessed of means, and compare these with those which would have arisen for the good of the masses from an equal sum distributed by Mr. Cooper in his lifetime in the form of wages, which is the highest form of distribution, being for work done and not for charity, we can form some estimate of the possibilities for the improvement of the race which lie embedded in the present law of the accumulation of wealth. Much of this sum, if distributed in small quantities among the people, would have been wasted in the indulgence of appetite, some of it in excess, and it may be doubted whether even the part put to the best use, that of adding to the comforts of the home, would have yielded results for the race, as a race, at all comparable to those which are flowing and are to flow from the Cooper Institute from generation to generation. Let the advocate of violent or radical change ponder well this thought.

15 We might even go so far as to take another instance, that of Mr. Tilden's[3] bequest of five millions of dollars for a free library in the city of New York, but in referring to this one cannot help saying involuntarily, How much better if Mr. Tilden had devoted the last years of his own life to the proper administration of this immense sum; in which case neither legal contest nor any other cause of delay could have interfered with his aims. But let us assume that Mr. Tilden's millions finally became the means of giving to this city a noble public library, where the treasures of the world contained in books will be open forever, without money and without price. Considering the good of that part of the race which congregates in and around Manhattan Island, would its permanent benefit have been better promoted had these millions been allowed to circulate in small sums through the hands of the masses? Even the most strenuous advocate of Communism must entertain a doubt upon this subject. Most of those who think will probably entertain no doubt whatever.

Poor and restricted are our opportunities in this life; narrow our horizon; our best work most imperfect; but rich men should be thankful for one inestimable boon. They have it in their power during their lives to busy themselves in organizing benefactions from which the masses of their fellows will derive lasting advantage, and thus dignify their own lives. The highest life is probably to be reached, not by such

---

[2] Cooper Institute was founded in 1857–1859 by Peter Cooper (1791–1883), an American inventor and philanthropist, as a tuition-free school for industrial design and the advancement of science and art.

[3] Samuel Tilden (1814–1886) was a lawyer and governor of New York who lost a highly disputed presidential election to Rutherford B. Hayes in 1876 by one electoral vote; he left his fortune to the establishment of a free library in New York City.

imitation of the life of Christ as Count Tolstoï gives us, but, while animated by Christ's spirit, by recognizing the changed conditions of this age, and adopting modes of expressing this spirit suitable to the changed conditions under which we live; still laboring for the good of our fellows, which was the essence of his life and teaching, but laboring in a different manner.

This, then, is held to be the duty of the man of Wealth: First, to set an example of modest, unostentatious living, shunning display or extravagance; to provide moderately for the legitimate wants of those dependent upon him; and after doing so to consider all surplus revenues which come to him simply as trust funds, which he is called upon to administer, and strictly bound as a matter of duty to administer in the manner which, in his judgment, is best calculated to produce the most beneficial results for the community—the man of wealth thus becoming the mere agent and trustee for his poorer brethren, bringing to their service his superior wisdom, experience, and ability to administer, doing for them better than they would or could do for themselves.

We are met here with the difficulty of determining what are moderate sums to leave to members of the family; what is modest, unostentatious living; what is the test of extravagance. There must be different standards for different conditions. The answer is that it is as impossible to name exact amounts or actions as it is to define good manners, good taste, or the rules of propriety; but, nevertheless, these are verities, well known although undefinable. Public sentiment is quick to know and to feel what offends these. So in the case of wealth. The rule in regard to good taste in the dress of men or women applies here. Whatever makes one conspicuous offends the canon. If any family be chiefly known for display, for extravagance in home, table, equipage, for enormous sums ostentatiously spent in any form upon itself,—if these be its chief distinctions, we have no difficulty in estimating its nature or culture. So likewise in regard to the use or abuse of its surplus wealth, or to generous, free-handed coöperation in good public uses, or to unabated efforts to accumulate and hoard to the last, whether they administer or bequeath. The verdict rests with the best and most enlightened public sentiment. The community will surely judge, and its judgments will not often be wrong.

The best uses to which surplus wealth can be put have already been indicated. Those who would administer wisely must, indeed, be wise, for one of the serious obstacles to the improvement of our race is indiscriminate charity. It were better for mankind that the millions of the rich were thrown into the sea than so spent as to encourage the slothful, the drunken, the unworthy. Of every thousand dollars spent in so called charity to-day, it is probable that $950 is unwisely spent; so spent, indeed, as to produce the very evils which it proposes to mitigate or cure. A well-known writer of philosophic books admitted the other day that he had given a quarter of a dollar to a man who approached him as he was coming to visit the house of his friend. He knew nothing of the habits of this beggar; knew not the use that would be made of this money, although he had every reason to suspect that it would be spent improperly. This man professed to be a disciple of Herbert Spencer; yet the quarter-dollar given that night will probably work more injury than all the money which its thoughtless donor will ever be able to give in true charity will do good. He only gratified his own feelings, saved himself from annoyance,—and this was probably one of the most selfish and very worst actions of his life, for in all respects he is most worthy.

20   In bestowing charity, the main consideration should be to help those who will help themselves; to provide part of the means by which those who desire to improve may do so; to give those who desire to rise the aids by which they may rise; to assist, but rarely or never to do all. Neither the individual nor the race is improved by alms-giving. Those worthy of assistance, except in rare cases, seldom require assistance. The really valuable men of the race never do, except in cases of accident or sudden change. Every one has, of course, cases of individuals brought to his own knowledge where temporary assistance can do genuine good, and these he will not overlook. But the amount which can be wisely given by the individual for individuals is necessarily limited by his lack of knowledge of the circumstances connected with each. He is the only true reformer who is as careful and as anxious not to aid the unworthy as he is to aid the worthy, and, perhaps, even more so, for in alms-giving more injury is probably done by rewarding vice than by relieving virtue.

The rich man is thus almost restricted to following the examples of Peter Cooper, Enoch Pratt of Baltimore, Mr. Pratt of Brooklyn, Senator Stanford, and others, who know that the best means of benefiting the community is to place within its reach the ladders upon which the aspiring can rise—parks, and means of recreation, by which men are helped in body and mind; works of art, certain to give pleasure and improve the public taste, and public institutions of various kinds, which will improve the general condition of the people;—in this manner returning their surplus wealth to the mass of their fellows in the forms best calculated to do them lasting good.

Thus is the problem of Rich and Poor to be solved. The laws of accumulation will be left free; the laws of distribution free. Individualism will continue, but the millionaire will be but a trustee for the poor; intrusted for a season with a great part of the increased wealth of the community, but administering it for the community far better than it could or would have done for itself. The best minds will thus have reached a stage in the development of the race in which it is clearly seen that there is no mode of disposing of surplus wealth creditable to thoughtful and earnest men into whose hands it flows save by using it year by year for the general good. This day already dawns. But a little while, and although, without incurring the pity of their fellows, men may die sharers in great business enterprises from which their capital cannot be or has not been withdrawn, and is left chiefly at death for public uses, yet the man who dies leaving behind him millions of available wealth, which was his to administer during life, will pass away "unwept, unhonored, and unsung," no matter to what uses he leaves the dross which he cannot take with him. Of such as these the public verdict will then be: "The man who dies thus rich dies disgraced."

Such, in my opinion, is the true Gospel concerning Wealth, obedience to which is destined some day to solve the problem of the Rich and the Poor, and to bring "Peace on earth, among men Good-Will."

For Journals

Describe what you think your standard of living is.

For Discussion

1. To what factors do you think Carnegie attributes his assertion that the standard of living is higher than ever before in history? How would you compare the American standard of living now to what Carnegie describes?

2. How do you think Carnegie would define civilization? In what ways, if any, is his definition a particularly American one?

3. According to Carnegie, what social price do we pay for the advantages of modern life? What price do you think we pay today for the modern advantages we enjoy?

4. How do you respond to Carnegie's argument that a great fortune in the hands of a few people can do society more good than a little money spread around among many people? How can a man who started with nothing argue that it's better for a few people to have a lot of money?

For Writing

1. Carnegie gives three possible models for how great American wealth should be distributed: rich people could leave it to their children; they could leave money in their wills for public purposes; or they could spend their money philanthropically during their lifetimes. Assume that you have found yourself in control of a great deal of money—and that you have already gratified your personal whims and those of your family. Write an essay arguing in favor of one of Carnegie's suggestions.

2. Assume that you have a great fortune; write a creative proposal explaining how you plan to spend that fortune for the public good. Make some specific suggestions for projects you would support, and be explicit about the American values or virtues you think your plan would encourage.

3. Carnegie said that, as a rule, individuals worthy of assistance don't need assistance, and that philanthropists should build parks, donate art, and create public institutions to improve the general condition of the people. On your own, or with other students, make plans to visit a homeless shelter to interview a counselor or social worker there. Then ask that worker to set up an interview between you and an individual or family receiving assistance from that institution. Write a summary of the interviews. Alternately, arrange a visit to your local parks department or to a museum that has a children's program; interview the administrator, and, if possible, some of the children who come to the program. In either case, conclude with your own evaluation of whether the service is an effective use of money for the public good.

∽ *California, the Cornucopia of the World* (1889)

The following poster was designed at a time when the population of California was smaller than that of Mississippi. What is now Los Angeles was a relatively small city consisting mostly of orange groves and palm trees. This poster is displayed in the Ellis Island Museum, located in the building where millions of immigrants first set foot on American soil.

For Journals

When you think of California, what images come to your mind? How many of them are represented in this poster?

For Discussion

1. Who do you think was the intended audience for this poster? What guesses can you make about their educational level? Their occupations? Their goals and dreams?

2. What does the artist want the audience to learn about California? What kinds of positive facts are incorporated into the picture? What does the artist want the audience to overlook or remain ignorant of?

3. The central image in the poster is the cornucopia overflowing with fruits, vegetables, and flowers. Why do you think this image was chosen? What associations does it bring to mind?

4. There are gaps in the information provided by this poster. For example, what does "untaken" land mean if Native Americans and Mexicans are living there? How can California be the cornucopia of the world if so many millions of its acres are still unfarmed? What other gaps can you find? What other kinds of information do you think the audience would want? Is this kind of advertising fair or unfair to the audience, and why?

For Writing

1. Look through some travel magazines for advertisements about a particular American place to visit. Be sure there are both pictures and text. Then write an essay answering discussion questions 1–4. You could begin with a visual exercise: look at the picture, close your eyes, and try to visualize it again; then look at it again, put it away, and try to write down everything you remember about it. What you remember— even incorrectly—will be a good guide to what made the biggest impression on you and will help you organize your ideas. Use examples from the text and images in the advertisement to support whatever conclusions you draw.

2. In his cultural history of California, *Inventing the Dream,* historian Kevin Starr says that developments and transformations in California set the standard for the rest of the nation and that California, particularly southern California and Hollywood, has a fixed place in the "daydream of America." Write an essay analyzing this idea. Here are some questions to consider: What are your mental images of California? What examples (such as movies, television, and music) portray the California dream Starr speaks of? How much do you identify the idea of California with the idea of the American dream?

∞ *In the Land of the Free* (ca. 1900)

SUI SIN FAR

Sui Sin Far (1865–1914) was the Chinese name of the daughter of an English father and a Chinese mother; her English name was Edith Eaton. She is the first Asian American whose fiction was published in the United States. This story is from a collection, Mrs. Spring Fragrance, *published in 1912.*

1

"See, Little One—the hills in the morning sun. There is thy home for years to come. It is very beautiful and thou wilt be very happy there."

The Little One looked up into his mother's face in perfect faith. He was engaged in the pleasant occupation of sucking a sweetmeat; but that did not prevent him from gurgling responsively.

"Yes, my olive bud; there is where thy father is making a fortune for thee. Thy father! Oh, wilt thou not be glad to behold his dear face. 'Twas for thee I left him."

The Little One ducked his chin sympathetically against his mother's knee. She lifted him on to her lap. He was two years old, a round, dimple-cheeked boy with bright brown eyes and a sturdy little frame.

"Ah! Ah! Ah! Ooh! Ooh! Ooh!" puffed he, mocking a tugboat ₅ steaming by.

San Francisco's waterfront was lined with ships and steamers, while other craft, large and small, including a couple of white transports from the Philippines, lay at anchor here and there off shore. It was some time before the *Eastern Queen* could get docked, and even after that was accomplished, a lone Chinaman who had been waiting on the wharf for an hour was detained that much longer by men with the initials U.S.C. on their caps, before he could board the steamer and welcome his wife and child.

"This is thy son," announced the happy Lae Choo.

Hom Hing lifted the child, felt of his little body and limbs, gazed into his face with proud and joyous eyes; then turned inquiringly to a customs officer at his elbow.

"That's a fine boy you have there," said the man. "Where was he born?"

"In China," answered Hom Hing, swinging the Little One on his ₁₀ right shoulder, preparatory to leading his wife off the steamer.

"Ever been to America before?"

"No, not he," answered the father with a happy laugh.

The customs officer beckoned to another.

"This little fellow," said he, "is visiting America for the first time." The other customs officer stroked his chin reflectively. ₁₅

"Good day," said Hom Hing.

"Wait!" commanded one of the officers. "You cannot go just yet."

"What more now?" asked Hom Hing.

"I'm afraid," said the customs officer, "that we cannot allow the boy to go ashore. There is nothing in the papers that you have shown us— your wife's papers and your own—having any bearing upon the child."

"There was no child when the papers were made out," returned ₂₀ Hom Hing. He spoke calmly; but there was apprehension in his eyes and in his tightening grip on his son.

"What is it? What is it?" quavered Lae Choo, who understood a little English.

The second customs officer regarded her pityingly.

"I don't like this part of the business," he muttered.

The first officer turned to Hom Hing and in an official tone of voice, said:

"Seeing that the boy has no certificate entitling him to admission to ₂₅ this country you will have to leave him with us."

"Leave my boy!" exclaimed Hom Hing.

"Yes; he will be well taken care of, and just as soon as we can hear from Washington he will be handed over to you."

"But," protested Hom Hing, "he is my son."

"We have no proof," answered the man with a shrug of his shoulders; "and even if so we cannot let him pass without orders from the Government."

30   "He is my son," reiterated Hom Hing, slowly and solemnly. "I am a Chinese merchant and have been in business in San Francisco for many years. When my wife told to me one morning that she dreamed of a green tree with spreading branches and one beautiful red flower growing thereon, I answered her that I wished my son to be born in our country, and for her to prepare to go to China. My wife complied with my wish. After my son was born my mother fell sick and my wife nursed and cared for her; then my father, too, fell sick, and my wife also nursed and cared for him. For twenty moons my wife care for and nurse the old people, and when they die they bless her and my son, and I send for her to return to me. I had no fear of trouble. I was a Chinese merchant and my son was my son."

"Very good, Hom Hing," replied the first officer. "Nevertheless, we take your son."

"No, you not take him; he my son too."

It was Lae Choo. Snatching the child from his father's arms she held and covered him with her own.

The officers conferred for a few moments; then one drew Hom Hing aside and spoke in his ear.

35   Resignedly Hom Hing bowed his head, then approached his wife. "'Tis the law," said he, speaking in Chinese, "and 'twill be but for a little while—until tomorrow's sun arises."

"You, too," reproached Lae Choo in a voice eloquent with pain. But accustomed to obedience she yielded the boy to her husband, who in turn delivered him to the first officer. The Little One protested lustily against the transfer; but his mother covered her face with her sleeve and his father silently led her away. Thus was the law of the land complied with.

2

Day was breaking. Lae Choo, who had been awake all night, dressed herself, then awoke her husband.

"'Tis the morn," she cried. "Go, bring our son."

The man rubbed his eyes and arose upon his elbow so that he could see out of the window. A pale star was visible in the sky. The petals of a lily in a bowl on the windowsill were unfurled.

40   "'Tis not yet time," said he, laying his head down again.

"Not yet time. Ah, all the time that I lived before yesterday is not so much as the time that has been since my Little One was taken from me."

The mother threw herself down beside the bed and covered her face.

Hom Hing turned on the light, and touching his wife's bowed head with a sympathetic hand inquired if she had slept.

"Slept!" she echoed, weepingly. "Ah, how could I close my eyes with my arms empty of the little body that has filled them every night for more than twenty moons! You do not know—man—what it is to miss the feel of the little fingers and the little toes and the soft round limbs of your little one. Even in the darkness his darling eyes used to shine up to mine, and often have I fallen into slumber with his pretty babble at my ear. And now, I see him not; I touch him not; I hear him not. My baby, my little fat one!"

"Now! Now! Now!" consoled Hom Hing, patting his wife's shoul- 45 der reassuringly; "there is no need to grieve so; he will soon gladden you again. There cannot be any law that would keep a child from its mother!"

Lae Choo dried her tears.

"You are right, my husband," she meekly murmured. She arose and stepped about the apartment, setting things to rights. The box of presents she had brought for her California friends had been opened the evening before; and silks, embroideries, carved ivories, ornamental lacquer-ware, brasses, camphorwood boxes, fans, and chinaware were scattered around in confused heaps. In the midst of unpacking the thought of her child in the hands of strangers had overpowered her, and she had left everything to crawl into bed and weep.

Having arranged her gifts in order she stepped out on to the deep balcony.

The star had faded from view and there were bright streaks in the western sky. Lae Choo looked down the street and around. Beneath the flat occupied by her and her husband were quarters for a number of bachelor Chinamen, and she could hear them from where she stood, taking their early morning breakfast. Below their dining-room was her husband's grocery store. Across the way was a large restaurant. Last night it had been resplendent with gay colored lanterns and the sound of music. The rejoicings over "the completion of the moon," by Quong Sum's firstborn, had been long and loud, and had caused her to tie a handkerchief over her ears. She, a bereaved mother, had it not in her heart to rejoice with other parents. This morning the place was more in accord with her mood. It was still and quiet. The revellers had dispersed or were asleep.

A roly-poly woman in black sateen, with long pendant earrings in 50 her ears, looked up from the street below and waved her a smiling greeting. It was her old neighbor, Kuie Hoe, the wife of the gold embosser, Mark Sing. With her was a little boy in a yellow jacket and lavender pantaloons. Lae Choo remembered him as a baby. She used to like to play with him in those days when she had no child of her own. What a long time ago that seemed! She caught her breath in a sigh, and laughed instead.

"Why are you so merry?" called her husband from within.

"Because my Little One is coming home," answered Lae Choo. "I am a happy mother—a happy mother."

She pattered into the room with a smile on her face.

The noon hour had arrived. The rice was steaming in the bowls and a fragrant dish of chicken and bamboo shoots was awaiting Hom Hing. Not for one moment had Lae Choo paused to rest during the morning hours; her activity had been ceaseless. Every now and again, however, she had raised her eyes to the gilded clock on the curiously carved mantelpiece. Once, she had exclaimed:

55   "Why so long, oh! why so long?" Then, apostrophizing herself: "Lae Choo, be happy. The Little One is coming! The Little One is coming!" Several times she burst into tears, and several times she laughed aloud.

Hom Hing entered the room; his arms hung down by his side.

"The Little One!" shrieked Lae Choo.

"They bid me call tomorrow."

With a moan the mother sank to the floor.

60   The noon hour passed. The dinner remained on the table.

3

The winter rains were over: the spring had come to California, flushing the hills with green and causing an ever-changing pageant of flowers to pass over them. But there was no spring in Lae Choo's heart, for the Little One remained away from her arms. He was being kept in a mission. White women were caring for him, and though for one full moon he had pined for his mother and refused to be comforted he was now apparently happy and contented. Five moons or five months had gone by since the day he had passed with Lae Choo through the Golden Gate; but the great Government at Washington still delayed sending the answer which would return him to his parents.

Hom Hing was disconsolately rolling up and down the balls in his abacus box when a keen-faced young man stepped into his store.

"What news?" asked the Chinese merchant.

"This!" The young man brought forth a typewritten letter. Hom Hing read the words:

65   "Re Chinese child, alleged to be the son of Hom Hing, Chinese merchant, doing business at 425 Clay Street, San Francisco.

"Same will have attention as soon as possible."

Hom Hing returned the letter, and without a word continued his manipulation of the counting machine.

"Have you anything to say?" asked the young man.

"Nothing. They have sent the same letter fifteen times before. Have you not yourself showed it to me?"

"True!" The young man eyed the Chinese merchant furtively. He 70 had a proposition to make and was pondering whether or not the time was opportune.

"How is your wife?" he inquired solicitously—and diplomatically. Hom Hing shook his head mournfully.

"She seems less every day," he replied. "Her food she takes only when I bid her and her tears fall continually. She finds no pleasure in dress or flowers and cares not to see her friends. Her eyes stare all night. I think before another moon she will pass into the land of the spirits."

"No!" exclaimed the young man, genuinely startled.

"If the boy not come home I lose my wife sure," continued Hom 75 Hing with bitter sadness.

"It's not right," cried the young man indignantly. Then he made his proposition.

The Chinese father's eyes brightened exceedingly.

"Will I like you to go to Washington and make them give you the paper to restore my son?" cried he. "How can you ask when you know my heart's desire?"

"Then," said the young fellow, "I will start next week. I am anxious to see this thing through if only for the sake of your wife's peace of mind."

"I will call her. To hear what you think to do will make her glad," 80 said Hom Hing.

He called a message to Lae Choo upstairs through a tube in the wall.

In a few moments she appeared, listless, wan, and hollow-eyed; but when her husband told her the young lawyer's suggestion she became electrified; her form straightened, her eyes glistened; the color flushed to her cheeks.

"Oh," she cried, turning to James Clancy. "You are a hundred man good!"

The young man felt somewhat embarrassed; his eyes shifted a little under the intense gaze of the Chinese mother.

"Well, we must get your boy for you," he responded. "Of course"— 85 turning to Hom Hing—"it will cost a little money. You can't get fellows to hurry the Government for you without gold in your pocket."

Hom Hing stared blankly for a moment. Then: "How much do you want, Mr. Clancy?" he asked quietly.

"Well, I will need at least five hundred to start with."

Hom Hing cleared his throat.

"I think I told to you the time I last paid you for writing letters for me and seeing the Custom boss here that nearly all I had was gone!"

90   "Oh well then we won't talk about it, old fellow. It won't harm the boy to stay where he is, and your wife may get over it all right."

"What that you say?" quavered Lae Choo.

James Clancy looked out of the window.

"He says," explained Hom Hing in English, "that to get our boy we have to have much money."

"Money! Oh, yes."

95   Lae Choo nodded her head.

"I have not got the money to give him."

For a moment Lae Choo gazed wonderingly from one face to the other; then, comprehension dawning upon her, with swift anger, pointing to the lawyer, she cried: "You not one hundred man good; you just common white man."

"Yes, ma'am," returned James Clancy, bowing and smiling ironically.

Hom Hing pushed his wife behind him and addressed the lawyer again: "I might try," said he, "to raise something; but five hundred—it is not possible."

100   "What about four?"

"I tell you I have next to nothing left and my friends are not rich."

"Very well!"

The lawyer moved leisurely toward the door, pausing on its threshold to light a cigarette.

"Stop, white man; white man, stop!"

105   Lae Choo, panting and terrified, had started forward and now stood beside him, clutching his sleeve excitedly.

"You say you can go to get paper to bring my Little One to me if Hom Hing give you five hundred dollars?"

The lawyer nodded carelessly; his eyes were intent upon the cigarette which would not take the fire from the match.

"Then you go get paper. If Hom Hing not can give you five hundred dollars—I give you perhaps what more that much."

She slipped a heavy gold bracelet from her wrist and held it out to the man. Mechanically he took it.

110   "I go get more!"

She scurried away, disappearing behind the door through which she had come.

"Oh, look here, I can't accept this," said James Clancy, walking back to Hom Hing and laying down the bracelet before him.

"It's all right," said Hom Hing, seriously, "pure China gold. My wife's parent give it to her when we married."

"But I can't take it anyway," protested the young man.

115   "It is all same as money. And you want money to go to Washington," replied Hom Hing in a matter-of-fact manner.

"See, my jade earrings—my gold buttons—my hairpins—my comb of pearl and my rings—one, two, three, four, five rings; very good—very good—all same much money. I give them all to you. You take and bring me paper for my Little One."

Lae Choo piled up her jewels before the lawyer.

Hom Hing laid a restraining hand upon her shoulder. "Not all, my wife," he said in Chinese. He selected a ring—his gift to Lae Choo when she dreamed of the tree with the red flower. The rest of the jewels he pushed toward the white man.

"Take them and sell them," said he. "They will pay your fare to Washington and bring you back with the paper."

For one moment James Clancy hesitated. He was not a sentimental 120 man; but something within him arose against accepting such payment for his services.

"They are good, good," pleadingly asserted Lae Choo, seeing his hesitation.

Whereupon he seized the jewels, thrust them into his coat pocket, and walked rapidly away from the store.

4

Lae Choo followed after the missionary woman through the mission nursery school. Her heart was beating so high with happiness that she could scarcely breathe. The paper had come at last—the precious paper which gave Hom Hing and his wife the right to the possession of their own child. It was ten months now since he had been taken from them—ten months since the sun had ceased to shine for Lae Choo.

The room was filled with children—most of them wee tots, but none so wee as her own. The mission woman talked as she walked. She told Lae Choo that little Kim, as he had been named by the school, was the pet of the place, and that his little tricks and ways amused and delighted every one. He had been rather difficult to manage at first and had cried much for his mother; "but children so soon forget, and after a month he seemed quite at home and played around as bright and happy as a bird."

"Yes," responded Lae Choo. "Oh, yes, yes!" 125

But she did not hear what was said to her. She was walking in a maze of anticipatory joy.

"Wait here, please," said the mission woman, placing Lae Choo in a chair. "The very youngest ones are having their breakfast."

She withdrew for a moment—it seemed like an hour to the mother—then she reappeared leading by the hand a little boy dressed in blue cotton overalls and white-soled shoes. The little boy's face was round and dimpled and his eyes were very bright.

"Little One, ah, my Little One!" cried Lae Choo.

130   She fell on her knees and stretched her hungry arms toward her son.
But the Little One shrunk from her and tried to hide himself in the
folds of the white woman's skirt.

"Go 'way, go 'way!" he bade his mother.

For Journals

There's an idea of America as a melting pot and another of America as
a tossed salad; which one do you think better describes the mix of cultures in this country?

For Discussion

1.   In the first sentence of this story, Lae Choo, arriving in San Francisco
with her infant son, expresses her dream for his happy future in America: "See, Little One—the hills in the morning sun. There is thy home for
years to come. It is very beautiful and thou wilt be very happy there."
But things don't work out exactly as planned; in fact, in each of the four
parts of this story, dreams are derailed, if not destroyed. What are these
dreams, whose are they, and how are they changed by circumstances?

2.   How does the involvement of white Americans in the lives of Hom
Hing, Lae Choo, and their child highlight cultural differences between
the Chinese and the white American characters? Do these involvements
have positive or negative consequences? What are the intentions of the
Americans?

3.   Earlier in this chapter you saw a poster advertising California,
printed roughly at the time this story was written. What elements of life
in California are left out of the poster, yet would affect the dreams of
people like Hom Hing and Lae Choo?

4.   The classic image of the immigrant experience in America is the
melting pot, in which everyone becomes part of the larger American
community. Does Sui Sin Far's representation of the Chinese immigrant
experience support this idea? What examples can you find in the text
that best convey her sense of what the Chinese immigrants' attitude is
toward assimilation and the larger American culture?

5.   What do you think of the story's title? What does it tell you about
expectation and reality in the lives of the Chinese characters?

For Writing

1.   Write an essay in which you look at this story from the point of view
of the missionary lady. How do you think she would have depicted the
last scene in the story, when Lae Choo finally gets her son back? Do you
think her dreams for him will be fulfilled? What dreams might the son

himself have? To find evidence for your essay, reread the last scene and look at the various exchanges: between Lae Choo and the missionary lady, Lae Choo and her son, and the son and the missionary lady.

2.   Compare Amy Tan's *The Joy Luck Club,* from the previous chapter, with this story. Be sure to include the following points: the attitudes of the native-born Chinese American women to their immigrant mothers; the attitude of the mothers toward raising children in America; Tan's descriptions of contemporary life in San Francisco's Chinatown.

3.   Research and write a report on one of the following topics: the cultural life in San Francisco's Chinatown at the turn of the century; the anti-Chinese immigration laws, including the prohibition of marriage; the role of Chinese laborers in building the transcontinental railroad; the prevalence of Chinese medicine and the unavailability of American health care in Chinatown; the way the Chinese in America were portrayed around 1900 in American newspapers, such as the *New York Times* and the *San Francisco Chronicle,* and in tabloids, such as the *Police Gazette* (see Chapter 9).

∞ *Let America Be America Again* (1938)

LANGSTON HUGHES

Langston Hughes (1902–1967) was one of the premier figures of the Harlem Renaissance—that jubilant outpouring of black art and culture in New York City in the 1920s. Hughes uses the rhythms of jazz, blues, and gospel music to celebrate and probe the role of black people in American society. His collections of verse include The Dream Keeper *(1932),* The Way of White Folks *(1934),* Shakespeare in Harlem *(1941), and* Montage of a Dream Deferred *(1951).*

Let America be America again.
Let it be the dream it used to be.
Let it be the pioneer on the plain
Seeking a home where he himself is free.

(America never was America to me.)   5

Let America be the dream the dreamers dreamed—
Let it be that great strong land of love
Where never kings connive nor tyrants scheme
That any man be crushed by one above.

(It never was America to me.)   10

O, let my land be a land where Liberty
Is crowned with no false patriotic wreath,
But opportunity is real, and life is free,
Equality is in the air we breathe.

15   (There's never been equality for me,
        Nor freedom in this "homeland of the free.")

        Say who are you that mumbles in the dark?
        And who are you that draws your veil across the stars?

        I am the poor white, fooled and pushed apart,
20   I am the red man driven from the land.
        I am the refugee clutching the hope I seek—
        But finding only the same old stupid plan

        Of dog eat dog, of mighty crush the weak.
        I am the Negro, "problem" to you all.
25   I am the people, humble, hungry, mean—
        Hungry yet today despite the dream.
        Beaten yet today—O, Pioneers!
        I am the man who never got ahead,
        The poorest worker bartered through the years.
30   Yet I'm the one who dreamt our basic dream
        In that Old World while still a serf of kings,
        Who dreamt a dream so strong, so brave, so true,
        That even yet its mighty daring sings
        In every brick and stone, in every furrow turned
35   That's made America the land it has become.
        O, I'm the man who sailed those early seas
        In search of what I meant to be my home—
        For I'm the one who left dark Ireland's shore,
        And Poland's plain, and England's grassy lea,
40   And torn from Black Africa's strand I came
        To build a "homeland of the free."

        The free?
        Who said the free? Not me?
        Surely not me? The millions on relief today?
45   The millions who have nothing for our pay
        For all the dreams we've dreamed
        And all the songs we've sung
        And all the hopes we've held
        And all the flags we've hung,
50   The millions who have nothing for our pay—
        Except the dream we keep alive today.

O, let America be America again—
The land that never has been yet—
And yet must be—the land where every man is free.
The land that's mine—the poor man's, Indian's, Negro's, ME—   55
Who made America,
Whose sweat and blood, whose faith and pain,
Whose hand at the foundry, whose plow in the rain,
Must bring back our mighty dream again.

    O, yes,   60
    I say it plain,
    America never was America to me,
And yet I swear this oath
America will be!

For Journals

What do you know about the America of the 1930s and the Great Depression? What do you think they have to do with the subject of the poem?

For Discussion

1.   With whom, or with what, does Hughes identify the America that is "the dream it used to be" (line 2)? In the first three stanzas, which examples of the dream does he celebrate?

2.   Beginning with line 52, Hughes gives examples of the people he thinks of as the real source of the American dream, a dream that must be "the poor man's, Indian's, Negro's, ME" (line 55) in order to be valid. How can this viewpoint coexist with the idea of an America exemplified by the founding fathers, including Benjamin Franklin (see Chapter 6)?

3.   Analyze the poem as an argument. What are the two sides? What are they fighting over? What points does each side make? Where does the poem "turn"? How would you describe the tone of the speaker? Optimistic? Cheerful? Bitter? What do you consider the most persuasive part of the poem?

4.   What does it mean for America to be America again, as the title says, if it never was in the first place? Since the population of America is almost all descended from people who came from somewhere else, including all the nationalities Hughes mentions, is there any evidence in the poem to support the possibility of change? Where would it come from?

5.   Considering how much of the American dream revolves around success, how do you respond to the fact that Hughes identifies the dream with examples of people who are not successful—"I am the man

who never got ahead, / The poorest worker bartered through the years" (lines 28–29)? Do you think he is distorting the definition of the dream, or redefining it? Why?

For Writing

1.   Write an essay that provides a persuasive answer to the following questions: If the people who originated the American dream are left out of it, what about the dream is still worthwhile to them? Why do they still want it? Read several newspaper or magazine articles about the problems and attitudes that prospective immigrants to America currently encounter. Support your essay with examples and, if possible, with actual quotations from immigrants about their desires to come to this country.

2.   Hughes was active as a writer both during and after the Harlem Renaissance. Research and write an essay on one of the following: the historical and social background for the Harlem Renaissance; the work of any of the artists, musicians, and writers involved in the Renaissance, for example, Jean Toomer, Zora Neale Hurston, Duke Ellington, Richard Wright, Countee Cullen, or Lou Jones; the history of the Cotton Club and the entertainers who worked there; the story of the Apollo Theater; or other work by Langston Hughes, including his great collection of short stories, *The Best of Simple.*

∞ *There's No Way like the American Way* (1937)

MARGARET BOURKE-WHITE

Margaret Bourke-White (1904–1971) was a photojournalist who covered major news stories for Life *magazine when that publication was home to the world's best photographers. As well as the work she did on the Great Depression, she is famous for her photographs of the invasion of Russia in World War II and the liberation of concentration camps.*

One of Bourke-White's most famous photographs is this picture of Americans in 1937, during the Great Depression, standing in line at an emergency relief station in the aftermath of an Ohio flood that killed hundreds of people and left thousands of others homeless.

For Journals

What do you know about the Great Depression of the 1930s? Was anyone in your family affected by it?

For Discussion

1.   From looking at this photo, what would you say was the image of the ideal American family in 1937? How is that image affected by the fact that in 1937 the Depression was in full force, with roughly 15 million Americans out of work?

2.   There are two verbal assertions in this photograph, both of them slogans on the billboard. How does the rest of the photograph, including the line of people, support or refute those statements?

3.   How do you suppose the people in the line would respond to the billboard behind them? What is your response to it?

4.   The composition of a great photograph is never accidental. Since the line of people was longer than the billboard, what do you think were Bourke-White's reasons for taking a photograph of those particular people under that particular billboard? Would it have a different impact if the flood victims were white? Is their color or their economic situation more important?

5.   If you had to translate this photo into a verbal assertion about life in America in 1937, what would it be? What details of the photograph would you choose to support your statement?

For Writing

1.   Today America still has problems of homelessness and unemployment. Look in recent newspapers or magazines for a picture or pictures of homeless or unemployed Americans. Write a reflective essay in which you consider the following: whether you could imagine yourself or your family in a similar situation and whether your choice of your major in school is affected by your concerns for the future.

2.   Bourke-White took this photograph from a particular point of view. Using back copies of magazines, contemporary magazines, or books of photographs, find an American photograph from a historic event—for example, the Civil War, the Great Depression, one of the world wars, a political assassination, the civil rights struggle in the South, a presidential campaign—in which the photographer makes a judgment about the event through the image. Research the background of the event to be sure you understand the historical context. Then write an essay in which you respond to the following questions: What is the photo's impact on you? Has the meaning of the photo changed over time? What biases or values or assumptions do you think the photographer is expressing? What details in the photograph support your assertions?

∞ *Early Success* (1937)

F. SCOTT FITZGERALD

While still in his twenties, F. Scott Fitzgerald (1897–1940) was already famous for his stories and novels. An extremely careful prose stylist, he was never prolific, but he had to produce a lot of short stories for magazines to pay for the expensive lifestyle that he and his wife had become accustomed to. By the time he died in 1940 of a heart attack, he had survived years of alcoholism and the decline of his reputation. But he had produced three remarkable novels: The Great Gatsby, Tender Is the Night, *and the unfinished* The Last Tycoon. *Since his death, he has become one of the most widely read and written-about American authors. This selection is an article from* The Crack-Up, *a collection of Fitzgerald's articles, letters, and notes in which he writes, with devastating honesty, about his early success, his later disintegration, and how he put himself back together.*

October, 1937

Seventeen years ago this month I quit work or, if you prefer, I retired from business. I was through—let the Street Railway Advertising Company carry along under its own power. I retired, not on my profits, but on my liabilities, which included debts, despair, and a broken engagement and crept home to St. Paul to "finish a novel."

That novel, begun in a training camp late in the war, was my ace in the hole. I had put it aside when I got a job in New York, but I was as constantly aware of it as of the shoe with cardboard in the sole, during all one desolate spring. It was like the fox and goose and the bag of beans. If I stopped working to finish the novel, I lost the girl.

So I struggled on in a business I detested and all the confidence I had garnered at Princeton and in a haughty career as the army's worst aide-de-camp melted gradually away. Lost and forgotten, I walked quickly from certain places—from the pawn shop where one left the field glasses, from prosperous friends whom one met when wearing the suit from before the war—from restaurants after tipping with the last nickel, from busy cheerful offices that were saving the jobs for their own boys from the war.

Even having a first story accepted had not proved very exciting. Dutch Mount and I sat across from each other in a car-card slogan advertising office, and the same mail brought each of us an acceptance from the same magazine—the old *Smart Set*.

"My check was thirty—how much was yours?"   5

"Thirty-five."

The real blight, however, was that my story had been written in college two years before, and a dozen new ones hadn't even drawn a personal letter. The implication was that I was on the down-grade at twenty-two. I spent the thirty dollars on a magenta feather fan for a girl in Alabama.

My friends who were not in love or who had waiting arrangements with "sensible" girls, braced themselves patiently for a long pull. Not I—I was in love with a whirlwind and I must spin a net big enough to catch it out of my head, a head full of trickling nickels and sliding dimes, the incessant music box of the poor. It couldn't be done like that, so when the girl threw me over I went home and finished my novel. And then, suddenly, everything changed, and this article is about that first wild wind of success and the delicious mist it brings with it. It is a short and precious time—for when the mist rises in a few weeks, or a few months, one finds that the very best is over.

It began to happen in the autumn of 1919 when I was an empty bucket, so mentally blunted with the summer's writing that I'd taken a job repairing car roofs at the Northern Pacific shops. Then the postman rang, and that day I quit work and ran along the streets, stopping automobiles to tell friends and acquaintances about it—my novel *This Side of Paradise* was accepted for publication. That week the postman rang and rang, and I paid off my terrible small debts, bought a suit, and woke up every morning with a world of ineffable toploftiness and promise.

10   While I waited for the novel to appear, the metamorphosis of amateur into professional began to take place—a sort of stitching together of your whole life into a pattern of work, so that the end of one job is automatically the beginning of another. I had been an amateur before; in October, when I strolled with a girl among the stones of a southern graveyard, I was a professional and my enchantment with certain things that she felt and said was already paced by an anxiety to set them down in a story—it was called *The Ice Palace* and it was published later. Similarly, during Christmas week in St. Paul, there was a night when I had stayed home from two dances to work on a story. Three friends called up during the evening to tell me I had missed some rare doings: a well-known man-about-town had disguised himself as a camel and, with a taxi-driver as the rear half, managed to attend the wrong party. Aghast with myself for not being there, I spent the next day trying to collect the fragments of the story.

"Well, all I can say is it was funny when it happened." "No, I don't know where he got the taxi-man." "You'd have to know him well to understand how funny it was."

In despair I said:

"Well, I can't seem to find out exactly what happened but I'm going to write about it as if it was ten times funnier than anything you've said." So I wrote it, in twenty-two consecutive hours, and wrote it "funny," simply because I was so emphatically told it was funny. *The Camel's Back* was published and still crops up in the humorous anthologies.

With the end of the winter set in another pleasant pumped-dry period, and, while I took a little time off, a fresh picture of life in America began to form before my eyes. The uncertainties of 1919 were over—there seemed little doubt about what was going to happen—America was going on the greatest, gaudiest spree in history and there was going to be plenty to tell about it. The whole golden boom was in the air—its splendid generosities, its outrageous corruptions and the tortuous death struggle of the old America in prohibition. All the stories that came into my head had a touch of disaster in them—the lovely young creatures in my novels went to ruin, the diamond mountains of my short stories blew up, my millionaires were as beautiful and damned as Thomas Hardy's peasants. In life these things hadn't happened yet, but I was pretty sure living wasn't the reckless, careless business these people thought—this generation just younger than me.

For my point of vantage was the dividing line between the two 15 generations, and there I sat—somewhat self-consciously. When my first big mail came in—hundreds and hundreds of letters on a story about a girl who bobbed her hair—it seemed rather absurd that they should come to me about it. On the other hand, for a shy man it was nice to be somebody except oneself again: to be "the Author" as one had been "the Lieutenant." Of course one wasn't really an author any more than one had been an army officer, but nobody seemed to guess behind the false face.

All in three days I got married and the presses were pounding out *This Side of Paradise* like they pound out extras in the movies.

With its publication I had reached a stage of manic depressive insanity. Rage and bliss alternated hour by hour. A lot of people thought it was a fake, and perhaps it was, and a lot of others thought it was a lie, which it was not. In a daze I gave out an interview—I told what a great writer I was and how I'd achieved the heights. Heywood Broun,[1] who was on my trail, simply quoted it with the comment that I seemed to be a very self-satisfied young man, and for some days I was notably poor company. I invited him to lunch and in a kindly way told him that it was too bad he had let his life slide away without accomplishing anything. He had just turned thirty and it was about then that I wrote a line which certain people will not let me forget: "She was a faded but still lovely woman of twenty-seven."

In a daze I told the Scribner Company that I didn't expect my novel to sell more than twenty thousand copies and when the laughter died away I was told that a sale of five thousand was excellent for a first novel. I think it was a week after publication that it passed the twenty thousand mark, but I took myself so seriously that I didn't even think it was funny.

---

[1] Broun (1888–1939) was a journalist and critic.

These weeks in the clouds ended abruptly a week later when Princeton turned on the book—not undergraduate Princeton but the black mass of faculty and alumni. There was a kind but reproachful letter from President Hibben, and a room full of classmates who suddenly turned on me with condemnation. We had been part of a rather gay party staged conspicuously in Harvey Firestone's car of robin's-egg blue, and in the course of it I got an accidental black eye trying to stop a fight. This was magnified into an orgy and in spite of a delegation of undergraduates who went to the board of Governors, I was suspended from my club for a couple of months. The *Alumni Weekly* got after my book and only Dean Gauss had a good word to say for me. The unctuousness and hypocrisy of the proceedings was exasperating and for seven years I didn't go to Princeton. Then a magazine asked me for an article about it and when I started to write it, I found I really loved the place and that the experience of one week was a small item in the total budget. But on that day in 1920 most of the joy went out of my success.

20   But one was now a professional—and the new world couldn't possibly be presented without bumping the old out of the way. One gradually developed a protective hardness against both praise and blame. Too often people liked your things for the wrong reasons or people liked them whose dislike would be a compliment. No decent career was ever founded on a public and one learned to go ahead without precedents and without fear. Counting the bag, I found that in 1919 I had made $800 by writing, that in 1920 I had made $18,000, stories, picture rights and book. My story price had gone from $30 to $1,000. That's a small price to what was paid later in the Boom, but what it sounded like to me couldn't be exaggerated.

The dream had been early realized and the realization carried with it a certain bonus and a certain burden. Premature success gives one an almost mystical conception of destiny as opposed to will power—at its worst the Napoleonic delusion. The man who arrives young believes that he exercises his will because his star is shining. The man who only asserts himself at thirty has a balanced idea of what will power and fate have each contributed, the one who gets there at forty is liable to put the emphasis on will alone. This comes out when the storms strike your craft.

The compensation of a very early success is a conviction that life is a romantic matter. In the best sense one stays young. When the primary objects of love and money could be taken for granted and a shaky eminence had lost its fascination, I had fair years to waste, years that I can't honestly regret, in seeking the eternal Carnival by the Sea. Once in the middle twenties I was driving along the High Corniche Road through the twilight with the whole French Riviera twinkling on the sea below. As far ahead as I could see was Monte Carlo, and though it was out of season and there were no Grand Dukes left to gamble and E. Phillips

Oppenheim[2] was a fat industrious man in my hotel, who lived in a bathrobe—the very name was so incorrigibly enchanting that I could only stop the car and like the Chinese whisper: "Ah me! Ah me!" It was not Monte Carlo I was looking at. It was back into the mind of the young man with cardboard soles who had walked the streets of New York. I was him again—for an instant I had the good fortune to share his dreams, I who had no more dreams of my own. And there are still times when I creep up on him, surprise him on an autumn morning in New York or a spring night in Carolina when it is so quiet that you can hear a dog barking in the next county. But never again as during that all too short period when he and I were one person, when the fulfilled future and the wistful past were mingled in a single gorgeous moment—when life was literally a dream.

For Journals

If, like Fitzgerald, you could become famous for something while you are still very young, what would it be?

For Discussion

1. What dream does Fitzgerald start with? Based on this essay, how would you describe his version of the American dream he found himself living?

2. Fitzgerald couldn't marry his girlfriend until he wrote a book that made money, and he wrote about money often: not having any, suddenly having a lot, losing it. How significant a role do you think money does or doesn't play in achieving success in this country, either in work or in love or in both?

3. Fitzgerald was able to speak ironically about himself even in his worst moments. Looking closely at the text, what examples can you find of irony and self-mockery? How persuasive are these examples in suggesting the changes Fitzgerald underwent in the process of going from an unknown to a famous writer?

4. What argument does Fitzgerald make in favor of later achievement rather than the kind of early fame that he enjoyed? How convincing are his assertions about the effects of fame on character? What examples can you think of concerning contemporary writers, actors, musicians, and so on who became very successful early and later had difficulties handling the results? What in Fitzgerald's experience could be extrapolated to help in such circumstances?

---

[2] Oppenheim (1866–1946) was an English author who wrote over 100 novels.

For Writing

1. Read the other essays in *The Crack-Up*, which Fitzgerald wrote about his own breakdown and subsequent recovery. Write an essay in which you examine the following questions: How does "Early Success" fit in this group? In what ways, if any, does Fitzgerald achieve success after his professional and personal failures?

2. Fitzgerald's most famous remark about success and money was an opening line to one of his stories, written in 1926: "Let me tell you about the very rich. They are different from you and me." Answering Fitzgerald, in a story as well, Ernest Hemingway responded, "Yes, they have more money." Write an essay in which you argue either that Fitzgerald was correct—that possession of a lot of money creates deep differences psychologically as well as culturally—or that Hemingway was right. Give your own interpretation of both remarks. You can use other selections in this book—by Andrew Carnegie, Benjamin Franklin, Gloria Steinem, and others—as well as your own observations and experience to support your assertions.

∞ *Win a Houseful of Beautiful Furniture!*

PLEDGE FURNITURE SWEEPSTAKES ADVERTISEMENT
(1967)

For Journals

In what ways do you think the idea of what constitutes desirable possessions has changed from your parents' generation to your own?

For Discussion

1. Have you ever entered or known anyone who entered a contest or a sweepstakes, or bought a lottery ticket? What desires or interests do these contests appeal to in order to encourage people to invest in what they know they have no realistic chance of winning?

2. If the houseful of furniture is supposed to be a dream come true, what dream is it? Would the objects in the picture be desirable to you? Why or why not?

3. If you were redoing this 1960's ad to appeal to a contemporary audience, what changes would you make, and why?

For Writing

1. Look through some contemporary magazines or newspapers and find an advertisement that shows how you can enjoy the best that money can buy without being rich. For example, credit card companies advertise how many products you can buy if you get one of their credit cards. Once you find an advertisement promoting consumption, write an essay in which you analyze it, addressing the following: What is the ad trying to sell you? What choices did the photographer or the designer make—composition, light and shadow, color, the appearance and attractiveness of the people or objects in the ad, the placement of words, the language used, and so on—to convince you?

2. In her book *The Overspent American*, writer Naomi Schor states that Americans no longer want to keep up with the Joneses when it comes to buying things; instead, they look at celebrities, or characters they see on television, and therefore come to expect to have more expensive possessions. Write an essay in which you assess, as honestly as you can, your idea of what possessions you want to have, either now or in the near future, and what it would take to satisfy you: sports equipment?

cars? houses? computers? travel? all of the above? Where do you think your ideas of what you need come from?

∞ *I Have a Dream* (1963)

MARTIN LUTHER KING, JR.

Martin Luther King, Jr. (1929–1968) was the leader of the nonviolent civil rights struggle. A minister from a family of ministers, he became a public figure while still in his twenties when he led a bus boycott in Montgomery, Alabama. Frequently threatened or arrested, he was the main organizer of sit-ins and marches in segregated southern towns and cities, particularly Birmingham, Alabama, in 1963. That summer he addressed a huge audience of civil rights workers who had marched in protest in Washington, D.C. His speech, delivered from the steps of the Lincoln Memorial, is one of the most famous of the century. King received the Nobel Peace Prize in 1964, the youngest person ever to do so. He was assassinated in Memphis, Tennessee, in 1968.

Five score years ago, a great American, in whose symbolic shadow we stand, signed the Emancipation Proclamation. This momentous decree came as a great beacon light of hope to millions of Negro slaves who had been seared in the flames of withering injustice. It came as a joyous daybreak to end the long night of captivity.

But one hundred years later, we must face the tragic fact that the Negro is still not free. One hundred years later, the life of the Negro is still sadly crippled by the manacles of segregation and the chains of discrimination. One hundred years later, the Negro lives on a lonely island of poverty in the midst of a vast ocean of material prosperity. One hundred years later, the Negro is still languishing in the corners of American society and finds himself an exile in his own land. So we have come here today to dramatize an appalling condition.

In a sense we have come to our nation's Capitol to cash a check. When the architects of our republic wrote the magnificent words of the Constitution and the Declaration of Independence, they were signing a promissory note to which every American was to fall heir. This note was a promise that all men would be guaranteed the unalienable rights of life, liberty, and the pursuit of happiness.

It is obvious today that America has defaulted on this promissory note insofar as her citizens of color are concerned. Instead of honoring this sacred obligation, America has given the Negro people a bad check; a check which has come back marked "insufficient funds." But we refuse to believe that the bank of justice is bankrupt. We refuse to believe that there are insufficient funds in the great vaults of opportunity of this nation. So we have come to cash this check—a check that will give us upon demand the riches of freedom and the security of justice. We have also come to this hallowed spot to remind America of the fierce urgency of *now*. This is no time to engage in the luxury of cooling off or to take the tranquilizing drug of gradualism. *Now* is the time to make real the promises of Democracy. *Now* is the time to rise from the dark and desolate valley of segregation to the sunlit path of racial justice. *Now* is the time to open the doors of opportunity to all of God's children. *Now* is the time to lift our nation from the quicksands of racial injustice to the solid rock of brotherhood.

It would be fatal for the nation to overlook the urgency of the moment and to underestimate the determination of the Negro. This sweltering summer of the Negro's legitimate discontent will not pass until there is an invigorating autumn of freedom and equality. 1963 is not an end, but a beginning. Those who hope that the Negro needed to blow off steam and will now be content will have a rude awakening if the nation returns to business as usual. There will be neither rest nor tranquility in America until the Negro is granted his citizenship rights. The whirlwinds of revolt will continue to shake the foundations of our nation until the bright day of justice emerges.

But there is something I must say to my people who stand on the warm threshold which leads into the palace of justice. In the process of gaining our rightful place we must not be guilty of wrongful deeds. Let us not seek to satisfy our thirst for freedom by drinking from the cup of bitterness and hatred. We must forever conduct our struggle on the high plane of dignity and discipline. We must not allow our creative protest to degenerate into physical violence. Again and again we must rise to the majestic heights of meeting physical force with soul force. The marvelous new militancy which has engulfed the Negro community must not lead us to a distrust of all white people, for many of our white brothers, as evidenced by their presence here today, have come to realize that their destiny is tied up with our destiny and their freedom is inextricably bound to our freedom. We cannot walk alone.

And as we walk, we must make the pledge that we shall march ahead. We cannot turn back. There are those who are asking the devotees of civil rights, "When will you be satisfied?" We can never be satisfied as long as the Negro is the victim of the unspeakable horrors of police brutality. We can never be satisfied as long as our bodies, heavy with the fatigue of travel, cannot gain lodging in the motels of the highways and the hotels of the cities. We cannot be satisfied as long as the Negro's basic mobility is from a smaller ghetto to a larger one. We can never be satisfied as long as a Negro in Mississippi cannot vote and a Negro in New York believes he has nothing for which to vote. No, no, we are not satisfied, and we will not be satisfied until justice rolls down like waters and righteousness like a mighty stream.

I am not unmindful that some of you have come here out of great trials and tribulations. Some of you have come fresh from narrow jail cells. Some of you have come from areas where your quest for freedom left you battered by the storms of persecution and staggered by the winds of police brutality. You have been the veterans of creative suffering. Continue to work with the faith that unearned suffering is redemptive.

Go back to Mississippi, go back to Alabama, go back to South Carolina, go back to Georgia, go back to Louisiana, go back to the slums and ghettoes of our northern cities, knowing that somehow this situation can and will be changed. Let us not wallow in the valley of despair.

10   I say to you today, my friends, that in spite of the difficulties and frustrations of the moment I still have a dream. It is a dream deeply rooted in the American dream.

I have a dream that one day this nation will rise up and live out the true meaning of its creed: "We hold these truths to be self-evident; that all men are created equal."

I have a dream that one day on the red hills of Georgia the sons of former slaves and the sons of former slaveowners will be able to sit down together at the table of brotherhood.

I have a dream that the state of Mississippi, a desert state sweltering with the heat of injustice and oppression, will be transformed into an oasis of freedom and justice.

I have a dream that my four little children will one day live in a nation where they will not be judged by the color of their skin but by the content of their character.

15   I have a dream today.

I have a dream that the state of Alabama, whose governor's lips are presently dripping with the words of interposition and nullification, will be transformed into a situation where little black boys and black girls will be able to join hands with little white boys and white girls and walk together as sisters and brothers.

I have a dream today.

I have a dream that one day every valley shall be exalted, every hill and mountain shall be made low, the rough places will be made plain, and the crooked places will be made straight, and the glory of the Lord shall be revealed, and all flesh shall see it together.

This is our hope. This is the faith with which I return to the South. With this faith we will be able to hew out of the mountain of despair a stone of hope. With this faith we will be able to transform the jangling discords of our nation into a beautiful symphony of brotherhood. With this faith we will be able to work together, to pray together, to struggle together, to go to jail together, to stand up for freedom together, knowing that we will be free one day.

This will be the day when all of God's children will be able to sing 20 with new meaning.

My country, 'tis of thee
Sweet land of liberty,
    Of thee I sing:
Land where my fathers died,
Land of the pilgrims' pride,
From every mountainside
    Let freedom ring.

And if America is to be a great nation this must become true. So let freedom ring from the prodigious hilltops of New Hampshire. Let freedom ring from the mighty mountains of New York. Let freedom ring from the heightening Alleghenies of Pennsylvania!

Let freedom ring from the snowcapped Rockies of Colorado!

Let freedom ring from the curvaceous peaks of California!

But not only that; let freedom ring from Stone Mountain of Georgia!

Let freedom ring from Lookout Mountain of Tennessee!   25

Let freedom ring from every hill and molehill of Mississippi. From every mountainside, let freedom ring.

When we let freedom ring, when we let it ring from every village and every hamlet, from every state and every city, we will be able to speed up that day when all of God's children, black men and white men, Jews and Gentiles, Protestants and Catholics, will be able to join hands and sing in the words of the old Negro spiritual, "Free at last! free at last! thank God almighty, we are free at last!"

For Journals

What have you heard or read about the civil rights movement? About Martin Luther King, Jr.? If you have seen film or newsreels of the struggle between civil rights advocates and segregationists, how did you react to them?

For Discussion

1.   What is King trying to convince African Americans they should do about segregation? What is he trying to convince white Americans to do?

2.   King gave this speech at the Lincoln Memorial. Aside from the obvious location, why does he begin with a line reminiscent of the beginning of Lincoln's Gettysburg Address, "Four score and seven years ago"? What associations might he be trying to raise in the minds of his audience?

3.   In order to identify the consequences of racial injustice in American life, King uses both unusual figures of speech, like the promissory note of equality (paragraph 3), and examples of the effects of prejudice in or-

dinary life, like not being able to get into a hotel (paragraph 7). Look for some more examples of both unusual language and ordinary experience. What do you think he gains from using both kinds of examples? How do the two together help make his argument more persuasive?

4. King says his dream is deeply rooted in the American dream. But he also uses Judeo-Christian references that are part of his background as a minister. Divide the speech into sections based on these two themes; with two of your peers, look through the speech for examples of religious and biblical language and references to the American dream. What values or ideas are expressed in those examples, as you see it?

5. King addresses the frustrated dreams of African Americans in the civil rights movement who thought progress was too slow and the irritation of northerners who thought it was too fast. Look at the section of the speech starting with, "We have also come to this hallowed spot to remind America of the fierce urgency of *now*" (the middle of paragraph 4). What examples does he use to address each group? Which examples advocate patience, and which ones express determination? Do you recognize the sources of any of his metaphorical examples?

6. The video of King's speech is available in many college libraries. If it is in yours, watch it in class. If not, read the speech out loud in class. In the last and most famous part of the speech, King begins paragraphs with the words, "I have a dream," and then "Let freedom ring." What kinds of fulfillment does he dream about in these passages? You might want to paraphrase his language to see how many kinds of dreams he evokes here.

For Writing

1. King gave this speech in the summer of 1963. Using contemporary newspaper and magazine reports and at least one biography of King or a history of the civil rights movement (Taylor Branch's *Parting the Waters* is a good example), write a researched paper on the circumstances that preceded the march. Some points to include: Who was against it? Why were there fears about what would happen at the march? What was the response of the audience? The press? What was the aftermath? Did people who heard King's speech talk about their own dreams for America in response?

2. This speech is remarkable for the number of other texts it borrows from, rephrases, or uses for its own purposes—the Bible, the Declaration of Independence, the Gettysburg Address, Shakespeare, spirituals, and others. Write an essay in which you identify at least three examples of these borrowed texts, and explain why you think King picked them, what point they were used to make, and how persuasive you think they are. Then try to come up with examples of contemporary texts or songs that you would borrow from if you were delivering this speech today.

∞ *Tomorrowland* (1997)

WITOLD RYBCZYNSKI

Witold Rybczynski (1943–), the Martin and Margy Myerson Professor of Urbanism at the University of Pennsylvania, has written in-depth, thoughtful works on urban architecture, housing, and the uses of technology. His books include Taming the Tiger *(1983),* Looking Around: A Journey Through Architecture *(1993), and* City Life *(1995). This selection is an article he wrote in 1997 for the* New Yorker.

Famous firsts are recorded by sports statisticians, academic journals, and the Guinness Book. Everyday firsts are not. I've never heard of a statue to the suburbanite who sprinted through the first mall, or to the person who punched into the first ATM. I have these thoughts while I'm standing in front of 931 Jasmine Street. It is unlikely that there will ever be a commemorative plaque here, but perhaps there should be. The building itself, while attractive, is unremarkable. It is a one-story house of a type that is not uncommon in the South. The hipped roof extends over a deep front veranda. The walls are clapboard; the double-hung windows are shuttered. There is a U-Haul van in the driveway. I'm standing on the sidewalk watching Larry Haber move into his new home. He is a good sport and pauses so that I can take a photograph. Larry and his wife, Terri, and their two young children are the first residents of an unusual town: a town that is being built by an organization whose chief business is storytelling and make-believe—the Walt Disney Company.

It was Walt himself who had the idea of building a town. Exactly thirty years ago, he announced that he was going to create a showcase for advanced technology—a kind of urban laboratory. It would be called EPCOT, for Experimental Prototype Community of Tomorrow, and it would be an actual community. But Disney died before he could realize his vision of a city of the future, and his successors were unable to reconcile his coercive brand of social engineering with the demands of American home buyers. When EPCOT finally opened, in 1982, it did feature futuristic technology, but there were no residents. It was a theme park.

EPCOT is situated in Walt Disney World, on the enormous tract of land—twenty-eight thousand acres—that Disney owns outside Orlando, in central Florida. There are two other theme parks there—the Magic Kingdom and the Disney-MGM Studios—and a fourth, Disney's Animal Kingdom, is slated to open in 1998. Even so, about a third of the land remained unused. The idea of building a residential community had lingered on in the Disney Company's corporate memory, and when a master plan was being prepared under the aegis of the current C.E.O., Michael Eisner, it was determined that it was finally time to implement Walt's vision. There were also practical considerations: highway access to the theme parks and various wetlands restrictions made residential use attractive. "At that point, we could have gone in any direction," says Disney's Tom Lewis, who oversaw planning during the first five years of the project. "It could have been a second-home community or a resort or a retirement village. Instead, we decided that it would be a place where families would have their primary residences. We wanted it to be a real town."

The notion that Disney World could be a setting for real life will strike most people as improbable. Yet the town promises not only to be real but to be a model for others to follow. Celebration, as it is called, is not a theme park. It is an unincorporated town under the rule of Osceola County. There will be a school, a health campus, and an office park. Planned recreational facilities include a golf course, a lake, and miles of walking trails and bike paths. The town center will have restaurants, shops, offices, a supermarket, a bank, a small inn, and a cinema. When Celebration is completed, in ten or fifteen years, it could have as many as twenty thousand inhabitants. It is the most comprehensively planned new town since Columbia, Maryland, and Reston, Virginia, were built, in the mid-sixties.

5   Celebration's temporary preview center opened last August. Although no houses—not even a model home—had actually been built, twenty thousand people visited the site during the next two months. So many of them expressed an interest in buying homes there that it was decided that the only fair way to sell lots was to draw names out of a hat. (Entrants were not screened, and Disney employees were not given preference.) About twelve hundred prospective residents put down refundable deposits of up to a thousand dollars for the chance to become one of three hundred and fifty-one home buyers or a hundred and twenty apartment renters in Celebration's first phase. Lots were drawn that November. "Things have moved very quickly," I was told by Don Killoren, who is the general manager of the Celebration Company, a Disney subsidiary. "But I'm not really surprised. We did a lot of research. We knew the type of houses that people wanted."

Killoren is being slightly disingenuous. Undoubtedly, one reason people wanted the houses was that they were *Disney* houses. (A 1990 international study identified the five brand names that were most widely recognized and most highly esteemed around the world. They were Coca-Cola, Sony, Mercedes-Benz, Kodak, and Disney.) The house that the Habers are moving into was built by David Weekley Homes, of Houston—one of two home builders chosen by Disney after an exhaustive national selection process. House prices range from about a hundred and thirty thousand dollars for a town house to more than three hundred thousand dollars for the largest detached house. A rigorous selection process was also used to arrive at eight local builders who are building more expensive, one-of-a-kind houses, which constitute a quarter of the total in the first phase. Prices for these custom-built houses start at around four hundred and twenty-five thousand dollars.

You would look in vain for manifestations of any of the current vogues in high-fashion architecture. There is no free-form deconstructivism here, no corrugated-metal high tech. Instead, there are gable roofs with dormers, bay windows and porches, balustrades and columns. Like all houses built commercially in the United States today, these houses favor distinctly traditional styles. The Habers' house, on Jasmine Street, is an example of Coastal, which is a loose interpretation of the type of house that was built in the South Carolina low country. It is a style characterized by deep one- or two-story porches, high ceilings, full-length windows, and first floors raised off the ground. Coastal is one of six—and only six—architectural styles permissible in Celebration; the others are Classical, Victorian, Colonial Revival, Mediterranean, and French. The six styles are defined in a pattern book, which insures that the builders achieve a degree of architectural clarity that is missing in most builder homes. Unusual, too, is Celebration's approach to parking. Alleys running behind the houses give access to garages in the rear, and many of these garages have rooms above them. Larry Haber has built a suite for his mother-in-law above his garage.

Leaving the Habers' house, I drive down Campus Street, which has town houses on one side and the site of the future school on the other. The town houses are still under construction, but ahead of me is a group of about twenty completed buildings: the downtown. Most of them are three stories high, fronting narrow streets. There's not a pedestrian mall in sight. The buildings seem vaguely familiar, like the sort of small-town architecture that is found across America—or used to be, for this looks, at first glance, like a nineteenth-century downtown, and actually recalls Disneyland's Main Street, U.S.A. The buildings line up to the sidewalk, and I can't see any parking lots. (I later discover that the lots are shoehorned into the center of the blocks, behind the buildings.) The sidewalks are shaded by trees; the main street—Market Street—is lined with palm trees. At the base of Market Street is a small lake. The street beside the water is called Front Street, as it is in many old river towns. The downtown doesn't really feel historical, however, for there is no consistency to the architecture. There is a plain office block that might be of the late eighteen-hundreds, a two-screen cinema—the only building not quite finished—that looks as if it might turn out to be Art Deco, and a bank with colored horizontal streamlining stripes that are straight out of the nineteen-twenties. There are also buildings—including the town hall, the post office, and a visitor center—that look quite modern.

Michael Eisner is an architecture buff who has previously commissioned such world-famous architects as Arata Isozaki, Michael Graves, Frank Gehry, and Aldo Rossi to design buildings for Disney. Celebration, too, has a cast of celebrated architects: Graves designed the post office, Philip Johnson the town hall, Robert Venturi and Denise Scott Brown the bank, Cesar Pelli the cinema, and the late Charles Moore the visitor center. I dislike the town hall: as with so much of Johnson's work, it tries to be monumental and manages to be merely bombastic. Most of the other signature buildings appear to me to be lacklustre rather than inspired; Graves's post office, though, is delightful, and Pelli's cinema will be appropriately dramatic. But I am most impressed by what architects call the "background buildings"—the ordinary buildings that give character to a town. Here they manage to be both unpretentious and charming, which is more difficult to achieve than it sounds. They are all the work of either Robert A. M. Stern or Jaquelin Robertson, of Cooper, Robertson & Partners.

10   Stern and Robertson are also the planners of the town, although the credits for the design of Celebration resemble those of a Hollywood screenplay. (With an estimated cost of two and a half billion dollars, however, Celebration is much more expensive than any movie.) First, in 1987, Disney held a design competition. It invited Andres Duany and Elizabeth Plater-Zyberk, whose concept of traditional neighborhood development is a major influence on Celebration's residential areas, along with Charles Gwathmey, of Gwathmey Siegel & Associates, and Stern to submit plans. Then, instead of choosing a winner, Disney asked the architects to work together to develop a consensus design. An expanded program, including more commercial uses and a new expressway, required a revised plan, which was prepared collaboratively by Skidmore, Owings & Merrill, and Cooper, Robertson & Partners. And, ultimately, Stern and Robertson were commissioned to prepare the final master plan, and also to design the health campus (Stern), the golf clubhouse (Robertson), and all the background buildings downtown.

The downtown buildings are owned by Disney and are leased to retail tenants. But there is no Banana Republic here. Instead of major national chains, Disney has chosen only local and regional shops and restaurants. The intention is to attract the public by creating an experience different from that found in a typical shopping mall, Don Killoren told me. Though a downtown like Celebration's, with but a single landlord, does resemble a shopping mall, there is one crucial difference here: this is a commercial area where people will also live. All hundred and twenty apartments are in the downtown area, many of them above shops or restaurants. As I walk around, I see construction workers putting finishing touches on four apartment buildings; the tenants are due to start moving in this month. When the bank, the post office, and the town hall open to the public, which will be in August (the formal opening of the downtown is scheduled for November), the mixture of tourists, shoppers, residents, and office workers should provide precisely the sort of daylong activity that is the hallmark of a successful downtown.

A lively downtown, apartments above shops, front porches, houses close to the street, and out-of-sight garages all add up to an old-fashioned sort of place. But there is more to Celebration than nostalgia and tradition. What families like the Habers really want—what most Americans really want—has less to do with architecture and urban design than with good schools, health care, safe neighborhoods, and a sense of community. "We understand that community is not something that we can engineer," I was assured by Todd Mansfield, who is an executive vice-president of Disney Imagineering, the division that oversees the design and construction of all the company's enterprises. "But we think that it's something we can foster." Despite Disney's reputation for obsessively leaving nothing to chance, fostering has not meant controlling. The Celebration school (kindergarten through twelfth grade) will be owned and operated not by Disney but by the Osceola County School District. The school will open next year and will eventually serve about fourteen hundred students—from the surrounding county as well as from the town. What is unusual about the school, apart from pedagogical innovations, is that it's in the center of the town. Children will be able to walk and bike to class. This fall will see the opening of the Teaching Academy, a teacher-training facility that is owned by Disney, run by Disney and Stetson University, and housed in a handsome building designed by William Rawn, who is also the architect of the school.

The health campus, now under construction on the outskirts of town, is a large facility belonging to Florida Hospital and including outpatient surgery, advanced diagnostics, primary-care physicians, and a fitness center. A fibre-optic network will eventually link both the school and the health facility to individual homes. This is just the sort of technological innovation that Walt Disney imagined would be the cornerstone of life in the future. But Michael Eisner's Celebration is actually the opposite of Walt Disney's urban vision. Walt Disney imagined a world in which problems would be solved by science and technology. Celebration puts technology in the background and concentrates on putting in place the less tangible civic infrastructure that is a prerequisite for community. Home buyers agree to be governed by their own homeowners' association and by a set of restrictive deed covenants whose purpose is to strike a balance between individual freedom and communal responsibility. You can park your cars in front of your house, for example, but no more than two cars. You can sublet your house—or your garage apartment—but you can't lease individual rooms. You can hold a garage sale, but only once a year. Writers and artists can work out of their homes, but not dentists—unless they live in the "home business district," where professional offices are allowed. A real sense of community can't develop in a vacuum, however, and Disney seems to have gone out of its way to insure that Celebration will not become a hermetic place. It is neither walled nor gated, unlike many recent master-planned communities. None of the streets are private. Policing is by the county sheriff's office, not by hired security guards (although the home-owners' association may hire additional security if it chooses to). The golf course, designed by the Robert Trent Joneses—father and son—is a public daily-fee facility, not a private club.

Yet, in spite of these efforts to make Celebration open to the outside world, much of the public assumes—or, at least, hopes—that a Disney town will be a perfect town. "It's one of my fears," says Todd Mans-field, who is himself going to build a house in Celebration. "We have people who have purchased houses who think they're moving to Utopia. We keep having to remind them that we can't provide safe-guards for all the ills of society. We will have everything that happens in any community." He's right. I'm confident that despite the advanced Honeywell security systems there will be break-ins. Despite the fibre-optic networks, there will be children with learning problems. Despite the state-of-the-art medical technology, there will be sickness. And, de-spite the sociable appearance of the front porches, there will be neigh-borly disputes. If there weren't, Celebration would not be the real place that Disney says it will become.

15   Charles E. Fraser has thought a great deal about creating real places. He is the creator of Sea Pines Plantation, on Hilton Head Island, in South Carolina; between 1956 and 1982, he oversaw the building of about thirty-four hundred homes there. Fraser pioneered the post–Second World War application of many of the concepts such as deed covenants, architectural-review boards, and neighborhood planning which are to-day standard practice in master-planned communities. I ask him how a sense of community was created at Sea Pines. "My wife and I gave a party every Saturday night for the first ten years," Fraser says. "We in-vited all the new residents and second-home owners who were on va-cation. I was only twenty-seven and not very knowledgeable, but I knew it was important to introduce people to each other." It was a good idea: by the time there were two thousand residents, Sea Pines had as many as two hundred clubs and social groups. Modern mobility means that the process of neighborhood creation, which previously took decades, must be "jump-started." Fraser adds, "I've come to the con-clusion that relatively small groups—two hundred or three hundred

families—that share a common responsibility such as a swimming pool or a park are the answer." At Celebration, where he has been a consultant for the past seven years, innovative covenants have been written to permit the creation of precisely such small sub-neighborhoods.

According to census projections, the population of the United States will increase by more than twenty-six million people during this decade. Most of this growth, Fraser points out, is now occurring randomly in metropolitan areas that are too large to have a single focus, like the old center-city downtown. What is needed, he suggests, is smaller planned communities at the edges of urban areas, which can offer people a sense of belonging. "Celebration is a model of such a smaller-size town," he says. "It can offer the range of neighborhood services and amenities— schools, churches, shops—that used to be the benefits of small-town living."

After leaving Celebration, I drive to Winter Park, which is just the sort of small town that Fraser has in mind. Winter Park, with a population of about twenty-five thousand, is not far from greater Orlando. It started life in the eighteen-eighties, as a master-planned community. The main commercial street, Park Avenue, was laid out beside a twelve-acre strip of green, named—what else?—Central Park. The focus of the park was a railroad depot, which was the chief place of arrival for winter visitors. The surrounding residential neighborhoods have comfortably shaded curved streets and a variety of houses. Park Avenue is lined with low buildings containing shops and restaurants with offices and apartments above. I'm sitting in a bar that opens out onto the sidewalk. It's five o'clock, and people are stopping by for a drink before going home. The bar is noisy, bustling, and convivial. People appear to know one another. It isn't hard to imagine that this is what Celebration will be like. More than thirty years ago, the developer James Rouse (who went on to build the town of Columbia, Maryland) called Disneyland "the outstanding piece of urban design in the United States." Disneyland radically transformed the amusement park. Celebration, with its curious mixture of old-fashioned values and newfangled organization, is a far cry from Walt Disney's vision of the future. Still, it will change the way we think about planning new communities, which is, after all, what Uncle Walt had in mind in the first place.

For Journals

When you see the name Disney, what immediate associations come to your mind? How many of them come from your childhood?

For Discussion

1. Since Celebration looks like a traditional community, why does Rybczynski call the article "Tomorrowland"? Why not "Yesterdayland"?

2. How would you paraphrase this selection's central thesis about Celebration? What examples does the author give to support it, and which do you find the most convincing?

3. Why do you think the Disney Company called its town Celebration? What ideas and values is it celebrating? What emotional appeal do you think the town and its houses are intended to make in order to attract prospective buyers?

4. Look up the meaning of the word *nostalgia* in the dictionary. In what ways does Celebration play upon that concept? Why?

5. What assumptions about the idea of a Disney town did Rybczynski have when he came to see Celebration? Find examples of them in the text. What assumptions did you start with?

6. When you finished reading this article, were you convinced that Celebration was in fact as close as possible to an ideal community? Why would or wouldn't you want to live there?

7. Since early in this century, most Americans have lived in cities. What, if any, features of Celebration could be adapted to improve city living?

For Writing

1. Write an essay in which you set forth your idea of an ideal community—its appearance, its size, its neighborhoods, its values, and the kinds of people who would live there.

2. Listen to the Disney song "Tomorrowland," and write an essay in which you compare the world described in the lyrics with the community described in Rybczynski's article.

3. There's a long history of both writing about ideal communities and attempting to establish them: Plato's *Republic*, Thomas More's *Utopia*, and various real-life experiments. Research and write a paper on one of the following American attempts to set up an ideal place to live: Brook Farm, the Oneida Community, the Shakers, or the recent effort in Colorado to form a self-sustaining community within a bubble.

∽ *United Shareholders of America* (1998)

JACOB WEISBERG

Jacob Weisberg is the chief political correspondent for the on-line magazine Slate. *This article is from an issue of the* Sunday New York Times *devoted entirely to Americans and their relationship to money.*

A political milestone passed without comment last fall when President Clinton was trying unsuccessfully to persuade Congress to renew his fast-track-negotiating authority. "If it passes," the President told reporters, "I think it will have a very positive impact on the stock market here and around the world."

No one present thought this comment especially significant. The *Times* didn't even quote it the next morning. Yet it speaks to an astonishing transformation. What President has ever made such a blatant appeal to stock owners? Even a Republican like Ronald Reagan would have seen the need to spin advantages for the investing class as conducive to a prosperity that would trickle down to the wage-earning middle class. Much has changed. What Bill Clinton, who is blessed with the political equivalent of sonar, may have sensed is that we have quietly become a society of shareholders. The investing class now includes the middle class.

According to an October NBC News/Wall Street Journal poll, 51 percent of adults say they own stock shares or mutual funds. Among registered voters, shareholders outnumber those not in the market 53 percent to 43 percent. These statistics help to explain not only Clinton's comment but Washington's increasing obsequiousness toward Wall Street in general. For the voting public, the level of the Dow has become a pocketbook issue.

This may be the least appreciated economic, cultural and political development of recent years. Over the last decade and a half, as the Dow has ascended from 800 to 8,000, luring tens of millions of middle-class Americans into the market, we have developed a mass culture of investing, the first to exist anywhere in the world. American democratic capitalism has brought about the *democratization* of capitalism.

In many obvious ways, this is a positive development. The stock-   5
market boom expresses the health of our economy. For millions of people, the rising Dow means an unanticipated degree of prosperity and bodes well for an earlier and more secure retirement. The mania for investing is also likely to ameliorate the country's chronic shortfall in private savings.

That said, it is nonetheless worth pausing to fret over the distortions that the rising market brings to our political and cultural life. A soaring Dow does not necessarily mean a healthy society. Even as a rising market makes many of us richer, it exacerbates inequality. By setting up speculative riches as an aspiration, it belittles the traditional virtues of industry and thrift. As a nation increasingly obsessed with stock prices, we are on the verge of becoming a society of Silas Marners, one in which too many of us spend too much time in the lonely and unrewarding pursuit of counting our money. . . .

But the market is not a simple way to save. To choose among thousands of stocks and mutual funds, you must assess your goals, determine an appropriate level of risk, know something about fund companies and fund managers and comparison-shop for the lowest fees. The problem is not that small investors are unable to handle complications or make prudent decisions. The problem is resource allocation. If you want to avoid getting nest egg on your face, you must spend a great deal of time superintending your investments. What begins as a healthy curiosity and natural self-interest can easily turn into a chore and a preoccupation. Thanks to cable TV and the Internet, it's possible to spend an inordinate amount of time in the mesmerizing but pointless activity of watching your balance ebb and flow. . . .

The din of business noise contributes to a paradox for individual investors. The goal of buying stocks is freedom, as the brokerage ads portraying lone, rugged baby boomers on scenic mountaintops remind us. Investing wisely means comfort, ease and a lack of worry about putting the kids through college. Yet in reality, investing in stocks means constant anxiety. Instead of liberation, rising values mean more money to manage. Time spent watching one's investments is not only time away from slower-paced and more rewarding forms of leisure; it also spoils you for them by doing violence to your attention span.

And once in, it is psychologically almost impossible to get out. Why abandon an investment that has out-performed the market, especially if doing so means paying taxes? An investment that has lagged or fallen may be just about to recoup. One often sells stocks with relief but seldom without a tinge of regret.

10   This anxiety among Americans about stocks is nothing new. Touring America in the 1880's, the British diplomat and historian James Bryce was struck by the popular passion for stocks and also the "high nervous tension" among stockholders. What is new is that stock angst has become a mass condition.

Business books, which a few years ago dwelled heavily on personal motivation and self-fulfillment, have given way to works promising personal enrichment through enrichment. "The Seven Habits of Highly Effective People" and "What Color Is Your Parachute?" are still selling, but the big business books at the moment are "Don't Worry, Make Money" (message: don't stress—invest), "The Millionaire Next Door" (message: spend less, invest more) and "Buffettology" (message: Warren Buffett did, you can too). There are dozens more. The successor to the book club as urban cultural phenomenon is the women's investment club, modeled on the Beardstown Ladies of Beardstown, Ill., who published a book about their successful approach to stock picking (message: invest where the parking lots are full).

Among men, casual conversation is now more likely to be about the market and less likely to be about sports. The transition from one topic to the other is seamless. Stock watching offers the statistical pleasures of baseball and football—the ability to parse information countless clever ways—along with a competitive element. But instead of being a democratic leveler, investment talk is a solipsistic divider.

*   *   *

There is enough puritan spirit left in politics that you occasionally still hear a Congressman railing against the vice of gambling. In the case of the market, however, the old prejudices have been not just banished but reversed. Political leaders now tend to defer to the market, behaving as if its continued exponential rise and the health of the country were synonymous.

This seems especially odd when you consider all the aspects of social and political health that the market reads as sickness and vice versa. The Dow typically responds badly to lower unemployment because of the threat of incrementally higher inflation. It frowns at increases in wages because they may squeeze corporate profits. (Rising inequality, on the other hand, does not trouble investors.) In foreign policy, the market prefers avoiding conflict to what may be necessary confrontation; this was reportedly a consideration in the President's recent deliberations over what to do about Iraq.

Inflated stock prices also create their own, gratuitous threats to the economy. Exaggerated valuations create a risk of a sudden collapse, possibly leading to recession. It is just more than a year since Alan Greenspan tried to inject caution into the market with his comment about "irrational exuberance." In the seven months that followed, the Dow rose almost 2,000 points. Before the 554-point "correction" in October, there was some concern about how new investors would react to a substantial drop. By and large, they did not engage in panic selling, having absorbed the wisdom that every dip is merely a buying opportunity in disguise. The market erased the loss in a matter of weeks. At this point, the risk may be less that investors will flee the market at the first sign of trouble than that they won't respond to any signal.

An economy growing at 3 percent a year cannot sustain stockmarket gains of 20 percent and 30 percent a year forever. But instead of dampening speculative fervor and unreasonable expectations, Congress is preoccupied with measures to spur stocks further upward. The tax code, which best promotes economic efficiency when it does not favor one type of earnings over another, now strongly tilts toward investors over wage earners. As a result of the 1997 budget bill, stockmarket profits are treated far more leniently than income. The basic rate on capital gains is 20 percent versus a top rate of nearly 40 percent on earned income. This creates an incentive to set up tax shelters and engage in other kinds of economically unproductive fiddling. But more troubling than the economic wrongheadedness is the ethical signal that such a differential sends: a dollar gained beats a dollar earned.

Other big favors to the market (seldom cast as such) are in the offing. One consequence, whether intended or otherwise, of most of the ideas about reforming Social Security would be to sustain otherwise unsustainable flows into equities. Under various plans being discussed, the money that must be put aside for the baby boomers' retirement would find its way into the stock market. The pressure to do this comes partly from the securities industry itself and partly from its satisfied customers; the more habituated people become to double-digit returns, the worse a bargain Social Security seems.

One suggestion is that the Government could itself put all or part of the surpluses accumulating in the Social Security trust fund into the stock market. No one has figured out how this would work. The magnitude of the sums invested would mean Government ownership of industry—socialism through the back door. It's also hard to comprehend how Washington might begin withdrawing those funds in 2013, as it will have to do to support retiring boomers, without sponsoring a crash. . . .

The problem is, once again, inequality. Even as average income has risen in recent years, the difference between those at the top and those at the bottom has grown more pronounced. With half the country in the market, the gap is no longer just between those with incomes going up and those with stagnant incomes. It's between those with a steadily escalating net worth multiplying in the market and those who have little prospect of building any net worth. It makes the separation between haves and have-nots seem more like a division between will-always-haves and won't-ever-haves.

20   The market creates a powerful argument for ignoring inequality. It does so not just by highlighting the self-interest of the investing majority but also by fostering political values based on the market. At a basic level, Wall Street is drawing the majority of Americans into a very different idea of citizenship and a very different experience of democracy than the one the country has long been familiar with.

There are superficial similarities between political democracy and shareholder democracy. Shareholders elect management to run a company in their interest. If management fails, the majority of owners can vote them out. But a publicly held company is a democracy without any care for equality. Shareholders have voting rights, but they do not all have the same rights. Voting power is proportionate to one's ownership stake. In a corporation, the majority owners owe no special obligation to the minority. To expend resources on the interests of nonshareholders—by analogy the nation or society as a whole—would be a breach of fiduciary responsibility.

As Alexander Hamilton noted, economic institutions do teach civic lessons, and the experience of voting one's shares as opposed to voting one's conscience has affected the mind-set and the rhetoric of American politics. Ronald Reagan was the first to pose a challenge to an incumbent President in terms of narrow, personal self-interest. "Are you better off now than you were four years ago?" he asked in 1980, implying that voters should assess management's performance in quantitative terms. The citizen's position in relation to the country is increasingly referred to as an ownership stake—the view taken by the C.E.O. candidate Ross Perot in 1992. Results overwhelm questions of democratic legitimacy.

There is no longer any real reluctance to accept the need for a professional manager—the chairman of the Federal Reserve—to run the economy with only the most attenuated form of accountability, at least when his performance is as good as Greenspan's.

The shareholder-citizen in whose image politics is being remade is not a new player on the American stage. In fact, he is the reincarnation of an old character. The new ideal of the financially autonomous individual, who manages his own investments so as not to be dependent on government, the community or institutions, embodies the eternal American aspiration to individualism and self-sufficiency. Investing man is a successor to the Jeffersonian ideal of the yeoman farmer, whose ability to satisfy his own modest needs was taken as an underpinning of democratic health.

But the contemporary shareholder-citizen is at the same time an 25 impoverished embodiment of that ideal, concentrating on material aspects of independence while largely excluding the experience of community and cultivation of civic virtue. An idea of material sufficiency that might have seemed appropriate just a few years ago has been supplanted by an ever-rising standard of how much is necessary for true happiness. Rather than fostering the kind of democratic citizen who can be trusted to govern, as Jefferson's ideal did, the market ideal of citizenship is about developing the means to withdraw from unsatisfactory common institutions—public schools, the Social Security system, even the need to work. The explicit version of this ideology, libertarianism, has been gaining adherents and credibility in recent years. It is the political philosophy fostered by the stock market.

The citizen-investor serves his fellow citizens badly by his inclination to withdraw from the community. He tends to serve himself badly as well. He does so by focusing his pursuit of happiness on something that very seldom makes people happy in the way they expect it to.

A hundred years ago, during another popular spasm of enthusiasm for investment, a President was more likely to remind the country of this human truth than to indulge its fascination with the market. In his 1893 Fourth of July proclamation, President Grover Cleveland warned the nation to "guard against the sordid struggle for unearned wealth" and to "hold fast to the American idea that work is honorable and economy a virtue." He viewed getting rich in the stock market as a dismal aspiration, not just for America but for Americans.

For Journals

What kinds of appeals do you find in advertisements that encourage people to invest in the stock market? How important do you think investing is to your own future?

For Discussion

1. While Weisberg clearly is uneasy with the American middle-class obsession with the stock market, he also recognizes that it has some positive effects. What would you identify as the most persuasive economic arguments in favor of ordinary people investing a lot of their money in the stock market?

2. Analyze Weisberg's argument that a soaring Dow Jones index does not necessarily mean a healthy society. What significant American values does he think get lost in a market-driven America? How does what he calls "a shareholder America" seem different to him from an America in which people earn money through their own work?

3. How does using language reminiscent of the Declaration of Independence—the "pursuit of happiness"—and phrases like "citizen-investor" strengthen Weisberg's argument against the stock-market mentality?

4. How do you respond to Weisberg's assertion that Americans find it more personal to talk about money than to talk about sex?

5. Weisberg's definition of the American dream is a middle-class standard of living for all. How would your personal definition of the American dream compare with his? With the definitions held by your friends or relatives?

For Writing

1. Look at an edition of *Money* magazine or any other popular financial magazine, and find one or two articles that favor stock-market investment as a good idea for Americans. Write an essay in which you consider the following questions: What appeals do the writers make to you on the subject of investing? What assumptions do they express, explicitly or implicitly, about Americans and their attitudes toward money?

2. Write an essay on an incident from your own life that you think best illustrates your attitude toward money and toward the issues of responsibility, selfishness, and involvement that Weisberg raises. As objectively as possible, analyze your own relationship to money and what you think it can and cannot do for you.

3. Write a review of one of the books Weisberg mentions in the article—*Don't Worry, Make Money, The Millionaire Next Door,* or another.

∞ Structured Appeal: Let America Be America Again (1997)

CHRIS COUNTRYMAN

Chris Countryman is a college student from California who wrote this essay as part of his second-quarter writing class. His assignment was to analyze a persuasive text, and he chose this Langston Hughes poem from his course text.

Not all arguments come in the form of emotional speeches or legalistic essays: cartoons, newspaper articles, and even photographs can persuade as well, and sometimes much more efficiently. Poetry exemplifies this type of argumentation. Because many forms of verse follow a less restrictive format than the typical essay, poets have much more freedom to arrange elements of structure to enhance the argumentative nature of a work. In his poem "Let America Be America Again" Langston Hughes uses evocative language and structural techniques to help emphasize the separation he feels underclass Americans experience in a country they helped create.

From the beginning Hughes crafts the structure of his poem to match the nature of his thesis. The first section of his poem alternates between four-line stanzas and short sentences in parentheses. The use of these two stylistically different forms creates individual voices which present the division Hughes sees in American society. Hughes's word choice enhances this contrast. In the opening lines Hughes chooses slow, balanced sentences: "Let America be America again. / Let it be the dream it used to be. / Let it be the pioneer on the plain / Seeking a home where he himself is free" (lines 1–4). These lines resound with confidence and grandeur, and evoke a powerful patriotic image of the rugged frontiersman representing America in search of a land to claim in the name of freedom. Hughes contrasts this formal stanza with a short, much more personal line set off in parentheses: "(America never was America to me)" (line 5). Several techniques come into play here. The line's physical separation from the narrative highlights the separation in viewpoint, and the enclosure in parentheses suggests an unequal relationship and differing viewpoints, the dominant majority's American dream and the submissive minority's American reality. Hughes's parenthetical interjection mimics the structure of the first line, but in replacing "again" in line 1 with "to me" he shifts the focus from past glory to present, and very personal, isolation.

The second and third verse paragraphs, up through line 10, follow the same pattern. Again, the first stanza employs highly connotative words in balanced structures, including the repetition of "dream" in the first line and the images of conniving kings and scheming tyrants (lines

6, 8). By repeating the formula of four-line stanza followed by interjection, Hughes creates a dialogue emphasizing the fact that all of these paragraphs address the same subject, America's deviation from the ideal. Hughes's formatting changes and word choice, however, give each speaker an entirely different message. One voice calls for a return to past greatness, the other claims that greatness never existed.

As the poem progresses Hughes alters his word choice and structure in order to bring about a reversal in this dialogue. After the short couplet in italics Hughes's speakers switch roles: the previously parenthetical voice gains new strength and the old narrator fades away. Hughes now indicates forcefulness by printing the second voice in normal text. In the stanza starting at line 19 Hughes has his second voice imitate the first, employing the same type of balanced sentence structure but with a twist. Instead of "America" he substitutes "I," emphasizing the isolation of the underprivileged from their own country.

5   In the next section Hughes concentrates on the collective identity, history, and struggle of the various groups that compose the American underclass, and his choice of imagery and structure reflects this move toward unity. Having established the stereotypical vision of the American foundational experience in his earlier stanzas, Hughes falls back on these emotionally charged images to retell American history in terms of the role of currently underprivileged minorities. Now the Negroes, poor whites, and red men are the "Pioneers"; it is they who are the "serf[s] of kings" (lines 19–31). Hughes also returns to images and phrases from earlier in the poem. The modern-day victims of America "dreamt our basic dream" and built a "homeland of the free" (lines 30, 41). Hughes inserts more parallel constructions near the end of the paragraph to emphasize the shared trials of the true American pioneers: ". . . all the dreams we've dreamed / And all the songs we've sung / And all the hopes we've held / And all the flags we've hung" (lines 46–49). In addition the structure of the poem as a whole changes to reflect Hughes's argumentative tactic. Instead of individual stanzas, Hughes casts this section of the poem in a single unified paragraph, mirroring the unified cause of Hughes's unsung American patriots.

In many ways poetry as an argumentative form bears a closer resemblance to photography or other artwork than to essays. While structural concerns certainly occupy an essay's author, the incredible flexibility of poetry allows the poet to balance phrases and order stanzas much like a photographer might arrange objects in a scene to create a certain effect. Poetry also relies heavily on visual language. Although poetic arguments may tend toward emotional appeals, they are no less valid than pathos appeals in essays, and can be much more effective. Certainly in Hughes's "Let America Be America Again" these images, combined with a carefully planned structure, create a powerful, and ultimately convincing, argument.

For Journals

Do you read poetry on your own? Do you think of it as a vehicle for intellectual expression?

For Discussion

1. What is Countryman's thesis about the use of poetry or other forms of art to make an argument or appeal?

2. Countryman does a very close reading of this poem to explain how the argument is constructed. What are the crucial voices and dialogues in the poem? What points of view do they express?

3. Given the different voices, how do the historical references to pioneers help structure the unity achieved at the end of the poem between various excluded groups like poor white, black, and red Americans?

4. How persuasive is Countryman's point that poetry resembles photography? What other arts do you think can pose an argument the way poetry can?

For Writing

"Let America Be America Again" was one of a series of poems Hughes wrote about his disappointment and hope for the realization of his country's potential. Pick another poem from the series, and apply Countryman's analytical structure to it: What appeal is Hughes making in the poem? How many different voices can you find, and what points of view can you identify? Pay attention to individual words, especially pronouns, to help establish the various voices. Finally, be sure to look for the argument that the language of the poem conveys, and rephrase it in your own words.

∞ *Film: Avalon* (1990)

The subject of this film is the story of a Jewish American family, taking place mostly in the late 1940s and 1950s in Baltimore. It begins and ends with the memory of Sam's arrival as an immigrant from Russia in 1914, and focuses on his wife, son, daughter-in-law, and grandson Michael. (126 minutes)

For Journals

Do any of the traditions in this family—large Thanksgiving dinners, a family circle, time spent with cousins during childhood, tension between a mother-in-law and her daughter-in-law, a relationship with a beloved grandparent—remind you of your own family? How?

For Discussion

1.   Who do you think is the hero of this film? What does this character do or represent that qualifies him for that status? In what ways is he central to the film's meaning?

2.   Why does the film begin and end with Sam's arrival in the United States on the Fourth of July, 1914? Why is the Fourth of July also the day of the fire? Why do you think holidays like the Fourth of July and Thanksgiving play such a prominent role in this film?

3.   What kinds of changes in the meaning of the Fourth of July have taken place in the film between Sam's first impressions of the holiday and the day his son makes a commercial for his discount store by advertising an Independence Day sale that promises independence from high prices?

4.   When the family earns enough money to move from a city neighborhood to the suburbs, Michael asks, "Is this a good thing?" Is it? What do they gain and what do they give up in the move?

5.   Look at the following scenes: the robbery and stabbing of Jules; the fight between Sam and his brother, Gabriel, first at Thanksgiving and then at the family circle; the time the family spends at the country club. What role does money play in the way the family begins to split up? Where else in the movie do you see the effects of money, both positive and negative?

For Writing

1.   Write an essay in which you trace the development of the three main male characters in the film—Sam, the grandfather; Jules, the son; and Michael, the grandson. Pick one or two scenes to examine closely, which you think best illustrate their relationships (for example, Michael confessing that he thinks he burned the store down; Sam taking Michael and his cousins to sleep out on the Fourth of July; Michael coming to visit Sam in the nursing home and bringing his son with him).

2.   Referring back to discussion item 2, write an essay about all the times in this film that the Fourth of July is the focus for some significant event in the family members' lives. Comment on closeness, disintegration, assimilation, growing up, or any other major themes you observe.

3.   The writer and director of the film, Barry Levinson, is from Baltimore and has set much of his work there. Look at one of his other films, such as *Diner* or *Tin Men*, or an episode of his television series, *Homicide*, and write an essay in which you compare the different ways he portrays life in Baltimore. What constitutes a family or a family substitute? What do family members fight about? What do they consider their most valuable relationships and traditions?

4.   Look up the original meaning of the place name Avalon. What kind of place was it supposed to be? Write a paper in which you describe Avalon and explain why that title is meaningful for this movie, its themes, and one or two of the main characters.

Writing Assignments

1.   Find an advertisement in a magazine or newspaper that uses examples of American symbols directly (for example, advertising U.S. savings bonds by showing the emblem of the American bald eagle) or indirectly (e.g., savings bank using Benjamin Franklin's portrait as a logo, or a jeans company that embroiders an American flag on the pocket). There are many such examples; you also might want to look at CD covers and movie advertisements. Write an analysis of the ad in which you consider the following questions: Who is the audience? Why do you think that advertiser included an example of American symbolism in the ad? Why was the particular example chosen? How effective is that example in conveying American values? How successful or unsuccessful do you think this approach is?

2.   The selections in this chapter each express some element of the American dream. Write an essay in which you argue for your own idea of what the American dream means—both what you think it means to most Americans and what it means to you. How do you see the American dream in members of your family? In yourself? What elements are crucial to it? Because you are dealing with a broad idea, it is especially important to include specific examples of what you believe the dream to be and how it manifests itself in you and your family. Do not confine yourself to generalizations like "My parents want me to have a better life than they have." Use your examples to explain their lives, including disappointments or worries, and to show what you really dream of for yourself.

3.   Langston Hughes was vitally interested in the promise of the American dream and in the importance of making it accessible to all Americans. With his work in mind, listen to and read the lyrics of contemporary songs, including rap lyrics, that talk about American dreams and nightmares. Write an analytical essay in which you discuss the vision of American life, especially urban life, set forth in these songs, including what they say about dreams for the future. Cite examples from the lyrics to support your assertions. You can use Hughes as a point of comparison if you want to.

4.   Imagine that you have to explain the American dream to an English-speaking visitor from another country and that you have to compose a popular culture curriculum featuring contemporary materials that would make the dream clearer to a stranger. Prepare a list of examples for this visitor drawn from each of the following categories: four movies to see; two to four musicians to listen to; two works of fiction and two works of nonfiction to read; and two magazines to read. After each selection, write a paragraph explaining why this particular example says something about the American dream, and what that is.

5.   Go to the newsstand or your library and pick up the following: one issue of what is usually known as a women's magazine (*Family Circle, Ladies' Home Journal,* and so on), one issue of a magazine addressed to different women's interests (*Cosmopolitan, Mademoiselle,* and so on), and one issue of a magazine addressed largely to men (*GQ, Esquire,* and so on). Be sure that the magazines you choose have *at least one article apiece* on the home (entertaining at home, decorating the home, cooking for friends or family, spending time with children at home, and so on). Write an essay comparing the images of house and home you find in these publications. What dreams of American home life do you think they advertise? Do the dreams of home revealed in articles in a men's magazine differ from those in the articles for women? If so, in what ways? Are any of the articles more informative than others? If they include photographs, how do the illustrations support the articles' points of view and persuade readers to accept them?

5
∞

Images of Gender and Family

At the core of American identities and American dreams lies the family. Whether a colonial-era farm household, an immigrant extended family, a native clan or tribe, an urban domestic partnership, or a suburban nuclear family, families serve as a connection between the individual and the outside world. The individual's identity, his or her dreams, in large part depend on the family of origin or a family of choice. The individual is shaped through beliefs, values, and assumptions that the family holds about the world and that are based on the family members' experiences and collective memory. The family itself, in turn, derives its value from the social, cultural, political, and philosophical assumptions and beliefs and the economic needs of the larger culture.

Questions about the family are pervasive in contemporary American society: What is the "definition" of a family? Who can belong to a family? What are appropriate gender roles within families? What restraints does the concept of family place on women? On men? On children? What happens to a society in which the nuclear family is no longer the dominant configuration? What are "family values"? Are they positive beliefs and aspirations that optimize growth and diversity for all, or narrow-minded strictures and intolerances that seek to shut out differences of approach or opinion? The debates over these issues are becoming increasingly rancorous.

And yet this kind of conflict is not altogether new. The history of our country is one of uneasy inequality between men and women. Revolutionary-era rhetoric depended heavily on a philosophy that was based on equality and on political rights, but those concepts applied to men only. Industrialization brought with it not only manufacturing jobs and manufactured goods but also exploitation of children for labor. World War I saw tremendous support for the war effort and for social services from women, but although women finally gained the vote in 1920, they received few additional rights thereafter. World War II brought new and demanding jobs for women to support the war effort, but as soon as the men returned from war, society's needs for employment for men and for social stability issued a new message to women:

go home, stay home, and raise children. The civil rights and women's movements of the sixties and seventies brought attention to gross civil injustices, but the Equal Rights Amendment failed to pass. Women have made some strides in business and government, but cries from the media, to politicians, to the religious right have declared that feminism and women's liberation have brought women in particular and society in general nothing but grief.

Despite this inequality of the sexes, the idea of the stable American family—and, concomitantly, a stable American society—has been with us for a long time. Recent debates decry the "decline" of the family and blame societal ills on a perceived lack of family stability. But to some degree we have idealized the family of the past. The current divorce rate is 50 percent of first marriages within forty years, but in the colonial era, marriages averaged only twelve years or less because of the death of one spouse. We deplore the numbers of absentee parents, but up to half of all colonial-era children lost at least one parent before the age of twenty-one, and before the 1920s, divorced fathers had no legal obligation to pay child support. We are rightfully concerned about problems in educating youth, but in the 1940s fewer than half of the students entering high school were able to finish. We mourn the death of the extended family, yet children are now more likely than at any earlier time in our history to have living grandparents and to be in contact with them. Many factories in the nineteenth century employed children under the age of eleven, and during the early industrial period, from 1850 to 1885, children worked at home, in tenement sweatshops, in mines and mills. Domestic workers supported middle-class nurturing and mothering, but their own children frequently served as maids or garment workers. During the years of the Great Depression, in the 1930s, families united for their own collective survival, but incompatible people who were stuck together in this manner, with few resources and little hope, would sometimes produce phenomena all too familiar in other eras: withdrawn or violent men; exhausted, overextended women; children with no resources with which to face the future.

Gender and Family in American History

Early recorded history of the colonies and the Revolution suggests that while the United States was founded on principles of equality, women were either invisible or were assumed to absorb the political views of their husbands or male relatives, just as their husbands were able to absorb their property upon marriage. They were expected to support economic embargoes against Britain and to supply provisions and support for the war, and they could be tried for treason during the Revolution. Men were expected to carry out the public duties of government and commerce. Some early Republicans and philosophers may have noticed the contradictions in promoting arguments about equal rights while restricting those rights to male landowners, but few questioned assumptions that women's work should be restricted to the home (though in the largely rural society, work at home was substantial). Women's sphere was the domestic arena; men participated in and ruled the public domain and debated affairs of state. One way to cope with this dichotomy was to state that the two realms were different but equal. As we examine this discussion, we will question just how equal those realms truly were, both in actuality and in perception.

The first selection in the chapter, the etching *Keep Within Compass*, comes from the early post-Revolutionary period and taps into the notion of dual spheres for men and women. As such, it is part of a long-standing tradition of defining women's roles by circumscribing them and fostering a desire for stability. One change that did result from the Revolution, however, was that divorce was slightly easier for women to obtain, which may help explain why the etching contrasts the contented "virtuous woman" with images of what can happen to her if she steps outside her role. For a far more graphic example of the consequences that befell one young woman who was victimized for failing to stay within traditional lines of demarcation, read the dissent of Judge Wilner in *Rusk* v. *State*. This late-twentieth-century case makes a somewhat frightening companion piece to *Keep Within Compass*.

In the nineteenth century, little challenged the assumptions of the twin spheres of domesticity and public realm, though domestic life, particularly in rural areas, certainly entailed labor, since families generally produced their own food and household goods and sometimes bartered for other needed commodities. Industrialization brought with it goods produced outside the home or farm, and along with increasing industry came the need for cheap labor. Immigrants, women, and children became part of that massive workforce. In the mid–nineteenth century, as household production decreased, wage labor and professional occupations developed, giving rise to an increasing middle class. Upper- and middle-class women could maintain a role focused on domesticity while men earned the family income, but the cost was borne by the laborers, often slaves and other men, women, and children, in mills, fields, and factories.

The second decade of the twentieth century saw worldwide turmoil brought about by World War I and social turmoil as U.S. women agitated for the vote, which they finally obtained in 1920. In a society in which women were assumed to carry on the emotional, sentimental, and moral needs of society as men pursued individualistic and public pursuits, women were to give love and nurturing freely, uncontaminated by the market forces of the newly industrialized society.

In addition to their role as breadwinners, men were assumed to be strong heroes and the protectors of women and children. War-era rhetoric and propaganda in particular appealed to manly attributes such as physical strength and a muscular build.

The World War I recruiting poster included in this chapter, *Enlist: On Which Side of the Window Are YOU?* makes a graphic statement about proper spheres for men and women, goading the male viewer into taking his rightful place in the public domain by using shame as a persuasive technique. The Charles Atlas body-building advertisement, published in 1944 during the height of America's involvement in World War II, uses classic appeals focusing on the shame of weakness and on men's desire to be real "red-blooded" Americans—with fame, and the admiration of women, as the ultimate prize.

Some advertisers took the next logical step and showcased both the woman/prize and the resulting offspring in a manner that clearly defined every role within the nuclear family. In the Edsel advertisement "They'll Know You've Arrived," gender and family roles are clearly delineated: the father and son are "action" figures in the foreground, next to the car, while the mother and daughter are relegated to watching from the sidelines. No competent wartime factory workers or Rosie Riveters here—women are back to the domestic sphere.

In the years that followed the civil rights and free speech movements of the 1960s, the women's movement increasingly argued for equality for women in society, especially in the home and workplace. Progress was slow, and even within liberal or left-wing social and political movements, such as the Student Nonviolent Coordinating Committee, male leaders typically assigned women to clerical or support duties rather than leadership roles. Increasing numbers of women in the workplace, relative to the postwar era of the 1950s and early 1960s, brought changes in the stable (to some, but stultifying to others) nuclear family. Long-standing assumptions that the nuclear family is the core of American communities underlie much of mainstream culture and affect how some Americans perceive cultures that differ from mainstream family values.

Assumptions and values about what a family is or should be extend even to the zoning codes of local communities. The attorney Keenan Peck, arguing from personal experience as well as from statutes and other legal evidence, articulates the hidden assumptions and challenges their applicability and their role in determining what does, and what does not, constitute a legal family. His essay "When 'Family' Is Not a Household Word" argues that not only two-parent married couples with children but also people who are not blood relatives yet care about and support each other constitute a family. Historically, unrelated people often lived together; boardinghouses, to cite just one example, often brought strangers into a household. The term "alternative family" has been gaining currency among some Americans, but assumptions about marriage and family run deep, and, as Peck points out, change can be frightening.

Assumptions also run deep about what is and is not appropriate behavior, particularly in women. We began this chapter with a look at an eighteenth-century etching exhorting women to stay in their place. Almost two hundred years later, in a famous "date rape" legal case, *Rusk v. State,* we see that if a woman doesn't "keep to her place" she is in essence putting herself in harm's way. Judge Wilner, the author of the minority opinion included in this chapter, articulates some of these assumptions as he argues against overturning the conviction of the rapist in this case. Ultimately the conviction was reinstated, but the case represents a sobering look at the assumptions and values that we take with us into policy and legal arenas.

Assumptions about work and class pervade the memoir "Bricklayer's Boy," by reporter Alfred Lubrano, who presents a portrait of what is likely considered a rather traditional American family. Yet even this family must struggle with change, in this case the upward mobility of members of the younger generation, who strive to retain the warmth and connection of their blue-collar background even as they make their way in the American middle-class, white-collar arena.

In the late 1980s and early 1990s, on the heels of the social changes of the previous two decades, gay and lesbian rights movements further challenged the concept and value of the heterosexual nuclear family; moreover, they brought the debate over homosexual marriages into the open. Thomas Stoddard, attorney and gay rights leader, argues that "Marriage Is a Fundamental Right" and that same-gender marriages are a civil rights issue. Attorney Bruce Fein's essay, "Reserve Marriage for Heterosexuals," cites legal precedent, as does Stoddard's, but also draws on our fears for children and our beliefs about two-parent families to make Fein's case.

As the century has progressed, women have appeared to make gains in politics, economics, the workplace, and society generally. But despite these gains—or, according to author Susan Faludi, because of them—women don't "have it all." In fact, women have never been worse off, in her view. Faludi reports on her extensive study of the negative reaction to women's modest gains of the 1970s and 1980s in her book *Backlash: The Undeclared War Against American Women.* In the introduction to the book, entitled "Blame It on Feminism," Faludi articulates the assumptions made by those who castigate the ill effects of feminism and then challenges them with reasoning as well as evidence and statistics.

The post–civil rights movement era also shows increasing concern over the needs of children. Some 20 percent of children still grow up in poverty, abuse, and neglect; some are born addicted to drugs and alcohol. In one battle for children's rights being fought through the courts, child advocates are arguing for increased legal rights for young people. An adult who has worked on behalf of children's rights for years, child advocate and Children's Defense Fund founder Marian Wright Edelman, explains the values, assumptions, and beliefs that led her to her life's work on behalf of children. Edelman's essay, "A Family Legacy," describes the family and extended family of community from which she learned the values of hard work, discipline, doing for others, and repaying the privileges of intellectual and material gifts by serving the community. Both Faludi, as a feminist author, and Edelman, as the leader of the Children's Defense Fund, address concerns related to those of Dr. Mary Pipher, author of *Reviving Ophelia: Saving the Selves of Adolescent Girls.* Pipher asks us to consider why young girls in our culture feel the need to stifle their voices, their energy, their creativity, and to ponder a corollary to this process—the incidence of depression, eating disorders, addictions, and suicide attempts. These young girls existing in a difficult culture are, she suggests, "Saplings in the Storm," and our society needs to look long and hard at what we are doing to them.

While some ethnic cultures within American society sometimes appear to have resolved problems that others find perplexing, image is not necessarily reality, and easy generalizations can flatten out layers of complexity. The final reading in the chapter looks at an image of Asian American families. In a researched essay, "Making and Unmaking the 'Model Minority,'" student writer John Wu studies a label once applied to Jewish immigrants and now applied to Asian Americans. He analyzes assumptions and beliefs about the values transmitted through families about family, work, and success, and about the values assumed by society to be held by American families of Asian descent. This chapter's film selection, *Mi familia (My Family)*, reflects in a visual medium the assumptions, values, and conflicts of a multigenerational Mexican American family coping with the differing assumptions, values, and conflicts of the dominant culture.

As you read the following selections, reflect on your own image of family and what the role of each member within it should be. Try also to identify and articulate the deeper assumptions on which these ideas are based. Do you think your images and assumptions are typical for an American? Are you comfortable with the fact that other Americans may have different family values?

∞ *Keep Within Compass* (ca. 1790)

A metaphor that surfaces decade after decade in conveying social worlds is that of the circle, or in some cases, the three-dimensional sphere. Sometimes referring to a social class, other times to occupations, the image is frequently used, from the late eighteenth century through the twentieth century, to describe the designated and circumscribed roles for men and women: men's world of greater economic, industrial, and political society, and women's world of the home.

This etching draws upon a centuries-old tradition of emblems, which combine visual elements and a moral lesson. Combining a didactic picture with a textual moral statement, the etching depicts four unpleasant scenes with which the "virtuous" woman is threatened if she does not remain within her own sphere or circle: raising a child in poverty and misery, working as a domestic or tavern worker, selling in the street, and prostituting herself to soldiers. Such scenes contrast with the well-dressed, happy-looking gentlewoman depicted next to flowers and a large home.

For Journals

Write about what you imagine to be the daily life of eighteenth-century American women: women of means, with landed or wealthy families, and women without family or financial support.

For Discussion

1. What is your overall impression of the etching? What draws your eye? What is emphasized? Why do you think the etching was drawn to create this impression and this emphasis? Relative to the entire circle, how much space is allotted to the virtuous woman?

2. Who are the intended audiences? Do different elements of the etching appeal to different audiences? To different audience concerns?

3. Why do you think the artist used a compass to make his point? In the late eighteenth century, who would have been likely to wield a compass? Who, then, would be setting the limits on women?

4. Analyze the etching as a moral lesson or argument with supporting subtopics and evidence, including the smaller pictures and the additional printed messages. Write out a text outline of the argument. What is inside the compass? What are "good" women supposed to do? What is outside the compass? What are women not supposed to do? Is this what you would expect?

5. Why is it important that a woman be "a crown to her husband"? Do you think the authors of this etching would expect a man to be a crown to his wife? What associations does the crown bring to mind?

6. In what ways might the assumptions apparent in this etching be relevant today? Do you see any connections between this two-hundred-year-old image and arguments about date rape today? (See the legal arguments regarding the noted "date rape" case later in this chapter.)

For Writing

1. In what ways are gender roles still restricted today? Draw a contemporary version of this etching for men or for women. Then write an essay explaining your diagram.

2. Argue that women are no longer restricted by gender roles—or that men are more restricted in their choices and behavior than women are.

3. Do research in art or literature of the American colonial period to examine the role of women or home life. Examine art books from your library, primary materials such as diaries if they are available, or secondary sources about the period. What do you conclude about women's or men's role in the home or in society during this period? Write a documented essay reporting your conclusions.

∞ Enlist: On Which Side of the Window Are YOU? (1917)

This American poster (see page 228), based on an earlier British poster, uses an approach that differs from the positive appeals to ethos and pathos that characterize many other war recruitment posters. You may want to review Chapter 1 for additional information on posters as a medium of persuasion.

For Journals

Do you believe men and women have an equal responsibility to participate in military service?

For Discussion

1. Examine the elements of the poster. What first catches your eye? What next? Is the man inside the window confined in any way? Where does he seem to belong? What is the argument of the poster? What are the appeals used to persuade the audience? How do light and shading affect the message?

2. Look closely at the man, his appearance, and his posture; then, look at the soldiers. What differences do you notice? What is implied by those differences?

3. Compare and contrast this image to that of *Keep Within Compass*. What do you infer about a woman's proper role? What is, conversely, a man's proper sphere? In what ways did women's and men's roles change, or remain constant, between 1790 and 1917? In what ways have they changed, and in what ways remained constant, since 1917?

For Writing

1. Review all the war era images in this book. What are the common themes and appeals? How do their strategies differ? Select two posters and write an essay comparing and contrasting them. Alternatively, select some other focus—appeals to ethos, for example—and develop an essay drawing evidence from the posters.

2. Using books of posters, a library collection, or a museum brochure, research other war era posters. You might look for particular ways in which the posters portray "the enemy" or particular kinds of appeals in posters from different countries.

✇ *Fame Instead of Shame* (1944)

*Charles Atlas (1893–1972) was a bodybuilder who made a fortune in the mail or-
der business promoting his techniques for developing a muscular male body. Appealing to men's desire to be "real red-blooded men" and using shame among other tactics,
Atlas's beach anecdote of the muscle man kicking sand in a skinny man's face became
the classic example of male-to-male bullying and competition—and of a cultural
stereotype of manliness.*

For Journals

What kinds of appeals dominate advertisements for men in the magazines you read?

For Discussion

1. List several assumptions that the author of this advertisement
makes about the readers. Do such assumptions seem realistic? What is
assumed about what men want? About what women want in a man?
About attractiveness, maturity, competition? What expectations of men
are conveyed?

2. How does Atlas define "a real man"? Examine the language, the phy-
sique of the cartoon figures, the appeals to emotion, the appeals to au-
thority. How persuasive do you think this advertisement was in 1944?
To what degree is it significant that the ad appeared during World War
II? Do you think the ad would be effective today? Why or why not?
How would an advertisement for a similar product be marketed today?

3. The advertisement contains a number of enthymemes (concise deductive arguments with conclusions that depend on the assumptions of
the audience in order to make sense). (For a fuller discussion of enthymemes, see Chapter 1.) Identify one or two; state them and supply
the missing assumption.

4. Do you detect any appeals to logos, or logic, in the text? What are
they? What is the evidence supplied to support the appeals? (See discussion of appeals to logos in Chapter 1.)

5. Considering both images and text, compare and contrast the stereotypical roles conveyed in *Keep Within Compass* and in this advertisement. Which gender seems to have a more narrowly defined role in
society? Have times changed for either gender?

For Writing

1. Write an essay arguing that expectations for men and their role in
American society have, or have not, changed since this advertisement

was published. You can focus on this advertisement, or you can find a related contemporary advertisement and compare and contrast the two.

2. Review a variety of magazines from the 1920s through the 1960s, looking for advertisements that convey gender roles or expectations. What is suggested in them about men's and women's roles? About children or children's gender roles? Write an essay developing your position. If possible, include photocopies of the advertisements you use.

∞ *They'll Know You've Arrived* (1958)

FORD MOTOR CO.

The Edsel car was one of the most embarrassing debacles in the automotive industry generally, and for the Ford Motor Company specifically, in the 1950s. Decades later, middle-aged and older Americans still allude to the Edsel in describing a colossal mistake, particularly in product development. But as the advertisement here suggests, the Edsel was marketed as a part of post–World War II prosperity, and ads such as this appeared in mainstream, middle-class magazines.

They'll know you've *arrived*

when you drive up in an Edsel

Step into an Edsel and you'll learn where the excitement is this year. Other drivers spot that classic vertical grille a block away—and never fail to take a long look at this year's most exciting car.

On the open road, your Edsel is watched eagerly for its already-famous performance.

And parked in front of your home, your Edsel always gets even more attention—because it always says a lot about you. It says you chose elegant styling, luxurious comfort and such exclusive features as Edsel's famous Teletouch Drive—only shift that puts the buttons where they belong, on the steering-wheel hub.

Your Edsel also means you made a wonderful buy. For of all medium-priced cars, this one really new car is actually priced the lowest.* See your Edsel Dealer this week.

Based on comparison of suggested retail delivered prices of the Edsel Ranger and similarly equipped cars in the medium-price field.

Above: Edsel Citation 2-door Hardtop. Engine: the E-475, with 10.5 to one compression ratio, 345 hp, 475 ft.-lb. torque. Transmission: Automatic with Teletouch Drive. Suspension: Ball-joint with optional air suspension. Brakes: self-adjusting.

EDSEL DIVISION · FORD MOTOR COMPANY

1958 EDSEL

Of all medium-priced cars, the one that's really new is the lowest-priced, too!

For Journals

What kinds of advertisements do you find most appealing? Do some types draw your eyes more than others? Do some appeal to your desire for status and success?

For Discussion

1. Who are the active people in the advertisement? Who are the passive onlookers? Where are the people in the photograph relative to the product being displayed? What do these positions in the photograph convey to you about gender roles, power, and targeted audiences for the advertisement?

2. The headline plays on the word *arrived* to indicate not only transportation but also status and success. Examine the smaller text at the bottom of the ad. In what ways does it reinforce the connection made in the headline between success, money, and consumption?

3. What assertions does the advertisement make about success? What appeals to ethos, or credibility and shared values; to pathos, or emotions; to logos, or logic, do the text and photograph make? Do both parts of the ad rely on the same types of appeals?

4. The Edsel became a notoriously unpopular car and the butt of many jokes. Is there a car or other type of product today that you think may become the "Edsel" of tomorrow despite currently being considered a status symbol?

For Writing

1. In her article "You've Come a Long Way, Madison Avenue" in *Lear's* magazine, author Betsy Sharkey has argued that ads sell sex to men and style to women. Browse through some current popular magazines, and find several advertisements you think are directed at men and several directed at women. Does the evidence you find support or refute Sharkey's assertion? Develop an argument in which you agree or disagree with Sharkey, drawing on the visual and textual evidence of the advertisements to support your view.

2. For many years, cigarettes were advertised for their ability to help depress the appetite and even for their good health side effects. Lucky Strike, for example, used to run an ad that said, "Reach for a Lucky—instead of a sweet" and "It's toasted—No Throat Irritation—No Cough." Find an advertisement that you think is particularly misleading or unrealistic, and write an essay in which you analyze the elements of the ad.

3. In *Satisfaction Guaranteed,* her book on American consumerism,

Susan Strasser says that Americans had to be trained to want products and to believe that they needed them so that they would go out and buy things and spend money. Based on your own observations and experience, do you agree or disagree with Strasser? Develop your argument into an essay supported by examples and details you have observed or experienced.

∞ Rusk v. State

Court of Special Appeals of Maryland, 406 A.2d 624 (1979)

JUDGE WILNER

This legal opinion comes from the second of three parts in a court proceeding. In the first part, Mr. Rusk was convicted of rape and sentenced to ten years in prison. In the second part, he appealed for his conviction to be overturned, and he won. Judge Wilner served on the appeals court panel that heard Mr. Rusk's request, but unlike the majority of the court, he felt that Mr. Rusk's original sentence was correct. In the minority opinion presented here, he explains why he thinks Mr. Rusk was in fact guilty of rape. (In the third phase, Mr. Rusk's victim appealed for his conviction to be reinstated and the court agreed, relying for its decision on Wilner's reasoning in this earlier appeal.)

Wilner, Judge, dissenting.

With the deepest respect for the generally superior wisdom of my colleagues who authored or endorsed the majority Opinion, but with the equally profound conviction that, in this case, they have made a serious mistake, I record this dissent. . . .

Md. Annot. Code art. 27, § 463(a) considers three types of conduct as constituting second degree rape. We are concerned only with the first: a person is guilty of rape in the second degree if he (1) engages in vaginal intercourse with another person, (2) by force or threat of force, (3) against the will, and (4) without the consent of the other person. There is no real question here as to the first, third, or fourth elements of the crime. The evidence was certainly sufficient to show that appellant had vaginal intercourse with the victim, and that such act was against her will and without her consent. The point at issue is whether it was accomplished by force or threat of force; and I think that in viewing the evidence, that point should remain ever clear. *Consent is not the issue here, only whether there was sufficient evidence of force or the threat of force.*

Unfortunately, courts, including in the present case a majority of this one, often tend to confuse these two elements—force and lack of consent—and to think of them as one. They are not. They mean, and require, different things. See *State* v. *Studham,* 572 P.2d 700 (Utah, 1977). What seems to cause the confusion—what, indeed, has become a common denominator of both elements—is the notion that the victim must actively resist the attack upon her. If she fails to offer sufficient resistance (sufficient to the satisfaction of the judge), a court is entitled, or at least presumes the entitlement, to find that there was no force or threat of force, or that the act was not against her will, or that she actually consented to it, or some unarticulated combination or synthesis of these elements that leads to the ultimate conclusion that the victim was not raped. Thus it is that the focus is almost entirely on the extent of resistance—*the victim's acts, rather than those of her assailant.* Attention is directed not to the wrongful stimulus, but to the victim's reactions to it. Right or wrong, that seems to be the current state of the Maryland law; and, notwithstanding its uniqueness in the criminal law, and its illogic, until changed by statute or the Court of Appeals, I accept it as binding.

5   But what is required of a woman being attacked or in danger of attack? How much resistance must she offer? Where is that line to be drawn between requiring that she either risk serious physical harm, perhaps death, on the one hand, or be termed a willing partner on the other? Some answers are given in *Hazel* v. *State,* 221 Md. 464, 157 A.2d 922 (1960), although, as in so many cases, they were stated in the context of both the requirement of force and the lack of consent. The Court said, at pp. 469, 470, 157 A.2d at p. 925:

"Force is an essential element of the crime and to justify a conviction, the evidence must warrant a conclusion either that the victim resisted and her resistance was overcome by force or that she was prevented from resisting by threats to her safety. But no particular amount of force, either actual or constructive, is required to constitute rape. Necessarily that fact must depend upon the prevailing circumstances. As in this case force may exist without violence. *If the acts and threats of the defendant were reasonably calculated to create in the mind of the victim—having regard to the circumstances in which she was placed—a real apprehension, due to fear, of imminent bodily harm, serious enough to impair or overcome her will to resist, then such acts and threats are the equivalent of force. . . .*

"With respect to the presence or absence of the element of consent, it is true, of course, that however reluctantly given, consent to the act at any time prior to penetration deprives the subsequent intercourse of its criminal character. *There is, however, a wide difference between consent and a submission to the act. Consent may involve submission, but submission does not necessarily imply consent. Furthermore, submission to a compelling force, or as a result of being put in fear, is not consent. . . .*

"The authorities are by no means in accord as to what degree of resistance is necessary to establish the absence of consent. However, the generally accepted doctrine seems to be that a female—who was conscious and possessed of her natural, mental and physical powers when the attack took place—must have resisted to the extent of her ability at the time, unless it appears that she was overcome by numbers or was so terrified by threats as to overpower her will to resist. . . . Since resistance is necessarily relative, the presence or absence of it must depend on the facts and circumstances in each case. . . . *But the real test, which must be recognized in all cases, is whether the assault was committed without the consent and against the will of the prosecuting witness.*

"The kind of fear which would render resistance by a woman unnecessary to support a conviction of rape includes, but is not necessarily limited to, a fear of death or serious bodily harm, or a fear so extreme as to preclude resistance, or a fear which would well nigh render her mind incapable of continuing to resist, or a fear that so overpowers her that she does not dare resist." (Citations omitted.) (Emphasis supplied.)

From these pronouncements in *Hazel*, this Court has articulated what the majority refers to as a "rule of reason"—*i.e.*, that "where the victim's story could not be corroborated by wounds, bruises or disordered clothing, the lack of consent could be shown by fear based upon reasonable apprehension." *Winegan* v. *State*, 10 Md.App. 196, 200, 268 A.2d 585, 588 (1970); *Goldberg* v. *State*, 41 Md.App. 58, 395 A.2d 1213 (1979). *As so phrased*, I do not consider this to be a rule of reason at all; it is highly unreasonable, and again mixes the element of consent with that of force. But what I do accept is what the Court of Appeals said in *Hazel*: (1) if the acts and threats of the defendant were reasonably calculated to create in the mind of the victim—having regard to the circumstances in which she was placed—a real apprehension, due to fear, of imminent bodily harm, serious enough to impair or overcome her will to resist, then such acts and threats are the equivalent of force; (2) submission is not the equivalent of consent; and (3) the real test is whether the assault was committed without the consent and against the will of the prosecuting witness.[1]

Upon this basis, the evidence against appellant must be considered. Judge Thompson recounts most, but not quite all, of the victim's story. The victim—I'll call her Pat—attended a high school reunion. She had arranged to meet her girlfriend Terry there. The reunion was over at 9:00, and Terry asked Pat to accompany her to Fell's Point.[2] Pat had

---

[1] Other courts have stated the rule this way: A rape victim is not required to do more than her age, strength, surrounding facts and all attending circumstances make it reasonable for her to do to manifest her opposition. See *Dinkens* v. *State*, 92 Nev. 74, 546 P.2d 228 (1976); *State* v. *Studham*, 572 P.2d 700 (Utah 1977). See also *Schrum* v. *Com.*, 219 Va. 168, 246, S.E.2d 893 (1978). [Author's note]

[2] Fell's Point is an old section of Baltimore City adjacent to the harbor. It has been extensively renovated as part of urban renewal and, among refurbished homes and shops, hosts a number of cafes and discotheques. It is part of the City's night scene. [Author's note]

gone to Fell's Point with Terry on a few prior occasions, explaining in court: "I've never met anybody [there] I've gone out with. I met people in general, talking in conversation, most of the time people that Terry knew, not that I have gone down there, and met people as dates." She agreed to go, but first called her mother, who was babysitting with Pat's two-year-old son, to tell her that she was going with Terry to Fell's Point, and that she would not be home late. It was just after 9:00 when Pat and Terry, in their separate cars, left for Fell's Point, alone.[3]

They went to a place called Helen's and had one drink. They stayed an hour or so and then walked down to another place (where they had another drink), stayed about a half hour there, and went to a third place. Up to that point, Pat conversed only with Terry, and did not strike up any other acquaintanceships. Pat and Terry were standing against a wall when appellant came over and said hello to Terry, who was conversing with someone else at the time. Appellant then began to talk with Pat. They were both separated, they both had young children; and they spoke about those things. Pat said that she had been ready to leave when appellant came on the scene, and that she only talked with him for five or ten minutes. It was then about midnight. Pat had to get up with her baby in the morning and did not want to stay out late.

Terry wasn't ready to leave. As Pat was preparing to go, appellant asked if she would drop him off on her way home.[4] She agreed because she thought he was a friend of Terry's. She told him, however, as they walked to her car, "I'm just giving a ride home, you know, as a friend, not anything to be, you know, thought of other than a ride." He agreed to that condition.

Pat was completely unfamiliar with appellant's neighborhood. She had no idea where she was. When she pulled up to where appellant said he lived, she put the car in park, but left the engine running. She said to appellant, "Well, here, you know, you are home." Appellant then asked Pat to come up with him and she refused. He persisted in his request, as did she in her refusal. She told him that even if she wanted to come up, she dared not do so. She was separated and it might cause marital problems for her. Finally, he reached over, turned off the ignition, took her keys, got out of the car, came around to her side, opened the door, and said to her, "Now, will you come up?"

15   It was at this point that Pat followed appellant to his apartment, and it is at this point that the majority of this Court begins to substitute its judgment for that of the trial court and jury. We know nothing about

---

[3] Pat said that Terry and she lived at opposite ends of town and that Fell's Point was sort of midway between their respective homes. [Author's note]

[4] Her testimony about this, on cross-examination, was: "I said I was leaving. I said, excuse me. It's nice meeting you; but I'm getting ready to leave; and he said, 'which way are you going;' and I told him; at that time, he said, 'Would you mind giving me a lift?'" [Author's note]

Pat and appellant. We don't know how big they are, what they look like, what their life experiences have been. We don't know if appellant is larger or smaller than she, stronger or weaker. We don't know what the inflection was in his voice as he dangled her car keys in front of her. We can't tell whether this was in a jocular vein or a truly threatening one. We have no idea what his mannerisms were. The trial judge and the jury could discern some of these things, of course, because they could observe the two people in court and could listen to what they said and how they said it. But all we know is that, between midnight and 1:00 A.M., in a neighborhood that was strange to Pat, appellant took her car keys, demanded that she accompany him, and most assuredly implied that unless she did so, at the very least, she might be stranded.

Now, let us interrupt the tale for a minute and consider the situation. Pat did not honk the horn; she did not scream; she did not try to run away. Why, she was asked. "I was scared. I didn't think at the time what to do." Later, on cross-examination: "At that point, because I was scared, because he had my car keys. I didn't know what to do. I was someplace I didn't even know where I was. It was in the city. I didn't know whether to run. I really didn't think, at that point, what to do. Now, I know that I should have blown the horn. I should have run. There were a million things I could have done. I was scared, at that point, and I didn't do any of them." What, counsel asked, was she afraid of? "Him," she replied. What was she scared that he was going to do? "Rape me, but I didn't say that. It was the way he looked at me, and said, 'Come on up, come on up;' and when he took the keys, I knew that was wrong. I just didn't say, are you going to rape me."

So Pat accompanied appellant to his apartment. As Judge Thompson points out, appellant left her in his apartment for a few minutes.[5] Although there was evidence of a telephone in the room, Pat said that, at the time, she didn't notice one. When appellant returned, he turned off the light and sat on the bed. Pat was in a chair. She testified: "I asked him if I could leave, that I wanted to go home, and I didn't want to come up. I said, 'Now, I came up. Can I go?'" Appellant, who, of course, still had her keys, said that he wanted her to stay. He told her to get on the bed with him, and, in fact, took her arms and pulled her on to the bed. He then started to undress her; he removed her blouse and bra and unzipped her pants. *At his direction,* she removed his clothes. She then said:

> "I was still begging him to please let, you know, let me leave. I said, 'you can get a lot of other girls down there, for what you want,' and he

---

[5] On direct examination, she twice said that he left the room "for a minute" after telling her to sit down. On cross-examination, she said she couldn't remember how long he was gone, but, at counsel's suggestion, said that it was not longer than five minutes. [Author's note]

just kept saying, 'no;' and then I was really scared, because I can't describe, you know, what was said. It was more the look in his eyes; and I said, at that point—I didn't know what to say; and I said, 'If I do what you want, will you let me go without killing me?' Because I didn't know, at that point, what he was going to do; and I started to cry; and when I did, he put his hands on my throat, and started lightly to choke me; and I said, 'If I do what you want, will you let me go?' And he said, yes, and at that time, I proceeded to do what he wanted me to."

He "made me perform oral sex, and then sexual intercourse." Following that:

20   "I asked him if I could leave now, and he said, 'Yes;' and I got up and got dressed; and he got up and got dressed; and he walked me to my car, and asked if he could see me again; and I said, 'Yes;' and he asked me for my telephone number; and I said, 'No, I'll see you down Fell's Point sometime,' just so I could leave."[6]

At this point, appellant returned her car keys and escorted her to her car. She then drove off:

"I stopped at a gas station, that I believe was Amoco or Exon (sic), and went to the ladies' room. From there I drove home. I don't know—I don't know if I rode around for a while or not; but I know I went home, pretty much straight home and pulled up and parked the car.
     "I was just going to go home, and not say anything."
     Q. "Why?"
25   A. *"Because I didn't want to go through what I'm going through now."*
     Q. "What, in fact, did you do then?"
     A. "I sat in the car, thinking about it a while, and I thought I wondered what would happen if I hadn't of done what he wanted me to do. So I thought the right thing to do was to go report it, and I went from there to Hillendale to find a police car." (Emphasis supplied.)

How does the majority Opinion view these events? It starts by noting that Pat was a 21-year-old mother who was separated from her husband but not yet divorced, as though that had some significance. To me, it has none, except perhaps (when coupled with the further characterization that Pat and Terry had gone "bar hopping") to indicate an underlying suspicion, for which there is absolutely no support in the record, that Pat was somehow "on the make." Even more alarming, and unwarranted, however, is the majority's analysis of Pat's initial reflections on whether to report what had happened. Ignoring completely her statement that she "didn't want to go through what I'm going through now," the majority, in footnote 1, cavalierly and without any foundation whatever, says:

"If, in quiet contemplation after the act, she had to wonder what would have happened, her submission on the side of prudence seems

---

[6] Pat explained this last comment further: "I didn't know what else to say. I had no intention of meeting him again." [Author's note]

hardly justified. Indeed, if *she* had to wonder afterward, how can a fact finder reasonably conclude that she was justifiably in fear sufficient to overcome her will to resist, at the time." (Emphasis in the original.)

It is this type of reasoning—if indeed "reasoning" is the right word 30 for it—that is particularly distressing. The concern expressed by Pat, made even more real by the majority Opinion of this Court, is one that is common among rape victims, and largely accounts for the fact that most incidents of forcible rape go unreported by the victim. See *F.B.I. Uniform Crime Reports* (1978), p. 14; *Report of Task Force on Rape Control,* Baltimore County (1975); *The Treatment of Rape Victims in the Metropolitan Washington Area,* Metropolitan Washington Council of Governments (1976), p. 4. See also *Rape and Its Victims: A Report for Citizens, Health Facilities, and Criminal Justice Agencies,* LEAA (1975). If appellant had desired, and Pat had given, her wallet instead of her body, there would be no question about appellant's guilt of robbery. Taking the car keys under those circumstances would certainly have supplied the requisite threat of force or violence and negated the element of consent. No one would seriously contend that because she failed to raise a hue and cry she had consented to the theft of her money. Why then is such life-threatening action necessary when it is her personal dignity that is being stolen?

For Journals

What is your understanding of the crime of rape? What are your biases or attitudes toward survivors of rape?

For Discussion

1.   Much of Judge Wilner's argument rests on a clear definition. What is the subject of his definition? What kinds of evidence does he use to substantiate his definition? Which kind is most effective?

2.   Judge Wilner recounts, from the majority opinion, the story of "Pat," the woman who was raped by a man she had met in a bar. Why do you think he did so? What attitude toward her story did he have? What do you infer was the attitude toward Pat's story of the majority justices (who overturned the rape conviction)?

3.   Examine the etching *Keep Within Compass* presented earlier in this chapter. Do you sense any connection between the values and attitudes conveyed in the etching and in this court case? Explain. You could look, for example, at Judge Wilner's comment about the selection of details in the majority opinion, such as that "Pat" was a 21-year-old mother who was separated but not divorced and had gone "bar-hopping" with a friend.

For Writing

1. Judge Wilner's argument refutes the majority opinion in *Rusk* v. *State*. Using discussion item 3 as a starting point, examine the assumptions held by the majority and opposing views, perhaps comparing and contrasting them with the message of the etching.

2. Research the other arguments in this case: the majority opinion in *Rusk* v. *State,* and the arguments in the *State* v. *Rusk* (the original conviction). You could select one argument to analyze in depth, examining types of appeals, use of evidence, or arguments. Or select one particular type of appeal (such as appeal to ethos) and examine the ways in which it is used in the series of arguments.

∽ When "Family" Is Not a Household Word (1988)

KEENAN PECK

Keenan Peck (1960–1990), attorney, activist, and member of The Progressive *editorial board, was educated at the University of Wisconsin where he received his bachelor's degree and law degree. He also served as counsel to Senator Herbert Kohl (D-Wisconsin) and was chair of his local chapter of the American Civil Liberties Union. Peck's articles for* The Progressive *include an exposé of the Federal Emergency Management Agency. Peck, who worked diligently on behalf of human and civil rights, died of an aneurysm at the age of twenty-nine. The article that follows was published in September 1988, also in* The Progressive, *and draws from Peck's personal experience as well as from his research.*

If my friends had been married, the three of us could have lived in peace. Instead, the authorities ordered us to vacate our home. In my neighborhood, it turned out, three unrelated people could not live together legally. Never mind that we were good, quiet neighbors. Never mind that we enjoyed the area. No marriage license, no occupancy. There might as well have been a sign at the end of our street: ALTERNATIVE FAMILIES, KEEP OUT.

I was sharing a three-bedroom house in Madison, Wisconsin, with an unmarried couple—a man and a woman who intended to make a life together but didn't want to get married just yet. Our arrangement was illegal because Madison, like many other cities, prohibits occupancy by more than two unrelated persons in neighborhoods designated for families. It's called "single-family zoning," and it's a pernicious form of discrimination against those in loving but unorthodox relationships.

When Madison told us to move, we sued the city. We argued that the ordinance violated our right to associate with one another. We pointed out that it in no way advanced the admirable goals of residential stability and tranquility. A person's marital status has nothing to do with his or her compatibility with the neighbors, we said. Consanguinity and lawn mowing are not connected. The city should regulate the *use* of dwellings, not the users.

We lost in the trial court (the case is now on appeal), but the experience offered a lesson in civil rights. We discovered that we were part of a growing legal debate over the definition of "family." Increasingly, Americans who live in groupings they regard as families but who are not related by blood, marriage, or adoption are pressing courts, legislatures, and employers for the same rights claimed by traditional families. Although the media have concentrated on the steamy (or contagious) aspects of the sexual revolution, that revolution has also led to a struggle over such mundane but important matters as insurance, housing, and inheritance.

In our case, my roommates and I asserted the simple right to live   5 where and with whom we wanted. But in 1974, the U.S. Supreme Court had held that the Constitution does not stop municipalities from restricting households composed of unrelated persons. The strength of one's rights in these situations turns on the interpretation of each state's constitution by its own judiciary. The high courts of New Jersey, California, New York, and Michigan have used their states' constitutions to protect alternative families; courts in Missouri, New Hampshire, and Hawaii have ruled against nontraditional living arrangements.

To reach their decisions, all of the courts grappled with the same essential questions: When does a household become, in lawyer's jargon, the "functional equivalent" of a family? And should the law treat the functional equivalent the same as the real item? The rise of the alternative family makes it essential to find answers.

The term "alternative family" refers to several kinds of living situations, the most common of which is the unmarried heterosexual couple. In 1980, the year of the last census, some 1.8 million Americans were living as cohabitating couples, a 300 percent increase from the number in 1970. The Census Bureau called them POSSLQs—Persons of Opposite Sex Sharing Living Quarters. According to two University of Wisconsin sociologists, Larry Bumpass and James Sweet, the proportion of persons cohabitating before their first marriage has quadrupled (to 44 percent) over the past two decades.

"Cohabitation has not simply become increasingly common," they said upon the release of their $4.5 million study. "If recent trends continue, it will soon be the majority experience."

"Alternative family" also encompasses gay and lesbian couples and the dependents of all unmarried couples. In all, there are about ten million people in the United States who can be classified as belonging to alternative families, reports Steven Ruggles, a demographer at the University of Minnesota. Looked at from the other side of the numbers, fewer than 30 percent of us live in a traditional nuclear family, defined as a married couple with children.

10   The law has lagged behind changes in our lifestyle. Twenty states have repealed laws against adultery, but cohabitators in some states still live under the threat of prosecution. Only one state, Wisconsin, prohibits discrimination on the basis of sexual orientation, and no state permits persons of the same sex to marry. Thus, gay and lesbian couples are denied the legal benefits of marriage, such as the automatic passing of property to the surviving partner when the other one dies without a will. To make matters worse, the U.S. Supreme Court ruled in 1986 that Georgia could enforce a law against "homosexual sodomy." (Actually, the law prohibited anal intercourse between men and women as well, but the homophobic majority ignored that fact.)

Like state governments, employers and insurance companies often refuse to treat unmarried or unadopted loved ones as family for the purposes of various benefits. A union contract can help, but only if the union is enlightened enough to deal with the problem in the first place.

Law professor Barbara Cox, writing in the *Wisconsin Women's Law Journal,* has catalogued the entitlements that are extended to nuclear families but withheld from alternative families: "They include the opportunity to live in neighborhoods zoned for single families; receive employment-based health insurance, bereavement and sick leave, pensions, moving expenses, library and recreational privileges, and low-cost day care and travel packages; sue for loss of consortium, worker's compensation or unemployment compensation; visit family members in hospitals and authorize their emergency medical treatment; and receive low-cost family rates from organizations such as health clubs, museums, and art centers."

What is the motive for perpetuating such discrimination? In the field of housing, opposition to alternative families is often really bias against college students who, local governments fear, will wreak havoc in communes. This was the unspoken justification for Madison's ordinance, and it figures in much of the litigation over zoning (including the 1974 U.S. Supreme Court case).

College students, to be sure, can put strain on a family-oriented neighborhood. Still, in the words of a recent New Jersey court opinion, students should not be "required to govern their lifestyle to meet the dictates of those who disapprove of their ways." The same judge hinted at another reason behind hostility toward alternative families: the generation gap. People who set rules and policies are likely to hark back to an era when sexual taboos limited alternative living arrangements. And homophobia afflicts politicians and employers, too. Employers and insurance companies, moreover, don't want to spend the money to cover children and lovers who are deemed family in expanded benefits plans.

But there seems to be a more fundamental concern behind the op- 15 position to alternative families—the feeling that the *nuclear* family forms society's bedrock. New types of loving relationships are perceived as a threat to the very order of things. The problem with this objection is that it ignores the negative attributes of nuclear families and the positive characteristics of alternative families. Something in the nuclear family is wrong if almost half of new marriages end in divorce; and what is wrong with an alternative relationship that's lasting and loving?

Steven Ruggles, the Minnesota demographer, found no significant differences between married and unmarried couples "in terms of sat isfaction, commitment, sexual satisfaction, communication, or psychological adjustment." What's more, half of the cohabitants in the University of Wisconsin study married within three years, suggesting that an alternative status is frequently temporary.

A happy or sad, healthy or abusive relationship will not be made less or more so with a marriage certificate. The law should focus on the societal interest, which is in long-term, supportive relationships. Although blood relation, marriage, and adoption have served as useful shorthands for "family," the legal establishment must now find categories that can accommodate new living arrangements without losing all definition.

Two cities have attempted to do so. In Santa Cruz, California, city workers and their loved ones may sign an "Affidavit of Domestic Partnership" to qualify the partners for health benefits. Under penalty of perjury, the two affirm, "We are each other's sole domestic partner and intend to remain so indefinitely and are responsible for our common welfare." The Santa Cruz personnel department indicates that 2 percent of the municipal work force has signed on the dotted line.

In West Hollywood, California, domestic partners can swear out a form indicating that they "share the common necessities of life," "are each other's sole domestic partner," and "agree to be responsible for each other's welfare." In addition to providing benefits for partners of municipal workers, the ordinance also requires hospitals and jails to permit visitation by partners. About 15 percent of the work force has signed up in West Hollywood, which has a large gay population.

Following the example of the California cities, a member of the 20 Madison Common Council proposed a similar plan. Partners would be allowed to file an affidavit with the city stating that they are in a relationship of "mutual support, caring, and commitment." The form would make partners and dependents eligible for the benefits given to nuclear families. Despite the support of the Madison Equal Opportunities Commission, however, the proposal encountered resistance in the usually liberal town. As of this writing, the plan has not been adopted.

When I try to fathom why the Madison plan fell flat—and, for that matter, why the city tried to oust three people from their home—one word comes to mind: fright. The powers that be are frightened by the prospect of yet another unfamiliar constituency demanding legal recognition. In Madison and elsewhere, officials are whispering, "Enough is enough." To them, alternative families don't need to live in family-oriented neighborhoods; gay couples don't need to marry; partners don't need benefits that accrue to their lovers.

By the same token, though, blacks didn't need to ride in the front of the bus; women didn't need membership in formerly all-male clubs; poor people didn't need the vote. But in each of those instances, the aggrieved segment of the population persuaded the rest of us that "equal rights" means what it says. In the coming years, many Americans will be asking for equal rights for the ten million members of alternative families.

In the meantime, I'll be asking for nothing more than the right to live with unmarried friends in a house of my choosing.

For Journals

Should there be regulations about who lives in your neighborhood—about unmarried couples living together, or domestic partners, or groups of unrelated people?

For Discussion

1. Study Peck's introduction. Why do you think he begins with a personal anecdote? With this particular anecdote?

2. What is the fundamental issue in controlling residents based on marital status? How does it relate to society's assumptions about marriage and families? How does it reflect assumptions about nonmarried people living together? Why are the courts involved in this issue? To what extent do society's needs or interests dictate the rules and regulations governing cohabitation?

3. Analyze the support the author uses to convince his readers of his assertion. What types of evidence and appeals seem most convincing? Consider statistics, personal experience, definition, analogy, comparison and contrast, cites to authorities, appeals to emotion and to ethos, or values and beliefs.

4. How does Peck define family? In what ways is it like, or unlike, your own definition of family? On what assumptions is Peck's definition based? On what assumptions is your definition based? What does Peck's community appear to believe about what creates a family? In what ways is Peck's small group like, and unlike, a family?

5. Do you agree with Peck's assertion that laws restricting alternative families exist, in large part, to restrict college students? Or do you believe they are a result of a more pervasive bias or fear in society of non–nuclear family relationships?

6. Are you convinced by Peck's argument that fostering long-term, stable relationships of various kinds is in society's best interest? Would Thomas Stoddard agree? What about Bruce Fein? (Both selections appear later in this chapter.)

For Writing

1. Stoddard and Peck both cite civil rights to support their arguments. Compare and contrast the readings, examining the persuasiveness and appropriateness of the premise that their issues are civil rights issues, keeping in mind their audiences: Stoddard—general readers and lawyers; Fein—lawyers; Peck—the liberal readership of *The Progressive*. (Alternatively, argue that Peck's case is, or is not, a civil rights issue.)

2. Research zoning laws pertaining to group or alternative-family housing in your college community. You could get in touch with city hall offices or other local authorities, or your campus housing office may have such information about the campus and nearby areas. Do the regulations support only traditional nuclear families, or do they allow for alternative arrangements? Write a documented essay based on your findings and share it with your classmates. If your campus housing office does not already have this information, they may be interested in getting a copy of your report.

3. Argue that communities do, or do not, have a right to enforce the kind of restrictions against which Peck is arguing. Examine the assumptions on which you are basing your argument. Be sure to support your assertion with reasons, evidence, and examples.

∞ *Bricklayer's Boy* (1989)

ALFRED LUBRANO

Alfred Lubrano is a reporter for New York Newsday *and is a contributor to* Gentleman's Quarterly, *where this essay originally appeared. Lubrano frequently writes about personal relationships and family life. In the memoir that follows, he writes about the family and work values gained from his blue-collar upbringing and how they are, or are not, reconciled with his adult way of life.*

My father and I were college buddies back in the mid 1970s. While I was in class at Columbia, struggling with the esoterica du jour, he was on a bricklayer's scaffold not far up the street, working on a campus building.

Sometimes we'd hook up on the subway going home, he with his tools, I with my books. We didn't chat much about what went on during the day. My father wasn't interested in Dante, I wasn't up on arches. We'd share a *New York Post* and talk about the Mets.

My dad has built lots of places in New York City he can't get into: colleges, condos, office towers. He makes his living on the outside. Once the walls are up, a place takes on a different feel for him, as if he's not welcome anymore. It doesn't bother him, though. For my father, earning the dough that paid for my entrée into a fancy, bricked-in institution was satisfaction enough, a vicarious access.

We didn't know it then, but those days were the start of a branching off, a redefining of what it means to be a workingman in our family. Related by blood, we're separated by class, my father and I. Being the white-collar son of a blue-collar man means being the hinge on the door between two ways of life.

5   It's not so smooth jumping from Italian old-world style to U.S. yuppie in a single generation. Despite the myth of mobility in America, the true rule, experts say, is rags to rags, riches to riches. According to Bucknell University economist and author Charles Sackrey, maybe 10 percent climb from the working to the professional class. My father has had a tough time accepting my decision to become a mere newspaper reporter, a field that pays just a little more than construction does. He wonders why I haven't cashed in on that multi-brick education and taken on some lawyer-lucrative job. After bricklaying for thirty years, my father promised himself I'd never pile bricks and blocks into walls for a living. He figured an education—genielike and benevolent—would somehow rocket me into the consecrated trajectory of the upwardly mobile, and load some serious loot into my pockets. What he didn't count on was his eldest son breaking blue-collar rule No. 1: Make as much money as you can, to pay for as good a life as you can get.

He'd tell me about it when I was nineteen, my collar already fading to white. I was the college boy who handed him the wrong wrench on help-around-the-house Saturdays. "You better make a lot of money," my blue-collar handy dad wryly warned me as we huddled in front of a disassembled dishwasher I had neither the inclination nor the aptitude to fix. "You're gonna need to hire someone to hammer a nail into a wall for you."

In 1980, after college and graduate school, I was offered my first job, on a now-dead daily paper in Columbus, Ohio. I broke the news in the kitchen, where all the family business is discussed. My mother wept as if it were Vietnam. My father had a few questions: "Ohio? Where the hell is Ohio?"

I said it's somewhere west of New York City, that it was like Pennsylvania, only more so. I told him I wanted to write, and these were the only people who'd take me.

"Why can't you get a good job that pays something, like in advertising in the city, and write on the side?"

"Advertising is lying," I said, smug and sanctimonious, ever the 10 unctuous undergraduate. "I wanna tell the truth."

"The truth?" the old man exploded, his face reddening as it does when he's up twenty stories in high wind. "What's truth?" I said it's real life, and writing about it would make me happy. "You're happy with your family," my father said, spilling blue-collar rule No. 2. "That's what makes you happy. After that, it all comes down to dollars and cents. What gives you comfort besides your family? Money, only money."

During the two weeks before I moved, he reminded me that newspaper journalism is a dying field, and I could do better. Then he pressed advertising again, though neither of us knew anything about it, except that you could work in Manhattan, the borough with the water-beading high gloss, the island polished clean by money. I couldn't explain myself, so I packed, unpopular and confused. No longer was I the good son who studied hard and fumbled endearingly with tools. I was hacking people off.

One night, though, my father brought home some heavy tape and that clear, plastic bubble stuff you pack your mother's second-string dishes in. "You probably couldn't do this right," my father said to me before he sealed the boxes and helped me take them to UPS. "This is what he wants," my father told my mother the day I left for Columbus in my grandfather's eleven-year-old gray Cadillac. "What are you gonna do?" After I said my good-byes, my father took me aside and pressed five $100 bills into my hands. "It's okay," he said over my weak protests. "Don't tell your mother."

When I broke the news about what the paper was paying me, my father suggested I get a part-time job to augment the income. "Maybe you could drive a cab." Once, after I was chewed out by the city editor for something trivial, I made the mistake of telling my father during a visit home. "They pay you nothin', and they push you around too much in that business," he told me, the rage building. "Next time, you gotta grab the guy by the throat and tell him he's a big jerk."

"Dad, I can't talk to the boss like that."   15

"Tell him. You get results that way. Never take any shit." A few years before, a guy didn't like the retaining wall my father and his partner had built. They tore it down and did it again, but the guy still bitched. My father's partner shoved the guy into the freshly laid bricks. "Pay me off," my father said, and he and his partner took the money and walked. Blue-collar guys have no patience for office politics and corporate bile-swallowing. Just pay me off and I'm gone. Eventually, I moved on to a job in Cleveland, on a paper my father has heard of. I think he looks on it as a sign of progress, because he hasn't mentioned advertising for a while.

When he was my age, my father was already dug in with a trade, a wife, two sons and a house in a neighborhood in Brooklyn not far from where he was born. His workaday, family-centered life has been very much in step with his immigrant father's. I sublet what the real-estate people call a junior one-bedroom in a dormlike condo in a Cleveland suburb. Unmarried and unconnected in an insouciant, perpetual-student kind of way, I rent movies during the week and feed single women in restaurants on Saturday nights. My dad asks me about my dates, but he goes crazy over the word "woman." "A girl," he corrects. "You went out with a girl. Don't say 'woman.' It sounds like you're takin' out your grandmother."

I've often believed blue-collaring is the more genuine of lives, in greater proximity to primordial manhood. My father is provider and protector, concerned only with the basics: food and home, love and progeny. He's also a generation closer to the heritage, a warmer spot nearer the fire that forged and defined us. Does heat dissipate and light fade further from the source? I live for my career, and frequently feel lost and codeless, devoid of the blue-collar rules my father grew up with. With no baby-boomer groomer to show me the way, I've been choreographing my own tentative shuffle across the wax-shined dance floor on the edge of the Great Middle Class, a different rhythm in a whole new ballroom.

I'm sure it's tough on my father, too, because I don't know much about bricklaying, either, except that it's hell on the body, a daily sacrifice. I idealized my dad as a kind of dawn-rising priest of labor, engaged in holy ritual. Up at five every day, my father has made a religion of responsibility. My younger brother, a Wall Street white-collar guy with the sense to make a decent salary, says he always felt safe when he heard Dad stir before him, as if Pop were taming the day for us. My father, fifty-five years old, but expected to put out as if he were three decades stronger, slips on machine-washable vestments of khaki cotton without waking my mother. He goes into the kitchen and turns on the radio to catch the temperature. Bricklayers have an occupational need to know the weather. And because I am my father's son, I can recite the five-day forecast at any given moment.

20   My father isn't crazy about this life. He wanted to be a singer and actor when he was young, but that was frivolous doodling to his Italian family, who expected money to be coming in, stoking the stove that kept hearth fires ablaze. Dreams simply were not energy-efficient. My dad learned a trade, as he was supposed to, and settled into a life of pre-scripted routing. He says he can't find the black-and-white publicity glossies he once had made.

Although I see my dad infrequently, my brother, who lives at home, is with the old man every day. Chris has a lot more blue-collar in him than I do, despite his management-level career; for a short time, he wanted to be a construction worker, but my parents persuaded him to go to Columbia. Once in a while he'll bag a lunch and, in a nice wool suit, meet my father at a construction site and share sandwiches of egg salad on semolina bread.

It was Chris who helped my dad most when my father tried to change his life several months ago. My dad wanted a civil-service bricklayer foreman's job that wouldn't be so physically demanding. There was a written test that included essay questions about construction work. My father hadn't done anything like it in forty years. Why the hell they needed bricklayers to write essays I have no idea, but my father sweated it out. Every morning before sunrise, Chris would be ironing a shirt, bleary-eyed, and my father would sit at the kitchen table and read aloud his practice essays on how to wash down a wall, or how to build a tricky corner. Chris would suggest words and approaches.

It was so hard for my dad. He had to take a Stanley Kaplan–like prep course in a junior high school three nights a week after work for six weeks. At class time, the outside men would come in, twenty-five construction workers squeezing themselves into little desks. Tough blue-collar guys armed with No. 2 pencils leaning over and scratching out their practice essays, cement in their hair, tar on their pants, their work boots too big and clumsy to fit under the desks.

"Is this what finals felt like?" my father would ask me on the phone when I pitched in to help long-distance. "Were you always this nervous?" I told him yes. I told him writing's always difficult. He thanked Chris and me for the coaching, for putting him through school this time. My father thinks he did okay, but he's still awaiting the test results. In the meantime, he takes life the blue-collar way, one brick at a time.

When we see each other these days, my father still asks how the money is. Sometimes he reads my stories; usually he likes them, although he recently criticized one piece as being a bit sentimental: "Too schmaltzy," he said. Some psychologists say that the blue-white-collar gap between fathers and sons leads to alienation, but I tend to agree with Dr. Al Baraff, a clinical psychologist and director of the Men-Center in Washington, D.C. "The core of the relationship is based on emotional and hereditary traits," Baraff says. "Class [distinctions] just get added on. If it's a healthful relationship from when you're a kid, there's a respect back and forth that'll continue."

Nice of the doctor to explain, but I suppose I already knew that. Whatever is between my father and me, whatever keeps us talking and keeps us close, has nothing to do with work and economic class.

During one of my visits to Brooklyn not long ago, he and I were in the car, on our way to buy toiletries, one of my father's weekly routines.

25

"You know, you're not as successful as you could be," he began, blue-collar blunt as usual. "You paid your dues in school. You deserve better restaurants, better clothes." Here we go, I thought, the same old stuff. I'm sure every family has five or six similar big issues that are replayed like well-worn videotapes. I wanted to fast-forward this thing when we stopped at a red light.

Just then my father turned to me, solemn and intense. His knees were aching and his back muscles were throbbing in clockable intervals that registered in his eyes. It was the end of a week of lifting fifty-pound blocks. "I envy you," he said quietly. "For a man to do something he likes and get paid for it—that's fantastic." He smiled at me before the light changed, and we drove on. To thank him for the understanding, I sprang for the deodorant and shampoo. For once, my father let me pay.

For Journals

What did you learn from your family, implicitly or explicitly, about class and money?

For Discussion

1.   What is your response to the voice and tone of the essay? Do the author and his family seem like people you would like to meet? Do any of his family members have values that you share?

2.   Lubrano directly addresses issues of class, comparing blue-collar and white-collar lifestyles. What does he suggest is typical of each lifestyle?

3.   The author mentions "blue-collar" rules. What do you think would be his "white-collar" rules? Do the "rules" lead to conflict in this family?

4.   The essay is full of rich language and metaphor. Select some of the more vivid metaphors, and discuss ways in which they underscore and reinforce Lubrano's assertions about values.

5.   What is the myth of mobility discussed in this essay? What is the connection of this myth to class values?

For Writing

1.   Develop your journal writing into a reflective essay on the ways in which your family taught you values, attitudes, and beliefs. You could focus on a specific area, such as work or education.

2. Research and develop an expository essay on the myth of mobility and the notion of "rags to riches." Do you find evidence to support Lubrano's claim that the usual scenario is "rags to rags"?

✑ Marriage Is a Fundamental Right (1989)

THOMAS STODDARD

Thomas Stoddard (1948–) is an attorney and serves as executive director of the Lambda Defense and Education Fund, a gay rights organization. He is the author of The Rights of Gay People *(1983) and frequently speaks out on gay civil rights issues. In the essay that follows, which first appeared in the* New York Times, *Stoddard argues on behalf of a controversial but fundamental issue: the rights of same-gender couples to marry.*

"In sickness and in health, 'til death do us part." With those words, millions of people each year are married, a public affirmation of a private bond that both society and the newlyweds hope will endure. Yet for nearly four years, Karen Thompson was denied the company of the one person to whom she had pledged life-long devotion.

Her partner is a woman, Sharon Kowalski, and their home state of Minnesota, like every other in the United States, refuses to permit same-sex marriages.

Karen Thompson and Sharon Kowalski are spouses in every respect except the legal. They exchanged vows and rings. They lived together until November 13, 1983—when Kowalski, as the result of an automobile accident, was rendered unable to walk and barely able to speak.

Thompson sought a ruling granting her guardianship over her partner, but Kowalski's parents opposed the petition and obtained sole guardianship. They then moved Kowalski to a nursing home 300 miles away from Thompson and forbade all visits between the two women.

In February 1989, in the wake of a reevaluation of Kowalski's mental competence, Thompson was permitted to visit her partner again. But the prolonged injustice and anguish inflicted on both women hold a moral for everyone. 5

Marriage, the Supreme Court declared in 1967 in *Loving* v. *Virginia*, is "one of the basic civil rights of man" (and, presumably, of woman as well). The freedom to marry, said the Court, is "essential to the orderly pursuit of happiness."

Marriage is far more than a symbolic state. It can be the key to survival—emotional and financial. Marriage triggers a universe of rights, privileges and presumptions. In every jurisdiction in this country, a married person can share in a spouse's estate even when there is no will. She typically has access to the group insurance and pension programs offered by the spouse's employer, and she enjoys tax advantages.

The decision whether or not to marry belongs properly to individuals, not to the government. While marriage historically has required a male and a female partner, history alone cannot sanctify injustice.

If tradition were the only measure, most states still would limit matrimony to partners of the same race. As recently as 1967, before the Supreme Court declared in *Loving* that miscegenation statutes are unconstitutional, sixteen states still prohibited marriages between a white person and a black person. When all the excuses were stripped away, it was clear that the only purpose of those laws was to maintain white supremacy.

10   Those who argue against reforming the marriage statutes because they believe that same-sex marriage would be "anti-family" overlook the obvious: Marriage creates families and promotes social stability. In an increasingly loveless world, those who wish to commit themselves to a relationship founded upon devotion should be encouraged, not scorned. Government has no legitimate interest in how that love is expressed.

And it can no longer be argued—if it ever could—that marriage is fundamentally a procreative unit. Otherwise, states would forbid marriage between those who, by reason of age or infertility, cannot have children, as well as those who elect not to.

The case of Sharon Kowalski and Karen Thompson demonstrates that sanctimonious illusions can lead directly to the suffering of others. Denied the right to marry, these women were left to the whims and prejudices of others, and of the law.

It is time for the marriage statutes to incorporate fully the concept of equal protection of the law by extending to the many millions of gay Americans the right to marry.

For Journals

Freewrite for five or ten minutes on your assumptions about or biases toward same-gender marriages or domestic partnerships.

For Discussion

1.   Why do you think Stoddard begins with an anecdote? Why do you think he focuses on women? On the issue of caring for sick loved ones? How does this strategy shift the focus of the debate?

2.   How does Stoddard's introductory strategy counter his readers' assumptions about the issue of gay marriage?

3. Stoddard's assertion is that same-gender marriage is not anti-family, as some have charged, but rather pro-family. Does he adequately counter the anti-family arguments? Does he adequately support his assertions that same-gender marriage "creates families and promotes social stability" (paragraph 10)? In what ways is he transforming traditional definitions of family to do so?

4. What appeals to values and beliefs does Stoddard make? What appeals to emotion? To logic? Which do you find most persuasive?

5. Although this essay was first published in the *New York Times,* a newspaper with a general rather than legal audience, Stoddard (who is an attorney) is comfortable citing legal precedent to support his argument. Do you think his evidence is convincing to a diverse audience? Stoddard's article was later reprinted in the *Journal of the American Bar Association.* Do you think that audience is more, or less, likely to accept the arguments he makes?

For Writing

1. Write a rebuttal to Stoddard, arguing with the specific points he makes, challenging his assumptions or premises, and making any additional points to support the opposing view. You may develop your argument using appeals to ethos, pathos, or logos, or appeals to values and beliefs, to emotion and empathy, to logic and evidence. (See Chapter 1, "Reading and Analyzing Arguments," on ethos, pathos, and logos.) Or you may wish to integrate evidence from outside sources into your arguments. If you do, be sure to read about both sides of the issue and to use your evidence to represent the opposing views fairly and ethically and in accord with the author's intended meaning. (See Chapter 2, "Writing and Research," for additional information on research.)

2. With a peer or in groups, write a dialogue between two people debating this topic or another controversial social issue. Then exchange dialogues with another peer or group. Evaluate the assumptions, premises, and appeals used in the dialogues. Summarize your findings, and share them with your class.

✑ Reserve Marriage for Heterosexuals (1990)

BRUCE FEIN

Bruce Fein, an attorney living in Washington, D.C., is the author of Significant Decisions of the Supreme Court *(1979–1980). He has contributed articles to the* National Review *and* American Legion Magazine. *Fein's article first appeared in the* Journal of the American Bar Association, *which also reprinted the preceding selection by Thomas Stoddard.*

Authorizing the marriage of homosexuals, like sanctioning polygamy, would be unenlightened social policy. The law should reserve the celebration of marriage vows for monogamous male-female attachments to further the goal of psychologically, emotionally and educationally balanced offspring.

As Justice Oliver Wendell Holmes noted, the life of the law has not been logic, it has been experience. Experience confirms that child development is skewed, scarred or retarded when either a father or mother is absent in the household.

In the area of adoption, married couples are favored over singles. The recent preferences for joint child-custody decrees in divorce proceedings tacitly acknowledge the desirability of child intimacies with both a mother and father.

As Supreme Court Justice Byron White recognized in *Taylor* v. *Louisiana* (1975): "[T]he two sexes are not fungible; a community made up exclusively of one is different from a community of both; the subtle interplay of influence one on the other is among the imponderables" (quoting from *Ballard* v. *United States*).

5   A child receives incalculable benefits in the maturing process by the joint instruction, consolation, oversight and love of a father and mother— benefits that are unavailable in homosexual households. The child enjoys the opportunity to understand and respect both sexes in a uniquely intimate climate. The likelihood of gender prejudice is thus reduced, an exceptionally worthy social objective.

The law should encourage male-female marriage vows over homosexual attachments in the interests of physically, mentally, and psychologically healthy children, the nation's most valuable asset.

Crowning homosexual relationships with the solemnity of legal marriage would wrongly send social cues that male-female marriages are not preferable. And there is no constitutional right to homosexual marriage since homosexual sodomy can be criminalized. See *Bowers* v. *Hardwick* (1986).

The fact that some traditional marriages end in fractious divorce, yield no offspring, or result in families with mistreated children does not discredit limiting marriage to monogamous female-male relationships. Anti-polygamy laws are instructive. They seek to discourage female docility, male autocracy, and intra-family rancor and jealousies that are promoted by polygamous marriages. That some might not exhibit such deplorable characteristics is no reason for their repeal or a finding of constitutional infirmity.

To deny the right of homosexual marriage is not an argument for limiting other rights to gays, because of community animosity or vengeance. These are unacceptable policy motivations if law is to be civilized.

Several states and localities protect homosexuals against discrimi- 10
nation in employment or housing. In New York, a state law confers on a homosexual the rent-control benefits of a deceased partner. Other jurisdictions have eschewed special legal rights for homosexuals, and the military excludes them. Experience will adjudge which of the varied legal approaches to homosexual rights has been the most enlightened.

Sober debate over homosexual rights is in short supply. The subject challenges deep-rooted and passionately held images of manhood, womanhood and parenthood, and evokes sublimated fears of community ostracism or degradation.

Each legal issue regarding homosexuality should be examined discretely with the recognition that time has upset many fighting faiths and with the goal of balancing individual liberty against community interests. With regard to homosexual marriage, that balance is negative.

For Journals

Freewrite for five to ten minutes on the assumptions about marriage you had as a child and now have as an adult. How do children fit into the image you have in mind?

For Discussion

1. What kinds of appeals does Fein make? Consider particularly his core assertion: that children will suffer from same-gender marriages. What assumptions about the purpose of marriage does his argument rest on? Is the argument that children are the key consideration in marriage laws one that would be as persuasive to general audiences as Fein believes it will be to lawyers?

2. In addition to citing legal cases, Fein cites authorities such as Oliver Wendell Holmes. But he then states that "experience confirms that child development is skewed, scarred or retarded when either a father or mother is absent in the household" (paragraph 2). Are you persuaded by his citing of "experience"? If not, what additional evidence could he offer that might be more convincing?

3. Fein's overall organizational pattern is direct: he asserts and then supports. How might writing for an audience of lawyers have dictated this pattern? Would it have been equally effective writing for a general audience?

4. Fein also argues by making an analogy to polygamous marriages. How convincing is the analogy? How appropriate is it to the argument?

5.   Fein differentiates and separates this issue from other civil rights issues. Do you accept his premise that marriage rights differ fundamentally from other civil rights?

6.   Examine the logic of Fein's arguments, such as the one in paragraph 7. It may be helpful to outline the premises and conclusion for each argument he makes. Which of his arguments stand up to the analysis? Which ones are weak? Which ones could be strengthened with evidence?

For Writing

1.   Write a letter of rebuttal to Fein. Use a different approach and different arguments than Thomas Stoddard (this chapter) uses in "Marriage Is a Fundamental Right." Keep in mind the biases and assumptions you wrote about in your journal assignment for the Stoddard article.

2.   Compare and contrast Fein's and Stoddard's arguments, focusing on the effectiveness of their appeals, their use of evidence, and their patterns of development. Which argument makes more appeals to emotion? To logic? To traditions, values, beliefs? Keeping in mind your own biases and attitudes toward the topic, which argument seems more sound?

∞ *Blame It on Feminism* (1991)

SUSAN FALUDI

Susan Faludi (1959–) graduated summa cum laude from Harvard University in 1981. Ten years later she won the Pulitzer Prize for an article about the leveraged buyout of Safeway supermarkets and the National Book Critics Circle Award for Backlash: The Undeclared War Against American Women *(1991), an extensive study of the social and political reaction against feminism and women's modest progress toward equal rights. Faludi is a regular contributor to the magazines* Ms. *and* Mother Jones, *and her writing sometimes skeptically examines the status of women in contemporary society. She describes* Backlash *as a book that "arms women with information and a good dose of cynicism," adding, "It's also very large, so it can be thrown at misogynists."*

To be a woman in America at the close of the 20th century—what good fortune. That's what we keep hearing, anyway. The barricades have fallen, politicians assure us. Women have "made it," Madison Avenue cheers. Women's fight for equality has "largely been won," *Time* magazine announces. Enroll at any university, join any law firm, apply for credit at any bank. Women have so many opportunities now, corporate leaders say, that we don't really need equal opportunity policies. Women are so equal now, lawmakers say, that we no longer need an Equal Rights Amendment. Women have "so much," former President Ronald Reagan says, that the White House no longer needs to appoint them to higher office. Even American Express ads are saluting a woman's freedom to charge it. At last, women have received their full citizenship papers.

And yet . . .

Behind this celebration of the American woman's victory, behind the news, cheerfully and endlessly repeated, that the struggle for women's rights is won, another message flashes. You may be free and equal now, it says to women, but you have never been more miserable.

This bulletin of despair is posted everywhere—at the newsstand, on the TV set, at the movies, in advertisements and doctors' offices and academic journals. Professional women are suffering "burnout" and succumbing to an "infertility epidemic." Single women are grieving from a "man shortage." The *New York Times* reports: Childless women are "depressed and confused" and their ranks are swelling. *Newsweek* says: Unwed women are "hysterical" and crumbling under a "profound crisis of confidence." The health advice manuals inform: High-powered career women are stricken with unprecedented outbreaks of "stress-induced disorders," hair loss, bad nerves, alcoholism, and even heart attacks. The psychology books advise: Independent women's loneliness represents "a major mental health problem today." Even founding feminist Betty Friedan has been spreading the word: she warns that women now suffer from a new identity crisis and "new 'problems that have no name.'"

How can American women be in so much trouble at the same time 5 that they are supposed to be so blessed? If the status of women has never been higher, why is their emotional state so low? If women got what they asked for, what could possibly be the matter now?

The prevailing wisdom of the past decade has supported one, and only one, answer to this riddle: it must be all that equality that's causing all that pain. Women are unhappy precisely *because* they are free. Women are enslaved by their own liberation. They have grabbed at the gold ring of independence, only to miss the one ring that really matters. They have gained control of their fertility, only to destroy it. They have pursued their own professional dreams—and lost out on the greatest female adventure. The women's movement, as we are told time and again, has proved women's own worst enemy.

"In dispensing its spoils, women's liberation has given my generation high incomes, our own cigarette, the option of single parenthood, rape crisis centers, personal lines of credit, free love, and female gynecologists," Mona Charen, a young law student, writes in the *National Review,* in an article titled "The Feminist Mistake." "In return it has effectively robbed us of one thing upon which the happiness of most women rests—men." The *National Review* is a conservative publication, but such charges against the women's movement are not confined to its pages. "Our generation was the human sacrifice" to the women's movement, *Los Angeles Times* feature writer Elizabeth Mehren contends in a *Time* cover story. Baby-boom women like her, she says, have been duped by feminism: "We believed the rhetoric." In *Newsweek,* writer Kay Ebeling dubs feminism "the Great Experiment That Failed" and asserts "women in my generation, its perpetrators, are the casualties." Even the beauty magazines are saying it: *Harper's Bazaar* accuses the women's movement of having "lost us [women] ground instead of gaining it."

In the last decade, publications from the *New York Times* to *Vanity Fair* to the *Nation* have issued a steady stream of indictments against the women's movement, with such headlines as WHEN FEMINISM FAILED, OR THE AWFUL TRUTH ABOUT WOMEN'S LIB. They hold the campaign for women's equality responsible for nearly every woe besetting women, from mental depression to meager savings accounts, from teenage suicides to eating disorders to bad complexions. The "Today" show says women's liberation is to blame for bag ladies. A guest columnist in the *Baltimore Sun* even proposes that feminists produced the rise in slasher movies. By making the "violence" of abortion more acceptable, the author reasons, women's rights activists made it all right to show graphic murders on screen.

At the same time, other outlets of popular culture have been forging the same connection: in Hollywood films, of which *Fatal Attraction* is only the most famous, emancipated women with condominiums of their own slink wild-eyed between bare walls, paying for their liberty with an empty bed, a barren womb. "My biological clock is ticking so loud it keeps me awake at night," Sally Field cries in the film *Surrender,* as, in an all too common transformation in the cinema of the '80s, an actress who once played scrappy working heroines is now showcased groveling for a groom. In prime-time television shows, from *thirtysomething* to *Family Man,* single, professional, and feminist women are humiliated, turned into harpies, or hit by nervous breakdowns; the wise ones recant their independent ways by the closing sequence. In popular novels, from Gail Parent's *A Sign of the Eighties* to Stephen King's *Misery,* unwed women shrink to sniveling spinsters or inflate to fire-breathing she-devils; renouncing all aspirations but marriage, they beg for wedding bands from strangers or swing axes at reluctant bachelors. We "blew it by waiting," a typically remorseful careerist sobs in Freda Bright's *Singular Women;* she and her sister professionals are "condemned to be childless forever." Even Erica Jong's high-flying independent heroine literally crashes by the end of the decade, as the author supplants *Fear of Flying*'s saucy Isadora Wing, a symbol of female sexual emancipation in the '70s, with an embittered careerist-turned-recovering-"co-dependent" in *Any Woman's Blues*—a book that is intended, as the narrator bluntly states, "to demonstrate what a deadend the so-called sexual revolution had become, and how desperate so-called free women were in the last few years of our decadent epoch."

Popular psychology manuals peddle the same diagnosis for con- 10 temporary female distress. "Feminism, having promised her a stronger sense of her own identity, has given her little more than an identity *crisis*," the best-selling advice manual *Being a Woman* asserts. The authors of the era's self-help classic *Smart Women/Foolish Choices* proclaim that women's distress was "an unfortunate consequence of feminism," because "it created a myth among women that the apex of self-realization could be achieved only through autonomy, independence, and career."

In the Reagan and Bush years, government officials have needed no prompting to endorse this thesis. Reagan spokeswoman Faith Whittlesey declared feminism a "straitjacket" for women, in the White House's only policy speech on the status of the American female population—entitled "Radical Feminism in Retreat." Law enforcement officers and judges, too, have pointed a damning finger at feminism, claiming that they can chart a path from rising female independence to rising female pathology. As a California sheriff explained it to the press, "Women are enjoying a lot more freedom now, and as a result, they are committing more crimes." The U.S. Attorney General's Commission on Pornography even proposed that women's professional advancement might be responsible for rising rape rates. With more women in college and at work now, the commission members reasoned in their report, women just have more opportunities to be raped.

Some academics have signed on to the consensus, too—and they are the "experts" who have enjoyed the highest profiles on the media circuit. On network news and talk shows, they have advised millions of women that feminism has condemned them to "a lesser life." Legal scholars have railed against "the equality trap." Sociologists have claimed that "feminist-inspired" legislative reforms have stripped women of special "protections." Economists have argued that well-paid working women have created "a less stable American family." And demographers, with greatest fanfare, have legitimated the prevailing wisdom with so-called neutral data on sex ratios and fertility trends; they say they actually have the numbers to prove that equality doesn't mix with marriage and motherhood.

Finally, some "liberated" women themselves have joined the lamentations. In confessional accounts, works that invariably receive a hearty greeting from the publishing industry, "recovering Superwomen" tell all. In *The Cost of Loving: Women and the New Fear of Intimacy,* Megan

Marshall, a Harvard-pedigreed writer, asserts that the feminist "Myth of Independence" has turned her generation into unloved and unhappy fast-trackers, "dehumanized" by careers and "uncertain of their gender identity." Other diaries of mad Superwomen charge that "the hard-core feminist viewpoint," as one of them puts it, has relegated educated executive achievers to solitary nights of frozen dinners and closet drinking. The triumph of equality, they report, has merely given women hives, stomach cramps, eye-twitching disorders, even comas.

But what "equality" are all these authorities talking about?

15   If American women are so equal, why do they represent two-thirds of all poor adults? Why are more than 80 percent of full-time working women making less than $20,000 a year, nearly double the male rate? Why are they still far more likely than men to live in poor housing and receive no health insurance, and twice as likely to draw no pension? Why does the average working woman's salary still lag as far behind the average man's as it did twenty years ago? Why does the average female college graduate today earn less than a man with no more than a high school diploma (just as she did in the '50s)—and why does the average female high school graduate today earn less than a male high school dropout? Why do American women, in fact, face the worst gender-based pay gap in the developed world?

If women have "made it," then why are nearly 80 percent of working women still stuck in traditional "female" jobs—as secretaries, administrative "support" workers and salesclerks? And, conversely, why are they less than 8 percent of all federal and state judges, less than 6 percent of all law partners, and less than one half of 1 percent of top corporate managers? Why are there only three female state governors, two female U.S. senators, and two Fortune 500 chief executives? Why are only nineteen of the four thousand corporate officers and directors women—and why do more than half the boards of Fortune 500 companies still lack even one female member?

If women "have it all," then why don't they have the most basic requirements to achieve equality in the work force? Unlike virtually all other industrialized nations, the U.S. government still has no family-leave and child care programs—and more than 99 percent of American private employers don't offer child care either. Though business leaders say they are aware of and deplore sex discrimination, corporate America has yet to make an honest effort toward eradicating it. In a 1990 national poll of chief executives at Fortune 1000 companies, more than 80 percent acknowledged that discrimination impedes female employees' progress—yet, less than 1 percent of these same companies regarded *remedying* sex discrimination as a goal that their personnel departments should pursue. In fact, when the companies' human resource officers were asked to rate their department's priorities, women's advancement ranked last.

If women are so "free," why are their reproductive freedoms in greater jeopardy today than a decade earlier? Why do women who want to postpone childbearing now have fewer options than ten years ago? The availability of different forms of contraception has declined, research for new birth control has virtually halted, new laws restricting abortion—or even *information* about abortion—for young and poor women have been passed, and the U.S. Supreme Court has shown little ardor in defending the right it granted in 1973.

Nor is women's struggle for equal education over; as a 1989 study found, three-fourths of all high schools still violate the federal law banning sex discrimination in education. In colleges, undergraduate women receive only 70 percent of the aid undergraduate men get in grants and work-study jobs—and women's sports programs receive a pittance compared with men's. A review of state equal-education laws in the late '80s found that only thirteen states had adopted the minimum provisions required by the federal Title IX law—and only seven states had anti-discrimination regulations that covered all education levels.

Nor do women enjoy equality in their own homes, where they still 20 shoulder 70 percent of the household duties—and the only major change in the last fifteen years is that now middle-class men *think* they do more around the house. (In fact, a national poll finds the ranks of women saying their husbands share equally in child care shrunk to 31 percent in 1987 from 40 percent three years earlier.) Furthermore, in thirty states, it is still generally legal for husbands to rape their wives; and only ten states have laws mandating arrest for domestic violence— even though battering was the leading cause of injury of women in the late '80s. Women who have no other option but to flee find that isn't much of an alternative either. Federal funding for battered women's shelters has been withheld and one third of the 1 million battered women who seek emergency shelter each year can find none. Blows from men contributed far more to the rising numbers of "bag ladies" than the ill effects of feminism. In the '80s, almost half of all homeless women (the fastest growing segment of the homeless) were refugees of domestic violence.

The word may be that women have been "liberated," but women themselves seem to feel otherwise. Repeatedly in national surveys, majorities of women say they are still far from equality. Nearly 70 percent of women polled by the *New York Times* in 1989 said the movement for women's rights had only just begun. Most women in the 1990 Virginia Slims opinion poll agreed with the statement that conditions for their sex in American society had improved "a little, not a lot." In poll after poll in the decade, overwhelming majorities of women said they needed equal pay and equal job opportunities, they needed an Equal Rights Amendment, they needed the right to an abortion without government interference, they needed a federal law guaranteeing maternity leave, they needed decent child care services. They have none of these. So how exactly have we "won" the war for women's rights?

Seen against this background, the much ballyhooed claim that feminism is responsible for making women miserable becomes absurd—and irrelevant. . . . The afflictions ascribed to feminism are all myths. From "the man shortage" to "the infertility epidemic" to "female burnout" to "toxic day care," these so-called female crises have had their origins not in the actual conditions of women's lives but rather in a closed system that starts and ends in the media, popular culture, and advertising—an endless feedback loop that perpetuates and exaggerates its own false images of womanhood.

Women themselves don't single out the women's movement as the source of their misery. To the contrary, in national surveys 75 to 95 percent of women credit the feminist campaign with *improving* their lives, and a similar proportion say that the women's movement should keep pushing for change. Less than 8 percent think the women's movement might have actually made their lot worse.

What actually is troubling the American female population, then? If the many ponderers of the Woman Question really wanted to know, they might have asked their subjects. In public opinion surveys, women consistently rank their own *inequality*, at work and at home, among their most urgent concerns. Over and over, women complain to pollsters about a lack of economic, not marital, oppportunities; they protest that working men, not working women, fail to spend time in the nursery and the kitchen. The Roper Organization's survey analysts find that men's opposition to equality is "a major cause of resentment and stress" and "a major irritant for most women today." It is justice for their gender, not wedding rings and bassinets, that women believe to be in desperately short supply. When the *New York Times* polled women in 1989 about "the most important problem facing women today," job discrimination was the overwhelming winner; none of the crises the media and popular culture had so assiduously promoted even made the charts. In the 1990 Virginia Slims poll, women were most upset by their lack of money, followed by the refusal of their men to shoulder child care and domestic duties. By contrast, when the women were asked where the quest for a husband or the desire to hold a "less pressured" job or to stay at home ranked on their list of concerns, they placed them at the bottom.

25   As the last decade ran its course, women's unhappiness with inequality only mounted. In national polls, the ranks of women protesting discriminatory treatment in business, political, and personal life climbed sharply. The proportion of women complaining of unequal employment opportunities jumped more than ten points from the '70s, and the number of women complaining of unequal barriers to job ad-

vancement climbed even higher. By the end of the decade, 80 percent to 95 percent of women said they suffered from job discrimination and unequal pay. Sex discrimination charges filed with the Equal Employment Opportunity Commission rose nearly 25 percent in the Reagan years, and charges of general harassment directed at working women climbed 208 percent. In the decade, complaints of sexual harassment jumped 70 percent. At home, a much increased proportion of women complained to pollsters of male mistreatment, unequal relationships, and male efforts to, in the words of the Virginia Slims poll, "keep women down." The share of women in the Roper surveys who agreed that men were "basically kind, gentle, and thoughtful" fell from almost 70 percent in 1970 to 50 percent by 1990. And outside their homes, women felt more threatened, too: in the 1990 Virginia Slims poll, 72 percent of women said they felt "more afraid and uneasy on the streets today" than they did a few years ago. Lest this be attributed only to a general rise in criminal activity, by contrast only 49 percent of men felt this way.

While the women's movement has certainly made women more cognizant of their own inequality, the rising chorus of female protest shouldn't be written off as feminist-induced "oversensitivity." The monitors that serve to track slippage in women's status have been working overtime since the early '80s. Government and private surveys are showing that women's already vast representation in the lowliest occupations is rising, their tiny presence in higher-paying trade and craft jobs stalled or backsliding, their minuscule representation in upper management posts stagnant or falling, and their pay dropping in the very occupations where they have made the most "progress." The status of women lowest on the income ladder has plunged most perilously; government budget cuts in the first four years of the Reagan administration alone pushed nearly 2 million female-headed families and nearly 5 million women below the poverty line. And the prime target of government rollbacks has been one sex only: one-third of the Reagan budget cuts, for example, came out of programs that predominantly serve women—even more extraordinary when one considers that all these programs combined represent only 10 percent of the federal budget.

The alarms aren't just going off in the work force. In national politics, the already small numbers of women in both elective posts and political appointments fell during the '80s. In private life, the average amount that a divorced man paid in child support fell by about 25 percent from the late '70s to the mid '80s (to a mere $140 a month). Domestic-violence shelters recorded a more than 100 percent increase in the numbers of women taking refuge in their quarters between 1983 and 1987. And government records chronicled a spectacular rise in sexual violence against women. Reported rapes more than doubled from the early '70s—at nearly twice the rate of all other violent crimes and four times the overall crime rate in the United States. While the homicide rate declined, sex-related murders rose 160 percent between 1976 and 1984. And these murders weren't simply the random, impersonal by-product of a violent society; at least one-third of the women were killed by their husbands or boyfriends, and the majority of that group were murdered just after declaring their independence in the most intimate manner—by filing for divorce and leaving home.

By the end of the decade, women were starting to tell pollsters that they feared their sex's social status was once again beginning to slip. They believed they were facing an "erosion of respect," as the 1990 Virginia Slims poll summed up the sentiment. After years in which an increasing percentage of women had said their status had improved from a decade earlier, the proportion suddenly shrunk by 5 percent in the last half of the '80s, the Roper Organization reported. And it fell most sharply among women in their thirties—the age group most targeted by the media and advertisers—dropping about ten percentage points between 1985 and 1990.

Some women began to piece the picture together. In the 1989 *New York Times* poll, more than half of black women and one-fourth of white women put it into words. They told pollsters they believed men were now trying to retract the gains women had made in the last twenty years. "I wanted more autonomy," was how one woman, a thirty-seven-year-old nurse, put it. And her estranged husband "wanted to take it away."

30   The truth is that the last decade has seen a powerful counterassault on women's rights, a backlash, an attempt to retract the handful of small and hard-won victories that the feminist movement did manage to win for women. This counterassault is largely insidious: in a kind of pop-culture version of the Big Lie, it stands the truth boldly on its head and proclaims that the very steps that have elevated women's position have actually led to their downfall.

The backlash is at once sophisticated and banal, deceptively "progressive" and proudly backward. It deploys both the "new" findings of "scientific research" and the dime-store moralism of yesteryear; it turns into media sound bites both the glib pronouncements of pop-psych trend-watchers and the frenzied rhetoric of New Right preachers. The backlash has succeeded in framing virtually the whole issue of women's rights in its own language. Just as Reaganism shifted political discourse far to the right and demonized liberalism, so the backlash convinced the public that women's "liberation" was the true contemporary American scourge—the source of an endless laundry list of personal, social, and economic problems.

But what has made women unhappy in the last decade is not their "equality"—which they don't yet have—but the rising pressure to halt, and even reverse, women's quest for that equality. The "man shortage" and the "infertility epidemic" are not the price of liberation; in fact, they do not even exist. But these chimeras are the chisels of a society-wide backlash. They are part of a relentless whittling-down process—much of it amounting to outright propaganda—that has served to stir women's private anxieties and break their political wills. Identifying feminism as women's enemy only furthers the ends of a backlash against women's equality, simultaneously deflecting attention from the backlash's central role and recruiting women to attack their own cause.

Some social observers may well ask whether the current pressures on women actually constitute a backlash—or just a continuation of American society's long-standing resistance to women's rights. Certainly hostility to female independence has always been with us. But if fear and loathing of feminism is a sort of perpetual viral condition in our culture, it is not always in an acute stage; its symptoms subside and resurface periodically. And it is these episodes of resurgence, such as the one we face now, that can accurately be termed "backlashes" to women's advancement. If we trace these occurrences in American history . . . , we find such flare-ups are hardly random; they have always been triggered by the perception—accurate or not—that women are making great strides. These outbreaks are backlashes because they have always arisen in reaction to women's "progress," caused not simply by a bedrock of misogyny but by the specific efforts of contemporary women to improve their status, efforts that have been interpreted time and again by men—especially men grappling with real threats to their economic and social well-being on other fronts—as spelling their own masculine doom.

The most recent round of backlash first surfaced in the late '70s on the fringes, among the evangelical right. By the early '80s, the fundamentalist ideology had shouldered its way into the White House. By the mid '80s, as resistance to women's rights acquired political and social acceptability, it passed into the popular culture. And in every case, the timing coincided with signs that women were believed to be on the verge of breakthrough.

Just when women's quest for equal rights seemed closest to achieving its objectives, the backlash struck it down. Just when a "gender gap" at the voting booth surfaced in 1980, and women in politics began to talk of capitalizing on it, the Republican party elevated Ronald Reagan and both political parties began to shunt women's rights off their platforms. Just when support for feminism and the Equal Rights Amendment reached a record high in 1981, the amendment was defeated the following year. Just when women were starting to mobilize against battering and sexual assaults, the federal government stalled funding for battered-women's programs, defeated bills to fund shelters, and shut down its Office of Domestic Violence—only two years after opening it in 1979. Just when record numbers of younger women were supporting feminist goals in the mid '80s (more of them, in fact, than older women) and a majority of all women were calling themselves feminists, the media declared the advent of a younger "postfeminist generation" that supposedly reviled the women's movement. Just when women racked up their largest percentage ever supporting the right to abortion, the U.S. Supreme Court moved toward reconsidering it.

In other words, the antifeminist backlash has been set off not by women's achievement of full equality but by the increased possibility that they might win it. It is a preemptive strike that stops women long before they reach the finish line. "A backlash may be an indication that women really have had an effect," feminist psychiatrist Dr. Jean Baker Miller has written, "but backlashes occur when advances have been small, before changes are sufficient to help many people. . . . It is almost as if the leaders of backlashes use the fear of change as a threat before major change has occurred." In the last decade, some women did make substantial advances before the backlash hit, but millions of others were left behind, stranded. Some women now enjoy the right to legal abortion—but not the 44 million women, from the indigent to the military work force, who depend on the federal government for their medical care. Some women can now walk into high-paying professional careers—but not the more than 19 million still in the typing pools or behind the department store sales counters. (Contrary to popular myth about the "have-it-all" baby-boom women, the largest percentage of women in this generation remain typists and clerks.)

As the backlash has gathered force, it has cut off the few from the many—and the few women who have advanced seek to prove, as a social survival tactic, that they aren't so interested in advancment after all. Some of them parade their defection from the women's movement, while their working-class peers founder and cling to the splintered remains of the feminist cause. While a very few affluent and celebrity women who are showcased in news articles boast about having "found my niche as Mrs. Andy Mill" and going home to "bake bread," the many working-class women appeal for their economic rights—flocking to unions in record numbers, striking on their own for pay equity and establishing their own fledgling groups for working women's rights. In 1986, while 41 percent of upper-income women were claiming in the Gallup poll that they were not feminists, only 26 percent of low-income women were making the same claim.

Women's advances and retreats are generally described in military terms; battles won, battles lost, points and territory gained and surrendered. The metaphor of combat is not without its merits in this context and, clearly, the same sort of martial accounting and vocabulary is already surfacing here. But by imagining the conflict as two battalions neatly arrayed on either side of the line, we miss the entangled nature, the locked embrace, of a "war" between women and the male culture they inhabit. We miss the reactive nature of a backlash, which, by definition, can exist only in response to another force.

In times when feminism is at a low ebb, women assume the reactive role—privately and most often covertly struggling to assert themselves against the dominant cultural tide. But when feminism itself becomes the tide, the opposition doesn't simply go along with the reversal: it digs in its heels, brandishes its fists, builds walls and dams. And its resistance creates countercurrents and treacherous undertows.

The force and furor of the backlash churn beneath the surface, 40 largely invisible to the public eye. On occasion in the last decade, they have burst into view. We have seen New Right politicians condemn women's independence, antiabortion protesters fire-bomb women's clinics, fundamentalist preachers damn feminists as "whores" and "witches." Other signs of the backlash's wrath, by their sheer brutality, can push their way into public consciousness for a time—the sharp increase in rape, for example, or the rise in pornography that depicts extreme violence against women.

More subtle indicators in popular culture may receive momentary, and often bemused, media notice, then quickly slip from social awareness: A report, for instance, that the image of women on prime-time TV shows has suddenly degenerated. A survey of mystery fiction finding the numbers of female characters tortured and mutilated mysteriously multiplying. The puzzling news that, as one commentator put it, "So many hit songs have the B-word [bitch] to refer to women that some rap music seems to be veering toward rape music." The ascendancy of virulently misogynist comics like Andrew Dice Clay—who called women "pigs" and "sluts" and strutted in films in which women were beaten, tortured, and blown up—or radio hosts like Rush Limbaugh, whose broadsides against "femi-Nazi" feminists made his syndicated program the most popular radio talk show in the nation. Or word that in 1987, the American Women in Radio & Television couldn't award its annual prize for ads that feature women positively: it could find no ad that qualified.

These phenomena are all related, but that doesn't mean they are somehow coordinated. The backlash is not a conspiracy, with a council dispatching agents from some central control room, nor are the people who serve its ends often aware of their role: some even consider themselves feminists. For the most part, its workings are encoded and internalized, diffuse and chameleonic. Not all of the manifestations of the backlash are of equal weight or significance either; some are mere ephemera, generated by a culture machine that is always scrounging for a "fresh" angle. Taken as a whole, however, these codes and cajolings, these whispers and threats and myths, move overwhelmingly in one direction: they try to push women back into their "acceptable" roles—whether as Daddy's girl or fluttery romantic, active nester or passive love object.

Although the backlash is not an organized movement, that doesn't make it any less destructive. In fact, the lack of orchestration, the absence of a single string-puller, only makes it harder to see—and perhaps more effective. A backlash against women's rights succeeds to the degree that it appears *not* to be political, that it appears not to be a struggle at all. It is most powerful when it goes private, when it lodges inside a woman's mind and turns her vision inward, until she imagines the pressure is all in her head, until she begins to enforce the backlash, too—on herself.

In the last decade, the backlash has moved through the culture's secret chambers, traveling through passageways of flattery and fear. Along the way, it has adopted disguises: a mask of mild derision or the painted face of deep "concern." Its lips profess pity for any woman who won't fit the mold, while it tries to clamp the mold around her ears. It pursues a divide-and-conquer strategy: single versus married women, working women versus homemakers, middle- versus working-class. It manipulates a system of rewards and punishments, elevating women who follow its rules, isolating those who don't. The backlash remarkets old myths about women as new facts and ignores all appeals to reason. Cornered, it denies its own existence, points an accusatory finger at feminism, and burrows deeper underground.

45   *Backlash* happens to be the title of a 1947 Hollywood movie in which a man frames his wife for a murder he's committed. The backlash against women's rights works in much the same way: its rhetoric charges feminists with all the crimes it perpetrates. The backlash line blames the women's movement for the "feminization of poverty"—while the backlash's own instigators in Washington pushed through the budget cuts that helped impoverish millions of women, fought pay equity proposals, and undermined equal opportunity laws. The backlash line claims the women's movement cares nothing for children's rights—while its own representatives in the capital and state legislatures have blocked one bill after another to improve child care, slashed billions of dollars in federal aid for children, and relaxed state licensing standards for day care centers. The backlash line accuses the women's movement of creating a generation of unhappy single and childless women—but its purveyors in the media are the ones guilty of making single and childless women feel like circus freaks.

To blame feminism for women's "lesser life" is to miss entirely the point of feminism, which is to win women a wider range of experience. Feminism remains a pretty simple concept, despite repeated—and enormously effective—efforts to dress it up in greasepaint and turn its proponents into gargoyles. As Rebecca West wrote sardonically in 1913, "I myself have never been able to find out precisely what feminism is: I only know that people call me a feminist whenever I express sentiments that differentiate me from a doormat."

The meaning of the word "feminist" has not really changed since it first appeared in a book review in the *Athenaeum* of April 27, 1895, describing a woman who "has in her the capacity of fighting her way back to independence." It is the basic proposition that, as Nora put it in Ibsen's *A Doll's House* a century ago, "Before everything else I'm a human being." It is the simply worded sign hoisted by a little girl in the 1970 Women's Strike for Equality: I AM NOT A BARBIE DOLL. Feminism asks the world to recognize at long last that women aren't decorative ornaments, worthy vessels, members of a "special-interest group." They are half (in fact, now more than half) of the national population, and just as deserving of rights and opportunities, just as capable of participating in the world's events, as the other half. Feminism's agenda is basic: It asks that women not be forced to "choose" between public justice and private happiness. It asks that women be free to define themselves—instead of having their identity defined for them, time and again, by their culture and their men.

The fact that these are still such incendiary notions should tell us that American women have a way to go before they enter the promised land of equality.

For Journals

How do you define the term *feminism*?

For Discussion

1. According to Faludi, what is the real reason for women's unhappiness in contemporary American society? What role do men play in this reason?

2. Reread the first two paragraphs of the selection. In what ways does the introduction set the approach, direction, and tone for the rest of the argument?

3. Faludi's basic assertion is that there has been a backlash, or resistance, against gains in women's rights. Examine her key points and supporting evidence. Are you persuaded by her assertions and her supporting evidence that there is, indeed, a backlash? Explain the reasons for your answer.

4. What are the implications for the American family of what Faludi is discussing? For example, she cites recent reports in the popular press about a "man shortage," an "infertility epidemic," and "hysterical" unwed women (paragraph 4). To what degree are concerns about the future and stability of families feeding the backlash? Do you think those fears are unfounded or appropriate?

5. Faludi cites a range of sources, first to summarize the backlash argument that it is "all that equality that's causing all the pain" (paragraph 6) and then to question what "equality" is under discussion. Analyze Faludi's use of statistics and sources, in both her representation of the opposing view and in support of her own assertions.

6. Faludi cites Mona Charen, writing in the conservative *National Review,* who says that feminism has effectively "robbed us of one thing upon which the happiness of most women rests—men" (paragraph 7). Do you think a male writer would be likely to make such an assertion about feminism?

For Writing

1. Write a dialogue between Faludi and either the originator of *Keep Within Compass* or Charles Atlas, asserting arguments consistent with each person's position and refuting the opposing view in the way you think each one might. Considering the various viewpoints represented in the chapter, to what degree have the arguments over women's and men's roles changed over the years?

2. The author cites Rebecca West, who wrote in 1913 that "people call me a feminist whenever I express sentiments that differentiate me from a doormat" (paragraph 46). Drawing from your journal writings, this article, other readings you have done, or conversations and experiences you have had, define what you mean by "feminist" and argue that feminism is, or is not, ultimately beneficial to women, men, and families.

∞ *A Family Legacy* (1992)

MARIAN WRIGHT EDELMAN

Marian Wright Edelman (1939–), attorney and founding president of the Children's Defense Fund, is one of five children of a Baptist minister. She graduated from Spelman College, a historically black institution, and Yale Law School; she was the first woman to pass the state bar exam in Mississippi. Edelman has spent her professional life as an activist for disadvantaged Americans, especially children. She has received many honors and awards, and her writings include Children out of School in America *(1974),* Black and White Children in America *(1980), and* Families in Peril: An Agenda for Social Change *(1987). The essay that follows is the first chapter of her book* The Measure of Our Success: A Letter to My Children and Yours.

South Carolina is my home state and I am the aunt, granddaughter, daughter, and sister of Baptist ministers. Service was as essential a part of my upbringing as eating and sleeping and going to school. The church was a hub of Black children's social existence, and caring Black adults were buffers against the segregated and hostile outside world that told us we weren't important. But our parents said it wasn't so, our teachers said it wasn't so, and our preachers said it wasn't so. The message of my racially segregated childhood was clear: let no man or woman look down on you, and look down on no man or woman.

We couldn't play in public playgrounds or sit at drugstore lunch counters and order a Coke, so Daddy built a playground and canteen behind the church. In fact, whenever he saw a need, he tried to respond. There were no Black homes for the aged in Bennettsville, so he began one across the street for which he and Mama and we children cooked and served and cleaned. And we children learned that it was our responsibility to take care of elderly family members and neighbors, and that everyone was our neighbor. My mother carried on the home after Daddy died, and my brother Julian has carried it on to this day behind our church since our mother's death in 1984.

Finding another child in my room or a pair of my shoes gone was far from unusual, and twelve foster children followed my sister and me and three brothers as we left home.

Child-rearing and parental work were inseparable. I went everywhere with my parents and was under the watchful eye of members of the congregation and community who were my extended parents. They kept me when my parents went out of town, they reported on and chided me when I strayed from the straight and narrow of community expectations, and they basked in and supported my achievements when I did well. Doing well, they made clear, meant high academic achievement, playing piano in Sunday school or singing or participating in other church activities, being helpful to somebody, displaying good manners (which is nothing more than consideration toward others), and reading. My sister Olive reminded me recently that the only time our father would not give us a chore ("Can't you find something constructive to do?" was his most common refrain) was when we were reading. So we all read a lot! We learned early what our parents and extended community "parents" valued. Children were taught—not by sermonizing, but by personal example—that nothing was too lowly to do. I remember a debate my parents had when I was eight or nine as to whether I was too young to go with my older brother, Harry, to help clean the bed and bedsores of a very sick, poor woman. I went and learned just how much the smallest helping hands and kindness can mean to a person in need.

The ugly external voices of my small-town, segregated childhood 5 (as a very young child I remember standing and hearing former South Carolina Senator James Byrnes railing on the local courthouse lawn about how Black children would never go to school with whites) were tempered by the internal voices of parental and community expectation and pride. My father and I waited anxiously for the *Brown* v. *Board of Education* decision in 1954. We talked about it and what it would mean for my future and for the future of millions of other Black children. He died the week before *Brown* was decided. But I and other children lucky enough to have caring and courageous parents and other adult role models were able, in later years, to walk through the new and heavy doors that *Brown* slowly and painfully opened—doors that some are trying to close again today.

The adults in our churches and community made children feel valued and important. They took time and paid attention to us. They struggled to find ways to keep us busy. And while life was often hard and resources scarce, we always knew who we were and that the measure of our worth was inside our heads and hearts and not outside in our possessions or on our backs. We were told that the world had a lot of problems; that Black people had an extra lot of problems, but that we were able and obligated to struggle and change them; that being poor was no excuse for not achieving; and that extra intellectual and material gifts brought with them the privilege and responsibility of sharing with others less fortunate. In sum, we learned that service is the rent we pay for living. It is the very purpose of life and not something you do in your spare time.

When my mother died, an old white man in my hometown of Bennettsville asked me what I do. In a flash I realized that in my work at the Children's Defense Fund I do exactly what my parents did—just on a different scale. My brother preached a wonderful sermon at Mama's funeral, but the best tribute was the presence in the back pew of the town drunk, whom an observer said he could not remember coming to church in many years.

The legacies that parents and church and teachers left to my generation of Black children were priceless but not material: a living faith reflected in daily service, the discipline of hard work and stick-to-it-ness, and a capacity to struggle in the face of adversity. Giving up and "burnout" were not part of the language of my elders—you got up every morning and you did what you had to do and you got up every time you fell down and tried as many times as you had to to get it done right. They had grit. They valued family life, family rituals, and tried to be and to expose us to good role models. Role models were of two kinds: those who achieved in the outside world (like Marian Anderson, my namesake) and those who didn't have a whole lot of education or fancy clothes but who taught us by the special grace of their lives the message of Christ and Tolstoy and Gandhi and Heschel and Dorothy Day and Romero and King that the Kingdom of God was within—in what you are, not what you have. I still hope I can be half as good as Black church and community elders like Miz Lucy McQueen, Miz Tee Kelly, and Miz Kate Winston, extraordinary women who were kind and patient and loving with children and others and who, when I went to Spelman College, sent me shoeboxes with chicken and biscuits and greasy dollar bills.

It never occurred to any Wright child that we were not going to college or were not expected to share what we learned and earned with the less fortunate. I was forty years old before I figured out, thanks to my brother Harry's superior insight, that my Daddy often responded to our requests for money by saying he didn't have any change because he *really* didn't have any rather than because he had nothing smaller than a twenty dollar bill.

I was fourteen years old the night my Daddy died. He had holes in 10 his shoes but two children out of college, one in college, another in divinity school, and a vision he was able to convey to me as he lay dying in an ambulance that I, a young Black girl, could be and do anything; that race and gender are shadows; and that character, self-discipline, determination, attitude, and service are the substance of life.

I have always believed that I could help change the world because I have been lucky to have adults around me who did—in small and large ways. Most were people of simple grace who understood what Walker Percy wrote: You can get all As and still flunk life.

Life was not easy back in the 1940s and 1950s in rural South Carolina for many parents and grandparents. We buried children who died from poverty (and I can't stand it that we still do). Little Johnny Harrington, three houses down from my church parsonage, stepped on and died from a nail because his grandmother had no doctor to advise her, nor the money to pay for health care. (Half of all low-income urban children under two are still not fully immunized against preventable childhood diseases like tetanus and polio and measles.) My classmate, Henry Munnerlyn, broke his neck when he jumped off the bridge into the town creek because only white children were allowed in the public swimming pool. I later heard that the creek where Blacks swam and fished was the hospital sewage outlet. (Today thousands of Black children in our cities and rural areas are losing their lives to cocaine and heroin and alcohol and gang violence because they don't have enough constructive outlets.) The migrant family who collided with a truck on the highway near my home and the ambulance driver who refused to take them to the hospital because they were Black still live in my mind every time I hear about babies who die or are handicapped from birth when they are turned away from hospitals in emergencies or their mothers are turned away in labor because they have no health insurance and cannot pay pre-admission deposits to enter a hospital. I and my brothers and sister might have lost hope—as so many young people today have lost hope—except for the stable, caring, attentive adults in our family, school, congregation, civic and political life who struggled with and for us against the obstacles we faced and provided us positive alternatives and the sense of possibility we needed.

At Spelman College in Atlanta, I found my Daddy and Mama's values about taking responsibility for your own learning and growth reinforced in the daily (except Saturday) chapel service. Daily chapel attendance was compulsory and enforced by the threat of points taken off one's earned grade average as a result of truancy. For all my rebellion then, I remember now far more from the chapel speakers who came to talk to us about life and the purpose of education than from any class. And during my tenure as chairwoman of Spelman's board, I advocated reinstitution of some compulsory assemblies (monthly, not daily!) so our young women would have to hear what we adults think is important.

Many of my mentors and role models, such as Dr. Benjamin Mays, then president of Morehouse College, Whitney Young, dean of the School of Social Work at Atlanta University and later National Urban League head, M. Carl Holman, a professor at Clark College, later head of the National Urban Coalition, Dr. Howard Thurman, dean of the Chapel at Boston University, and Dr. King, all conveyed the same message as they spoke in Sisters Chapel at Spelman: education is for improving the lives of others and for leaving your community and world better than you found it. Other important influences during my Spelman years—Ella Baker, Septima Clark, Howard Zinn, Charles E. Merrill, Jr., and Samuel Dubois Cook—stretched my vision of the future and of one person's ability to help shape it. I'm still trying to live up to their teachings and to the examples of the extraordinary ordinary people whom I had the privilege to serve and learn from after law school during my civil rights sojourn in Mississippi between 1963 and 1968.

15 Fannie Lou Hamer, Amzie Moore, Winson and Dovie Hudson, Mae Bertha Carter, school desegregation and voting rights pioneers in Mississippi, and Unita Blackwell, who rose from sharecropper to mayor of rural Mayersville, Mississippi—and countless courageous men and women who gave their voices and homes and lives to get the right to vote and to secure for their children a better life than they had—guide and inspire me still. Those largely unknown and usually unlettered people of courage and commitment, along with my parents, remind me each day to keep trying and to let my little light shine, as Mrs. Hamer sang and did through her inspiring life. In a D.C. neighborhood church, I recently saw a banner that reminded me "there is not enough darkness in the world to snuff out the light of even one small candle."

I have always felt extraordinarily blessed to live in the times I have. As a child and as an adult—as a Black woman—I have had to struggle to understand the world around me. Most Americans remember Dr. King as a great leader. I do too. But I also remember him as someone able to admit how often he was afraid and unsure about his next step. But faith prevailed over fear and uncertainty and fatigue and depression. It was his human vulnerability and his ability to rise above it that I most remember. In this, he was not different from many Black adults whose credo has been to make "a way out of no way."

The Children's Defense Fund was conceived in the cauldron of Mississippi's summer project of 1964 and in the Head Start battles of

1965, where both the great need for and limits of local action were apparent. As a private civil rights lawyer, I learned that I could have only limited, albeit important, impact on meeting epidemic family and child needs in that poor state without coherent national policy and investment strategies to complement community empowerment strategies. I also learned that critical civil and political rights would not mean much to a hungry, homeless, illiterate child and family if they lacked the social and economic means to exercise them. And so children—my own and other people's—became the passion of my personal and professional life. For it is they who are God's presence, promise, and hope for humankind.

For Journals

How do you think American families measure their success? What kinds of achievements or possessions are often used to measure success?

For Discussion

1. The subtitle of Edelman's book, of which this selection is the first chapter, is "A Letter to My Children and Yours." Why do you believe Edelman is addressing her remarks to these audiences? How do the audiences shape her message?

2. Edelman and the children of her community grew up knowing that they were valued and important. How did the adults of the community transmit these beliefs? What were the adults' expectations of the children? What did the children assume about their role in the community?

3. Edelman writes of the legacies from her family and community— of service, of doing for others, of making the most of intellectual and material gifts. How have such legacies changed her life? How have they influenced her work?

4. Edelman concludes, "Service is the rent we pay for living" (paragraph 6). What are the assumptions on which she bases this statement?

5. Edelman's community served as an extended family in supporting her and other children. In what ways was her upbringing like, and unlike, that of children growing up in the 1980s and 1990s? What has changed for the better? For the worse? What has not changed?

6. Edelman writes that her father died with "holes in his shoes but two children out of college, one in college, another in divinity school, and a vision" (paragraph 10). How does Edelman's measure of her father's success compare to, and contrast with, statements of family values and beliefs evident in other readings in this book? (Look, for example, at Martin Luther King, Jr.'s "I Have a Dream," in Chapter 4,

and at "Bricklayer's Boy" and "Making and Unmaking the 'Model Minority,'" both in Chapter 5.

For Writing

1.   Write an essay examining, and explaining, the values and beliefs with which you were raised. What did you learn about your role in the family? In the community? What were the expectations of your parents and any extended family you have? You could focus on education, community involvement, music, or some other aspect of your youth.

2.   Research a current issue in children's rights—for example, health care, legal protection, or issues of abuse. In addition to drawing on books, periodicals, and government documents, try to interview people in your community who work on behalf of children in the area you are researching. What are the controversies? Write up your research in a documented essay.

3.   Write a letter to the children you have or expect to have, or to nieces or nephews or other relatives. Explain to them the legacies that you grew up with and that you hope you will pass on to them.

∽ *Saplings in the Storm* (1994)

MARY PIPHER

Mary Pipher, Ph.D., is a clinical psychologist in private practice in Lincoln, Nebraska. She teaches part-time at the University of Nebraska and Nebraska Wesleyan University. Dr. Pipher is also a commentator for Nebraska Public Radio. This selection is from her book Reviving Ophelia: Saving the Selves of Adolescent Girls.

When my cousin Polly was a girl, she was energy in motion. She danced, did cartwheels and splits, played football, basketball and baseball with the neighborhood boys, wrestled with my brothers, biked, climbed trees and rode horses. She was as lithe and as resilient as a willow branch and as unrestrained as a lion cub. Polly talked as much as she moved. She yelled out orders and advice, shrieked for joy when she won a bet or heard a good joke, laughed with her mouth wide open, argued with kids and grown-ups and insulted her foes in the language of a construction worker.

We formed the Marauders, a secret club that met over her garage. Polly was the Tom Sawyer of the club. She planned the initiations, led the spying expeditions and hikes to haunted houses. She showed us the rituals to become blood "brothers" and taught us card tricks and how to smoke.

Then Polly had her first period and started junior high. She tried to keep up her old ways, but she was called a tomboy and chided for not acting more ladylike. She was excluded by her boy pals and by the girls, who were moving into makeup and romances.

This left Polly confused and shaky. She had temper tantrums and withdrew from both the boys' and girls' groups. Later she quieted down and reentered as Becky Thatcher. She wore stylish clothes and watched from the sidelines as the boys acted and spoke. Once again she was accepted and popular. She glided smoothly through our small society. No one spoke of the changes or mourned the loss of our town's most dynamic citizen. I was the only one who felt that a tragedy had transpired.

Girls in what Freud called the latency period, roughly age six or 5 seven through puberty, are anything but latent. I think of my daughter Sara during those years—performing chemistry experiments and magic tricks, playing her violin, starring in her own plays, rescuing wild animals and biking all over town. I think of her friend Tamara, who wrote a 300-page novel the summer of her sixth-grade year. I remember myself, reading every children's book in the library of my town. One week I planned to be a great doctor like Albert Schweitzer. The next week I wanted to write like Louisa May Alcott or dance in Paris like Isadora Duncan. I have never since had as much confidence or ambition.

Most preadolescent girls are marvelous company because they are interested in everything—sports, nature, people, music and books. Almost all the heroines of girls' literature come from this age group— Anne of Green Gables, Heidi, Pippi Longstocking and Caddie Wood-lawn. Girls this age bake pies, solve mysteries and go on quests. They can take care of themselves and are not yet burdened with caring for others. They have a brief respite from the female role and can be tomboys, a word that conveys courage, competency and irreverence.

They can be androgynous, having the ability to act adaptively in any situation regardless of gender role constraints. An androgynous person can comfort a baby or change a tire, cook a meal or chair a meeting. Research has shown that, since they are free to act without worrying if their behavior is feminine or masculine, androgynous adults are the most well adjusted.

Girls between seven and eleven rarely come to therapy. They don't need it. I can count on my fingers the girls this age whom I have seen: Coreen, who was physically abused; Anna, whose parents were divorcing; and Brenda, whose father killed himself. These girls were courageous and resilient. Brenda said, "If my father didn't want to stick around, that's his loss." Coreen and Anna were angry, not at themselves, but rather at the grown-ups, who they felt were making mistakes. It's amazing how little help these girls needed from me to heal and move on.

A horticulturist told me a revealing story. She led a tour of junior-high girls who were attending a math and science fair on her campus. She showed them side oats grama, bluestem, Indian grass and trees—redbud, maple, walnut and willow. The younger girls interrupted each other with their questions and tumbled forward to see, touch and smell everything. The older girls, the ninth-graders, were different. They hung back. They didn't touch plants or shout out questions. They stood primly to the side, looking bored and even a little disgusted by the enthusiasm of their younger classmates. My friend asked herself, What's happened to these girls? What's gone wrong? She told me, "I wanted to shake them, to say, 'Wake up, come back. Is anybody home at your house?'"

10   Recently I sat sunning on a bench outside my favorite ice-cream store. A mother and her teenage daughter stopped in front of me and waited for the light to change. I heard the mother say, "You have got to stop blackmailing your father and me. Every time you don't get what you want, you tell us that you want to run away from home or kill yourself. What's happened to you? You used to be able to handle not getting your way."

The daughter stared straight ahead, barely acknowledging her mother's words. The light changed. I licked my ice-cream cone. Another mother approached the same light with her preadolescent daughter in tow. They were holding hands. The daughter said to her mother, "This is fun. Let's do this all afternoon."

Something dramatic happens to girls in early adolescence. Just as planes and ships disappear mysteriously into the Bermuda Triangle, so do the selves of girls go down in droves. They crash and burn in a social and developmental Bermuda Triangle. In early adolescence, studies show that girls' IQ scores drop and their math and science scores plummet. They lose their resiliency and optimism and become less curious and inclined to take risks. They lose their assertive, energetic and "tomboyish" personalities and become more deferential, self-critical and depressed. They report great unhappiness with their own bodies.

Psychology documents but does not explain the crashes. Girls who rushed to drink in experiences in enormous gulps sit quietly in the corner. Writers such as Sylvia Plath, Margaret Atwood and Olive Schreiner have described the wreckage. Diderot, in writing to his young friend Sophie Volland, described his observations harshly: "You all die at 15."

Fairy tales capture the essence of this phenomenon. Young women eat poisoned apples or prick their fingers with poisoned needles and fall asleep for a hundred years. They wander away from home, encounter great dangers, are rescued by princes and are transformed into passive and docile creatures.

15   The story of Ophelia, from Shakespeare's *Hamlet,* shows the destructive forces that affect young women. As a girl, Ophelia is happy

and free, but with adolescence she loses herself. When she falls in love with Hamlet, she lives only for his approval. She has no inner direction; rather she struggles to meet the demands of Hamlet and her father. Her value is determined utterly by their approval. Ophelia is torn apart by her efforts to please. When Hamlet spurns her because she is an obedient daughter, she goes mad with grief. Dressed in elegant clothes that weigh her down, she drowns in a stream filled with flowers.

Girls know they are losing themselves. One girl said, "Everything good in me died in junior high." Wholeness is shattered by the chaos of adolescence. Girls become fragmented, their selves split into mysterious contradictions. They are sensitive and tenderhearted, mean and competitive, superficial and idealistic. They are confident in the morning and overwhelmed with anxiety by nightfall. They rush through their days with wild energy and then collapse into lethargy. They try on new roles every week—this week the good student, next week the delinquent and the next, the artist. And they expect their families to keep up with these changes.

My clients in early adolescence are elusive and slow to trust adults. They are easily offended by a glance, a clearing of the throat, a silence, a lack of sufficient enthusiasm or a sentence that doesn't meet their immediate needs. Their voices have gone underground—their speech is more tentative and less articulate. Their moods swing widely. One week they love their world and their families, the next they are critical of everyone. Much of their behavior is unreadable. Their problems are complicated and metaphorical—eating disorders, school phobias and self-inflicted injuries. I need to ask again and again in a dozen different ways, "What are you trying to tell me?"

Michelle, for example, was a beautiful, intelligent seventeen-year-old. Her mother brought her in after she became pregnant for the third time in three years. I tried to talk about why this was happening. She smiled a Mona Lisa smile to all my questions. "No, I don't care all that much for sex." "No, I didn't plan this. It just happened." When Michelle left a session, I felt like I'd been talking in the wrong language to someone far away.

Holly was another mystery. She was shy, soft-spoken and slow-moving, pretty under all her makeup and teased red hair. She was a Prince fan and wore only purple. Her father brought her in after a suicide attempt. She wouldn't study, do chores, join any school activities or find a job. Holly answered questions in patient, polite monosyllables. She really talked only when the topic was Prince. For several weeks we talked about him. She played me his tapes. Prince somehow spoke for her and to her.

Gail burned and cut herself when she was unhappy. Dressed in 20 black, thin as a straw, she sat silently before me, her hair a mess, her ears, lips and nose all pierced with rings. She spoke about Bosnia and the hole in the ozone layer and asked me if I liked rave music. When I asked about her life, she fingered her earrings and sat silently.

My clients are not different from girls who are not seen in therapy. I teach at a small liberal arts college and the young women in my classes have essentially the same experiences as my therapy clients. One student worried about her best friend who'd been sexually assaulted. Another student missed class after being beaten by her boyfriend. Another asked what she should do about crank calls from a man threatening to rape her. When stressed, another student stabbed her hand with paper clips until she drew blood. Many students have wanted advice on eating disorders.

After I speak at high schools, girls approach me to say that they have been raped, or they want to run away from home, or that they have a friend who is anorexic or alcoholic. At first all this trauma surprised me. Now I expect it.

Psychology has a long history of ignoring girls this age. Until recently adolescent girls haven't been studied by academics, and they have long baffled therapists. Because they are secretive with adults and full of contradictions, they are difficult to study. So much is happening internally that's not communicated on the surface.

Simone de Beauvoir believed adolescence is when girls realize that men have the power and that their only power comes from consenting to become submissive adored objects. They do not suffer from the penis envy Freud postulated, but from power envy.

25　　She described the Bermuda Triangle this way: Girls who were the subjects of their own lives became the objects of others' lives. "Young girls slowly bury their childhood, put away their independent and imperious selves and submissively enter adult existence." Adolescent girls experience a conflict between their autonomous selves and their need to be feminine, between their status as human beings and their vocation as females. De Beauvoir says, "Girls stop being and start seeming."

Girls become "female impersonators" who fit their whole selves into small, crowded spaces. Vibrant, confident girls become shy, doubting young women. Girls stop thinking, "Who am I? What do I want?" and start thinking, "What must I do to please others?"

This gap between girls' true selves and cultural prescriptions for what is properly female creates enormous problems. To paraphrase a Stevie Smith poem about swimming in the sea, "they are not waving, they are drowning." And just when they most need help, they are unable to take their parents' hands.

Olive Schreiner wrote of her experiences as a young girl in *The Story of an African Farm.* "The world tells us what we are to be and shapes us by the ends it sets before us. To men it says, work. To us, it says, seem. The less a woman has in her head the lighter she is for carrying." She described the finishing school that she attended in this way: "It was a machine for condensing the soul into the smallest possible area. I have seen some souls so compressed that they would have filled a small thimble."

Margaret Mead believed that the ideal culture is one in which there is a place for every human gift. By her standards, our Western culture is far from ideal for women. So many gifts are unused and unappreciated. So many voices are stilled. Stendhal wrote: "All geniuses born women are lost to the public good."

Alice Miller wrote of the pressures on some young children to deny   30 their true selves and assume false selves to please their parents. *Reviving Ophelia* suggests that adolescent girls experience a similar pressure to split into true and false selves, but this time the pressure comes not from parents but from the culture. Adolescence is when girls experience social pressure to put aside their authentic selves and to display only a small portion of their gifts.

This pressure disorients and depresses most girls. They sense the pressure to be someone they are not. They fight back, but they are fighting a "problem with no name." One girl put it this way: "I'm a perfectly good carrot that everyone is trying to turn into a rose. As a carrot, I have good color and a nice leafy top. When I'm carved into a rose, I turn brown and wither."

Adolescent girls are saplings in a hurricane. They are young and vulnerable trees that the winds blow with gale strength. Three factors make young women vulnerable to the hurricane. One is their developmental level. Everything is changing—body shape, hormones, skin and hair. Calmness is replaced by anxiety. Their way of thinking is changing. Far below the surface they are struggling with the most basic of human questions: What is my place in the universe, what is my meaning?

Second, American culture has always smacked girls on the head in early adolescence. This is when they move into a broader culture that is rife with girl-hurting "isms," such as sexism, capitalism and lookism, which is the evaluation of a person solely on the basis of appearance.

Third, American girls are expected to distance from parents just at the time when they most need their support. As they struggle with countless new pressures, they must relinquish the protection and closeness they've felt with their families in childhood. They turn to their none-too-constant peers for support.

Parents know only too well that something is happening to their   35 daughters. Calm, considerate daughters grow moody, demanding and distant. Girls who loved to talk are sullen and secretive. Girls who liked to hug now bristle when touched. Mothers complain that they can do nothing right in the eyes of their daughters. Involved fathers bemoan their sudden banishment from their daughters' lives. But few parents realize how universal their experiences are. Their daughters are entering a new land, a dangerous place that parents can scarcely comprehend. Just when they most need a home base, they cut themselves loose without radio communications.

Most parents of adolescent girls have the goal of keeping their daughters safe while they grow up and explore the world. The parents' job is to protect. The daughters' job is to explore. Always these different tasks have created tension in parent-daughter relationships, but now it's even harder. Generally parents are more protective of their daughters than is corporate America. Parents aren't trying to make money off their daughters by selling them designer jeans or cigarettes, they just want them to be well adjusted. They don't see their daughters as sex objects or consumers but as real people with talents and interests. But daughters turn away from their parents as they enter the new land. They befriend their peers, who are their fellow inhabitants of the strange country and who share a common language and set of customs. They often embrace the junk values of mass culture.

This turning away from parents is partly for developmental reasons. Early adolescence is a time of physical and psychological change, self-absorption, preoccupation with peer approval and identity formation. It's a time when girls focus inward on their own fascinating changes.

It's partly for cultural reasons. In America we define adulthood as a moving away from families into broader culture. Adolescence is the time for cutting bonds and breaking free. Adolescents may claim great independence from parents, but they are aware and ashamed of their parents' smallest deviation from the norm. They don't like to be seen with them and find their imperfections upsetting. A mother's haircut or a father's joke can ruin their day. Teenagers are furious at parents who say the wrong things or do not respond with perfect answers. Adolescents claim not to hear their parents, but with their friends they discuss endlessly all parental attitudes. With amazing acuity, they sense nuances, doubt, shades of ambiguity, discrepancy and hypocrisy.

Adolescents still have some of the magical thinking of childhood and believe that parents have the power to keep them safe and happy. They blame their parents for their misery, yet they make a point of not telling their parents how they think and feel; they have secrets, so things can get crazy. For example, girls who are raped may not tell their parents. Instead, they become hostile and rebellious. Parents bring girls in because of their anger and out-of-control behavior. When I hear about this unexplainable anger, I ask about rape. Ironically, their parents should have known about the danger and been more protective; afterward, they should have sensed the pain and helped.

40   Most parents feel like failures during this time. They feel shut out, impotent and misunderstood. They often attribute the difficulties of this time to their daughters and their own failings. They don't understand that these problems go with the developmental stage, the culture and the times.

Parents experience an enormous sense of loss when their girls enter this new land. They miss the daughters who sang in the kitchen, who read them school papers, who accompanied them on fishing trips and to ball games. They miss the daughters who liked to bake cookies, play Pictionary and be kissed goodnight. In place of their lively, affectionate daughters they have changelings—new girls who are sadder, angrier and more complicated. Everyone is grieving.

Fortunately adolescence is time-limited. By late high school most girls are stronger and the winds are dying down. Some of the worst problems—cliques, a total focus on looks and struggles with parents— are on the wane. But the way girls handle the problems of adolescence can have implications for their adult lives. Without some help, the loss of wholeness, self-confidence and self-direction can last well into adulthood. Many adult clients struggle with the same issues that overwhelmed them as adolescent girls. Thirty-year-old accountants and realtors, forty-year-old homemakers and doctors, and thirty-five-year-old nurses and schoolteachers ask the same questions and struggle with the same problems as their teenage daughters.

Even sadder are the women who are not struggling, who have forgotten that they have selves worth defending. They have repressed the pain of their adolescence, the betrayals of self in order to be pleasing. These women come to therapy with the goal of becoming even more pleasing to others. They come to lose weight, to save their marriages or to rescue their children. When I ask them about their own needs, they are confused by the question.

Most women struggled alone with the trauma of adolescence and have led decades of adult life with their adolescent experiences unexamined. The lessons learned in adolescence are forgotten and their memories of pain are minimized. They come into therapy because their marriage is in trouble, or they hate their job, or their own daughter is giving them fits. Maybe their daughter's pain awakens their own pain. Some are depressed or chemically addicted or have stress-related illnesses—ulcers, colitis, migraines or psoriasis. Many have tried to be perfect women and failed. Even though they followed the rules and did as they were told, the world has not rewarded them. They feel angry and betrayed. They feel miserable and taken for granted, used rather than loved.

Women often know how everyone in their family thinks and feels 45 except themselves. They are great at balancing the needs of their co-workers, husbands, children and friends, but they forget to put themselves into the equation. They struggle with adolescent questions still unresolved: How important are looks and popularity? How do I care for myself and not be selfish? How can I be honest and still be loved? How can I achieve and not threaten others? How can I be sexual and not a sex object? How can I be responsive but not responsible for everyone?

As we talk, the years fall away. We are back in junior high with the cliques, the shame, the embarrassment about bodies, the desire to be accepted and the doubts about ability. So many adult women think they are stupid and ugly. Many feel guilty if they take time for themselves. They do not express anger or ask for help.

We talk about childhood—what the woman was like at ten and at fifteen. We piece together a picture of childhood lost. We review her own particular story, her own time in the hurricane. Memories flood in. Often there are tears, angry outbursts, sadness for what has been lost. So much time has been wasted pretending to be who others wanted. But also, there's a new energy that comes from making connections, from choosing awareness over denial and from the telling of secrets.

We work now, twenty years behind schedule. We reestablish each woman as the subject of her life, not as the object of others' lives. We answer Freud's patronizing question "What do women want?" Each woman wants something different and particular and yet each woman wants the same thing—to be who she truly is, to become who she can become.

Many women regain their preadolescent authenticity with menopause. Because they are no longer beautiful objects occupied primarily with caring for others, they are free once again to become the subjects of their own lives. They become more confident, self-directed and energetic. Margaret Mead noticed this phenomenon in cultures all over the world and called it "pmz," postmenopausal zest. She noted that some cultures revere these older women. Others burn them at the stake.

50   Before I studied psychology, I studied cultural anthropology. I have always been interested in that place where culture and individual psychology intersect, in why cultures create certain personalities and not others, in how they pull for certain strengths in their members, in how certain talents are utilized while others atrophy from lack of attention. I'm interested in the role cultures play in the development of individual pathology.

For a student of culture and personality, adolescence is fascinating. It's an extraordinary time when individual, developmental and cultural factors combine in ways that shape adulthood. It's a time of marked internal development and massive cultural indoctrination.

I want to try in this book to connect each girl's story with larger cultural issues—to examine the intersection of the personal and the political. It's a murky place; the personal and political are intertwined in all of our lives. Our minds, which are shaped by the society in which we live, can oppress us. And yet our minds can also analyze and work to change the culture.

An analysis of the culture cannot ignore individual differences in women. Some women blossom and grow under the most hostile conditions while others wither after the smallest storms. And yet we are more alike than different in the issues that face us. The important question is, Under what conditions do most young women flower and grow?

Adolescent clients intrigue me as they struggle to sort themselves out. But I wouldn't have written this book had it not been for these last few years when my office has been filled with girls—girls with eating disorders, alcohol problems, posttraumatic stress reactions to sexual or physical assaults, sexually transmitted diseases (STDs), self-inflicted injuries and strange phobias, and girls who have tried to kill themselves or run away. A health department survey showed that 40 percent of all girls in my midwestern city considered suicide last year. The Centers for Disease Control in Atlanta reports that the suicide rate among children age ten to fourteen rose 75 percent between 1979 and 1988. Something dramatic is happening to adolescent girls in America, something unnoticed by those not on the front lines.

At first I was surprised that girls were having more trouble now. 55 After all, we have had a consciousness-raising women's movement since the sixties. Women are working in traditionally male professions and going out for sports. Some fathers help with the housework and child care. It seems that these changes would count for something. And of course they do, but in some ways the progress is confusing. The Equal Rights Amendment was not ratified, feminism is a pejorative term to many people and, while some women have high-powered jobs, most women work hard for low wages and do most of the "second shift" work. The lip service paid to equality makes the reality of discrimination even more confusing.

Many of the pressures girls have always faced are intensified in the 1990s. Many things contribute to this intensification: more divorced families, chemical addictions, casual sex and violence against women. Because of the media, which Clarence Page calls "electronic wallpaper," girls all live in one big town—a sleazy, dangerous tinsel town with lots of liquor stores and few protected spaces. Increasingly women have been sexualized and objectified, their bodies marketed to sell tractors and toothpaste. Soft- and hard-core pornography are everywhere. Sexual and physical assaults on girls are at an all-time high. Now girls are more vulnerable and fearful, more likely to have been traumatized and less free to roam about alone. This combination of old stresses and new is poison for our young women.

Parents have unprecedented stress as well. For the last half-century, parents worried about their sixteen-year-old daughters driving, but now, in a time of drive-by shootings and car-jackings, parents can be panicked. Parents have always worried about their daughters' sexual behavior, but now, in a time of date rapes, herpes and AIDS, they can be sex-phobic. Traditionally parents have wondered what their teens were doing, but now teens are much more likely to be doing things that can get them killed.

This book will tell stories from the front lines. It's about girls because I know about girls. I was one, I see them in therapy, I have a teenage daughter and I teach primarily young women. I am not writing about boys because I have had limited experience with them. I'm not saying that girls and boys are radically different, only that they have different experiences.

I am saying that girls are having more trouble now than they had thirty years ago, when I was a girl, and more trouble than even ten years ago. Something new is happening. Adolescence has always been hard, but it's harder now because of cultural changes in the last decade. The protected place in space and time that we once called childhood has grown shorter. There is an African saying, "It takes a village to raise a child." Most girls no longer have a village.

60 Parents, teachers, counselors and nurses see that girls are in trouble, but they do not realize how universal and extreme the suffering is. This book is an attempt to share what I have seen and heard. It's a hurricane warning, a message to the culture that something important is happening. This is a National Weather Service bulletin from the storm center.

For Journals

Think back to what your life was like when you were ten years old, then at age fifteen. In what ways did you change the way you thought of yourself? Of your role as a young woman or young man?

For Discussion

1. What is the "storm" that the author writes about? Who are the "saplings"?

2. Pipher quotes the writer Diderot as saying to a young woman, "You all die at 15." What do you think Diderot means? Do you agree or disagree? Cite examples from the text, or from your own observation or experience, to support your view.

3. The author integrates several different types of evidence—specific cases, literary examples, assertions, and authority—to support her key assertions. Which do you find most persuasive, and why?

For Writing

1. Using your journal writing as a starting point, write a reflective essay on your own passage into adolescence. Use a specific anecdote or examples to illustrate your essay.

2.   Research rites of passage for adolescence in American cultures or in other countries and cultures. Be sure to focus your topic so that you can develop the paper well in the space available.

3.   Write a response to Pipher. If you agree with her, provide a case example that supports her view. If you disagree, offer convincing evidence that refutes her assertion.

∞ Making and Unmaking the "Model Minority" (1994)

JOHN WU

John Wu is a college student who was born in Taipei, Taiwan, and lived there until 1983. His family then moved to Arcadia, California, where they still live. Wu hopes to pursue a career in film and television; his parents still hope that he will go into law. Wu wrote this researched essay in response to a writing assignment asking him to examine assumptions about his identity and his family values.

Asians in America used to be the "yellow peril" and were considered unassimilable. Today, Asian Americans are the "model minority" and are seemingly assimilating into the white, middle-class mainstream. This change in public perception affirms the improving fortune of Asian Americans as a group in recent years. Rosy pictures, however, do not capture the full realities facing this diverse and aggregate population under the rubric of "Asian American." Labeling an entire group overlooks the individuality of its members. Labels lead to generalizations and stereotypes. Generalizations and stereotypes lead to prejudice. And prejudice is the seed of racism. For this reason, many Asian Americans reject the model minority label despite its complimentary nature.

Whether celebrated or renounced, the model minority label carries with it expectations that are uncomfortably familiar to second-generation Asian Americans whose immigrant parents want nothing less for their children than for them to be the "model minority." This familiarity is the source of unease and ambivalence about the outright rejection of the model minority image. Because the sense of familial duty and filial piety is deeply embedded in most Asian cultures, second-generation Asian Americans often feel obligated to live up to the visions of the immigrant parents and to fulfill the American dream.

There are many explanations for why the model minority story emerged. Bob Suzuki, in what is considered the first major rebuttal to the model minority thesis, titled "Education and the Socialization of

Asian Americans: A Revisionist Analysis of the 'Model Minority' Thesis," suggests that the timing, which coincided with the racial crisis of the sixties, was not accidental. He writes: "The activists charged that the actual status of Asian Americans was being deliberately distorted to fit the 'model minority' image in an attempt to discredit the protests and demands for social justice of other minority groups by admonishing them to follow the 'shining example' set by Asian Americans" (Suzuki 24). The concept of model minority absolves the guilt of the white majority for the bleak condition which other minority groups face. It permits white Americans to feel better about America and its history of flagrant racial discrimination and botched race relations.

More important, the model minority story keeps the American dream alive. Americans hold dear the idea that an individual, regardless of any disadvantaged background, can succeed in this society as long as he or she works hard. Commenting on the need of the model minority myth, Ronald Takaki, professor of ethnic studies at the University of California at Berkeley, explains: "Here is a society that is very nervous about the black underclass and gloomy about the economy. These are tough economic times . . . you need a model minority to reassure people, they need to be told the American dream still works . . . 'look at these immigrants, they can still do it'" (qtd. in Kamen). Thus the success of Asian Americans reassures the dominant culture that the American dream is still realizable.

5   Within the Asian American community, the current debate is no longer whether Asian Americans are the model minority; rather, it is over whether we should completely discard the label or take pride in its positive aspects. What almost all commentators agree on is that the expectations brought about by the model minority stereotype present problems for Asian Americans. Consider the following description in the *Washington Post*: "Armed with little more than a will to succeed, they open stores where no other entrepreneur will venture. They streak to the top in the technical worlds of computers and mathematics. Their workers are the most dedicated and tireless, their children are the smartest. They are wealthy and self-sufficient" (Kamen). This near-mythical description is an example of the overall depiction of Asian Americans by the media "as industrious and intelligent, enterprising and polite, with good values and strong families, equally successful as children in school and as adults in business and medicine and science and engineering" (Shaw).

These popular media stereotypes create expectations of how Asian Americans are supposed to be. Ironically, these expectations are the same ones that immigrant parents often have of their children. In school, Asian American students are expected to excel. Placing much hope on education as the key to success, parents want and expect their children to work extra hard in school. They accept nothing but the best marks and the highest scores as evidence of hard work and success. Educators also expect Asian American students to be brilliant in the classroom, particularly in math and science. These two sources of high expectations create an enormous pressure for Asian American students. Those who cannot deliver perfect scores and top marks often suffer from low self-esteem and low confidence. Some community activists believe that the expectations of the society and the parents are a contributing factor to an increase in suicides among Asian American youth (Kamen).

As adults, Asian Americans have limited career choices because of the model minority label and of parental expectations. Stereotypes of Asian Americans as good in technical fields are not bad in and of themselves. The implication, though, is that Asian Americans are not good in anything else. Hence we see few successful Asian Americans in areas like politics, sports, and entertainment. In fact, many doors to nontechnical fields are virtually dead-bolted to Asian Americans. This limited career track is also enforced by many Asian parents who push their children in certain directions. Having self-sacrificed by leaving a familiar home, immigrant parents place all of their hopes on their children to succeed, to be better than they. They tend to encourage their children to stick to safe fields where success is rewarded by hard work and not by luck.

Asian Americans are also seen as people who "do not rock the boat." This expectation is usually entangled with the stereotype of being quiet and unassertive. Many non-Asians regard Asian Americans as people who are easy to work with but are not leaders, which may explain why few Asian Americans are in the top management level despite the high percentage of professionals in the corporate world. The emphasis on stoicism in many Asian cultures is the other source for the "do not rock the boat" expectation. Immigrant parents usually teach their children not to fight back against harassment or not to complain about academic pressures (Lee). In the same way, the society expects Asian Americans to overcome any obstacles of racism and discrimination. As Leonard Downie, managing editor of the *Washington Post*, observes, "These are just quiet people who come here, go to work and go to school and do a good job and don't ask for coverage and don't make themselves very visible in the community" (qtd. in Shaw).

Beyond these expectations, the dominant culture and new immigrants share one more thing in common—the American dream. The dominant culture, still embracing the American dream, wishes to believe that American society is colorblind and that individualism is a practicable principle (Chan 171). The model minority tale grants them that wish: Asian Americans are living the American dream because they have the initiative and they work hard. Children of immigrant parents are well aware of the American dream. It is the reason, at least partially, many Asian immigrants have come to the United States. They come in search of better opportunities. With expectations of success conjured by the American dream, immigrant parents self-sacrifice so their children can have a better education, a better career, and a better life. Knowing the sacrifices of the immigrant parents, second-generation Asian Americans feel obligated to work hard to meet the expectations and, in a way, repay the first generation. These are the same expectations as those of the society on Asian Americans in general as a model minority.

10   These expectations exact a psychological toll on Asian Americans. Suzuki explains that "over-anxious attempts by Asian Americans to gain acceptance have stripped them of their dignity and have caused many of them to suffer from severe psychological disorders characterized by lack of confidence, low self-esteem, expressive conformity and alienation" (25). This situation is especially acute among Asian American students. Feeling obligated to succeed, they work extremely hard in school. Their diligence, though praised by teachers, is frowned upon by non-Asian peers. As a result, Asian American students often feel isolated and alienated. This situation is compounded when Asian American students cannot meet the expectations demanded of them. In essence, they are "doubly burdened" (Shaw). On the one hand, they are attempting to meet the standards of their parents and end up feeling isolated from the peer community. On the other, their inability to meet those standards distances them from their parents.

Because of the pluralist nature of American society, every minority group member feels as if he or she is serving as a model for the group as a whole. As Asian Americans, we constantly feel as if we have to prove ourselves to white Americans that we are just as "good." Perhaps we have achieved our goal because we are now a model minority. But because we do not have our individuality, we are not as "good" as they.

Labels and stereotypes hinder individuality. The model minority myth precludes the possibility that some Asian Americans may not be upwardly mobile and successful. Yet our parents expect us to become upwardly mobile and successful. Our parents' expectations personalize the society's model minority expectations for us. For second-generation Asian Americans, the Asian sense of duty to the family and filial piety still run strong. We feel obligated to live up to the goals of our parents. At the same time, we want to be our own person; we want to be successful on our own terms. We want to reject the labels and the stereotypes but we cannot deny the positive achievements of Asian Americans. We are in a schizophrenic state of trying to become the "model minority" for our parents while trying to unmake the "model minority" of white America.

Works Cited

Chan, Sucheng. *Asian Americans: An Interpretive History.* Boston: Twayne, 1991.

Kamen, Al. "Myth of 'Model Minority' Haunts Asian Americans." *Washington Post,* 22 June 1992: Al.

Lee, Felicia. "'Model Minority' Label Taxes Asian Youths." *New York Times,* 20 Mar. 1990: B1.

Shaw, David. "Asian-Americans Chafe Against Stereotype of 'Model Citizen.'" *Los Angeles Times,* 11 Dec. 1990: A31.

Suzuki, Bob. "Education and the Socialization of Asian Americans: A Revisionist Analysis of the 'Model Minority' Thesis." *Amerasia* 4.2 (1977): 23–51.

For Journals

Do people make assumptions about you, based on your ethnicity or gender?

For Discussion

1. Identify the main idea and key supporting points in Wu's essay. To what extent do his own assumptions link and support the evidence to his main idea?

2. What assumptions of society is Wu questioning? Of white American society? Of Asian Americans and their families?

3. To what extent are the values Wu writes about transmitted through families? Through society?

4. If you were to exchange drafts with Wu in peer review, what suggestions would you make for a revision?

For Writing

1. Select a social issue of concern and interest to you and, as Wu does, challenge the assumptions with reasoning and evidence.

2. Do others make assumptions about your family values and beliefs? Write an essay explaining your value system to others with the goal of clarifying misperceptions and communicating what you consider to be a true picture of your value system.

∞ *Film:* Mi familia *(My Family)* (1995)

This film's subject is the story and struggles of the three-generation Sanchez family, seen through the eyes of the eldest son, a writer. The narrative includes the father's journey on foot from Mexico to California in the 1920s, a brother's tragic death in the 1950s, and social and economic struggles in contemporary America. (121 minutes)

For Journals

What do you expect from a film about a Mexican American family? If you are Mexican American, what themes or issues do you think are likely to appear in this film?

For Discussion

1.   In what ways is the Sanchez family similar to your own family? In what ways is it different?

2.   The film begins, and ends, with images of the bridges connecting East Los Angeles with Los Angeles. What is the significance of those bridges? What do they mean to the members of the Sanchez family?

3.   Jose Sanchez comes to California to find a relative who was born in California "when it was still Mexico." Discuss the political implications of this situation in terms of people who are, and are not, considered "American."

4.   Mrs. Sanchez suffers extreme difficulties in order to be reunited with her husband and children. Discuss the ways in which this element of the film, as well as other particular examples, conveys values and beliefs about family.

5.   Compare and contrast the values and beliefs that the parents and children have about work and money.

For Writing

1.   Write a review of this film for your campus newspaper, or write a letter to a friend urging him or her to see the film (or not). If you are unfamiliar with the genre of film reviews, read several from your local newspaper. The review captures reader interest, makes a claim about the film's merit or lack thereof, and usually briefly summarizes the film in a way that does not give away the plot or any surprises. The reader should be able to make an informed decision about viewing the film based on your review.

2.   Select one scene in the film and write about how it illuminates a larger theme or idea that the film as a whole suggests (for example, the father's journey, the mother's river crossing, the wedding scene, one of the scenes in which a new romantic partner is introduced to the family).

3.   Research and write a documented essay about one of the actual or historical events or situations referred to in the film, such as forced re-

location of American citizens who "looked Mexican" during the Great Depression of the 1930s.

Writing Assignments

1. Select a reading in this chapter, and diagram the assumptions on which it rests. Put the main point in a box at the top of the page and then draw boxes and connecting lines showing the supporting assumptions and reasons. How do you think the writer knew which assumptions to state explicitly and which ones would be understood or automatically accepted by the audience?

2. Examine a piece of artwork or other visual image that appears in another chapter in this book. Articulate the implicit and explicit assumptions and values on which it is based, and write an essay analyzing what such assumptions tell us about the audiences for which the image was intended.

3. Develop your own argument on the subject of women's or men's proper role in society, on same-gender domestic partnerships, on interracial adoption, or on some other social issue of concern to you. Exchange essays with a peer, preferably one who has taken an opposing view or has written on a different subject. Write refutations of each other's essays, and turn in both originals and refutations. Did you find yourselves refuting primarily the assumptions, the reasons, the conclusions drawn, or some of each part of the argument in equal amounts?

4. Examine your own values and beliefs about family and gender. Do some private freewriting, reflecting on how you have come to hold those values. What are your assumptions about family life? The work ethic? Dating roles? Parental roles? Friendship between genders? Marriage or partnership roles? Write a reflective essay exploring the process through which you have come to hold these particular beliefs.

5. Interview your parents or grandparents or other people of their generations; ask them about the expectations they grew up with about dating, gender roles, or family and parental duties. Do they still hold those assumptions? What do they think of current customs? Write an essay summarizing your findings and share it with other class members. Alternatively, compare the assumptions held by the people you interviewed with those you hold, and analyze the similarities and differences.

6. In a group, and if everyone is willing to share, put up butcher paper around the classroom and have everyone write his or her name, ethnic background, parents' and grandparents' occupations, and any sayings, proverbs, legacies (ideas they've passed down to you or possessions that represent these ideas). After everyone has finished, silently review the material, looking for connections, themes, values, or assumptions that emerge. Discuss them as a class, or write up your reflections privately or to share.

7. Design a flyer to inform an audience about a social issue. Write an essay explaining your design, focusing on the assumptions you made about your audience and the premises on which your flyer is based.

6

Work and Play

The relationship of Americans to work is one of the most complicated dynamics in our culture. The ethics of worth, beliefs about
wealth and the importance of money, and ways of measuring success
for ourselves and others all come into the discussion. Work, like religion, family, the American dream, and other deeply rooted beliefs, is
closely identified with who we are, how we value ourselves, and how
we in turn are valued, or not valued, by society.

Americans believe that everyone deserves at least the chance to be
successful; perhaps that's how most would interpret the Declaration of
Independence's guarantee of the pursuit of happiness. But they have
never agreed on how success is to be achieved or measured and are torn
between the Protestant work ethic—a belief in hard work and diligence
rewarded by middle-class prosperity—and the fantasy of wealth
gained without any work, through the blind luck of buying a winning
lottery ticket or marrying the boss's only child.

Between those two extremes, Americans have historically entertained a variety of beliefs about work, some of them mutually inconsistent. The Calvinist theology that prevailed in early New England
included the belief that God chooses to save some unworthy souls as a
sign of infinite mercy; these fortunate few are called the elect. Gradually that austere tenet of faith came to include an assumption that someone living the comfortable life must be doing it with God's help; thus,
outward success was viewed as proof of good work habits and God's
favor. Calvinism has long since ceased to dominate our country's religious life, but the connection of high pay, status, and success with personal self-worth has remained embedded in American culture and
consciousness.

Industrialization, especially after the Civil War, brought factory
jobs and long hours. The fortunate few—the elect of industrial America—were known as the robber barons. Many of these railroad, mine,
and factory owners came from poor or ordinary backgrounds and
made inconceivably vast amounts of money. Poorer Americans both resented and worshipped them; low pay and terrible working conditions
were the reality for most Americans, and their highest goal was to

become middle class. But secretly they dreamed that perhaps their children would do better—much better.

Part of the reward system for doing better and entering the middle class was the opportunity to enjoy a privilege that was once reserved for the rich—leisure time in which to engage in a pleasurable activity such as a sport or a craft, to be a spectator at professional sports events, to go to the theater or to a musical performance, or even to travel. Well-off Victorian America offered baseball, tennis, boating, parlor games and card games, and bicycling. For the very poor, of course, leisure was still a rare luxury, but some sports, such as baseball and boxing, were more generally available to everyone. Baseball was probably the most democratized sport of all, played before the Civil War, spread by prisoners on both sides during the Civil War, played in cities, by immigrants as well as native-born Americans, by blacks as well as whites. However, when baseball, like other American institutions, embraced segregation in the late nineteenth century, it established what would eventually become a truism about sports in America—they represented a microcosm of the country as a whole, and, in this case, a tragic reflection of inequalities in other areas of American life.

Baseball was significant in another way too. It became the first American sport to turn into a business, and big business at that. Eventually, other sports that were originally strictly amateur—football and basketball, for example—followed its lead. College stars went on to play on professional teams, with salaries, owners, fans, local pride, local economies, and a lot of money at stake. The area of athletics that remained amateur the longest (that is, with no real money involved) was women's college sports. Many of them—track and field, field hockey, softball—still draw women for the love of the sport alone. But others—women's tennis, golf, and particularly basketball—now imitate men's sports in the sense that the best college athletes can now join professional tours or leagues. At the same time, the Olympics highlight sports in which women are particularly well established, such as gymnastics and figure skating, and a gold medal means endorsements and high salaries, not to mention product advertisements, celebrity, and pictures of the champion emblazoned on Wheaties boxes.

These changes certainly signal a definite move toward equality and recognition that great women athletes are as interesting, if not more interesting, to watch than men. But these opportunities are not an unalloyed blessing: now some women athletes experience the problems of commercialization and overmarketing that were previously the preserve of men alone. Whether women's sports handle those problems any differently remains to be seen.

The most significant American writing about work and play is both a response to and a reflection of the values behind them and the national experience that shaped them. The selections in this chapter sample a spectrum of those values, examine various kinds of work and play, and offer possibilities for combining the two. They also raise related issues: the tenuousness of life in this country for those who lack paying work or whose work is unfulfilling and poorly paid; the corruption of the amateur ideal by the reality of sports finances; the questionable status of women in a culture in which husbands work outside and supply the paychecks and wives work at home but do not earn money; the significance of work and money as satisfying, nongendered activities; the benefits of athletic competition and the dangers of completely commercialized sports. Finally, this chapter raises the question of balance—between work and play, between amateur and professional, between the lives of working men and women, between Americans' faith in the redeeming possibilities of work as well as their desire to escape it.

Work and Play Through History

The selections in this chapter revolve around two areas: work and play. Work-related issues include needing a job, having a job and getting the most out of it, looking for job security, or dealing with the trauma of losing it. Play includes both sports and a less determinate but valuable category called leisure—the time and the freedom to choose a night out, a vacation, a stay at home, or nothing at all.

Benjamin Franklin worked at many jobs in his lifetime—some for money, some for science, some for public service—but his overall brilliance makes it difficult to know where his work ended and his leisure began. He seems to have enjoyed working as a printer—a vocation which made him wealthy, gratified his early ambitions, and enabled him to retire very early. But he also seems to have enjoyed swimming, teaching himself languages while playing chess, and finding ways to establish the first circulating library in the country, the fire department, the American Philosophical Society, and the University of Pennsylvania. And if he sometimes found diplomacy with France stressful, he so charmed the French that they followed him around as if he were a rock star. In the first selection, taken from the *Autobiography*, we see him making a go of his printing work, competing for business, and embarking on the first of innumerable and successful public projects, all with an energy and humor that make him, still, the most remarkable of Americans.

In another part of his *Autobiography*, Franklin reports on a widow who proved infinitely more successful at running a printing business than her late husband had been. Franklin's conclusion—that women should be educated about money, accounting, and business transactions—was far ahead of its time, and it fell on deaf ears. But it found an echo, more than a century later, in the groundbreaking work of Charlotte Perkins Gilman. Gilman knew from personal experience what it meant to be a well-brought up Victorian woman suffocated by conventions and restrictions. She wrote a remarkable story, "The Yellow Wallpaper," about a young mother who has a breakdown that is exacerbated by the condescending and wrong-headed ministrations of her doctor and husband. Gilman's understanding of what it meant for married women to have no legal or financial independence led to her innovative study *Women and Economics*, which is excerpted here. It made her the first professional American woman economist.

Well-off Americans were spared the grinding poverty exposed in Jacob Riis's famous photograph of women sewing in a tenement around 1907 (although Gilman would have understood the economic extremities that brought it about). In the early part of this century, Riis documented the lives of immigrants in New York's Lower East Side, letting the images of sweatshops, illness, crowded living conditions, and desperate determination speak for themselves. At the same time, Americans who were poorer than Gilman but much better off than the women in Riis's photograph, namely blue- and white-collar workers, were beginning to enjoy a variety of relatively inexpensive pleasures such as amusement parks, vaudeville shows, early movie theaters (called picture palaces), and inner-city baseball parks. In his social history *Going Out*, David Nasaw explains how the beginnings of American mass entertainment came into being, who got to enjoy it and who didn't, and how the growth of the big cities and the development of electric lights made that entertainment possible.

For those more prosperous Americans whose income enabled them to travel, the favorite destination was Europe, particularly London and Paris. But as the 1914 Hawaiian postcard of famous swimmer and surfer Duke Kahanamoku shows, the idea of being an American tourist in America was beginning to take shape, especially if the destination could be shown as exotic and attractive. Hawaii was certainly far enough from the mainland and unknown enough to qualify as practically a foreign place to most Americans, and the postcard wisely plays up the different pleasures it has to offer.

Equally welcoming—and equally powerful in its representation of the body as an object of worship—is the 1927 cover of Bernarr Macfadden's highly successful magazine, *Physical Culture*. The young woman on the cover, like Duke Kahanamoku, is emblematic of American health and energy, consciously developed and energetically pursued. Just as Duke is an advertisement for Hawaii, the cover girl promotes Macfadden's somewhat eccentric ideology, in which a healthy body is a necessary precondition to moral excellence. And a blooming female body, scantily dressed by 1927 standards, isn't a bad idea for attracting readers.

Woody Guthrie's "Union Maid" and Studs Terkel's interview with the stonemason, Mr. Bates, also glorify their subjects, but here the object of discussion is getting or having a good job. Guthrie's sympathies were perpetually with the underdog, the dispossessed, and the poor, and this song is one of many he wrote to honor and empower ordinary people who suffered from poor working conditions, low wages, and the sometimes violent efforts of companies to discourage the formation of unions. It is unusual, though, in that it is dedicated to women workers. Mr. Bates, on the fortunate end of the employment spectrum, is a man who has worked steadily and for many years at a job of which he is extremely proud and that gives him tremendous satisfaction. His delight in his craft, his sense of having made something which lasts, is almost as palpable as the stone with which he works.

Gloria Steinem, writing when the women's movement had begun to realign men's and women's perceptions of the role of work in their lives, takes on a topic that grows in significance as more choices become available: the difficulty women have in admitting that they work because they like it—not only because they have to, not only because they need the money, but because, like Mr. Bates, they enjoy the sense of accomplishment and satisfaction that comes with doing a job well and being recognized for it.

The next two selections deal with problems arising from the presence or absence of true amateurism in sports, and the difficulties that develop when money, rather than the activity itself, becomes the reward. Leonard Koppett writes about college sports programs that are supposed to be amateur, but that in fact have so much at stake in television contracts and professional possibilities that amateurism becomes a byword for corruption. Susan Cahn addresses the recent professionalization of women's sports and the question of whether that development produces independent women athletes or women who are co-opted, athletically and morally, by the preexisting male sports establishment. And the film *Jerry Maguire,* a comedy about the disillusionment and moral recovery of a sports agent, provides another look at the sports/work/ethics dilemma. Jorge Flores's essay on the displacement of Mexican American workers during the Great Depression explains how difficult times can deprive some people of their work and others of their sense of fairness; and an advertisement for Motrin headache medicine reminds us, in a witty and poignant way, that doing an ordinary job honestly and well can be the hardest work of all.

∞ FROM *Autobiography* (1771)

BENJAMIN FRANKLIN

Benjamin Franklin (1706–1790) had established himself as a printer, writer, and public servant in Philadelphia by the time he was twenty-four years old. He was so

successful that he retired from business at the age of forty-two and spent the next
forty-two years of his life in the service of philanthropy, science, and the young coun-
try he had helped to found. Franklin wrote his Autobiography *in 1771. The excerpt*
that follows describes how he started his printing business, with type shipped over
from London, and how he built the business, his reputation, and his fortune. It also
shows him in one of his many experiments—this one personal rather than scientific—
which he recounts with characteristic self-mockery.

We had not been long return'd to Philadelphia, before the New
Types arriv'd from London—We settled with Keimer, & left him by his
Consent before he heard of it.—We found a House to hire near the Market, and took it. To lessen the Rent, (which was then but 24£ a Year tho'
I have since known it let for 70) We took in Tho§Godfrey a Glazier, & his
Family, who were to pay a considerable Part of it to us, and we to board
with them. We had scarce opened our Letters & put our Press in Order,
before George House, an Acquaintance of mine, brought a Countryman
to us; whom he had met in the Street enquiring for a Printer. All our
Cash was now expended in the Variety of Particulars we had been
obliged to procure, & this Countryman's Five Shillings, being our First
Fruits & coming so seasonally, gave me more Pleasure than any Crown
I have since earn'd; and from the Gratitude I felt towards House, has
made me often more ready than perhaps I should otherwise have been
to assist young Beginners. . . .

Brientnal particularly procur'd us from the Quakers, the Printing
40 Sheets of their History, the rest being to be done by Keimer: and
upon this we work'd exceeding hard, for the Price was low. . . . I compos'd of it a Sheet a Day, and Meredith work'd it off at Press. It was
often 11 at Night and sometimes later, before I had finish'd my Distribution for the next days Work: For the little Jobbs sent in by our
other Friends now & then put us back. But so determin'd I was to continue doing a Sheet a Day of the Folio, that one Night when having
impos'd my Forms, I thought my Days Work over, one of them by
accident was broken and two Pages reduc'd to Pie. I immediately distributed & compos'd it over again before I went to bed. And this Industry visible to our Neighbours began to give us Character and Credit;
particularly I was told, that mention being made of the new Printing
Office at the Merchants Every-night-Club, the general Opinion was that
it must fail, there being already two Printers in the Place, Keimer &
Bradford; but Doctor Baird . . . gave a contrary Opinion; for the Industry of that Franklin, says he, is superior to any thing I ever saw of the
kind: I see him still at work when I go home from Club; and he is at
Work again before his Neighbours are out of bed. This struck the rest,
and we soon after had Offers from one of them to supply us with Stationary. But as yet we did not chuse to engage in Shop Business.

I soon after obtain'd, thro' my Friend Hamilton, the Printing of the NewCastle Paper Money, another profitable Jobb, as I then thought it; small Things appearing great to those in small Circumstances. And these to me were really great Advantages, as they were great Encouragements.—He procured me also the Printing of the Laws and Votes of that Government which continu'd in my Hands as long as I follow'd the Business.—

I now open'd a little Stationer's Shop. I had in it Blanks of all Sorts the correctest that ever appear'd among us, being assisted in that by my Friend Brientnal; I had also Paper, Parchment, Chapmen's Books, &c. One Whitemash a Compositor I had known in London, an excellent Workman now came to me & work'd with me constantly & diligently, and I took an Apprentice the Son of Aquila Rose. I began now gradually to pay off the Debt I was under. . . . In order to secure my Credit and Character as a Tradesman, I took care not only to be in *Reality* Industrious & frugal, but to avoid all *Appearances* of the Contrary. I drest plainly; I was seen at no Places of idle Diversion; I never went out a-fishing or shooting; a Book, indeed, sometimes debauch'd me from my Work; but that was seldom, snug, & gave no Scandal: and to show that I was not above my Business, I sometimes brought home the Paper I purchas'd at the Stores, thro' the Streets on a Wheelbarrow. Thus being esteem'd an industrious thriving young Man, and paying duly for what I bought, the Merchants who imported Stationary solicited my Custom, others propos'd supplying me with Books, & I went on swimmingly.—In the mean time Keimer's Credit & Business declining daily, he was at last forc'd to sell his Printing-house to satisfy his Creditors. He went to Barbadoes, & there lived some Years, in very poor Circumstances.

But now another Difficulty came upon me, which I had never the 5 least Reason to expect. Mr. Meredith's Father, who was to have paid for our Printing House according to the Expectations given me, was able to advance only one Hundred Pounds, Currency, which had been paid, & a Hundred more was due to the Merchant; who grew impatient & su'd us all. We gave Bail, but saw that if the Money could not be rais'd in time, the Suit must come to a Judgment & Execution, & our hopeful Prospects must with us be ruined, as the Press & Letters must be sold for Payment, perhaps at half-Price.—In this Distress two true Friends whose Kindness I have never forgotten nor ever shall forget while I can remember any thing, came to me separately unknown to each other, and without any Application from me, offering each of them to advance me all the Money that should be necessary to enable me to take the whole Business upon my self if that should be practicable, but they did not like my continuing the Partnership with Meredith, who as they said was often seen drunk in the Streets, & playing at low Games in Alehouses, much to our Discredit. These two Friends were *William Coleman & Robert Grace.* I told them I could not propose a Separation while any Prospect remain'd of the Merediths fulfilling their Part of our Agreement. Because I thought my self under great Obligations to them for what they had done & would do if they could. But if they finally fail'd in their Performance, & our Partnership must be dissolv'd, I should then think myself at Liberty to accept the Assistance of my Friends. Thus the matter rested for some time. When I said to my Partner, perhaps your Father is dissatisfied at the Part you have undertaken in this Affair of ours, and is unwilling to advance for you & me what he would for you alone: If that is the Case, tell me, and I will resign the whole to you & go about my Business. No—says he, my Father has really been disappointed and is really unable; and I am unwilling to distress him farther. I see this is a Business I am not fit for. I was bred a Farmer, and it was a Folly in me to come to Town & put my self at 30 Years of Age an Apprentice to learn a new Trade. Many of our Welsh People are going to settle in North Carolina where Land is cheap: I am inclin'd to go with them, & follow my old Employment. You may find Friends to assist you. If you will take the Debts of the Company upon you, return to my Father the hundred Pound he has advanc'd, pay my little personal Debts, and give me Thirty Pounds & a new Saddle, I will relinquish the Partnership & leave the whole in your Hands. I agreed to this Proposal. It was drawn up in Writing, sign'd & seal'd immediately. I gave him what he demanded & he went soon after to Carolina; from whence he sent me next Year two long Letters, containing the best Account that had been given of that Country, the Climate, Soil, Husbandry, &c. for in those Matters he was very judicious. I printed them in the Papers, and they gave grate Satisfaction to the Publick.

As soon as he was gone, I recurr'd to my two Friends; and because I would not give an unkind Preference to either, I took half what each had offered & I wanted, of one, & half of the other; paid off the Company Debts, and went on with the Business in my own Name, advertising that the Partnership was dissolved. I think this was in or about the Year 1729. . . .

It was about this time that I conceiv'd the bold and arduous Project of arriving at moral Perfection. I wish'd to live without committing any Fault at any time; I would conquer all that either Natural Inclination, Custom, or Company might lead me into. As I knew, or thought I knew, what was right and wrong, I did not see why I might not *always* do the one and avoid the other. But I soon found I had undertaken a Task of more Difficulty than I had imagined: While my Care was employ'd in guarding against one Fault, I was often surpriz'd by another. . . .

The Precept of *Order* requiring that *every Part of my Business should have its allotted Time*, one Page in my little Book contain'd the following Scheme of Employment for the Twenty-four Hours of a natural Day,

The Morning Question, What Good shall I do this Day?	5 6 7 8	Rise, wash, and address *Powerful Goodness;* contrive Day's Business and take the Resolution of the Day; prosecute the present Study: and breakfast. —
	9 10 11	Work.
	12 1	Read, or overlook my Accounts, and dine.
	2 3 4 5	Work.
	6 7 8 9	Put Things in their Places, Supper, Musick, or Diversion, or Conversation, Examination of the Day.
Evening Question, What Good have I done to-day?	10 11 12 1 2 3 4	Sleep. —

. . . My Scheme of Order, gave me the most Trouble, and I found, that tho' it might be practicable where a Man's Business was such as to leave him the Disposition of his Time, that of a Journey-man Printer for instance, it was not possible to be exactly observ'd by a Master, who must mix with the World, and often receive People of Business at their own Hours.—*Order* too, with regard to Places for Things, Papers, &c. I found extreamly difficult to acquire. I had not been early accustomed to it, & having an exceeding good Memory, I was not so sensible of the Inconvenience attending Want of Method. This Article therefore cost me so much painful Attention & my Faults in it vex'd me so much, and I made so little Progress in Amendment, & had such frequent Relapses, that I was almost ready to give up the Attempt, and content my self with a faulty Character in that respect. Like the Man who in buying an Ax of a Smith my Neighbour, desired to have the whole of its Surface as bright as the Edge; the Smith consented to grind it bright for him if he would turn the Wheel. He turn'd while the Smith press'd the broad Face of the Ax hard & heavily on the Stone, which made the Turning of it very fatiguing. The Man came every now & then from the Wheel to see how the Work went on; and at length would take his Ax as it was without farther Grinding. No, says the Smith, Turn on, turn on; we shall have it bright by and by; as yet 'tis only speckled. Yes, says the Man; but—*I think I like a speckled Ax best.*—And I believe this may have been the Case with many who having for want of some such Means as I employ'd found the Difficulty of obtaining good, & breaking bad Habits, in other Points of Vice & Virtue, have given up the Struggle, & concluded that *a speckled Ax was best.* . . . In Truth I found myself incorrigible with respect to *Order;* and now I am grown old, and my Memory bad, I feel very sensibly the want of it. But on the whole, tho' I never arrived at the Perfection I had been so ambitious of obtaining, but fell far short of it, yet I was by the Endeavour made a better and a happier Man than I otherwise should have been, if I had not attempted it.

For Journals

Do you think Franklin would succeed in a business today if he were starting one? Would his skills still be useful?

For Discussion

1. How would you describe Franklin's work ethic? Why does he work hard? What does he get out of his efforts? What are his own assertions about work? Look for supporting evidence in the text—either quotations or accounts of his work experience.

2. What role does friendship play in Franklin's ability to build a business? What assumptions do you think his friends make about him when they bring him business or loan him money? Do you think his experiences with friends were only helpful in an open society with relatively little competition, like colonial America? Would any of the same patterns be helpful to a businessperson today?

3. Franklin was very open about promoting his reputation as a hardworking and industrious young man. He says, "In order to secure my Credit and Character as a Tradesman, I took care not only to be in *Reality* Industrious & frugal, but to avoid all *Appearances* of the Contrary" (paragraph 4). What relationship do you think there is between his public advertisement of his hard work and his private success? Could he have one without the other? If he did, would that make his achievements less valuable to him? To you?

4. What do you think was Franklin's attitude toward success? How do you think he would have defined it? Would you define it differently? How much of Franklin's definition do you think has to do with money? Would you describe Franklin's idea of success as typically American? Atypically? Why?

5. How does the anecdote Franklin tells about the man who took his ax to a smith to be polished, but eventually took it back partly polished, support or not support the assertions he makes about self-improvement? Why would Franklin tell this story about himself?

6. Franklin believed, at least for a while, that he could get rid of all his bad habits and develop good ones instead. Look at his chart of how he wanted to spend his time every day. How much of this activity do you regard as work?

For Writing

1. Write an essay about your own work ethic. Whatever assertions you make about what you think of work and why it is or isn't important to you, try to be aware of the assumptions you are basing your ideas on. Consider the following questions: How important is making money to you? Is that why you work? Would you work if you didn't need the money? What would you do instead? It might be interesting to make up a chart like Franklin's, using your own assessment of how your time should be divided up daily for you to get the most out of it.

2. Starting with Franklin's *Autobiography,* research and write a paper on Philadelphia in the eighteenth century. Consider, for example, what people did for a living, what cultural institutions there were (aside from the ones that Franklin started himself), the role of the Quaker community, what food people ate, and what houses looked like and how they were furnished.

∞ FROM *Women and Economics* (1898)

CHARLOTTE PERKINS GILMAN

Born in Hartford, Connecticut, in 1860, Charlotte Perkins Gilman supported herself as an artist, teacher, and governess before discovering her gift for writing. In the 1890s she escaped destitution by publishing short stories like "Similar Cases" and "The Yellow Wallpaper," the latter a harrowing fictionalization of her own experience of nervous breakdown. Women and Economics *appeared in 1898 and was hailed as the most important work of its kind since John Stuart Mill's* Subjugation of Women. *Gilman committed suicide in 1934. She is recognized as one of the intellectual leaders of the women's movement in American history.*

What we do modifies us more than what is done to us. The freedom of expression has been more restricted in women than the freedom of impression, if that be possible. Something of the world she lived in she has seen from her barred windows. Some air has come through the purdah's[1] folds, some knowledge has filtered to her eager ears from the

---

[1] Purdah is the Hindu word for hiding or concealing women from strangers by means of a veil or a curtain.

talk of men. Desdemona learned somewhat of Othello. Had she known more, she might have lived longer. But in the ever-growing human impulse to create, the power and will to make, to do, to express one's new spirit in new forms,—here she has been utterly debarred. She might work as she had worked from the beginning,—at the primitive labors of the household; but in the inevitable expansion of even those industries to professional levels we have striven to hold her back. To work with her own hands, for nothing, in direct body-service to her own family,—this has been permitted,—yes, compelled. But to be and to do anything further from this she has been forbidden. Her labor has not been limited in kind, but in degree. Whatever she has been allowed to do must be done in private and alone, the first-hand industries of savage times. . . .

It is painfully interesting to trace the gradual cumulative effect of these conditions upon women: first, the action of large natural laws, acting on her as they would act on any other animal; then the evolution of social customs and laws (with her position as the active cause), following the direction of mere physical forces, and adding heavily to them; then, with increasing civilization, the unbroken accumulation of precedent, burnt into each generation by the growing force of education, made lovely by art, holy by religion, desirable by habit; and, steadily acting from beneath, the unswerving pressure of economic necessity upon which the whole structure rested. These are strong modifying conditions indeed.

The process would have been even more effective and far less painful but for one important circumstance. Heredity has no Salic law.[2] Each girl child inherits from her father a certain increasing percentage of human development, human power, human tendency; and each boy as well inherits from his mother the increasing percentage of sex-development, sex-power, sex-tendency. The action of heredity has been to equalize what every tendency of environment and education made to differ. This has saved us from such a female as the gypsy moth. It has held up the woman, and held down the man. It has set iron bounds to our absurd effort to make a race with one sex a million years behind the other. But it has added terribly to the pain and difficulty of human life,—a difficulty and a pain that should have taught us long since that we were living on wrong lines. Each woman born, re-humanized by the current of race activity carried on by her father and re-womanized by her traditional position, has had to live over again in her own person the same process of restriction, repression, denial; the smothering "no" which crushed down all her human desires to create, to discover, to learn, to express, to advance. . . .

To the young man confronting life the world lies wide. Such pow-

---

[2] Law prohibiting a woman from ascending a throne.

ers as he has he may use, must use. If he chooses wrong at first, he may choose again, and yet again. Not effective or successful in one channel, he may do better in another. The growing, varied needs of all mankind call on him for the varied service in which he finds his growth. What he wants to be, he may strive to get. What he wants to get, he may strive to get. Wealth, power, social distinction, fame,—what he wants he can try for.

To the young woman confronting life there is the same world be- 5
yond, there are the same human energies and human desires and ambition within. But all that she may wish to have, all that she may wish to do, must come through a single channel and a single choice. Wealth, power, social distinction, fame,—not only these, but home and happiness, reputation, ease and pleasure, her bread and butter,—all, must come to her through a small gold ring. This is a heavy pressure. It has accumulated behind her through heredity, and continued about her through environment. It has been subtly trained into her through education, till she herself has come to think it a right condition, and pours its influence upon her daughter with increasing impetus. Is it any wonder that women are oversexed? But for the constant inheritance from the more human male, we should have been queen bees, indeed, long before this. But the daughter of the soldier and the sailor, of the artist, the inventor, the great merchant, has inherited in body and brain her share of his development in each generation, and so stayed somewhat human for all her femininity.

For Journals

What is your response to Gilman's first assertion: "What we do modifies us more than what is done to us" (paragraph 1)?

For Discussion

1. According to Gilman, what different kinds of conditions have combined to make women dependent? Do you agree with her? If you do not, would you substitute other reasons to support her conclusion?

2. How do you respond to Gilman's views on heredity and its consequences for creativity in both men and women? Identify her central assertion about heredity, and rephrase it in your own terms. Do you accept her reasoning? What evidence do you have, personal or otherwise, to support or deny it?

3. What assertions does Gilman make about the effect of marriage on women's independence? Why is a gold wedding ring such a heavy burden to her? What do you think she would consider a successful woman's life?

4. Gilman is talking about the situation of middle- and upper-middle-class Victorian women. How valid or invalid do you find her assertions about women, independence, and the need for work today? How do you think women who work entirely in the home today feel about their independence or the value of their work?

5. What is your evaluation of Gilman's belief that a young man confronting life can try for anything he wants, do any kind of work he wants, and keep getting new opportunities if the work he is doing doesn't suit him? Do you agree? Why or why not?

6. In her book on the history of American housework, *Never Done*, Susan Strasser writes, "When Charlotte Perkins Gilman described the food of her ideal future, she envisioned kitchenless houses; individuals and families would patronize establishments that served hot cooked food ready to eat, produced according to the industrial principles of the division of labor and economies of scale. Eighty years later her dream has come true at McDonald's." From what you have read of Gilman and what you know of McDonald's, how valid is Strasser's assertion?

For Writing

1. Write an essay in which you analyze a major compromise made by your mother, another female relative, a friend, or you for the sake of financial security. The choice can be personal or professional, and you can argue either for or against it, but, even if you disagree with the result, try to be objective. What reasons or assertions were given or assumed in making the trade-off? What values or beliefs supported it? What pressures, economic or otherwise, were brought to bear on the person who made the compromise?

2. Research and write a report to share with your peers about a Victorian American woman who found a way to combine work and marriage, or one who chose work over marriage (for example, political activists Susan B. Anthony and Carrie Chapman Catt, or writers such as Harriet Beecher Stowe, Louisa May Alcott, Kate Chopin, and Edith Wharton). Pay special attention to the economic and social obstacles these women had to struggle with in order to find fulfilling work.

∞ *Two Women Sewing* (ca. 1907)

JACOB RIIS

Jacob Riis (1849–1914) was born in Denmark and emigrated to the United States as a young man. He became famous as a reporter and social crusader whose books about immigrant life in New York at the turn of the century helped mobilize public opinion and educate his readers about the shocking working conditions and poverty in which many immigrants were forced to live. Riis was active in the movements to build small parks and playgrounds and to reform tenement houses and schools. His books include How the Other Half Lives *(1890),* The Children of the Poor *(1892),* Children of the Tenements *(1903), and* The Making of an American *(1901). This photograph is from* Children of the Tenements.

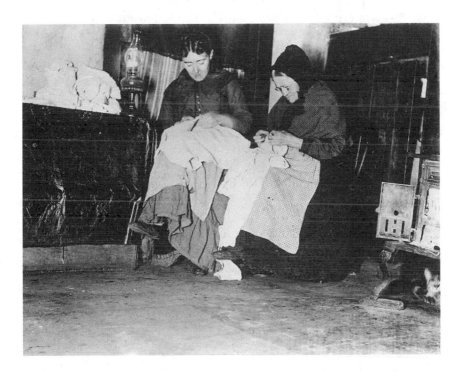

For Journals

What other documentary photographs, war photographs, or historical photographs have you seen? What made the greatest impression on you, and why?

For Discussion

1. With no other information except the picture itself, what can you deduce about the working conditions depicted in this photograph? Which details in this picture are the most persuasive in expressing the women's poverty or misery?

2. Describe the contents of this photograph in detail. How similar or different are the two women? How would you describe their body language? Why does including both of them create a more powerful image than just one figure would?

3. If this picture were in color instead of black and white, what colors do you think would predominate? What are the advantages of using only black and white for documentary pictures? How might color change the overall effect?

For Writing

Jacob Riis was one of the most famous documentary photographers of his time. Look at a book on immigrant life (such as Irving Howe's *World of Our Fathers,* for example), and find another picture by Riis, by Alfred Stieglitz, or by any of the photographers who took pictures of immigrant workers in order to document the conditions under which they lived. Write an essay in which you compare and contrast the Riis picture here with another image of immigrant labor—sweatshop workers, immigrant neighborhoods in New York, street peddlers, and so on. Examine how the figures are arranged, how the background (other people, objects, or interiors) is composed, and how those details contribute to the overall impression. If you think the photographer is exposing an injustice, discuss what the injustice is, how you deduced its nature and seriousness from the photograph, and how persuasive the photograph is to you.

∞ FROM *Going Out* (1994)

DAVID NASAW

David Nasaw (1945–) is a professor of history at the College of Staten Island of the City University of New York. He is the author of Schooled to Order: A Social History of Public Schooling in the United States *(1972) and* Children of the City: At Work and at Play *(1985). This selection is from* Going Out *(1994), a social history of American popular entertainment—vaudeville, amusement parks, etc.— before World War II.*

. . . The rise of public amusements was a by-product of the enormous expansion of the cities. Commercial entertainments were, in this period at least, an urban phenomenon. Their rise and fall were inevitably and inextricably linked to the fortunes of the cities that sustained them.

Between 1870 and 1920, American cities flourished as never before. The urban population of the nation increased from under ten to over fifty-four million people. Per capita income and free time expanded as well. Between 1870 and 1900, real income for nonfarm employees increased by more than 50 percent, while the cost of living, as measured by the consumer price index, decreased by 50 percent. This increase in wages was accompanied by a steady decrease in work hours. The average manufacturing worker worked three and a half hours less in 1910 than in 1890; for many blue-collar workers, unionized employees, and white-collar workers, the decrease in the workweek was even more dramatic. It also was in this period that the Saturday half-holiday and the "vacation habit" arrived in the American city. Although . . . most workers still had to finance their own vacations, increasing numbers of white-collar employees were beginning to take days, even a week or more, off during the warm-weather months.

As Roy Rosenzweig and a generation of labor and social historians have argued, the quest for leisure time "reverberated through the labor struggles of the late nineteenth and early twentieth centuries. As a compositor told the U.S. Senate Committee on Relations Between Labor and Capital in 1883: 'A workingman wants something besides food and clothes in this country. . . . He wants recreation.'" "Going out" was more than an escape from the tedium of work, it was the gateway into a privileged sphere of everyday life. The ability to take time out from work for recreation and public sociability was the dividing line between old worlds and new. Peasants and beasts of burden spent their lives at work; American workers and citizens went out at night and took days off in the summer.

Recreation and play were not luxuries but necessities in the modern city. As Daniel Rodgers has noted, the workday had been shortened by "squeezing periods of relaxation and amusement out of working hours, by trading long hours of casual work for shorter, more concentrated workdays." Instead of the older "interfusion of free and work time," there was now "an increasing segregation of work and play into distinct categories." The fear of idle time as the devil's workshop gave way to a reverence for play, promoted alike by middle-class reformers and working-class organizers. As the Yiddish *Tageblatt* advised its Jewish readers in the spring of 1907, "He who can enjoy and does not enjoy commits a sin."

While all the city's workers, even its most recent immigrants, [5] joined the assembling public for commercial amusements, it was the workers in white collars who constituted the critical element in the construction of the new "nightlife." As the white-collar sector of the work force increased in size in the late nineteenth and early twentieth centuries, so did the potential audience for the new public amusements. In 1880, there had been 5,000 typists and stenographers in the nation. By 1910, the number had increased sixtyfold to 300,000, while the overall clerical work force had risen from 160,000 to more than 1.7 million. From a negligible 2.4 percent of the total work force in 1870, the number of clerical and sales workers grew to a substantial 11 percent by

1920. In the big cities, the percentage of white-collar workers was even greater: 24 percent of the Chicago work force in 1920 were white-collar workers, a large number of them women.

The city's white-collar workers were the most avid consumers of the commercial pleasures. Their work was increasingly regimented, concentrated, and tedious, creating a need for recreation. And, compared to that of blue-collar workers, it provided them with sufficient time, resources, and energy to go out at night. For factory, mill, and manual workers who had to get up at five in the morning to be at work by six, the consequences of a night "out" were considerable. Clerical and sales workers could, on the other hand, stay out late, get a good night's sleep, and still get to work on time.

The new amusements were "public" and "commercial" as well as urban. The terms, in this period at least, became almost interchangeable, as the city's showmen, learning the new calculus of public entertainments, lowered prices to welcome the largest possible audience to their establishments. Although in the long run, it was growth in the demand, not the supply, side that would prompt the expansion of commercial entertainments, the showmen played a considerable role in assembling the new urban public. To succeed in the show business (as it was called throughout this period), the amusement entrepreneurs had to do more than build theaters; they had to provide commercial amusements and amusement sites that were public in the sense that they belonged to no particular social groups, exciting enough to appeal to the millions, and respectable enough to offend no one.

Leisure time remained a contested terrain, an arena of social life of such critical importance that the city's social, political, cultural, and religious elites dared not abandon it to the whims of consumers and the marketplace. To keep their critics at bay and attract an audience from the diverse social groups in the city, the show businessmen had to mold and maintain a revised moral taxonomy of shows and audiences. Vaudeville had to be certified as a decent entertainment for mixed audiences, with no relation to the male-only variety show that had preceded it; the amusement parks had to be promoted as "clean" outdoor shows for the whole family; the moving-picture theaters had to be distinguished from the penny arcades and peep shows. The envelope in which it was delivered mattered as much as the content of the show. An otherwise "indecent" act became "decent" when presented in an amusement site certified as "respectable." It was permissible to stare at gyrating belly dancers on the world's fair midways, if the dancers in question were performing "authentic" foreign dances; women in tights or tight-fitting bathing suits could appear on the vaudeville stage, if they were billed as acrobats or championship swimmers; holding onto a member of the opposite sex was acceptable at the amusement park, if it happened "accidentally" on the cyclone.

*   *   *

No matter how hungry city folk might have been for cheap amuse-ments or how eager the show businessmen were to provide them, the expansion in commercial amusements could not have occurred without accompanying advances in technology, in particular the electrification of the metropolis . . . the lighting of the city by electricity, the sine qua non for the expansion of urban "nightlife" in the late nineteenth and early twentieth centuries.

Incandescent lighting transformed the city from a dark and treacher-   10
ous netherworld into a glittering multicolored wonderland. Nineteenth-century authors had described city streets after dark as sinister and filled with danger. The gas lamps did not "light" up the night as much as cast into shadow the disreputable doings and personages of slum, tenderloin, and levee. In *New York by Gas-Light*, first published in 1850, George Foster, the *New-York Tribune* reporter and best-selling author, described in lurid detail "the fearful mysteries of darkness in the me-tropolis—the festivities of prostitution, the orgies of pauperism, the haunts of theft and murder, the scenes of drunkenness and beastly de-bauch, and all the sad realities that go to make up the lower stratum—the under-ground story—of life in New York!"

Fifty years after Foster wrote his account, Theodore Dreiser pub-lished *Sister Carrie*, an account of city life that turned upside-down the sunshine/shadow, light/dark, day/night tropes used by Foster and other nineteenth-century authors. For Dreiser, it was in daylight, not af-ter dark, that the city was at its grayest, cruelest, and most distressing. The coming of the night was a sign of promise, not depravity. "Ah, the promise of the night. . . . What old illusion of hope is not here forever re-peated! Says the soul of the toiler to itself, 'I shall soon be free. I shall be in the ways and the hosts of the merry. The streets, the lamp, the lighted chamber set for dining are for me. The theaters, the halls, the parties, the ways of rest and the paths of song—these are mine in the night.'" Only after dark, when the "street lamps" shone brightly with their "merry twinkle," did joy return to the city as the "artificial fires of mer-riment" dispelled the gloom and chill, providing "light and warmth."

The sparkling city that Sister Carrie traveled to was Chicago in 1900, when electric lighting was still new and wondrous. A Chicago journal-ist, writing in 1900, declared that "he had witnessed a profound change in the city's lighting, a revolution 'little short of marvelous. The field where but yesterday the flickering gas flame held full sway now blazes nightly in the glow of myriads of electric lamps, aggregating in inten-sity the illuminating power of 15,000,000 candles.'" By 1903, the new Commonwealth Edison of Chicago turbogenerator was producing over 5,000 times more energy than the dynamos that had powered Edison's 1882 Pearl Street station. Electricity had, in the words of the historian Wolfgang Schivelbusch, "begun to permeate modern, urban life."

Unlike gas lamps, which were highly flammable, electric lamps could be kept on all night. The street lamps illuminated not simply the lamppost beneath but both sides of the street with a clear, bright white light, not the sooty gray of the gas lamps. The commercial lights of restaurants, shops, and theaters added the merry twinkle that gave the "nocturnal round of business, pleasure and illumination . . . we think of as night life . . . its own special atmosphere."

The artificially illuminated streets provided city residents with an added incentive to leave their darkened or gas-lit flats to go out at night "when all the shop fronts are lighted, and the entrances to the theaters blaze out on the sidewalk like open fireplaces." As the journalist Richard Harding Davis wrote of Broadway in 1892, "It is at this hour that the clerk appears, dressed in his other suit, the one which he keeps for the evening, and the girl bachelor, who . . . has found her hall bedroom cold and lonely after the long working day behind a counter or at a loom and the loneliness tends to homesickness . . . puts on her hat and steps down a side-street and loses herself in the unending processions of Broadway, where, though she knows no one, and no one wants to know her, there is light and color, and she is at least not alone."

15   Earlier in the nineteenth century, young people who walked the streets after dark would have been admonished for placing themselves in mortal danger of moral contamination. But the electric street lights had gone a long way toward purging "nightlife" of its aura of licentiousness. Although there were no accurate statistics to prove the case, it was taken for granted that the electric street lamps were removing much of the danger that had lurked in the dark. A 1912 article in *The American City* listed first among "the advantages accruing from ornamental street lighting [a decrease in] lawlessness and crime . . . 'A light is as good as a policeman' . . . A criminologist of world-wide fame, and one who is considered an authority, says that he would rather have plenty of electric lights and clean streets than all the law and order societies in existence."

Electricity was not simply providing power to light the urban landscape but was reconfiguring it into a fairyland of illuminated shapes, signs, and brightly colored, sometimes animated, messages and images—forty-foot green pickles, gigantic pieces of chewing gum, Roman chariots racing on top of a hotel. The lights of the city created "a new kind of visual text," a new landscape of modernity. They foregrounded the city's illuminated messages, its theaters, tall buildings, hotels, restaurants, department stores, and "Great White Ways," while erasing its "unattractive areas and cast[ing] everything unsightly into an impenetrable darkness. If by day poor or unsightly sections called out for social reform, by night the city was a purified world of light, simplified into a spectacular pattern, interspersed with now-unimportant blanks."

The lights "marked" the city as a "sight" worthy of respect, even admiration. But they also focused attention on the city as a source of amusement. The lighting of the lights signaled that the workday was over and the time for play at hand. As the editorial in the February 1904 issue of *The Four-Track News* declared, "It is an old, old theme, and an oft told tale—but when the lights are on, and the season is in full swing, as it is now, any evening, that great thoroughfare, with its business activity, its wonderful social life, its rialto with its tragic comedians and its comic tragedians . . . when Broadway is really itself, it is a continuous vaudeville that is worth many times the 'price of admission'— especially as no admission price is asked. Where else is there such a free performance—such a festive panorama of gay life as Broadway 'puts up' when the lights are on."

Electrification made going out at night not only safer and more exciting but easier and cheaper than ever before. The dynamos and generators that lit the street lamps also powered the trolleys that tied together the city and its neighborhoods. Between 1890 and 1902, investment in electric and cable cars quadrupled, track mileage tripled, and fare passengers doubled. In 1890, only 15 percent of all American streetcars had been electrified, and the remainder were connected to horses. By 1902, 94 percent were electric. The flat nickel fare and free transfers between lines made streetcar travel accessible to more city residents and workers.

In connecting the city's business and residential districts, the electric streetcars fostered the growth—and transformation—of "downtown" into a central shopping and entertainment district. In Chicago, as Sam Bass Warner has written, the Loop, tied by electric streetcar to outlying neighborhoods, prospered as never before. "The downtown district became *the* city for Chicagoans. It was a place of work for tens of thousands, a market for hundreds of thousands, a theater for thousands more."

The new "downtowns" were defined geographically by the con- 20 vergence of the railroad and trolley lines and framed architecturally by the mammoth new terminals that welcomed out-of-towners into the heart of the city. The majority of those who resided temporarily in the nearby hotels had come for business purposes: to buy, sell, insure, inspect, or display their goods. Before, after, and sometimes even during business hours, however, they expected to be entertained. They were joined in this pursuit by white-collar workers who stayed "downtown" after work; by city residents who worked and lived in outlying residential neighborhoods but rode the streetcar to the theater district; and by suburbanites who were linked by electric "interurban" to the city and its nighttime pleasures. For all of them, the city was becoming as much a place of play as a place of work.

For Journals

Do you think of leisure as an entitlement? A privilege? A right? Why?

For Discussion

1.   In your own words, state Nasaw's thesis about the development of leisure time in America. Which social and technological evidence does he present to describe this radical change in the lives of working people?

2.   How does Nasaw explain the connection between work and leisure time for ordinary Americans? Is it more of a reward for working or a proof of success? Is it a status symbol or a physical necessity? Why shouldn't it continue to be reserved, as it previously had been, for wealthy people to enjoy?

3.   What leisure activities that Americans pursue now are the modern parallels for the vaudeville shows and amusement parks that Nasaw describes? What needs do you think those activities fulfill for us now that distinguish us from the Americans whom Nasaw discusses?

4.   What do you and your friends spend your leisure time on? Do you think of it as an opportunity to go out, or are you more likely to watch television? How active or passive is your use of free time, and why?

For Writing

1.   Write an essay in which you respond to discussion question 4. Explain what your leisure time is for and how you spend it. Use Nasaw's thesis about leisure in America as a basis for comparison. In what ways do your ideas about leisure for Americans in general and for you in particular substantiate or contradict his argument?

2.   If you have ever been to Disneyland, Disney World, Universal Studios, Las Vegas, Atlantic City, or any similar place that millions of Americans visit for leisure or vacation, write a description of your visit. Include your observations on who goes there and why, how they behave, whether you thought the entertainment and atmosphere were in good taste, and your own response to the experience. Support your conclusions with details from your own visit.

∞ *Duke Kahanamoku* (1914)

HAWAIIAN TOURIST BOARD

Duke Paoa Kahanamoku (1890–1968) was the greatest swimmer of his time. The winner of three Olympic gold medals, he set three world records in the 100-meter freestyle. After he retired from swimming he acted occasionally in movies, became the sheriff of Honolulu, and was a perpetually popular symbol of the Hawaiian islands.

For Journals

What would be your idea of a perfect place to spend a vacation? Describe in detail your idea of the ideal leisure environment.

For Discussion

1. What image does this postcard give you of Hawaii? Of Duke himself? On what details do you base your impressions?

2. This postcard has an inner picture and an outer border with scenery; how do these two strengthen the card's impact? What adjectives would you use to describe the mood or emotion that results from their interplay?

3. How would you describe Duke's pose—his tense body, clenched fists, and big smile? Is it welcoming? Challenging? Competitive? How does his pose contribute to the impression the tourist board wants to create?

4. Look at the text on the card; how does it tell a tourist that he or she would have a good time in Hawaii? Which American tourist audience do you think would be most attracted by this postcard? What other images of Hawaii might succeed in attracting visitors?

For Writing

This postcard is an early-twentieth-century American manifestation of the leisure postcard, advertising various forms of play and vacations accessible to the middle class. Find a current poster (for example, in a travel agency), a postcard, or a magazine advertisement that promotes sports and leisure in Hawaii or anywhere else—Bermuda, the Rockies, New York City, and so on. Write an essay in which you describe the picture, compare it to Duke's postcard, and decide how much, if anything, has changed over seventy-five years in promoting leisure travel. What lifestyle is being advertised? What activity or kind of entertainment? Who is the presumed audience? Does the ad portray an idea of leisure that you find attractive?

∞ *Physical Culture* (1927)

Physical Culture *magazine was edited by Bernarr Macfadden (1868–1955), who took it over in 1899. Macfadden was part showman, part entrepreneur, and he*

*had a sensational career in marketing health products and promoting himself as a
health guru. He raised the circulation of this monthly magazine from three thousand
to one hundred thousand subscribers, partly by using somewhat revealing pictures
of women. He also established "healthatoriums" and called himself a professor of
psyscultopathy and brain breathing.*

For Journals

How important are exercise and leisure in your own life?

For Discussion

1.   Judging from the appearance of the young woman on the cover and what she is wearing, what sport or sports is she supposed to be engaged in? Since she is a standard-bearer for health and exercise, why isn't she shown sweating or working hard?

2.   Look at some contemporary exercise and self-improvement magazines, featuring young women on the cover. How is their image of a healthy woman exercising similar to or different from the way this 1927 cover presents the same subject?

3.   How do you respond to this opinion of the editor of *Physical Culture:* "the individual was always solely responsible for his or her own condition—economic, social, or medical. If taken by some serious disease, people had only themselves to blame"? What attitude do you take toward the idea that you can control the state of your own well-being through your choices and behavior?

4.   Look at the articles listed on the front of the ad; how many of these would be of interest to you? Which ones address concerns relevant to your own experience?

For Writing

Referring back to discussion item 2, look at the covers of several contemporary magazines that advertise youth, health, and attractiveness: *Cosmopolitan, Self, Esquire,* a men's or women's fashion magazine, and so on. Pick one cover, and write an essay in which you compare it with the cover of *Physical Culture.* Look for the rhetorical strategies that underlie each. What is each ad trying to sell? What points do you think the magazine wants to convey to you about the connections between health and attractiveness? Health and youth? How are the topics of the articles listed on the cover of the contemporary magazine similar to or different from those on the *Physical Culture* cover?

∞ *Union Maid* (1940)

WOODY GUTHRIE

Woody Guthrie (1912–1967) was probably the greatest of all American folksingers and composers. A native of Oklahoma, he spent most of his life on the road, hitching rides on freight trains or living in migrant worker camps. In hundreds of songs, he detailed the experiences of Americans caught in the throes of economic dislocation

during the Great Depression: migrant workers, union organizers, wanderers and ho-
bos, and particularly people forced to move from Oklahoma by the terrible dust storms
of the 1930s. His most famous song, "This Land Is Your Land," has become a sort of
informal national anthem.

There once was a union maid
Who never was afraid
Of goons and ginks and company finks
And the deputy sheriffs who made the raids;
She went to the union hall   5
When a meeting it was called,
And when the company boys came 'round
She always stood her ground.

CHORUS:
Oh, you can't scare me.   10
I'm sticking to the union,
I'm sticking to the union,
I'm sticking to the union.
Oh, you can't scare me.
I'm sticking to the union,   15
I'm sticking to the union
Till the day I die.

This union maid was wise
To the tricks of company spies.
She never got fooled by a company stool,   20
She'd always organize the guys.
She always got her way
When she struck for higher pay,
She'd show her union card to the company guard
And this is what she'd say: 25

You gals who want to be free,
Just take a little tip from me:
Get you a man who's a union man
And join the Ladies' Auxiliary;
Married life ain't hard   30
When you've got a union card,
A union man has a happy life
When he's got a union wife.

For Journals

What songs do you associate with a specific event, cause, or place in
your life?

For Discussion

1.   Describe the intended audience for this song. Is it aimed at people similar to the characters in the song? Where can you imagine Guthrie singing it, and why?

2.   Given the subject matter, why do you think the song is written from the point of view of a woman rather than a man? In what ways is a woman's perspective presented in the song as similar to or different from a man's? Would using a female narrator broaden or lessen its appeal to its intended audience?

3.   Judging from the lyrics, what tactics were involved in discouraging the formation of unions? Guthrie made no secret of where his sympathies lay. How does he convey them to you? How does he characterize the other side? How persuasive is he?

For Writing

1.   A lot of Guthrie's music was based on specific historical situations, such as the battle between pro- and anti-union forces or the effects of the Great Depression on farmers in the Midwest. But many of the songs have entered the larger culture. If you can get a tape or CD of Guthrie's music, listen to some of his other songs, such as "This Land Is Your Land." Pick two or three of the most popular songs, and write an essay in which you comment on their message, the effectiveness of the lyrics, and your description of the intended audience. What emotions is he expressing? In what sense is his evocation of America one that you recognize?

2.   Songs are invariably associated with crucial developments in American history. Research the music related to one event—for example, the Civil War, World War I or II, the Great Depression, the Vietnam War. Write an essay in which you explain the circumstances in which it was written or became popular, the positive and negative reactions of audiences, the cause or event with which it was associated, and the ideas it represented.

⮞ FROM *Working* (1972)

STUDS TERKEL

Studs Terkel (1912–) grew up and still lives in Chicago. Having worked as a disc jockey and a sports commentator, among other jobs, he has for many years hosted a daily interview program, which is broadcast all over the country; for a writer to be interviewed by Mr. Terkel is considered a great honor. Mr. Terkel is the author of several books, including Division Street: America *(1967),* The Good War *(1984), and* Hard Times *(1970). All of them use interviews with Americans from all walks of life to reveal the effect of historic events, like the Depression and World War II, on the lives of individuals. The following selection is from his book about Americans and what they do for a living, called* Working *(1974).*

The Mason

Carl Murray Bates

We're in a tavern no more than thirty yards from the banks of the Ohio. Toward the far side of the river, Alcoa smokestacks belch forth: an uneasy coupling of a bucolic past and an industrial present. The waters are polluted, yet the jobs out there offer the townspeople their daily bread.

He is fifty-seven years old. He's a stonemason who has pursued his craft since he was seventeen. None of his three sons is in his trade.

As far as I know, masonry is older than carpentry, which goes clear back to Bible times. Stone mason goes back way *before* Bible time: the pyramids of Egypt, things of that sort. Anybody that starts to build anything stone, rock, or brick, start on the northeast corner. Because when they built King Solomon's Temple, they started on the northeast corner. To this day, you look at your courthouses, your big public buildings, you look at the cornerstone, when it was created, what year, it will be on the northeast corner. If I was gonna build a septic tank, I would start on the northeast corner. (Laugh.) Superstition, I suppose.

With stone we build just about anything. Stone is the oldest and best building material that ever was. Stone was being used even by the cavemen that put it together with mud. They built out of stone before they even used logs. He got him a cave, he built stone across the front. And he learned to use dirt, mud, to make the stones lay there without sliding around—which was the beginnings of mortar, which we still call mud. The Romans used mortar that's almost as good as we have today.

Everyone hears these things, they just don't remember 'em. But me being in the profession, when I hear something in that line, I remember it. Stone's my business. I, oh, sometimes talk to architects and engineers that have made a study and I pick up the stuff here and there.

Every piece of stone you pick up is different, the grain's a little different and this and that. It'll split one way and break the other. You pick up your stone and look at it and make an educated guess. It's a pretty good day layin' stone or brick. Not tiring. Anything you like to do isn't tiresome. It's hard work; stone is heavy. At the same time, you get interested in what you're doing and you usually fight the clock the other way. You're not lookin' for quittin'. You're wondering you haven't got enough done and it's almost quittin' time. (Laughs.) I ask the hod carrier what time it is and he says two thirty. I say, "Oh, my Lord, I was gonna get a whole lot more than this."

5   I pretty well work by myself. On houses, usually just one works. I've got the hod carrier there, but most of the time I talk to myself, "I'll get my hammer and I'll knock the chip off there." (Laughs.) A good hod carrier is half your day. He won't work as hard as a poor one. He knows what to do and make very move count makin' the mortar. It has to be so much water, so much sand. His skill is to see that you don't run out of anything. The hod carrier, he's above the laborer. He has a certain amount of prestige.

I think a laborer feels that he's the low man. Not so much that he works with his hands, it's that he's at the bottom of the scale. He always wants to get up to a skilled trade. Of course he'd make more money. The main thing is the common laborer—even the word *common* laborer—just sounds so common, he's at the bottom. Many that works with his hands takes pride in his work.

I get a lot of phone calls when I get home: how about showin' me how and I'll do it myself? I always wind up doin' it for 'em. (Laughs.) So I take a lot of pride in it and I do get, oh, I'd say, a lot of praise or whatever you want to call it. I don't suppose anybody, however much he's recognized, wouldn't like to be recognized a little more. I think I'm pretty well recognized.

One of my sons is an accountant and the other two are bankers. They're mathematicians, I suppose you'd call 'em that. Air-conditioned offices and all that. They always look at the house I build. They stop by and see me when I'm aworkin'. Always want me to come down and fix somethin' on their house, too. (Laughs.) They don't buy a house that I don't have to look at it first. Oh sure, I've got to crawl under it and look on the roof, you know . . .

I can't seem to think of any young masons. So many of 'em before, the man lays stone and his son follows his footsteps. Right now the only one of these sons I can think of is about forty, fifty years old.

10   I started back in the Depression times when there wasn't any apprenticeships. You just go out and if you could hold your job, that's it. I was just a kid then. Now I worked real hard and carried all the blocks I could. Then I'd get my trowel and I'd lay one or two. The second day the boss told me: I think you could lay enough blocks to earn your wages. So I guess I had only one day of apprenticeship. Usually it takes about three years of being a hod carrier to start. And it takes another ten or fifteen years to learn the skill.

I admired the men that we had at that time that were stonemasons. They knew their trade. So naturally I tried to pattern after them. There's been very little change in the work. Stone is still stone, mortar is still the same as it was fifty years ago. The style of stone has changed a little. We use a lot more, we call it golf. A stone as big as a baseball up to as big as a basketball. Just round balls and whatnot. We just fit 'em in the wall that way.

Automation has tried to get in the bricklayer. Set 'em with a crane. I've seen several put up that way. But you've always got in-between the windows and this and that. It just doesn't seem to pan out. We do have a power saw. We do have an electric power mix to mix the mortar, but the rest of it's done by hand as it always was.

In the old days they all seemed to want it cut out and smoothed. It's harder now because you have no way to use your tools. You have no way to use a string, you have no way to use a level or a plumb. You just have to look at it because it's so rough and many irregularities. You have to just back up and look at it.

All construction, there's always a certain amount of injuries. A scaffold will break and so on. But practically no real danger. All I ever did do was work on houses, so we don't get up very high—maybe two stories. Very seldom that any more. Most of 'em are one story. And so many of 'em use stone for a trim. They may go up four, five feet and then paneling or something. There's a lot of skinned fingers or you hit your finger with a hammer. Practically all stone is worked with hammers and chisels. I wouldn't call it dangerous at all.

Stone's my life. I daydream all the time, most times it's on stone. 15 Oh, I'm gonna build me a stone cabin down on the Green River. I'm gonna build stone cabinets in the kitchen. That stone door's gonna be awful heavy and I don't know how to attach the hinges. I've got to figure out how to make a stone roof. That's the kind of thing. All my dreams, it seems like it's got to have a piece of rock mixed in it.

If I got some problem that's bothering me, I'll actually wake up in the night and think of it. I'll sit at the table and get a pencil and paper and go over it, makin' marks on paper or drawin' or however . . . this way or that way. Now I've got to work this and I've only got so much. Or they decided they want it that way when you already got it fixed this way. Anyone hates tearing his work down. It's all the same price but you still don't like to do it.

These fireplaces, you've got to figure how they'll throw out heat, the way you curve the fireboxes inside. You have to draw a line so they reflect heat. But if you throw out too much of a curve, you'll have them smoke. People in these fine houses don't want a puff of smoke coming out of the house.

The architect draws the picture and the plans, and the draftsman and the engineer, they help him. They figure the strength and so on. But when it comes to actually makin' the curves and doin' the work, you've got to do it with your hands. It comes right back to your hands.

When you get into stone, you're gettin' away from the prefabs, you're gettin' into the better homes. Usually at this day and age they'll start into sixty to seventy thousand and run up to about half a million. We've got one goin' now that's mighty close, three or four hundred thousand. That type of house is what we build.

20   The lumber is not near as good as it used to be. We have better fabricating material, such as plywood and sheet rock and things of that sort, but the lumber itself is definitely inferior. Thirty, forty years ago a house was almost entirely made of lumber, wood floors . . . Now they have vinyl, they have carpet, everything, and so on. The framework wood is getting to be of very poor quality.

But stone is still stone and the bricks are actually more uniform than they used to be. Originally they took a clay bank . . . I know a church been built that way. Went right on location, dug a hole in the ground and formed bricks with their hands. They made the bricks that built the building on the spot.

Now we've got modern kilns, modern heat, the temperature don't vary. They got better bricks now than they used to have. We've got machines that make brick, so they're made true. Where they used to, they were pretty rough. I'm buildin' a big fireplace now out of old brick. They run wide, long, and it's a headache. I've been two weeks on that one fireplace.

The toughest job I ever done was this house, a hundred years old plus. The lady wanted one room left just that way. And this doorway had to be closed. It had deteriorated and weathered for over a hundred years. The bricks was made out of broken pieces, none of 'em were straight. If you lay 'em crooked, it gets awful hard right there. You spend a lifetime tryin' to learn to lay bricks straight. And it took a half-day to measure with a spoon, to try to get the mortar to match. I'd have so much dirt, so much soot, so much lime, so when I got the recipe right I could make it in bigger quantity. Then I made it with a coffee cup. Half a cup of this, half a cup of that . . . I even used soot out of a chimney and sweepin's off the floor. I was two days layin' up a little doorway, mixin' the mortar and all. The boss told the lady it couldn't be done. I said, "Give me the time, I believe I can do it." I defy you to find where that door is right now. That's the best job I ever done.

There's not a house in this country that I haven't built that I don't look at every time I go by. (Laughs.) I can set here now and actually in my mind see so many that you wouldn't believe. If there's one stone in there crooked, I know where it's at and I'll never forget it. Maybe thirty years, I'll know a place where I should have took that stone out and re-done it but I didn't. I still notice it. The people who live there might not notice it, but I notice it. I never pass that house that I don't think of it. I've got one house in mind right now. (Laughs.) That's the work of my hands. 'Cause you see, stone, you don't prepaint it, you don't camouflage it. It's there, just like I left it forty years ago.

25   I can't imagine a job where you go home and maybe go by a year

later and you don't know what you've done. My work, I can see what I did the first day I started. All my work is set right out there in the open and I can look at it as I go by. It's something I can see the rest of my life. Forty years ago, the first blocks I ever laid in my life, when I was seventeen years old. I never go through Eureka—a little town down there on the river—that I don't look thataway. It's always there.

Immortality as far as we're concerned. Nothin' in this world lasts forever, but did you know that stone—Bedford limestone, they claim—deteriorates one-sixteenth of an inch every hundred years? And it's around four or five inches for a house. So that's gettin' awful close. (Laughs.)

For Journals

What skills or knowledge of a craft do you have or would you like to have?

For Discussion

1. Usually the word *professional* is used to describe jobs that require a college education or advanced degrees. Judging from the text of this interview, explain Mr. Bates's sense of pride in his job. In what ways is he a professional?

2. What do you think of the status hierarchy Mr. Bates sets up among levels of workers? Between him and his own sons who have white-collar jobs?

3. How does Terkel's decision to call this interview "The Mason" instead of "Mr. Bates" establish his attitude toward Mr. Bates and his work? How does it affect your own attitude toward Mr. Bates?

4. Looking at the text, identify the assertions Mr. Bates makes to connect the history of masonry and the possibilities for achieving immortality. Are those possibilities affected by the fact that no young masons are following in his footsteps? Is that irrelevant? Why or why not?

For Writing

1. In the excerpt from his *Autobiography* at the beginning of this chapter, Franklin mentions how much he loved watching craftsmen do their work. Write an essay in which you compare Franklin's attitude toward work, pride in one's occupation, ambition, and excellence with Mr. Bates's ideas on the same subjects or on other work-related issues you find in the two texts. Use specific references and quotations from each to support your points.

2. Do an interview with someone who you know who works hard at his or her job. Pick someone, in or outside the home, whose work you admire or are curious about. If you can, use a tape recorder for accuracy and show the person a copy of what you've written. Encourage this person to show you or tell you exactly what he or she does, how meaningful the work is or isn't, and what the most rewarding parts of it are. Be sure that whoever you interview understands that you are treating his or her work with respect.

∝ The Importance of Work (1983)

GLORIA STEINEM

Born in Toledo, Ohio, Gloria Steinem (1934–) was educated at Smith College and went on to study at the University of Delhi and the University of Calcutta, India. She was the editor and cofounder of Ms. *magazine and has played an important part in the women's movement. Steinem's works include* Outrageous Acts and Everyday Rebellions *(1983),* Revolution from Within *(1992), and* Moving Beyond Words *(1994). In her essay "The Importance of Work," she examines the relationship between personal and professional fulfillment.*

Toward the end of the 1970s, the *Wall Street Journal* devoted an eight-part front-page series to "the working woman"—that is, the influx of women into the paid-labor force—as the greatest change in American life since the Industrial Revolution.

Many women readers greeted both the news and the definition with cynicism. After all, women have always worked. If all the productive work of human maintenance that women do in the home were valued at its replacement cost, the gross national product of the United States would go up by 26 percent. It's just that we are now more likely than ever before to leave our poorly rewarded, low-security, high-risk job of homemaking (though we're still trying to explain that it's a perfectly good one and that the problem is male society's refusal both to do it and to give it an economic value) for more secure, independent and better-paid jobs outside the home.

Obviously, the real work revolution won't come until all productive work is rewarded—including child rearing and other jobs done in the home—and men are integrated into so-called women's work as well as vice versa. But the radical change being touted by the *Journal* and other media is one part of that long integration process: the unprecedented flood of women into salaried jobs, that is, into the labor force as it has been male-defined and previously occupied by men. We are already more than 41 percent of it—the highest proportion in history. Given the fact that women also make up a whopping 69 percent of the "discouraged labor force" (that is, people who need jobs but don't get counted in the unemployment statistics because they've given up looking), plus an official female unemployment rate that is substantially higher than men's, it's clear that we could expand to become fully half of the national work force by 1990.

Faced with this determination of women to find a little independence and to be paid and honored for our work, experts have rushed to ask: "Why?" It's a question rarely directed at male workers. Their basic motivations of survival and personal satisfaction are taken for granted. Indeed, men are regarded as "odd" and therefore subjects for sociological study and journalistic reports only when they *don't* have work, even if they are rich and don't need jobs or are poor and can't find them. Nonetheless, pollsters and sociologists have gone to great expense to prove that women work outside the home because of dire financial need, or if we persist despite the presence of a wage-earning male, out of some desire to buy "little extras" for our families, or even out of good old-fashioned penis envy.

Job interviewers and even our own families may still ask salaried 5 women the big "Why?" If we have small children at home or are in some job regarded as "men's work," the incidence of such questions increases. Condescending or accusatory versions of "What's a nice girl like you doing in a place like this?" have not disappeared from the workplace.

How do we answer these assumptions that we are "working" out of some pressing or peculiar need? Do we feel okay about arguing that it's as natural for us to have salaried jobs as for our husbands whether or not we have young children at home? Can we enjoy strong career ambitions without worrying about being thought "unfeminine"? When we confront men's growing resentment of women competing in the work force (often in the form of such guilt-producing accusations as "You're taking men's jobs away" or "You're damaging your children"), do we simply state that a decent job is a basic human right for everybody?

I'm afraid the answer is often no. As individuals and as a movement, we tend to retreat into some version of a tactically questionable defense: "Womenworkbecausewehaveto." The phrase has become one word, one key on the typewriter—an economic form of the socially "feminine" stance of passivity and self-sacrifice. Under attack, we still tend to present ourselves as creatures of economic necessity and familial devotion. "Womenworkbecausewehaveto" has become the easiest thing to say.

Like most truisms, this one is easy to prove with statistics. Economic need *is* the most consistent work motive—for women as well as men. In 1976, for instance, 43 percent of all women in the paid-labor force were single, widowed, separated, or divorced, and working to support themselves and their dependents. An additional 21 percent were married to men who had earned less than ten thousand dollars in the previous year, the minimum then required to support a family of four. In fact, if you take men's pensions, stocks, real estate, and various forms of accumulated wealth into account, a good statistical case can be made that there are more women who "have" to work (that is, who have neither the accumulated wealth, nor husbands whose work or wealth can support them for the rest of their lives) than there are men with the same need. If we were going to ask one group "Do you really need this job?" we should ask men.

But the first weakness of the whole "have to work" defense is its deceptiveness. Anyone who has ever experienced dehumanized life on welfare or any other confidence-shaking dependency knows that a paid job may be preferable to the dole, even when the handout is coming from a family member. Yet the will and self-confidence to work on one's own can diminish as dependency and fear increase. That may explain why—contrary to the "have to" rationale—wives of men who earn less than three thousand dollars a year are actually *less* likely to be employed than wives whose husbands make ten thousand dollars a year or more.

10   Furthermore, the greatest proportion of employed wives is found among families with a total household income of twenty-five to fifty thousand dollars a year. This is the statistical underpinning used by some sociologists to prove that women's work is mainly important for boosting families into the middle or upper middle class. Thus, women's incomes are largely used for buying "luxuries" and "little extras": a neat double-whammy that renders us secondary within our families, and makes our jobs expendable in hard times. We may even go along with this interpretation (at least, up to the point of getting fired so a male can have our job). It preserves a husbandly ego-need to be seen as the primary breadwinner, and still allows us a safe "feminine" excuse for working.

But there are often rewards that we're not confessing. As noted in *The Two-Career Couple,* by Francine and Douglas Hall: "Women who hold jobs by choice, even blue-collar routine jobs, are more satisfied with their lives than are the full-time housewives."

In addition to personal satisfaction, there is also society's need for all its members' talents. Suppose that jobs were given out on only a "have to work" basis to both women and men—one job per household. It would be unthinkable to lose the unique abilities of, for instance, Eleanor Holmes Norton, the distinguished chair of the Equal Employment Opportunity Commission. But would we then be forced to question the important work of her husband, Edward Norton, who is also a distinguished lawyer? Since men earn more than twice as much as women on the average, the wife in most households would be more likely to give up her job. Does that mean the nation could do as well without millions of its nurses, teachers, and secretaries? Or that the rare man who earns less than his wife should give up his job?

It was this kind of waste of human talents on a society-wide scale that traumatized millions of unemployed or underemployed Americans during the Depression. Then, a one-job-per-household rule seemed somewhat justified, yet the concept was used to displace women workers only, create intolerable dependencies, and waste female talent that the country needed. That Depression experience, plus the energy and example of women who were finally allowed to work during the manpower shortage created by World War II, led Congress to reinterpret the meaning of the country's full-employment goal in its Economic Act of 1946. Full employment was officially defined as "the employment of those who want to work, without regard to whether their employment is, by some definition, necessary. This goal applies equally to men and women." Since bad economic times are again creating a resentment of employed women—as well as creating more need for women to be employed—we need such a goal more than ever. Women are again being caught in a tragic double bind: We are required to be strong and then punished for our strength.

Clearly, anything less than government and popular commitment to this 1946 definition of full employment will leave the less powerful groups, whoever they may be, in danger. Almost as important as the financial penalty paid by the powerless is the suffering that comes from being shut out of paid and recognized work. Without it, we lose much of our self-respect and our ability to prove that we are alive by making some difference in the world. That's just as true for the suburban woman as it is for the unemployed steel worker.

But it won't be easy to give up the passive defense of "weworkbe- 15
causewehaveto."

When a woman who is struggling to support her children and grandchildren on welfare sees her neighbor working as a waitress, even though that neighbor's husband has a job, she may feel resentful; and the waitress (of course, not the waitress's husband) may feel guilty. Yet unless we establish the obligation to provide a job for everyone who is willing and able to work, that welfare woman may herself be penalized by policies that give out only one public-service job per household. She and her daughter will have to make a painful and divisive decision about which of them gets that precious job, and the whole household will have to survive on only one salary.

A job as a human right is a principle that applies to men as well as women. But women have more cause to fight for it. The phenomenon of the "working woman" has been held responsible for everything from an increase in male impotence (which turned out, incidentally, to be attributable to medication for high blood pressure) to the rising cost of steak (which was due to high energy costs and beef import restrictions, not women's refusal to prepare the cheaper, slower-cooking cuts). Unless we see a job as part of every citizen's right to autonomy and personal fulfillment, we will continue to be vulnerable to someone else's idea of what "need" is, and whose "need" counts the most.

In many ways, women who do not have to work for simple survival, but who choose to do so nonetheless, are on the frontier of asserting this right for all women. Those with well-to-do husbands are dangerously easy for us to resent and put down. It's easier still to resent women from families of inherited wealth, even though men generally control and benefit from that wealth. (There is no Rockefeller Sisters Fund, no J. P. Morgan & Daughters, and sons-in-law may be the ones who really sleep their way to power.) But to prevent a woman whose husband or father is wealthy from earning her own living, and from gaining the self-confidence that comes with that ability, is to keep her needful of that unearned power and less willing to disperse it. Moreover, it is to lose forever her unique talents.

Perhaps modern feminists have been guilty of a kind of reverse snobbism that keeps us from reaching out to the wives and daughters of wealthy men; yet it was exactly such women who refused the restrictions of class and financed the first wave of feminist revolution.

20   For most of us, however, "womenworkbecausewehaveto" is just true enough to be seductive as a personal defense.

If we use it without also staking out the larger human right to a job, however, we will never achieve that right. And we will always be subject to the false argument that independence for women is a luxury affordable only in good economic times. Alternatives to layoffs will not be explored, acceptable unemployment will always be used to frighten those with jobs into accepting low wages, and we will never remedy the real cost, both to families and to the country, of dependent women and a massive loss of talent.

Worst of all, we may never learn to find productive, honored work as a natural part of ourselves and as one of life's basic pleasures.

For Journals

Why do you believe women work? Do they work for different reasons than men do?

For Discussion

1.   Steinem writes that "the real work revolution won't come until all productive work is rewarded—including child rearing and other jobs done in the home—and men are integrated into so-called women's work as well as vice versa" (paragraph 3). Do you believe that, a decade later, this revolution has begun? If so, to what do you attribute the change? If not, why not? Specify the assumptions and evidence on which you are basing your assertion.

2. Steinem takes issue with the "womenworkbecausewehaveto" (paragraph 7) rejoinder that has so often answered those who criticize women for holding down paid jobs outside the home. What is her counterassertion, and how does she support it? Do you find her argument convincing?

3. Do you believe the "womenworkbecausewehaveto" (paragraph 7) argument is valid? Support your point of view with specific examples, narrative, or other support.

4. Consider the following two quotations, the first from Gilman's *Women and Economics* (this chapter):

> But all that she may wish to have, all that she may wish to do, must come through a single channel and a single choice. Wealth, power, social distinction, fame—not only these, but home and happiness, reputation, ease, and pleasure, her bread and butter,—all, must come to her through a gold ring. (paragraph 5)

the second from Steinem's essay:

> "Womenworkbecausewehaveto." The phrase has become one word, one key on the typewriter—an economic form of the socially "feminine" stance of passivity and self-sacrifice. Under attack, we still tend to present ourselves as creatures of economic necessity and familial devotion. (paragraph 7)

Compare these two quotations by examining the different assumptions behind them, the evidence the authors provide to support them, and the extent to which they represent gender and work issues of their respective times.

5. Analyze the evidence on which Steinem bases her assertions. Do you agree with the conclusions she draws? Do you accept the evidence she cites?

For Writing

1. What is the importance of work to you? Write an essay arguing that the role and value of work is, or is not, determined by gender.

2. Compare the assertions about work and gender that Steinem makes with those that Gilman makes. You may want to create a dialogue between the two writers in responding to the assignment.

∝ FROM *Sports Illusion, Sports Reality* (1994)

LEONARD KOPPETT

Leonard Koppett (1926–) has been a sports reporter for the New York Times *and the* New York Post. *The author of ten books about sports, he is one of this country's greatest experts on professional and amateur sports, as well as sports journalism. He is a member of the writers' division of both the Baseball Hall of Fame and the Basketball Hall of Fame.*

The Poison of Amateurism

One concept peculiar to sports deserves condemnation.

It is called *amateurism*. Amateurism has been pumping a poisonous hypocrisy through American society for more than a century, and continues to do so. Almost all the harmful effects of the sports establishment can be traced to this misnamed "ideal." And it's a virus that touches everyone everywhere, even those who have no apparent connection to sports.

Amateurism, as it has come to be defined and interpreted by the worldwide sports community, is evil *in principle*. That amateur "rules" are widely violated in practice is generally accepted, with a wink, or a sigh, or indignation, or indifference. And it is also well understood that tolerating these violations is hypocritical. What is rarely considered however, is that the amateur ideal—if perfectly observed and policed— is incompatible with any decent modern society, especially American society. In many twentieth-century cultures, it is simply an inapplicable term. In others, where its definition can be put into some sort of correspondence with reality, it reflects and promotes concepts those very societies renounce.

In short, amateurism doesn't work anywhere; if it did work, it would be a bad thing; and since it can't work and shouldn't, institutionalizing its respectability (through the American school system, primarily) corrupts the intellect as well as the ethical sense. . . . Why make such a designation as "amateur" in the first place? And why consider it a virtue?

5   In ordinary usage, *amateur*, as distinguished from *professional*, connotes less proficiency. As Tevye says about poverty in *Fiddler on the Roof*, it's no disgrace, but it's no great honor, either. When we speak of a musician (or any artist) as an amateur, we don't imply moral superiority, or even praise. We are explaining the artist's status, either as a justification for lack of skill or as something to marvel at, if the skill is of professional quality. Do you know of anyone who prefers to be treated by an amateur doctor? Or defended by an amateur lawyer, before an amateur judge?

Note, incidentally, that this demarcation has nothing to do with talent. Professionalism is the cultivation of a talent through time, training, and dedication. An amateur may actually be more talented, in native aptitude, than a polished professional, but he or she hasn't developed that talent to the same degree.

In sports, unlike the arts, medicine, or law, the activity consists of pitting one competitor against another, for the express purpose of finding out which one will win. It would make admirable sense, therefore, to ensure fair competition by grading the participants, so that only those of reasonably equal abilities are brought together. And that's exactly what's done with weight classes in boxing or wrestling, age designations in Little League, major-league and minor-league affiliations among professional teams, and varsity and intramural distinctions in schools.

But what is the essential ingredient in developing athletic talent to the highest, world-class levels of proficiency? Time. Time to train, practice, concentrate, and gain competitive experience. So it would make perfect sense to separate amateurs from professionals on the basis of time and effort devoted to becoming proficient. The term *professional* itself signifies someone who has completed a rigorous, accepted program of preparation, and who makes the practiced activity his chief occupation.

But that is not how sports amateurism is defined. It is defined exclusively in terms of *remuneration*. . . .

This concept of sports organization, which didn't exist before the 10 1800s, and evolved in the England of Queen Victoria, wasn't pointless in the culture of that time. That was a time when "gentlemen" still didn't soil their hands with "commerce," if they could help it; when hereditary privilege was still the backbone of social status; when work performed for pay was considered vaguely degrading, if sometimes necessary; when affiliation to club or caste or family was still considered more important than personal worth or eccentricity.

It was also a time when the facilities and leisure time for sports activity were generally unavailable to ordinary or working-class people. The golf course, the running oval, the polo field, the cricket ground, the newly designed tennis court were the provinces of the upper class. (The working-class game was football—soccer—and it became openly professional without much fuss, throughout Europe and soon throughout the world.)

But athletic games are mastered by muscle, determination, reflexes, and alertness—commodities not restricted to "nice" people. In fact, since the lower classes were so much more numerous and generally less inhibited, they could certainly overwhelm club members if they could compete under equal conditions for any extended period of time. So elevating the lack of remuneration to a symbol of moral purity was in tune with the social climate; and it was very, very convenient. In plain language, it kept the riff-raff out. For a while, that is.

At this point, someone is sure to ask about the ancient Greeks and their ideals. The ancient Olympics, which inspired the modern Games, had no cash prizes and were also our model for democracy and citizen participation, weren't they? No, they weren't. Ancient Greek "democracy," where it did exist briefly, was a slave-based society that supported a small upper layer of citizens. Professionalism was plentiful in the ancient Olympics, and prizes of great value were heaped upon winners by their communities. (Even at Olympia, the promoters knew how to avoid putting up expensive awards themselves.)

In any case, the social forces of mid-Victorianism had nothing to do with American life, even then. But the practices and frames of reference that became codified in the financial definition of amateurism were grafted onto American culture too.

15   The messages embedded in such concepts can be paraphrased thus:

- Since athletic excellence can be achieved only through full-time application, and since tangible rewards for the fruits of this effort are forbidden, there must be something wrong with honest pay for honest work.

- Since superior achievement is honored but cannot be rewarded directly (as it can for the artist or the surgeon), and since part-time effort can't achieve the goal, it must be all right to accept sponsorship, openly or covertly.

- Since everyone has to eat, and since only the "authorities" can determine whether you have complied with rules only the independently wealthy could live up to, it must be proper to lie (at worst) or pervert logic (at best) and stay eligible.

But what if every single individual in America were a paragon of integrity, and lies and subterfuge did not exist? Would we want a system that restricts competition to amateurs drawn only from a leisure class? That brands compensation for honest work as somehow dirty? That cheats a performer of a decent share of the tangible rewards his performances generate for those authorities who sell tickets and television rights, have salaried staffs, and share profits with ancillary businesses?

We would not want it, and we don't have it. In practice, everyone sees that value is given for value received in amateur sports. The high school athlete is rewarded with college admission he might not get otherwise—a ticket to upward mobility. The college athlete gets a free ride (worth thousands of dollars a year) and is in a position to obtain advantageous postgraduate opportunities through alumni and publicity. . . .

By subscribing to this definition, uncritically, American society has been infected with a debilitating disease. The entire school system, which forms the backbone of America's athletic programs, insists on an amateur posture. But the high school football or basketball star is perfectly aware of the tangible reward he is playing for: a free college education. And the college player knows he is getting it. His coaches know. And his teachers. And the school administrators. And his parents and family. And his nonplaying classmates. And his out-of-school friends. And all the neighbors and local businessmen who congratulate him on his athletic success. And he knows they know. And they know he knows.

A more pervasive institutionalization of hypocrisy is hard to imagine, and it is at work every single day, in millions of cases. The lesson is inescapable: It is all right to do one thing while professing its opposite. It's not only all right, it is warmly endorsed and fostered by the leaders of society and all the authority figures who fashion a child's values: parents, clergy, teachers, and government officials.

If you accept the idea that remuneration is O.K. when it is properly 20 disguised, you cripple your moral sensibilities. If you accept the disguises at face value and say they are not really remuneration, you cripple your capacity to think straight. And for three generations, *everyone* who has been to school in America, not just the athletes, has been exposed to this moral flabbiness and intellectual dishonesty. The athlete, at least, earns his keep by actual effort, but everyone else sees—and enjoys and profits from, in many cases—the hypocrisy that is being accepted.

None of this, please note, involves *violations* of the serpentine rules. Those also abound, come to the attention of millions, and are usually accepted. When, in some particular instance, punishment is inflicted and self-righteous horror is expressed, the rarity and quixotic nature of the incident merely heightens everyone's perception of injustice. The violations, which can't be kept secret from those who participate in them, even if they are never uncovered officially, compound the problem but don't alter its basic nature.

The problem is that upholding amateurism as an ideal in an industrialized world guarantees daily indoctrination in false values. Work *should* be rewarded. World-class athletic performance, for the entertainment of millions of paying customers, is *work*. A privileged leisure class, which could afford to play just for the love of it, is what Western civilization has been rejecting for the last two hundred years, in capitalistic countries no less than in socialistic ones.

In reality, there are millions of true amateurs playing sports everywhere—but not in front of ticket-buying audiences, for the purpose of mass entertainment. It's the deliberate confusion of two distinct functions—play and entertainment—that does the damage.

Why, then, does modern democratic society cling to the old definition? Cheap labor. The professional is controlled by whoever pays him: he must perform when and where and how the employer decides. But before he agrees, he can command a high price for his services (that is, a significant fraction of the income he generates for the promoter). The amateur, on the other hand, is controlled by *eligibility*. And that can't be negotiated. It's completely in the hands of the promoter—the school, club, IOC,[1] or whatever. To stay eligible, the amateur must accept what's offered: scholarship, books, room, training table, expense money, free equipment, lionization, promises, or even the products of cheating. These awards are substantial in themselves, but they add up to a smaller fraction of the promoter's budget than negotiated fees would.

25   Just as it suits the socialist world to have a no-money definition of amateurism imposed on market-exchange societies, it suits school and amateur-sports authorities to have the same definition imposed on the performers they "hire" so indirectly. You couldn't get away with that if you presented it openly. If nothing else, the antitrust laws would get in the way, but aside from that, the illusion of glamour, which draws spectators, would be tarnished by acknowledged cheapness.

So the package is wrapped in high-sounding morality. Amateurs are presented as "pure," "noble," "disinterested in profit," and "motivated by love of sport." Professionals are grubby, greedy, commerce-soiled mercenaries. And of course professionals must never, never, *never* be allowed to compete against amateurs, because they would show up the amateurs for what they really are—less proficient—and would destroy the amateurs' gate appeal.

There is only one appropriate word for such a system: *sick.*

For Journals

Do you participate or have you ever wanted to participate in any team or individual sports? Do you consider yourself a fan? Why or why not?

For Discussion

1.   *Poison* is a very strong word to use. How does it fit Koppett's argument as he makes his case that amateurism, as it is practiced in America, is both hypocritical and unethical? Is use of such a strong word justified?

2.   In another part of his book, Koppett suggests that in a modern, affluent, high-technology society, watching sports provides a vicarious and pleasurable thrill without any personal danger. Do you agree? What are other reasons for watching athletes compete, either as amateurs or professionals?

3.   Koppett says that any sport pursued as the work of a lifetime is in fact work and should be rewarded as such. Does that explain the enormous salaries that professional athletes get paid? What other factors can you think of?

4.   If you had a chance to go to college on a full athletic scholarship, what arguments could you make to justify your position to a nonathlete

---

[1] International Olympic Committee.

who had to work twenty hours a week to qualify for an ordinary scholarship?

For Writing

1.   The old definition of *amateur* is "one who participates and always has participated in sport as an avocation without material gain of any kind." Based on Koppett's article, write an essay in which you either argue in support of this definition or make up one of your own. Incorporate your own experience as a spectator or as a participant.

2.   Elsewhere in his book, Koppett notices the tendency of many writers to use sports metaphors in writing about topics that have nothing to do with sports, such as business or politics. For example, X can't get to first base with that customer; Hertz is number one; the candidates are going for the knockout punch in their debate. Find a newspaper or magazine article which uses this kind of language and rewrite it in terms that do not refer to sports at all. Either omit those terms altogether or substitute typical terminology or slang from a different field, such as the military. Then write an assessment of how the change in language affects the tone and overall effect of the article.

3.   Research and write a paper on one of the following topics: the decision to allow professional athletes to compete in the Olympic Games; the salaries of professional athletes; charges of corruption or payoffs in the National Collegiate Athletic Association. For your sources, check newspaper and magazine articles, the work of sportswriters such as Koppett or Roger Angell, and, if you have access to it, the Internet.

∞ FROM *Coming on Strong* (1994)

SUSAN K. CAHN

Susan K. Cahn is a member of the faculty at the State University of New York at Buffalo. This excerpt comes from her book about sports and gender in the twentieth century.

You've Come a Long Way, Maybe

. . . In addition to issues of participation, leadership, sexual stigma, and racial discrimination, two other issues with roots in a more distant era have become of critical importance in the contemporary situation of women athletes. Today matters of money and problems surrounding the control and regulation of the female body have assumed a new prominence in shaping female athletic experience.

For most of women's athletic history, financial matters remained uncomplicated because of the simple fact that there was so little money available. Women's sports took place in schools, community centers, low-budget athletic clubs, and ritzier country clubs in which women's athletic activities received but a small portion of the moneys set aside for athletic activities. Only a few sports promoters attempted to finance professional women's ventures, and those that did tended to sponsor low-budget barnstorming operations like the touring All-American Red Heads basketball team. Small-time professional and semipro women's sports did not differ significantly from many similar ventures in men's athletics.

However, as sports have developed over the last half-century, corporate sponsorship has become central not only to professional sport but to financing amateur events like college athletics and the Olympic Games. Both in the form of direct sponsorship and indirect backing through television and advertising arrangements, private industry makes the wheels spin in the contemporary sports world. More than ever before, decision making in sports revolves around the marketplace: which sports will sell tickets, which activities can attract advertisers, and which marketing strategies enhance a sport's commercial viability.

The priority given to profit making often means that women's events simply do not receive financial support. Professional basketball and softball leagues of the 1970s and early 1980s failed to attract enough paying fans or advertisers to break even, much less turn a profit. When women's events do attract corporate sponsorship, investors concerned with selling their product often decide that what sells the best is not women's athletic ability but their "sex appeal."

5   . . . While selling big-time women's sports is of minor concern to most members of the commercialized sporting world, selling sports and fitness to ordinary women has become critical to the industry's financial growth. The fitness boom of the 1970s and 1980s spurred millions of American women to take up jogging, aerobics, walking, weight training, bicycling, swimming and a variety of team and individual sports in pursuit of better physical and mental health. For the many women who felt nothing but alienation from team and competitive sports, fitness activities like jogging or swimming provided an entrée into physical activity and the pleasures that can accompany it. Aerobics classes—first called "jazzercise"—seemed more like dance than sport, attracting women who were initially more comfortable with a classically "feminine" form of physical exercise. Because classes were scheduled around women's workday, and because they attracted a predominantly female clientele, aerobics became a way for busy women to fit exercise into their lives in a comfortable, even social gathering of women.

However, while many women found that exercise contributed to a confident and healthy body, the fitness boom also capitalized on widespread, almost obsessive, anxieties women felt about their body weight. By the 1980s the ideal "look" for women had gone beyond thin to a sculpted, fatless body—a kind of curveless, hard-edged, taut-skinned ideal most women found unattainable. But they didn't stop trying. Diet products and weight-control clinics became a multi-billion-dollar industry; eating disorders reached almost epidemic proportions among young women; and studies found that a majority of girls under ten years old had already begun dieting. As women turned to sport and exercise to shed dreaded pounds, the fitness industry both benefited from and incited women's preoccupation with weight control.

The impulse to use exercise systems to control the body is not new. Early in the twentieth century, physical educators introduced European exercise regimens designed to strengthen the bodies of female students while instilling greater physical control over a female body thought to be unpredictable, even hysterical. By contrast today's sporting boom occurred within the context of a popular culture that has emphasized pleasure, release, and the relaxation of controls over mind and body. The concept of liberation from coercive controls took on political overtones when sports advocates linked the boom in women's athletics to the freeing of the female body from traditional constraints.

Although many women do indeed experience sport as a form of physical liberation, the all-consuming concern with fitness and thinness forms a distinct countercurrent to that goal. It has evolved into a new form of physical coercion in which the body is no longer controlled by external forms of discipline and supervision but by an internalized surveillance system. Women constantly patrol their own bodies for signs of age, cellulite, and lapses of self-control. Under the rubric of health and physical enjoyment, they endure grueling exercise routines and punishing diets that do not liberate as much as regulate the female body to fit an ideal most women have little voice in creating and little success in attaining.

The tension between physical empowerment and coercive bodily regulation extends to sport as well as fitness activities. Two sports that have gained tremendous popularity since the early 1970s—gymnastics and bodybuilding—illustrate the new athleticism's contradictory influences on the female body.

Since Olga Korbut charmed her way into the public's heart during 10 the 1972 Olympics, gymnastics has been one of the most popular and fastest-growing sports in the United States. The sport's required combination of strength, agility, flexibility, grace, explosive power, and risk enthralls audiences and inspires reverence for its young stars. Yet the daring moves originated by the slight, girlish Korbut and her 1976 successor Nadia Comaneci introduced fundamental changes into gymnastic routines and officiating standards. Judges now place the greatest value on high-risk maneuvers suited to prepubescent girls' highly flexible bodies and low fat ratios. By their late teens most female gymnasts lose this advantage, and their careers go into decline.

That teenage girls have become heroes in a sporting culture that boasts of empowering women contains a certain irony. The 1970s, when gymnastics first burst onto the scene, were years in which a broad-based feminist movement was demanding access to power, in the process threatening the status quo in sports, politics, and business. It was precisely at this moment that the public fastened onto a sport whose heroes were little girls noted for their "tiny" bodies, "cute" looks, and coquettish demeanor. These teenage "pixies" were typically coached by middle-aged adult men who combined the roles of surrogate parent and stern taskmaster. The athletes' childlike bodies and childish relationships to adults seemed to offer some unconscious reassurance to a public who looked with anxiety on the growing power of adult women.

However, as their bodies matured and grew less able to perform the high-risk stunts that won competitions, Korbut, Comaneci, and other young gymnasts fell from grace—figuratively and literally. Comaneci took the logical step of trying to prevent the physical changes that would spell the end of her career; she stopped eating, developing a severe anorexic condition. This phenomenon grew so common among competitive gymnasts that insiders in the sport called it the Nadia syndrome. Eating disorders remain common in gymnastics and have been detected in other sports as well. A 1986 study of female college athletes in the Midwest found that 74 percent of gymnasts—and 33.3 percent of all women athletes—practiced potentially dangerous weight-control methods, including vomiting, laxatives, and diet pills.

As one of the nation's most popular sports, gymnastics illustrates the private and public contradictions of women's athleticism in the late twentieth century. Privately gymnastics can offer great physical confidence and personal satisfaction to a developing athlete, yet the sport all too frequently turns into a nightmare of starvation and self-doubt. To the public it presents at once a virtuoso performance of spectacular athletic beauty and a reassuring picture of the athlete as a tiny, juvenile figure who cloaks her athletic skills in a coy sexuality and girlish cuteness to please her adult coaches, judges, and audience.

Bodybuilding, at first glance, appears to present the exact opposite image. In packed auditoriums women parade their large, well-sculpted muscles before admiring fans who whoop gleefully with every carefully orchestrated pose, each one designed to show off the definition and size of a particular muscle group. By celebrating female bulk and muscularity, bodybuilding rewards women's strength and their ability to take on a look that, until recently, was limited to and definitive of masculine posture. Yet bodybuilding shares with gymnastics many of the same tensions around the control and emancipation of the gendered body.

15   For years the sport's leaders divided over judging standards, a minority claiming that women should be evaluated by the same criteria used in male competitions, while the majority advanced the familiar athletic

double standard that a woman's performance ought to weigh strength and definition alongside evidence of attractive femininity. The emphasis on muscular build without "masculine bulk" has put great pressure on women to reduce fat levels in order to heighten muscle definition. Many female bodybuilders have, consequently, fallen into a dangerous routine of strenuous dieting, exchanging food intake for the consumption of anabolic steroids that aid muscular growth and sharpen definition. The impressive power and bravado of top contenders is the outcome of vigilant, potentially harmful, forms of self-denial and chemical ingestion.

Bodybuilding also encourages women to sculpt their bodies as objects for public display and evaluation. Like Miss America contestants, bikini-clad competitors strut their tanned, hairless bodies before a panel of judges to show off their physical beauty, only in this case they are judged for conventionally masculine attributes rather than classically feminine ones. Yet for all its similarities to entrenched forms of sexual objectification, the exhibitionism of bodybuilding also contains a more subversive element. Where female gymnasts disrupt the traditional opposition between femininity and athletic strength, power, and control, in bodybuilding the combination of traditionally "feminine" ritual and dress with "masculine" muscles and posturing operates as an even-more-daring form of gender provocation. Bodybuilders engage in a playful performance that blends polarities—tiny bikinis and enormous muscles—and transgresses athletic boundaries through a celebration of women inhabiting a "male" sport and posture. In doing so they disturb assumptions about what the culture understands to be masculine and feminine in the human body.

Bodybuilding, gymnastics, and the fitness boom are all elements within a thriving corporate-dominated sport culture that affords women multiple opportunities for physical enjoyment and development. Yet that very culture also serves as a conduit for broader cultural pressures on women continually to shape and monitor their bodies to meet social standards of body size and personal attractiveness. In these activities as in other women's sports, the possibilities for physical pleasure and empowerment compete with entrenched but ever-changing forms of physical constraint that fundamentally undercut women's personal and societal power.

In late-twentieth-century America, a skilled adult woman striving for athletic recognition or a young girl just starting out in a local sports program will each find competitive opportunities, athletic resources, and media interest far beyond the typical scenario of earlier times. In all likelihood she will not face the ridicule, rejection, or blatant disregard that earlier women athletes met with time and again.

Yet the path is not clear of obstacles. Even as contemporary definitions of femininity have grown to include athleticism, sporting institutions and resources continue to be dominated by men, while the sports world as a whole continues to reflect a set of deeply inscribed sexist values and meanings which are hostile to women's full participation and enjoyment. Moreover, while women are permitted and even encouraged or pressured to take up sport and fitness activities, sport leaders, corporate sponsors, and the commercial media consistently attempt to regulate women's bodies, their outward appearance, and their sexuality. Sport remains a key cultural location for male dominance, a site where traditional patriarchal values are upheld and transformed in response to changes in the broader society.

20   Yet, far from being discouraged, women are approaching these barriers with a sense of entitlement, buttressed by the broader inroads of feminism into American society and energized by the personal pleasures and power they experience through their own sporting involvement. It is this sense of entitlement and determination that stamps the recent period of sport history and provides hope for a future in which adequate leisure, athletic pleasures, and physical power are available to all women.

In its fullest expression, the demand for opportunity and equality in the athletic world involves more than asking men to move over and make room for female competitors. It means insisting that men relinquish privilege—most obviously their monopoly on athletic skill and enjoyment. Women's athletic freedom requires that certain attributes long defined as masculine—skill, strength, speed, physical dominance, uninhibited use of space and motion—become human qualities and not those of a particular gender.

This seemingly simple shift would have radical consequences, for the "masculine" attributes of sport are also the very qualities that define manhood in American society. Sport turns boys into men and endows them with the physical strength and social confidence to assume positions of power. The centrality of sport in contemporary culture makes it integral to the way American society organizes and evaluates gender relations—the everyday conventions that govern male and female activities; our images and ideals of masculinity and femininity; and the social hierarchies that have historically granted men greater authority in political, economic, religious, family, and athletic matters.

Ultimately women's efforts to attain meaningful leisure, unrestricted access to sport, and athletic self-determination will be part and parcel of transforming the broader social relations of gender within which sporting life takes place.

For Journals

Why do you think Cahn picked this particular title for her article?

For Discussion

1.   According to Cahn, in what ways were women's sports better off when they were amateur and involved little money?

2. What evidence does Cahn provide to prove her assertion that as women's sports succeed in becoming a multi-billion-dollar business, they also are losing much of their benefit to women? Which areas are of particular concern to her?

3. In your own terms, rephrase Cahn's argument against the turn women's gymnastics has taken since Olga Korbut won the Olympics in the 1970s. Why does she not see the changes in that sport as a sign of women's advances toward athletic equality?

4. Which sports do you consider especially female or feminine? Why? How do your choices provide support for or against Cahn's argument about the ways exercise and fitness for women have been forced into certain patterns?

For Writing

1. The Mattel Toy Company, manufacturers of the Barbie doll, have recently come out with a WNBA (Women's National Basketball Association) Barbie doll, shooting a basketball. Go to a toy store, and examine the range of Barbie dolls being offered. Write a paper in which you compare the differing images of young womanhood they represent. Use the dolls themselves—their clothing, activities, physical structure—as evidence for your comparison. You can also argue for or against Cahn's assertions about the way women's bodies are perceived.

2. Interview the athletic director at your college or at a local high school, and write up the interview with a view toward answering at least two of the following questions: What women's sports are available, and why? Which are the most popular, and how is money spent on these programs? What kind of facilities do women have, compared to men? Alternatively, interview women on a sports team at your school or another school: ask if you can spend time watching them practice, and write up your observations. Keep Cahn's arguments in mind, particularly in terms of the women's image of an ideal woman athlete's body.

∞ *Motrin Spoken Here* (1998)

MAGAZINE ADVERTISEMENT

One of the hardest jobs in advertising is finding clever ways of publicizing utilitarian and unglamorous products. This ad, from a recent Life *magazine, is a witty solution that relies on a photograph and the viewer's ability to empathize with the tired waitress to make its point.*

For Journals

What was the best or worst job you ever had?

For Discussion

1. This photograph advertises Motrin, a pain-relief medicine. Why is this ad a clever way to advertise the product without ever showing it in the picture itself?

2. What about this ad attracts your attention first, and why? What adjectives would you use to describe the mood of this photograph? What details in the picture support your choice of words? What effect is conveyed by the waitress's expression? Her clothing? Her posture? Look at the background of the picture; how does the sign that says "Walk, Don't Run" affect your assessment of it?

3.   If you have ever worked in a restaurant, how accurate does this picture seem to you? If the ad had been intended to attract customers to an enjoyable restaurant instead of to market a pain reliever, how would you change this photo to present a more attractive image of waitressing?

4.   Look again at the picture of the sweatshop workers earlier in this chapter. Each of these pictures expresses different aspects of working life in America. Which do you think is the most successful in conveying its point, and why?

For Writing

1.   Referring back to discussion question 4, write an essay in which you compare and contrast the Motrin advertisement with the sweatshop picture in this chapter. Consider the angle of the picture, the placement of the figure or figures, the presence or absence of light and shadow, the facial expressions, and the objects and background of each in your comparison.

∽ From Necessary to Unwanted (1997)

An Analysis on the Anti–Mexican American Movement During the Great Depression

JORGE FLORES

Jorge Flores is a student at a western university.

In the early half of the twentieth century, America experienced a considerable economic boost as a direct result of its increasingly market-driven society. The Industrial Revolution, which surfaced and rapidly gained strength in the early eighteenth and nineteenth centuries, significantly changed preexisting ways of life in the United States. The Age of Reason and Scientific Progress introduced immense technological advancements that reshaped America's economic structure from an agricultural one to a more industrial one. The establishment of wage labor, along with the development of working classes and new social identities, directly resulted from industrialism. Eric R. Wolf, an expert on the influences of capitalism on society, elaborates on the massive restructuring of society caused by industrial growth. Industry and plantation growth which relied on the mass amounts of land caused the *mobilization* of people from all over to supply the growing demand for a labor force (Wolf 2). Increasing farm production in California and the Southwest, along with the new railway system which was being developed, called for the mass migration of ethnic groups mainly from Mexico and Asia. America's economic prosperity caused the opening of its borders and allowed for thousands of immigrants to leave their native lands and freely enter this country in search of work.

Although it was difficult in the early 1900s to adjust and assimilate into the American culture, many of these Mexican and Asian immigrant families survived in the predominantly white society without any major conflicts. However, when the Great Depression devastated the U.S. economy, unemployment became rampant nationwide, and Americans desperately tried to cope with poverty and starvation. Widespread feelings existed among the white American population that Mexican immigrants were taking away their few remaining jobs. An "anti-immigrant hysteria" which grew out of desperation led to the need for Americans to find something or someone to blame (3). Consequently, the Mexican immigrant and Mexican American population of the Southwest became a scapegoat, and white Americans led by the federal government felt that they should take prompt action and rectify the situation.

During the 1930s, when the Great Depression was taking its toll on American society, the "Mexican Problem" became a means for people to justify the devastated economy. Repatriation, it was argued, would solve the problem and alleviate harsh economic strains. The economic situation of the 1930s, combined with haunting racist views which were once again resurfacing since the era of "Manifest Destiny" of the mid-1800s, increasingly alienating non-Anglo Americans and immigrants, ultimately led to the unjust treatment of a significant part of this country's social and economic structure.

In order to better understand why such actions were taken against the Mexican American population, we must first analyze the earliest part of Mexican American history, which began in 1848 at the end of the Mexican-American War.

5   ... The belief in "Manifest Destiny," first named by John O'Sullivan, was gaining strong popularity throughout the country and played an enormous role in starting the war. "Manifest Destiny" was a great motivational instrument for promoting territorial expansion. But what did this term really mean? Historian Frederick Merk defined Manifest Destiny as "a free, confederated, self-governed republic on a continued scale—Manifest Destiny meant freedom" (Merk 29). The term, however, also entailed racist implications. Many Americans like Frederick

Merk felt that Manifest Destiny also meant "the duty of the U.S. to regenerate backward peoples of the continent" (33). The belief that the Anglo-Saxon American race was dominant over all the others in the western hemisphere was also widespread. The editor of the New Orleans paper, *The Picayune*, wrote on January 1848:

> We may argue against the tendencies of a race of men of higher organization, bolder hearts, more enterprising minds, of superior thaws and muscles, and stouter wills, to supplant weak and emasculated tribes . . . but no scrap of philosophy, nor moral essay, no political disquisition can countervail the dangerous odor of fields in perennial blossom to an army of Anglo-Saxons. (154)

Clearly from this example, one can see how sentiments of racial superiority could continue to be expressed even at the turn of the twentieth century, and affect minority groups both socially and economically.

After the U.S. ceded a large area of land in 1848, the several thousand Mexicans who remained in the area automatically became American citizens. These new Americans had to overcome the difficult task of assimilation. But prejudice views against the Mexican American population would prove to make it very difficult for them to fully incorporate into American society. Even in the early 1900s feelings of racial superiority still stood strong in the U.S., making it hard on the newly formed Mexican American population to feel accepted. Historian Camille Guerin-Gonzales cites an example of this racial prejudice which serves as evidence. In a time when Mexicans sought economic advancements through higher-paying jobs, racial prejudice prevented most Mexican farm worker children from obtaining an education which in turn would have given them the proper skills to acquire high-wage jobs (102). Dr. George P. Clemens, who managed the Los Angeles Chamber of Commerce's Agricultural Department for over twenty years, went as far as to say that "the tasks of agriculture were those to which the oriental and Mexican due to their crouching and bending habits are fully adapted, while the white is physically unable to adapt himself to them" (Hoffman 10).

. . . With the discovery of gold in California in the 1850s and with a growing industrial economy which called for the creation of this country's railway system, jobs emerged in abundant numbers for Mexican Americans and Mexican immigrants. With the U.S. immigration policy "basically being an open door deal more or less until 1880," the number of Mexican immigrants entering the U.S. in search of work increased in alarming numbers (Carreras de Velasco 32). Both economic and political reasons caused this large influx of Mexican immigrants primarily into the Southwest. Historian Abraham Hoffman states that there was a great demand for Mexicans to fill up menial positions and unskilled jobs such as working in steel mills, mines, meat-packing plants, brickyards, canneries, but most importantly in agriculture (4). Mexican labor was in high demand in Southwestern agricultural fields because Mexicans were cheap and reliable workers.

Mexicans were best suited for agricultural jobs for several reasons. First, the Immigration Act of 1917 prevented further immigrants from Europe and Asia from entering the U.S., thus preventing a source of cheap labor from working in the fields. Second, the southern Negro potential labor force was moving away from agricultural areas into larger northern cities to work in factories. Third, the Immigration Act of 1917, which did not apply to Mexican immigrants, perhaps best demonstrates the great importance of Mexican labor in the U.S., since this labor was responsible for the large agricultural profits (Hoffman 9). Hoffman quoted a spokesman for agriculture and industry during the 1920s admitting their dependence on Mexican labor, whether they be Mexican Americans or immigrants: "To put it quite simply, he comes to us because he wants to, and also because we want him to come . . . the Mexican is the preferred of all labor available in the Southwest" (9).

Mexico's political and economic situation during the administration of President Porfirio Diaz, highlighted by Mexican historian Mercedes Carreras de Velasco, caused a great exodus of Mexican nationals from Mexico (25). According to Velasco, in a drastic attempt to reshape Mexico's economic structure, President Diaz encouraged foreign migration, for he saw it necessary to improve the Mexican population of the U.S. in both quality and quantity (25). By the turn of the century, the Mexican government estimated that nearly 100,400 Mexicans resided in the U.S. while foreign residents in Mexico only totaled 51,000 (25). Porfirio Diaz proved to be too radical and his economic changes only seemed to favor wealthy *hacienda* owners, therefore making the poor poorer. Instability soon plagued Mexico and revolution broke out between the rich and the poor. As a result, as Carreras de Velasco suggests, thousands of Mexicans left their native country from 1910 to 1930 for two reasons: Mexican workers were in search of higher wages; Mexicans feared great political and economic difficulties which resulted from the revolution.

10   The fact that Mexican labor was an essential part of production in California, Texas, and the rest of the Southwest has been made quite clear. However, the relationship between Mexican Americans and Mexican immigrants and American industry was solely dependent on the economic prosperity of the time. When the Great Depression hit in 1930 and economic prosperity ended abruptly, America turned its back on the Mexican labor force. Whereas before Mexicans were openly invited to come in and work, now with the loss of thousands of jobs, Mexicans were the first to go. Consequently, an overproduction of goods led to a rapid decline in prices. Producers acted accordingly and reduced not only the production of goods, but also personnel.

Now racist presumptions, which had been put away during the several years in which a lower class of people were needed, once again shed light. Mexicans became a scapegoat to the economic downfall. Feelings by the American public that Mexicans were taking away American jobs became widespread. In a time of desperation, more and more Americans were becoming aware of the "Mexican Problem," and realized their need to step in and attempt to alleviate the crisis. What ensued was repatriation. The question is, why??? In order to try and answer this question, we must first make an attempt to define what is meant by the "Mexican Problem." Historian Alberto Camarillo, an expert in this era of Mexican American history, best defines this term in his *History of Mexican Americans in California*:

> As the volume of that migration peaked, the visibility of Mexicans in the public eye also increased. Mexican American neighborhoods were being formed in all major cities such as Los Angeles, San Diego, and Riverside. . . . Recognition of the Mexicans' desire to remain in the U.S. focused public attention. Californians by the late 1920's began questioning the notion that Mexicans were a temporary population— that they would stay long enough to earn money and then return back to Mexico. (43)

Camarillo stresses the fact that Mexican workers were not expected to permanently establish their homes in America. Californians only invited immigrant workers to assist its mass production of goods, and expected them to go back to their native lands when their services were no longer needed.

. . . Here we are confronted with the main argument: if a large number of the Mexican population in the Southwest were American citizens themselves, why then did people claim that "American" jobs were being taken away? Abraham Hoffman suggests that the reason is that the Americans viewed all Mexicans as immigrants. "Unlike immigrants from Europe," Hoffman points out, "the Mexican was considered a permanent foreigner, and his American-born children were considered equally foreign" (vii). In his book *Ethnic Conflict in Californian History*, Charles Wollenberg suggests that Mexicans had been "relatively isolated in twentieth-century California." Mexicans, according to Wollenberg, lacked any "natural bridges of access" to the larger American society. Anglos and Mexicans were stuck in a "cultural stalemate," where the Mexican American finds that he is "completely at opposite poles" from the larger American society. In the eyes of America, Mexicans could not be both Mexican and American; they had to choose one or the other (57).

Once the blame was put on the Mexican population in the U.S., measures were quickly taken to try to prevent further migration north from Mexico. A conspicuous anti-immigrant, or anti-Mexican, movement was initiated. Congress passed stricter immigration enforcement laws and implemented new deportation methods. In 1924, Congress created the border patrol in order to prevent the illegal entry of the Mexicans to the U.S., and the U.S. government initiated a form of deportation which they called "voluntary departure" in which people received an invitation from the Mexican government to leave the U.S. (Carreras de Velasco 57). The Harris Bill which was brought to Congress in 1930 promised tighter enforcement of the borders, and restriction on further Mexican immigration (Beals 51). The California legislature passed a law which made it illegal for American contractors to employ Mexicans for public jobs.

These new government policies towards immigrants were in many ways too severe. The methods of deportation used in many instances violated fundamental human rights of all those involved, and in instances where Mexican American citizens were involved, their rights were ignored. As a result a "Deportation Terror" arose in which unjust methods of apprehending suspected Mexican immigrants were used by officials (Oppenheimer 231). In 1930, a commission met with the purpose to report on the enforcement of the deportation laws of the United States in order to analyze the legitimacy of enforcement procedures and show whether or not the repatriation being carried out by government agencies was a breach of human rights, and civil rights guaranteed to all American citizens.

The Wickersham Report brought to light many instances in which government agencies were acting unlawfully. . . .

15   . . . Such abuses included these: a massive deportation program of Mexicans from urban areas such as Los Angeles disregarded following protocol, and in many instances people were apprehended without proper warrants. Immigration officials understood implied regulations and said that any suspected of being illegally in the United States could be detained. Because many immigrants hardly knew English, they became susceptible to extortion and blackmail from people seeking to take advantage of them. In many cases, the economic situations in which many detained immigrants found themselves did not allow for them to be represented by a lawyer or legal advisor in their hearings. As a result, it became easy to convict detained suspects, therefore facilitating their deportation back to Mexico (Oppenheimer 232–233).

The Report made people aware that many violations did take place during the Repatriation movement in the early 1930s. According to Reuben Oppenheimer, "a leading metropolitan paper exclaimed regarding the Wickersham report 'America's sense of mercy and justice is dead'" (231). These concerns were prevalent throughout the nation, and people soon started asking questions. . . . How could America forget that Mexican Americans were rightfully here, either by birth or by invitation? Robert N. McLean expressed his sentiments towards the deportation ordeal in a 1930 magazine article when he stated:

> Every industry has been dependent upon [the Mexican]. And as is always the case with the common laborer, he has put much in and taken little out. Today, under the strain of economic adversity, we forget that during these years the Mexican has become part of our community life. . . . We forget that he has given his best years to our industries and in doing so has forfeited his place in his own land. We forget that by the sweat of his brow he has earned a place in our economic life. We are sending him home. There is little gratitude in our hearts. (166)

In essence, McLean sums up the Mexican American experience during the early 1900s. In a time of economic growth, since industry and agriculture needed large numbers of workers, Mexicans were openly invited to come in and work these jobs. In times of "economic adversity" Mexican hardships, the strenuous hours of labor put into production, are forgotten and the workers forcefully sent back to where they came from.

The Great Depression certainly marked a sad period of American history. The early 1930s caused great suffering and desperation among millions of Americans. It is important for people to understand why, in a time of desperation, certain actions can take place against a whole group of people who are seen as the "problem." People must understand that ethnic differences and feelings of racial distinctions among Anglo Americans dating back to Manifest Destiny have always played significant roles in the shaping of what is known as Mexican American history (Garcia 295). America has always been a nation of immigrants, as has been demonstrated countlessly in history books. However, anti-immigrant sentiments still run rampant in the U.S. and these sentiments lead to insidious comments and actions against Mexicans and other immigrant groups that ultimately demean their sense of being human individuals. The treatment of Mexican Americans in the United States, during the 1930s especially, marked a terrible and unforgettable period of history for all those involved. Sadly, this period is most often ignored and rarely even mentioned in history texts. As a result, people tend to forget that injustices such as repatriation did take place, and what we get is resurfacing anti-immigrant and anti-Mexican sentiments even in the 1990s. It seems that prejudiced views will always keep being perpetuated through history.

Works Cited

Beals, Carleton. "Mexico and the Harris Bill." *The Nation* 9 July 1930: 51–52.

Camarillo, Albert. *Chicanos in California: A History of Mexican Americans in California.* San Francisco: Boyd & Fraser, 1984.

Carreras de Velasco, Mercedes. *Los Mexicanos Que Devolvio La Crisis.* Tlatelolco, Mexico: Secretaria De Relaciones Exteriores, 1974.

Flores, Jorge. "The True Causes of the Mexican War." Thesis written in 1995 for A.P. U.S. History class.

Garcia, Mario T. *Mexican Americans.* New Haven: Yale UP, 1989.

Guerin-Gonzales, Camille. *Cycles of Immigration and Repatriation.* Ann Arbor: University Microfilms International, 1986.

Hoffman, Abraham. *The Repatriation of Mexican Nationals.* Ann Arbor: Xerox University Microfilms, 1976.

McLean, Robert N. "The Mexican Return." *The Nation* 24 Aug. 1932: 165–66.

Merk, Frederick. *Manifest Destiny and Mission in American History.* New York: Knopf, 1963.

Oppenheimer, Reuben. "The Deportation Terror." *The New Republic* 12 Jan. 1932: 231–34.

Wolf, Eric R. "The New Laborers." Berkeley: U of California P, 1982.

Wollenberg, Charles, ed. *Ethnic Conflict in California History.* Los Angeles: Tinnon-Brown, 1970.

For Journals

How do you respond to the point that in difficult times one group of Americans can act unfairly toward another? What experience of your own or your family's can you think of to prove or disprove this idea?

For Discussion

1. Restate Flores's thesis, and find two or three pieces of evidence that support that restatement.

2. What are Flores's feelings about this subject? What particulars in his language demonstrate what his feelings are? Would this paper be stronger or weaker to you if it were written in a completely objective tone? Why?

3. What other kinds of evidence would you like to see included in this paper (anecdotes, interviews, and so on), and why? How would the addition of any of these elements change the effect of the paper on you as a reader?

For Writing

1. Most Americans have a dual heritage: Irish Americans, Italian Americans, Mexican Americans, African Americans, and so on. All of them have had encounters with prejudice. Choose one ethnic group— your own or someone else's—and research its experience with and search for acceptance. For example, look at the early history of the Irish in Boston, the Italians or Jews in New York, or the Japanese in California. Write a paper that explores and documents how one of these groups was first treated—or mistreated.

2. This is a paper written by a student like yourself; as an exercise, rewrite this paper using as much of Flores's language as you want to and changing whatever you think would make it even more effective. He has a lot of source material in his citations; see what additional information you can find on his topic; look particularly for the kinds of additional evidence mentioned in discussion question 3.

∞ Film: Jerry Maguire (1997)

Jerry Maguire is a film about a sports agent who, in a tired moment, writes an unexpectedly honest memorandum about how hypocritical and greedy his profession has become. As a result he is fired by his employer and deserted by all but one of his clients—a mediocre football player who provides him with one last chance to truly help and inspire an athlete and redeem himself. (126 minutes)

For Journals

Does this film give you a higher or lower opinion of professional sports? What did you think before you saw this film, and on what were you basing your opinion?

For Discussion

1. What image of sports agents does the film communicate, particularly in the scenes at the office after Jerry sends around his mission statement? What do you think a sports agent is supposed to do?

2. Jerry Maguire can't express intimate feelings but is good at his job, and Rod Tidwell is good at personal intimacy but not so good at his job. What scenes in the film are crucial, in your opinion, to the gradual change in both men? How do they affect and help one another?

3. In what ways does this film portray sports as a business? What and who is marketed? What does success mean in this context? Look for specific scenes or exchanges of dialogue to prove your point.

4. The most famous line in this movie is "Show me the money!" But the end of the film is more sentimental than financial in impact. How well does the director lay the groundwork for this change? In what scenes does he prepare us to accept a kinder, gentler resolution of the problems the movie raises? Where, in particular, do you see Jerry Maguire changing his behavior?

For Writing

1. Watch the movie *Field of Dreams*, and write an essay in which you analyze at least two of the following issues: the pure pleasure of sport; baseball as the ultimate game of American mythology; nostalgia for an earlier America that we think was simpler than the America we live in; the powers of memory; impractical idealism versus cold business practices. Look for scenes in which these issues appear, and examine them

for crucial dialogue or character development. Give specific examples from them as evidence for your conclusions.

2. The salaries of major league sports figures are much higher, even for average professional athletes, than they were ten years ago. In fact, Rod Tidwell's successful bid for a higher salary from his team would no longer be considered a great deal. Research and write a paper explaining the causes and effects of the enormous jump in major league salaries in either baseball or football. To find a range of facts and opinions, check the writings of Leonard Koppett, Roger Noll, Harry Edwards, or any other sports expert who has written extensively about the issue. Also, use the Internet to locate other articles on this subject.

Writing Assignments

1. Why do people work? Or more specifically, why do you or will you work? After brainstorming, reading, discussing, and recollecting some of the points made in class and in your readings, develop a core assertion as to the meaning, value, or purpose of work—to people in your family, to people of a certain class, to people of a certain ethnic culture or gender. Avoid vague generalizations. Focus on a specific assertion, and offer strong support for it.

2. Research advertisements or political cartoons from times gone by—from nineteenth-century publications to back issues of *Life* or other popular magazines from the 1940s. Analyze the values implied and the assertions made about work or play in the images. Alternatively, view one or two television comedies from the 1950s and 1960s, and analyze the values, assumptions, and assertions they convey, particularly those about work and gender, or play and gender.

3. Record oral histories of three different workers talking about what work means to them. Draft several questions to get your interview started and to suggest a focus. After the interviews, compare and contrast the views of your interviewees, looking for common and diverse threads among the histories. Develop a core claim or thesis, using the material from the interviews and, if you want, from the readings in this chapter and your own experience to support your view. Alternatively, do the same assignment, but by interviewing three people who are committed to a sport or sports on a regular basis.

4. Examine the assertions made about blue-collar work or the importance of work in women's lives by this chapter's authors, especially Gilman and Steinem. Do particular types of factual assertions, evaluative assertions, or proposals dominate either topic or selection? Which types are most persuasive? Write an analytical paper discussing your findings.

5.   Write a proposal for change in a program at your college or in your community: a change in the curriculum, such as revising the language or writing requirements; a change in scholarship or work-study funding; a change in alcohol policy in your residence; or a campus or community recycling program. Write the proposal in the form of a letter to the appropriate administrator, or for a more general audience, as a letter to the editor.

6.   Write an argumentative essay asserting your own view of the value of work, success, money, education, or some other belief that you hold. Pay special attention to the assumptions you are making and the evidence you are selecting to support your view, and be sure to back up any assumptions you make that your audience may not share or accept.

7

Justice and Civil Liberties

E very morning, millions of American schoolchildren recite the
pledge of allegiance to the flag, which ends, "With liberty and justice for all." That phrase refers to more people today than it has in the
past; today it includes women, children, ethnic minorities, the aged,
and the disabled. This is a country proudly self-conscious that its political system was established to be something new, that it offered a re-
adjustment of rights and privileges more profound than anything that
had ever been attempted before. So standards and expectations for justice and civil liberties have always been higher here, at least in theory,
than anywhere else.

Given our ideals, however, the fact that for 250 years African Americans were bought and sold like furniture could not be easily explained,
nor could the denial of their civil rights into modern times. So, more often than not, a consideration of social justice in America starts with
racial justice.

Many of the high and low points associated with racial justice involve attempts of whites to deny or to correct past wrongs, and the attempts of African Americans to claim the promise of liberty and the
American dream from which they had been excluded. At times, individual leaders—like Frederick Douglass—have taken upon themselves
the role of spokespersons and protest leaders. Their job has been simultaneously to educate white Americans about the everyday injustices
in African American life and to organize their constituencies to effect
change.

The fact that laws did not change quickly, or that the laws did but
attitudes did not, has led to a continuing and sometimes violent debate
over what justice is, who is entitled to justice (and how much), and
whether there is a way to compensate citizens for past wrongs. These
issues raise profound questions for Americans about the depth of their
commitment to ideals of freedom, opportunity, and political participation.

Race is not the only social struggle in America. As the definitions of
justice and freedom became gradually more inclusive in the nineteenth
century, one of the offshoots of the first struggle for civil rights was the

increased consciousness in other segments of the population that they too were discriminated against. Foremost among these other groups were women—mostly white and middle-class—who began organizing for the right to vote. Many of them had been abolitionists, and they turned the self-confidence and political skills they had honed during the fight against slavery to the fight for universal suffrage.

In Victorian America, however, constrained expectations of women as domestic goddesses who knew their place (at home with husband and children) meant that most men and many women were horrified by the open political participation of women and criticized them for being disobedient, unfeminine, and threatening to the status quo. Like African Americans who demanded to be treated equally, the suffragists were viewed as unnatural and ungrateful deviants from the norm who had forgotten their traditional virtues of deference and meekness.

In recent decades the gay rights movement has gained considerable momentum, though its members too have often been castigated as deviants from the norm who should stay in their place and not demand equal rights. Although gays have essentially secured civil liberties in arenas such as housing and employment, the ongoing debate about their presence in the armed forces indicates that the struggle is not fully resolved.

Indeed, complete civil liberties for ethnic and sexual minorities and women are still a long way from being assured as the twentieth century draws to a close. Unpopular causes and new ideas frequently make audiences angry, and while we all demand the right to say what we want, we are better at defending the speech of people who agree with us than that of people we think are wrong, misguided, extreme, disloyal, or simply very different. Fortunately, however, at all points in our history, this country has been graced by the presence of Americans who were willing to stand up—by themselves, if necessary—to defend the civil liberties in which they believed, particularly the freedoms of speech and press guaranteed by the First Amendment to the Constitution.

Justice and Civil Liberties Through History

The writers and artists in this chapter all engaged in an ongoing argument in which the interpretations about the extent of civil liberties and the meaning of justice in America have varied wildly. The values in question were established first in the Declaration of Independence in 1776, then in the Constitution and the Bill of Rights in 1787, in the subsequent amendments to the Constitution, in two hundred years of legal decisions, in reform movements and political debates, in the trauma of a Civil War in which 618,000 Americans died at each other's hands, and in the words and lives of individuals who have made civil liberties and justice their personal business.

But the issues and rights that found their way into our government's defining documents did not spring full-blown from the founding fathers' heads. By the time the Revolution began, discussion of the question of individual rights already had a relatively long history in what was still a very young country. For example, in 1735, John Peter Zenger, a publisher, was put on trial for having printed articles critical of the British colonial government. His lawyer, Andrew Hamilton, based his ultimately successful defense of Zenger on the nature and importance of freedom of the press. That defense, which is the first selection in this chapter, is one of the crucial early cases in the establishment of basic American freedoms.

The men who dominated the American Revolution do not fit the usual image of revolutionaries. They were not poverty-stricken peasants revolting against an insensitive aristocracy but established, educated, and powerful men whose earliest loyalties were to England. Over time, however, they had come to feel capable of managing their own government; finally, they began to think of themselves differently—as Americans. But if they were not radical in the traditional sense, their great contribution to political history, a representative democracy headed by an elected leader, was a radical political development, and its first major expression, the Declaration of Independence, is a remarkable document. Like the Constitution that followed it eleven years later, it is written with such foresight and flexibility that it has stretched to accommodate the needs of later generations and previously excluded constituencies. Much of subsequent American political argument refers back to it or to its promise. Whenever the subject of justice, equality, and civil liberties comes up, either the phrases of the Declaration or the spirit—or both—hover over the discussion. For example, in the years before the Civil War, issues of equality and freedom were slowly if inexorably working their way to the forefront of American political consciousness, and some Americans were more sensitive than others to the impossibility of supporting slavery in a growing democracy with continental ambitions. Among those Americans were Henry David Thoreau and Frederick Douglass. Examples of their work in this chapter are, to differing degrees, early warning signals for the conflagration of the coming Civil War. Henry David Thoreau had a direct sense of the evils of slavery, and he interpreted the Declaration not only as an ideal for collective rebellion against injustice but as an injunction to every single American to heed his or her conscience, even if that meant disobeying the government. Thoreau's most famous piece on dissent, *Civil Disobedience,* which first appeared in 1849, has been a prod to American complacency and self-satisfaction ever since.

Thoreau spoke publicly against slavery because he was an abolitionist—a member of the movement that campaigned for the immediate end to slavery. The abolitionist movement was considered a collection of radicals by most northerners, but like all other campaigns it depended on good speakers to attract attention, audiences, and public support. Thoreau was not in the same class as Frederick Douglass as an orator—nobody was—although he was once called upon to substitute for Douglass at a meeting in Boston.

Douglass, a former slave and a brilliant activist and writer, also had a charismatic presence as a speaker. His powerful intellect and emotion come through intensely in his 1851 Independence Day speech in Rochester, New York, in which he forcefully reminded his white audience of the meaninglessness of the phrase "all men are created equal" for Americans who were enslaved.

Once the Civil War was over, racial division remained, but the political energy that had previously been concentrated on the abolition of slavery began to find its way into other protest movements, particularly the movement for women's right to vote. The intellectual leader and spokesperson of the suffrage movement, Susan B. Anthony, gave her famous speech, "Women's Right to Vote," after she was arrested for trying to register to vote in a presidential election. Like Douglass, also a supporter of women's rights, she was adept at turning the language of the Declaration of Independence and the Constitution back on her audience to prove her point.

By 1896, all the southern states had passed segregation laws against African Americans for the explicit purpose of undoing the civil rights they had won as a result of the Civil War, especially the Thirteenth, Fourteenth, and Fifteenth Amendments to the Constitution, which ended slavery and granted equal protection under the law and the right to vote. The Supreme Court undermined those amendments when, in 1896, it sided with the state of Louisiana in a case called *Plessy* v. *Ferguson*, and declared that black Americans who were forced to ride in separate train cars from whites were not being deprived of equal protection under the law. This is what became known as the "separate but equal" doctrine. Technically, the *Plessy* decision applied only to railroads, but its real effect was to institutionalize segregation in every area of southern public life: transportation, restaurants, beaches, churches, schools. The lone dissenter to the Court's ruling in *Plessy* was Justice John Harlan, a former slave owner who foresaw the tragic consequences of the decision very clearly.

The Supreme Court's interpretation of any case becomes the law of the land, until or unless the law changes or the interpretation changes. In the case of *Plessy*, the worst effects of segregation continued to make themselves felt everywhere in the ordinary experience, the psyches, and the economic suffering of African Americans in the South.

Perhaps the single most striking visual representation of that suffering is a series of photographs taken by the great southern writer Eudora Welty, in rural Mississippi during the worst days of segregation as well as the Depression. One of them is reproduced here: a photograph, called "Dolls," of two little African American girls, wearing their Sunday-best clothes and clutching two white dolls. In this picture Welty condenses the effects of the prejudice that the Supreme Court would eventually confront. In an entirely different mood, and with a very different purpose in mind—to remind Americans in World War II of what they were fighting for—Norman Rockwell's famous 1943 painting *Freedom of Speech*, which appeared on the cover of the *Saturday Evening Post*, offers a small-town New England, almost Jeffersonian image of our most cherished freedom being fully exercised by ordinary Americans.

Roughly half a century, two world wars, and a depression after *Plessy*, Justice Harlan's lonely dissent was finally vindicated in what is probably the most famous Supreme Court decision of the twentieth century, *Brown* v. *Board of Education* (1954). In *Brown*, the Warren Court declared, in an unusual unanimous decision, that the "separate but equal" standard approved in *Plessy* is a contradiction in terms. Like *Plessy*, *Brown* was technically about only one kind of public segregation—in this instance, public schools. Like *Plessy*, however, it had a domino effect: the outlawing of segregation of children at school began, slowly, to dismantle segregation in the South.

But resistance to integration was fierce, and change was irregular and slow, opposed at every step by southern legislatures, governors, sheriffs, and private citizens who met peaceful efforts to integrate public facilities with hatred and often violence. The medium through which most Americans became acquainted with southern segregation and the civil rights movement was television. Pictures of police turning water cannons or attack dogs on unarmed marchers, including elderly men and women, or on college students asking for service at a lunch counter or a drink of water at a fountain marked "WHITES ONLY," made a powerful impression on Americans who had never been south of the Mason Dixon line and whose only image of the South probably came from watching *Gone with the Wind*.

Martin Luther King, Jr., the leader of the civil rights movement, was frequently arrested. During one incarceration in Birmingham, Alabama, King took the opportunity to respond to some of his critics, who had taken out an advertisement in the local paper criticizing him and his followers. Ironically, these particular opponents were not Ku Klux Klan members or other white supremacists but southern clergymen—and mostly black clergymen at that. King's answer, "Letter from Birmingham Jail," immediately became an unofficial primer for the ideology of nonviolent resistance.

In the 1970s and later, a whole new series of arguments about justice and individual rights arose: for or against the Vietnam War, a new wave of the feminist movement, sex education in schools, gays in the military. Probably one of the most incendiary civil liberties issues to emerge in recent years is the question of what can and should be allowed on the Internet. A recent *Time* magazine article gives an overview of the immense possibilities of Internet access, the dangers of pornography on the Internet, and the legislative attempts to protect children from it without violating everyone else's freedom of speech. Finally, the film *The Long Walk Home* brings the issue of civil liberties back to where it started, in a story about the effects of the Montgomery bus boycott on two families, one black and one white.

As long as Americans continue to believe in the ideals of the Declaration of Independence and the Constitution, they will recognize, intermittently and with considerable discomfort, that justice and civil liberty are easy to support but hard to practice. The tension between equality and conformity, individuality and difference, can lead to prejudice. Americans do not always welcome the artists, writers, or political leaders who remind them of the American promise or of how much they have fallen short. Yet even for its harshest critics, America's promise of justice for all survives.

∽ In Defense of Freedom of the Press (1735)

ANDREW HAMILTON

Andrew Hamilton (1676–1741) was a native of Scotland who came to colonial America around 1700, remarkably enough not as a free man, but as an indentured servant. By 1735, he had been a teacher, studied law in London, served as a representative in the Maryland Assembly, and become one of the most famous lawyers in the country. In 1735, he defended John Peter Zenger, who had been arrested for criticizing the colonial British governor in his newspaper. This selection, the first major American defense of freedom of the press, is from Hamilton's argument before the jury.

May it please your honors, I agree with Mr. Attorney [Richard Bradley] that government is a sacred thing, but I differ very widely from him when he would insinuate that the just complaints of a number of men, who suffer under a bad administration, is libeling that administration. Had I believed that to be law, I should not have given the court the trouble of hearing anything that I could say in this cause. . . .

There is heresy in law as well as in religion, and both have changed very much; and we well know that it is not two centuries ago that a man would have burned as a heretic for owning such opinions in matters of religion as are publicly written and printed at this day. They were fallible men, it seems, and we take the liberty, not only to differ from them in religious opinion, but to condemn them and their opinions too; and I must presume that in taking these freedoms in thinking and speaking about matters of faith or religion, we are in the right; for, though it is said there are very great liberties of this kind taken in New York, yet I have heard of no information preferred by Mr. Attorney for any offenses of this sort. From which I think it is pretty clear that in New York a man may make very free with his God, but he must take special care what he says of his Governor. It is agreed upon by all men that this is a reign of liberty, and while men keep within the bounds of truth, I hope they may with safety both speak and write their sentiments of the conduct of men of power; I mean of that part of their conduct only which affects the liberty or property of the people under their administration; were this to be denied, then the next step may make them slaves. For what notions can be entertained of slavery beyond that of suffering the greatest injuries and oppressions without the liberty of complaining; or if they do, to be destroyed, body and estate, for so doing?

It is said, and insisted upon by Mr. Attorney, that government is a sacred thing; that it is to be supported and reverenced; it is government that protects our persons and estates; that prevents treasons, murders, robberies, riots, and all the train of evils that overturn kingdoms and states and ruin particular persons; and if those in the administration, especially the supreme magistrates, must have all their conduct censured by private men, government cannot subsist. This is called a licentiousness not to be tolerated. It is said that it brings the rulers of the people into contempt so that their authority is not regarded, and so that in the end the laws cannot be put in execution. These, I say, and such as these, are the general topics insisted upon by men in power and their advocates. But I wish it might be considered at the same time how often it has happened that the abuse of power has been the primary cause of these evils, and that it was the injustice and oppression of these great men which has commonly brought them into contempt with the people. The craft and art of such men are great, and who that is the least acquainted with history or with law can be ignorant of the specious pretenses which have often been made use of by men in power to introduce arbitrary rule and destroy the liberties of a free people. . . .

If a libel is understood in the large and unlimited sense urged by Mr. Attorney, there is scarce a writing I know that may not be called a libel, or scarce any person safe from being called to account as a libeler, for Moses, meek as he was, libeled Cain; and who is it that has not libeled the devil? For, according to Mr. Attorney, it is not justification to say one has a bad name. Eachard has libeled our good King William; Burnet has libeled, among many others, King Charles and King James; and Rapin has libeled them all. How must a man speak or write, or what must he hear, read, or sing? Or when must he laugh, so as to be secure from being taken up as a libeler? I sincerely believe that were some persons to go through the streets of New York nowadays and read a part of the Bible, if it were not known to be such, Mr. Attorney, with the help of his innuendoes, would easily turn it into a libel. As for instance: Isaiah 11:16: "The leaders of the people cause them to err, and they that are led by them are destroyed." But should Mr. Attorney go about to make this a libel, he would read it thus: "The leaders of the people" (*innuendo,* the Governor and council of New York) "cause them" (*innuendo,* the people of this province) "to err, and they" (the Governor and council meaning) "are destroyed" (*innuendo,* are deceived into the loss of their liberty), "which is the worst kind of destruction." Or if some person should publicly repeat, in a manner not pleasing to his betters, the tenth and the eleventh verses of the fifty-sixth chapter of the same book, there Mr. Attorney would have a large field to display his skill in the artful application of his innuendoes. The words are: "His watchmen are blind, they are ignorant," etc. "Yea, they are greedy dogs, they can never have enough." But to make them a libel, there is, according to Mr. Attorney's doctrine, no more wanting but the aid of his skill in the right adapting his innuendoes. . . .

5   The loss of liberty to a generous mind is worse than death; and yet we know there have been those in all ages who, for the sakes of preferment or some imaginary honor, have freely lent a helping hand to oppress, nay, to destroy, their country. This brings to my mind that saying of the immortal Brutus, when he looked upon the creatures of Caesar, who were very great men, but by no means good men: "You Romans," said Brutus, "if yet I may call you so, consider what you are doing; remember that you are assisting Caesar to forge those very chains which one day he will make yourselves wear." This is what every man that values freedom ought to consider; he should act by judgment and not by affection or self-interest; for where those prevail, no ties of either country or kindred are regarded; as, upon the other hand, the man who loves his country prefers its liberty to all other considerations, well knowing that without liberty life is a misery. . . .

Power may justly be compared to a great river; while kept within its bounds, it is both beautiful and useful, but when it overflows its banks, it is then too impetuous to be stemmed; it bears down all before it, and brings destruction and desolation wherever it comes. If, then, this be the nature of power, let us at least do our duty, and, like wise men who value freedom, use our utmost care to support liberty, the only bulwark against lawless power, which, in all ages, has sacrificed to its wild lust and boundless ambition the blood of the best men that ever lived.

I hope to be pardoned, sir, for my zeal upon this occasion. It is an old and wise caution that "when our neighbor's house is on fire, we ought to take care of our own." For though, blessed be God, I live in a government where liberty is well understood and freely enjoyed, yet experience has shown us all (I am sure it has to me) that a bad precedent in one government is soon set up for an authority in another; and therefore I cannot but think it mine and every honest man's duty that, while we pay all due obedience to men in authority, we ought, at the same time, to be upon our guard against power wherever we apprehend that it may affect ourselves or our fellow subjects.

I am truly very unequal to such an undertaking, on many accounts. And you see I labor under the weight of many years and am borne down with great infirmities of body; yet old and weak as I am, I should think it my duty, if required, to go to the utmost part of the land, where my service could be of any use in assisting to quench the flame of prosecutions upon informations, set on foot by the government to deprive a people of the right of remonstrating, and complaining too, of the arbitrary attempts of men in power. Men who injure and oppress the people under their administration provoke them to cry out and complain, and then make that very complaint the foundation for new oppressions and prosecutions. I wish I could say there were no instances of this kind. But, to conclude, the question before the court, and you, gentlemen of the jury, is not of small nor private concern; it is not the cause of a poor printer, nor of New York alone, which you are now trying. No! It may, in its consequence, affect every free man that lives under a British government on the main continent of America. It is the best cause; it is the cause of liberty; and I make no doubt that your upright conduct, this day, will not only entitle you to the love and esteem of your fellow citizen, but every man who prefers freedom to a life of slavery will bless and honor you as men who have baffled the attempt of tyranny, and, by an impartial and uncorrupt verdict, have laid a noble foundation for securing to ourselves, our posterity, and our neighbors that to which nature and the laws of our country have given us a right—the liberty of both exposing and opposing arbitrary power (in these parts of the world at least) by speaking and writing truth. . . .

For Journals

If you were to write a letter to a newspaper on an issue that really mattered to you, what would it be about? How free would you feel to say what you wanted to?

For Discussion

1. Libel is, very loosely defined, a printed statement that has the effect of damaging a person's standing in the community. The crucial legal principle Hamilton established here is that truth is always a defense to libel. Why does that make sense, and in what situations, if any, can you imagine this ruling being a protection for you?

2. Hamilton is worried about what lawyers call the slippery slope—once a freedom is endangered, a process of further erosion begins, which is as hard to stop as sliding down a slippery slope. What specific harms will follow, and who will be hurt, if freedom of the press is not upheld in this case?

3. John Peter Zenger, the defendant, was arrested for publishing articles critical of the British colonial government. What argument does the government make to justify the arrest? Do you think a government is ever justified in stopping someone from speaking or writing? If so, under what circumstances? If not, why not?

4. What is the logic behind Hamilton's argument that if what Zenger did is libelous, then it's hard to find anyone who isn't? How does he strengthen his argument by including examples such as Moses and Isaiah of the Bible and Julius Caesar and Brutus of ancient Rome?

For Writing

1. Go to the supermarket and buy or look at a tabloid newspaper. Pick out one or two articles directed at either the government or a famous person, and write an essay in which you explain why they might be considered libelous and why the writers of those articles should or should not be protected from prosecution. Remember that truth is a defense to libel, but an untrue statement is not. Two techniques of Hamilton's you could imitate in your paper are use of historical references to support an argument and stating the other side's argument before attacking it.

2. The Constitutional question of preventing publication of documents damaging to the government has continued to come up in American history. Research and write a paper about the circumstances surrounding the publication of the Pentagon Papers in the *New York Times* during the Vietnam War. You can consult books written about this case (which was decided by the U.S. Supreme Court), published court opinions, and the Pentagon Papers themselves, which have been published with an introduction. The Internet may also serve as a source for material about this case and the issues raised by it.

∽ *The Declaration of Independence* (1776)

THOMAS JEFFERSON

The author of the Declaration was thirty-two-year-old Thomas Jefferson (1743–1826) who could, in the words of a contemporary, "break a horse, play the violin, dance the minuet" and of whom the usually acerbic John Adams said, he had a "reputation for literature, science, and a happy talent of composition. His writings

were remarkable for their felicity of expression." Jefferson was, in succession, a mem-
ber of the Continental Congress, governor of Virginia, ambassador to France, the first
secretary of state, vice-president, and then president for two terms, during which he
authorized the Louisiana Purchase, doubling the size of the United States. He founded
the University of Virginia; designed it and his home, Monticello; and collected the
books that formed the basis for the Library of Congress.

In 1962, when President Kennedy invited a group of Nobel Prize winners to din-
ner, he said it was the greatest concentration of intellect in the White House since the
evenings when Thomas Jefferson dined there alone. Jefferson died on July 4, 1826—
fifty years to the day after the signing of the Declaration of Independence. In the text
that follows, the underlined words and phrases were in the first draft but were re-
moved in the final draft. The words and phrases in the margin are those that appeared
in the final version.

A DECLARATION BY THE REPRESENTATIVES OF THE UNITED STATES
OF AMERICA, IN GENERAL CONGRESS ASSEMBLED.

When in the course of human events, it becomes necessary for one
people to dissolve the political bands which have connected them with
another, and to assume among the powers of the earth the separate and
equal station to which the laws of nature and of nature's God entitle
them, a decent respect to the opinions of mankind requires that they
should declare the causes which impel them to the separation.

We hold these truths to be self evident: that all men are created
equal, that they are endowed by their Creator with <u>inherent and</u> un- *certain*
alienable rights; that among these are life, liberty, and the pursuit of
happiness; that to secure these rights, governments are instituted
among men, deriving their just powers from the consent of the governed; that whenever any form of government becomes destructive of
these ends, it is the right of the people to alter or to abolish it, and to institute new government, laying its foundation on such principles, and
organizing its powers in such form, as to them shall seem most likely to
effect their safety and happiness. Prudence, indeed, will dictate that
governments long established should not be changed for light and tran-
sient causes; and accordingly all experience hath shown that mankind
are more disposed to suffer while evils are sufferable, than to right
themselves by abolishing the forms to which they are accustomed. But
when a long train of abuses and usurpations, <u>begun at a distinguished</u>
<u>period and</u> pursuing invariably the same object, evinces a design to re-
duce them under absolute despotism, it is their right, it is their duty to
throw off such government, and to provide new guards for their future
security. Such has been the patient sufferance of these colonies; and
such is now the necessity which constrains them to <u>expunge</u> their for- *alter*
mer systems of government. The history of the present king of Great
Britain is a history of <u>unremitting</u> injuries and usurpations, <u>among</u> *repeated*
<u>which appears no solitary fact to contradict the uniform tenor of the</u> *all having*
<u>rest, but all have</u> in direct object the establishment of an absolute

tyranny over these states. To prove this, let facts be submitted to a candid world for the truth of which we pledge a faith yet unsullied by falsehood.

He has refused his assent to laws the most wholesome and necessary for the public good.

5 He has forbidden his governors to pass laws of immediate and pressing importance, unless suspended in their operation till his assent should be obtained; and, when so suspended, he has utterly neglected to attend to them.

He has refused to pass other laws for the accommodation of large districts of people, unless those people would relinquish the right of representation in the legislature, a right inestimable to them, and formidable to tyrants only.

He has called together legislative bodies at places unusual, uncomfortable, and distant from the depository of their public records, for the sole purpose of fatiguing them into compliance with his measures.

He has dissolved representative houses repeatedly and continually for opposing with manly firmness his invasions on the rights of the people.

He has refused for a long time after such dissolutions to cause others to be elected, whereby the legislative powers, incapable of annihilation, have returned to the people at large for their exercise, the state remaining, in the meantime, exposed to all the dangers of invasion from without and convulsions within.

10 He has endeavored to prevent the population of these states: for that purpose obstructing the laws for naturalization of foreigners, refusing to pass others to encourage their migrations hither, and raising the conditions of new appropriations of lands.

He has suffered the administration of justice totally to cease in some of these states refusing his assent to laws for establishing judiciary powers. obstr by

He has made our judges dependent on his will alone for the tenure of their offices, and the amount and payment of their salaries.

He has erected a multitude of new offices, by a self-assumed power and sent hither swarms of new officers to harass our people and eat out their substance.

He has kept among us in times of peace standing armies and ships of war without the consent of our legislatures.

15 He has affected to render the military independent of, and superior to, the civil power.

He has combined with others to subject us to a jurisdiction foreign to our constitutions and unacknowledged by our laws, giving his assent to their acts of pretended legislation for quartering large bodies of armed troops among us; for protecting them by a mock trial from punishment for any murders which they should commit on the inhabitants of these states; for cutting off our trade with all parts of the world; for imposing taxes on us without our consent; for depriving us [   ] of *[in many cases]* the benefits of trial by jury; for transporting us beyond seas to be tried for pretended offenses; for abolishing the free system of English laws in a neighboring province, establishing therein an arbitrary government, *[in many cases]* and enlarging its boundaries, so as to render it at once an example and fit instrument for introducing the same absolute rule into these states; *[colonies]* for taking away our charters, abolishing our most valuable laws, and altering fundamentally the forms of our governments; for suspending our own legislatures, and declaring themselves invested with power to legislate for us in all cases whatsoever.

He has abdicated government here withdrawing his governors, and declaring us out of his allegiance and protection. *[by declaring us out of his protection and waging war against us]*

He has plundered our seas, ravaged our coasts, burnt our towns, and destroyed the lives of our people.

He is at this time transporting large armies of foreign mercenaries to complete the works of death, desolation and tyranny already begun with circumstances of cruelty and perfidy [   ] unworthy the head of a civilized nation. *[scarcely paralleled in the most barbarous ages, and totally]*

20   He has constrained our fellow citizens taken captive on the high seas, to bear arms, against their country, to become the executioners of their friends and brethren, or to fall themselves by their hands.

He has [   ] endeavored to bring on the inhabitants of our frontiers, the merciless Indian savages, whose known rule of warfare is an undistinguished destruction of all ages, sexes and conditions of existence. *[excited domestic insurrection among us, and has]*

He has incited treasonable insurrections of our fellow citizens, with the allurements of forfeiture and confiscation of our property.

He has waged cruel war against human nature itself, violating its most sacred rights of life and liberty in the persons of a distant people who never offended him, captivating and carrying them into slavery in another hemisphere, or to incur miserable death in their transportation thither. This piratical warfare, the opprobrium of INFIDEL powers, is the warfare of the CHRISTIAN king of Great Britain. Determined to keep open a market where MEN should be bought and sold, he has prostituted his negative for suppressing every legislative attempt to prohibit or to restrain this execrable commerce. And that this assem-blage of horrors might want no fact of distinguished die, he is now exciting those very people to rise in arms among us, and to purchase that liberty of which he has deprived them, by murdering the people on whom he also obtruded them: thus paying off former crimes committed against the LIBERTIES of one people, with crimes which heurges them to commit against the LIVES of another.

In every stage of these oppressions we have petitioned for redress in the most humble terms: our repeated petitions have been answered only by repeated injuries.

25   A prince whose character is thus marked by every act which may define a tyrant is unfit to be the ruler of a [   ] people who mean to be *[free]*

free. Future ages will scarcely believe that the hardiness of one man adventured, within the short compass of twelve years only, to lay a foundation so broad and so undisguised for tyranny over a people fostered and fixed in principles of freedom.

Nor have we been wanting in attentions to our British brethren. We have warned them from time to time of attempts by their legislature to extend a jurisdiction over these our states. We have reminded them of the circumstances of our emigration and settlement here, no one of which would warrant so strange a pretension: that these were effected at the expense of our own blood and treasure, unassisted by the wealth or the strength of Great Britain: that in constituting indeed our several forms of government, we had adopted one common king, thereby laying a foundation for perpetual league and amity with them: but that submission to their parliament was no part of our constitution, nor ever in idea, if history may be credited: and, we [   ] appealed to their native justice and magnanimity as well as to the ties of our common kindred to disavow these usurpations which were likely to interrupt our connection and correspondence. They too have been deaf to the voice of justice and of consanguinity, and when occasions have been given them, by the regular course of their laws, of removing from their councils the disturbers of our harmony, they have, by their free election, reestablished them in power. At this very time too, they are permitting their chief magistrate to send over not only soldiers of our common blood, but Scotch and foreign mercenaries to invade and destroy us. These facts have given the last stab to agonizing affection, and manly spirit bids us to renounce forever these unfeeling brethren. We must endeavor to forget our former love for them, and hold them as we hold the rest of mankind, enemies in war, in peace friends. We might have been a free and a great people together; but a communication of grandeur and of freedom, it seems, is below their dignity. Be it so, since they will have it. The road to happiness and to glory is open to us, too. We will tread it apart from them, and acquiesce in the necessity which denounces our eternal separation [   ]!

We therefore the representatives of the United States of America in General Congress assembled, do in the name, and by the authority of the good people of these states reject and renounce all allegiance and subjection to the kings of Great Britain and all others who may hereafter claim by, through or under them; we utterly dissolve all political connection which may heretofore have subsisted between us and the people or parliament of Great Britain: and finally we do assert and declare these colonies to be free and independent states, and that as free and independent states, they have full power to levy war, conclude peace, contract alliances, establish commerce, and to do all other acts and things which independent states may of right do.

And for the support of this declaration, we mutually pledge to each other our lives, our fortunes, and our sacred honor.

We, therefore, the representatives of the United States of America in General Congress assembled, appealing to the supreme judge of the world for the rectitude of our intentions, do in the name, and by the authority of the good people of these colonies, solemnly publish and declare, that these united colonies are, and of right ought to be free and independent states; that they are absolved from all allegiance to the British crown, and that all political connection between them and the state of Great Britain is, and ought to be, totally dissolved; and that as free and independent states, they have full power to levy war, conclude peace, contract alliances, establish commerce, and to do all other acts and things which independent states may of right do.

And for the support of this declaration, with a firm reliance on the 30 protection of divine providence, we mutually pledge to each other our lives, our fortunes, and our sacred honor.

For Journals

Is the content of the Declaration of Independence what you expected it would be? What parts of it, if any, were familiar to you?

For Discussion

1. Read the entire Declaration out loud, with each person in the class reading part of it. Then do five minutes worth of freewriting. Using your freewriting as a basis, compare your thoughts about the Declaration with those of your peers.

2. The Declaration was the justification for the idea of a democratic republic when no such republic had ever existed before. Working with someone else in your class, find three good examples of Jefferson's argument for the form of government he wants. What is the main point in each example? What is the supporting evidence? What is the conclusion?

3. The two most famous phrases in the Declaration of Independence declare that "all men are created equal" and that we are endowed by our Creator with the rights to "life, liberty, and the pursuit of happiness." What do you think those particular phrases mean? What does it mean to be created equal? Equal in what way? Equal spiritually? Equal legally? Equal intellectually? How do you think an American pursues happiness?

4. Jefferson, who was trained as a lawyer, was accustomed to framing arguments. Reread the Declaration as though you were a member of a jury listening to a trial lawyer's closing statement on behalf of his client. How does he refute the idea that George III is a just king and that Americans owe him their loyalty under any circumstances? What kind of evidence does he present about the injustices committed by the king and Great Britain to prove that Americans are entitled to decide on their own?

5. Many Americans did not support the Revolution and remained loyal to the English government. What arguments do you think they might have made to refute Jefferson's assertions? What holes would they have tried to find in his argument?

6. What do you think Jefferson wanted an American audience to take away from the Declaration? What do you think he wanted a British audience to learn?

For Writing

1. Look at the underlined phrases that were in the first version of the Declaration but were eliminated or changed in the final version; then examine the words in the margin that replaced them. For example, in the first draft, Jefferson included a long denunciation of slavery; in the final draft it is taken out because the southern slaveholders would not vote for a document that included it. Write an essay in which you respond to the following: What changes were the most surprising to you? Are there any cases in which you prefer the first version over the final one? Which ones do you think present a stronger argument against British injustice? Why?

2. There were many lawyers among the founding fathers; yet although they all opposed British rule, at least one of them was willing to defend British soldiers in court in the name of justice and civil liberties. Research and write a documented paper on the story of how John Adams defended British soldiers accused of murdering five colonials during the Boston Massacre. Include his reasons for taking on the case, what the colonial community thought of Adams's decision, and your own reaction.

∞ FROM *Civil Disobedience* (1850)

HENRY DAVID THOREAU

Henry David Thoreau (1817–1862) spent almost his entire life in and around Concord, Massachusetts, and found there all the subject matter he needed. An ardent abolitionist, diarist, nature writer, and natural scientist, he challenged American materialism and complacency as no other writer has before or since. Always an individualist, he wrote his most famous book, Walden *(1854), while living alone for two years at Walden Pond, where he said he could live a life of "simplicity, independence, magnanimity, trust." It was at Walden that he was arrested—willingly—and spent a night in jail for having refused to pay taxes supporting slavery and the Mexican-American War.* Civil Disobedience, *which explains Thoreau's theory of passive resistance, challenged his neighbors—and us—to examine our lives and our ethics, and to act.*

I heartily accept the motto—"That government is best which governs least"; and I should like to see it acted up to more rapidly and systematically. Carried out, it finally amounts to this, which also I believe,—"That government is best which governs not at all"; and when men are prepared for it, that will be the kind of government which they will have. Government is at best but an expedient; but most governments are usually, and all governments are sometimes, inexpedient. The objections which have been brought against a standing army, and they are many and weighty, and deserve to prevail, may also at last be brought against a standing government. The standing army is only an arm of the standing government. The government itself, which is only the mode which the people have chosen to execute their will, is equally liable to be abused and perverted before the people can act through it. Witness the present Mexican war, the work of comparatively a few individuals using the standing government as their tool; for, in the outset, the people would not have consented to this measure.

This American government,—what is it but a tradition, though a recent one, endeavoring to transmit itself unimpaired to posterity, but each instant losing some of its integrity? It has not the vitality and force of a single living man; for a single man can bend it to his will. It is a sort of wooden gun to the people themselves; and, if ever they should use it in earnest as a real one against each other, it will surely split. But it is not the less necessary for this; for the people must have some complicated machinery or other, and hear its din, to satisfy that idea of government which they have. Governments show thus how successfully men can be imposed on, even impose on themselves, for their own advantage. It is excellent, we must all allow; yet this government never of itself furthered any enterprise, but by the alacrity with which it got out of its way. *It* does not keep the country free. *It* does not settle the West. *It* does not educate. The character inherent in the American people has done all that has been accomplished; and it would have done somewhat more, if the government had not sometimes got in its way. For government is an expedient by which men would fain succeed in letting one another alone; and, as has been said, when it is most expedient, the governed are most let alone by it. Trade and commerce, if they were not made of india rubber, would never manage to bounce over the obstacles which legislators are continually putting in their way; and, if one were to judge these men wholly by the effects of their actions, and not partly by their intentions, they would deserve to be classed and punished with those mischievous persons who put obstructions on the railroads.

But, to speak practically and as a citizen, unlike those who call themselves no-government men, I ask for, not at once no government, but *at once* a better government. Let every man make known what kind of government would command his respect, and that will be one step toward obtaining it.

After all, the practical reason why, when the power is once in the hands of the people, a majority are permitted, and for a long period continue, to rule, is not because this seems fairest to the minority, but because they are physically the strongest. But a government in which the majority rule in all cases cannot be based on justice, even as far as men understand it. Can there not be a government in which majorities do not virtually decide right and wrong, but conscience?—in which majorities decide only those questions to which the rule of expediency is applicable? Must the citizen ever for a moment, or in the least degree, resign his conscience to the legislator? Why has every man a conscience, then? I think that we should be men first, and subjects afterward. It is not desirable to cultivate a respect for the law, so much as for the right. The only obligation which I have a right to assume, is to do at any time what I think right. . . .

5   How does it become a man to behave toward this American government to-day? I answer that he cannot without disgrace be associated with it. I cannot for an instant recognize that political organization as *my* government which is the *slave's* government also.

All men recognize the right of revolution; that is, the right to refuse allegiance to and to resist the government, when its tyranny or its inefficiency are great and unendurable. But almost all say that such is not the case now. But such was the case, they think, in the Revolution of '75. If one were to tell me that this was a bad government because it taxed certain foreign commodities brought to its ports, it is most probable that I should not make an ado about it, for I can do without them; all machines have their friction; and possibly this does enough good to counterbalance the evil. At any rate, it is a great evil to make a stir about it. But when the friction comes to have its machine, and oppression and robbery are organized, I say, let us not have such a machine any longer. In other words, when a sixth of the population of a nation which has undertaken to be the refuge of liberty are slaves, and a whole country is unjustly overrun and conquered by a foreign army, and subject to military law, I think that it is not too soon for honest men to rebel and revolutionize. What makes this duty the more urgent is the fact, that the country so overrun is not our own, but ours is the invading army. . . .

Practically speaking, the opponents to a reform in Massachusetts are not a hundred thousand politicians at the South, but a hundred thousand merchants and farmers here, who are more interested in commerce and agriculture than they are in humanity, and are not prepared to do justice to the slave and to Mexico, *cost what it may*. I quarrel not with far-off foes, but with those who, near at home, co-operate with, and do the bidding of those far away, and without whom the latter would be harmless. We are accustomed to say, that the mass of men are unprepared; but improvement is slow, because the few are not materially wiser or better than the many. It is not so important that many should be as good as you, as that there be some absolute goodness somewhere; for that will leaven the whole lump. There are thousands who are *in opinion* opposed to slavery and to the war, who yet in effect do nothing to put an end to them; who, esteeming themselves children of Washington and Franklin, sit down with their hands in their pockets, and say that they know not what to do, and do nothing; who even postpone the question of freedom to the question of free-trade, and quietly read the prices-current along with the latest advices from Mexico, after dinner, and, it may be, fall asleep over them both. . . .

The American has dwindled into an Old Fellow,—one who may be known by the development of his organ of gregariousness, and a manifest lack of intellect and cheerful self-reliance; whose first and chief concern, on coming into the world, is to see that the alms-houses are in good repair; and, before yet he has lawfully donned the virile garb, to collect a fund for the support of the widows and orphans that may be; who, in short, ventures to live only by the aid of the mutual insurance company, which has promised to bury him decently. . . .

Unjust laws exist: shall we be content to obey them, or shall we endeavor to amend them, and obey them until we have succeeded, or shall we transgress them at once? Men generally, under such a government as this, think that they ought to wait until they have persuaded the majority to alter them. They think that, if they should resist, the remedy would be worse than the evil. But it is the fault of the government itself that the remedy *is* worse than the evil. *It* makes it worse. Why is it not more apt to anticipate and provide for reform? Why does it not cherish its wise minority? Why does it cry and resist before it is hurt? Why does it not encourage its citizens to be on the alert to point out its faults, and *do* better than it would have them? Why does it always crucify Christ, and excommunicate Copernicus and Luther, and pronounce Washington and Franklin rebels? . . .

If the injustice is part of the necessary friction of the machine of 10 government, let it go, let it go: perchance it will wear smooth,—certainly the machine will wear out. If the injustice has a spring, or a pulley, or a rope, or a crank, exclusively for itself, then perhaps you may consider whether the remedy will not be worse than the evil; but if it is of such a nature that it requires you to be the agent of injustice to another, then, I say, break the law. Let your life be a counter friction to stop the machine. What I have to do is to see, at any rate, that I do not lend myself to the wrong which I condemn.

As for adopting the ways which the State has provided for remedying the evil, I know not of such ways. They take too much time, and a man's life will be gone. I have other affairs to attend to. I came into this world, not chiefly to make this a good place to life [*sic*], but to live in it, be it good or bad. A man has not everything to do, but something; and because he cannot do *every thing*, it is not necessary that he should do *something* wrong. It is not my business to be petitioning the governor or the legislature any more than it is theirs to petition me; and if they should not hear my petition, what should I do then? But in this case the

State has provided no way: its very Constitution is the evil. This may seem to be harsh and stubborn and unconciliatory; but it is to treat with the utmost kindness and consideration the only spirit that can appreciate or deserves it. So is all change for the better, like birth and death which convulse the body.

I do not hesitate to say, that those who call themselves abolitionists should at once effectually withdraw their support, both in person and property, from the government of Massachusetts, and not wait till they constitute a majority of one, before they suffer the right to prevail through them, I think that it is enough if they have God on their side, without waiting for that other one. Moreover, any man more right than his neighbors constitutes a majority of one already. . . .

Under a government which imprisons any unjustly, the true place for a just man is also in prison. The proper place to-day, the only place which Massachusetts has provided for her freer and less desponding spirits, is in her prisons, to be put out and locked out of the State by her own act, as they have already put themselves out by their principles. It is there that the fugitive slave, and the Mexican prisoner on parole, and the Indian come to plead the wrongs of his race, should find them; on that separate, but more free and honorable ground, where the State places those who are not *with* her, but *against* her,—the only house in a slave-state in which a free man can abide with honor. If any think that their influence would be lost there, and their voices no longer afflict the ear of the State, that they would not be as an enemy within its walls, they do not know by how much truth is stronger than error, nor how much more eloquently and effectively he can combat injustice who has experienced a little in his own person. Cast your whole vote, not a strip of paper merely, but your whole influence. A minority is powerless while it conforms to the majority; it is not even a minority then; but it is irresistible when it clogs by its whole weight. If the alternative is to keep all just men in prison, or give up war and slavery, the State will not hesitate which to choose. If a thousand men were not to pay their tax-bills this year, that would not be a violent and bloody measure, as it would be to pay them, and enable the State to commit violence and shed innocent blood. This is, in fact, the definition of a peaceable revolution, if any such is possible. If the tax-gatherer, or any other public officer, asks me, as one has done, "But what shall I do?" my answer is, "If you really wish to do anything, resign our office." When the subject has refused allegiance, and the officer has resigned his office, then the revolution is accomplished. But even suppose blood should flow. Is there not a sort of blood shed when the conscience is wounded? Through this wound a man's real manhood and immortality flow out, and he bleeds to an everlasting death. I see this blood flowing now. . . .

I have paid no poll-tax for six years. I was put into a jail once on this account, for one night; and, as I stood considering the walls of solid stone, two or three feet thick, the door of wood and iron, a foot thick, and the iron grating which strained the light, I could not help being struck with the foolishness of that institution which treated me as if I were mere flesh and blood and bones, to be locked up. I wondered that it should have concluded at length that this was the best use it could put me to, and had never thought to avail itself of my services in some way. I saw that, if there was a wall of stone between me and my townsmen, there was a still more difficult one to climb or break through, before they could get to be as free as I was. I did not for a moment feel confined, and the walls seemed a great waste of stone and mortar. I felt as if I alone of all my townsmen had paid my tax. They plainly did not know how to treat me, but behaved like persons who are underbred. In every threat and in every compliment there was a blunder; for they thought that my chief desire was to stand the other side of that stone wall. I could not but smile to see how industriously they locked the door on my meditations, which followed them out again without let or hindrance, and *they* were really all that was dangerous. As they could not reach me, they had resolved to punish my body; just as boys, if they cannot come at some person against whom they have a spite, will abuse his dog. I saw that the State was half-witted, that it was timid as a lone woman with her silver spoons, and that it did not know its friends from its foes, and I lost all my remaining respect for it, and pitied it.

Thus the State never intentionally confronts a man's sense, intellec- 15 tual or moral, but only his body, his senses. It is not armed with superior wit or honesty, but with superior physical strength. I was not born to be forced. I will breathe after my own fashion. Let us see who is the strongest. What force has a multitude? They only can force me who obey a higher law than I. They force me to become like themselves. I do not hear of *men* being *forced* to live this way or that by masses of men. What sort of life were that to live? When I meet a government which says to me, "Your money or your life," why should I be in haste to give it my money? It may be in a great strait, and not know what to do: I cannot help that. It must help itself; do as I do. It is not worth the while to snivel about it. I am not responsible for the successful working of the machinery of society. I am not the son of the engineer. I perceive that, when an acorn and a chestnut fall side by side, the one does not remain inert to make way for the other, but both obey their own laws, and spring and grow and flourish as best they can, till one, perchance, overshadows and destroys the other. If a plant cannot live according to its nature, it dies; and so a man. . . .

I do not wish to quarrel with any man or nation. I do not wish to split hairs, to make fine distinctions, or set myself up as better than my neighbors. I seek rather, I may say, even an excuse for conforming to the laws of the land. I am but too ready to conform to them. Indeed I have reason to suspect myself on his head; and each year, as the tax-gatherer comes round, I find myself disposed to review the acts and position of the general and state governments, and the spirit of the people, to discover a pretext for conformity. I believe that the State will soon be able to take all my work of this sort out of my hands, and then I shall be no better a patriot than my fellow-countrymen. Seen from a lower point of view, the Constitution, with all its faults, is very good; the law and the courts are very respectable; even this State and this American government are, in many respects, very admirable and rare things, to be thankful for, such as a great many have described them; but seen from a point of view a little higher, they are what I have described them; seen from a higher still, and the highest, who shall say that they are, or that they are worth looking at or thinking of at all?

However, the government does not concern me much, and I shall bestow the fewest possible thoughts on it. It is not many moments that I live under a government, even in this world. If a man is thought-free, fancy-free, imagination-free, that which *is not* never for a long time appearing *to be* to him, unwise rulers or reformers cannot fatally interrupt him. . . .

The authority of government, even such as I am willing to submit to,—for I will cheerfully obey those who know and can do better than I, and in many things even those who neither know nor can do so well,—is still an impure one: to be strictly just, it must have the sanction and consent of the governed. It can have no pure right over my person and property but what I concede to it. The progress from an absolute to a limited monarchy, from a limited monarchy to a democracy, is a progress toward a true respect for the individual. Is a democracy, such as we know it, the last improvement possible in government? Is it not possible to take a step further towards recognizing and organizing the rights of man? There will never be a really free and enlightened State, until the State comes to recognize the individual as a higher and independent power, from which all its own power and authority are derived, and treats him accordingly. I please myself with imagining a State at last which can afford to be just to all men, and to treat the individual with respect as a neighbor, which even would not think it inconsistent with its own repose, if a few were to live aloof from it, not meddling with it, nor embraced by it, who fulfilled all the duties of neighbors and fellowmen. A State which bore this kind of fruit, and suffered it to drop off as fast as it ripened, would prepare the way for a still more perfect and glorious State, which also I have imagined, but not yet anywhere seen.

For Journals

Thoreau states that the government which governs best is the one which governs least. What functions does he seem to think government should stay out of? Which areas today would you want government to stay out of, and which do you think it should pursue more actively?

For Discussion

1. What is your response to Thoreau's ideas that an individual American following his or her conscience is a majority of one, and that fighting injustice by persuading the majority to change the law takes too long? What traditional ideas of good government and citizenship does he refute in these statements?

2. Thoreau says that the government does not keep the country free, that it does not settle the West, that it does not educate. In his opinion, then, what does it do?

3. Democracy is supposed to be governed by the rule of the majority, but Thoreau says that his only obligation is "to do what I think is right." How do you respond to this assertion? Do you think that the two principles—majority rule and individual conscience—are compatible or mutually incompatible? Why?

4. Thoreau refused to pay a poll tax as a protest against slavery and the war America was waging against Mexico. Do you find withholding taxes or going to jail reasonable ways of protesting injustice? If not, what would you say to refute Thoreau's belief in civil disobedience? Are there any principles for which you would be willing to break the law, go to jail, or otherwise practice civil disobedience yourself?

5. What does Thoreau think constitute the responsibilities of a good citizen? Why does he think most Americans, even the ones opposed to slavery, are not truly good citizens?

6. How would the government function if everyone followed his or her conscience the way Thoreau did? Do you see him as an extremist? A patriot? Both?

For Writing

1. Write an essay in which you compose your own definition of patriotism. Be sure to identify the principles—political, personal, or ethical—on which your definition is based. You can refer to Thoreau, the Declaration, or any other readings, and either refute these arguments or draw on them to support your own views.

2. Read one of Thoreau's other works—for example, *Walden*, the diary of his year-long adventure of living alone and being self-sufficient; or *A Week on the Concord and Merrimack Rivers*, an account of his canoeing trip in the American wilderness. Write a review critiquing Thoreau's skill as a naturalist and observer, and share the review with your peers; you should use secondary library sources (articles, biographies, and so on) if possible.

∞ Independence Day Speech at Rochester (1852)

FREDERICK DOUGLASS

At the time Frederick Douglass gave this speech, he had been living in Rochester, New York, for several years and editing his abolitionist newspaper, the Northern Star. *His autobiography had been published in 1845, after he escaped from slavery, and he subsequently spent two years in England lecturing and earning money to buy his freedom so that he could not be captured and returned to the South. He had a remarkable career as a diplomat, civil rights leader before and after the Civil War, marshal of the District of Columbia, organizer of black combat units, campaigner for women's rights, newspaper editor, and writer. He was asked to deliver the Fourth of July speech in Rochester in 1852. Fourth of July speeches were already an old American political tradition. Like parades and fireworks, the speeches on such occasions are usually celebratory, uncritical, and immediately forgettable. Douglass's speech, made nine years before the start of the Civil War, is the exception.*

Fellow citizens, pardon me, allow me to ask, why am I called upon to speak here today? What have I, or those I represent, to do with your national independence? Are the great principles of political freedom and of natural justice, embodied in that Declaration of Independence, extended to us? and am I, therefore, called upon to bring our humble offering to the national altar, and to confess the benefits and express devout gratitude for the blessings resulting from your independence to us?

Would to God, both for your sakes and ours, that an affirmative answer could be truthfully returned to these questions! Then would my task be light, and my burden easy and delightful. For who is there so cold that a nation's sympathy could not warm him? Who so obdurate and dead to the claims of gratitude that would not thankfully acknowledge such priceless benefits? Who so stolid and selfish that would not give his voice to swell the hallelujahs of a nation's jubilee, when the chains of servitude had been torn from his limbs? I am not that man. In a case like that the dumb might eloquently speak and the "lame man leap as an hart."[1]

But such is not the state of the case. I say it with a sad sense of the disparity between us. I am not included within the pale of this glorious anniversary! Your high independence only reveals the immeasurable distance between us. The blessings in which you, this day, rejoice are not enjoyed in common. The rich inheritance of justice, liberty, prosperity, and independence bequeathed by your fathers is shared by you, not by me. The sunlight that brought light and healing to you has brought stripes and death to me. This Fourth of July is yours, not mine. You may

---

[1] From the Bible, Isaiah 35:6.

rejoice, I must mourn. To drag a man in fetters into the grand illuminated temple of liberty, and call upon him to join you in joyous anthems, were inhuman mockery and sacrilegious irony. Do you mean, citizens, to mock me by asking me to speak today? If so, there is a parallel to your conduct. And let me warn you that it is dangerous to copy the example of a nation whose crimes, towering up to heaven, were thrown down by the breath of the Almighty, burying that nation in irrevocable ruin! I can today take up the plaintive lament of a peeled and woe-smitten people![2]

"By the rivers of Babylon, there we sat down. Yea! we wept when we remembered Zion. We hanged our harps upon the willows in the midst thereof. For there, they that carried us away captive, required of us a song; and they who wasted us required of us mirth, saying, Sing us one of the songs of Zion. How can we sing the Lord's song in a strange land? If I forget thee, O Jerusalem, let my right hand forget her cunning. If I do not remember thee, let my tongue cleave to the roof of my mouth."[3]

Fellow citizens, above your national, tumultuous joy, I hear the mournful wail of millions! whose chains, heavy and grievous yesterday, are, today, rendered more intolerable by the jubilee shouts that reach them. If I do forget, if I do not faithfully remember those bleeding children of sorrow this day, "may my right hand forget her cunning, and may my tongue cleave to the roof of my mouth"! To forget them, to pass lightly over their wrongs, and to chime in with the popular theme would be treason most scandalous and shocking, and would make me a reproach before God and the world. My subject, then, fellow citizens, is *American slavery*. I shall see this day and its popular characteristics from the slave's point of view. Standing there identified with the American bondman, making his wrongs mine. I do not hesitate to declare with all my soul that the character and conduct of this nation never looked blacker to me than on this Fourth of July! Whether we turn to the declarations of the past or to the professions of the present, the conduct of the nation seems equally hideous and revolting. America is false to the past, false to the present, and solemnly binds herself to be false to the future. Standing with God and the crushed and bleeding slave on this occasion, I will, in the name of humanity which is outraged, in the name of liberty which is fettered, in the name of the Constitution and the Bible which are disregarded and trampled upon, dare to call in question and to denounce, with all the emphasis I can command, everything that serves to perpetuate slavery—the great sin and shame of America! "I will not equivocate, I will not excuse"; I will use

---

[2] In 586 B.C.E., the near eastern kingdom of Babylon invaded Judea, burned the first temple in Jerusalem, and took the population into captivity.

[3] Psalm 137:1–6. This is the lament of the Judean exiles.

the severest language I can command; and yet not one word shall escape me that any man, whose judgment is not blinded by prejudice, or who is not at heart a slaveholder, shall not confess to be right and just.

But I fancy I hear someone of my audience say, "It is just in this circumstance that you and your brother abolitionists fail to make a favorable impression on the public mind. Would you argue more and denounce less, would you persuade more and rebuke less, your cause would be much more likely to succeed." But, I submit, where all is plain, there is nothing to be argued. What point in the antislavery creed would you have me argue? On what branch of the subject do the people of this country need light? Must I undertake to prove that the slave is a man? That point is conceded already. Nobody doubts it. The slaveholders themselves acknowledge it in the enactment of laws for their government. They acknowledge it when they punish disobedience on the part of the slave. There are seventy-two crimes in the state of Virginia which, if committed by a black man (no matter how ignorant he be), subject him to the punishment of death; while only two of the same crimes will subject a white man to the like punishment. What is this but the acknowledgment that the slave is a moral, intellectual, and responsible being? The manhood of the slave is conceded. It is admitted in the fact that the Southern statute books are covered with enactments forbidding, under severe fines and penalties, the teaching of the slave to read or to write. When you can point to any such laws in reference to the beasts of the field, then I may consent to argue the manhood of the slave. When the dogs in your streets, when the fowls of the air, when the cattle on your hills, when the fish of the sea and the reptiles that crawl shall be unable to distinguish the slave from a brute, then will I argue with you that the slave is a man!

For the present, it is enough to affirm the equal manhood of the Negro race. Is it not astonishing that, while we are plowing, planting, and reaping, using all kinds of mechanical tools, erecting houses, constructing bridges, building ships, working in metals of brass, iron, copper, silver, and gold; that, while we are reading, writing, and ciphering, acting as clerks, merchants, and secretaries, having among us lawyers, doctors, ministers, poets, authors, editors, orators, and teachers; that, while we are engaged in all manner of enterprises common to other men, digging gold in California, capturing the whale in the Pacific, feeding sheep and cattle on the hillside, living, moving, acting, thinking, planning, living in families as husbands, wives, and children, and, above all, confessing and worshiping the Christian's God, and looking hopefully for life and immortality beyond the grave, we are called upon to prove that we are men!

Would you have me argue that man is entitled to liberty? That he is the rightful owner of his own body? You have already declared it. Must I argue the wrongfulness of slavery? Is that a question for republicans?

Is it to be settled by the rules of logic and argumentation, as a matter beset with great difficulty, involving a doubtful application of the principle of justice, hard to be understood? How should I look today, in the presence of Americans, dividing and subdividing a discourse, to show that men have a natural right to freedom? speaking of it relatively and positively, negatively and affirmatively? To do so would be to make myself ridiculous and to offer an insult to your understanding. There is not a man beneath the canopy of heaven that does not know that slavery is wrong for him.

What, am I to argue that it is wrong to make men brutes, to rob them of their liberty, to work them without wages, to keep them ignorant of their relations to their fellow men, to beat them with sticks, to flay their flesh with the lash, to load their limbs with irons, to hunt them with dogs, to sell them at auction, to sunder their families, to knock out their teeth, to burn their flesh, to starve them into obedience and submission to their masters? Must I argue that a system thus marked with blood, and stained with pollution, is wrong? No! I will not. I have better employment for my time and strength than such arguments would imply.

What, then, remains to be argued? Is it that slavery is not divine; that God did not establish it; that our doctors of divinity are mistaken? There is blasphemy in the thought. That which is inhuman cannot be divine! Who can reason on such a proposition? They that can may; I cannot. The time for such argument is past.

At a time like this, scorching iron, not convincing argument, is needed. O! had I the ability, and could I reach the nation's ear, I would today pour out a fiery stream of biting ridicule, blasting reproach, withering sarcasm, and stern rebuke. For it is not light that is needed, but fire; it is not the gentle shower, but thunder. We need the storm, the whirlwind, and the earthquake. The feeling of the nation must be quickened; the conscience of the nation must be roused; the propriety of the nation must be startled; the hypocrisy of the nation must be exposed; and its crimes against God and man must be proclaimed and denounced.

What, to the American slave, is your Fourth of July? I answer: a day that reveals to him, more than all other days in the year, the gross injustice and cruelty to which he is the constant victim. To him, your celebration is a sham; your boasted liberty, an unholy license; your national greatness, swelling vanity; your sounds of rejoicing are empty and heartless; your denunciation of tyrants, brass-fronted impudence; your shouts of liberty and equality, hollow mockery; your prayers and hymns, your sermons and thanksgivings, with all your religious parade and solemnity, are, to Him, mere bombast, fraud, deception, impiety, and hypocrisy—a thin veil to cover up crimes which would disgrace a nation of savages. There is not a nation of savages. There is not a nation on the earth guilty of practices more shocking and bloody than are the people of the United States at this very hour.

Go where you may, search where you will, roam through all the monarchies and despotisms of the Old World, travel through South America, search out every abuse, and when you have found the last, lay your facts by the side of the everyday practices of this nation, and you will say with me that, for revolting barbarity and shameless hypocrisy, America reigns without a rival.

For Journals

Was Independence Day an appropriate time for Douglass to make his speech? Why or why not?

For Discussion

1. What do you think were the expectations of Douglass's audience when he began his speech? At what point in the speech do you think he begins to move toward his real topic?

2. Review Douglass's speech with one or two other people in your class, and identify the main points of his argument. (You might begin by identifying the crucial sentence in each paragraph.) What are his conclusions? What do you think he wants his audience to take away with them?

3. Refutation in Douglass's case is not only logically precise but full of emotion. Where in this speech do you find examples of Douglass's anger? Irony? Sarcasm? To what purpose does he express these? How do they help him make his point?

4. What evidence does Douglass accumulate to justify his conclusion that a slave is indeed a man? How would the argument be weaker without this proof? Are there any pieces of evidence that you would add?

5. Which phrases does Douglass quote or paraphrase from the language of the Declaration of Independence? How does he make use of those quotations to support his argument against slavery and to refute the idea that he should be celebrating the Fourth of July?

6. Douglass uses the technique of raising objections his audience might bring up and then refuting them himself. Find two or three examples of this strategy. Why do you think he employs it? In what ways is it effective in strengthening his argument?

For Writing

1. Douglass revised his autobiography, *The Life and Times of Frederick Douglass*, three times, adding information each time. For example, the first version, written before the Civil War, gives very few details about the people who helped him escape from slavery because Douglass didn't want to jeopardize anyone. The last version of the book, written many years later, is much more explicit. Write a research paper in which you compare elements of one version with another—for example, Douglass's childhood, his experiences as a slave, his education, his escape, or his relations with the Auld family. Consider these questions: What did Douglass add about a certain episode? Which version do you think is more effective? How was your initial response to the injustices Douglass fought against affected by reading the later version?

2. Following the pattern of Douglass's speech, write a speech, for delivery at a formal occasion, about a political or social cause you believe in and which your audience may be hostile to or not enthusiastic about. Be sure to identify your audience—your parents, the people who came to your high school graduation, a historical figure (living or dead), a friend or acquaintance. Begin by making the conventional remarks expected on the occasion, and then focus on what you really want to speak about. Anticipate the objections of your audience, and then refute these objections.

∽ *Women's Right to Vote* (1873)

SUSAN B. ANTHONY

Susan B. Anthony (1820–1906) grew up in a Quaker family with strong abolitionist beliefs. A campaigner for women's rights even as a teenager, she was an early advocate of equal pay for women teachers and of coed education. At a time when women had almost no legal rights, she helped a bill through the New York legislature that gave women some control over their children and their earnings: both had previously been controlled by the husband. She supported the emancipation of slaves and was an active abolitionist, but devoted her life mainly to the fight for women's right to vote. In 1872, during a presidential election, she decided to test whether the Fourteenth Amendment to the Constitution—equal protection under the law—applied to women. She tried to register and was arrested and fined; the fine was never collected. This is the speech she gave to explain her views.

I stand before you under indictment for the alleged crime of having voted at the last presidential election, without having a lawful right to vote. It shall be my work this evening to prove to you that in thus doing, I not only committed no crime, but instead simply exercised my citizen's rights, guaranteed to me and all United States citizens by the National Constitution beyond the power of any State to deny.

Our democratic-republican government is based on the idea of the natural right of every individual member thereof to a voice and a vote in making and executing the laws. We assert the province of government to be to secure the people in the enjoyment of their inalienable rights. We throw to the winds the old dogma that government can give rights. No one denies that before governments were organized each individual possessed the right to protect his own life, liberty and property. When 100 to 1,000,000 people enter into a free government they do not barter away their natural rights; they simply pledge themselves to protect each other in the enjoyment of them through prescribed judicial and legislative tribunals. They agree to abandon the methods of brute force in the adjustment of their differences and adopt those of civilization. . . . The Declaration of Independence, the United States Constitution, the constitutions of the several States and the organic laws of the Territories, all alike propose to *protect* the people in the exercise of their God-given rights. Not one of them pretends to bestow rights.

> All men are created equal, and endowed by their Creator with certain inalienable rights. Among these are life, liberty and the pursuit of happiness. To secure these, governments are instituted among men, deriving their just powers from the consent of the governed.

Here is no shadow of government authority over rights, or exclusion of any class from their full and equal enjoyment. Here is pronounced the right of all men, and "consequently," as the Quaker preacher said, "of all women," to a voice in the government. And here, in this first paragraph of the Declaration, is the assertion of the natural right of all to the ballot; for how can "the consent of the governed" be given, if the right to vote be denied? . . . The women, dissatisfied as they are with this form of government, that enforces taxation without representation—that compels them to obey laws to which they never have given their consent—that imprisons and hangs them without a trial by a jury of their peers—that robs them, in marriage, of the custody of their own persons, wages, and children—are this half of the people who are left wholly at the mercy of the other half, in direct violation of the spirit and letter of the declarations of the framers of this government, every one of which was based on the immutable principle of equal rights to all. By these declarations, kings, popes, priests, aristocrats, all were alike dethroned and placed on a common level, politically, with the lowliest born subject or serf. By them, too, men, as such, were deprived of their divine right to rule and placed on a political level with women. By the practice of these declarations all class and caste distinctions would be abolished, and slave, serf, plebeian, wife, woman, all alike rise from their subject position to the broader platform of equality.

The preamble of the Federal Constitution says:

We, the people of the United States, in order to form a more perfect union, establish justice, insure domestic tranquillity, provide for the common defence, promote the general welfare and secure the blessings of liberty to ourselves and our posterity, do ordain and establish this Constitution for the United States of America.

It was we, the people, not we, the white male citizens, nor we, the 5 male citizens; but we, the whole people, who formed this Union. We formed it not to give the blessings of liberty but to secure them; not to the half of ourselves and the half of our prosperity, but to the whole people—women as well as men. It is downright mockery to talk to women of their enjoyment of the blessings of liberty while they are denied the only means of securing them provided by this democratic-republican government—the ballot. . . .

When, in 1871, I asked [Senator Charles Sumner] to declare the power of the United States Constitution to protect women in their right to vote—as he had done for black men—he handed me a copy of all his speeches during that reconstruction period, and said:

Put "sex" where I have "race" or "color," and you have here the best and strongest argument I can make for woman. There is not a doubt but women have the constitutional right to vote, and I will never vote for a Sixteenth Amendment to guarantee it to them. I voted for both the Fourteenth and Fifteenth under protest; would never have done it but for the pressing emergency of that hour; would have insisted that the power of the original Constitution to protect all citizens in the equal enjoyment of their rights should have been vindicated through the courts. But the newly-made freedmen had neither the intelligence, wealth nor time to await that slow process. Women do possess all these in an eminent degree, and I insist that they shall appeal to the courts and through them establish the powers of our American magna charta to protect every citizen of the republic.

But, friends, when in accordance with Senator Sumner's counsel I went to the ballot-box, last November, and exercised my citizen's right to vote, the courts did not wait for me to appeal to them—they appealed to me, and indicted me on the charge of having voted illegally. . . .

For any State to make sex a qualification, which must ever result in the disfranchisement of one entire half of the people, is to pass a bill of attainder, an ex post facto law, and is therefore a violation of the supreme law of the land. By it the blessings of liberty are forever withheld from women and their female posterity. For them, this government has no just powers derived from the consent of the governed. For them this government is not a democracy; it is not a republic. It is the most odious aristocracy ever established on the face of the globe. An oligarchy of wealth, where the rich govern the poor; an oligarchy of learning, where the educated govern the ignorant; or even an oligarchy of race, where the Saxon rules the African, might be endured; but this oligarchy of sex which makes father, brothers, husband, sons, the oligarchs over the mother and sisters, the wife and daughters of every household; which ordains all men sovereigns, all women subjects—carries discord and rebellion into every home of the nation. . . .

It is urged that the use of the masculine pronouns *he, his* and *him* in all the constitutions and laws, is proof that only men were meant to be included in their provisions. If you insist on this version of the letter of the law, we shall insist that you be consistent and accept the other horn of the dilemma, which would compel you to exempt women from taxation for the support of the government and from penalties for the violation of laws. There is no *she* or *her* or *hers* in the tax laws, and this is equally true of all the criminal laws.

10 Take for example, the civil rights law which I am charged with having violated; not only are all the pronouns in it masculine, but everybody knows that it was intended expressly to hinder the rebel men from voting. It reads, "If any person shall knowingly vote without *his* having a lawful right.". . . I insist if government officials may thus manipulate the pronouns to tax, fine, imprison and hang women, it is their duty to thus change them in order to protect us in our right to vote. . . .

Though the words persons, people, inhabitants, electors, citizens, are all used indiscriminately in the national and State constitutions, there was always a conflict of opinion, prior to the war, as to whether they were synonymous terms, but whatever room there was for doubt, under the old regime, the adoption of the Fourteenth Amendment settled that question forever in its first sentence:

> All persons born or naturalized in the United States, and subject to the jurisdiction thereof, are citizens of the United States, and of the State wherein they reside.

The second settles the equal status of all citizens:

> No State shall make or enforce any law which shall abridge the privileges or immunities of citizens of the United States; nor shall any State deprive any person of life, liberty or property without due process of law, or deny to any person within its jurisdiction the equal protection of the laws.

The only question left to be settled now is: Are women persons? I scarcely believe any of our opponents will have the hardihood to say they are not. Being persons, then, women are citizens, and no State has a right to make any new law, or to enforce any old law, which shall abridge their privileges or immunities. Hence, every discrimination against women in the constitutions and laws of the several States is today null and void, precisely as is every one against negroes.

Is the right to vote one of the privileges or immunities of citizens? I think the disfranchised ex-rebels and ex-State prisoners all will agree that it is not only one of them, but the one without which all the others are nothing. Seek first the kingdom of the ballot and all things else shall be added, is the political injunction. . . .

However much the doctors of the law may disagree as to whether 15 people and citizens, in the original Constitution, were one and the same, or whether the privileges and immunities in the Fourteenth Amendment include the right of suffrage, the question of the citizen's right to vote is forever settled by the Fifteenth Amendment. "The right of citizens of the United States to vote shall not be denied or abridged by the United States, or by any State, on account of race, color or previous condition of servitude." How can the State deny or abridge the right of the citizen, if the citizen does not possess it? There is no escape from the conclusion that to vote is the citizen's right, and the specifications of race, color or previous condition of servitude can in no way impair the force of that emphatic assertion that the citizen's right to vote shall not be denied or abridged. . . .

If, however, you will insist that the Fifteenth Amendment's emphatic interdiction against robbing United States citizens of their suffrage "on account of race, color or previous condition of servitude," is a recognition of the right of either the United States or any State to deprive them of the ballot for any or all other reasons, I will prove to you that the class of citizens for whom I now plead are, by all the principles of our government and many of the laws of the States, included under the term "previous conditions of servitude."

Consider first married women and their legal status. What is servitude? "The condition of a slave." What is a slave? "A person who is robbed of the proceeds of his labor; a person who is subject to the will of another." By the laws of Georgia, South Carolina and all the States of the South, the negro had no right to the custody and control of his person. He belonged to his master. If he were disobedient, the master had the right to use correction. If the negro did not like the correction and ran away, the master had the right to use coercion to bring him back. By the laws of almost every State in this Union today, North as well as South, the married woman has no right to the custody and control of her person. The wife belongs to the husband; and if she refuse obedience he may use moderate correction, and if she do not like his moderate correction and leave his "bed and board," the husband may use moderate coercion to bring her back. The little word "moderate," you see, is the saving clause for the wife, and would doubtless be overstepped should her offended husband administer his correction with the "cat-o'-nine-tails," or accomplish his coercion with blood-hounds.

Again the slave had no right to the earnings of his hands, they belonged to his master; no right to the custody of his children, they belonged to his master; no right to sue or be sued, or to testify in the courts. If he committed a crime, it was the master who must sue or be sued. In many of the States there has been special legislation, giving married women the right to property inherited or received by bequest, or earned by the pursuit of any avocation outside the home; also giving them the right to sue and be sued in matters pertaining to such separate property; but not a single State of this Union has ever secured the wife in the enjoyment of her right to equal ownership of the joint earnings of the marriage copartnership. And since, in the nature of things, the vast majority of married women never earn a dollar by work outside their families, or inherit a dollar from their fathers, it follows that from the day of their marriage to the day of the death of their husbands not one of them ever has a dollar, except it shall please her husband to let her have it. . . .

Is anything further needed to prove woman's condition of servitude sufficient to entitle her to the guarantees of the Fifteenth Amendment? Is there a man who will not agree with me that to talk of freedom without the ballot is mockery to the women of this republic, precisely as New England's orator, Wendell Phillips, at the close of the late war declared it to be to the newly emancipated black man? I admit that, prior to the rebellion, by common consent, the right to enslave, as well as to disfranchise both native and foreign born persons, was conceded to the States. But the one grand principle settled by the war and the reconstruction legislation, is the supremacy of the national government to protect the citizens of the United States in their right to freedom and the elective franchise, against any and every interference on the part of the several States; and again and again have the American people asserted the triumph of this principle by their overwhelming majorities for Lincoln and Grant.

20   The one issue of the last two presidential elections was whether the Fourteenth and Fifteenth Amendments should be considered the irrevocable will of the people; and the decision was that they should be, and that it is not only the right, but the duty of the national government to protect all United States citizens in the full enjoyment and free exercise of their privileges and immunities against the attempt of any State to deny or abridge. . . .

It is upon this just interpretation of the United States Constitution that our National Woman Suffrage Association, which celebrates the twenty-fifth anniversary of the woman's rights movement next May in New York City, has based all its arguments and action since the passage of these amendments. We no longer petition legislature or Congress to give us the right to vote, but appeal to women everywhere to exercise their too long neglected "citizen's right." We appeal to the inspectors of election to receive the votes of all United States citizens, as it is their duty to do. We appeal to United States commissioners and marshals to arrest, as is their duty, the inspectors who reject the votes of United

States citizens, and leave alone those who peform their duties and accept these votes. We ask the juries to return verdicts of "not guilty" in the cases of law-abiding United States citizens who cast their votes, and inspectors of election who receive and count them.

We ask the judges to render unprejudiced opinions of the law, and wherever there is room for doubt to give the benefit to the side of liberty and equal rights for women, remembering that, as Sumner says, "The true rule of intepretation under our National Constitution, especially since its amendments, is that anything *for* human rights is constitutional, everything *against* human rights unconstitutional." It is on this line that we propose to fight our battle for the ballot—peaceably but nevertheless persistently—until we achieve complete triumph and all United States citizens, men and women alike, are recognized as equals in the government.

For Journals

What was your reaction to the first sentence in Anthony's speech?

For Discussion

1.   Almost all men in Victorian America, and many women, thought that women should not have the right to vote. What would you guess the arguments were against women's suffrage? What would the opponents of suffrage have been worried about if women did secure the right to vote?

2.   How do Anthony's references to the language of the Declaration of Independence, the Constitution, and the Fourteenth and Fifteenth Amendments help her refute the belief that women should not be allowed to vote? Why do you think she chooses those particular quotations?

3.   How does Anthony see the political condition of women in her own time as compared to the role of American men in the Revolution? As compared to the condition of former slaves? Considering your own knowledge, how valid do you find her comparisons?

4.   Evaluate Anthony's argument that if laws refer only to "he" and "him," women shouldn't have to pay taxes to support the government or go to jail for breaking the law. What are the strengths and weaknesses of this argument? How would you make it stronger? What would Thoreau think of it?

5.   Anthony argues that women are "persons" within the legal meaning stated by the Constitution. In an earlier selection in this chapter, Douglass argued that African Americans are men. Look back at Douglass's

argument and compare it to Anthony's. Do they argue in similar ways or differently? Why do they feel compelled to argue these points at all?

6. Like Douglass, Anthony poses questions in her argument and then refutes them. What do you think are the advantages or disadvantages of this strategy? Which of her own questions do you think she answers best? In her place, what other questions would you ask? How would you answer them?

For Writing

1. Write a paper in which you argue either for or against one of the following:

a. An American teenager today has as much right to emancipation from parental control as a married woman in Anthony's time had with respect to her husband's control.

b. Women should be allowed to serve in combat units in the armed forces.

c. The women's movement has become too aggressive and does more harm than good.

Whichever issue or side you take, follow Anthony's example in using the Constitution and the Declaration of Independence for your argument. Keep in mind what someone who disagrees with you would say, so that you can anticipate some of the serious objections and refute them.

2. Using recent biographies of Anthony or *The Life and Works of Susan B. Anthony*, write a documented paper on one of the following topics:

a. The influence of her Quaker upbringing on her activism; her early fights for equal pay for women teachers.

b. Her support of emancipation during the Civil War.

c. Her refusal to support the vote for freed slaves because it did not include a vote for women.

d. The circumstances surrounding her attempt to register to vote and her subsequent arrest.

∽ *Plessy* v. *Ferguson* (1894)

U.S. SUPREME COURT

After the Civil War and Reconstruction, southern legislatures began passing Jim Crow laws, which instituted segregation against African Americans. In an earlier decision, the Court had repealed the Civil Rights Act of 1875, and the majority decision in Plessy *effectively made discrimination legal. Justice John Harlan, who had grown up as a slaveholder but who had become one of a long line of distinguished Supreme Court dissenters, was the only justice to vote against the decision.*

Majority Opinion (by Justice Henry Billings Brown)

Mr. Justice Brown, . . . delivered the opinion of the court.

This case turns upon the constitutionality of an Act of the general assembly of the state of Louisiana, passed in 1890, providing for separate railway carriages for the white and colored races.

The first section of the statute enacts "that all railway companies carrying passengers in their coaches in this state, shall provide equal but separate accommodations for the white, and colored races."

. . . [Plessy argued that he] was seven-eighths Caucasian and one-eighth African blood; that the mixture of colored blood was not discernible in him; and that he was entitled to every right, privilege, and immunity secured to citizens of the United States of the white race; and that, upon such theory, he took possession of a vacant seat in a coach where passengers of the white race were accommodated, and was ordered by the conductor to vacate said coach and take a seat in another, assigned to persons of the colored race, and, having refused to comply with such demand, he was forcibly ejected, with the aid of a police officer, and imprisoned in the parish jail to answer a charge of having violated the above act.

The constitutionality of this act is attacked upon the ground that it 5 conflicts both with the Thirteenth Amendment of the Constitution abolishing slavery, and the Fourteenth Amendment, which prohibits certain restrictive legislation on the part of the states.

1. That it does not conflict with the Thirteenth Amendment, which abolished slavery and involuntary servitude, except as a punishment for crime, is too clear for argument. Slavery implies involuntary servitude,—a state of bondage; the ownership of mankind as a chattel, or, at least, the control of the labor and services of one man for the benefit of another, and the absence of a legal right to the disposal of his own person, property, and services.

. . . "It would be running the slavery question into the ground," said Mr. Justice Bradley, "to make it apply to every act of discrimination which a person may see fit to make as to the guests he will entertain, or as to the people he will take into his coach or cab or car, or admit to his concert or theater, or deal with in other matters of intercourse or business."

A statute which implies merely a legal distinction between the white and colored races—a distinction which is founded in the color of the two races, and which must always exist so long as white men are distinguished from the other race by color—has no tendency to destroy the legal equality of the two races, or re-establish a state of involuntary servitude. . . .

2. By the Fourteenth Amendment, all persons born or naturalized in the United States, and subject to the jurisdiction thereof, are made citizens of the United States and of the state wherein they reside; and the states are forbidden from making or enforcing any law which . . . shall deprive any person of life, liberty, or property without due process of law, or deny to any person . . . equal protection of the laws.

10   The object of the Amendment was undoubtedly to enforce the absolute equality of the two races before the law, but in the nature of things, it could not have been intended to abolish distinctions based upon color, or to enforce social, as distinguished from political, equality, or a commingling of the two races upon terms unsatisfactory to either. Laws permitting, and even requiring, their separation, in places where they are liable to be brought into contact, do not necessarily imply the inferiority of either race to the other. . . . The most common instance of this is connected with the establishment of separate schools for white and colored children. . . .

So far, then, as a conflict with the Fourteenth Amendment is concerned, the case reduces itself to the question whether the statute of Louisiana is a reasonable regulation, and with respect to this there must necessarily be a large discretion on the part of the legislature. In determining the question of reasonableness, it is at liberty to act with reference to the established usages, customs, and traditions of the people, and with a view to the promotion of their comfort, and the preservation of the public peace and good order. Gauged by this standard, we cannot say that a law which authorizes or even requires the separation of the two races in public conveyances is unreasonable, or more obnoxious to the Fourteenth Amendment than the acts of Congress requiring separate schools for colored children in the District of Columbia, the constitutionality of which does not seem to have been questioned, or the corresponding acts of state legislatures.

We consider the underlying fallacy of the plaintiff's argument to consist in the assumption that the enforced separation of the two races stamps the colored race with a badge of inferiority. If this be so, it is not by reason of anything found in the act, but solely because the colored race chooses to put that construction upon it. The argument necessarily assumes that if, as has been more than once the case, and is not unlikely to be so again, the colored race should become the dominant power in the state legislature, and should enact a law in precisely similar terms, it would thereby relegate the white race to an inferior position. We imagine that the white race, at least, would not acquiesce in this assumption. The argument also assumes that social prejudices may be overcome by legislation, and that equal rights cannot be secured to the Negro except by an enforced commingling of the two races. We cannot accept this proposition. If the two races are to meet upon terms of social equality, it must be the result of natural affinities, a mutual appreciation of each other's merits, and a voluntary consent of individuals. . . . Legislation is powerless to eradicate racial instincts, or to abolish distinctions based upon physical differences, and the attempt to do so can only result in accentuating the difficulties of the present situation. If the civil and political rights of both races be equal, one cannot be inferior to the other civilly or politically. If one race be inferior to the other socially, the Constitution of the United States cannot put them upon the same plane.

Dissenting Opinion (by Justice John Harlan)

. . . In respect of civil rights common to all citizens, the Constitution of the United States does not, I think, permit any public authority to know the race of those entitled to be protected in the enjoyment of such rights. Every true man has pride of race, and under appropriate circumstances when the rights of others, his equals before the law, are not to be affected, it is his privilege to express such pride and to take such action based upon it as to him seems proper. But I deny that any legislative body or judicial tribunal may have regard to the race of citizens when the civil rights of those citizens are involved. Indeed, such legislation, as that here in question, is inconsistent not only with the equality of rights which pertains to citizenship, national and state, but with the personal liberty enjoyed by every one within the United States. . . .

The white race deems itself to be the dominant race in this country. And so it is, in prestige, in achievements, in education, in wealth and in power. So, I doubt not, it will continue to be for all time, if it remains true to its great heritage and holds fast to the principles of constitutional liberty. But in view of the Constitution, in the eye of the law, there is in this country no superior, dominant, ruling class of citizens. There is no caste here. Our Constitution is color-blind, and neither knows nor tolerates classes among citizens. In respect of civil rights, all citizens are equal before the law. The humblest is the peer of the most powerful. The law regards man as man, and takes no account of his surroundings or of his color when his civil rights as guaranteed by the supreme law of the land are involved. It is, therefore, to be regretted that this high tribunal, the final expositor of the fundamental law of the land, has reached the conclusion that it is competent for a State to regulate the enjoyment by citizens of their civil rights solely upon the basis of race. . . .

The arbitrary separation of citizens, on the basis of race, while they are on a public highway, is a badge of servitude wholly inconsistent with the civil freedom and the equality before the law established by the Constitution. It cannot be justified upon any legal grounds.

If evils will result from the commingling of the two races upon public highways established for the benefit of all, they will be infinitely less than those that will surely come from state legislation regulating the enjoyment of civil rights upon the basis of race. We boast of the freedom enjoyed by our people above all other peoples. But it is difficult to reconcile that boast with a state of the law which, practically, puts the brand of servitude and degradation upon a large class of our fellow-citizens, our equals before the law. The thin disguise of "equal" accommodations for passengers in railroad coaches will not mislead anyone, nor atone for the wrong this day done.

For Journals

In your own words, what did the Court decide in this case? Who won? Who lost?

For Discussion

1. Mr. Plessy argued that denying him the right to ride in the white railway carriage was a violation of the Thirteenth Amendment, which prohibits slavery, and the Fourteenth Amendment, which grants equal protection under the law. What reasons does Justice Brown give to refute Plessy's argument? Why does he think the two amendments do not apply to this case?

2. How does the Court define "separate but equal"?

3. In the majority opinion, Justice Brown says that equality before the law doesn't have to mean social equality. Do you think it is possible to be equal before the law but not in any other way? What is your definition of equality?

4. How would you refute the Court's statement that if blacks felt inferior because they were forced to ride in a separate railway carriage, it was their fault because they chose to look at it that way?

5. In his minority opinion, what does Justice Harlan think is the real meaning of the separate-but-equal laws as far as the future of black–white relations is concerned? What kinds of injustices does he foresee in a segregated South?

6. Why do you think Harlan sees dangers to other minorities besides African Americans in the *Plessy* decision? What does he mean when he says that the decision would not mislead anyone and not atone for the wrong done? Do you agree with him?

For Writing

1. Research the term "Jim Crow." Write a documented paper in which you discuss the origins of the term and how Jim Crow laws affected the

lives of southern blacks (give specific examples of segregation in every-day life). If you know someone who had firsthand experience with the Jim Crow laws, interview him or her for your paper.

2.   Both Justice Harlan in *Plessy* and Thoreau in *Civil Disobedience* believed, with very different results, that legislation is not a good way to change people's behavior. Write an essay in which you argue for or against the proposition that injustice cannot be changed through legislation and that trying to eradicate differences through legislation can only make a situation worse. Focus your argument around an injustice you think needs changing. Use Thoreau, *Plessy,* or both to back up your assertions.

∽ *Dolls* (1935)

EUDORA WELTY

Eudora Welty (1909–) was born in Mississippi. She is most famous as a writer of novels and short stories, including Delta Wedding *(1946),* Golden Apples *(1949), and* Losing Battles *(1970); and she won the Pulitzer Prize for* The Optimist's Daughter *(1972). In her fiction, which is set in the South she knows so well, she often writes about familial conflicts and people who don't know themselves or those close to them as well as they should. In her photography, which also revolves mainly around Mississippi, she provides a compassionate and extraordinarily perceptive record of the lives of ordinary people, particularly the poor southern blacks whose dignity she portrays and respects. This photograph is one of a series she took in the 1930s, when she was hired by the Works Progress Administration to interview poor people and see how they coped with the additional burden of the Depression. Many of her greatest photographs, taken in the rural South, New York City, and Ireland, among other places, have been collected in a book called* Welty Photographs *(1989).*

For Journals

What is your most or least favorite childhood photograph of yourself? What does it remind you of?

For Discussion

1.   Until recently, almost no dolls were manufactured with a skin color other than white. What do you think was the effect on the children in this picture of having only blond dolls to play with? Why would there be a connection between the toys and the way they see themselves?

2.   This picture is usually called "Dolls." Based on your own first impressions of it, what new title would you give that would be more descriptive of its emotional impact? Why do you think Welty did not pick a more emotional title?

3.   A photograph can establish a point of view, make an argument, or assert a moral viewpoint. Welty said that her photographs were facts. She took this photograph when life in the South was completely segregated and southern blacks lacked the most basic civil rights. Looking at the details of this picture—how the girls hold the dolls, the girls' facial expressions, the background, how the children and the dolls are dressed, and so on—explain in your own words what Welty was trying to communicate in this picture, and how well you think she succeeded.

For Writing

1.   Bring to class a childhood photograph of yourself that brings back strong memories or a photograph of children from a magazine. Trade that photograph with someone else in class. Write an essay on the other person's photograph, analyzing it closely, as you did with Welty's photo. Make up a history for it: describe the mood it conveys, what happened just before and after the picture was taken, and so on. Use details from the photo as evidence for your interpretation. Then trade essays with your peer and compare the results; write follow-up notes on how accurate or inaccurate your interpretations were.

2.   Eudora Welty said her photographs were facts. Select another photograph from her book, and write an essay in which you evaluate and compare it with "Dolls," in the light of Welty's statement. Do you think she points a finger at injustice? Do you find her photos of black southern life under segregation objective? Sympathetic? Depressing? Refer directly to the photographs to support your argument.

∞ *Freedom of Speech* (1943)

NORMAN ROCKWELL

Norman Rockwell (1894–1978) was born in New York City. An artist and illustrator who specialized in portraying the archetypal American small town, he was best known for the covers he illustrated for the Saturday Evening Post. *He was famous for creating visual images that told stories and communicated detailed, if sometimes idealized, images of American life. This picture is from one of his best-known series,* The Four Freedoms, *which he painted in 1943, in the middle of World War II.*

For Journals

Have you ever made a speech at a public gathering? How comfortable are you with the idea of getting up to speak in a possibly hostile or indifferent setting?

For Discussion

1.   What would you think is the economic level or job status of the man who is speaking? How do you think it compares to that of the other people in the audience? How can you tell that he's not accustomed to making speeches? Given the title of the painting, what purpose could Rockwell have had in making that particular person the central figure?

2.   Four words are visible on the papers held by the man in the forefront of the picture: *Annual Report, town,* and *Vermont.* Why do you think Rockwell chose a small-town setting? How might this painting be different if the setting were a poor city neighborhood? A middle-class suburb?

3.   Rockwell wanted to make a patriotic statement about the freedoms that American soldiers in World War II were fighting to preserve. There are no American flags and we don't know what the subject matter is, so

what makes this picture a persuasively patriotic statement in favor of freedom of speech?

4.   What are the ages, postures, and expressions of the people listening to the speaker? How would you describe the clothing and expression of the older man to his right? In what ways do his reaction and those of other audience members indicate the speaker's success?

For Writing

1.   If your library or local bookstore has a book on Rockwell, look at the other three pictures he did in the series *The Four Freedoms,* portray-

ing freedom from want, freedom from fear, and freedom of worship. Pick one or two of them, and write an analysis in which you examine the theme of the painting as it is expressed in individual figures, their clothing, body language, expressions, and so on; the relationship between them and the background, surrounding buildings and objects, and so on. Alternatively, choose a different painting by Rockwell that deals with a different aspect of American life, such as the World War II poster in Chapter 1, or such as family life, children playing, or adults doing their work.

∝ Brown v. Board of Education (1954)

U.S. SUPREME COURT

Brown v. Board of Education *is the landmark decision of the Supreme Court, under Chief Justice Earl Warren, in this century. Its official result was to declare segregation in public schools unconstitutional and to overturn the* Plessy *doctrine of "separate but equal" facilities. It followed on the heels of other cases that had outlawed segregation in professional schools. Its effect was to take away the legal underpinnings of segregation in all areas, and it began a process of dismantling segregation that has had a profound effect on American life.*

These cases come to us from the states of Kansas, South Carolina, Virginia, and Delaware. They are premised on different facts and different local conditions, but a common legal question justifies their consideration together in this consolidated opinion.

In each of the cases, minors of the Negro race, through their legal representatives, seek the aid of the courts in obtaining admission to the public schools of their community on a nonsegregated basis. In each instance, they have been denied admission to schools attended by white children under laws requiring or permitting segregation according to race. This segregation was alleged to deprive the plaintiffs of the equal protection of the laws under the Fourteenth Amendment. In each of the cases other than the Delaware case, a three-judge federal district court denied relief to the plaintiffs on the so-called "separate but equal" doctrine announced by this Court in *Plessy* v. *Ferguson....* Under that doctrine, equality of treatment is accorded when the races are provided substantially equal facilities, even though these facilities be separate. . . .

The plaintiffs contend that segregated public schools are not "equal" and cannot be made "equal," and that hence they are deprived of the equal protection of the laws. Because of the obvious importance of the question presented, the Court took jurisdiction. . . .

There are findings below that the Negro and white schools involved have been equalized, or are being equalized, with respect to buildings, curricula, qualifications and salaries of teachers, and other "tangible" factors. Our decision, therefore, cannot turn on merely a comparison of these tangible factors in the Negro and white schools involved in each of the cases. We must look instead to the effect of segregation itself on public education.

5   In approaching this problem, we cannot turn the clock back to 1868 when the Amendment was adopted, or even to 1896 when *Plessy* v. *Ferguson* was written. We must consider public education in the light of its full development and its present place in American life throughout the nation. Only in this way can it be determined if segregation in public schools deprives these plaintiffs of the equal protection of the laws.

Today, education is perhaps the most important function of state and local governments. Compulsory school attendance laws and the great expenditures for education both demonstrate our recognition of the importance of education to our democratic society. It is required in the performance of our most basic public responsibilities, even service in the armed forces. It is the very foundation of good citizenship. Today it is a principal instrument in awakening the child to cultural values, in preparing him for later professional training, and in helping him to adjust normally to his environment. In these days, it is doubtful that any child may reasonably be expected to succeed in life if he is denied the opportunity of an education. Such an opportunity, where the state has undertaken to provide it, is a right which must be made available to all on equal terms.

We come then to the question presented: Does segregation of children in public schools solely on the basis of race, even though the physical facilities and other "tangible" factors may be equal, deprive the children of the minority group of equal educational opportunities? We believe that it does.

In *Sweatt* v. *Painter*, . . . in finding that a segregated law school for Negroes could not provide them equal educational opportunities, this Court relied in large part on "those qualities which are incapable of objective measurement but which make for greatness in a law school." In *McLaurin* v. *Oklahoma State Regents*, . . . the Court, in requiring that a Negro admitted to a white graduate school be treated like all other students, again resorted to intangible considerations: ". . . his ability to study, to engage in discussions and exchange views with other students, and, in general, to learn his profession." Such considerations apply with added force to children in grade and high schools. To separate them from others of similar age and qualifications solely because of their race generates a feeling of inferiority as to their status in the community that may affect their hearts and minds in a way unlikely ever to be undone. The effect of this separation on their educational opportunities was well stated by a finding in the Kansas case by a court which nevertheless felt compelled to rule against the Negro plaintiffs:

> Segregation of white and colored children in public schools has a detrimental effect upon the colored children. The impact is greater when it has the sanction of the law; for the policy of separating the races is usually interpreted as denoting the inferiority of the Negro group. A sense of inferiority affects the motivation of a child to learn. Segregation with the sanction of law, therefore, has a tendency to retard the educational and mental development of Negro children and to deprive them of some of the benefits they would receive in a racially integrated school system.

Whatever may have been the extent of psychological knowledge at the time of *Plessy* v. *Ferguson*, this finding is amply supported by modern authority. Any language in *Plessy* v. *Ferguson* contrary to this finding is rejected.

We conclude that in the field of public education the doctrine of "separate but equal" has no place. Separate educational facilities are inherently unequal. Therefore, we hold that the plaintiffs and others similarly situated for whom the actions have been brought are, by reason of the segregation complained of, deprived of the equal protection of the laws guaranteed by the Fourteenth Amendment. . . .

For Journals

Summarize the decision in the case. In your own words, write what you think the essence of the decision was.

For Discussion

1.   In American law, precedent—what has been determined in previous legal decisions—is very important, so refuting the ruling of *Plessy* after almost fifty years required considerable justification. How does the Warren Court in *Brown* get around the fact that *Plessy* had stood since it was declared good law in 1896?

2.   What are the Court's main points in its argument that education today and education right after the Civil War that a new interpretation of *Plessy* is appropriate?

3.   Analyze what the Court says about the harmful effects of segregated schooling on black children. What injustice does the Court in *Brown* see in segregation that the Court in *Plessy* did not? Why wouldn't a school for black children do as good a job as an integrated school?

4.   The decision of a court is called a ruling. In refuting *Plessy*, the Warren Court made a ruling that separate public schools could not also be

equal. Why did the Court think that separate but equal was a contradiction?

5. If you had to pick the most crucial sentence from this ruling, what would it be? Why?

6. The Court says that if it only took into account "tangible" factors like buildings and curriculum for segregated schools, it would fail to see the situation in its entirety. What kinds of "intangibles" do you think the Warren Court considered in reaching its decision in *Brown?*

For Writing

1. Research one of the following and, in a documented essay, discuss its significance for civil liberties in the United States:

a. The life and career of Thurgood Marshall, who argued *Brown* and later became solicitor general of the United States and then the first African American justice of the Supreme Court.

b. Marshall's strategy, as leading attorney for the NAACP, in challenging segregation through the courts instead of in state legislatures, and in picking elementary school education as the point of attack.

c. The significance of the cases before *Brown* that are mentioned by Chief Justice Warren, especially *Sweatt* v. *Painter* and *McLaurin* v. *Oklahoma State Regents.*

2. Chief Justice Warren wrote that we must look at the intangibles to get a complete picture. Write an essay in which you compare the *Brown* decision and its use of intangible factors to either Douglass's Independence Day speech or Anthony's "Women's Right to Vote" speech. What tangible evidence and intangibles do the authors consider in arguing against injustice? Which category is more important to them? Which do you think is more important? Use examples from the selections as proof for your conclusions.

∽ *Letter from Birmingham Jail* (1963)

MARTIN LUTHER KING, JR.

The strategy developed by the modern civil rights movement and its leader, the young Atlanta minister Martin Luther King, Jr. (see Chapter 4), was the policy of nonviolent resistance. Based on the teachings of the Bible, Mahatma Gandhi, and Thoreau, it revolved around peaceful marches, sit-ins at lunch counters, and economic boycotts of buses and businesses. In 1963, while leading demonstrations in Montgomery, Alabama, King was arrested. In jail he wrote a letter of justification and explanation addressed to eight southern clergymen who had issued a public state-ment objecting to the demonstrations King led and to demonstrations as a method for dealing with racial problems. Both letters are reprinted here.

Clergymen's Letter

We the undersigned clergymen are among those who, in January, issued "An Appeal for Law and Order and Common Sense," in dealing with racial problems in Alabama. We expressed understanding that honest convictions in racial matters could properly be pursued in the courts, but urged that decisions of those courts should in the meantime be peacefully obeyed.

Since that time there had been some evidence of increased forbear-ance and a willingness to face facts. Responsible citizens have under-taken to work on various problems which cause racial friction and unrest. In Birmingham, recent public events have given indication that we all have opportunity for a new constructive and realistic approach to racial problems.

However, we are now confronted by a series of demonstrations by some of our Negro citizens, directed and led in part by outsiders. We recognize the natural impatience of people who feel that their hopes are slow in being realized. But we are convinced that these demonstrations are unwise and untimely.

We agree rather with certain local Negro leadership which has called for honest and open negotiation of racial issues in our area. And we believe this kind of facing of issues can best be accomplished by cit-izens of our own metropolitan area, white and Negro, meeting with their knowledge and experience of the local situation. All of us need to face that responsibility and find proper channels for its accomplishment.

Just as we formerly pointed out that "hatred and violence have ⁵ no sanction in our religious and political traditions," we also point out that such actions as incite to hatred and violence, however technically peaceful those actions may be, have not contributed to the resolution of our local problems. We do not believe that these days of new hope are days when extreme measures are justified in Birmingham.

We commend the community as a whole, and the local news media and the law enforcement officials in particular, on the calm manner in which these demonstrations have been handled. We urge the public to continue to show restraint should the demonstrations continue, and the law enforcement officials to remain calm and continue to protect our city from violence.

We further strongly urge our own Negro community to withdraw support from these demonstrations, and to unite locally in working peacefully for a better Birmingham. When rights are consistently denied, a cause should be pressed in the courts and in negotiations among local leaders, and not in the streets. We appeal to both our white and Negro citizenry to observe the principles of law and order and common sense.

Signed by:

C. C. J. *Carpenter*, D.D., LL.D., Bishop of Alabama

Joseph A. Durick, D.D., Auxiliary Bishop, Diocese of Mobile, Birmingham

Milton L. Grafman, Rabbi, Temple Emanu-El, Birmingham, Alabama

Paul Hardin, Bishop of the Alabama–West Florida Conference of the Methodist Church

Nolan B. Harmon, Bishop of the North Alabama Conference of the Methodist Church

George M. Murray, D.D., LL.D., Bishop Coadjutor, Episcopal Diocese of Alabama

Edward V. Ramage, Moderator, Synod of the Alabama Presbyterian Church in the United States

Earl Stallings, Pastor, First Baptist Church, Birmingham, Alabama

King's Letter

April 16, 1963

My Dear Fellow Clergymen:

While confined here in the Birmingham city jail, I came across your recent statement calling my present activities "unwise and untimely." Seldom do I pause to answer criticism of my work and ideas. If I sought to answer all the criticisms that cross my desk, my secretaries would have little time for anything other than such correspondence in the course of the day, and I would have no time for constructive work. But since I feel that you are men of genuine good will and that your criticisms are sincerely set forth, I want to try to answer your statement in what I hope will be patient and reasonable terms.

I think I should indicate why I am here in Birmingham, since you have been influenced by the view which argues against "outsiders coming in." I have the honor of serving as president of the Southern Christian Leadership Conference, an organization operating in every southern state, with headquarters in Atlanta, Georgia. We have some eighty-five affiliated organizations across the South, and one of them is the Alabama Christian Movement for Human Rights. Frequently we share staff, educational and financial resources with our affiliates. Several months ago the affiliate here in Birmingham asked us to be on call to engage in a nonviolent direct-action program if such were deemed necessary. We readily consented, and when the hour came we lived up to our promise. So I, along with several members of my staff, am here because I was invited here. I am here because I have organizational ties here.

But more basically, I am in Birmingham because injustice is here. 10 Just as the prophets of the eighth century B.C. left their villages and carried their "thus saith the Lord" far beyond the boundaries of their home towns, and just as the Apostle Paul left his village of Tarsus and carried the gospel of Jesus Christ to the far corners of the Greco-Roman world, so am I compelled to carry the gospel of freedom beyond my own home town. Like Paul, I must constantly respond to the Macedonian call for aid.

Moreover, I am cognizant of the interrelatedness of all communities and states. I cannot sit idly by in Atlanta and not be concerned about what happens in Birmingham. Injustice anywhere is a threat to justice everywhere. We are caught in an inescapable network of mutuality, tied in a single garment of destiny. Whatever affects one directly, affects all indirectly. Never again can we afford to live with the narrow, provincial "outside agitator" idea. Anyone who lives inside the United States can never be considered an outsider anywhere within its bounds.

You deplore the demonstrations taking place in Birmingham. But your statement, I am sorry to say, fails to express a similar concern for the conditions that brought about the demonstrations. I am sure that none of you would want to rest content with the superficial kind of social analysis that deals merely with effects and does not grapple with underlying causes. It is unfortunate that demonstrations are taking place in Birmingham, but it is even more unfortunate that the city's white power structure left the Negro community with no alternative.

In any nonviolent campaign there are four basic steps: collection of the facts to determine whether injustices exist; negotiation; self-purification; and direct action. We have gone through all these steps in Birmingham. There can be no gainsaying the fact that racial injustice engulfs this community. Birmingham is probably the most thoroughly segregated city in the United States. Its ugly record of brutality is widely known. Negroes have experienced grossly unjust treatment in the courts. There have been more unsolved bombings of Negro homes and churches in Birmingham than in any other city in the nation. These are the hard, brutal facts of the case. On the basis of these conditions, Negro leaders sought to negotiate with the city fathers. But the latter consistently refused to engage in good-faith negotiation.

Then, last September, came the opportunity to talk with leaders of Birmingham's economic community. In the course of the negotiations, certain promises were made by the merchants—for example, to remove the stores' humiliating racial signs. On the basis of these promises, the Reverend Fred Shuttlesworth and the leaders of the Alabama Christian Movement for Human Rights agreed to a moratorium on all demonstrations. As the weeks and months went by, we realized that we were the victims of a broken promise. A few signs, briefly removed, returned; the others remained.

15   As in so many past experiences, our hopes had been blasted, and the shadow of deep disappointment settled upon us. We had no alternative except to prepare for direct action, whereby we would present our very bodies as a means of laying our case before the conscience of the local and the national community. Mindful of the difficulties involved, we decided to undertake a process of self-purification. We began a series of workshops on nonviolence, and we repeatedly asked ourselves: "Are you able to accept blows without retaliating?" "Are you able to endure the ordeal of jail?" We decided to schedule our direct-action program for the Easter season, realizing that except for Christmas, this is the main shopping period of the year. Knowing that a strong economic-withdrawal program would be the by-product of direct action, we felt that this would be the best time to bring pressure to bear on the merchants for the needed change.

Then it occurred to us that Birmingham's mayoral election was coming up in March, and we speedily decided to postpone action until after election day. When we discovered that the Commissioner of Public Safety, Eugene "Bull" Connor, had piled up enough votes to be in the run-off, we decided again to postpone action until the day after the run-off so that the demonstrations could not be used to cloud the issues. Like many others, we waited to see Mr. Connor defeated, and to this end we endured postponement after postponement. Having aided in this community need, we felt that our direct-action program could be delayed no longer.

You may well ask: "Why direct action? Why sit-ins, marches and so forth? Isn't negotiation a better path?" You are quite right in calling for negotiation. Indeed, this is the very purpose of direct action. Nonviolent direct action seeks to create such a crisis and foster such a tension that a community which has constantly refused to negotiate is forced to confront the issue. It seeks so to dramatize the issue that it can no longer be ignored. My citing the creation of tension as part of the work of the nonviolent-resister may sound rather shocking. But I must confess that I am not afraid of the word "tension." I have earnestly opposed violent tension, but there is a type of constructive, nonviolent tension which is necessary for growth. Just as Socrates felt that it was necessary to create a tension in the mind so that individuals could rise from the bondage of myths and half-truths to the unfettered realm of creative analysis and objective appraisal, so must we see the need for nonviolent gadflies to create the kind of tension in society that will help men rise from the dark depths of prejudice and racism to the majestic heights of understanding and brotherhood.

The purpose of our direct-action program is to create a situation so crisis-packed that it will inevitably open the door to negotiation. I therefore concur with you in your call for negotiation. Too long has our

beloved Southland been bogged down in a tragic effort to live in mono-
logue rather than dialogue.

One of the basic points in your statement is that the action that I
and my associates have taken in Birmingham is untimely. Some have
asked: "Why didn't you give the new city administration time to act?"
The only answer that I can give to this query is that the new Birmingham administration must be prodded about as much as the outgoing
one, before it will act. We are sadly mistaken if we feel that the election
of Albert Boutwell as mayor will bring the millennium to Birmingham.
While Mr. Boutwell is a much more gentle person than Mr. Connor,
they are both segregationists, dedicated to maintenance of the status
quo. I have hope that Mr. Boutwell will be reasonable enough to see the
futility of massive resistance to desegregation. But he will not see this
without pressure from devotees of civil rights. My friends, I must say to
you that we have not made a single gain in civil rights without determined legal and nonviolent pressure. Lamentably, it is an historical fact
that privileged groups seldom give up their privileges voluntarily. Individuals may see the moral light and voluntarily give up their unjust
posture; but, as Reinhold Niebuhr has reminded us, groups tend to be
more immoral than individuals.

We know through painful experience that freedom is never volun-   20
tarily given by the oppressor; it must be demanded by the oppressed.
Frankly, I have yet to engage in a direct-action campaign that was "well
timed" in the view of those who have not suffered unduly from the disease of segregation. For years now I have heard the word "Wait!" It
rings in the ear of every Negro with piercing familiarity. This "Wait"
has almost always meant "Never." We must come to see, with one of
our distinguished jurists, that "justice too long delayed is justice denied."

We have waited for more than three hundred forty years for our
constitutional God-given rights. The nations of Asia and Africa are
moving with jetlike speed toward gaining political independence, but
we still creep at horse-and-buggy pace toward gaining a cup of coffee
at a lunch counter. Perhaps it is easy for those who have never felt the
stinging darts of segregation to say, "Wait." But when you have seen vi-
cious mobs lynch your mothers and fathers at will and drown your sisters and brothers at whim; when you have seen hate-filled policemen
curse, kick, and even kill your black brothers and sisters; when you see
the vast majority of your twenty million Negro brothers smothering in
an airtight cage of poverty in the midst of an affluent society; when you
suddenly find your tongue twisted and your speech stammering as you
seek to explain to your six-year-old daughter why she can't go to the
public amusement park that has just been advertised on television, and
see tears welling up in her eyes when she is told that Funtown is closed
to colored children, and see ominous clouds of inferiority beginning to

form in her little mental sky, and see her beginning to distort her personality by developing an unconscious bitterness toward white people; when you have to concoct an answer for a five-year-old son who is asking: "Daddy, why do white people treat colored people so mean?"; when you take a cross-country drive and find it necessary to sleep night after night in the uncomfortable corners of your automobile because no motel will accept you; when you are humiliated day in and day out by nagging signs reading "white" and "colored"; when your first name becomes "nigger," your middle name becomes "boy" (however old you are) and your last name becomes "John," and your wife and mother are never given the respected title "Mrs."; when you are harried by day and haunted by night by the fact that you are a Negro, living constantly at tiptoe stance, never quite knowing what to expect next, and are plagued with inner fears and outer resentments; when you are forever fighting a degenerating sense of "nobodiness"—then you will understand why we find it difficult to wait. There comes a time when the cup of endurance runs over, and men are no longer willing to be plunged into the abyss of despair. I hope, sirs, you can understand our legitimate and unavoidable impatience.

You express a great deal of anxiety over our willingness to break laws. This is certainly a legitimate concern. Since we so diligently urge people to obey the Supreme Court's decision of 1954 outlawing segregation in the public schools, at first glance it may seem rather paradoxical for us consciously to break laws. One may well ask: "How can you advocate breaking some laws and obeying others?" The answer lies in the fact that there are two types of laws: just and unjust. I would be the first to advocate obeying just laws. One has not only a legal but a moral responsibility to obey just laws. Conversely, one has a moral responsibility to disobey unjust laws. I would agree with St. Augustine that "an unjust law is no law at all."

Now, what is the difference between the two? How does one determine whether a law is just or unjust? A just law is a man-made code that squares with the moral law or the law of God. An unjust law is a code that is out of harmony with the moral law. To put it in the terms of St. Thomas Aquinas: An unjust law is a human law that is not rooted in eternal law and natural law. Any law that uplifts human personality is just. Any law that degrades human personality is unjust. All segregation statutes are unjust because segregation distorts the soul and damages the personality. It gives the segregator a false sense of superiority and the segregated a false sense of inferiority. Segregation, to use the terminology of the Jewish philosopher Martin Buber, substitutes an "I–it" relationship for an "I–thou" relationship and ends up relegating persons to the status of things. Hence, segregation is not only politically, economically and sociologically unsound, it is morally wrong and sinful. Paul Tillich has said that sin is separation. Is not segregation an existential expression of man's tragic separation, his awful estrangement, his terrible sinfulness? Thus it is that I can urge men to obey the 1954 decision of the Supreme Court, for it is morally right; and I can urge them to disobey segregation ordinances, for they are morally wrong.

Let us consider a more concrete example of just and unjust laws. An unjust law is a code that a numerical or power majority group compels a minority group to obey but does not make binding on itself. This is *difference* made legal. By the same token, a just law is a code that a majority compels a minority to follow and that it is willing to follow itself. This is *sameness* made legal.

Let me give another explanation. A law is unjust if it is inflicted on   25 a minority that, as a result of being denied the right to vote, had no part in enacting or devising the law. Who can say that the legislature of Alabama which set up that state's segregation laws was democratically elected? Throughout Alabama all sorts of devious methods are used to prevent Negroes from becoming registered voters, and there are some counties in which, even though Negroes constitute a majority of the population, not a single Negro is registered. Can any law enacted under such circumstances be considered democratically structured?

Sometimes a law is just on its face and unjust in its application. For instance, I have been arrested on a charge of parading without a permit. Now, there is nothing wrong in having an ordinance which requires a permit for a parade. But such an ordinance becomes unjust when it is used to maintain segregation and to deny citizens the First-Amendment privilege of peaceful assembly and protest.

I hope you are able to see the distinction I am trying to point out. In no sense do I advocate evading or defying the law, as would the rabid segregationist. That would lead to anarchy. One who breaks an unjust law must do so openly, lovingly, and with a willingness to accept the penalty. I submit that an individual who breaks a law that conscience tells him is unjust, and who willingly accepts the penalty of imprisonment in order to arouse the conscience of the community over its injustice, is in reality expressing the highest respect for law.

Of course, there is nothing new about this kind of civil disobedience. It was evidenced sublimely in the refusal of Shadrach, Meshach and Abednego to obey the laws of Nebuchadnezzar, on the ground that a higher moral law was at stake. It was practiced superbly by the early Christians, who were willing to face hungry lions and the excruciating pain of chopping blocks rather than submit to certain unjust laws of the Roman Empire. To a degree, academic freedom is a reality today because Socrates practiced civil disobedience. In our own nation, the Boston Tea Party represented a massive act of civil disobedience.

We should never forget that everything Adolf Hitler did in Germany was "legal" and everything the Hungarian freedom fighters did in Hungary was "illegal." It was "illegal" to aid and comfort a Jew in

Hitler's Germany. Even so, I am sure that, had I lived in Germany at the time, I would have aided and comforted my Jewish brothers. If today I lived in a Communist country where certain principles dear to the Christian faith are suppressed I would openly advocate disobeying that country's antireligious laws.

30   I must make two honest confessions to you, my Christian and Jewish brothers. First, I must confess that over the past few years I have been gravely disappointed with the white moderate. I have almost reached the regrettable conclusion that the Negro's great stumbling block in his stride toward freedom is not the White Citizen's Counciler or the Ku Klux Klanner, but the white moderate, who is more devoted to "order" than to justice; who prefers a negative peace which is the presence of tension to a positive peace which is the presence of justice; who constantly says: "I agree with you in the goal you seek, but I cannot agree with your methods of direct action"; who paternalistically believes he can set the timetable for another man's freedom; who lives by a mythical concept of time and who constantly advises the Negro to wait for a "more convenient season." Shallow understanding from people of good will is more frustrating than absolute misunderstanding from people of ill will. Lukewarm acceptance is much more bewildering than outright rejection.

I had hoped that the white moderate would understand that law and order exist for the purpose of establishing justice and that when they fail in this purpose they become the dangerously structured dams that block the flow of social progress. I had hoped that the white moderate would understand that the present tension in the South is a necessary phase of the transition from an obnoxious negative peace, in which the Negro passively accepted his unjust plight, to a substantive and positive peace, in which all men will respect the dignity and worth of human personality. Actually, we who engage in nonviolent direct action are not the creators of tension. We merely bring to the surface the hidden tension that is already alive. We bring it out in the open, where it can be seen and dealt with. Like a boil that can never be cured so long as it is covered up but must be opened with all its ugliness to the natural medicines of air and light, injustice must be exposed, with all the tension its exposure creates, to the light of human conscience and the air of national opinion before it can be cured.

In your statement you assert that our actions, even though peaceful, must be condemned because they precipitate violence. But is this a logical assertion? Isn't this like condemning a robbed man because his possession of money precipitated the evil act of robbery? Isn't this like condemning Socrates because his unswerving commitment to truth and his philosophical inquiries precipitated the act by the misguided populace in which they made him drink hemlock? Isn't this like condemning Jesus because his unique God-consciousness and never-ceasing devotion to God's will precipitated the evil act of crucifixion? We must come to see that, as the federal courts have consistently affirmed, it is wrong to urge an individual to cease his efforts to gain his basic constitutional rights because the quest may precipitate violence. Society must protect the robbed and punish the robber.

I had also hoped that the white moderate would reject the myth concerning time in relation to the struggle for freedom. I have just received a letter from a white brother in Texas. He writes: "All Christians know that the colored people will receive equal rights eventually, but it is possible that you are in too great a religious hurry. It has taken Christianity almost two thousand years to accomplish what it has. The teachings of Christ take time to come to earth." Such an attitude stems from a tragic misconception of time, from the strangely irrational notion that there is something in the very flow of time that will inevitably cure all ills. Actually, time itself is neutral; it can be used either destructively or constructively. More and more I feel that the people of ill will have used time much more effectively than have the people of good will. We will have to repent in this generation not merely for the hateful words and actions of the bad people but for the appalling silence of the good people. Human progress never rolls in on wheels of inevitability; it comes through the tireless efforts of men willing to be co-workers with God, and without this hard work, time itself becomes an ally of the forces of social stagnation. We must use time creatively, in the knowledge that the time is always ripe to do right. Now is the time to make real the promise of democracy and transform our pending national elegy into a creative psalm of brotherhood. Now is the time to lift our national policy from the quicksand of racial injustice to the solid rock of human dignity.

You speak of our activity in Birmingham as extreme. At first I was rather disappointed that fellow clergymen would see my nonviolent efforts as those of an extremist. I began thinking about the fact that I stand in the middle of two opposing forces in the Negro community. One is a force of complacency, made up in part of Negroes who, as a result of long years of oppression, are so drained of self-respect and a sense of "somebodiness" that they have adjusted to segregation; and in part of a few middle-class Negroes who, because of a degree of academic and economic security and because in some ways they profit by segregation, have become insensitive to the problems of the masses. The other force is one of bitterness and hatred, and it comes perilously close to advocating violence. It is expressed in the various black nationalists groups that are springing up across the nation, the largest and best-known being Elijah Muhammad's Muslim movement. Nourished by the Negro's frustration over the continued existence of racial discrimination, this movement is made up of people who have lost faith in America, who have absolutely repudiated Christianity, and who have concluded that the white man is an incorrigible "devil."

35   I have tried to stand between these two forces, saying that we need emulate neither the "do-nothingism" of the complacent nor the hatred and despair of the black nationalist. For there is the more excellent way of love and nonviolent protest. I am grateful to God that, through the influence of the Negro church, the way of nonviolence became an integral part of our struggle.

If this philosophy had not emerged, by now many streets of the South would, I am convinced, be flowing with blood. And I am further convinced that if our white brothers dismiss as "rabble-rousers" and "outside agitators" those of us who employ nonviolent direct action, and if they refuse to support our nonviolent efforts, millions of the Negroes will, out of frustration and despair, seek solace and security in black-nationalist ideologies—a development that would inevitably lead to a frightening racial nightmare.

Oppressed people cannot remain oppressed forever. The yearning for freedom eventually manifests itself, and that is what has happened to the American Negro. Something within has reminded him of his birthright of freedom, and something without has reminded him that it can be gained. Consciously or unconsciously, he has been caught up by the *Zeitgeist,* and with his black brothers of Africa and his brown and yellow brothers of Asia, South America and the Caribbean, the United States Negro is moving with a sense of great urgency toward the promised land of racial justice. If one recognizes this vital urge that has engulfed the Negro community, one should readily understand why public demonstrations are taking place. The Negro has many pent-up resentments and latent frustrations, and he must release them. So let him march; let him make prayer pilgrimages to the city hall; let him go on freedom rides—and try to undertand why he must do so. If his repressed emotions are not released in nonviolent ways, they will seek expression through violence; this is not a threat but a fact of history. So I have not said to my people: "Get rid of your discontent." Rather, I have tried to say that this normal and healthy discontent can be channeled into the creative outlet of nonviolent direct action. And now this approach is being termed extremist.

But though I was initially disappointed at being categorized as an extremist, as I continued to think about the matter I gradually gained a measure of satisfaction from the label. Was not Jesus an extremist for love: "Love your enemies, bless them that curse you, do good to them that hate you, and pray for them which despitefully use you, and persecute you." Was not Amos an extremist for justice: "Let justice roll down like waters and righteousness like an ever-flowing stream." Was not Paul an extremist for the Christian gospel: "I bear in my body the marks of the Lord Jesus." Was not Martin Luther an extremist: "Here I stand; I cannot do otherwise, so help me God." And John Bunyan: "I will stay in jail to the end of my days before I make a butchery of my conscience." And Abraham Lincoln: "This nation cannot survive half slave and half free." And Thomas Jefferson: "We hold these truths to be self-evident, that all men are created equal. . . ." So the question is not whether we will be extremists, but what kind of extremists we will be. Will we be extremists for hate or for love? Will we be extremists for the preservation of injustice or for the extension of justice? In that dramatic scene on Calvary's hill three men were crucified. We must never forget that all three were crucified for the same crime—the crime of extremism. Two were extremists for immorality, and thus fell below their environment. The other, Jesus Christ, was an extremist for love, truth and goodness, and thereby rose above his environment. Perhaps the South, the nation and the world are in dire need of creative extremists.

I had hoped that the white moderate would see this need. Perhaps I was too optimistic; perhaps I expected too much. I suppose I should have realized that few members of the oppressor race can understand the deep groans and passionate yearnings of the oppressed race, and still fewer have the vision to see that injustice must be rooted out by strong, persistent and determined action. I am thankful, however, that some of our white brothers in the South have grasped the meaning of this social revolution and committed themselves to it. They are still all too few in quantity, but they are big in quality. Some—such as Ralph McGill, Lillian Smith, Harry Golden, James McBride Dabbs, Ann Braden and Sarah Patton Boyle—have written about our struggle in eloquent and prophetic terms. Others have marched with us down nameless streets of the South. They have languished in filthy, roach-infested jails, suffering the abuse and brutality of policemen who view them as "dirty nigger-lovers." Unlike so many of their moderate brothers and sisters, they have recognized the urgency of the moment and sensed the need for powerful "action" antidotes to combat the disease of segregation.

Let me take note of my other major disappointment. I have been 40 so greatly disappointed with the white church and its leadership. Of course, there are some notable exceptions. I am not unmindful of the fact that each of you has taken some significant stands on this issue. I commend you, Reverend Stallings, for your Christian stand on this past Sunday, in welcoming Negroes to your worship service on a nonsegregated basis. I commend the Catholic leaders of this state for integrating Spring Hill College several years ago.

But despite these notable exceptions, I must honestly reiterate that I have been disappointed with the church. I do not say this as one of those negative critics who can always find something wrong with the church. I say this as a minister of the gospel, who loves the church; who was nurtured in its bosom; who has been sustained by its spiritual blessings and who will remain true to it as long as the cord of life shall lengthen.

When I was suddenly catapulted into the leadership of the bus protest in Montgomery, Alabama, a few years ago, I felt we would be supported by the white church. I felt that the white ministers, priests and rabbis of the South would be among our strongest allies. Instead, some have been outright opponents, refusing to understand the freedom movement and misrepresenting its leaders; all too many others have been more cautious than courageous and have remained silent behind the anesthetizing security of stained-glass windows.

In spite of my shattered dreams, I came to Birmingham with the hope that the white religious leadership of this community would see the justice of our cause and, with deep moral concern, would serve as the channel through which our just grievances could reach the power structure. I had hoped that each of you would understand. But again I have been disappointed.

I have heard numerous southern religious leaders admonish their worshipers to comply with a desegregation decision because it is the law, but I have longed to hear white ministers declare: "Follow this decree because integration is morally right and because the Negro is your brother." In the midst of blatant injustices inflicted upon the Negro, I have watched white churchmen stand on the sideline and mouth pious irrelevancies and sanctimonious trivialities. In the midst of a mighty struggle to rid our nation of racial and economic injustice, I have heard many ministers say: "Those are social issues, with which the gospel has no real concern." And I have watched many churches commit themselves to a completely otherworldly religion which makes a strange, un-Biblical distinction between body and soul, between the sacred and the secular.

45   I have traveled the length and breadth of Alabama, Mississippi and all the other southern states. On sweltering summer days and crisp autumn mornings I have looked at the South's beautiful churches with their lofty spires pointing heavenward. I have beheld the impressive outlines of her massive religious-education buildings. Over and over I have found myself asking: "What kind of people worship here? Who is their God? Where were their voices when the lips of Governor Barnett dripped with words of interposition and nullification? Where were they when Governor Wallace gave a clarion call for defiance and hatred? Where were their voices of support when bruised and weary Negro men and women decided to rise from the dark dungeons of complacency to the bright hills of creative protest?"

Yes, these questions are still in my mind. In deep disappointment I have wept over the laxity of the church. But be assured that my tears have been tears of love. There can be no deep disappointment where there is not deep love. Yes, I love the church. How could I do otherwise? I am in the rather unique position of being the son, the grandson, and the great-grandson of preachers. Yes, I see the church as the body of Christ. But, oh! How we have blemished and scarred that body through social neglect and through fear of being nonconformists.

There was a time when the church was very powerful—in the time when the early Christians rejoiced at being deemed worthy to suffer for what they believed. In those days the church was not merely a thermometer that recorded the ideas and principles of popular opinion; it was a thermostat that transformed the mores of society. Whenever the early Christians entered a town, the people in power became disturbed and immediately sought to convict the Christians for being "disturbers of the peace" and "outside agitators." But the Christians pressed on, in the conviction that they were "a colony of heaven," called to obey God rather than man. Small in number, they were big in commitment. They were too God-intoxicated to be "astronomically intimidated." By their effort and example they brought an end to such ancient evils as infanticide and gladiatorial contests.

Things are different now. So often the contemporary church is a weak, ineffectual voice with an uncertain sound. So often it is an archdefender of the status quo. Far from being disturbed by the presence of the church, the power structure of the average community is consoled by the church's silent—and often even vocal—sanction of things as they are.

But the judgment of God is upon the church as never before. If today's church does not recapture the sacrificial spirit of the early church, it will lose its authenticity, forfeit the loyalty of millions, and be dismissed as an irrelevant social club with no meaning for the twentieth century. Every day I meet young people whose disappointment with the church has turned into outright disgust.

Perhaps I have once again been too optimistic. Is organized religion 50 too inextricably bound to the status quo to save our nation and the world? Perhaps I must turn my faith to the inner spiritual church, the church within the church, as the true *ekklesia* and the hope of the world. But again I am thankful to God that some noble souls from the ranks of organized religion have broken loose from the paralyzing chains of conformity and joined us as active partners in the struggle for freedom. They have left their secure congregations and walked the streets of Albany, Georgia, with us. They have gone down the highways of the South on tortuous rides for freedom. Yes, they have gone to jail with us. Some have been dismissed from their churches, have lost the support of their bishops and fellow ministers. But they have acted in the faith that right defeated is stronger than evil triumphant. Their witness has been the spiritual salt that has preserved the true meaning of the gospel in these troubled times. They have carved a tunnel of hope through the dark mountain of disappointment.

I hope the church as a whole will meet the challenge of this decisive hour. But even if the church does not come to the aid of justice, I have no despair about the future. I have no fear about the outcome of our struggle in Birmingham, even if our motives are at present misunderstood. We will reach the goal of freedom in Birmingham and all over the nation, because the goal of America is freedom. Abused and scorned though we may be, our destiny is tied up with America's destiny. Before the pilgrims landed at Plymouth, we were here. Before the pen of Jefferson etched the majestic words of the Declaration of Independence across the pages of history, we were here. For more than two centuries our forebears labored in this country without wages; they made cotton king; they built the homes of their masters while suffering gross injustice and shameful humiliation—and yet out of a bottomless vitality they continued to thrive and develop. If the inexpressible cruelties of slavery could not stop us, the opposition we now face will surely fail. We will win our freedom because the sacred heritage of our nation and the eternal will of God are embodied in our echoing demands.

Before closing I feel impelled to mention one other point in your statement that has troubled me profoundly. You warmly commended the Birmingham police force for keeping "order" and "preventing violence." I doubt that you would have so warmly commended the police force if you had seen its dogs sinking their teeth into unarmed, nonviolent Negroes. I doubt that you would so quickly commend the policemen if you were to observe their ugly and inhumane treatment of Negroes here in the city jail; if you were to watch them push and curse old Negro women and young Negro girls; if you were to see them slap and kick old Negro men and young boys; if you were to observe them, as they did on two occasions, refuse to give us food because we wanted to sing our grace together. I cannot join you in your praise of the Birmingham police department.

It is true that police have exercised a degree of discipline in handling the demonstrators. In this sense they have conducted themselves rather "nonviolently" in public. But for what purpose? To preserve the evil system of segregation. Over the past few years I have consistently preached that nonviolence demands that the means we use must be as pure as the ends we seek. I have tried to make clear that it is wrong to use immoral means to attain moral ends. But now I must affirm that it is just as wrong, or perhaps even more so, to use moral means to preserve immoral ends. Perhaps Mr. Connor and his policemen have been rather nonviolent in public, as was Chief Pritchett in Albany, Georgia, but they have used the moral means of nonviolence to maintain the immoral end of racial injustice. As T. S. Eliot has said: "The last temptation is the greatest treason: To do the right deed for the wrong reason."

I wish you had commended the Negro sit-inners and demonstrators of Birmingham for their sublime courage, their willingness to suffer and their amazing discipline in the midst of great provocation. One day the South will recognize its real heroes. They will be the James Merediths, with the noble sense of purpose that enables them to face jeering and hostile mobs, and with the agonizing loneliness that characterizes the life of the pioneer. They will be old, oppressed, battered Negro women, symbolized in a seventy-two-year-old woman in Montgomery, Alabama, who rose up with a sense of dignity and with her people decided not to ride segregated buses, and who responded with ungrammatical profundity to one who inquired about her weariness: "My feets is tired, but my soul is at rest." They will be the young high school and college students, the young ministers of the gospel and a host of their elders, courageously and nonviolently sitting in at lunch counters and willingly going to jail for conscience' sake. One day the South will know that when these disinherited children of God sat down at lunch counters, they were in reality standing up for what is best in the American dream and for the most sacred values in our Judaeo-Christian heritage, thereby bringing our nation back to those great wells of democracy which were dug deep by the founding fathers in their formulation of the Constitution and the Declaration of Independence.

Never before have I written so long a letter. I'm afraid it is much too 55 long to take your precious time. I can assure you that it would have been much shorter if I had been writing from a comfortable desk, but what else can one do when he is alone in a narrow jail cell, other than write long letters, think long thoughts and pray long prayers?

If I have said anything in this letter that overstates the truth and indicates an unreasonable impatience, I beg you to forgive me. If I have said anything that understates the truth and indicates my having a patience that allows me to settle for anything less than brotherhood, I beg God to forgive me.

I hope this letter finds you strong in faith. I also hope that circumstances will soon make it possible for me to meet each of you, not as an integrationist or a civil-rights leader but as a fellow clergyman and a Christian brother. Let us all hope that the dark clouds of racial prejudice will soon pass away and the deep fog of misunderstanding will be lifted from our fear-drenched communities, and in some not too distant tomorrow the radiant stars of love and brotherhood will shine over our great nation with all their scintillating beauty.

Yours for the cause of Peace and Brotherhood
MARTIN LUTHER KING, JR.

For Journals

What does King mean, in response to accusations that the civil rights demonstrations have not come to Birmingham at the right time, that he has "yet to engage in a direct-action movement that was 'well timed'" (paragraph 20)?

For Discussion

1. Why do you think the black clergymen opposed to King were so worried about the civil rights activists? Since they were subject to the

same prejudice as King, why wouldn't they join in the demonstrations themselves?

2. How does King refute the accusations that he is an outsider in Birmingham?

3. What is your response to King's argument that there are legitimate reasons for breaking the law if it is unjust? What are his criteria for deciding if a law is unjust? What basis would you use to decide if a law is unjust?

4. King says that one reason injustice is so powerful is not the actions of bad people but the "appalling silence of the good people" (paragraph 33). Do you think he is right? What is the responsibility of ordinary people when faced with an evil in their society?

5. Why do you think it pleases King to be referred to by his religious opponents as an extremist?

6. What do King's criticisms of the contemporary church tell you about what he thinks the role an effective clergy should be in promoting justice in American society? How does King refute the idea that an uninvolved clergy is better than an active one? How does he make the transition from discussing unheroic clergy to heroic activists?

For Writing

1. Write an essay or a speech on a public topic that makes you angry. Use Douglass and King as models. Be very explicit about who your audience is; you can choose to address any audience you want. State the point of view that you disagree with; then refute it. If you want, write your essay as a letter to the editor of a local newspaper; mail it to the newspaper for possible publication.

2. Like Thoreau, King spent time in jail for his beliefs, although Thoreau was never in danger of being killed and King was. Review Thoreau's *Civil Disobedience,* and write an essay in which you discuss the way both men approach and implement political resistance. Include a consideration of the following questions: What is Thoreau's definition of nonviolent resistance, and how does it compare with King's? What does King owe Thoreau in the development of his own philosophy? How does each man argue for the need to sometimes go to jail?

∞ Unshackling Net Speech (1997)

JOSHUA QUITTNER

Joshua Quittner is coauthor of the book Speeding the Net: The Inside Story of Netscape and How It Challenged Microsoft *(1998). This article appeared in the July 7, 1997 issue of* Time *magazine.*

One of the key ideas behind the Internet was to build a computer network that could withstand a nuclear holocaust. Last week the Net proved its resilience in the face of another sort of attack. The Communications Decency Act, signed into law by President Clinton last year, was designed to protect children by prohibiting "indecent" speech or images from being sent through cyberspace. But even before Congress passed the legislation, free-speech advocates were blasting it as an unacceptable infringement on the First Amendment.

Now the Supreme Court has agreed that the CDA is precisely that. The court, while disagreeing about some issues in the case, unanimously concluded that reducing online communication to a safe-for-kids standard is unconstitutional. "The interest in encouraging freedom of expression in a democratic society," wrote Justice John Paul Stevens, "outweighs any theoretical but unproven benefit of censorship."

It was a decisive—though not unexpected—victory for civil libertarians. Opponents of the CDA, led by the American Civil Liberties Union and the American Library Association as well as dozens of other plaintiffs, including Planned Parenthood and Human Rights Watch, had argued that the statute was so vaguely worded and ill defined that discussions in online chat rooms about abortion or contraception could have attracted the vice squad. Says Ira Glasser, executive director of the A.C.L.U.: "It would have criminalized all sorts of speech that would never have been criminalized before."

And that, said the court, could have crippled the Internet, which now has some 50 million users. Indeed, wrote Stevens in his 15-page opinion, the CDA threatened "to torch a large segment of the Internet community." Clearly the Justices, like many newbies before them, were swept up in the global reach and boundless potential of the medium. "Any person with a phone line can become a town crier with a voice that resonates farther than it could from any soap-box," Stevens observed.

Minutes after the ruling was handed down, the court could have 5 seen that phenomenon in action. At the click of a mouse, the text of the opinion was piped across the Net and plastered on computer sites from New York City to Australia. A laptop computer in New York was used to "Netcast" the audio portion of an A.C.L.U. press conference to all corners of the earth. Chat rooms and message boards were choked with

Net folk weighing in about what it all meant. Computer jocks even ventured forth into the sunlight for real-time, nonvirtual victory parties. "Let today be the first day of a new American Revolution—a Digital American Revolution!" said Mike Godwin, attorney for the Electronic Frontier Foundation, addressing a crowd of revelers in San Francisco.

CDA proponents were every bit as vociferous in defeat as their counterparts were in victory. Members of the anti-porn group Enough is Enough, led by former Gary Hart co-scandalist Donna Rice Hughes, demonstrated outside the Supreme Court with signs that read HONK IF YOU HATE PORN and CHILD MOLESTERS ARE LOOKING FOR VICTIMS ON THE INTERNET.

Legislators seized the moment as well. "Parents are going to have to realize that a computer without any restrictions to children is just as dangerous to their minds and development as a triple-X store," said retiring Indiana Senator Dan Coats, co-author of the CDA. "The court has ignored the clear will of the Executive Branch and the Congress and the clear will of the American people."

In fact, though, the court did not rule that government cannot regulate the Internet. Nor did it alter the long-standing legal prohibition against obscenity, which remains unprotected speech, both on and off the Net. It simply said that the CDA as written was fatally flawed because in trying to protect children it would also keep adults from getting material they have a legal right to see. That gives CDA forces hope that they'll be able to revisit the issue. "The opinion gives us a good road map to what the courts will allow," says Bob Flores, senior counsel of the National Law Center for Children and Families. Vows Don Hodel, the recently installed president of the Christian Coalition: "We won't accept this as the last word."

Nor, evidently, will the President. The White House began backing away from its support of the clearly doomed CDA months ago. But Administration officials have recently come at the problem from a new angle. They propose to fight technology with technology. This week President Clinton will convene a meeting of Internet providers, family groups and others during which he'll propose to protect kids from indecency with a software fix.

10   While the details have yet to be worked out, White House staff members hope to talk Website operators into a kind of universal rating system. Combining it with software browsers used to access much of the Net, parents could in theory set their own comfort level and filter out the naughty bits. "If we are to make the Internet a powerful resource for learning, we must give parents and teachers the tools they need to make the Internet safe for children," Clinton said last week. "With the right technology and rating systems, we can help ensure that our children don't end up in the red-light districts of cyber-space."

Good luck. Software filters and online ratings systems have been around since before the CDA was born, and they've always been beset with problems. Recently, for instance, when Microsoft began backing a ratings standard known as RSACI and started including the filter as part of its browser, Internet Explorer, the company quickly found that the "solution" could keep large numbers of viewers away from its news site, MSNBC. Microsoft quietly removed the rating. The problem should have been foreseen. News, after all, frequently covers violent, adult-oriented subjects, which puts many news stories into the same verboten range as porn. While RSACI officials have proposed offering a news exemption, it's hard to see how that could work. Readers of the sex-oriented newspaper *Screw,* for instance, might well consider it just as newsworthy as the *New York Times.*

Still, the First Amendment notwithstanding, many Americans feel that parents have a legitimate right to protect their kids from inappropriate material. "You can't connect every high school in America to the Net unless there's some way to ensure that kids won't see what they're not supposed to," says Lawrence Lessig, a Harvard Law School professor and author of an essay, "Reading the Constitution in Cyberspace," that was cited repeatedly by Justice O'Connor in a minority opinion. "It can't be the case that Congress has no power to regulate here."

It can be the case, however, that Congress's power is largely symbolic. Even if the government figures out a constitutional way to impose limited censorship online, these rules can apply only within the U.S.—and the Internet is international. If parents want to control what their children see, they'll probably have to resort to an old-fashioned, low-tech solution: they'll have to supervise their kids' time online.

For Journals

What dangers did your family try to protect you from when you were a child? Was there anything you were not allowed to read or to watch on television?

For Discussion

1. The Supreme Court decided that the Communications Decency Act was unconstitutional. According to the author, what were the Court's main points in reaching that decision? What was wrong with the CDA?

2. People who were pleased with the Court's decision said it was the dawn of a Digital American Revolution. How persuasive is this analogy to you? In what ways do you think the Internet does or doesn't change American life as profoundly as the political results of the American Revolution?

3. Obscene speech is not protected on or off the Internet. The Court has defined obscenity as that which lacks any literary, artistic, political, or social value—a deliberately general definition. What do you think are the problems, both logical and political, with trying to decide, as an individual, what constitutes permissible or obscene content? What standards would members of your community apply? What standards do you think you or your friends would apply?

4. If you surf the Net, would you recommend any restrictions on what you could have access to in terms of subject matter or content? On what your little brother or sister could have access to? What rights do you think are involved here? How much access, if any, would you be willing to give up permanently so that children couldn't be exposed to pornography?

5. Those who supported the CDA said that it could be redrawn with a combination of a universal rating system and browsing software to help parents set their own comfort level. The author, however, says the best thing would be for parents to restrict how much time their kids could spend on the Internet. What do you think are the parameters of parental responsibility in this conflict?

For Writing

1. The Constitution says that Congress shall make no laws abridging freedom of speech, but that statement has always been interpreted so that some kinds of speech are protected and some aren't. For example, Justice Oliver Wendell Holmes said that no one has the right to yell "Fire!" in a crowded theater when there is no fire, just to see what would happen. Write an essay in which you argue the limits of freedom of speech or freedom of the press; use the argumentative points in this article or in the Hamilton selection at the beginning of this chapter.

2. Referring back to discussion item 4, write an essay in which you argue to support your own assessment of what should or should not be allowed on the Internet. Keep in mind that the legal issue is freedom of speech, and the question is whether certain restrictions on it are permissible for the purpose of protecting one part of the population—in this case, children—from possible harm. Be honest about what you think your own rights are or ought to be.

3. If you have access to the Internet, look up the category of Internet and freedom of speech. Pick an entry which has a view different from your own, and write an essay in which you argue against it. Start with your strongest point, and give examples to illustrate any general statements you make about free speech. For an example of a good legal argument, look at the first selection in this chapter, Hamilton's defense of freedom of the press.

∞ Film: The Long Walk Home (1995)

In 1955, the American South was completely segregated. In one of the turning points of the civil rights movement, Rosa Parks, an African American woman who rode the bus to work every day in Montgomery, Alabama refused for once to give her seat to a white person and go sit in the back of the bus. She was arrested; in protest, a twenty-six-year-old minister from Atlanta, Martin Luther King, Jr., organized a bus boycott by African Americans in Montgomery. This film is about the effect of those events on two women: a black woman named Odessa Carter, who works as a housekeeper for a white family and decides to join the boycott, even though that means walking nine painful miles to and from work; and the middle-class white woman, Miriam Thompson, for whom she works and who begins to sympathize with what Odessa is doing. (98 minutes)

For Journals

Before you saw this film, what did you know about the Montgomery bus boycott?

For Discussion

1.   This famous event is reported in movie newsreels, television news, and documentaries. Why do you think the writer and director told this story from the point of view of ordinary people on both sides, instead of looking at the larger political picture? What did they have to gain by sticking with the effects on just two families?

2.   How differently does Odessa behave when she's working from the way she behaves at home? For specific examples, examine the humiliating scene in the park, the apology of the policeman to Miriam Thompson, and the Christmas dinner at which Mr. Thompson's mother makes racist remarks while Odessa is in the room.

3.   Late in the film, the white husband who is opposed to his wife's driving Odessa to work says that Odessa is a wonderful maid but that's not who she is and they will never know what she's really like. How well does Mrs. Thompson in fact get to know her? What bonds are formed between the two women? What are those bonds based on?

4.   In the climactic scene in the movie, the attack by white men on the carpoolers' parking lot, the behavior of both Odessa and Miriam—facing the crowd and joining hands—suggests a positive resolution, but also ends the movie rather abruptly. What do you think will be the personal consequences for each woman? What questions are left unanswered?

For Writing

1.   Research the history of the Montgomery boycott and write about one aspect of it: the role of Martin Luther King, Jr.; the economic and personal effect of the boycott on the black community; the decision by the city of Montgomery to capitulate; or any other aspect that you find particularly interesting. Two sources you might check are the documentary book *Eyes on the Prize* and the Pulitzer Prize–winning history *Parting the Waters* by Taylor Branch.

2.   Write a comparison of this film and "Letter from Birmingham Jail" by Martin Luther King, Jr., which you read earlier in this chapter. For example, the film does not deal with King's efforts in overcoming the resistance of more conservative black clergy and businessmen who were uneasy about rocking the boat, but King's letter specifically addresses that issue. Other possible contrasts include the film's attention to private unknown people and King's need to reach both immediate and distant audiences; and the fact that in his letter King describes discrimination and nonviolent resistance, whereas in the film Odessa and her family experience them.

Writing Assignments

1.   Write an analytical essay comparing Frederick Douglass's Independence Day speech with Martin Luther King, Jr.'s "Letter from Birmingham Jail." Consider the audience each man was addressing; the way in which each criticizes his audience and why; the sources of their anger; and how successful each one is at refuting the argument of his opponents. Do Douglass and King have any persuasive or argumentative points in common? Do they evoke in you similar or different responses?

2.   Investigate some of the Victorian stereotypes about women's behavior, weakness, and dependence that Susan B. Anthony had to refute in her efforts to secure the vote. Use periodicals and books, but, if they are available at your library, also look at nineteenth-century women's magazines, etiquette books, and so on. Write an essay on your findings.

3.   Visit the nearest federal, state, or city courthouse, and sit in on a trial for a couple of hours. Call or write the court clerk in advance so that you will know what kinds of trials are scheduled for that week and can pick a case that interests you. Family court and juvenile court, for example, deal in emotional issues that are both immediate and comprehensible. Take notes on what you see and hear: the behavior of the judge and attorneys, the demeanor of the defendants, the issues being

raised. Write a paper analyzing the experience: what you saw and learned, whether the trial was different from what you've learned to expect from television, and how effectively each attorney refuted the other's arguments.

4. Devise your own favorite example of American individualism coming up against either government regulations or majority opinion—anything from whether the government can make you fight a war to whether it can force you to wear a helmet when you're riding a motorcycle. Write an argumentative paper in favor of your opinion, and include quotations or ideas from *Civil Disobedience* as support for your refutation.

5. During the Civil War, Frederick Douglass petitioned President Lincoln for the formation of black army units. Eventually the Fifty-Fourth Regiment was formed, and two of Douglass's sons fought in it. Write a documented research paper on the history of this unit or on Douglass's role in getting it established. Alternatively, compare the results of your research with the way the unit is developed in the film *Glory*. Does the film support or refute the version you found during your research? Why or why not?

6. The U.S. armed forces remained officially segregated until President Truman integrated them by executive order in 1947. Research this decision, and write a paper on your findings. What were the arguments against integration? What ideas were advanced to refute them? What was the immediate reaction of the military? How was integration put into practice?

8

War and the Enemy

In the introduction to the film *Faces of the Enemy*, narrator Sam Keen notes, "Before we make war, even before we make weapons, we make an idea of the enemy." As we make an image of the enemy, we clarify who we are and set ourselves in opposition to that enemy: we are good, they are evil; our cause is just, theirs is unjust; we are human, they are animals. There is a certain peace of mind accompanying that clarity: suicide rates go down in wartime, people feel they have a common purpose, citizens rally to the cause, gray tones disappear in an increasingly black and white world where there is a good side (us) and a bad side (them).

As we identify and characterize an enemy, we more clearly establish our own national identity. Our leaders then appeal to that identity and to the desire to belong in order to rally the nation to support the war effort. In encouraging the citizenry to identify with national goals and in vilifying the enemy, politicians and officials, and often private commercial interests, use primarily appeals to ethos and pathos. Appeals to *ethos* commonly establish a sense of values and ideals to which true Americans would subscribe; those wishing to be considered real Americans support the efforts identified as essential to the common good. Leaders can also appeal to ethos to establish their credibility and their sense of leadership and authority, to appear "presidential" and offer an image of stability and steadfastness in the face of potential chaos.

Appeals to *pathos* convince us to suffer for the common good. On the home front, such appeals urge us to support the war politically, to work in factories, to conserve petroleum products, to do without luxuries, and sometimes necessities, to support the war effort in any way possible. Even more difficult can be the appeal to offer one's time and loss of independence and income through military service. Along with such service comes the risk of losing one's life, and appeals must be strong indeed to urge men and women to be prepared to give their lives for their country and the "American way of life."

War and the Enemy Through History

Throughout recorded history on the American continent, conflicts between economic forces, between cultures and ways of life, and between competing claims on the land have created divergent views about whose rights to the land, to the resources, to political and economic power, should be superior. White settlements intruded on the indigenous peoples of America, and European settlers from various countries fought over land and resources.

Most notable in mainstream American history is the Revolutionary War against Britain. In the first selection, Thomas Paine writes persuasively about the kind of American who Americans would not want to be—the "summer soldier and sunshine patriot"—and the kind with whom they want to identify—"he whose heart is firm, and whose conscience approves his conduct, will pursue his principles unto death." Intertwined with his appeals to support American independence in its most desperate hour are his descriptions of the enemy, "A sottish, stupid, stubborn, worthless, brutish man." In setting up oppositions—of supporting America or not, of courage or fear—Paine relies on parallel phrasing and balanced sentences to outline and reinforce the choices Americans will need to make.

Speaking about the Civil War—a war that many argue was primarily economic yet pitted "brother against brother"—Abraham Lincoln sought, in "The Gettysburg Address," not to divide but to unite, by linking the themes of birth and death, the deaths of Gettysburg in exchange for "a new birth of freedom." Lincoln predicted in his address that "the world will little note nor long remember what we say here," but about that he was wrong: The world rightly sees "The Gettysburg Address" as a perhaps unparalleled statement of the poignance of war.

Just as each side in the Civil War saw itself as the rightful victor, so do we frequently need to see ourselves as good and the other side as bad; we need to avoid seeing the enemy as anything but dangerous and worthy of extinction. Mark Twain, a sharp if humorous critic of American society, lacerates the tendency to simplify the waging of war in "The War Prayer," a short satirical piece countering piety with the grim reminder that victory for one side brings with it defeat and blighted lives for the other.

Once we have created an image of an enemy and determined the need to go to war, and once society has endorsed that war, popular culture often takes on the selling of that war back to society, through posters, advertisements, opinion pieces, and other media that implore us to enlist, to conserve, to contribute. In the same media, we see not advertisers selling the war but war selling the products, whether or not such products have anything to do with the war effort. In *"We Smash 'Em HARD,"* an advertisement published in 1918, we see association, innuendo, and appeals to the emotion of hatred as well as an appeal to the desire to be manly and the association of masculinity with tobacco products. A very different image, an anti-Nazi poster entitled *"Deliver Us from Evil,"* appeals to emotion and to values in order to move its audience—not merely to buy bonds but to sacrifice for the innocent victims of war.

The act of asking Congress to declare war is probably the most solemn occasion at which a sitting president can speak, and President Franklin Delano Roosevelt's "Pearl Harbor Address" on December 8, 1941, after the bombings of Pearl Harbor and other bases on Oahu, Hawaii, is a prime example of a difficult rhetorical situation and the ways in which a nation's leader can use such an occasion to unite citizens against a common enemy. In asking for a formal declaration of war, Roosevelt's speech required appeals to patriotism and a strong characterization of a treacherous enemy.

Sometimes in creating an enemy, we see something of ourselves in the enemy and something of the enemy in ourselves. The two Vietnam War–era photographs included in this chapter illustrate contradictions of that war. In "Saigon Execution," Americans are brought painfully close to the actuality of the war and to the confusion about friends and enemies that characterized it. In "The Terror of War," war's most horrifying damage—to innocent children—challenged political arguments and domino theories of spreading communism and had a profound effect on Americans' perceptions of the war.

Simple, straightforward narratives of war hold their own compelling power as well and can teach us something memorable about suffering. Jacqueline Navarra Rhoads's narrative, "Nurses in Vietnam," is a story of healing in the midst of massive casualties and war waging. Rhoads's account of her tour of duty in Vietnam also reminds us of the power of the personal voice in bringing the pain and tragedy of massive warfare to an individual level.

Language is one of the weapons of war and a means of justifying it. Author Jeff Zorn, addressing fellow English teachers in a professional journal, argues that after a history of mutual, partial acceptance based on self-interest, both Iraq and the United States shifted to demonizing the enemy through language and image—not because the enemy was suddenly "bad," but for each country's own political, strategic, or economic gain.

These selections can provide an illuminating perspective on the use of persuasion before, during, and after a war to identify the "good" side and the "bad" side, to recruit troops and rally the home front, and to write the history of the war and set it in the context of America's image of itself. Student writer Jeremy Kassis looks, from his vantage point of the 1990s, at the rhetorical strategies Roosevelt used to bring America into World War II and to unite all Americans in support for that war, while Peter Douglas looks at the propaganda that not only promoted the war but transformed our cultural sensibilities.

Creating War and the Enemy Through Persuasive Language

Each of the selections in this chapter is an argument: to unite against a common threat; to renounce an enemy; to embrace a former enemy and "bind up the nation's wounds"; to unite as a people to defeat a treacherous foe; to challenge our assumptions about who our political friends and enemies are. The arguments about war, and about waging war, appeal to the ethos of Americans—to fair play, to leadership in the free world, to protecting the innocent—and to logic—to protecting American and allies' interests. They also appeal to pathos—to empathy for the weak and hurt, to manliness and virility, to hatred of the less-than-human enemy. These appeals are made through language: word choice, syntax or sentence structure, emphasis, and allusions or references that evoke images to which we respond. (See Chapter 1 for further explanation.)

The authors in this chapter are all highly attentive to the power of language to move people's emotions and to move them to action. The discussion after the reading selections will help you to analyze persuasive language in what you read, to develop persuasive strategies of language in your own writing, and to appreciate the power of language to unite and to divide.

As you read and reflect on the selections in this chapter, consider the changes, even over your own lifetime, that have created the context in which questions about war must now be asked. In the last years of the twentieth century, given the changing world political order that has resulted from the breakup of the Soviet Union and the end of the Cold War, Americans increasingly look upon war—and this nation's role in establishing and maintaining world peace—with skepticism. There may no longer be a clearly definable, monolithic "enemy"—communism, for example—but there are nevertheless desperate, devastating ethnic, political, and religious struggles all over the globe, from the Middle East to Bosnia to Rwanda to Haiti. Acutely aware of our own democratic problems—a soaring national deficit, inadequate health care coverage, unacceptable levels of poverty, illiteracy, unemployment, and perceived deterioration of standards of living—we increasingly decline to commit our national involvement and American lives to the affairs of other nations, no matter how grievous the situation. The questions, then, intensify: What are America's vital interests? When is war not merely justifiable but necessary? Are there problems so grave that it is our moral imperative to wage war to eradicate them?

∽ These Are the Times That Try Men's Souls (1776)

THOMAS PAINE

Thomas Paine (1737–1809) came to America from England in 1774. A political radical and active writer and supporter of the American Revolution, Paine worked in a variety of occupations and held several official posts in the colonies, but it is for his crusades on behalf of democratic principles and rights, both in America and abroad, that he is best remembered. Paine's writings include Common Sense *(1776),* The American Crisis *(1776–1783),* Public Good *(1780),* The Rights of Man *(1791–1792), and* The Age of Reason *(1794–1796), a book for which he was denounced as an atheist.* The American Crisis, *a series of sixteen pamphlets supporting the American Revolution, was widely distributed in the American colonies. The selection that follows is from the famous first pamphlet in the series, which was read to American troops on the eve of the Battle of Trenton by order of General Washington.*

These are the times that try men's souls. The summer soldier and the sunshine patriot will, in this crisis, shrink from the service of his country; but he that stands it NOW, deserves the love and thanks of man and woman. Tyranny, like hell, is not easily conquered: yet we have this consolation with us, that the harder the conflict, the more glorious the triumph. What we obtain too cheap, we esteem too lightly: 'tis dearness only that gives every thing its value. Heaven knows how to put a proper price upon its goods: and it would be strange indeed, if so celestial an article as FREEDOM should not be highly rated. Britain, with an army to enforce her tyranny, has declared that she has a right (*not only to* TAX) but "to BIND *us in* ALL CASES WHATSOEVER," and if being *bound in that manner,* is not slavery, then is there no such a thing as slavery upon earth. Even the expression is impious, for so unlimited a power can belong only to God. . . .

I have as little superstition in me as any man living, but my secret opinion has ever been, and still is, that God Almighty will not give up a people to military destruction, or leave them unsupportedly to perish, who have so earnestly and so repeatedly sought to avoid the calamities of war, by every decent method which wisdom could invent. Neither have I so much of the infidel in me, as to suppose that He has relinquished the government of the world, and given us up to the care of devils, and as I do not, I cannot see on what grounds the king of Britain can look up to Heaven for help against us: a common murderer, a high wayman, or a housebreaker, has as good a pretence as he. . . .

I call not upon a few, but upon all: not on *this* state or *that* state, but on *every* state; up and help us; lay your shoulders to the wheel; better have too much force than too little, when so great an object is at stake. Let it be told to the future world, that in the depth of winter, when nothing but hope and virtue could survive, that the city and the country, alarmed at one common danger, came forth to meet and to repulse it. Say not that thousands are gone, turn out your tens of thousands: throw not the burden of the day upon Providence, but *"show your faith by your works,"* that God may bless you. It matters not where you live, or what rank of life you hold, the evil or the blessing will reach you all. The far and the near, the home counties and the back, the rich and the poor, will suffer or rejoice alike. The heart that feels not now, is dead: the blood of his children will curse his cowardice, who shrinks back at a time when a little might have saved the whole, and made *them* happy. I love the man that can smile in trouble, that can gather strength from distress, and grow brave by reflection. 'Tis the business of little minds to shrink; but he whose heart is firm, and whose conscience approves his conduct, will pursue his principles unto death. My own line of reasoning is to myself as straight and clear as a ray of light. Not all the treasures of the world, so far as I believe, could have induced me to support an offensive war, for I think it murder; but if a thief breaks into my house, burns and destroys my property, and kills or threatens to kill me, or those that are in it, and to *"bind me in all cases whatsoever,"* to his absolute will, am I to suffer it? What signifies it to me, whether he who does it is a king or a common man; my countryman or not my countryman: whether it be done by an individual villain, or an army of them? If we reason to the root of things we shall find no difference: neither can any just cause be assigned why we should punish in the one case and pardon in the other. Let them call me rebel, and welcome, I feel no concern from it; but I should suffer the misery of devils, were I to make a whore of my soul by swearing allegiance to one whose character is that of a sottish, stupid, stubborn, worthless, brutish man. I conceive likewise a horrid idea in receiving mercy from a being, who at the last day shall be shrieking to the rocks and mountains to cover him, and fleeing with terror from the orphan, the widow, and the slain of America.

There are cases which cannot be overdone by language, and this is one. There are persons too who see not the full extent of the evil which threatens them, they solace themselves with hopes that the enemy, if they succeed, will be merciful. It is the madness of folly, to expect mercy from those who have refused to do justice; and even mercy, where conquest is the object, is only a trick of war; the cunning of the fox is as murderous as the violence of the wolf; and we ought to guard equally against both. . . .

5   I thank God that I fear not. I see no real cause for fear. I know our situation well, and can see the way out of it. . . . By perseverance and fortitude we have the prospect of a glorious issue: by cowardice and submission, the sad choice of a variety of evils—a ravaged country— a depopulated city—habitations without safety, and slavery without hope—our homes turned into barracks and bawdy-houses for Hes-

sians, and a future race to provide for, whose fathers we shall doubt of. Look on this picture and weep over it! and if there yet remains one thoughtless wretch who believes it not, let him suffer it unlamented. . . .

For Journals

Have you heard someone use the expression in the title of this selection? What did it mean to you? If you haven't heard it before, freewrite about your initial reactions to it.

For Discussion

1. A number of the phrases in this essay became well-known expressions over time. Which ones have you heard before? Did you know they came from the Revolutionary War era? What did they mean to you when you first heard them? What emotions did they inspire in you?

2. How does Paine characterize the kind of Americans who will answer the call? In what ways does he appeal to his audience so that they will want to support the cause of independence?

3. How does Paine characterize the enemy? What evidence does he offer to support his characterization? Cite examples of vivid language and concrete images.

4. Paine develops his argument with parallelism, or grammatically similar phrases; and antithesis, or the setting up of a statement that begins with what is *not* true and then states what *is* true; for example, "I call not upon a few, but upon all." Identify specific examples of these and other stylistic strategies that you believe are particularly effective, and analyze what they contribute to the argument.

5. Compare this selection with the Franklin woodcut *Join, or Die* (Chapter 3). What common themes and appeals do you find?

For Writing

1. Using discussion question 2 as a starting point, develop an essay on Paine's ideal heroic American.

2. Look up some of Paine's other pamphlets from *The American Crisis*. Study several selections, and write an essay analyzing the most common strategies of language in his writings.

∞ *The Gettysburg Address* (1863)

ABRAHAM LINCOLN

The son of a pioneer, Abraham Lincoln was born in Hodgesville, Kentucky, in 1809 and moved to Illinois in 1831. After brief experiences as a clerk, postmaster, and county surveyor, he studied law and was elected to the state legislature in 1834. A prominent member of the newly organized Republican Party, Lincoln became president on the eve of the Civil War. In 1862, after the Union victory at Antietam, Lincoln issued the Emancipation Proclamation freeing the slaves—the crowning achievement of an illustrious presidency. He delivered "The Gettysburg Address," one of his greatest speeches, at the dedication of the Gettysburg National Cemetery in 1863. Lincoln was assassinated by John Wilkes Booth in 1865, shortly after Robert E. Lee's surrender and the end of the Civil War.

Four score and seven years ago our fathers brought forth on this continent, a new nation, conceived in Liberty, and dedicated to the proposition that all men are created equal.

Now we are engaged in a great civil war, testing whether that nation, or any nation so conceived and so dedicated, can long endure. We are met on a great battlefield of that war. We have come to dedicate a portion of that field as a final resting-place for those who here gave their lives that that nation might live. It is altogether fitting and proper that we should do this.

But, in a larger sense, we cannot dedicate—we cannot consecrate—we cannot hallow—this ground. The brave men, living and dead, who struggled here have consecrated it, far above our poor power to add or detract. The world will little note, nor long remember, what we say here, but it can never forget what they did here. It is for us the living, rather, to be dedicated here to the unfinished work which they who fought here have thus far so nobly advanced. It is rather for us to be here dedicated to the great task remaining before us—that from these honored dead we take increased devotion to that cause for which they gave the last full measure of devotion; that we here highly resolve that these dead shall not have died in vain; that this nation, under God, shall have a new birth of freedom; and that government of the people, by the people, for the people, shall not perish from the earth.

For Journals

What phrases from "The Gettysburg Address" have you heard before? What did they mean to you when you first heard them?

For Discussion

1. After your first reading, do a slow, line-by-line reading out loud. Do you find that the address engages your intellect, or your emotions, or both? Discuss your answer.

2. Analyze what Lincoln leaves out of the speech as well as what he includes; for example, the address does not mention slavery, or the animosity between North and South. What is the effect of his careful selection of themes and words?

3. What key ideas does Lincoln evoke in the address? What images? How do they work together to support Lincoln's persuasive purpose?

4. In what ways does Lincoln weave the themes of birth and death? How does the style—the sentence structure, or syntax; the diction, or word choice—convey those themes?

5. The address is full of expressions we have heard in other contexts: for example, Martin Luther King, Jr.'s "I Have a Dream" (Chapter 4) echoes its opening, and countless military funerals have repeated the phrase "last full measure of devotion." Author Garry Wills wrote, "Hemingway claimed that all modern American novels are the offspring of *Huckleberry Finn*. It is no greater exaggeration to say that all modern political prose descends from 'The Gettysburg Address.'" Discuss this assertion in view of the examples and other prose you have heard or read that have sought to invoke "The Gettysburg Address."

For Writing

1. Do a close textual analysis of the address, considering sentence-level strategies as they relate to the larger theme or paradox of the address and to Lincoln's persuasive purpose in speaking. Consider the rhythm of the language, parallelism, pauses, and diction in your analysis.

2. Research the context of the Battle of Gettysburg or of the address itself, writing a documented essay that gives the reader an understanding of the significance of the battle and the context of the speech.

∞ *The War Prayer* (1904–1905)

MARK TWAIN

Mark Twain (1835–1910) is the pen name of Samuel Clemens. He was born in Florida, Missouri, and explored a variety of jobs—printer, riverboat pilot, gold prospector—before discovering success as a writer with the publication of The Celebrated Jumping Frog of Calaveras County and Other Sketches *(1867) and* The Innocents Abroad *(1869). Twain established his reputation as a humorist through his classic novels* The Adventures of Tom Sawyer *(1876) and* The Adventures of Huckleberry Finn *(1885). Twain was always a critic of American society—Huckleberry Finn attacks racism, for example—but in later years he grew especially somber, even pessimistic. "The War Prayer" exemplifies the darker side of his satire.*

It was a time of great and exalting excitement. The country was up in arms, the war was on, in every breast burned the holy fire of patriotism; the drums were beating, the bands playing, the toy pistols popping, the bunched firecrackers hissing and spluttering; on every hand and far down the receding and fading spread of roofs and balconies a fluttering wilderness of flags flashed in the sun; daily the young volunteers marched down the wide avenue gay and fine in their new uniforms, the proud fathers and mothers and sisters and sweethearts cheering them with voices choked with happy emotion as they swung by; nightly the packed mass meetings listened, panting, to patriot oratory which stirred the deepest deeps of their hearts, and which they interrupted at briefest intervals with cyclones of applause, the tears running down their cheeks the while; in the churches the pastors preached devotion to flag and country, and invoked the God of Battles, beseeching His aid in our good cause in outpouring of fervid eloquence which moved every listener. It was indeed a glad and gracious time, and the half dozen rash spirits that ventured to disapprove of the war and cast a doubt upon its righteousness straightway got such a stern and angry warning that for their personal safety's sake they quickly shrank out of sight and offended no more in that way.

Sunday morning came—next day the battalions would leave for the front; the church was filled; the volunteers were there, their young faces alight with martial dreams—visions of the stern advance, the gathering momentum, the rushing charge, the flashing sabers, the flight of the foe, the tumult, the enveloping smoke, the fierce pursuit, the surrender!—them home from the war, bronzed heroes, welcomed, adored, submerged in golden seas of glory! With the volunteers sat their dear ones, proud, happy, and envied by the neighbors and friends who had no sons and brothers to send forth to the field of honor, there to win for the flag, or, failing, die the noblest of noble deaths. The service proceeded; a war chapter from the Old Testament was read; the first prayer was said; it was followed by an organ burst that shook the building, and with one impulse the house rose, with glowing eyes and beating hearts, and poured out that tremendous invocation—

"God the all-terrible! Thou who ordainest,
Thunder thy clarion and lightning thy sword!"

Then came the "long" prayer. None could remember the like of it for passionate pleading and moving and beautiful language. The burden of its supplication was, that an ever-merciful and benignant Father of us all would watch over our noble young soldiers, and aid, comfort, and encourage them in their patriotic work; bless them, shield them in the day of battle and the hour of peril, bear them in His mighty hand, make them strong and confident, invincible in the bloody onset; help them to crush the foe, grant to them and to their flag and country imperishable honor and glory—

An aged stranger entered and moved with slow and noiseless step up the main aisle, his eyes fixed upon the minister, his long body clothed in a robe that reached to his feet, his head bare, his white hair descending in a frothy cataract to his shoulders, his seamy face unnaturally pale, pale even to ghastliness. With all eyes following him and wondering, he made his silent way; without pausing, he ascended to the preacher's side and stood there, waiting. With shut lids the preacher, unconscious of his presence, continued his moving prayer, and at last finished it with the words, uttered in fervent appeal, "Bless our arms, grant us the victory, O Lord our God, Father and Protector of our land and flag!"

The stranger touched his arm, motioned him to step aside—which the startled minister did—and took his place. During some moments he surveyed the spellbound audience with solemn eyes, in which burned an uncanny light; then in a deep voice he said:

"I come from the Throne—bearing a message from Almighty God!" 5
The words smote the house with a shock; if the stranger perceived it he gave no attention. "He has heard the prayer of His servant your shepherd, and will grant it if such shall be your desire after I, His messenger, shall have explained to you its import—that is to say, its full import. For it is like unto many of the prayers of men, in that it asks for more than he who utters it is aware of—except he pause and think.

"God's servant and yours has prayed his prayer. Has he paused and taken thought? Is it one prayer? No, it is two—one uttered, the other not. Both have reached the ear of Him Who heareth all supplications, the spoken and the unspoken. Ponder this—keep it in mind. If you would beseech a blessing upon yourself, beware! lest without intent you invoke a curse upon a neighbor at the same time. If you pray for the blessing of rain upon your crop which needs it, by that act you are possibly praying for a curse upon some neighbor's crop which may not need rain and can be injured by it.

"You have heard your servant's prayer—the uttered part of it. I am commissioned of God to put into words the other part of it—that part which the pastor—and also you in your hearts—fervently prayed silently. And ignorantly and unthinkingly? God grant that it was so! You heard these words: 'Grant us the victory, O Lord our God!' That is sufficient. The *whole* of the uttered prayer is compact into those pregnant words. Elaborations were not necessary. When you have prayed for victory you have prayed for many unmentioned results which follow victory—*must* follow it, cannot help but follow it. Upon the listening spirit of God the Father fell also the unspoken part of the prayer. He commandeth me to put it into words. Listen!

"O Lord our Father, our young patriots, idols of our hearts, go forth to battle—be Thou near them! With them—in spirit—we also go forth from the sweet peace of our beloved firesides to smite the foe. O Lord our God, help us to tear their soldiers to bloody shreds with our shells; help us to cover their smiling fields with the pale forms of their patriot dead; help us to drown the thunder of the guns with the shrieks of their wounded, writhing in pain; help us to lay waste their humble homes with a hurricane of fire; help us to wring the hearts of their unoffending widows with unavailing grief; help us to turn them out roofless with their little children to wander unfriended the wastes of their desolated land in rags and hunger and thirst, sports of the sun flames of summer and the icy winds of winter, broken in spirit, worn with travail, imploring Thee for the refuge of the grave and denied it—for our sakes who adore Thee, Lord, blast their hopes, blight their lives, protract their bitter pilgrimage, make heavy their steps, water their way with their tears, stain the white snow with the blood of their wounded feet! We ask it, in the spirit of love, of Him Who is the Source of Love, and Who is the ever-faithful refuge and friend of all that are sore beset and seek His aid with humble and contrite hearts. Amen."

(*After a pause*) "Ye have prayed it: if ye still desire it, speak! The messenger of the Most High waits."

10   It was believed afterward that the man was a lunatic, because there was no sense in what he said.

For Journals

Do you think of Mark Twain as a humorous writer? As a writer of satire or social commentary? Write about your expectations of this selection based on the title.

For Discussion

1. Examine the diction in the first two paragraphs. What tone and stance are established? Through which particular words and expressions?

2. What is your understanding of what the worshippers are praying for? Do you envision people on the other side of the conflict doing the same?

3. What does the messenger want the people in church to understand? How does he help them to do so? How does Twain convey to us the people's response to the message?

4. How does Twain show the irony of their prayer and their "spirit of love"? Examine the language, and cite specific examples that support your point.

5. How do you interpret the ending of the selection, particularly the last two sentences? How do you think the people hearing the stranger would respond? Would the other side respond any differently?

6. What is Twain's persuasive purpose in writing this selection? Why do you think he selected this genre and format for his purpose?

For Writing

1. Using discussion question 4 as a starting point, develop an analytical essay examining the style of this selection and the strategies Twain uses to convey irony.

2. Write a contemporary war prayer that pertains to a geopolitical situation in the middle to late twentieth century. Irony is not an easy writing technique, so aim for a subtle effect; get feedback from peers, and revise your language carefully.

∽ "*We Smash 'Em HARD*" (1918)

The advertisement that follows, which appeared in popular magazines in 1918, links a product—cigars—with the war effort of World War I. Although the battles were being fought in Europe, Americans at home were called upon to do their part to support the war, whether in military service or through conserving resources. Advertisements and posters for war bonds were abundant; this ad draws on an association with the war as a marketing ploy.

For Journals

What do you think are the most common types of appeals in advertisements? What causes you to want to buy something that you see or hear advertised?

For Discussion

1. What is your emotional response to the ad? What feelings does it evoke in you? How might the response of people in 1918 be similar to, or different from, your own?

2. Analyze the advertisement carefully, examining placement of pictures and text. What element in the advertisement gets the most emphasis? How does the emphasis contribute to persuasion?

3.   What appeals to pathos, ethos, and logos do you find in the advertisement? Which are most prominent? Give examples. Why do you
think the artist chose such appeals? How does the ad's depiction of the
enemy, the "Hun," contribute to the persuasive message?

For Writing

1.   The advertisement is an argument. Summarize the argument, and
then write an analysis of its logic.

2. Look through copies of popular magazines from World War I or II. Most college or large public libraries have collections of bound copies of such magazines as *Life, Look,* and *The New Yorker.* Do any advertisers in them use the war to sell their products? Write an essay analyzing the strategies for a particular type of product or a particular theme of war that is evident in advertising for a wide range of products.

∞ *"Deliver Us from Evil"* (ca. 1940)

This poster reveals a number of typical strategies used by poster artists to invoke American desire to support the war effort in Europe during both world wars —in this case, World War II. As you examine this selection and other visual materials in the chapter, consider what types of appeals are being made and which audiences are being targeted.

For Journals

What could convince you to work toward a war effort, whether by joining the military or contributing money? What are the most compelling ways in which a writer or artist could appeal to you?

For Discussion

1. What is your immediate emotional response to the image?

2. What draws your eye? What do the shades and shapes emphasize?

3. Of what ethnicity does the child seem to be? How does that affect the viewer's reaction to the image?

4. The headline is from a Christian prayer. What is the significance of using this allusion?

For Writing

Using your journal entry as a starting point, if that would be helpful, write an essay on the different types of strategies that poster artists could use to elicit different kinds of support (monetary, military) from different segments of American society in a time of war. Pay special attention to the kinds of images you think would be most persuasive.

∞ *Pearl Harbor Address* (1941)

FRANKLIN DELANO ROOSEVELT

Franklin Delano Roosevelt (1882–1945) was the thirty-second president of the United States and the only president ever elected to four consecutive terms in office. His innovative New Deal economic recovery plan guided America through the difficult years of the Great Depression, and his cooperation with Winston Churchill helped secure an Allied victory in World War II. He died in Warm Springs, Georgia, in 1945, ironically, three weeks before the Nazi surrender. Roosevelt's address to the House of Representatives after the Japanese attack on Pearl Harbor in 1941, with such ringing phrases as "a date which will live in infamy," remains a classic call to action.

To the Congress of the United States: Yesterday, December 7, 1941—a date which will live in infamy—the United States of America was suddenly and deliberately attacked by naval and air forces of the Empire of Japan.

The United States was at peace with that nation and, at the solicitation of Japan, was still in conversation with its government and its emperor looking toward the maintenance of peace in the Pacific. Indeed, one hour after Japanese air squadrons had commenced bombing in Oahu, the Japanese ambassador to the United States and his colleague delivered to the secretary of state a formal reply to a recent American message. While this reply stated that it seemed useless to continue the existing diplomatic negotiations, it contained no threat or hint of war or armed attack.

It will be recorded that the distance of Hawaii from Japan makes it obvious that the attack was deliberately planned many days or even weeks ago. During the intervening time the Japanese government had deliberately sought to deceive the United States by false statements and expressions of hope for continued peace.

The attack yesterday on the Hawaiian Islands has caused severe damage to American naval and military forces. I regret to tell you that very many American lives have been lost. In addition American ships have been reported torpedoed on the high seas between San Francisco and Honolulu.

Yesterday the Japanese government also launched an attack against 5 Malaya.

Last night Japanese forces attacked Hong Kong.

Last night Japanese forces attacked Guam.

Last night Japanese forces attacked the Philippine Islands.

Last night the Japanese attacked Wake Island.

This morning the Japanese attacked Midway Island.   10

Japan has, therefore, undertaken a surprise offensive extending throughout the Pacific area. The facts of yesterday speak for themselves. The people of the United States have already formed their opinions and well understand the implications to the very life and safety of our nation.

As commander in chief of the army and navy I have directed that all measures be taken for our defense.

Always will we remember the character of the onslaught against us.

No matter how long it may take us to overcome this premeditated invasion, the American people in their righteous might will win through to absolute victory.

15   I believe I interpret the will of the Congress and of the people when I assert that we will not only defend ourselves to the uttermost but will make very certain that this form of treachery shall never endanger us again.

Hostilities exist. There is no blinking at the fact that our people, our territory, and our interests are in grave danger.

With confidence in our armed forces—with the unbounded determination of our people—we will gain the inevitable triumph—so help us God.

I ask that the Congress declare that since the unprovoked and dastardly attack by Japan on Sunday, December 7, 1941, a state of war has existed between the United States and the Japanese Empire.

For Journals

Have your parents or grandparents ever talked about World War II or what they did in the war? Write for a few minutes on what you know about the war.

For Discussion

1.   Have you previously heard excerpts from this speech on television or radio? What was your reaction then? If you haven't heard the speech before, talk with people who heard the speech in 1941, and ask them about their reactions; share your findings with your peers, and compare accounts.

2.   How does Roosevelt seek to unite Americans? What sense of identity does he evoke? What themes does he dwell upon? What ethos appeals does he make? What pathos appeals?

3.   How does Roosevelt establish a sense of the enemy in his audience? What kinds of logos or other appeals does he use? How do syntax and diction reinforce the appeals? Look, for example, at his use of repetition in the series that opens "last night," at midspeech (paragraph 6).

4.   Examine the second-to-last sentence: "With confidence . . ." What effect does opening with a dependent phrase have on the emphasis in this sentence?

5.   Compare and contrast the rhetorical demands of a presidential address calling for war with an inaugural address or other presidential speech. Which type of speech do you believe would be the more difficult to write? Why?

For Writing

1.   Through library research or through taking oral histories, investigate reactions to this speech at the time it was given. You could examine newspaper commentaries and magazine articles and interview

older people about their memories of the occasion. In what ways were they affected, practically and emotionally, by the address? How did the journalistic accounts of the times view the speech? Write an essay summarizing your findings.

2. Write an essay discussing the ways in which Roosevelt seeks to unite the American people and how he develops an image of the enemy in the speech. Pay special attention to Roosevelt's use of language, syntax, and repetition.

∞ *Saigon Execution* (1969)

EDWARD T. ADAMS

The following photograph became one of the most famous images of the Vietnam War. Colonel Nguyen Ngoc Loan, South Vietnam's police chief, executes a Vietcong suspect in Saigon. The filmed version of this execution was shown on television all over the world. Adams's photograph won the Pulitzer Prize for News Photography in 1969.

For Journals

Describe the visual images that come to mind when you think of the Vietnam War.

For Discussion

1. Analyze the photograph. What is emphasized? Whose face is more visible, and how does that visibility affect how you react to the photograph? How are the respective figures dressed? Where are their hands? What do these details tell you about the relative power of each man? How do such elements of the photograph contribute to your logical, ethical, and emotional reactions to the image?

2. In what ways is this sort of event expected in wartime? In what ways is it surprising?

3. What effects would this photograph have on Americans' perceptions of their "friends" and "enemies" during the war?

For Writing

1. What impact do you think that this photograph, and others like it, may have had on the American public and their perception of the Vietnam War?

2. Research the Vietnam War in pictures and photographs, and see if you can discern changes over time in the ways in which the war was covered in the popular print media.

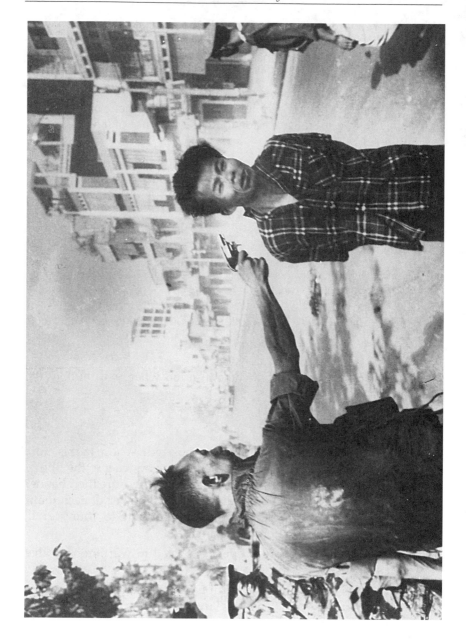

∞ The Terror of War (1973)

HUYNH CONG "NICK" UT

The following photograph, taken by Associated Press photographer Huynh Cong "Nick" Ut, brought with it the horrifying realization of the many civilian participants in, and victims of, the war in Vietnam. Napalm, a gel developed in World War II, was used widely in Vietnam in flame throwers and incendiary bombs; it burns hotly and rather slowly and sticks to its target. The children pictured were apparently the victims of napalm bombs dropped by the South Vietnamese air force. This photograph won the Pulitzer Prize for News Photography in 1973.

For Journals

Think about the truism that a picture is worth a thousand words. Do you agree?

For Discussion

1.   What are your immediate reactions to the photograph? Do you respond primarily on an emotional or intellectual level? What does your response tell you about the power of an image?

2.   Examine the composition and content of the photograph. What is being conveyed? Do you find it more reportorial or persuasive? Of what might a viewer of this photograph be persuaded?

3.   Who are the primary victims of war? To what extent do you think they are represented in war images? Do you think the image in the next photograph is more, or less, persuasive than images of young American men on the battlefield? Explain.

For Writing

1.   Write a report describing the event portrayed in this photograph, using precise, concrete language. Then, in view of your journal entry, analyze the relative power of visual images and language.

2.   Talk with people who remember the Vietnam War, and ask them about whom they perceived as America's friends and enemies during that war. Analyze the ways in which this photograph confirms or contradicts what you learned from your interviewees.

∞ Nurses in Vietnam (1987)

JACQUELINE NAVARRA RHOADS

Jacqueline Navarra Rhoads was born in 1948 in Albion, New York, resided for some time in San Antonio, and now lives in Albuquerque, New Mexico, where she is on the nursing faculty of the University of New Mexico. She served as an army nurse in Vietnam in 1970–1971 and spent most of her tour with the 18th Surgical Hospital in Quang Tri. Her personal account of her tour focuses the politically charged conflict on a personal level, dealing with both the pain and exhilaration of her work and the long-term effects it has had on her life.

We arrived in Vietnam on April 26, 1970, right in the middle of a rocket attack. We were ordered off the plane and everyone was supposed to lay down on the ground. So here I am with my dress uniform, stockings, shoes, and skirt, and suddenly I'm lying down on a cement pavement at Tan Son Nhut wondering, "My God, what did I get myself into?" The noise was so deafening. The heat—I remember how hot it was. We eventually got inside this terminal building where there were all these guys waiting to get on the plane to go home. They were whooping it up, running around with signs saying things like: "Only one hour and thirty-five minutes left!" They saw us coming and one of them said, "Cheer up, the worst is yet to come." We stayed there sixteen hours before we could get out. When we got on the bus, all the windows were screened. I learned from the bus driver that this was to prevent the Vietnamese from throwing grenades in through the windows. I said, "But I thought the enemy was up north somewhere." He told me, "No, the enemy is all around you here. You never know who you're fighting."

My first assignment was in Phu Bai. I was there for thirty days because they needed some emergency room nurses there. Then I was transferred to the 18th Surgical Hospital in Quang Tri, just a few miles from the DMZ. They had just put a MUST (Medical Unit Self-Transportable) unit in there from Camp Evans and they needed operating and emergency room nurses right away. I was there the remainder of my tour.

I was a very young twenty-one. At St. Mary's School of Nursing in Rochester (New York), I kept these Army recruiting posters all over my room. There was a big push at that time for nurses, and we had recruiters coming to the school constantly from the time I started in 1966. I don't know what it was, I loved nursing so much. I always thought—I know it sounds crazy—but I wanted to do something for my country. I just had a feeling that being a nurse in the Army was what I wanted to do. And of course my uncles were all in the Army in World War II. There were nine brothers in my mother's family, and they all went into the Army within six months of each other.

Everyone thought I was crazy. I remember my mother saying, "Jacque, do you know what you're getting yourself into?" Of course, when you're young you have no fear.

5   I did basic training at Fort Sam Houston in San Antonio. My main memory of that time is the parties, big parties. I never took basic training very seriously. It was only later I realized that I should have. What to do in case of a nuclear attack, what to do for chemical warfare, how to handle a weapon—these were things we laughed at. We went out to Camp Bullis and shot weapons, but as nurses we never thought that shooting a weapon was something we needed to know. True, we never had to fire weapons, but we had wounded who came in with weapons as splints, and they were loaded weapons. When that happened, I thought, "Why didn't I listen when they taught us how to take this weapon apart?" You know, an M-16 with a full magazine. We had a young guy come in, he had a grenade with the pin pulled wrapped in a handkerchief and stuffed into his fatigue pocket, a live grenade! I thought, "Gosh, if only I had listened."

I think the practice village out where we trained at Camp Bullis is still in existence. The bamboo sticks smeared with excrement, they were authentic. There was an instructor in black pajamas, camouflage makeup on his face. Well, we kind of laughed. We didn't take it seriously until we started seeing these kinds of injuries in Vietnam.

My first real exposure to the war came five days after I landed. It was at Phu Bai. We received twenty-five body bags in on this giant Chinook helicopter. You know, the Chinook is this great big helicopter, this two-blade deal that can carry one hundred to one hundred and fifty people. And this Chinook came in with twenty-five body bags aboard. One of the nurses' responsibilities was to look inside these body bags to determine cause of death. Of course, they couldn't release the doctors for such trivial work. What you had to do was open the bag, look inside and see what possibly could have killed this person, and then write down on the tag what you felt the cause of death was. It was so obvious most of the time. That's something I still have flashbacks about—unzipping those bags. It was my first exposure to maggots, something I had never seen before in my life.

One was a young guy who had had his face blown away, with hundreds of maggots eating away where his face used to be. Another one, he had his eyes wide open. He was staring up at me. I remember he had a large hole in his chest and I knew it was a gunshot wound or a grenade injury. It had blown his heart, his lungs, everything to shreds. He had nothing left but a rib cage. Evidently, they had lain out on the ground awhile before someone could get to them. The corpsmen were told to take care of the wounded first, instead of spending time getting the dead in the bags. There were GIs exposed to flame throwers or gas explosions. We used to call them "crispy critters" to keep from getting depressed. They'd come in and there would be nothing more than this shell of a person. That was a little easier to take, they didn't have a face. It could have been an animal's carcass for all you knew. But to have to go looking for the dog tags, to find the dog tags on a person, that bothered me. I remember the first time I looked in a body bag I shook so badly. One of the doctors was kind enough to help me through it, saying, "Come on, it's your duty and you're going to have to do this. It's just something that I'm going to help you through. It's just a dead person." It was such a close-knit group. We were considered the most beautiful women in the world. The guys treated us special. You could have been the ugliest woman in the world, but still you were treated special.

The mass-cal, that's mass-casualty situation, traditionally was anything more than ten or fifteen wounded. It was mass chaos, bordering on panic. There'd be a corpsman walking around saying, "Dust off just called and they're bringing in twenty-five wounded. Everybody get going." So we'd pull out all our supplies. The nurses would put extra tourniquets around their necks to get ready to clamp off blood vessels. The stretchers were all prepared, and we'd go down each row hanging IVs all plugged and ready to go. It was mass production. You'd start the IVs on those people where the doctor was able to say, "This one is saved, this one is saved." We put them in triage categories. The expectant ones were the ones who required too much care. We'd make them comfortable and allow them to die. I guess it was making us comfortable too.

I remember this guy named Cliff, a triple amputee we once had. He came in with mast-trousers on. Mast-trousers is an apparatus you inflate that puts pressure on the lower half of your body to allow adequate blood flow to your heart and brain. When Cliff came in, he was conscious, which was amazing. He looked like a stage dummy who'd been thrown haphazardly in a pile. One of his legs was up underneath his chin so that he was able to look down at the underside of his foot. His left arm was twisted behind his head in a horrible way. We couldn't even locate his second leg. He had stepped on a land mine. With his legs that bad, we knew there probably wasn't much backbone left. He was alive because of these trousers. The corpsman must have been right there when he got wounded. He had put him in this bag and inflated it. Cliff should have been dead.

It was really funny because he looked at two of us nurses there and said, "God, I think I've died and gone to heaven . . . a round-eye, an American, you look so beautiful." He was so concerned about the way he looked because of us standing there, "Gee, I must look a mess." But he was alert, he knew where he was. "Doc, take good care of me. I know my leg is pretty bad because I can see it, but take good care of me, doc." The docs couldn't put him in the expectant category and give him morphine to make him comfortable, because he was too alert. The docs had trouble letting go. So one of them finally said, "Well, let's get him into the operating room, deflate the bag, and let's get in there and see if we can't do something."

Well, we knew just by looking at him in that condition that he wasn't going to last, that as soon as we deflated the bag he'd bleed to death in a matter of seconds. Somehow, he knew it too. I remember I was getting blood prepared for him. He called me from across the room, "Jacque, come here quick." I went over to him and said, "What's the matter Cliff, what's wrong?" He said, "Just hold my hand and don't leave me." I said, "Why, Cliff? Are you in pain?" We always worried about pain, alleviating pain. We'd do anything to alleviate pain. He said, "I think I'm going to die and I don't want to be alone." So I stood there crying, with him holding my hand. And when we deflated the trousers, we lost him in seconds. We found no backbone, no lower part of his body. Really, he had been cut in half.

The leg that was folded underneath his neck was completely severed from his body. It was just there. The corpsmen had evidently bundled him together into the bag hoping maybe something would be there that was salvageable. And he just died. I remember he had blond hair, blue eyes—cute as a button. I had to take his body myself to graves registration. I just couldn't let him go alone. I just couldn't do that. I had to pry my hand away from his hand, because he had held on to my hand so tightly. I had to follow him to graves registration and put him in the bag myself. I couldn't let go of him. It was something I had to do.

Usually the expectants had massive head injuries. They were practically gone, they couldn't communicate with you. You were supposed to clean them up, call the chaplain. You did all that stuff, I guess, to make you feel as though you were helping them. To preserve their lives, you would've had to put them on a respirator and evac them to a neuro facility, which in our case would have been all the way to Da Nang, which was hours, miles away. I was an operating room nurse, but when there was a mass-cal, since there were only twelve of us, we'd be called into triage to work there. After that, I'd follow them into the operating room and help do the surgery. A lot of the shrapnel extractions we'd do ourselves, and a lot of the closures too. The docs would say, "Why don't you close? I got this next case in the next room." You didn't have to worry about it too much, if you got into trouble he'd be right there next door.

15   We wanted to save everyone. We had a lot of ARVNs (Army of the Republic of Vietnam), we called them "Marvin the ARVN." We tried to take care of the Americans first, but we also had to take care of whoever needed care—period, whether he was a Vietnamese, a POW, or whatever. In fact, when we tried to save Cliff, they brought in the Vietnamese who had laid the mine. He had an amputation. He was

bleeding badly and had to be treated right away. And we saved him. I guess in my heart I felt angry about what happened.

We were short on anesthesia and supplies. And we were giving anesthesia to this POW, which made me angry because I thought, "What if—what happens if someone comes in like Cliff and we don't have any anesthesia left because we gave it all to this POW?" Again, because I was very strongly Catholic, as soon as I heard myself thinking this, I thought, "God, how can you think that? The tables could be turned, and what if it was Cliff in the POW's place, and how would I feel if he received no anesthesia simply because he was an enemy?" First of all, it shocked me and embarrassed me. It made me think, "Gosh, I'm losing my values, what's happened to me?" I had been taught in nursing school to save everybody regardless of race, creed, color, ethnic background, whatever. Life is life. But suddenly I wasn't thinking that anymore. I was thinking, "I'm American, and they're the enemy. Kill the enemy and save the American."

Before I went to Vietnam, I was kind of bubbly, excited about life. I haven't changed that much really, I'm still that way. But back then, suddenly, I began questioning things, wondering about what we were doing there. I remember talking with the chaplain, saying, "What are we doing? For what purpose are we here?" We were training Vietnamese helicopter pilots to go out and pick up their wounded and take them to their hospitals. And we treated plenty of them at our hospitals, too. Yet when we'd call up and say, "We got a wounded soldier in Timbuktu," they'd say, "It's five o'clock and we don't fly at night." We had soldiers in the hospital shot by ten-year-old boys and girls. We had women who'd invite GIs to dinner—nice women—and they'd have someone come out from behind a curtain and shoot them all down dead. I mean, what kind of war was this?

The chaplain told me, "Hey Jacque, you can't condemn the American government. We can't say the American government is wrong to put us in this position here. We can't say, because there is so much we don't know." It was good advice at the time, it really helped me. I was thinking, "Here I am judging, and I'm saying what the heck are we doing here, look at all these lives lost, all these young boys and for what? And who am I to judge that? There has to be a reason." I guess I'm still trying to hold on to that belief, even though people laugh at me when I say it. They think I'm living in a dream world because I'm hoping there was a good reason.

I didn't really have much time to worry about right and wrong back then, because during these mass-cals we'd be up for thirty-six hours at a stretch. Nobody wanted to quit until the last surgery case was stabilized. By that time, we were emotionally and physically numb. You couldn't see clearly, you couldn't react. Sounds were distant. We kind of policed each other. When we saw each other reacting strangely or slowly, we'd say, "Hey, Jacque, get some sleep, someone will cover, go get some sleep." That's how close we were. That's how we coped with stress.

20   You didn't have time to think about how unhappy you were. It was afterwards, when you couldn't go to sleep . . . here you were without sleep for thirty-six hours, lying in your bed expecting sleep to overwhelm you, but you couldn't fall asleep because you were so tensed and stressed from what you saw. I knew I had a problem the day I was with a nurse I was training who was going to replace someone else. I remember I had completed this amputation and I had the soldier's leg under my arm. I was holding the leg because I had to dress it up and give it to graves registration. They'd handle all the severed limbs in a respectful manner. They wouldn't just throw them in the garbage pile and burn them. They were specially labeled and handled the good old government way.

I remember this nurse came in and she was scheduled to take the place of another nurse. When she saw me, I went to greet her and I had this leg under my arm. She collapsed on the ground in a dead faint. I thought, "What could possibly be wrong with her?" There I was trying to figure out what's wrong with her, not realizing that here I had this leg with a combat boot still on and half this man's combat fatigue still on, blood dripping over the exposed end. And I had no idea this might bother her.

We had a lot of big parties, too. The Army had all these rules about fraternization, how officers couldn't fraternize with enlisted. In Quang Tri, we were just one big family. You didn't worry about who had an E-2 stripe or who had the colonel's insignia. I'm not saying we didn't have problems with officers and enlisted people or things like insubordination. But everybody partied together.

I never had a sexual relationship over there. You have to remember how Catholic I was. Dating, well, you'd walk around bunkers and talk about home. Every hooch had a bunker, so you'd bring a bottle of wine and he'd bring glasses and—this sounds gross, I guess—you'd sit and watch the B-52s bomb across the DMZ. It produced this northern lights effect. The sky would light up in different colors and you'd sit and watch the fireworks. I know it sounds strange, watching somebody's village get blown up. We didn't want to think about the lives being lost.

The grunts always knew where the female nurses were. They all knew that at the hospital there was a good chance of seeing a "round-eye." Once, during monsoon season, we received a dust off call saying there'd been a truck convoy ambush involving forty or fifty guys. They were in bad shape but not far from the hospital, maybe seven or eight miles. We could stand on the tops of our bunkers and see flashes of light from where they were fighting the VC. One of these deuce-and-a-half trucks with a load of wounded came barreling up right into our triage area. Like I said, they all knew where the hospital was. The truck's canvas and wood back part were all on fire. Evidently they had just thrown the wounded in back and driven straight for us.

We were concerned about the truck, about getting it out of the way, but we were also trying to get to the wounded. There were two guys in the back, standing up. There was a third guy we couldn't see, and the first two were carrying him and shrieking at the top of their lungs. One was holding the upper part of his torso, under the arms, and the other held the legs. Their eyes were wild and they were screaming. I couldn't see what was wrong with the guy they were carrying. Everyone else on the truck was jumping off. We were shouting to these guys to get off too, that the truck was about to explode. We were screaming, "You're OK, you're at the hospital."

Two of the corpsmen got up in the truck, grabbing them to let go and get moving. The corpsmen literally had to pick them up and throw them off the truck. Once they were off, they sat down in a heap, still shrieking. It wasn't until then that I got a look at the wounded one. He didn't have a head. He must have been a buddy of theirs. The buddy system was very strong, and these two evidently weren't going to leave without their friend. We brought them to the docs and had them sedated. We didn't have any psychiatric facilities, so we got them evac'd to Da Nang. We never heard what happened to them.

After awhile in Vietnam, I guess I wasn't so young anymore. I was seeing things, doing things that I never imagined could happen to anyone. I had to do a lot of things on my own, making snap decisions that could end up saving someone or costing him his life. Like once, when I'd been there about seven months, they brought in this guy who'd been shot square in the face. It was the middle of the night and I was on duty with a medical corpsman, no doctors around at all. They were sleeping, saving their strength. We got the call from dust off that this guy was coming in. Apparently he'd been shot by a sniper. Amazingly enough, he was conscious when they brought him in. As a matter of fact, he was sitting up on the stretcher. It was incredible.

His face was a huge hole, covered with blood. You couldn't see his eyes, his nose, or his mouth. There was no support for his jaw and his tongue was just hanging. You could hear the sound of blood gurgling as he took a breath, which meant he was taking blood into his lungs. We were afraid he'd aspirate. The corpsman was this older guy, over 40 anyway, an experienced sergeant. I took a look at this guy and knew we'd have to do a trach on him pretty fast. He couldn't hear us and we couldn't get him to lie down.

I told the sergeant, "We gotta call the doc in." He told me we didn't have time for that. We had to stabilize him with a trach and ship him out to Da Nang. I told the corpsman that the only time I'd ever done a trach was on a goat back in basic training at Fort Sam Houston. The corpsman said, "If you don't do it, he'll die." So he put my gloves on for me, and handed me the scalpel. I was shaking so badly I thought I'd cut his throat. I remember making the incision, and hearing him cough. The blood came out of the hole, he was coughing out everything he was breathing in. The drops flew into my eyes, spotting my contact lenses. After the blood finished spurting out, we slid the tube in. He laid back and I worried, "What's going on?"

30   But he was breathing. He didn't have to fight or struggle for breath anymore. I could see the air was escaping from the trach, just like it was supposed to. It was a beautiful feeling, believe me. We packed his face with four-by-fours and roller gauze to stop the bleeding. We told him what we were doing and he nodded his head. When they finally loaded him up for the trip to Da Nang, I was shaking pretty badly. The whole thing had taken less than forty-five minutes, from the time dust off landed to the time we packed him off. We never did get his name.

But three months later, I was sitting in the mess hall in Da Nang, waiting to take a C-130 to Hong Kong for R&R. I'd been in country ten months by then, and I was in the mess hall alone, drinking coffee and eating lunch, still in my fatigues. Somebody tapped me on the shoulder. I remember turning around. You have to remember, I was used to guys being friendly. I saw this guy standing there in hospital pajamas, the green-gray kind with the medical corps insignia on it. He had blond hair on the sides, bald on top. His face was a mass of scars, and you could see the outline of a jaw and chin. He had lips and a mouth, but no teeth. He looked like he had been badly burned, with a lot of scar tissue. You couldn't really tell where his lips began and the scar tissue ended.

The rest of his body was fine, and he could talk. "Do you remember me?" I was used to that, too, people coming up to me and saying, "Hey, I drove that tank by you the other day. . . ." Then he pointed to his trach scar and I said, "You can't be the same guy." He said something like, "I'll never forget you." I asked him how he knew who I was, because, I mean, there had been nothing left of his face. Apparently, the shot had flipped this skin flap up over his eyes so he could still see through the corners. I couldn't believe it. They called my flight right then, so I started saying a hasty goodbye. He mumbled something about how they had taken his ribs from his ribcage and artificially made a jaw-bone, and reconstructed portions of his face, taking skin from the lower legs, the buttocks.

Well, they began calling my name over the loud speaker. I remember giving him a big hug, saying I wished I had more time to talk to him. I wanted to learn his name, but I don't think he ever said it. I wanted to go back to the hospital and tell the others, "Hey, you remember what's-his-name? He's from Arkansas and he's doing fine." We always wanted to put names to faces, but we rarely got a chance to do it. You kept believing that everyone who left the hospital actually lived. When you found out someone actually had survived, it helped staff morale.

I came back home on a Friday, on a Pan American flight that landed in Seattle. I remember how we were told not to wear our uniforms, not to go out into the streets with our uniforms on. That made us feel worthless. There was no welcome home, not even from the Army people who processed your papers to terminate your time in the service. That was something. I felt like I had just lost my best friend. I decided to fly home to upstate New York in my uniform anyway. Nobody said anything. There were no dirty looks or comments. I was kind of excited. I wanted to say to people, "I just got back from Vietnam." Nobody cared. When I got home, my parents had a big banner strung up across the garage, "Welcome Home, Jacque." But that was about it. My parents were proud of me, of course. But other civilians? "Oh, you were in Vietnam? That's right, I remember reading something in the newspaper about you going there. That's nice." And then they'd go on talking about something else.

You were hungry to talk about it. You wanted so badly to say, "Gee, 35 don't you want to hear about what's going on there, and what we did, and how proud you should be of your soldiers and your nurses and your doctors?" I expected them to be waiting there, waving the flag. I remember all those films of World War II, with the tape that flew from the buildings in New York City, the motorcades. Of course, I had my mother. My mom was always willing to listen, but of course she couldn't understand it when I started talking about "frag wounds" or "claymore mines." There was no way she could.

The first six months at home, I just wanted to go back to Vietnam. I wanted to go back to where I was needed, where I felt important. The first job I took was in San Francisco. It was awful. Nobody cared who I was. I remember the trouble I got into because I was doing more than a nurse was supposed to do. I got in trouble because I was a "mini-doctor." They kept saying, "You're acting like you're a doctor! You're doing all these things a doctor is supposed to do. What's the big idea? You're a nurse, not a doctor." And I thought, how can I forget all the stuff I learned—putting in chest tubes, doing trachs. True, doctors only do that, but how do you prevent yourself from doing things that came automatically to you for eighteen months? How do you stop the wheels, and become the kind of nurse you were before you left?

I was completely different. Even my parents didn't recognize me as the immature little girl who left Albion, New York, just out of nursing school. San Francisco was a bomb, and there wasn't an Army post for miles around Albion. So that's why I came back to San Antonio. All my friends were back in and around Fort Sam Houston, so I just naturally gravitated back toward my network. I came to San Antonio in 1974 to get my B.S. in nursing from Incarnate Word College. The best thing I did was to get into the reserve unit there. That's where I met my husband. It gave me a chance to share my feelings with other Vietnam veterans. It kept me in touch with Army life, the good things and the bad. It was like a family.

On weekends at North Fort Hood, we really do sit around the campfire and talk about 'Nam, about what we as reservists can do to be better prepared than we were back there. If there is another Vietnam-type war, God forbid, I just know I'd want to be part of it. I couldn't sit on the sidelines. We usually just talk about these things among ourselves. I think the reason a lot of people are hesitant to talk about it is that they don't know anyone who wants to listen. A lot of people don't want to hear those kinds of stories. A lot of people just want to forget that time altogether. I don't know why. I guess I'm just not like that.

I'm not saying you don't pay a price for your memories. Last year, I had an intense flashback while flying on a Huey (helicopter) around North Fort Hood. It was the last day of this reserve unit exercise and I was invited on this tour of the area. We were flying a dust off, a medevac helicopter, just like the ones we had back then. It was my first time up in a helicopter since. I thought ,"Gee, this is going to be great." One of the other nurses said to me, "Are you sure you want to do this? You're pretty tired." I brushed her aside, "No problem." We sat in back in seats strapped in next to where they held the litters. I was sitting in the seat, the helicopter was revving up . . . I don't know how to describe it. It was like a slide show, one of the old-fashioned kind where you go through this quick sequence . . . flick, flick, flick . . . now I know where they got the term flashback.

40   At first, it was as though I was daydreaming. What scared me to death was that I couldn't turn it off. I couldn't control my mind. The cow grazing in the field became a water buffalo. Fields marked off and cross-sectioned became cemeteries. We flew over this tent, it was the 114th (reserve hospital unit) and suddenly it became the 18th surg. I was scared. All I could do was grasp the hand of this friend of mine. We couldn't talk above the helicopter roar. I just started to cry, I couldn't control myself. I saw blood coming down onto the windshield and the wiper blades swishing over it. There was blood on the floor, all over the passenger area where we were sitting. The stretchers clicked into place had bodies on top of them. I was crying. The nurse next to me kept shouting about whether I was all right. My contacts were swimming around, I wanted the ride to end. I could see why GIs felt scared . . . I couldn't just turn around and open up to the nurse sitting next to me. How could you explain something like that?

I had had a flashback or two before, but the difference was I could control them. Even when the nurse started shaking me, I couldn't turn it off. I just looked past her toward the racks in the helicopter, with bodies on stretchers, body bags on the floor, blood everywhere. When we landed, everyone saw I was visibly upset. The pilot came over to see if I was OK. The only thing I could say was, "It brought back a lot of memories." How could I explain my feelings to these people at North Fort Hood. A lot of them were too young to remember Vietnam as anything more than some dim kind of image on the nightly news. I was scared to death, because all these feelings were brought back that I never knew I had.

I still try to think of the good memories from Vietnam, the people we were able to save. A flashback has certain negative connotations. It's a flashback when they can't think of another way of explaining it. I guess I'm lucky it took fourteen years for it to hit me like that. The one positive thing I can say about it is that it felt awfully good to come back and hover down to that red cross on the top of the tent. It felt good to come home.

For Journals

Do you know anyone who served in Vietnam? Do you know anyone who is a nurse or a nursing student? In what ways do they talk about their work?

For Discussion

1. What is your personal response to the story Rhoads tells and the ways in which she relates it? In what ways does her story confirm, or dispute, what you have heard about the Vietnam War?

2. Rhoads is a woman telling about an experience more often associated with men. In what ways do you think her perspective differs from or is similar to that of the men who served in Vietnam, leaving aside, for the moment, considerations of age and rank?

3. Doctors and nurses who serve in the military have in some ways a fundamentally different mission from the soldiers whose job, in the words of an army colonel, is to "kill people and break things." What kinds of personal conflicts do you imagine existed for the military health care workers in Vietnam? In what ways do you think they might have resolved this conflict?

4. The personal narrative can bring geopolitical conflict to a human scale. Examine the ways in which Rhoads clarifies your understanding of both the human cost of war and the painful homecoming of returning Vietnam veterans.

5. In what ways does Rhoads seem transformed by her experience? Do you sense a shift in her perspective, in her approach or attitudes, as she tells the story of her tour of duty?

For Writing

1. Interview someone who served in Vietnam or in some other war, using the oral history technique (see Studs Terkel's oral history in Chapter 6 as one possible model). Write up the oral history, and then compose a brief analysis that responds to the following questions: In what ways is the individual's story similar to, or different from, Rhoads's story? In what ways does your interviewee's language compare to Rhoads's style?

2. Research newspaper and magazine articles from the late sixties and early seventies, selecting articles and opinion pieces that covered the Vietnam War. Examine the language in which stories about Vietnam are conveyed, and write an essay analyzing the attitudes about the war, and about the Vietnam service personnel, in the press coverage.

∞ *Demonizing in the Gulf War*

Reading the Archetypes (1991)

JEFF ZORN

Jeffrey Zorn is an educator from the University of Santa Clara. He wrote the essay that follows for an audience of college and university English faculty.

Demonizing makes of one's political opposition pure, cartoonish evil, while making of oneself a heroic crusader for righteousness, justice, and progress. Both sides in the War in the Persian Gulf talked about the enemy in melodramatic demon-language of this kind, in each case important and successful propaganda in the campaign to win hearts and minds. Though this topic already begins to seem dated, the issues remain important for English teachers to consider—in their professional practice and as citizens.

We talked of Saddam Hussein as the "madman on the loose," an irrational aggressor out to conquer the region if not the world. His victim was Kuwait, the wealthy but innocent socialite. And we were its protector, nobly prepared to sacrifice for the highest principles: freedom, the integrity of established borders, the security of the economic order. Our job was like Dirty Harry's: to take on, or better yet, to "take out," the street scum of the world.

The other script featured the United States as "the Great Satan," the Western Imperialist infidel out to humiliate and dominate; Kuwait, Saudi Arabia, and Egypt as quisling traitor-states, betraying Arab and Islamic brotherhood; and Saddam Hussein as the Nasser of his era, boldly stepping forward to challenge the status quo, uniting Arabs and Muslims world-wide.

In each case one important effect of demonizing the other side was to rally the armed forces and the public alike, simultaneously drawing attention away from pressing and politically embarrassing problems at home. Another effect was to justify all forms of attack against the demon, under the general theory that "it's all the bastards understand."

The artificial, propagandistic quality of demonizing is best seen 5 through rapid changes in viewpoint, in many cases directly contradicting views held immediately before the campaign to demonize. George Orwell satirized this feature of demonizing brilliantly in *1984*: "Is Eurasia the enemy and Eastasia the ally or vice versa? It changes. . . ."

Until the last moment before his armies occupied Kuwait, Saddam Hussein had been to the US government "a man we can work with" (Morton Kondracke, 1990, "Saddamnation," *New Republic* 7 May: 10), this despite the appalling human rights record of the Baath Party regime since 1968. When Saddam Hussein became president in July 1979, his first act in office was to purge the government of anyone who might support him with substandard zeal; twenty-two Baathist leaders were executed, many of them political allies and personal friends of Saddam Hussein for decades (Marion Farouk-Sluglett and Peter Sluglett, 1987, *Iraq Since 1922*, London: Routledge, 209). Iraqi Communists and liberals, Kurdish nationalists, non-Baathist Arab nationalists, radical Shiite fundamentalists—all these and more heard the "knock on the door" from Saddam Hussein's dreaded Internal Security force, and all were taken away for good, their bodies never returned or returned to their families in pieces.

But two Reagan administrations had subsidized and armed the Saddam Hussein regime, and as late as May 7, 1990, a "top White House official" could be quoted as saying that President Bush "considers Saddam Hussein a bright tough guy . . . ; we want to downplay our negative comments" (Kondracke 9). Similarly on October 27, 1989, John Kelly, assistant secretary of state for Near Eastern and Southeast Asian affairs, stated, "Iraq is an important state with great potential. We want to broaden and deepen our relationship" (Kondracke 9).

When in 1988, members of Congress pushed for trade sanctions against Iraq after the Hussein regime had used poison gas against Kurdish citizens, the Bush administration resisted. Business as usual would continue, and we would neither withhold $500 million in agricultural credit guarantees nor block new loan guarantees from the Export-Import Bank. No "madman" talk here. Rather more typically, talk of even right and wrong had been subordinated to the pressures exerted by the farm lobby and the Department of Agriculture. What won the day, apparently, was the fact that Iraq purchased twenty-four percent of US rice exports (Kondracke 10).

Such mundane considerations of profit and loss, far removed from the gaudy, glaring tones of "demon" talk, brought Iraq and Kuwait to the edge of war and then over it. In the trail of the eight-year Iran-Iraq war, three important controversies had developed between Iraq and Kuwait. First, the Iraqis criticized Kuwait for raising oil production quotas, driving the price of oil down just when Iraq most needed money. Second, the Iraqis claimed that slant drilling at the Rumaila oil fields took oil from Iraqi territory, and they demanded $2.5 billion in repayment. And third, Iraq asked Kuwait to write off the debt it had incurred while fighting Iran, arguing that the threat of exported theocratic revolution posed by Iran applied equally to Iraq and the Gulf states, and so Iraq had fought Kuwait's war.

10   During the extended negotiations over these matters, Kuwait hardly resembled the demure debutante portrayed in our fairy-tale version of the Gulf War. Arab commentators noted surprise at how "very cocky" the Kuwaitis were (Milton Viorst, 1991, "The House of Hashem," *New Yorker* 7 Jan.: 43). An advisor of Jordan's King Hussein said of the Kuwaitis: "They told us officially that the United States would intervene if there was trouble with Iraq. . . . The Kuwaitis said they knew what they were doing. They seemed to think they were safe" (Viorst 43–44).

In July, Iraq sent thirty thousand troops to the Kuwait border, asserting that they would not advance so long as negotiations continued in good faith. At a key juncture Saddam Hussein summoned April Glaspie, the US ambassador in Baghdad, to explain the US reaction to the troop deployment; he was told this was an Arab, not an American affair (Viorst 44).

On August 1, talks at Jidda broke down entirely, and Iraq invaded the next morning, "to teach Kuwait a lesson" (Viorst 44). In crossing the frontier into Kuwait, Saddam Hussein seemed less a madman than a leader pursuing his country's and his own interests ruthlessly but quite rationally, given the standards for political rationality established by nation-states like England, France, the US, and the USSR, and given the relationship the US had forged with Saddam Hussein ever since he became president.

Reversals of position and inflammatory language on the other side were even more striking. During the Iran-Iraq War of the 1980s, Saddam Hussein had been called "the Great Satan" by the Islamic fundamentalists who now lionized him. Bleeding money, his initial, brutal sorties into Iran repulsed, Saddam Hussein had played his Israel card with great finesse. For the benefit of wealthy Arab audiences in the Persian Gulf states, Saddam Hussein had linked Iran and Zionism, making the war against him an international Jewish conspiracy aimed at the whole region. How he had been able to connect the Ayatollah to the Israelis was not clear, but perfectly clear was his former alignment with the very states he now made war upon and the leaders he now called "midgets, traitors, and fornicators" (Farouk-Sluglett and Sluglett 261).

By 1984, he had avidly courted additional US support and won it after re-opening full diplomatic relationships with the US. Instructively, these relationships had broken down in 1967 after the Six Day War, with Iraq claiming it "never again would speak in friendship with the imperialist power behind the Zionists." At this time, however, Iraq needed us, and so Tariq Aziz was dispatched to Washington, to tell lies. There he said on television, on December 2, 1984, "My country would support any just, honorable and lasting settlement between the Arab states and Israel. Iraq does not consider itself to be a direct party to the conflict, because Israel is not occupying any part of Iraqi soil" (Farouk-Sluglett and Sluglett 262).

Despite all these obvious contradictions and all the blatant, vulgar 15 exaggerations, demonizing played well in Peoria. Who talks about the savings and loan crisis these days? Or about Neil Bush, mooning over the "incredibly sweet deal" he got from the Silverado board of directors? Who criticizes the five-hundred-point gain in the stock market or the huge oil profits or the president's eighty-four-percent popularity rating? Who in Jordan and Algeria and the Palestinian camps reviles Saddam Hussein as the invader of an Islamic country, then an Arab country, or remembers him as Iraq's hated Director of Internal Security, or as the exterminator of the Iraqi Kurds?

The call to war against demons, I conclude, must appeal to something very deep in people: to an anger born of profound insecurity and spirit-scouring frustration, to the gall that Achilles described as "sweeter to a man by far than the dripping of honey." Its fairy-tale quality only adds to its attractiveness, providing a drama that can be understood by everyone and that has a hero's role for everyone, no matter how stupid or self-doubting or downtrodden.

We Americans can be sure we will be cast in the role of arch-villain by millions in the Arab world and elsewhere for a long time to come. The peacemakers among us must convince our fellow citizens and especially our government not to respond in kind. This will not be easy, as careful analysis and principled, effective foreign policy-making demand a great deal more than demonizing. The former requires intelligence and moral courage, the latter only a phrase-book and the will to injure.

For Journals

What is your image of the country Iran and of Saddam Hussein?

For Discussion

1.   This article was addressed to English teachers. Why do you think that the author makes his case to this audience? How might the topic be important in both their personal and professional lives?

2.	Zorn argues that demonizing the other side can rally both the armed forces and the public. Do you believe that this effect justifies demonizing the enemy? Why or why not?

3.	The author supports his point, that each side demonized the other in the Gulf War, with evidence of political interactions before the war that did not treat the other as an enemy, but that were, in fact, calculated and strategic. Why do you think the author gives such extensive, documented evidence to support his view? Do you find it persuasive?

For Writing

1.	Research the Gulf War by finding newspaper and magazine articles from the period immediately before, during, and after the war. Analyze news articles for bias and demonizing of the enemy. Does your research support Zorn's point?

2.	Argue that "demonizing the enemy" is justifiable in times of war. Be sure to consider opposing views, such as the belief that demonizing and dehumanizing the enemy makes it easier to wage war rather than to use diplomacy and that it fosters unnecessary cruelty in the postwar period.

3.	View the video *Faces of the Enemy* (producer: Bill Jersey; narrator: Sam Keen), and write a review for your classmates. Does the argument of the film pertain to U.S. politics in the Middle East?

∞ *Rhetorical Divisiveness in Nation-Building and War*

An Analysis of FDR's "Pearl Harbor Address" (1994)

JEREMY KASSIS

Jeremy Kassis is a college student who is interested in the emerging science of nanotechnology, among other topics. He wrote the essay that follows in response to chapter writing assignment 5 for his first-year writing course on the art of persuasion. As you read it, consider the ways in which he evaluated language as a vehicle for persuasion.

Franklin Delano Roosevelt's "Pearl Harbor Address" survives as a reflection of the national horror and outrage elicited by the Japanese bombing of Pearl Harbor. To what extent did his address actually create that outrage? Think of his words as a photograph of national sentiment, not innocently packed away in a photo album, but enlarged to propagandistic proportions. The national tide had shifted against Japan upon news of the bombing, but FDR's speech wove a subtle tapestry of logic and emotion with threads of American justice and history to whip public fervor against the Empire of Japan, to name it "enemy."

December 7, 1941, has been "a date that will live in infamy," as FDR predicted. But the date does not live alone. It lives inextricably joined to the phrase our thirty-second president coined to characterize it. Destiny, it would seem, formed an iron fist that day, holding the furiously scrawling pen that forced us to recognize that our national history, and future, was being determined before our eyes. It is FDR's clever use of double-appositional structure in these lines, emphasized by the certainty and timeliness of the response, that sends chills up our spines, preparing us for the incensed speech to follow.

In fact, analysis of FDR's first paragraph reveals careful integration and overview of all his subsequent themes. He continues, "The United States of America was suddenly and deliberately attacked by naval and air forces of the Empire of Japan." Drawing upon American notions of justice, FDR characterizes the United States as victim and Japan as aggressor, but not so simply. The Japanese are unsportsmanlike, as "suddenly" might suggest, and "deliberate" aggressors, which is to say that they are "premeditative murderers of the first degree" as per the American legal distinction in trials of homicide. Not only do they deserve punishment in this interpretation; they deserve death. We are inclined to perceive them as we perceive our criminals, as subhuman. The Japanese have already been reduced in the speech to barbarians or even animals, preying upon the vulnerable.

But mere barbarism is not descriptive enough. They are an organized people, intensifying the threat to Americans. They constitute an "Empire," a political system that would make any red-blooded, democratic, American patriot cringe with the notions of conquest and domination that the term evokes. This is not political convention; FDR might have referred to the Japanese nation merely as "Japan," as he does throughout the remainder of the speech. It is political manipulation, not of the kind that would be condemned, but manipulation nonetheless.

The balance of the address concretizes the themes already intro- 5 duced, and the second paragraph begins by explaining the scenario of deception. Roosevelt's reference to Japan as "that nation" effectively excommunicates it. Japan has become an unmentionable. "Indeed" of the next paragraph extends the scenario, as though to exclaim of the audacity of the trick.

FDR then asserts himself through the construction "It will be recorded," which bolsters the president's ethos by placing him in a position of command. His word shall be done, history shall be created, in an almost biblical sense. The paragraph concludes the scenario of deceit with an "awful truth" clincher line. "Makes it obvious that the attack was deliberately planned many days or even weeks ago" is an appeal to logos, calling for the audience to assimilate the information just received to determine for themselves the obviousness of the conclusion.

As a student of rhetoric, FDR knows that the appeal to logos does not complete the argument. He brings his personal ethos to bear by asserting an encapsulated conclusion, validating the one he has just asked his audience to produce, which improves his pathos. It is easy to follow a leader who makes you feel intelligent. "During the intervening time, the Japanese government had deliberately sought to deceive the United States by false statements and expressions of hope for continuing peace," he says. This shocking statement is followed by a list of consequences. Material casualty is followed by human casualty, delicately demonstrating his human sensitivity. But FDR ends the story of destruction again on a material note to provoke resolution and action, not the bitter sorrow that human death brings. He ends by turning anguish into anger and the Japanese into marauders, pirates "on the high seas."

He then pursues the point with relentless parallelism. Malaya, Hong Kong, Guam, the Philippines, Wake Island, and, finally, Midway. The last frightens us with its immediacy. Attacked the very morning of the speech, Midway reminds us that the violence continues and that every moment wasted in deliberation is a moment in which the Japanese advance.

Later, the speech evolves into a proclamation of manifest destiny: "American people in their righteous might will win through to absolute victory." In this case, "right" makes "might," and the Americans are, of course, right. The shift to use of the pronoun "we" emphasizes the collectivity of the action, and the invocation of the deity is the culmination of this statement of national purpose. God and our determination shall save us.

10   Finally, FDR makes a humble shift in tense. Persuasion is turned to request, one of burning intensity, sealing the fate of U.S. involvement in World War II. "I ask that the Congress declare that since the unprovoked and dastardly attack by Japan on Sunday, December 7, 1941, a State of War has existed between the United States and the Japanese Empire."

For Journals

Do you remember a memorable speech given in a time of crisis—by a public figure or by someone in your community or school? What do you think made it memorable?

For Discussion

1. What is Kassis's thesis? What does he assert about FDR's speech? Does his introduction lead into his assertion effectively? How well does his evidence support his thesis?

2. Examine Kassis's language. What tone, stance, and approach toward the topic are suggested? To what degree might he be creating a reaction in the way he asserts that Roosevelt does? Cite examples of specific words and phrases that support your assessment.

3. Identify the organizing principle Kassis uses to develop his essay. Is it appropriate for an analytical essay? What other methods of organization might have been suitable?

For Writing

1. Find and listen to a recording of Roosevelt's "Pearl Harbor Address." Are you more, or less, persuaded of Kassis's thesis after listening to the president?

2. In what ways does Kassis himself use appeals to ethos, pathos, and logos to support his view? Write an analysis of his analytical essay.

∞ *Intelligent Propaganda: Deliver Us from Evil* (1998)

PETER C. DOUGLAS

Peter C. Douglas is a student at a California university who is interested in politics and public policy. He wrote this essay for his expository writing class; his assignment was to analyze a persuasive text or image (see page 446).

Successful propaganda often highlights the strongest cultural values of the audience to which it is appealing. At the same time, such propaganda often transforms and adds to those cultural values in the process of invoking them. Many American World War II propaganda posters do both. The poignant and intelligently constructed images of these posters remain ingrained in the American consciousness despite the more than fifty years of cultural metamorphosis which have passed since that thankful day on which the final surrender was consummated. As the heart which pumped patriotism through the arteries of the American war effort, these propaganda posters both hyperbolically expressed and subtly created cultural values which to this day rival those fundamental symbols of America: apple pie, mom, and baseball. We all know all too well the "I Want YOU" poster, for it has become a cultural symbol, invoking and strengthening a plethora of American associations and sentiments in order to achieve its goal of recruiting young men for the U.S. Army. Similarly, the anti-Nazi poster "Deliver us from evil," a lesser known but equally well-designed piece of World

War II propaganda, intelligently appeals to logos, ethos, and pathos in order to achieve its aim of selling war bonds.

At first glance one's eyes rest sympathetically upon the disheveled girl at the center of the poster. The propagandist, in selecting this image, is most clearly making an appeal to pathos, to the emotional sensibilities, of the audience. The girl's expression is one of suffering—she seems on the "verge of tears." She is alone, abandoned in the middle of the poster—she seems to "want her mother." Her nose is red, perhaps from frostbite, and the effect on the viewer is figuratively chilling. On the most fundamental level this image seeks to make the audience say to themselves, "I can't just do nothing—what if this were my daughter?" In fact, the propagandist wants the viewer to see his or her own child as much as the one presented.

At the same time that it appeals to pathos, this image relies on the beliefs and values, the ethos, of "mainstream" American culture to awaken a protective attitude in its audience. As a young blonde, white girl, this child is an image of purity in traditional American culture. Her smudgy face, seemingly bleeding lips, greasy hair, and soiled boy's shirt turn her into an image of purity, violated. The slight show of skin between the two halves of her shirt might even be calculated to raise questions of specifically female violation—has she been raped?—and to appeal to the protective cultural ideal of masculinity. As a symbol both of violated American ideals and of violated feminine purity, the image of this girl is magnified to provoke a parentally, and possibly a sexually, protective response. Indeed, her eyes are raised up in a prayer-like supplication to God to send her a savior.

As one's eyes make their natural progression, however, to the swastika and the cloudy sky (heaven) behind the hopeful child, one is imbued with a sense that, as the girl prays to heaven, she is answered only by that forbidding symbol of Nazi terror. The swastika successfully obstructs the girl's view of heaven and hinders her ability to communicate with God. At the same time, on a particularly subtle level, the young girl, murdered by the Nazis, ascends into heaven. An appeal to both ethos and pathos is therefore made by the arrangement of the various elements, overlaid one on top of the other. Christianity and prayer are invoked, and on an emotional level, one is forced to ask oneself, "how could I let this child die?"

5   The Christian phrase "Deliver us from evil" descends, then, into one's focus. The propagandist, assuming a certain measure of religious homogeneity, of a common ethos, within his American audience, taps into a nondenominational prayer, "The Lord's Prayer," to cut across racial, ethnic, and socioeconomic divisions and to infuse the advertisement with divine authority. At the same time, this phrase places the American people in the "God" position. The prayer begins "Our Father, who art in heaven." The association through "Deliver us from evil" im-

plies, therefore, that the American viewer is the "Father," the almighty—the viewer has the ability to save the children and all Europeans. And from the perspective of a European on a war-wasted continent, the American passerby, living in the free, unscourged, and economically prosperous America, is practically "in heaven." But from what exactly is the viewer to save them? Although it may seem clear that the Nazis are the "evil," one must recognize that the designer of this poster is attempting, through this biblical phrase, to transform the Nazis into pure "evil," into Satan. Against the sky background, this supplicant phrase seeks to conjure up in the audience's mind an image of the omnipotent Americans sweeping in from above to destroy the Nazis (in the symbol of the swastika) and to cradle the young girl back up into the safety and prosperity of the sky, of peaceful America. On another level, this phrase implicitly conveys a sense that such a charitable act by the Americans would be ordained by God, that such an aggressor as the Nazi regime was precisely the type of evil Christ meant to destroy when he implored to his Father, "Deliver us from evil."

Finally, one's eyes scan down to the capitalized command "BUY WAR BONDS." A logical connection is established. "If I buy war bonds, I will deliver them from evil—I will save them." The capitalization of the phrase adds weight, of course, to the argument, but it also sends the viewer the subtle message of "Don't think, just see the suffering, hear the word of God and ACT." Furthermore, rather than offering an indirect appeal in the third person, such as "Deliver them from evil . . . BUY WAR BONDS," the propagandist connects the image of the war-dirtied girl with the text so that she implores the viewer directly, "Deliver (me) from evil . . . (please) BUY WAR BONDS." And assuming that the audience's eyes will follow the carefully planned progression of the poster, a build-up is created which climaxes in a commanding final order "BUY WAR BONDS."

Ultimately, we, in analyzing this poster as a piece of propaganda, must acknowledge that the image of the dirty, disheveled, suffering girl is a selective sample of the real situation in Europe, and if it weren't for the horrible truth which the image contains, such biased sampling would be condemned as purely manipulative propaganda. As well, the propagandist appeals to logos to connect the soiled and battered appearance of the girl with the Nazis, that is to say that the audience will assume that the Nazis have done this to the girl. Although this conclusion is probable, I believe it is important, in retrospect, to acknowledge that this girl might have been put into this state by the war at large—by the British and American bombings, by the animalistic tendencies of any of the competing armies, or by some other aspect of the war. However, looking back on World War II, one cannot help but approve of practically any propaganda strategies, excepting of course the racist and sexist trends of the decade, which the United States might have employed in order to raze the Nazi monolith which had cast its shadow over all of Europe.

In the same way that the "I Want YOU" poster became an entrenched image of patriotism in the American cultural spectrum, "Deliver us from evil," among many other anti-Nazi posters, helped to establish the swastika as the quintessential symbol of evil in America for the latter half of the twentieth century. Not only did these propaganda posters appeal to ethos, pathos, and logos, but they also added to those sensitivities through the creation of new and the transformation of existing cultural sensibilities. For example, if one were to consider the cultural images of the Cold War, which dominated American life for nearly fifty years, one might find that the ethos instilled in Americans by World War II propaganda posters permeated the formation of the American Cold War consciousness. Americans live and breathe these slogans and images to this day.

For Journals

Examine the images in this chapter. Which one evokes the strongest reaction for you? An alternate approach: What comes to mind when you hear the words "children" and "war"? Freewrite your associations of these words in your journal.

For Discussion

1. Douglas's essay analyzes the persuasive poster image found on page 446. Examine the image carefully. In what ways are your impressions similar to Douglas's? In what ways are they different? Explain.

2. What is Douglas's thesis or dominant point about the poster? Does he offer convincing evidence to support that thesis? Discuss.

3. How is developing and organizing an analytical essay about a visual argument different from writing one on a persuasive text? You might use as a starting point for discussion the Kassis essay (this chapter) as well as Douglas's.

For Writing

1. Write a response to Douglas, agreeing or disagreeing with his assessment of the persuasive strategies of the poster. Remember to develop a thesis or core point and to support it with evidence.

2. Select one of the visual images in this text or another source, perhaps reviewing propaganda posters on appropriate Web sites. While you may develop your own approach to the assignment, you may find it helpful to review Chapter 1 materials on visual media and on Kris Andeen's analysis of a Norman Rockwell image used in a poster for War Bonds.

∞ Film: Casablanca (1942)

During World War II, refugees from all over Europe gather in Casablanca, Northern Africa, while awaiting transit visas for America. Many of them frequent Rick's Café Americain, where unexpectedly Rick's former lover arrives with her husband, a leader of the resistance who recently escaped from a German concentration camp. Rick ultimately helps them to freedom, choosing to return to the fight against fascism. (102 minutes)

For Journals

What stories have you heard from relatives or in the popular culture about World War II and the reasons it was fought? What films have you seen? How did they depict the war?

For Discussion

1. What is the mood and flavor of this film? Does it strike you as a film with a message about war? About other ideas or beliefs? Articulate those ideas or values. What kind of message comes across? From which characters do the values emanate, and how does that affect how we feel about the message?

2. The enemy is characterized both explicitly and implicitly. Recount specific incidents from the film that convey images of the enemy.

3. The main character, Rick, changes both his attitudes and his behavior during the film. How does he start out, and how does his character seem to change? Cite examples from the film to support your view.

4. Set in the early 1940s, the film portrays social situations that most contemporary Americans would consider unenlightened at best and racist at worst. Can we nevertheless appreciate and value such films? In what ways are films from the past social and cultural markers for where we have been as a society?

For Writing

1. Analyze one of the characters in the film, and assess what he or she contributes to the film and to the assertions being made about war and the enemy.

2. Research immigration from Europe during World War II. You could focus on a particular country or part of Europe or a particular means of immigration. Alternatively, interview family members about their memories of some element of wartime or of their memory of this film's debut. How was it received?

3. Select a recent film, such as *Saving Private Ryan,* and write either a review or an essay in which you compare and contrast its portrayal of war with another film about World War II.

4. Write a film review for your campus paper, arguing that your peers should, or should not, rent the video.

Writing Assignments

1. Observe a simple or brief event at school, in class, at home—someone coming to class late, for example, or an argument at mealtime, or perhaps a traffic mishap. Write up the event in three ways: (1) positively biased toward the subject or main character, (2) negatively biased, and (3) as neutral as possible. Indicate an ostensible purpose for writing the report in each situation (i.e., for your friend who was driving the car; for the other driver, for a no-fault insurance report). Exchange assignments with a peer, and assess the differences in the three accounts. Did you change the passages by selecting different details to include or exclude? By changing nouns and verbs? By changing modifiers? Analyze the differences, and discuss them in class or in an analytical essay.

2. Select a political event or issue of current national interest. Then select three or four magazines, such as *National Review, U.S. News and World Report,* the *New Republic,* or the *Nation,* and read their coverage of the event or issue. Do a close textual analysis of the selections, and write an essay comparing and contrasting their styles.

3. Write a rallying cry to get fellow students or neighbors involved in an issue or plan of action. Revise the argument for a special interest magazine, an academic publication, or a broader audience. Submit both, with an explanation for the change you made in style for the different writing situations.

4. Write an argument on an issue you care about. Use every bit of persuasive, connotative language you can think of, every stylistic strategy you have learned. Then exchange essays with a peer, and write out your immediate, and then studied, responses to each other's essays. How effective was the language? How convincing the argument? Were you persuaded or put off by the language of the argument?

5. Analyze a persuasive speech or text from a war era, whether historical material from the world wars or Vietnam or more recent material. As do Zorn and Kassis in this chapter, watch for patterns of imagery or other tactics for creating an "us" and "them" system. How does the imagery help to unite? How does it divide?

9

∞

Frontiers

At the beginning of the nineteenth century, New York State was on the frontier, and most people thought it would take a hundred years to get to the Pacific, if in fact they ever thought in those terms at all. They certainly would have been surprised to learn that by 1849 Americans had moved across the entire continent, all the way to California, thanks to the political and economic charms of expansion and the incentive of the Gold Rush. What they would have found even more unlikely is that a hundred years after the frontier had ceased to exist as a geographic marker, Americans would still be so attached to it, or to what it represents, that the search for new frontiers—even technological ones—continues to occupy the American vocabulary and the American psyche.

The American idea of frontier is of an invisible border between settled and unsettled, civilized and uncivilized areas. It is recognized more by what it is not than by what it is: it's not civilization as you know it, it's not domesticated, it's not safe. Of course, the idea of the frontier was a reality only to the European settlers who saw themselves as the bearers of culture and developers of empty country, not to Native Americans who had their own indigenous cultures and knew the country wasn't empty because they were already there.

Whether or not everyone accepted the idea of a frontier—receding before the development of towns and farms but always out there somewhere, leading to newer undiscovered places—it became so embedded in our culture that it is what Americans think they know best about their own country, and it is the way we are identified by the rest of the world. In Germany, for example, there are vacation places complete with wigwams so tourists can play cowboys and Indians. Blue jeans, invented by young merchant Levi Strauss during the Gold Rush so prospectors could put ore in their pockets without tearing them, are an American national uniform and a status symbol in eastern Europe and Russia. American theme parks have frontier towns; movie studios have mock shoot-outs between good guys and bad guys; and Americans have been watching western movies as long as there have been movies to watch.

How much all of this re-creation has to do with what the frontier

477

was actually like seems to matter much less than what most people prefer to think it was like. Wherever Americans live, they infuse some sense of the centrality of the frontier into their image of the United States. Whatever changes are wrought in that image are the cause of pitched emotional and intellectual battles between groups with an interest in preserving the idea of the frontier. In the last forty or fifty years, many scholars have explored the difference between the actual American frontier and the frontier of the American imagination, and many Native Americans have campaigned successfully for reevaluations of the image of Indians in American history.

Frontiers Through History

Most Americans never saw the frontier, wherever it happened to be at the time. In the eighteenth and most of the nineteenth centuries, whether they lived in towns, on farms and in rural areas, or in the bigger eastern cities, they got their information about the frontier from newspaper reports, narratives—accurate or exaggerated, paintings by artists who had accompanied expeditions, and eventually from photographs.

The people who knew the frontier from firsthand experience were not only the settlers, trappers, hunters, and seekers for gold, and the frontier was not just the Far West. It existed as a permeable border between the white settlers and the Native Americans, or the Mexicans, or the English and the French, or wherever issues of control, power, and settlement arose, and it moved irregularly from the east coast to the west coast over a period of almost three hundred years; in the nineteenth century, as gold was discovered in California, the frontier receded with astonishing speed as far as it could go—to the Pacific Ocean and California.

One of the earliest and most interesting records we have of the frontier, however, is set not on the plains or in the Sierra Nevada, but in New England in the early eighteenth century. It is a journal written in 1704 by an unusually independent and entrepreneurial businesswoman named Sarah Kemble Wright. She traveled from Boston, which was then a small city, to Connecticut, to New York, and back, and her observations of manners and mores, terrible food and beautiful scenery, are an early and disconcertingly accurate part of the profile America was beginning to draw of itself.

The struggle between whites and Indians, which Mrs. Knight records in its earlier phases, continued throughout the eighteenth and nineteenth centuries and became the defining constituent of the mythology of the American West. But there were other significant conflicts with enormous cultural and political impact, and one of the most important was that between the American settlers and the indigenous Hispanic population in the Southwest and West. The military climax of that conflict was the Mexican-American War of 1848, which ended with the

Treaty of Guadalupe Hidalgo, an excerpt of which is presented here. In the treaty, Mexico essentially ceded the Southwest to the United States, but Congress never passed the provisions that guaranteed full civil rights to Mexicans in the territories, and the resultant economic and political hardship was severe (see Flores's essay in Chapter 6).

For a lucky few, the idea of the frontier was an adventure of absolutely glorious proportions, and no one left a record of a better time than the young Samuel Clemens, otherwise known as Mark Twain. In 1861, accompanying his brother, who had been appointed secretary to the governor of the Nevada Territory, Clemens saw the continent as few other people but the Native Americans had ever been privileged to see it—stagecoaches, the Pony Express, the Southwest, clear lakes full of fish, early San Francisco, silver mining in Nevada, even Hawaii. His early book, *Roughing It*, is ironic from title to finish, but Twain's irrepressible humor communicates the reality of the frontier at the same time that it embroiders and sustains the mythology.

Twain could find amusement in almost anything, but the trip was extremely difficult, and relations between settlers and Indians deteriorated in proportion to the number of settlers who arrived and the realization that they were not going to stop coming. Some settlers both feared and pitied the Indians, but for Americans back East the picture was less complicated. People who went through their entire lives without ever seeing an Indian believed in the popular image of crazed savages bent on destroying civilization. A more respectful image, Albert Bierstadt's spectacular painting *Giant Redwood Trees of California*, gives us a sense of the symbiotic relationship between the Indians and the landscape.

There were real instances of brutality as competition for diminishing natural resources raised the stakes on both sides. But the tabloid newspapers such as the *Police Gazette* knew their audience and catered to its prejudices. In a typical example, the *Gazette* gives its version of a clash between U.S. Cavalry and Indians in South Dakota, complete with headline (Indian Treachery and Bloodshed) and violent illustration.

By 1893, the frontier was essentially closed; Oklahoma would not become a state until 1912, but the Indians were no longer a factor, the railroad had long since become transcontinental, industrialization had transformed American cities and multiplied their populations, and people who wanted to see Indians could buy a ticket to Buffalo Bill's show—the great Indian chief Sitting Bull was one of his acts.

Chicago, the youngest of America's great cities, celebrated its status by holding a World's Fair in 1893. A brilliant young professor, Frederick Jackson Turner, took the opportunity to speak about the impact the closing of the frontier had on the American consciousness. The result, his essay "The Significance of the Frontier in American History," is the first and still the most famous analysis of the frontier. Turner's address had profound effects on the development of economics as a discipline, as well as on the study of American history, and the argument he started about the significance of the frontier to the development of American character and democracy has continued ever since. Richard Hofstadter's response that follows is the most famous, but it is only one of many.

Among the many tangible effects of the closing of the frontier was the confinement of Native Americans to reservations and, not coincidentally, the beginnings of what was to become the national parks system. As the actual frontier disappeared, and with it the real conflict between whites and Indians, the need to preserve some portion of a pristine landscape grew, with the West and Far West as the primary beneficiaries. A conservationist movement led by naturalist and writer John Muir successfully campaigned for Yosemite and the Sequoias in California, which were declared national parks in 1890.

The size of the parks system has gradually increased over the years, but not without debate about the need for development versus the need for open space. One western writer who dedicated much of his work to the significance of the wilderness in an industrialized America was the novelist and conservationist Wallace Stegner. In his famous "Coda: Wilderness Letter," Stegner argues not just for the wilderness but for the *idea* of the wilderness, even for Americans who have never seen it and don't really want to, except in the movies.

The idea of the West—as it once was, or as we believe it once was—is what fascinates Joan Didion, the novelist, essayist, political reporter, and screenwriter, who writes her own ancestral memory in "Notes of a Native Daughter." The great-grandchild of settlers who had come to the Sacramento Valley in the nineteenth century, she lives in a sophisticated world on both coasts, but the California of her memory hovers just outside of reach, a mixture of open fields and provincial relatives, a place whose only constant is perpetual change, a symbol of the frontier that lives more in memory than in reality.

For Native Americans, the idea of manifest destiny, the movement of settlers across the plains, and the industrialization of an increasingly powerful America marked not just the closing of the West but the destruction of their civilizations. Invisible in the power structure, they tended to be pictured more in movie westerns, usually in the act of being shot off their horses by cowboy heroes in general, and John Wayne in particular. In her poem "Dear John Wayne," Native American writer Louise Erdrich captures the ironic experience of American Indians who go to the drive-in movie to watch Hollywood movie versions of what happened to their ancestors.

If California is the romantic edge of the frontier, then the American Northwest, particularly Oregon and Washington State, has become a sort of refuge in the popular mind for people fleeing from California's crowds, development, and lost promise. Irritated natives have bumper stickers on their cars asking that their state not be "Californiacated"; loggers fight with environmentalists about jobs versus nature, work versus open land. Perhaps only someone who is not a westerner—English writer Jonathan Raban—could explain these conflicts, as he does in his article "The Last Frontier," about traveling in Washington State, Wyoming, and Montana. Like Sarah Kemble Knight almost two hundred years earlier, he is observant, curious, and a good listener, and the country he sees strikes him with all the force of a visit to an alien planet.

The last selection, Clint Eastwood's revisionist film about the frontier, *Unforgiven*, employs many of the elements of the traditional western, including the western hero, the gunslinger, good guy versus bad guy, ladies in distress, and the big gunfight at the end. But it turns many of those same elements on their heads: the good guy is a retired killer who can barely ride a horse and would rather be at home with his two small children; the ladies in distress are prostitutes who want revenge on the cowboy who mutilated one of them; the most brutal character in the film is the sheriff; and the afterword, which tells what happened to the gunslinger after he went home, is a comic undercutting of the whole premise. The result is a movie that simultaneously revises, criticizes, and yet validates the West of myth.

⌘ FROM *The Journal of Madam Knight* (1704)

SARAH KEMBLE KNIGHT

Sarah Kemble Knight (1666–1727) was a remarkable woman by any standards. At a time when women were not usually independent, she was, at various times, a court recorder (scrivener), the headmistress of a school that young Benjamin Franklin reportedly attended, and operator of a shop and a boardinghouse. She was thirty-eight years old in 1704 when she went on the hazardous six-month journey from Boston to Connecticut to New York and back, which she records with wit and intelligence.

Beginning the Journey

Monday, October the Second, 1704

About three o'clock afternoon, I began my journey from Boston to New Haven, being about two hundred miles. My kinsman, Capt. Robert Luist, waited on me as far as Dedham, where I was to meet the western post.

I visited the Rev. Mr. Belcher, the minister of the town, and tarried there till evening in hopes the post would come along. But he not coming, I resolved to go to Billingses where he used to lodge, being 12 miles further. But being ignorant of the way, Madam Belcher, seeing no persuasions of her good spouse's or hers could prevail with me to lodge there that night, very kindly went with me to the tavern, where I hoped to get my guide, and desired the hostess to inquire of her guests whether any of them would go with me.

Upon this, to my no small surprise, son John arose and gravely demanded what I would give him to go with me? "Give you," says I, "are you John?" "Yes," says he, for want of a better; and behold! this John looked as old as my host, and perhaps had been a man in the last century. "Well, Mr. John," says I, "make your demands." "Why, half a piece of eight and a dram," says John. I agreed, and gave him a dram (now) in hand to bind the bargain.

. . . His shade on his horse resembled a globe on a gate post. His habit, horse, and furniture, its looks and going incomparably answered the rest.

5   Thus jogging on with an easy pace, my guide telling me it was dangerous to ride hard in the night (which his horse had the sense to avoid), he entertained me with the adventures he had passed by late riding, and eminent dangers he had escaped, so that, remembering the heroes in *Parismus* and *The Knight of the Oracle,* I didn't know but I had met with a prince disguised.

When we had rid about an hour, we came into a thick swamp, which by reason of a great fog, very much startled me, it being now very dark. But nothing dismayed John: he had encountered a thousand and a thousand such swamps, having a universal knowledge in the woods; and readily answered all my inquiries, which were not a few.

In about an hour, or something more, after we left the swamp, we came to Billinges, where I was to lodge. My guide dismounted and very complacently helped me down and showed the door, signing to me with his hand to go in; which I gladly did—But had not gone many steps into the room, ere I was interrogated by a young lady I understood afterwards was the eldest daughter of the family, with these, or words to this purpose *(viz.),* "Law for me—what in the world brings you here at this time a night?—I never see a woman on the road so dreadful late, in all the days of my versal[1] life. Who are you? Where are you going? I'm scared out of my wits:—with much now of the same kind. I stood aghast, preparing to reply, when in comes my guide—to him madam turned, roaring out: "Lawful heart, John, is it you?—howdy do! Where in the world are you going with this woman? Who is she?" John made no answer but sat down in the corner, fumbled out his black junk,[2] and saluted that instead of Debb; she then turned

---

[1] Entire.
[2] Twist of tobacco.

again to me and fell anew into her silly questions, without asking me to sit down.

I told her she treated me very rudely, and I did not think it my duty to answer her unmannerly questions. But to get rid of them, I told her I came there to have the post's[3] company with me tomorrow on my journey, etc. Miss stared awhile, drew a chair, bid me sit, and then ran upstairs and put on two or three rings (or else I had not seen them before) and returning, set herself just before me, showing the way to reding,[4] that I might see her ornaments, perhaps to gain more respect. But her grandma's new rung sow, had it appeared, would [have] affected me as much. I paid honest John with money and dram according to contract, and dismissed him and prayed Miss to show me where I must lodge. She conducted me to a parlor in a little back leanto, which was almost filled with the bedstead, which was so high that I was forced to climb on a chair to get up to the wretched bed that lay on it; on which having stretched my tired limbs, and laid my head on a sad-colored pillow, I began to think on the transactions of the past day.

Tuesday, October the Third

About 8 in the morning, I with the post proceeded forward without observing anything remarkable; and about two, afternoon, arrived at the post's second stage, where the western post met him and exchanged letters. Here, having called for something to eat, the woman brought in a twisted thing like a cable, but something whiter; and laying it on the board, tugged for life to bring it into a capacity to spread; which having with great pains accomplished, she served in a dish of pork and cabbage, I suppose the remains of dinner. The sauce was of a deep purple, which I thought was boiled in her dye kettle; the bread was Indian and everything on the table service agreeable to these. I, being hungry, got a little down; but my stomach was soon cloyed, and what cabbage I swallowed served me for a cud the whole day after.

Having here discharged the ordinary[5] for self and guide (as I understood was the custom), about three, afternoon, went on with my third guide, who rode very hard; and having crossed Providence ferry, we came to a river which they generally ride through. But I dared not venture; so the post got a lad and canoe to carry me to t'other side, and he rid through and led my horse. The canoe was very small and shallow, so that when we were in, she seemed ready to take in water, which greatly terrified me, and caused me to be very circumspect, sitting with my hands fast on each side, my eyes steady, not daring so much as to lodge my tongue a hair's breadth more on one side of my mouth than

10

---

[3] Messenger.
[4] Showing off.
[5] Paid for the food.

t'other nor so much as think on Lot's wife,[6] for a wry thought would have overset our wherry;[7] but was soon put out of this pain, by feeling the canoe on shore, which I as soon almost saluted with my feet; and rewarding my sculler, again mounted and made the best of our way forwards. The road here was very even and the day pleasant, it being now near sunset. But the post told me we had near 14 miles to ride to the next stage (where we were to lodge). I asked him of the rest of the road, foreseeing we must travel in the night. He told me there was a bad river we were to ride through, which was so very fierce a horse could sometimes hardly stem it: but it was but narrow, and we should soon be over. I cannot express the concern of mind this relation set me in: no thoughts but those of the dangerous river could entertain my imagination, and they were as formidable as various, still tormenting me with blackest ideas of my approaching fate—sometimes seeing myself drowning, otherwhiles drowned, and at the best, like a holy sister just come out of a spiritual bath in dripping garments. . . .

Thus, absolutely lost in thought, and dying with the very thoughts of drowning, I came up with the post, who I did not see 'til even with his horse: he told me he stopped for me; and we rode on very deliberately a few paces, when we entered a thicket of trees and shrubs, and I perceived by the horse's going, we were on the descent of a hill, which, as we came nearer the bottom, 'twas totally dark with the trees that surrounded it. But I knew by the going of the horse we had entered the water, which my guide told me was the hazardous river he had told me of; and he, riding up close to my side, bid me not fear—we should be over immediately. I now rallied all the courage I was mistress of, knowing that I must either venture my fate of drowning, or be left like the children in the wood. So, as the post bid me, I gave reins to my nag; and sitting as steady as just before in the canoe, in a few minutes got safe to the other side, which he told me was the Narragansett country.

Here we found great difficulty in traveling, the way being very narrow, and on each side the trees and bushes gave us very unpleasant welcomes with their branches and boughs, which we could not avoid, it being so exceeding dark. My guide, as before so now, put on harder than I, with my weary bones, could follow; so left me and the way behind him. Now returned my distressed apprehensions of the place where I was; the dolesome woods, my company next to none, going I knew not whither, and encompassed with terrifying darkness; the least of which was enough to startle a more masculine courage. Adding to which the reflections, as in the afternoon of the day that my call was very questionable, which, til then I had not so prudently as I ought con-

---

[6] From Genesis 19:26. Lot's wife was turned into a pillar of salt when she stopped to look back at the destruction of Sodom and Gomorrah.
[7] Canoe.

sidered. Now, coming to the foot of a hill, I found great difficulty in ascending; but being got to the top, was there amply recompensed with the friendly appearance of the kind conductress of the night, just then advancing above the horizontal line. The raptures which the sight of that fair planet produced in me, caused me, for the moment, to forget my present weariness and past toils; and inspired me for most of the remaining way with very diverting thoughts, some of which, with other occurrences of the day, I reserved to note down when I should come to my stage. . . .

Being thus agreeably entertained without a thought of anything but thoughts themselves, I on a sudden was roused from these pleasing imaginations by the post's sounding his horn, which assured me he was arrived at the stage where we were to lodge; and that music was then most musical and agreeable to me.

Being come to Mr. Havens', I was very civilly received, and courteously entertained, in a clean comfortable house; and the good woman was very active in helping off my riding clothes, and then asked what I would eat. I told her I had some chocolate, if she would prepare it; which with the help of some milk, and a little clean brass kettle, she soon effected to my satisfaction. I then betook me to my apartment, which was a little room parted from the kitchen by a single board partition; where, after I had noted the occurrences of the past day, I went to bed, which, though pretty hard, yet neat and handsome. But I could get no sleep, because of the clamor of some of the town topers in next room, who were entered into a strong debate concerning the signification of the name of their country *(viz.)*, *Narragansett*. One said it was named so by the Indians, because there grew a brier there, of a prodigious height and bigness, the like hardly ever known, called by the Indians narragansett; and quotes an Indian of so barbarous a name for his author, that I could not write it. His antagonist replied no—it was from a spring it had its name, which he well knew where it was, which was extreme cold in summer, and as hot as could be imagined in the winter, which was much resorted to by the natives, and by them called Narragansett (hot and cold), and that was the original of their place's name—with a thousand impertinances not worth notice, which he uttered with such a roaring voice and thundering blows with the fist of wickedness on the table, that it pierced my very head. I heartily fretted, and wished 'um tonguetied. . . . They kept calling for t'other gill,[8] which while they were swallowing, was some intermission; but presently, like oil to fire, increased the flame. I set my candle on a chest by the bedside, and setting up, fell to my old way of composing my resentments, in the following manner:

---

[8] About a quarter pint.

I ask thy aid, O potent rum!
To charm these wrangling topers dumb.
Thou hast their giddy brains possessed—
The man confounded with the beast—
And I, poor I, can get no rest.
Intoxicate them with thy fumes:
O still their tongues til morning comes!

And I know not but my wishes took effect; for the dispute soon ended
with t'other dram; and so good night! . . .

15   There are everywhere, in the towns as I passed, a number of Indians, the natives of the country, and are the most savage of all the savages of that kind that I had ever seen: little or no care taken (as I heard
upon inquiry) to make them otherwise. They have in some places lands
of their own, and governed by laws of their own making;—they marry
many wives and at pleasure put them away, and on the least dislike or
fickle humor, on either side, saying "Stand away" to one another is sufficient divorce. And indeed those uncomely "Stand aways" are too
much in vogue among the English in this (indulgent colony) as their
records plentifully prove, and that on very trivial matters, of which
some have been told me, but are not proper to be related by a female
pen, tho some of that foolish sex have had too large a share in the story.

If the natives commit any crime on their own precincts among
themselves, the English takes no cognizance of. But if on the English
ground, they are punishable by our laws. They mourn for their dead by
blacking their faces, and cutting their hair, after an awkward and fright-
ful manner; but can't bear you should mention the names of their dead
relations to them. They trade most for rum, for which they'd hazard
their very lives; and the English fit them generally as well, by seasoning
it plentifully with water.

They give the title of merchant to every trader, who rate their goods
according to the time and specie they pay in: *viz.* Pay, money, pay as
money, and trusting. *Pay* is grain, pork, beef, etc., at the prices set by the
General Court that year; *money* is pieces of eight, riyals,[9] or Boston or
Bay shillings (as they call them) or good hard money, as sometimes silver coin is termed by them; also wampum, *viz.* Indian beads which
serves for change. *Pay as money* is provisions, as aforesaid, one third
cheaper than as the Assembly or General Court sets it; and *Trust* as they
and the merchant agree for time.

Now, when the buyer comes to ask for a commodity, sometimes before the merchant answers that he has it, he says, "is your pay ready?"
Perhaps the chap replies, "Yes"; "What do you pay in?" says the merchant. The buyer having answered, then the price is set; as suppose he

---

[9] Spanish coins.

wants a sixpenny knife, in pay it is 12d—in pay as money eight pence, and hard money its own price, *viz.* 6d. It seems a very intricate way of trade and what *Lex Mercatoria*[10] had not thought of.

Being at a merchant's house, in comes a tall country fellow, full of tobacco; for they seldom lose their cud, but keep chewing and spitting as long as their eyes are open,—he advanced to the middle of the room, made an awkward nod, and spitting a large deal of aromatic tincture, he gave a scrape with his shovel-like shoe, leaving a small shovelful of dirt on the floor, made a full stop, hugging his own pretty body with his hands under his arms, stood staring 'round him, like a cat let out of a basket. At last, like the creature Balaam rode on,[11] he opened his mouth and said: "have you any ribbon for hatbands to sell, I pray?" The questions and answers about the pay being past, the ribbon is bro't and opened. Bumpkin simpers, cries "it's confounded gay I vow"; and beckoning to the door, in comes Joan Tawdry, dropping about 50 curtsies, and stands by him; he shows her the ribbon. "Law you," says she, "it's right gent, do you, take it, 'tis dreadful pretty." Then she enquires, "have you any hood silk, I pray?" which being brought and bought, "Have you any thread to sew it with," says she, which being accommodated with, they departed. They generally stand after they come in a great while speechless, and sometimes don't say a word till they are asked what they want, which I impute to the awe they stand in of the merchants, who they are constantly almost indebted to; and must take what they bring without liberty to choose for themselves; but they serve them as well, making the merchants stay long enough for their pay.

We may observe here the great necessity and benefit both of education and conversation; for these people have as large a portion of mother wit, and sometimes larger, than those who have been brought up in cities; but for want of improvements, render themselves almost ridiculous, as above. I should be glad if they would leave such follies, and am sure all that love clean houses (at least) would be glad on't too.

They are generally very plain in their dress, throughout all the Colony, as I saw, and follow one another in their modes; that you may know where they belong, especially the women, meet them where you will.

Their chief red letter day is St. Election, which is annually observed according to charter, to choose their government: a blessing they can never be thankful enough for, as they will find, if ever it be their hard fortune to lose it. The present governor in Connecticut is the Honorable John Winthrop, Esq.: a gentleman of an ancient and honorable family, whose father was governor here sometime before, and his grandfather

20

---

[10] Law of business.
[11] Namely, an ass (Numbers 22–24).

had been governor of Massachusetts. This gentleman is a very courteous and affable person, much given to hospitality, and has by his good services gained the affection of the people as much as any who had been before him in that post.

For Journals

Knowing from Mrs. Knight's account how extremely uncomfortable colonial travel was, can you imagine taking such a trip, if you could? Why or why not?

For Discussion

1.   We usually think of the frontier as the West; what elements in Mrs. Knight's description of her journey fit your idea of a frontier adventure?

2.   Mrs. Knight's journal is a unique window into the manners and mores of her fellow colonists. Using evidence from the text, which parts of the trip—and which responses of Mrs. Knight—do you find the most admirable? The most humorous? The most revealing of her character?

3.   Look back at William Bradford's description of meetings with Indians in Plymouth Plantation (Chapter 4). How would you compare his attitude toward them with Mrs. Knight's? What changes, if any, seem to have occurred in the relationships between Indians and colonists since Bradford's time?

4.   Mrs. Knight is going from Boston to Connecticut to New York, but she describes what she sees with the curiosity of someone from another country. What are her impressions of the food? The traveling conditions? The natural obstacles? The manners of the people she meets?

For Writing

1.   Go back to Chapter 3, and reread the excerpt from Tocqueville's *Democracy in America*. Choosing two or three specific incidents from Mrs. Knight's adventure, write an essay comparing her assessments of American behavior with his. Tocqueville is still considered an extremely accurate guide to the American character; explain what points he and Mrs. Knight make about this country that still seem valid to you.

2.   Referring back to discussion question 4, write an essay in which you discuss Mrs. Knight's reaction to the following features of her journey: the food; the way other people did business; what houses, clothing, and customs were like away from Boston. What judgments does she make? What seem to be her criteria for manners? What are her own manners like?

3. Look at the etching in Chapter 5 called *Keep Within Compass*, and write an essay in which you assess the ways in which Mrs. Knight strays beyond the boundaries set for traditional female behavior. Use the text of her journal as proof.

∞ FROM *The Treaty of Guadalupe Hidalgo* (1848)

The Treaty of Guadalupe Hidalgo marked the end of the Mexican-American War in 1848. The result of the war was ultimately the addition of Texas, California, and what are now the southwestern states to the United States. The treaty was intended to guarantee the rights of the Mexicans living in the formerly disputed areas, but Congress passed only parts of the treaty and did not include the civil rights provisions, which were never subsequently enforced. This selection includes ratified Articles VIII through XII, plus the original version of Article IX.

Articles VIII–XII

Article VIII

Mexicans now established in territories previously belonging to Mexico, and which remain for the future within the limits of the United States, as defined by the present treaty, shall be free to continue where they now reside, or to remove at any time to the Mexican Republic, retaining the property which they possess in the said territories, or disposing thereof, and removing the proceeds wherever they please, without their being subjected, on this account, to any contribution, tax or charge whatever.

Those who shall prefer to remain in the said territories, may either retain the title and rights of Mexican citizens, or acquire those of citizens of the United States. But they shall be under the obligation to make their election within one year from the date of the exchange of ratifications of this treaty; and those who shall remain in the said territories, after the expiration of that year, without having declared their intention to retain the character of Mexicans, shall be considered to have elected to become citizens of the United States.

In the said territories, property of every kind, now belonging to Mexicans, not established there, shall be inviolably respected. The present owners, the heirs of these and all Mexicans who may hereafter acquire said property by contract, shall enjoy with respect to it, guarantees equally ample as if the same belonged to citizens of the United States.

Article IX

The Mexicans who, in the territories aforesaid, shall not preserve the character of citizens of the Mexican Republic, conformably with what is stipulated in the preceding article, shall be incorporated into the Union of the United States and be admitted, at the proper time (to be judged of by the Congress of the United States) to the enjoyment of all the rights of citizens of the United States according to the principles of the Constitution; and in the mean time shall be maintained and protected in the free enjoyment of their liberty and property, and secured in the free exercise of their religion without restriction.

[*One of the amendments of the Senate struck out Article 10.*]

Article XI

5 Considering that a great part of the territories which, by the present Treaty, are to be comprehended for the future within the limits of the United States, is now occupied by savage tribes, who will hereafter be under the exclusive control of the Government of the United States, and whose incursions within the territory of Mexico would be prejudicial in the extreme; it is solemnly agreed that all such incursions shall be forcibly restrained by the Government of the United States, whensoever this may be necessary; and that when they cannot be prevented, they shall be punished by the said Government, and satisfaction for the same shall be exacted; all in the same way, and with equal diligence and energy; as if the same incursions were meditated or committed within its own territory against its own citizens.

It shall not be lawful, under any pretext whatever, for any inhabitant of the United States, to purchase or acquire any Mexican or any foreigner residing in Mexico, who may have been captured by Indians inhabiting the territory of either of the two Republics, nor to purchase or acquiring horses, mules, cattle or property of any kind, stolen within Mexican territory by such Indians.

And, in the event of any person or persons, captured within Mexican Territory by Indians, being carried into the territory of the United States, the Government of the latter engages and binds itself in the most solemn manner, so soon as it shall know such captives being within its territory, and shall be able so to do, through the faithful exercise of its influence and power, to rescue them and return them to their country, or deliver them to the agent or representative of the Mexican Government. The Mexican Authorities will, as far as practicable, give to the Government of the United States notice of such captures; and its agent shall pay the expenses incurred in the maintenance and transmission of the rescued captives; who, in the mean time, shall be treated with the utmost hospitality by the American authorities at the place where they may be. But if the Government of the United States, before receiving such notice from Mexico, should obtain intelligence through any other channel, of the existence of Mexican captives within its territory, it will proceed forthwith to effect their release and delivery to the Mexican agent, as above stipulated.

For the purpose of giving to these stipulations the fullest possible efficacy, thereby affording the security and redress demanded by their true spirit and intent, the Government of the United States will now and hereafter pass, without unnecessary delay, and always vigilantly enforce, such laws as the nature of the subject may require. And finally, the sacredness of this obligation shall never be lost sight of by the said Government, when providing for the removal of the Indians from any portion of the said territories, or for its being settled by citizens of the United States; but on the contrary special care shall then be taken not to place its Indian occupants under the necessity of seeking new homes, by committing those invasions which the United States have solemnly obliged themselves to restrain.

Article XII

In consideration of the extension acquired by the boundaries of the United States, as defined in the fifth Article of the present treaty, the Government of the United States engages to pay to that of the Mexican Republic the sum of fifteen Millions of Dollars.

Immediately after this treaty shall have been duly ratified by the Government of the Mexican Republic, the sum of three millions of dollars shall be paid to the said Government by that of the United States at the city of Mexico, in the gold or silver coin of Mexico. The remaining twelve millions of dollars shall be paid at the same place and in the same coin, in annual instalments of three millions of dollars each, together with interest on the same at the rate of six per centum per annum. This interest shall begin to run upon the whole sum of twelve millions, from the day of the ratification of the present treaty by the Mexican Government, and the first of the instalments shall be paid at the expiration of one year from the same day. Together with each annual instalment, as it falls due, the whole interest accruing on such instalment from the beginning shall also be paid.

Article IX Before Senate Amendment

Article IX

The Mexicans who, in the territories aforesaid, shall not preserve the character of citizens of the Mexican Republic, conformably with what is stipulated in the preceding Article, shall be incorporated into the Union of the United States, and admitted as soon as possible, according to the principles of the Federal Constitution, to the enjoyment of all the rights of citizens of the United States. In the mean time, they shall be maintained and protected in the enjoyment of their liberty, their property, and the civil rights now vested in them according to the Mexican laws. With respect to political rights, their condition shall be on an equality with that of the inhabitants of the other territories of the United States and at least equally good as that of the inhabitants of Louisiana and the Floridas, when these provinces, by transfer from the French Republic and the Crown of Spain, became territories of the United States.

The same most ample guaranty shall be enjoyed by all ecclesiastics and religious corporations or communities, as well in the discharge of the offices of their ministry, as in the enjoyment of their property of every kind, whether individual or corporate. This guaranty shall embrace all temples, houses and edifices dedicated to the Roman Catholic worship; as well as all property destined to its support, or to that of schools, hospitals and other foundations for charitable or beneficent purposes. No property of this nature shall be considered as having become the property of the American Government, or as subject to be; by it, disposed of or diverted to other uses.

Finally, the relations and communication between the Catholics living in the territories aforesaid, and their respective ecclesiastical authorities shall be open, free and exempt from all hindrance whatever, even although such authorities should reside within the limits of the Mexican Republic, as defined by this treaty; and this freedom shall continue, so long as a new demarcation of ecclesiastical districts shall not have been made, conformably with the laws of the Roman Catholic Church.

For Journals

Many Americans know very little about the Mexican-American War; what military conflict in American history are you most familiar with, and how do you know about it?

For Discussion

1. The original version of Article IX of the treaty promised that Mexicans in the ceded areas could become American citizens as soon as possible. The Article IX that Congress passed was revised to read that they would be made citizens "at the proper time (to be judged of by the Congress of the United States)" (paragraph 4). In practical terms, why do you think this change is significant to both sides?

2. Restate in your own words what you think Article XI says. Why do you think a treaty with the Mexicans devotes so much space to discussing the Indians who still live in the newly ceded territories?

3.   Working in a group with two or three other members of your class, underline the words and phrases in each section of the treaty that you think are the most important; in effect, look for the thesis of each section and for choices of vocabulary that seem to you especially revealing. Compare your list with those of other members of your group, and discuss the reasons for your choices.

For Writing

1.   The American doctrine of Manifest Destiny expressed, among other ideas, the belief that the United States was destined to extend from coast to coast, regardless of who was already living there. We usually think of this doctrine in terms of Indians and white settlers, but it also profoundly affected the lives of Mexican Americans. Research and write a paper on one of the following topics: the development of the Manifest Destiny doctrine; the life of General Vallejo, the transitional figure in Mexican California; the economic role of Mexican Americans in the Southwest (see the article by Flores in Chapter 6 for possible research references).

2.   Write a version of discussion question 3: Pick out the words and phrases from the articles of the treaty that seem to you most significant, and write an essay in which you explain the function of those phrases in the treaty—for example, how they depict the future of the relationships between the Americans, Mexicans, and Indians living in the ceded territories.

3.   Write an essay in which you compare Article IX as it was ratified by Congress with the original version. Here are some questions to consider: What changes were made between the original and final versions? What do you think would have been the effect of those changes—why do they matter? What guesses can you make as to the reasons the original version was not passed?

∽ FROM *Roughing It* (1872)

MARK TWAIN

Mark Twain (pseudonym of Samuel Clemens, 1835–1910), humorist, novelist, satirist, and lecturer, is one of the foremost writers in American literature, and probably the most beloved. He grew up in Missouri before the Civil War and worked as a printer and a Mississippi riverboat pilot before accompanying his brother Orion to Nevada in 1862. Roughing It, *with its adventures, tall tales, and absolutely American voice, came out in 1872.*

By eight o'clock everything was ready, and we were on the other side of the river. We jumped into the stage, the driver cracked his whip, and we bowled away and left "the States" behind us. It was a superb summer morning, and all the landscape was brilliant with sunshine. There was a freshness and breeziness, too, and an exhilarating sense of emancipation from all sorts of cares and responsibilities, that almost made us feel that the years we had spent in the close, hot city, toiling and slaving, had been wasted and thrown away. We were spinning along through Kansas, and in the course of an hour and a half we were fairly abroad on the great Plains. Just here the land was rolling—a grand sweep of regular elevations and depressions as far as the eye could reach—like the stately heave and swell of the ocean's bosom after a storm. And everywhere were cornfields, accenting with squares of deeper green, this limitless expanse of grassy land. But presently this sea upon dry ground was to lose its "rolling" character and stretch away for seven hundred miles as level as a floor!

Our coach was a great swinging and swaying stage, of the most sumptuous description—an imposing cradle on wheels. It was drawn by six handsome horses, and by the side of the driver sat the "conductor," the legitimate captain of the craft; for it was his business to take charge and care of the mails, baggage, express matter, and passengers. We three were the only passengers, this trip. We sat on the back seat, inside. About all the rest of the coach was full of mail-bags—for we had three days' delayed mails with us. Almost touching our knees, a perpendicular wall of mail matter rose up to the roof. There was a great pile of it strapped on top of the stage, and both the fore and hind boots were full. We had twenty-seven hundred pounds of it aboard, the driver said—"a little for Brigham, and Carson, and 'Frisco, but the heft of it for the Injuns, which is powerful troublesome 'thout they get plenty of truck to read." But as he just then got up a fearful convulsion of his countenance which was suggestive of a wink being swallowed by an earthquake, we guessed that his remark was intended to be facetious, and to mean that we would unload the most of our mail matter somewhere on the Plains and leave it to the Indians, or whosoever wanted it.

We changed horses every ten miles, all day long, and fairly flew over the hard, level road. We jumped out and stretched our legs every time the coach stopped, and so the night found us still vivacious and unfatigued.

It was now just dawn; and as we stretched our cramped legs full length on the mail-sacks, and gazed out through the windows across the wide wastes of greensward clad in cool, powdery mist, to where there was an expectant look in the eastern horizon, our perfect enjoyment took the form of a tranquil and contented ecstasy. The stage whirled along at a spanking gait, the breeze flapping curtains and suspended coats in a most exhilarating way; the cradle swayed and swung luxuriously, the pattering of the horses' hoofs, the cracking of the driver's whip, and his "Hi-yi! g'lang!" were music; the spinning ground and the waltzing trees appeared to give us a mute hurrah as we went by, and then slack up and look after us with interest, or envy, or something; and as we lay and smoked the pipe of peace and compared all this luxury with the years of tiresome city life that had gone before it, we felt that there was only one complete and satisfying happiness in the world, and we had found it. . . .

Really and truly, two thirds of the talk of drivers and conductors 5 had been about this man Slade, ever since the day before we reached Julesburg. In order that the Eastern reader may have a clear conception of what a Rocky Mountain desperado is, in his highest state of development, I will reduce all this mass of Overland gossip to one straightforward narrative, and present it in the following shape.

Slade was born in Illinois, of good parentage. At about twenty-six years of age he killed a man in a quarrel and fled the country. At St. Joseph, Missouri, he joined one of the early California-bound emigrant trains, and was given the post of trainmaster. One day on the Plains he had an angry dispute with one of his wagon-drivers, and both drew their revolvers. But the driver was the quicker artist, and had his weapon cocked first. So Slade said it was a pity to waste life on so small a matter, and proposed that the pistols be thrown on the ground and the quarrel settled by a fist-fight. The unsuspecting driver agreed, and threw down his pistol—whereupon Slade laughed at his simplicity, and shot him dead!

He made his escape, and lived a wild life for a while, dividing his time between fighting Indians and avoiding an Illinois sheriff, who had been sent to arrest him for his first murder. It is said that in one Indian battle he killed three savages with his own hand, and afterward cut their ears off and sent them, with his compliments, to the chief of the tribe.

Slade soon gained a name for fearless resolution, and this was sufficient merit to procure for him the important post of Overland division-agent at Julesburg, in place of Mr. Jules, removed. For some time previously, the company's horses had been frequently stolen, and the coaches delayed, by gangs of outlaws, who were wont to laugh at the idea of any man's having the temerity to resent such outrages. Slade resented them promptly. The outlaws soon found that the new agent was a man who did not fear anything that breathed the breath of life. He made short work of all offenders. The result was that delays ceased, the company's property was let alone, and no matter what happened or who suffered, Slade's coaches went through, every time! True, in order to bring about this wholesome change, Slade had to kill several men— some say three, others say four, and others six—but the world was the richer for their loss. The first prominent difficulty he had was with the ex-agent Jules, who bore the reputation of being a reckless and desperate man himself. Jules hated Slade for supplanting him, and a good fair occasion for a fight was all he was waiting for. By and by Slade dared to employ a man whom Jules had once discharged. Next, Slade seized a team of stage-horses which he accused Jules of having driven off and hidden somewhere for his own use. War was declared, and for a day or two the two men walked warily about the streets, seeking each other, Jules armed with a double-barreled shotgun, and Slade with his history-creating revolver. Finally, as Slade stepped into a store, Jules poured the contents of his gun into him from behind the door. Slade was pluck, and Jules got several bad pistol wounds in return. Then both men fell, and were carried to their respective lodgings, both swearing that better aim should do deadlier work next time. Both were bedridden a long time, but Jules got on his feet first, and gathering his possessions together, packed them on a couple of mules, and fled to the Rocky Mountains to gather strength in safety against the day of reckoning. For many months he was not seen or heard of, and was gradually dropped out of the remembrance of all save Slade himself. But Slade was not the man to forget him. On the contrary, common report said that Slade kept a reward standing for his capture, dead or alive!

After a while, seeing that Slade's energetic administration had restored peace and order to one of the worst divisions of the road, the Overland Stage Company transferred him to the Rocky Ridge division in the Rocky Mountains, to see if he could perform a like miracle there. It was the very paradise of outlaws and desperadoes. There was absolutely no semblance of law there. Violence was the rule. Force was the only recognized authority. The commonest misunderstandings were settled on the spot with the revolver or the knife. Murders were done in open day, and with sparkling frequency, and nobody thought of inquiring into them. It was considered that the parties who did the killing had their private reasons for it; for other people to meddle would have been looked upon as indelicate. After a murder, all that Rocky Mountain etiquette required of a spectator was, that he should help the gentleman bury his game—otherwise his churlishness would surely be remembered against him the first time he killed a man himself and needed a neighborly turn in interring him.

10   Slade took up his residence sweetly and peacefully in the midst of this hive of horse-thieves and assassins, and the very first time one of them aired his insolent swaggerings in his presence he shot him dead! He began a raid on the outlaws, and in a singularly short space of time he had completely stopped their depredations on the stage stock, recovered a large number of stolen horses, killed several of the worst desperadoes of the district, and gained such a dread ascendancy over the rest that they respected him, admired him, feared him, obeyed him! He wrought the same marvelous change in the ways of the community that had marked his administration at Overland City. He captured two men who had stolen Overland stock, and with his own hands he hanged them. He was supreme judge in his district, and he was jury

and executioner likewise—and not only in the case of offences against his employers, but against passing emigrants as well. On one occasion some emigrants had their stock lost or stolen, and told Slade, who chanced to visit their camp. With a single companion he rode to a ranch, the owners of which he suspected, and opening the door, commenced firing, killing three, and wounding the fourth.

From a bloodthirstily interesting little Montana book* I take this paragraph:

> While on the road, Slade held absolute sway. He would ride down to a station, get into a quarrel, turn the house out of windows, and maltreat the occupants most cruelly. The unfortunates had no means of redress, and were compelled to recuperate as best they could. On one of these occasions, it is said, he killed the father of the fine little half-breed boy, Jemmy, whom he adopted, and who lived with his widow after his execution. Stories of Slade's hanging men, and of innumerable assaults, shootings, stabbings and beatings, in which he was a principal actor, form part of the legends of the stage line. As for minor quarrels and shootings, it is absolutely certain that a minute history of Slade's life would be one long record of such practices.

Slade was a matchless marksman with a navy revolver. The legends say that one morning at Rocky Ridge, when he was feeling comfortable, he saw a man approaching who had offended him some days before—observe the fine memory he had for matters like that—and, "Gentlemen," said Slade, drawing, "it is a good twenty-yard shot—I'll clip the third button on his coat!" Which he did. The bystanders all admired it. And they all attended the funeral, too.

On one occasion a man who kept a little whiskey-shelf at the station did something which angered Slade—and went and made his will. A day or two afterward Slade came in and called for some brandy. The man reached under the counter (ostensibly to get a bottle—possibly to get something else), but Slade smiled upon him that peculiarly bland and satisfied smile of his which the neighbors had long ago learned to recognize as a death-warrant in disguise, and told him to "none of that!—pass out the high-priced article." So the poor bar-keeper had to turn his back and get the high-priced brandy from the shelf; and when he faced around again he was looking into the muzzle of Slade's pistol. "And the next instant," added my informant, impressively, "he was one of the deadest men that ever lived."

The stage-drivers and conductors told us that sometimes Slade would leave a hated enemy wholly unmolested, unnoticed and unmentioned, for weeks together—had done it once or twice at any rate. And some said they believed he did it in order to lull the victims into

---

* *The Vigilantes of Montana*, by Prof. Thos. J. Dimsdale. [Author's note]

unwatchfulness, so that he could get the advantage of them, and others said they believed he saved up an enemy that way, just as a schoolboy saves up a cake, and made the pleasure go as far as it would by gloating over the anticipation. One of these cases was that of a Frenchman who had offended Slade. To the surprise of everybody Slade did not kill him on the spot, but let him alone for a considerable time. Finally, however, he went to the Frenchman's house very late one night, knocked, and when his enemy opened the door, shot him dead—pushed the corpse inside the door with his foot, set the house on fire and burned up the dead man, his widow and three children! I heard this story from several different people, and they evidently believed what they were saying. It may be true, and it may not. "Give a dog a bad name," etc.

15   Slade was captured, once, by a party of men who intended to lynch him. They disarmed him, and shut him up in a strong log-house, and placed a guard over him. He prevailed on his captors to send for his wife, so that he might have a last interview with her. She was a brave, loving, spirited woman. She jumped on a horse and rode for life and death. When she arrived they let her in without searching her, and before the door could be closed she whipped out a couple of revolvers, and she and her lord marched forth defying the party. And then, under a brisk fire, they mounted double and galloped away unharmed!

In the fulness of time Slade's myrmidons captured his ancient enemy Jules, whom they found in a well-chosen hiding-place in the remote fastnesses of the mountains, gaining a precarious livelihood with his rifle. They brought him to Rocky Ridge, bound hand and foot, and deposited him in the middle of the cattle-yard with his back against a post. It is said that the pleasure that lit Slade's face when he heard of it was something fearful to contemplate. He examined his enemy to see that he was securely tied, and then went to bed, content to wait till morning before enjoying the luxury of killing him. Jules spent the night in the cattle-yard, and it is a region where warm nights are never known. In the morning Slade practised on him with his revolver, nipping the flesh here and there, and occasionally clipping off a finger, while Jules begged him to kill him outright and put him out of his misery. Finally Slade reloaded, and walking up close to his victim, made some characteristic remarks and then dispatched him. The body lay there half a day, nobody venturing to touch it without orders, and then Slade detailed a party and assisted at the burial himself. But he first cut off the dead man's ears and put them in his vest pocket, where he carried them for some time with great satisfaction. That is the story as I have frequently heard it told and seen it in print in California newspapers. It is doubtless correct in all essential particulars.

In due time we rattled up to a stage station, and sat down to breakfast with a half-savage, half-civilized company of armed and bearded mountaineers, ranchmen and station employ[ees]. The most gentlemanly-appearing, quiet and affable officer we had yet found along the road in the Overland Company's service was the person who sat at the head of the table, at my elbow. Never youth stared and shivered as I did when I heard them call him SLADE!

Here was romance, and I sitting face to face with it!—looking upon it—touching it—hobnobbing with it, as it were! Here, right by my side, was the actual ogre who, in fights and brawls and various ways, *had taken the lives of twenty-six human beings*, or all men lied about him! I suppose I was the proudest stripling that ever traveled to see strange lands and wonderful people.

He was so friendly and so gentle-spoken that I warmed to him in spite of his awful history. It was hardly possible to realize that this pleasant person was the pitiless scourge of the outlaws, the raw-head-and-bloody-bones the nursing mothers of the mountains terrified their children with. And to this day I can remember nothing remarkable about Slade except that his face was rather broad across the cheek bones, and that the cheek bones were low and the lips peculiarly thin and straight. But that was enough to leave something of an effect upon me, for since then I seldom see a face possessing those characteristics without fancying that the owner of it is a dangerous man.

The coffee ran out. At least it was reduced to one tin-cupful, and 20 Slade was about to take it when he saw that my cup was empty. He politely offered to fill it, but although I wanted it, I politely declined. I was afraid he had not killed anybody that morning, and might be needing diversion. But still with firm politeness he insisted on filling my cup, and said I had traveled all night and better deserved it than he—and while he talked he placidly poured the fluid, to the last drop. I thanked him and drank it, but it gave me no comfort, for I could not feel sure that he would not be sorry, presently, that he had given it away, and proceed to kill me to distract his thoughts from the loss. But nothing of the kind occurred. We left him with only twenty-six dead people to account for, and I felt a tranquil satisfaction in the thought that in so judiciously taking care of No. 1 at that breakfast-table I had pleasantly escaped being No. 27. Slade came out to the coach and saw us off, first ordering certain rearrangements of the mail-bags for our comfort, and then we took leave of him.

For Journals

What had you previously read of Twain's works? What did you know about him or his work?

For Discussion

1. Tall tales are very characteristic of Twain and of western humor. Why do you think the frontier lent itself to such wildly exaggerated stories about people and places?

2. How do you respond to the idea that giving a biography to Slade or any other western character gives a history to a frontier that doesn't have any history of its own?

3. How does Twain's encounter with the real Slade make us revise our expectations of what he would be like?

4. What image of the frontier do you think Twain's eastern readers had? Does Twain's way of writing reinforce or revise that image?

5. How does Twain's humor contribute to his portrait of himself as a man who knows absolutely nothing about the frontier? Why do you think he chose that way of presenting himself?

For Writing

1. Read a couple of other chapters from *Roughing It*—for example, on Mono Lake, on an earthquake in San Francisco, on Hawaii, on the desert, on striking it rich for ten days in a silver mine—and write a paper on how these episodes support or contradict your own expectations of what the frontier was like, what frontier heroes were like, and what American values these heroes lived by.

2. Write an essay about a trip you took when you were younger to a place—a national park or a city, for example—that made a big impression on you at the time. Write a paragraph about it as you experienced it in childhood and a paragraph on the same experience as you recall it now. Analyze both paragraphs, and write an essay examining the ways you revised your understanding of your own experience.

∞ *Giant Redwood Trees of California* (1874)

ALBERT BIERSTADT

Albert Bierstadt (1830–1902), was born in Germany but became famous in America as a painter of western scenery. After traveling and sketching the mountains of Europe, he went on a trail-making expedition to the West in 1859. He painted huge grand canvases, whose subjects included a Shoshone village, the last of the buffalo, the Rocky Mountains, and Yosemite, and his work was extremely popular.

For Journals

Who do you think was the original audience for this painting? What was your own first reaction to it?

For Discussion

1. Why do you think Bierstadt includes human beings in the painting? How would the overall impression given by the sequoias be changed if there were no figures of people at all?

2. How would the dramatic impact of the picture be changed if the figures in it were white rather than Native American? Why do you think Bierstadt made the choice he did?

3. How would you describe the mood conveyed by this painting? How do its features—the angle from which you view it, the vertical placement of the trees, the subject matter—contribute to that mood?

4. Today Americans take the sequoias for granted, but in the nineteenth century many easterners, faced with the spectacular western scenery of paintings like Bierstadt's, couldn't believe their eyes until they saw photographs of the same places. What would be the advantages and disadvantages of viewing a photograph of a scene like this versus a painting of the same scene?

For Writing

1. Compare this painting with the *California, the Cornucopia of the World* poster in Chapter 4, and write an analysis of their respective persuasive strategies: who their intended audiences might have been; what they told their audiences about California; what details conveyed that information; which one you find most effective, and why.

2. John Muir was the founder of the modern conservationist movement; his campaigns on behalf of Yosemite led to its establishment as a national park. Read John Muir's descriptions of Yosemite and the sequoias. Write an essay in which you include your analysis of his appreciation of the landscape, the relevance of his concerns as conservation issues today, and the attempt in his writing to revise the idea of land development as an unquestioned good.

∞ *Indian Treachery and Bloodshed* (1891)

POLICE GAZETTE

The Police Gazette *was a popular and lurid newspaper that was begun in 1846 but was at its height—or depth—in the 1880s and 1890s. It specialized in stories about crime, prostitution, and sports, was copiously illustrated, never had a story without a melodramatic title, and freely expressed the biases of its publisher, James Fox, who entertained lifelong prejudices against Chinese, African Americans, Jews, Native Americans, ministers, and college students, among others.*

The Indian war in South Dakota, so long anticipated, has at last become a reality, and with it has come the death of a number of brave troops of the United States Cavalry. The leader of the warriors was Big Foot and he and his braves tricked the troops into ambush. Then a wholesale slaughter began, the Indians being nearly annihilated, those who were not killed seeking refuge in the Bad Lands, where they will be frozen or starved out. As soon as the troops had cornered the Indians they fell upon them with Hotchkiss guns. The Indians fell in heaps but, determined to the last, they fought to the death even after being sorely wounded.

The saddest scene of the carnage was the killing of Captain George D. Wallace of the Seventh Cavalry, who was brutally tomahawked. Captain Wallace was appointed to the Military Academy from South Carolina in 1868 and upon being graduated in 1872 was commissioned a second lieutenant in the Seventh. He received his promotion to first lieutenant in 1876 and was commissioned captain in September 1885.

It is said that General Sheridan first remarked that "a dead Indian is the best Indian" and the action of the soldiers appears to coincide with Little Phil's views. The action teaches the lesson that if the Sioux are of any use at all they should be fairly dealt with, and if not, that they should at once be given free passes to the happy hunting grounds. As they speak highly of the happy hunting grounds, it might be as well to start them on the journey in any case, and then, if the decision be found unjust, to write them an apology.

For Journals

How does the news style of the *Police Gazette* compare to that of contemporary tabloid newspapers?

For Discussion

1. How would you describe the author's attitude toward the Indians? What values do you think the writer places on the lives of both Indians and soldiers?

2. How closely do you think the contents of the article and the illustration are related? What would you describe as the theme of the article? Of the illustration?

3. Look at the headline of the article and then at the first paragraph. How does the article support or revise the sentiments in the headline? Given the headline, what would you have expected?

4. Look at the illustration, starting at the top and working down to the bottom. How successfully does each grouping convey violent action? If there were no headline for the picture and text, what headline would you supply?

5. Who do you think read the *Police Gazette*? What would its audience have to do with the kinds of articles it published?

6. Suppose that Indians were writing the article and drawing the illustrations. In what specific ways do you think they would have revised the results?

For Writing

1.   At the library, look at a book with copies of George Catlin's paintings of Native Americans—*North American Indians* or *Catlin's Indians*, for example—and write a paper in which you discuss and compare any two of the portraits. Among the points for you to consider: What is your impression of the character and personality of the Native Americans in the pictures? Exactly what in the paintings conveyed that impression to you—color, body posture, expression, background? What words would you use to describe the mood of the paintings? Your college library would be a good source of material on the history of the various tribes and on Catlin's artistry.

2.   Research the development of the idea of the reservation: how it was developed, what treaties surrounded the setting up of reservations, or what conditions prevail on reservations today. If you write about reservations today, focus on one area of the country or one or two reservations.

∞ The Significance of the Frontier in American History (1893)

FREDERICK JACKSON TURNER

Frederick Jackson Turner (1862–1932) was born in Wisconsin and taught at the University of Wisconsin and Harvard. He presented this paper during the Chicago World's Fair of 1893 before the American Historical Association. Although Jackson did not publish a great deal, this essay alone made him one of the most famous historians in American studies.

In a recent bulletin of the Superintendent of the Census for 1890 appear these significant words: "Up to and including 1880 the country had a frontier of settlement, but at present the unsettled area has been so broken into by isolated bodies of settlement that there can hardly be said to be a frontier line. In the discussion of its extent, its westward movement, etc., it can not therefore, any longer have a place in the census reports." This brief official statement marks the closing of a great historic movement. Up to our own day American history has been in a large degree the history of the colonization of the Great West. The existence of an area of free land, its continuous recession, and the advance of American settlement westward, explain American development.

Behind institutions, behind constitutional forms and modifications, lie the vital forces that call these organs into life and shape them to meet changing conditions. The peculiarity of American institutions is, the fact that they have been compelled to adapt themselves to the changes of an expanding people—to the changes involved in crossing a continent, in winning a wilderness, and in developing at each area of this progress out of the primitive economic and political conditions of the frontier into the complexity of city life. Said Calhoun in 1817, "We are great, and rapidly—I was about to say fearfully—growing!" So saying, he touched the distinguishing feature of American life. All peoples show development; the germ theory of politics has been sufficiently emphasized. In the case of most nations, however, the development has occurred in a limited area; and if the nation has expanded, it has met other growing peoples whom it has conquered. But in the case of the United States we have a different phenomenon. Limiting our attention to the Atlantic coast, we have the familiar phenomenon of the evolution of institutions in a limited area, such as the rise of representative government; the differentiation of simple colonial governments into complex organs; the progress from primitive industrial society, without division of labor, up to manufacturing civilization. But we have in addition to this a recurrence of the process of evolution in each western area reached in the process of expansion. Thus American development has exhibited not merely advance along a single line, but a return to primitive conditions on a continually advancing frontier line, and a new development for that area. American social development has been continually beginning over again on the frontier. This perennial rebirth, this fluidity of American life, this expansion westward with its new opportunities, its continuous touch with the simplicity of primitive society, furnish the forces dominating American character. The true point of view in the history of this nation is not the Atlantic coast, it is the great West. Even the slavery struggle, which is made so exclusive an object of attention by writers like Professor von Holst, occupies its important place in American history because of its relation to westward expansion.

In this advance, the frontier is the outer edge of the wave—the meeting point between savagery and civilization. Much has been written about the frontier from the point of view of border warfare and the chase, but as a field for the serious study of the economist and the historian it has been neglected.

The American frontier is sharply distinguished from the European frontier—a fortified boundary line running through dense populations. The most significant thing about the American frontier is, that it lies at the hither edge of free land. In the census reports it is treated as the margin of that settlement which has a density of two or more to the square mile. The term is an elastic one, and for our purposes does not need sharp definition. We shall consider the whole frontier belt, including the Indian country and the outer margin of the "settled area" of the census reports. This paper will make no attempt to treat the subject exhaustively; its aim is simply to call attention to the frontier as a fertile field for investigation, and to suggest some of the problems which arise in connection with it.

In the settlement of America we have to observe how European life entered the continent, and how America modified and developed that life and reacted on Europe. Our early history is the study of European germs developing in an American environment. Too exclusive attention has been paid by institutional students to the Germanic origins, too little to the American factors. The frontier is the line of most rapid and effective Americanization. The wilderness masters the colonist. It finds him a European in dress, industries, tools, modes of travel, and thought. It takes him from the railroad car and puts him in the birch canoe. It strips off the garments of civilization and arrays him in the hunting shirt and the moccasin. It puts him in the log cabin of the Cherokee and Iroquois and runs an Indian palisade around him. Before long he has gone to planting Indian corn and plowing with a sharp stick; he shouts the war cry and takes the scalp in orthodox Indian fashion. In short, at the frontier the environment is at first too strong for the man. He must accept the conditions which it furnishes, or perish, and so he fits himself into the Indian clearings and follows the Indian trails. Little by little he transforms the wilderness, but the outcome is not the old Europe, not simply the development of Germanic germs, any more than the first phenomenon was a case of reversion to the Germanic mark. The fact is, that here is a new product that is American. At first, the frontier was the Atlantic coast. It was the frontier of Europe in a very real sense. Moving westward, the frontier became more and more American. As successive terminal moraines result from successive glaciations, so each frontier leaves its traces behind it, and when it becomes a settled area the region still partakes of the frontier characteristics. Thus the advance of the frontier has meant a steady movement away from the influence of Europe, a steady growth of independence on American lines. And to study this advance, the men who grew up under these conditions, and the political, economic, and social results of it, is to study the really American part of our history. . . .

The Frontier Furnishes a Field for Comparative Study of Social Development

At the Atlantic frontier one can study the germs of processes repeated at each successive frontier. We have the complex European life sharply precipitated by the wilderness into the simplicity of primitive conditions. The first frontier had to meet its Indian question, its question of the disposition of the public domain, of the means of intercourse with older settlements, of the extension of political organization, of religious and educational activity. And the settlement of these and similar questions for one frontier served as a guide for the next. The

American student needs not to go to the "prim little townships of Sleswick" for illustrations of the law of continuity and development. For example, he may study the origin of our land policies in the colonial land policy; he may see how the system grew by adapting the statutes to the customs of the successive frontiers. He may see how the mining experience in the lead regions of Wisconsin, Illinois, and Iowa was applied to the mining laws of the Rockies, and how our Indian policy has been a series of experimentations on successive frontiers. Each tier of new States has found in the older ones material for its constitutions. Each frontier has made similar contributions to American character, as will be discussed farther on.

But with all these similarities there are essential differences, due to the place element and the time element. It is evident that the farming frontier of the Mississippi Valley presents different conditions from the mining frontier of the Rocky Mountains. The frontier reached by the Pacific Railroad, surveyed into rectangles, guarded by the United States Army, and recruited by the daily immigrant ship, moves forward at a swifter pace and in a different way than the frontier reached by the birch canoe or the pack horse. The geologist traces patiently the shores of ancient seas, maps their areas, and compares the older and the newer. It would be a work worth the historian's labors to mark these various frontiers and in detail compare one with another. Not only would there result a more adequate conception of American development and characteristics, but invaluable additions would be made to the history of society.

Loria, the Italian economist, has urged the study of colonial life as an aid in understanding the stages of European development, affirming that colonial settlement is for economic science what the mountain is for geology, bringing to light primitive stratifications. "America," he says, "has the key to the historical enigma which Europe has sought for centuries in vain, and the land which has no history reveals luminously the course of universal history." There is much truth in this. The United States lies like a huge page in the history of society. Line by line as we read this continental page from west to east we find the record of social evolution. It begins with the Indian and the hunter; it goes on to tell of the disintegration of savagery by the entrance of the trader, the pathfinder of civilization; we read the annals of the pastoral stage in ranch life; the exploitation of the soil by the raising of unrotated crops of corn and wheat in sparsely settled farming communities; the intensive culture of the denser farm settlement; and finally the manufacturing organization with city and factory system. This page is familiar to the student of census statistics, but how little of it has been used by our historians. Particularly in eastern States this page is a palimpsest. What is now a manufacturing State was in an earlier decade an area of intensive farming. Earlier yet it had been a wheat area, and still earlier the "range" had attracted the cattle herder. Thus Wisconsin, now developing manufacture, is a State with varied agricultural interests. But earlier it was given over to almost exclusive grain-raising, like North Dakota at the present time.

Each of these areas has had an influence in our economic and political history; the evolution of each into a higher stage has worked political transformations. But what constitutional historian has made any adequate attempt to interpret political facts by the light of these social areas and changes?

The Atlantic frontier was compounded of fisherman, fur-trader, 10 miner, cattle-raiser, and farmer. Excepting the fisherman, each type of industry was on the march toward the West, impelled by an irresistible attraction. Each passed in successive waves across the continent. Stand at Cumberland Gap and watch the procession of civilization, marching single file—the buffalo following the trail to the salt springs, the Indian, the fur-trader and hunter, the cattle-raiser, the pioneer farmer—and the frontier has passed by. Stand at South Pass in the Rockies a century later and see the same procession with wider intervals between. The unequal rate of advance compels us to distinguish the frontier into the trader's frontier, the rancher's frontier, or the miner's frontier, and the farmer's frontier. When the mines and the cow pens were still near the fall line the traders' pack trains were tinkling across the Alleghenies, and the French on the Great Lakes were fortifying their posts, alarmed by the British trader's birch canoe. When the trappers scaled the Rockies, the farmer was still near the mouth of the Missouri. . . .

Land

The exploitation of the beasts took hunter and trader to the west, the exploitation of the grasses took the rancher west, and the exploitation of the virgin soil of the river valleys and prairies attracted the farmer. Good soils have been the most continuous attraction to the farmer's frontier. The land hunger of the Virginians drew them down the rivers into Carolina, in early colonial days; the search for soils took the Massachusetts men to Pennsylvania and to New York. As the eastern lands were taken up migration flowed across them to the west. Daniel Boone, the great backwoodsman, who combined the occupations of hunter, trader, cattle-raiser, farmer, and surveyor—learning, probably from the traders, of the fertility of the lands on the upper Yadkin, where the traders were wont to rest as they took their way to the Indians, left his Pennsylvania home with his father, and passed down the Great Valley road to that stream. Learning from a trader whose posts were on the Red River in Kentucky of its game and rich pastures, he pioneered the way for the farmers to that region. Thence he passed to the frontier of Missouri, where his settlement was long a landmark on the frontier. Here again he helped to open the way for civilization, finding salt licks, and trails, and land. His son was among the earliest trappers in the passes of the Rocky Mountains, and his party are said to have been the first to camp on the present site of Denver. His grandson, Col. A. J. Boone, of Colorado, was a power among the Indians of the Rocky Mountains, and was appointed an agent by the Government. Kit Carson's mother was a Boone. Thus this family epitomizes the backwoodsman's advance across the continent. . . .

Composite Nationality

First, we note that the frontier promoted the formation of a composite nationality for the American people. The coast was preponderantly English, but the later tides of continental immigration flowed across to the free lands. This was the case from the early colonial days. The Scotch-Irish and the Palatine Germans, or "Pennsylvania Dutch," furnished the dominant element in the stock of the colonial frontier. With these peoples were also the freed indentured servants, or redemptioners, who at the expiration of their time of service passed to the frontier. Governor Spottswood of Virginia writes in 1717, "The inhabitants of our frontiers are composed generally of such as have been transported hither as servants, and, being out of their time, settle themselves where land is to be taken up and that will produce the necessarys of life with little labour." Very generally these redemptioners were of non-English stock. In the crucible of the frontier the immigrants were Americanized, liberated, and fused into a mixed race, English in neither nationality nor characteristics. The process has gone on from the early days to our own. Burke and other writers in the middle of the eighteenth century believed that Pennsylvania was "threatened with the danger of being wholly foreign in language, manners, and perhaps even inclinations." The German and Scotch-Irish elements in the frontier of the South were only less great. In the middle of the present century the German element in Wisconsin was already so considerable that leading publicists looked to the creation of a German state out of the commonwealth by concentrating their colonization. Such examples teach us to beware of misinterpreting the fact that there is a common English speech in America into a belief that the stock is also English.

Industrial Independence

In another way the advance of the frontier decreased our dependence on England. The coast, particularly of the South, lacked diversified industries, and was dependent on England for the bulk of its supplies. In the South there was even a dependence on the Northern colonies for articles of food. Governor Glenn, of South Carolina, writes in the middle of the eighteenth century: "Our trade with New York and Philadelphia was of this sort, draining us of all the little money and bills we could gather from other places for their bread, flour, beer, hams, bacon, and other things of their produce, all which, except beer, our new townships begin to supply us with, which are settled with very industrious and thriving Germans. This no doubt diminishes the number of shipping and the appearance of our trade, but it is far from being a detriment to us." Before long the frontier created a demand for merchants. As it retreated from the coast it became less and less possible for England to bring her supplies directly to the consumer's wharfs, and carry away staple crops, and staple crops began to give way to diversified agriculture for a time. The effect of this phase of the frontier action upon the northern section is perceived when we realize how the advance of the frontier aroused seaboard cities like Boston, New York, and Baltimore, to engage in rivalry for what Washington called "the extensive and valuable trade of a rising empire." . . .

Growth of Democracy

But the most important effect of the frontier has been in the promotion of democracy here and in Europe. As has been indicated, the frontier is productive of individualism. Complex society is precipitated by the wilderness into a kind of primitive organization based on the family. The tendency is anti-social. It produces antipathy to control, and particularly to any direct control. The tax gatherer is viewed as a representative of oppression. Professor Osgood, in an able article, has pointed out that the frontier conditions prevalent in the colonies are important factors in the explanation of the American Revolution, where individual liberty was sometimes confused with absence of all effective government. The same conditions aid in explaining the difficulty of instituting a strong government in the period of the confederacy. The frontier individualism has from the beginning promoted democracy.

The frontier States that came into the Union in the first quarter of a   15 century of its existence came in with democratic suffrage provisions, and had reactive effects of the highest importance upon the older States whose peoples were being attracted there. An extension of the franchise became essential. It was *western* New York that forced an extension of suffrage in the constitutional convention of that State in 1821; and it was *western* Virginia that compelled the tide-water region to put a more liberal suffrage provision in the constitution framed in 1830, and to give to the frontier region a more nearly proportionate representation with the tide-water aristocracy. The rise of democracy as an effective force in the nation came in with western preponderance under Jackson and William Henry Harrison, and it meant the triumph of the frontier—with all of its good and with all of its evil elements. . . .

So long as free land exists, the opportunity for a competency exists, and economic power secures political power. But the democracy born of free land, strong in selfishness and individualism, intolerant of administrative experience and education, and pressing individual liberty beyond its proper bounds, has its dangers as well as its benefits. Individualism in America has allowed a laxity in regard to governmental affairs which has rendered possible the spoils system and all the manifest evils that follow from the lack of a highly developed civic spirit. In this connection may be noted also the influence of frontier conditions in permitting lax business honor, inflated paper currency and wild-cat banking. The colonial and revolutionary frontier was the region whence emanated many of the worst forms of an evil currency. The West in the War of 1812 repeated the phenomenon on the frontier of that day, while the speculation and the wild-cat banking of the period of the crisis of 1837 occurred on the new frontier belt of the next tier of States. Thus each one of the periods of lax financial integrity coincides with periods when a new set of frontier communities had arisen, and coincides in area with these successive frontiers, for the most part. The recent Populist agitation is a case in point. Many a State that now declines any connection with the tenets of the Populists, itself adhered to such ideas in an earlier stage of the development of the State. A primitive society can hardly be expected to show the intelligent appreciation of the complexity of business interests in a developed society. The continual recurrence of these areas of paper-money agitation is another evidence that the frontier can be isolated and studied as a factor in American history of the highest importance. . . .

Intellectual Traits

From the conditions of frontier life came intellectual traits of profound importance. The works of travelers along each frontier from colonial days onward describe certain common traits, and these traits have, while softening down, still persisted as survivals in the place of their origin, even when a higher social organization succeeded. The result is that to the frontier the American intellect owes its striking characteristics. That coarseness and strength combined with acuteness and inquisitiveness; that practical, inventive turn of mind, quick to find expedients; that masterful grasp of material things, lacking in the artistic but powerful to effect great ends; that restless, nervous energy; that dominant individualism, working for good and for evil, and withal that buoyancy and exuberance which comes with freedom—these are traits of the frontier. Since the days when the fleet of Columbus sailed into the waters of the New World, America has been another name for opportunity, and the people of the United States have taken their tone from the incessant expansion which has not only been open but has even been forced upon them. He would be a rash prophet who should assert that the expansive character of American life has now entirely ceased. Movement has been its dominant fact, and, unless this training has no effect upon a people, the American energy will continually demand a wider field for its exercise. But never again will such gifts of free land offer themselves. For a moment, at the frontier, the bonds of custom are broken and unrestraint is triumphant. There is not *tabula rasa*. The stubborn American environment is there with its imperious summons to accept its conditions; the inherited ways of doing things are also there; and yet, in spite of environment, and in spite of custom, each frontier did indeed furnish a new field of opportunity, a gate of escape from the bondage of the past; and freshness, and confidence, and scorn of older society, impatience of its restraints and its ideas, and indifference to its lessons, have accompanied the frontier. What the Mediterranean Sea was to the Greeks, breaking the bond of custom, offering new experiences, calling out new institutions and activities, that, and more, the ever retreating frontier has been to the United States directly, and to the nations of Europe more remotely. And now, four centuries from the discovery of America, at the end of a hundred years of life under the Constitution, the frontier has gone, and with its going has closed the first period of American history.

For Journals

What is your own idea of what the American frontier represents? Cowboys and Indians? The Gold Rush? The space program? Movie westerns?

For Discussion

1.   Turner saw the existence of a frontier as crucial to the formation of the American character and American democracy. What are his premises in this argument? What evidence does he provide to support them?

2.   How do you respond to Turner's assertion that the frontier was the meeting point between civilization and savagery "the outer edge of the wave—" (paragraph 3)? How positively do you regard the idea of settlers moving through the frontier in order to create a different and distinctly American civilization?

3.   Why does Turner see the life of Daniel Boone as a prototype of the frontiersman? What combination of elements makes Boone, in Turner's thesis, so suitable an example of the positive side of westward expansion?

4.   How do you think Turner defines the idea of progress in American civilization? Progress from what to what? What do you think of as an example of progress in America?

5.   One writer has said that Turner's essay is not *an* explanation of American history but rather *the* explanation of American history. Why would an analysis of the frontier be an analysis of American history altogether?

6.   Turner said that the frontier had made the American character expansive, and that once the free land disappeared, Americans would have to find other ways of stretching their horizons. Where do you think Americans have turned to find psychological substitutions for the western frontier?

For Writing

1.   Watch a video of one of the following movies: *High Noon; Shane; A Fistful of Dollars; Little Big Man; She Wore a Yellow Ribbon; Unforgiven.* Then write an essay in which you address the following issues: What picture does the movie give of life in the West? How closely does that picture coincide with your own idea of that life? What are the primary ethical and social values expressed in the movie, and who in the film embodies them?

2.   Since it was written, there have been many revisions of Turner's thesis. Read one of them, such as David Potter's *People of Plenty,* and then write your own evaluation of whether the revision refutes all of Turner's claims effectively. Then write your own response to Turner's ideas.

∞ The Thesis Disputed (1949)

RICHARD HOFSTADTER

Richard Hofstadter (1916–1970) was a highly original American historian who spent his career at Columbia University. His amazingly diverse body of work paid particular attention to the importance of ideas in American history and to the development of political institutions. He won the Pulitzer Prize twice. When he wrote this essay, the most famous analysis of Frederick Jackson Turner's thesis on the role of the frontier in American history, the thesis had just undergone a period of attack by other historians. Hofstadter was able to appreciate the significance as well as the faults of Turner's theory.

American historical writing in the past century has produced two major theories or models of understanding, the economic interpretation of politics associated with Charles A. Beard, and the frontier interpretation of American development identified with Frederick Jackson Turner. Both views have had a pervasive influence upon American thinking, but Beard himself felt that Turner's original essay on the frontier had "a more profound influence on thought about American history than any other essay or volume ever written on the subject." It is the frontier thesis that has embodied the predominant American view of the American past. . . .

American evolution, Turner believed, had been a repeated return to primitive conditions on a continually receding frontier line, a constant repetition of development from simple conditions to a complex society. From this perennial rebirth and fluidity of American life, and from its continual re-exposure to the simplicity of primitive society, had come the forces dominant in the American character. And as the frontier advanced, society moved steadily away from European influences, grew steadily on distinctive American lines. To study this advance and the men who had been fashioned by it was "to study the really American part of our history."

Of all the effects of the frontier, the most important was that it promoted democracy and individualism. So long as free land existed, there was always opportunity for a man to acquire a competency, and economic power secured political power. Each succeeding frontier furnished "a new field of opportunity, a gate of escape from the bondage of the past." The lack of binding tradition and organized restraints promoted a distinctively American passion for individual freedom, antipathy to direct control from outside, aggressive self-interest, and intolerance of education and administrative experience. But by the year 1890, this process had come to an end; the frontier, the hither edge of unsettled land, no longer existed, and with its passing the first epoch of American history had closed. . . .

The initial plausibility of the Turner thesis lies in the patent fact that no nation could spend more than a century developing an immense continental empire without being deeply affected by it. Few critics question the great importance of the inland empire, or that Turner originally performed a service for historical writing by directing attention to it. Many accept Turner's emphasis on the frontier as one of several valid but limited perspectives on American history. But it has been forcefully denied that the frontier deserves any special preeminence among several major factors in "explaining" American development. The question has also been raised (and frequently answered in the negative) whether Turner analyzed the frontier process itself clearly or correctly.

It became plain, as new thought and research was brought to bear 5 upon the problem, that the frontier theory, as an analytic device, was a blunt instrument. The terms with which the Turnerians dealt—the frontier, the West, individualism, the American character—were vague at the outset, and as the Turnerian exposition developed, they did not receive increasingly sharp definition. Precisely because Turner defined the frontier so loosely ("the term," he said, "is an elastic one"), he could claim so much for it. At times he referred to the frontier literally as the edge of the settled territory having a population density of two to the square mile. But frequently he identified "the frontier" and "the West," so that areas actually long settled could be referred to as frontier. At times he spoke of both the "frontier" and the "West" not as places or areas, but as a social process: "The West, at bottom, is a form of society rather than an area." When this definition is followed to its logical conclusion, the development of American society is "explained" by "a form of society"—certainly a barren tautology. Again, at times Turner assimilated such natural resources as coal, oil, timber, to the idea of "the West"; in this way the truism that natural wealth has an important bearing upon a nation's development and characteristics was subtly absorbed into the mystique of the frontier and took on the guise of a major insight.

However, the central weakness of Turner's thesis was in its intellectual isolationism. Having committed himself to an initial overemphasis on the uniqueness of the historical development of the United States, Turner compounded the error by overemphasizing the frontier as a factor in this development. The obsession with uniqueness, the subtly demagogic stress on "the truly American part of our history," diverted the attention of historical scholarship from the possibilities of comparative social history; it offered no opportunity to explain why so many features of American development—for example, the rise of democracy in the nineteenth century—were parallel to changes in countries that did not have a contiguous frontier. Historians were encouraged to omit a host of basic influences common to both American and Western European development—the influence of Protestantism and the Protestant ethic, the inheritance from English republicanism, the growth of industrialism and urbanism. More than this, factors outside the frontier process that contributed to the singularity of American history were skipped over: the peculiar American federal structure, the slave system and the Southern caste complex, immigration and ethnic heterogeneity, the unusually capitalistic and speculative character of American agriculture, the American inheritance of *laissez faire*. The interpretation seems particularly weak for the corporate-industrial phase of American history that followed the Civil War. Indeed, if the historian's range of vision had to be limited to one explanatory idea, as it fortunately does not, one could easily argue that the business corporation was the dominant dynamic factor in American development during this period.

As a form of geographical determinism, the frontier interpretation is vulnerable on still another ground. If the frontier alone was a self-sufficient source of democracy and individualism, whatever the institutions and ideas the frontiersmen brought with them, frontiers elsewhere ought to have had a similar effect. The early frontier of seignorial French Canada, the South American frontier, and the Siberian frontier should have fostered democracy and individualism. The frontier should have forged the same kind of democracy when planters came to Mississippi as when yeomen farmers came to Illinois. Turner's dictum, "American democracy came out of the American forest," proved to be a questionable improvement upon the notion of his predecessors that it came out of the German forest. Plainly the whole complex of institutions, habits and ideas that men brought to the frontier was left out of his formula, and it was these things, not bare geography, that had been decisive. Turner's analysis, as George Warren Pierson aptly put it, hung too much on real estate, not enough on a state of mind. . . .

One of the most criticized aspects of Turner's conception of American history, the so-called safety-valve thesis, maintains that the availability of free land as a refuge for the oppressed and discontented has alleviated American social conflicts, minimized industrial strife, and contributed to the backwardness of the American labor movement. As Turner expressed it, the American worker was never compelled to accept inferior wages because he could "with a slight effort" reach free country and set up in farming. "Whenever social conditions tended to crystallize in the East, whenever capital tended to impede the freedom of the mass, there was this gate of escape to the free conditions of the frontier," where "free lands promoted individualism, economic equality, freedom to rise, democracy."

The expression "free land" is itself misleading. Land was relatively cheap in the United States during the nineteenth century, but the difference between free land and cheap land was crucial. Up to 1820 the basic price of land was $2.00 an acre, and for years afterward it was $1.25. Slight as it may seem, this represented a large sum to the Eastern worker, whose wage was generally about $1.00 a day. Economic historians have estimated that during the 1850s, $1,000 represented a fairly typical cost for setting up a farm on virgin prairie land, or buying an established one; and the cost of transporting a worker's family from, say, Massachusetts or New York to Illinois or Iowa was a serious additional burden. Farming, moreover, is no enterprise for an amateur, nor one at which he has a good chance of success. The value of "free land" in alleviating distress has been challenged by several writers who have pointed out that periods of depression were the very periods when it was most difficult for the Eastern worker to move. Scattered instances of working-class migration to the West can be pointed to, but detailed studies of the origins of migrants have failed to substantiate the Turner thesis. . . .

Finally, Turner acknowledged but failed to see the full importance 10 for his thesis of the fact that the United States not only had a frontier but was a frontier—a major outlet for the countries of Western Europe during the nineteenth century. From 1820 to 1929, the total European emigration to the United States was more than 37,500,000—a number only a million short of the entire population of the United States in 1870. In one decade alone, 1901–1910, 8,795,000 people came from Europe. If

Europe shared to such a major extent in this safety-valve economy, its uniqueness for American development must be considerably modified. The mingling of peoples that took place in the United States must be placed alongside the presence of "free land" in explaining American development; the closure of the American gates after the First World War becomes an historical event of broader significance than the disappearance of the frontier line in 1890. And the facts of immigration probably provide a better key to the character of the American labor movement than any speculation about the effects of "free land" upon workers who could not reach it.

It should be added, in justice to Turner, that his historical writing was better than his frontier thesis, and not least because he regularly made use in practice of historical factors which were not accounted for in his theory. Although he often stated his ideas with the vigor of a propagandist, his was not a doctrinaire mind, and he was willing, as time went on, to add new concepts to his analysis. In 1925 he went so far as to admit the need of "an urban reinterpretation of our history." "I hope," he frequently said, "to propagate inquiry, not to produce disciples." In fact he did both, but he propagated less inquiry among his disciples than among his critics.

For Journals

Hofstadter says he is revising Turner, but in effect he comes up with a thesis of his own. How would you state Hofstadter's central idea?

For Discussion

1.   What do you think Hofstadter means when he states that, as an analytic device, Turner's frontier theory is "a blunt instrument" (paragraph 5)? What kinds of problems in Turner's approach does that phrase suggest?

2.   Hofstadter accuses Turner of intellectual isolationism. In revising Turner's thesis, what kinds of evidence does he include that he says Turner failed to consider in developing his ideas?

3.   Hofstadter revises Turner but does not reject him. Where do you find points of agreement or overlap in their theories?

4.   Hofstadter thought that Turner overstated the significance of rural life in American history at the expense of the city. Which do you think—rural life or urban life—was more significant as a source of values? Of power?

5.   Based on your other readings in this book, what do you think of Hofstadter's assertion that emigration to America of millions of people from Europe is a better key to the American character than the idea of available free land in the West?

6. Look back over Turner's thesis and Hofstadter's revision. Which one is more satisfying to you? Intellectually, are they equally interesting? Which one coincides more with your own ideas about why America developed as it did?

For Writing

1. In your college library, look for primary and secondary materials, including books, periodicals, or photographs, as material for a research paper on one of the following topics: African American cowboys and the West; the great Mexican ranches of California; the Indian cultures of the Southwest; or any other group that is not a part of Turner's thesis. You could focus on an aspect of this group's life in frontier days (for example, influential individuals, significant events, or contributions to American culture). How does being aware of the group cause you to revise your image of the frontier?

2. Turner and Hofstadter are both interested in the idea of American progress. Write an essay about a change in American life that has come about in your own lifetime that you think represents real progress. Is it a result of technology, or of social and political change? Why do you think this change is important? For contrast, you might ask someone in your parents' generation what they think of as a major contribution to progress in America.

∞ *Coda: Wilderness Letter* (1960)

WALLACE STEGNER

Wallace Stegner (1909–1993) grew up in Canada and the American West, and much of his writing, including his novels and essays, reflects his love for the wilderness. Stegner was active in the conservationist movement, often working with photographer Ansel Adams to promote national parks and a balance between development and the preservation of open space. The recipient of both the National Book Award and the Pulitzer Prize, Stegner founded the Creative Writing Program at Stanford University.

Los Altos, Calif.
Dec. 3, 1960

David E. Pesonen
Wildland Research Center
Agricultural Experiment Station
243 Mulford Hall
University of California
Berkeley 4, Calif.

Dear Mr. Pesonen:

I believe that you are working on the wilderness portion of the Outdoor Recreation Resources Review Commission's report. If I may, I should like to urge some arguments for wilderness preservation that involve recreation, as it is ordinarily conceived, hardly at all. Hunting, fishing, hiking, mountain-climbing, camping, photography, and the enjoyment of natural scenery will all, surely, figure in your report. So will the wilderness as a genetic reserve, a scientific yardstick by which we may measure the world in its natural balance against the world in its man-made imbalance. What I want to speak for is not so much the wilderness uses, valuable as those are, but the wilderness *idea*, which is a resource in itself. Being an intangible and spiritual resource, it will seem mystical to the practical-minded—but then anything that cannot be moved by a bulldozer is likely to seem mystical to them.

I want to speak for the wilderness idea as something that has helped form our character and that has certainly shaped our history as a people. It has no more to do with recreation than churches have to do with recreation, or than the strenuousness and optimism and expansiveness of what historians call the "American Dream" have to do with recreation. Nevertheless, since it is only in this recreation survey that the values of wilderness are being compiled, I hope you will permit me to insert this idea between the leaves, as it were, of the recreation report.

Something will have gone out of us as a people if we ever let the remaining wilderness be destroyed; if we permit the last virgin forests to be turned into comic books and plastic cigarette cases; if we drive the few remaining members of the wild species into zoos or to extinction; if we pollute the last clear air and dirty the last clean streams and push our paved roads through the last of the silence, so that never again will Americans be free in their own country from the noise, the exhausts, the stinks of human and automotive waste. And so that never again can we have the chance to see ourselves single, separate, vertical and individual in the world, part of the environment of trees and rocks and soil, brother to the other animals, part of the natural world and competent to belong in it. Without any remaining wilderness we are committed wholly, without chance for even momentary reflection and rest, to a headlong drive into our technological termite-life, the Brave New World of a completely man-controlled environment. We need wilderness preserved—as much of it as is still left, and as many kinds—because it was the challenge against which our character as a people was formed. The reminder and the reassurance that it is still there is good for our spiritual health even if we never once in ten years set foot in it. It is good for us when we are young, because of the incomparable sanity it can bring briefly, as vacation and rest, into our insane lives. It is important to us when we are old simply because it is there—important, that is, simply as idea.

We are a wild species, as Darwin pointed out. Nobody ever tamed or domesticated or scientifically bred us. But for at least three millennia we have been engaged in a cumulative and ambitious race to modify and gain control of our environment, and in the process we have come close to domesticating ourselves. Not many people are likely, any more, to look upon what we call "progress" as an unmixed blessing. Just as surely as it has brought us increased comfort and more material goods, it has brought us spiritual losses, and it threatens now to become the Frankenstein that will destroy us. One means of sanity is to retain a hold on the natural world, to remain, insofar as we can, good animals. Americans still have that chance, more than many peoples; for while we were demonstrating ourselves the most efficient and ruthless environment-busters in history, and slashing and burning and cutting our way through a wilderness continent, the wilderness was working on us. It remains in us as surely as Indian names remain on the land. If the abstract dream of human liberty and human dignity became, in America, something more than an abstract dream, mark it down at least partially to the fact that we were in subtle ways subdued by what we conquered.

The Connecticut Yankee, sending likely candidates from King 5 Arthur's unjust kingdom to his Man Factory for rehabilitation, was over-optimistic, as he later admitted. These things cannot be forced, they have to grow. To make such a man, such a democrat, such a believer in human individual dignity, as Mark Twain himself, the frontier was necessary, Hannibal and the Mississippi and Virginia City, and reaching out from those the wilderness; the wilderness as opportunity and as idea, the thing that has helped to make an American different from and, until we forget it in the roar of our industrial cities, more fortunate than other men. For an American, insofar as he is new and different at all, is a civilized man who has renewed himself in the wild. The American experience has been the confrontation by old peoples and cultures of a world as new as if it had just risen from the sea. That gave us our hope and our excitement, and the hope and excitement can be passed on to newer Americans, Americans who never saw any phase of the frontier. But only so long as we keep the remainder of our wild as a reserve and a promise—a sort of wilderness bank.

As a novelist, I may perhaps be forgiven for taking literature as a reflection, indirect but profoundly true, of our national consciousness. And our literature, as perhaps you are aware, is sick, embittered, losing its mind, losing its faith. Our novelists are the declared enemies of their society. There has hardly been a serious or important novel in this century that did not repudiate in part or in whole American technological culture for its commercialism, its vulgarity, and the way in which it has dirtied a clean continent and a clean dream. I do not expect that the preservation of our remaining wilderness is going to cure this condition. But the mere example that we can as a nation apply some other criteria than commercial and exploitative considerations would be heartening to many Americans, novelists or otherwise. We need to demonstrate our acceptance of the natural world, including ourselves; we need the spiritual refreshment that being natural can produce. And one of the best places for us to get that is in the wilderness where the fun houses, the bulldozers, and the pavements of our civilization are shut out.

Sherwood Anderson, in a letter to Waldo Frank in the 1920s, said it better than I can. "Is it not likely that when the country was new and men were often alone in the fields and the forest they got a sense of bigness outside themselves that has now in some way been lost. . . . Mystery whispered in the grass, played in the branches of trees overhead, was caught up and blown across the American line in clouds of dust at evening on the prairies. . . . I am old enough to remember tales that strengthen my belief in a deep semi-religious influence that was formerly at work among our people. The flavor of it hangs over the best work of Mark Twain. . . . I can remember old fellows in my home town speaking feelingly of an evening spent on the big empty plains. It had taken the shrillness out of them. They had learned the trick of quiet. . . ."

We could learn it too, even yet; even our children and grandchildren could learn it. But only if we save, for just such absolutely non-recreational, impractical, and mystical uses as this, all the wild that still remains to us.

It seems to me significant that the distinct downturn in our literature from hope to bitterness took place almost at the precise time when the frontier officially came to an end, in 1890, and when the American way of life had begun to turn strongly urban and industrial. The more urban it has become, and the more frantic with technological change, the sicker and more embittered our literature, and I believe our people, have become. For myself, I grew up on the empty plains of Saskatchewan and Montana and in the mountains of Utah, and I put a very high valuation on what those places gave me. And if I had not been able periodically to renew myself in the mountains and deserts of western America I would be very nearly bughouse. Even when I can't get to the back country, the thought of the colored deserts of southern Utah, or the reassurance that there are still stretches of prairie where the world can be instantaneously perceived as disk and bowl, and where the little but intensely important human being is exposed to the five directions and the thirty-six winds, is a positive consolation. The idea alone can sustain me. But as the wilderness areas are progressively exploited or "improved," as the jeeps and bulldozers of uranium prospectors scar up the deserts and the roads are cut into the alpine timberlands, and as the remnants of the unspoiled and natural world are progressively eroded, every such loss is a little death in me. In us.

10   I am not moved by the argument that those wilderness areas which have already been exposed to grazing or mining are already deflow-

ered, and so might as well be "harvested." For mining I cannot say much good except that its operations are generally short-lived. The extractable wealth is taken and the shafts, the tailings, and the ruins left, and in a dry country such as the American West the wounds men make in the earth do not quickly heal. Still, they are only wounds; they aren't absolutely mortal. Better a wounded wilderness than none at all. And as for grazing, if it is strictly controlled so that it does not destroy the ground cover, damage the ecology, or compete with the wildlife it is in itself nothing that need conflict with the wilderness feeling or the validity of the wilderness experience. I have known enough range cattle to recognize them as wild animals; and the people who herd them have, in the wilderness context, the dignity of rareness; they belong on the frontier, moreover, and have a look of rightness. The invasion they make on the virgin country is a sort of invasion that is as old as Neolithic man, and they can, in moderation, even emphasize a man's feeling of belonging to the natural world. Under surveillance, they can belong; under control, they need not deface or mar. I do not believe that in wilderness areas where grazing has never been permitted, it should be permitted; but I do not believe either that an otherwise untouched wilderness should be eliminated from the preservation plan because of limited existing uses such as grazing which are in consonance with the frontier condition and image.

Let me say something on the subject of the kinds of wilderness worth preserving. Most of those areas contemplated are in the national forests and in high mountain country. For all the usual recreational purposes, the alpine and forest wildernesses are obviously the most important, both as genetic banks and as beauty spots. But for the spiritual renewal, the recognition of identity, the birth of awe, other kinds will serve every bit as well. Perhaps, because they are less friendly to life, more abstractly nonhuman, they will serve even better. On our Saskatchewan prairie, the nearest neighbor was four miles away, and at night we saw only two lights on all the dark rounding earth. The earth was full of animals—field mice, ground squirrels, weasels, ferrets, badgers, coyotes, burrowing owls, snakes. I knew them as my little brothers, as fellow creatures, and I have never been able to look upon animals in any other way since. The sky in that country came clear down to the ground on every side, and it was full of great weathers, and clouds, and winds, and hawks. I hope I learned something from knowing intimately the creatures of the earth; I hope I learned something from looking a long way, from looking up, from being much alone. A prairie like that, one big enough to carry the eye clear to the sinking, rounding horizon, can be as lonely and grand and simple in its forms as the sea. It is as good a place as any for the wilderness experience to happen; the vanishing prairie is as worth preserving for the wilderness idea as the alpine forests.

So are great reaches of our western deserts, scarred somewhat by prospectors but otherwise open, beautiful, waiting, close to whatever God you want to see in them. Just as a sample, let me suggest the Robbers' Roost country in Wayne County, Utah, near the Capitol Reef National Monument. In that desert climate the dozer and jeep tracks will not soon melt back into the earth, but the country has a way of making the scars insignificant. It is a lovely and terrible wilderness, such a wilderness as Christ and the prophets went out into; harshly and beautifully colored, broken and worn until its bones are exposed, its great sky without a smudge or taint from Technocracy, and in hidden corners and pockets under its cliffs the sudden poetry of springs. Save a piece of country like that intact, and it does not matter in the slightest that only a few people every year will go into it. That is precisely its value. Roads would be a desecration, crowds would ruin it. But those who haven't the strength or youth to go into it and live can simply sit and look. They can look two hundred miles, clear into Colorado; and looking down over the cliffs and canyons of the San Rafael Swell and the Robbers' Roost they can also look as deeply into themselves as anywhere I know. And if they can't even get to the places on the Aquarius Plateau where the present roads will carry them, they can simply contemplate the *idea,* take pleasure in the fact that such a timeless and uncontrolled part of earth is still there.

These are some of the things wilderness can do for us. That is the reason we need to put into effect, for its preservation, some other principle than the principles of exploitation or "usefulness" or even recreation. We simply need that wild country available to us, even if we never do more than drive to its edge and look in. For it can be a means of reassuring ourselves of our sanity as creatures, a part of the geography of hope.

Very sincerely yours,
Wallace Stegner

For Journals

Do you go hiking or camping in national parks or other wilderness areas? If not, do you nevertheless support the idea of saving wilderness?

For Discussion

1. Stegner says that he wants to argue not for the wilderness but for the idea of the wilderness (paragraph 1). What do you think he means by the idea as opposed to the reality of the wilderness? Why should the idea be protected?

2. How did you respond to Stegner's assertion that Americans—even Americans who have never set foot in the wilderness—will lose the wilderness if it is destroyed?

3. How does Stegner think the development of technology and urban life have affected Americans? What advantage does he feel Americans who were exposed to the frontier gained?

4. Why does Stegner think that the relatively undramatic prairies and the deserts are as worthy of preservation as the more spectacular forest and alpine areas? How does emphasizing them help or harm his thesis?

5. Stegner was always interested in conflicting attitudes toward nature and development. Where do his sympathies lie? Yours?

For Writing

1. Write an essay about an urban place you know—an open space, a part of an old neighborhood, a small city park, a favorite store, a place that a parent used to take you to or that you shared with a childhood friend—and you want to see preserved. Explain its emotional and spiritual value to you and why you would like it to stay the way it is. Your research may include firsthand observation, interviews with other people familiar with the place, and library research. For example, if you are interested in an old movie theater, look for source materials on historic preservation and old movie palaces.

2. Write a paper in which you compare Stegner's and Turner's ideas of the wilderness. How does each man think the idea of the wilderness has shaped Americans? What represents progress to each author? In which instances does Stegner sound like Turner? Revise Turner? How did reading Stegner revise your reading of Turner?

∞ *Notes from a Native Daughter* (1965)

JOAN DIDION

Joan Didion (1934–) was born and raised in Sacramento, California. This essay is drawn from a collection called Slouching Towards Bethlehem *(1968). Her nonfiction includes another essay collection,* The White Album *(1979), as well as two insightful books of political reporting,* Miami *(1987) and* Salvador *(1994); the novels* Play It as It Lays *(1970),* Democracy *(1984), and* The Last Thing He Wanted *(1996); and several screenplays.*

It is very easy to sit at the bar in, say, La Scala in Beverly Hills, or Ernie's in San Francisco, and to share in the pervasive delusion that California is only five hours from New York by air. The truth is that La Scala and Ernie's are only five hours from New York by air. California is somewhere else.

Many people in the East (or "back East," as they say in California, although not in La Scala or Ernie's) do not believe this. They have been to Los Angeles or to San Francisco, have driven through a giant redwood and have seen the Pacific glazed by the afternoon sun off Big Sur, and they naturally tend to believe that they have in fact been to California. They have not been, and they probably never will be, for it is a longer and in many ways a more difficult trip than they might want to undertake, one of those trips on which the destination flickers chimerically on the horizon, ever receding, ever diminishing. I happen to know about that trip because I come from California, come from a family, or a congeries of families, that has always been in the Sacramento Valley.

You might protest that no family has been in the Sacramento Valley for anything approaching "always." But it is characteristic of Californians to speak grandly of the past as if it had simultaneously begun, *tabula rasa,* and reached a happy ending on the day the wagons started west. *Eureka*—"I Have Found It"—as the state motto has it. Such a view of history casts a certain melancholia over those who participate in it; my own childhood was suffused with the conviction that we had long outlived our finest hour. In fact that is what I want to tell you about: what it is like to come from a place like Sacramento. If I could make you understand that, I could make you understand California and perhaps something else besides, for Sacramento *is* California, and California is a place in which a boom mentality and a sense of Chekhovian loss meet in uneasy suspension; in which the mind is troubled by some buried but ineradicable suspicion that things had better work here, because here, beneath that immense bleached sky, is where we run out of continent.

In 1847 Sacramento was no more than an adobe enclosure, Sutter's Fort, standing alone on the prairie; cut off from San Francisco and the sea by the Coast Range and from the rest of the continent by the Sierra Nevada, the Sacramento Valley was then a true sea of grass, grass so high a man riding into it could tie it across his saddle. A year later gold was discovered in the Sierra foothills, and abruptly Sacramento was a town, a town any moviegoer could map tonight in his dreams—a dusty collage of assay offices and wagonmakers and saloons. Call that Phase Two. Then the settlers came—the farmers, the people who for two hundred years had been moving west on the frontier, the peculiar flawed strain who had cleared Virginia, Kentucky, Missouri; they made Sacramento a farm town. Because the land was rich, Sacramento became eventually a rich farm town, which meant houses in town, Cadillac dealers, a country club. In that gentle sleep Sacramento dreamed until perhaps 1950, when something happened. What happened was that Sacramento woke to the fact that the outside world was moving in, fast and hard. At the moment of its waking Sacramento lost, for better or for worse, its character, and that is part of what I want to tell you about.

5   But the change is not what I remember first. First I remember running a boxer dog of my brother's over the same flat fields that our great-

great-grandfather had found virgin and had planted; I remember swimming (albeit nervously, for I was a nervous child, afraid of sink-holes and afraid of snakes, and perhaps that was the beginning of my error) the same rivers we had swum for a century: the Sacramento, so rich with silt that we could barely see our hands a few inches beneath the surface; the American, running clean and fast with melted Sierra snow until July, when it would slow down, and rattlesnakes would sun themselves on its newly exposed rocks. The Sacramento, the American, sometimes the Cosumnes, occasionally the Feather. Incautious children died every day in those rivers; we read about it in the paper, how they had miscalculated a current or stepped into a hole down where the American runs into the Sacramento, how the Berry Brothers had been called in from Yolo County to drag the river but how the bodies remained unrecovered. "They were from away," my grandmother would extrapolate from the newspaper stories. "Their parents had no *business* letting them in the river. They were visitors from Omaha." It was not a bad lesson, although a less than reliable one; children we knew died in the rivers too.

When summer ended—when the State Fair closed and the heat broke, when the last green hop vines had been torn down along the H Street road and the tule fog began rising off the low ground at night— we would go back to memorizing the Products of Our Latin American Neighbors and to visiting the great-aunts on Sunday, dozens of great-aunts, year after year of Sundays. When I think now of those winters I think of yellow elm leaves wadded in the gutters outside the Trinity Episcopal Pro-Cathedral on M Street. There are actually people in Sacramento now who call M Street Capitol Avenue, and Trinity has one of those featureless new buildings, but perhaps children still learn the same things there on Sunday mornings:

> Q. In what way does the Holy Land resemble the Sacramento Valley?
> A. In the type and diversity of its agricultural products.

And I think of the rivers rising, of listening to the radio to hear at what height they would crest and wondering if and when and where the lev-ees would go. We did not have as many dams in those years. The by-passes would be full, and men would sandbag all night. Sometimes a levee would go in the night, somewhere upriver; in the morning the ru-mor would spread that the Army engineers had dynamited it to relieve the pressure on the city.

After the rains came spring, for ten days or so; the drenched fields would dissolve into a brilliant ephemeral green (it would be yellow and dry as fire in two or three weeks) and the real-estate business would pick up. It was the time of year when people's grandmothers went to Carmel; it was the time of year when girls who could not even get into Stephens or Arizona or Oregon, let alone Stanford or Berkeley, would be sent to Honolulu, on the *Lurline*. I have no recollection of anyone going to New York, with the exception of a cousin who visited there (I cannot imagine why) and reported that the shoe salesmen at Lord & Taylor were "intolerably rude." What happened in New York and Washington and abroad seemed to impinge not at all upon the Sacramento mind. I remember being taken to call upon a very old woman, a rancher's widow, who was reminiscing (the favored conversational mode in Sacramento) about the son of some contemporaries of hers. "That Johnston boy never did amount to much," she said. Desultorily, my mother protested: Alva Johnston, she said, had won the Pulitzer Prize, when he was working for the *New York Times*. Our hostess looked at us impassively. "He never amounted to anything in Sacramento," she said.

Hers was the true Sacramento voice, and, although I did not realize it then, one not long to be heard, for the war was over and the boom was on and the voice of the aerospace engineer would be heard in the land. VETS NO DOWN! EXECUTIVE LIVING ON LOW FHA!

Later, when I was living in New York, I would make the trip back to Sacramento four and five times a year (the more comfortable the flight, the more obscurely miserable I would be, for it weighs heavily upon my kind that we could perhaps not make it by wagon), trying to prove that I had not meant to leave at all, because in at least one respect California—the California we are talking about—resembles Eden: it is assumed that those who absent themselves from its blessings have been banished, exiled by some perversity of heart. Did not the Donner-Reed Party, after all, eat its own dead to reach Sacramento?

10   I have said that the trip back is difficult, and it is—difficult in a way that magnifies the ordinary ambiguities of sentimental journeys. Going back to California is not like going back to Vermont, or Chicago; Vermont and Chicago are relative constants, against which one measures one's own change. All that is constant about the California of my childhood is the rate at which it disappears. An instance: on Saint Patrick's Day of 1948 I was taken to see the legislature "in action," a dismal experience; a handful of florid assemblymen, wearing green hats, were reading Pat-and-Mike jokes into the record. I still think of the legislators that way—wearing green hats, or sitting around on the veranda of the Senator Hotel fanning themselves and being entertained by Artie Samish's emissaries. (Samish was the lobbyist who said, "Earl Warren may be the governor of the state, but I'm the governor of the legislature.") In fact there is no longer a veranda at the Senator Hotel—it was turned into an airline ticket office, if you want to embroider the point— and in any case the legislature has largely deserted the Senator for the flashy motels north of town, where the tiki torches flame and the steam rises off the heated swimming pools in the cold Valley night.

It is hard to *find* California now, unsettling to wonder how much of it was merely imagined or improvised; melancholy to realize how much of anyone's memory is no true memory at all but only the traces of someone else's memory, stories handed down on the family network. I have an indelibly vivid "memory," for example, of how Prohibition affected the hop growers around Sacramento: the sister of a grower my family knew brought home a mink coat from San Francisco, and was told to take it back, and sat on the floor of the parlor cradling that coat and crying. Although I was not born until a year after Repeal, that scene is more "real" to me than many I have played myself.

I remember one trip home, when I sat alone on a night jet from New York and read over and over some lines from a W. S. Merwin poem I had come across in a magazine, a poem about a man who had been a long time in another country and knew that he must go home:

... But it should be
Soon. Already I defend hotly
Certain of our indefensible faults,
Resent being reminded; already in my mind
Our language becomes freighted with a richness
No common tongue could offer, while the mountains
Are like nowhere on earth, and the wide rivers.

You see the point. I want to tell you the truth, and already I have told you about the wide rivers.

It should be clear by now that the truth about the place is elusive, and must be tracked with caution. You might go to Sacramento tomorrow and someone (although no one I know) might take you out to Aerojet-General, which has, in the Sacramento phrase, "something to do with rockets." Fifteen thousand people work for Aerojet, almost all of them imported; a Sacramento lawyer's wife told me, as evidence of how Sacramento was opening up, that she believed she had met one of them, at an open house two Decembers ago. ("Couldn't have been nicer, actually," she added enthusiastically. "I think he and his wife bought the house next *door* to Mary and Al, something like that, which of course was how *they* met him.") So you might go to Aerojet and stand in the big vendors' lobby where a couple of thousand components salesmen try every week to sell their wares and you might look up at the electrical wallboard that lists Aerojet personnel, their projects and their locations at any given time, and you might wonder if I have been in Sacramento lately. MINUTEMAN, POLARIS, TITAN, the lights flash, and all the coffee tables are littered with airline schedules, very now, very much in touch.

But I could take you a few miles from there into towns where the banks still bear names like The Bank of Alex Brown, into towns where the one hotel still has an octagonal-tile floor in the dining room and dusty potted palms and big ceiling fans; into towns where everything—the seed business, the Harvester franchise, the hotel, the department store, and the main street—carries a single name, the name of the man who built the town. A few Sundays ago I was in a town like that, a town smaller than that, really, no hotel, no Harvester franchise, the bank burned out, a river town. It was the golden anniversary of some of my relatives and it was 110 degrees and the guests of honor sat on straight-backed chairs in front of a sheaf of gladioluses in the Rebekah Hall. I mentioned visiting Aerojet-General to a cousin I saw there, who listened to me with interested disbelief. Which is the true California? That is what we all wonder.

15   Let us try out a few irrefutable statements, on subjects not open to interpretation. Although Sacramento is in many ways the least typical of the Valley towns, it *is* a Valley town, and must be viewed in that context. When you say "the Valley" in Los Angeles, most people assume that you mean the San Fernando Valley (some people in fact assume that you mean Warner Brothers), but make no mistake: we are talking not about the valley of the sound stages and the ranchettes but about the real Valley, the Central Valley, the fifty thousand square miles drained by the Sacramento and the San Joaquin Rivers and further irrigated by a complex network of sloughs, cutoffs, ditches, and the Delta-Mendota and Friant-Kern canals.

A hundred miles north of Los Angeles, at the moment when you drop from the Tehachapi Mountains into the outskirts of Bakersfield, you leave Southern California and enter the Valley. "You look up the highway and it is straight for miles, coming at you, with the black line down the center coming at you and at you . . . and the heat dazzles up from the white slab so that only the black line is clear, coming at you with the whine of the tires, and if you don't quit staring at that line and don't take a few deep breaths and slap yourself hard on the back of the neck you'll hypnotize yourself."

Robert Penn Warren wrote that about another road, but he might have been writing about the Valley road, U.S. 99, three hundred miles from Bakersfield to Sacramento, a highway so straight that when one flies on the most direct pattern from Los Angeles to Sacramento one never loses sight of U.S. 99. The landscape it runs through never, to the untrained eye, varies. The Valley eye can discern the point where miles of cotton seedlings fade into miles of tomato seedlings, or where the great corporation ranches—Kern County Land, what is left of DiGiorgio—give way to private operations (somewhere on the horizon, if the place is private, one sees a house and a stand of scrub oaks), but such distinctions are in the long view irrelevant. All day long, all that moves is the sun, and the big Rainbird sprinklers.

Every so often along 99 between Bakersfield and Sacramento there is a town: Delano, Tulare, Fresno, Madera, Merced, Modesto, Stockton.

Some of these towns are pretty big now, but they are all the same at heart, one- and two- and three-story buildings artlessly arranged, so that what appears to be the good dress shop stands beside a W. T. Grant store, so that the big Bank of America faces a Mexican movie house. *Dos Peliculas, Bingo Bingo Bingo.* Beyond the downtown (pronounced *down-town*, with the Okie accent that now pervades Valley speech patterns) lie blocks of old frame houses—paint peeling, sidewalks cracking, their occasional leaded amber windows overlooking a Foster's Freeze or a five-minute car wash or a State Farm insurance office; beyond those spread the shopping centers and the miles of tract houses, pastel with redwood siding, the unmistakable signs of cheap building already blos-soming on those houses which have survived the first rain. To a stranger driving 99 in an air-conditioned car (he would be on business, I suppose, any stranger driving 99, for 99 would never get a tourist to Big Sur or San Simeon, never get him to the California he came to see), these towns must seems so flat, so impoverished, as to drain the imag-ination. They hint at evenings spent hanging around gas stations, and suicide pacts sealed in drive-ins.

But remember:

Q. *In what way does the Holy Land resemble the Sacramento Valley?*
A. *In the type and diversity of its agricultural products.*

U.S. 99 in fact passes through the richest and most intensely culti- 20
vated agricultural region in the world, a giant outdoor hothouse with a billion-dollar crop. It is when you remember the Valley's wealth that the monochromatic flatness of its towns takes on a curious meaning, suggests a habit of mind some would consider perverse. There is some-thing in the Valley mind that reflects a real indifference to the stranger in his air-conditioned car, a failure to perceive even his presence, let alone his thoughts or wants. An implacable insularity is the seal of these towns. I once met a woman in Dallas, a most charming and at-tractive woman accustomed to the hospitality and social hypersensitiv-ity of Texas, who told me that during the four war years her husband had been stationed in Modesto, she had never once been invited inside anyone's house. No one in Sacramento would find this story remark-able ("She probably had no *relatives* there," said someone to whom I told it), for the Valley towns understand one another, share a peculiar spirit. They think alike and they look alike. *I* can tell Modesto from Merced, but I have visited there, gone to dances there; besides, there is over the main street of Modesto an arched sign which reads:

WATER—WEALTH
CONTENTMENT—HEALTH

There is no such sign in Merced.

I said that Sacramento was the least typical of the Valley towns, and it is—but only because it is bigger and more diverse, only because it has had the rivers and the legislature; its true character remains the Valley character, its virtues the Valley virtues, its sadness the Valley sadness. It is just as hot in the summertime, so hot that the air shimmers and the grass bleaches white and the blinds stay drawn all day, so hot that August comes on not like a month but like an affliction; it is just as flat, so flat that a ranch of my family's with a slight rise on it, perhaps a foot, was known for the hundred-some years which preceded this year as "the hill ranch." (It is known this year as a subdivision in the making, but that is another part of the story.) Above all, in spite of its infusions from outside, Sacramento retains the Valley insularity.

To sense that insularity a visitor need do no more than pick up a copy of either of the two newspapers, the morning *Union* or the afternoon *Bee*. The *Union* happens to be Republican and impoverished and the *Bee* Democratic and powerful ("THE VALLEY OF THE BEES!" as the McClatchys, who own the Fresno, Modesto, and Sacramento *Bees*, used to headline their advertisements in the trade press. "ISOLATED FROM ALL OTHER MEDIA INFLUENCE!"), but they read a good deal alike, and the tone of their chief editorial concerns is strange and wonderful and instructive. The *Union*, in a county heavily and reliably Democratic, frets mainly about the possibility of a local takeover by the John Birch Society; the *Bee*, faithful to the letter of its founder's will, carries on overwrought crusades against phantoms it still calls "the power trusts." Shades of Hiram Johnson, whom the *Bee* helped elect governor in 1910. Shades of Robert La Follette, to whom the *Bee* delivered the Valley in 1924. There is something about the Sacramento papers that does not quite connect with the way Sacramento lives now, something pronouncedly beside the point. The aerospace engineers, one learns, read the San Francisco *Chronicle*.

The Sacramento papers, however, simply mirror the Sacramento peculiarity, the Valley fate, which is to be paralyzed by a past no longer relevant. Sacramento is a town which grew up on farming and discovered to its shock that land has more profitable uses. (The chamber of commerce will give you crop figures, but pay them no mind—what matters is the feeling, the knowledge that where the green hops once grew is now Larchmont Riviera, that what used to be the Whitney ranch is now Sunset City, thirty-three thousand houses and a country-club complex.) It is a town in which defense industry and its absentee owners are suddenly the most important facts; a town which has never had more people or more money, but has lost its *raison d'être*. It is a town many of whose most solid citizens sense about themselves a kind of functional obsolescence. The old families still see only one another, but they do not see even one another as much as they once did; they are closing ranks, preparing for the long night, selling their rights-of-way and living on the proceeds. Their children still marry one another, still play bridge and go into the real-estate business together. (There is no other business in Sacramento, no reality other than land—even I, when I was living and working in New York, felt impelled to take a University of California correspondence course in Urban Land Economics.) But late at night when the ice has melted there is always somebody now, some Julian English, whose heart is not quite in it. For out there on the outskirts of town are marshaled the legions of aerospace engineers, who talk their peculiar condescending language and tend their dichondra and plan to stay in the promised land; who are raising a new generation of native Sacramentans and who do not care, really do not care, that they are not asked to join the Sutter Club. It makes one wonder, late at night when the ice is gone; introduces some air into the womb, suggests that the Sutter Club is perhaps not, after all, the Pacific Union or the Bohemian; that Sacramento is not *the city*. In just such self-doubts do small towns lose their character.

I want to tell you a Sacramento story. A few miles out of town is a place, six or seven thousand acres, which belonged in the beginning to a rancher with one daughter. That daughter went abroad and married a title, and when she brought the title home to live on the ranch, her father built them a vast house—music rooms, conservatories, a ballroom. They needed a ballroom because they entertained: people from abroad, people from San Francisco, house parties that lasted weeks and involved special trains. They are long dead, of course, but their only son, aging and unmarried, still lives on the place. He does not live in the house, for the house is no longer there. Over the years it burned, room by room, wing by wing. Only the chimneys of the great house are still standing, and its heir lives in their shadow, lives by himself on the charred site, in a house trailer.

That is a story my generation knows; I doubt that the next will know it, the children of the aerospace engineers. Who would tell it to them? Their grandmothers live in Scarsdale, and they have never met a great-aunt. "Old" Sacramento to them will be something colorful, something they read about in *Sunset*. They will probably think that the Redevelopment has always been there, that the Embarcadero, down along the river, with its amusing places to shop and its picturesque fire houses turned into bars, has about the true flavor of the way it was. There will be no reason for them to know that in homelier days it was called Front Street (the town was not, after all, settled by the Spanish) and was a place of derelicts and missions and itinerant pickers in town for a Saturday-night drunk: VICTORIOUS LIFE MISSION, JESUS SAVES, BEDS 25¢ A NIGHT, CROP INFORMATION HERE. They will have lost the real past and gained a manufactured one, and there will be no way for them to know, no way at all, why a house trailer should stand alone on seven thousand acres outside town.

But perhaps it is presumptuous of me to assume that they will be missing something. Perhaps in retrospect this has been a story not about Sacramento at all, but about the things we lose and the promises we break as we grow older; perhaps I have been playing out unawares the Margaret in the poem:

> Margaret, are you grieving
> Over Goldengrove unleaving? . . .
> It is the blight man was born for,
> It is Margaret you mourn for.

For Journals

What area of the country would you most like to live in? Why?

For Discussion

1. The California state motto is "Eureka!"—I have found it! Aside from gold, what else do you think people have hoped to find in California?

2. What distinctions does Didion draw between the California sought by tourists and the California she knows from her childhood? Why are great natural wonders like Big Sur and the sequoias, which everyone recognizes as Californian, not as real in Didion's eyes as the Sacramento Valley?

3. Locate the main points of Didion's argument that it is harder to find the real California than other places because, unlike Chicago or Vermont, it changes all the time. How does the brief history Didion gives of the growth of Sacramento illustrate her point that change is the only constant in California?

4. How does Didion's statement that "things had better work here [in California], because here, beneath that immense bleached sky, is where we run out of continent" (paragraph 3) help explain why the idea of a new frontier is so important to Americans?

5. Several of the towns Didion described in the 1960s as full of small buildings, old frame houses, a bank, a Mexican move theater, and tract houses spreading outward, have become large cities with big populations. In what ways would the transformation of these old frontier towns into cities prove Didion's theory about the way history works in California?

For Writing

1. Look at the late-nineteenth-century poster in Chapter 4 entitled *California, the Cornucopia of the World.* It advertised the charms of California to prospective settlers. Write an essay in which you compare the qualities advertised in the poster to the kind of California Didion grew up in. Focus on these questions: Did her childhood experiences and the life of her family in the Sacramento Valley fulfill the promise of the poster? Did the poster offer a different, perhaps unattainable life?

2. Write a reflective essay about the place where you grew up, in which you use Didion's criteria: How much has it changed since you were a child? Did the people you grew up with have a distinct sense of identity and an attitude toward outsiders? What would a visiting tourist see, and how much of the place could be understood only by someone who grew up there?

∞ *Dear John Wayne* (1984)

LOUISE ERDRICH

Louise Erdrich (1954–) is a Native American novelist, poet, and essayist who teaches at Dartmouth College. She was born in Minnesota and grew up near a reservation in North Dakota, where her Native American mother and German father worked for the Bureau of Indian Affairs. She is the author of the novels Love Medicine *(1984),* The Beet Queen *(1986),* The Bingo Palace *(1994),* The Blue Jay's Dance *(1995), and* The Antelope Wife *(1998), as well as short stories and poems. She and her recently deceased husband, Michael Dorris, coauthored a novel,* The Crown of Columbus *(1991). "Dear John Wayne" is a wonderful example of Erdrich's ability to explore how differently white Americans and American Indians experience the mythology of the frontier.*

August and the drive-in picture is packed.
We lounge on the hood of the Pontiac
surrounded by the slow-burning spirals they sell
at the window, to vanquish the hordes of mosquitoes.
Nothing works. They break through the smoke-screen for blood.   5

Always the look-out spots the Indians first,
spread north to south, barring progress.
The Sioux, or Cheyenne, or some bunch
in spectacular columns, arranged like SAC missiles,
their feathers bristling in the meaningful sunset.   10

The drum breaks. There will be no parlance.
Only the arrows whining, a death-cloud of nerves
swarming down on the settlers
who die beautifully, tumbling like dust weeds
into the history that brought us all here   15
together: this wide screen beneath the sign of the bear.

The sky fills, acres of blue squint and eye
that the crowd cheers. His face moves over us,
a thick cloud of vengeance, pitted
20   like the land that was once flesh. Each rut,
each scar makes a promise: *It is*
not over, this fight, not as long as you resist.

Everything we see belongs to us.
A few laughing Indians fall over the hood
25   slipping in the hot spilled butter.
The eye sees a lot, John, but the heart is so blind.
How will you know what you own?
He smiles, a horizon of teeth
the credits reel over, and then the white fields
30   again blowing in the true-to-life dark.
The dark films over everything.
We get into the car
scratching our mosquito bites, speechless and small
as people are when the movie is done.
35   We are back in ourselves.

How can we help but keep hearing his voice,
the flip side of the sound-track, still playing:
Come on, boys, we've got them
where we want them, drunk, running.
40   *They will give us what we want, what we need:*
The heart is a strange wood inside of everything
we see, burning, doubling, splitting out of its skin.

For Journals

Where do your own ideas of the West come from? Movies? If so, which
ones? What other sources? Where else could you find information
about the West?

For Discussion

1.   Read the poem out loud, all the way through. Then go back to the
beginning, and in each stanza find three or four words that are either
unexpected or particularly effective. What do they contribute to the
theme of each stanza? How?

2.   Compare this poem with the article and illustration from the *Police
Gazette.* How does the view of Indians in the *Gazette* compare with the

portrayal of them in the John Wayne movie? With the Indians watching the movie at the drive-in?

3.   What values does the image of John Wayne usually represent? How does Erdrich's attitude toward him revise that image?

4.   How do you think Erdrich would see the settling of the West compared to the way Turner sees it? Whose evidence do you find more persuasive? Why?

5.   If the Indians had written the film script, how do you think they would write the battle scene? What kind of movie do you think they could make about whites and Indians on the frontier?

6.   How does Erdrich use ironic details like the drive-in movie and the fact that the American Indians have a car named for an Indian chief to suggest Indians' ambivalence toward American culture and their place in it? What other examples of this irony can you find in the poem?

For Writing

Investigate books and scholarly articles for material on the Battle of Little Big Horn. Write a documented paper in which you compare an earlier version of the story—from newspaper stories at the time of the battle, or older books about it—with recent versions, like Evan Connell's *Son of the Morning Star*. How have evaluations of Custer, his strategy, and the battle been revised?

∞ *The Next Last Frontier* (1993)

JONATHAN RABAN

Jonathan Raban (1942–) was born in Great Britain but lives in Seattle. He is the author of novels, literary criticism, and works of social commentary, travel, and exploration. This selection is from an article he wrote for Harper's *magazine, after he had traveled through the Northwest from Washington State to Idaho to Montana.*

In the spring of 1990 I packed up as much of my life in London as would fit into four tea chests and flew to Seattle to set up house. It was a selfish and irregular move. I had "met someone" and liked what I'd seen of the Pacific Northwest during a two-month stay there in the autumn of 1989: the aquarium lighting, the sawtooth alps forested with black firs, the compact cities encrusted in Romanesque stucco. Most of all, I liked the place's wateriness. At forty-seven I felt cracked and dry. My new home territory was as rainy as Ireland, puddled with lakes and veined with big rivers. Seattle was built out on pilings over the sea, and at high tide the whole city seemed to come afloat like a ship lifting free from a mud berth and swaying in its chains.

We took a house on the wrong side of Queen Anne, the innermost of Seattle's hilltop suburbs. The tall wooden house, built like a boat from massive scantlings of Douglas fir, carvel-planked with cedar, had been put up in 1906, in the wake of the Yukon gold rush, when the hill was logged. It had warped and settled through a string of minor earthquakes: the floors sloped, doors hung askew in their frames. In the silence of the night, the house groaned and whiffled like a sleeping dog.

Barely a mile from the new banking and insurance skyscrapers of downtown, the house felt hidden away in the woods. Shaggy conifers, survivors of the original forest, darkened the views from every window. The study looked down over the Ship Canal, where trawlers stalked through an avenue of poplars on their way to the Alaskan fishing grounds, eight hundred miles to the north. From the deck on the top floor, one could see out over the pale suburbs, like shell middens, to the serrated line of the Cascade mountains, still snowcapped in May.

For someone fresh off the plane from London, it was a big prospect to take in, and a hard one in which to make oneself at home. It had been fine to be a tourist in this landscape, when I had been enjoyably awed by its far-western heights and distances; but now that I'd signed up as a permanent resident, the view from the window seemed only to reflect my own displacement here.

5   Even the very near-at-hand was strange. I kept Peterson's *Western Birds* and the Audubon Society's *Western Forests* by the typewriter. I made lists, and pinned them to the wall. *Redwood, cedar, cypress, dogwood, laurel, madrona, maple,* I wrote, trying to distinguish individual personalities in the jumble of damp and muddy greens framed by the window. I took the tree book down to the garden and matched the real-life barks with their pictures; the peeling, fish-scale skin of the lodgepole pine, the frayed hemp rope of the coast redwood. It took a month, at least, to be able to see the black-crested Steller's jay in the madrona with something like the comfortable indifference with which I'd used to notice a song thrush in the sycamore in Battersea. It took a good deal longer to adjust to the way the rufous hummingbird, like a tiny thrashing autogiro, redisposed itself in space, zapping from point to point too fast for the eye to follow. Glancing up from the typewriter, stuck for a phrase, I'd sight a bald eagle, circling on a thermal over the Ship Canal on huge stiff ragged wings, and lose the logic of the sentence to another bout of ornithology.

The German word for "uncanny," as in Freud's famous essay on the Uncanny, is *unheimlich*—unhomely. The tourist thrives on the uncanny, moving happily through a phenomenal world of effects without causes. This world, in which he has no experience and no memory, is presented to him as a supernatural domain: the language of travel advertising hawks the uncanny as part of the deal. Experience the *magic* of Bali! the *wonders* of Hawaii! the *enchantment* of Bavaria!

But for the newly arrived immigrant, this magic stuff is like a curse. He's faced at every turn with the unhomelikeness of things, in an uncanny realm where the familiar house sparrows have all fled, to be replaced by hummingbirds and eagles. The immigrant needs to grow a memory, and grow it fast. Somehow or other, he must learn to convert the uncanny into the homely, in order to find a stable footing in his new land. . . .

November 1992 and the snow level, said Harry Wappler, our TV weatherman, was down to 3,500 feet and dropping fast. In a week the mountain passes would be tricky and the back roads closed for the winter. I dug out of storage my never-used box of tire chains and set off on a wide swing around the neighborhood.

It was high time to make the trip: though I had been living in Seattle for more than two years, I was still confused as to its whereabouts. I knew the city better than its cabdrivers (a very modest boast), but I'd barely begun to work out how Seattle fitted into the larger story. A long drive, on empty western roads where it's still possible to think with one's foot down, would, with luck, thread the oddly assorted bits of the Pacific Northwest onto one string and set them in narrative order.

The afternoon rush hour had started by the time I got away, and on   10 Interstate 90 heading east, the cars were locked bumper-to-bumper on the floating bridge over Lake Washington. The sky was lightless, and the windshield wipers scraped on the glass in the fall moisture, typical of these parts, that was something more than mist and less than rain. The traffic jam was typical of these parts, too: a ceremonious procession, like a funeral, of VWs with ski racks on their tops and I'D RATHER BE SAILING stickers on their rear ends. A lot of higher education was stuck on the bridge that afternoon. The names of the universities from which the drivers had graduated were posted in their back windows— faraway schools, mostly, like Syracuse, M.I.T., Columbia, Missouri, Michigan.

My own car, a low-slung, thirsty, black Dodge Daytona with a working ashtray, marked me out as a Yahoo among the Houyhnhnms—too old, dirty, and wasteful to pass as a member of Seattle's uniquely refined middle class. Stuffed into the book bag beside the work of the northwestern writers whom I had brought along for the ride (Richard Hugo, Ursula K. Le Guin, Raymond Carver, Katherine Dunn, William Stafford, Norman Maclean, James Welch, James Crumley) was a bottle of Teacher's, two-thirds full, which would have been okay by the northwestern writers but thought a very low touch by these northwestern drivers. In Seattle, a double shot of non-decaffeinated espresso was thought to be pushing the boat out farther than was wise.

In shifts and starts, we lurched into Eastside Seattle, Houyhnhnm country, where the VWs began to peel off to the Bellevue exits. Bellevue and its satellites were not suburbs so much as—in the rising term—an "edge city," with its own economy, sociology, and architecture. Things made on the Eastside were odorless, labor-intensive, and credit-card thin, like computer software and aerospace-related electronics gear. They were assembled in low, tree-shaded factories, whose grounds were known as "campuses"—for in Bellevue all work was graduate work, and the jargon of college leaked naturally into the workplace. Seen from an elevated-freeway distance, Bellevue looked like one of its own products: a giant circuit board of color-coded diodes and resistors, connected by a mazy grid of filaments.

During the presidential campaign, Bill Clinton had jetted around the country, calling for the advent of the "high-growth, high-wage, smart-work society"—a fair description of Bellevue, with its lightly rooted, highly trained workforce, its safe streets, its scented malls sprayed with composerless light orchestral music, its air of bland good conscience. Bellevue was the new and hopeful face of American capitalism, and it had a strongly Japanese cast to its features. The one- and two-story campuses with their radial walkways reflected a style of business management that was closer to the industrial collectives of Tokyo than to the moribund hierarchies of Detroit and the American Rust Belt.

The place looked like somebody's utopia, more a model city than an actual one, and it was inhabited by the kinds of people whom architects like to place as strolling figures in the foregrounds of watercolor sketches of their projects. Wherever the eye wandered in Bellevue, it lit on another 31¾-year-old, with a master's if not a doctorate, dressed for work in hiking shoes and chunky sweater. Thousands of these diagrammatic people were housed along I-90 in white-painted, shingled faux–New England condo blocks called "villages." Lakefront Village . . . Redwood Village . . . Olde Towne Village . . . communities in which the villagers met in the evenings at neighboring Exercycles in the village health club or at a pre-breakfast tee-off on the village driving range.

15 Eastside Seattle was a new kind of American city, though it had a lot in common with the long-established retirement paradises of Florida and southern California. People in their twenties and thirties were now moving (as their parents had done only toward the ends of their lives) for the sake of the climate and the natural amenities of a place rather than just for the jobs offered there. They were coming to Seattle in much the same way as people had gone to Venice, California, and to Miami Beach; the difference was that they were coming at the beginnings of their careers. So they arrived, as kayakers, hikers, balloon-

ists, bird-watchers, skiers, and mountain bikers who also happened to have degrees in math and marketing and computer science. Their Pacific Northwest was really a civic park, roughly the same size as France, equipped with golf courses, hiking trails, rock-climbing routes, boat-launch ramps, ski lifts, campgrounds, and scenic overlooks. This great migration of open-air hobbyists (which dated from about 1980—the early Reagan years) had won Seattle a curious niche in urban history, as the first big city to which people had fled in order to be closer to nature.

Sixteen miles out of Seattle the eastward march of the city was stopped in its tracks by the foothills of the Cascades. Beyond Issaquah the black cliffs of the forest began, and the social character of the road abruptly changed, as the last of the VWs melted into the last of the white condo blocks. Up till now I'd been in the fast lane; no longer. Mud-slathered pickups with jumbo tires charged past the Dodge wearing angry slogans on their tailgates: JOBS BEFORE OWLS. SUPPORT THE TIMBER INDUSTRY. SAVE A LOGGER—SHOOT AN OWL. Behind the glass of a cab window, a Zippo lighter flashed in the gloaming.

Small charcoal-colored clouds were snagged in the firs. We were climbing steadily now, the road wet, the light failing fast. Each bend in the road opened on another wall of Douglas fir, the trees as dense and regularly spaced as the bristles on a broom.

This wasn't true forest; it was a "tree farm"—a second- or third-growth plantation, now ready for "harvesting." The terms were those of the industry, and after two years of seeing them in use, I still found myself putting quotation marks around them in my head. To me, farm and harvest meant a two-acre wheat field in Essex, with rabbits scarpering from between the cornstalks, and the words refused to stick when I tried to attach them to a mountain range with 150-foot trees, where bears and cougars ran out in place of rabbits and twin-rotor helicopters served as baling machines. . . .

That night I put up at a motel in Forks, twelve miles inland, on the slope of the invisible Olympics. It was a timber town, and a minor classic in its genre. I had been driving through timber towns all day and seen them at every stage of their evolution. Forks was the most highly evolved version so far.

The lowest form of timber-industry social life was a camp of trailers parked in line along the roadside. It became a town with a name when the trailers were joined by three or four prefabricated ranch-style bungalows and a 7-Eleven convenience store with a gas pump out front. The next stage up the ladder required the addition of a gas station with a "deli" (which in these parts meant not a delicatessen but a basic horseshoe-counter diner, serving steak-and-egg breakfasts and sandwiches). Serious civic ambitions set in with the arrival of the video store and the motel. After that came the sculpture.

The sculpture was as formalized in its way as the statue of the bronze infantryman atop the war memorial in small English market towns. I'd seen a dozen variants of it in Oregon, Washington, and British Columbia. It was carved from a section of old-growth Douglas fir of massive diameter, and it represented, in heavy relief, sometimes painted and sometimes in bare varnished wood, a logger with an ax cutting down an old-growth Douglas fir.

The example outside the motel was a beauty, for Forks was the metropolis of the logging camps—a mile-long strip of neon business signs, with three stoplights and a string of tenebrous beer joints. But the carved and painted logger, a figure of heroic pastoral, was way out of tune with his real-life counterparts, who gloomed disconsolately over their drinks in the bars. None were Paul Bunyan types. The loggers were journeyman employees of billion-dollar outfits like the Weyerhaeuser Corporation, and they gave off the sour smell of years of negative profits, evaporating cash flows, and hard bottom lines.

They were now the endangered species. They put up homemade signs on their lawns that said THIS FAMILY LIVES ON TIMBER DOLLARS— and I'd find myself peering in at the windows of these houses as if, indeed, I might catch a glimpse of some rare owlish birds pecking at a tray of timber dollars while *Wheel of Fortune* played in the background.

The sculptures (and all the ones I saw were recently carved) were part of the counter-preservationist movement. They owed a lot to the carved totemic ravens and thunderbirds with which the local Indian tribes announced their special status. They made the assertion that timber-industry workers, like the Indians, had, in one of the hardest-worked American phrases of the late twentieth century, a unique and historic *culture*. Deny me my job, and you deny me my culture, my past, my ethnic identity. So the logging communities were busy manufacturing craft objects that gave them a tribal history and the right to be regarded as yet another beleaguered minority threatened with extinction.

25   It took some imaginative effort to identify the Weyerhaeuser forklift operators and helicopter crews with the carved figures of lone brawny woodsmen swinging axes. The sculptures seemed to me to be self-defeating: they came across as sentimental tributes to a past so long gone that it was far beyond the reach of preservation.

I picked at a meal in an overlit, almost empty restaurant. The view through the window was of pickups and logging trucks plowing through the wet and dark. The chicken and French fries tasted of sawdust and wood pulp. The only other customer removed his teeth and pocketed them after he'd finished dining. Forks in the rain was an unlovely place.

An elderly blue VW Beetle was stopped at the light. Its back end was pasted over with slogans that looked misplaced in Forks: anti-nuke, Clinton/Gore, and the brightest piece of folk wisdom that I'd yet seen on the tribulations of the timber industry, SAVE A LOGGER & A WHALE — SINK A JAPANESE SHIP.

For Journals

What is your reaction to the idea of limiting logging as a livelihood in order to preserve a natural setting? To save a species?

For Discussion

1. The author is an Englishman who moved to Seattle from London. How does his status as an outsider help him assess the beliefs and experiences of loggers and conservationists? Is he in any way at a disadvantage in trying to understand them?

2. Explain the title of the essay; does it undercut or support the notion of the American frontier? How many frontiers do you think there have been or will be in the future?

3. Compare the arguments of Wallace Stegner versus those of the loggers in Raban's article; what are the most persuasive points each makes? Try to consider both arguments in their own terms—that is, based on the different assumptions about environment and livelihood that each side starts out with.

4. Protest sculptures of loggers felling Douglas firs remind Raban of Indian totems; in what way is this an ironic comparison, and how do you think the loggers would respond to it?

For Writing

1. Going back to discussion question 2, write an essay in which you compare and contrast Wallace Stegner's passionate letter for preservation of the wilderness with the loggers' equally passionate stance against conservationists. Try to present each side in the best possible light before you evaluate them.

2. Raban mentions that Paul Bunyan, a logger, used to be a folklore hero. Write an essay in which you address the following issues: Why did the logger go from being a larger-than-life hero to a larger-than-life villain? What ideas and myths about the frontier did his character represent to most Americans in the past? What does his image seem to represent now?

∞ *Film: Unforgiven* (1993)

Two retired, down-on-their luck outlaws pick up their guns one last time to collect a bounty offered by the vengeful prostitutes of the remote Wyoming town of Big Whiskey. (131 minutes)

For Journals

Why do you think this movie is called *Unforgiven*? How many people are unforgiven, and for what?

For Discussion

1. In older westerns the good guys wore white hats and the bad guys wore black hats, so the audience would always know who was who. In this movie, the hero is a killer; what does Eastwood, both as director and as actor, do with the character to make him heroic?

2. Two young people have significant parts in this movie: a near-sighted gunslinger who pretends he is an experienced killer, and a nearsighted writer who is enchanted with the idea of meeting a real killer. In a way, both become accomplices to what happens. Look closely at the scenes in which they appear: Who is the more innocent? Who is more corrupted by the West? What kind of harm does each of them do?

3. There are considerable comic touches in the film: Will Monny can't ride a horse well, and the Scofield Kid can't see what he's shooting at. How do these touches play against the usual stereotypes of western gunslingers? What parts of the movie reinforce those images?

4. The movie begins and ends with a peaceful scene of Will's farm, accompanied by words on the screen. Look at what the words say in the beginning and in the end; who do you think is supposed to be the author of those words? Why does it sound like part of a novel? What point do you think Eastwood is making about the fictionalization of the frontier?

For Writing

1. View one of Eastwood's earlier spaghetti westerns or one of his early American westerns, such as *A Fistful of Dollars* (1964), *For a Few Dollars More* (1966), *Hang 'Em High* (1968), and *The Good, the Bad, and the Ugly* (1967). Take two or three scenes from one of those films and two or three scenes from *Unforgiven*, and write an essay in which you compare them for the presence or absence of the following themes: guilt, conscience, memory, or a frontier ethic. How has Eastwood's archetype of the western hero evolved since the earlier films?

2. The western is one of the primary American film traditions; that has made it a target for humor and satire. Look at Mel Brooks's *Blazing Saddles* (1974), the single most parodic version of a western ever made. Write an essay in which you identify as many stereotypes as you can, and how Brooks treats them; for example—cowboys and Indians, whites and blacks, the gunslinger, the crooked politician.

Writing Assignments

1. Write an essay on an issue you feel strongly about, but take a stand absolutely against your usual position. Analyze a poem, take a side of a debate, or examine an advertisement from the perspective of someone with a background or gender different from yours. Your paper can be research oriented, expository, or narrative. Then write a reflective essay on how the change in perspective affected your writing process and your conclusions, and whether or how it caused you to revise your previous certainties on the topic.

2. Go through copies of old magazines—*Century* or *McClure's* from the early twentieth century, or *Colliers, Harper's, Saturday Evening Post* through the 1950s and 1960s—and look for images of Native Americans in advertisements. Write a paper in which you include your reflections on the following questions: What are the Native Americans being used to sell? If there are any whites in the ads, what is the relationship between them and the Native Americans? What stereotypes or clichés do you find in these ads? If you were writing any of these advertisements, how would you revise the pictures or the text, or both?

3. Try to locate any of the following: the old television series on Daniel Boone and Davy Crockett (starring, incidentally, the same actor, Fess Parker, as though these historical figures were interchangeable) or the musical based on the life of Annie Oakley, *Annie Get Your Gun*. How does the image of these figures put forth by articles and books revise or coincide with the image of them in television and theater? What do you think is lost or gained when the revised versions of their lives become more important than the reality?

4. Write an essay in which you discuss the negative stereotyping of any group to which you belong: your gender, your racial heritage, the region of the country you come from, your religious affiliation, your love of computers. Consider the following questions: How do you think your group is perceived by others? What stereotyping, negative and positive, do you have to contend with? How would you revise the stereotype to make it a more accurate reflection of reality?

5. Research any American hero or heroine in sports, movies, politics, or some other area who has become the subject of a mythology. Some of the most obvious are Elvis Presley, Marilyn Monroe, F. Scott Fitzgerald, and JFK, but anyone who can persistently fascinate the American public and is the subject of endless restructuring and remaking would be a good subject. Concentrate on separating some of the reality from the subsequent revision or on the way your subject's standing is revised positively or negatively in people's estimation. What, would you argue, is the cultural significance of your subject to America?

Acknowledgments

Text

Kris Andreen, "End of the Tunnel." Reprinted with the permission of the author.

Susan K. Cahn, "You've Come a Long Way, Maybe" from *Coming on Strong: Gender and Sexuality in Twentieth-Century Women's Sport*. Copyright © 1994 by Susan K. Cahn. Reprinted with the permission of The Free Press, a division of Simon & Schuster.

Chris Countryman, "Structured Appeal: Let America Be America Again." Reprinted with the permission of the author.

Joan Didion, "Notes from a Native Daughter" from *Slouching Towards Bethlehem*. Copyright © 1965, 1968 by Joan Didion. Reprinted with the permission of Farrar, Straus & Giroux, Inc.

Peter Douglas, "Intelligent Propaganda! Deliver us from Evil." Reprinted with the permission of the author.

Marian Wright Edelman, "A Family Legacy" from *The Measure of Our Success: A Letter to My Children and Yours*. Copyright © 1992 by Marian Wright Edelman. Reprinted with the permission of Beacon Press, Boston.

Ralph Ellison, "Prologue" from *Invisible Man*. Copyright 1952 by Ralph Ellison. Reprinted with the permission of Random House, Inc.

Louise Erdrich, "Dear John Wayne" from *Jacklight*. Copyright © 1984 by Louise Erdrich. Reprinted with the permission of Henry Holt and Company, Inc.

Susan Faludi, "Blame It on Feminism" from *Backlash: The Undeclared War Against American Women*. Copyright © 1991 by Susan Faludi. Reprinted with the permission of Crown Publishers, Inc.

Bruce Fein, "Reserve Marriage for Heterosexuals" from *ABA Journal* (January 1990). Copyright © 1990 by the American Bar Association. Reprinted with the permission of *ABA Journal* and the author.

F. Scott Fitzgerald, "Early Success" from *The Crack-Up*. Copyright 1945 by New Directions Publishing Corporation. Reprinted with the permission of the publishers.

Jorge Flores, "From Unnecessary to Unwanted: An Analysis on the Anti–Mexican American Movement During the Great Depression." Reprinted with the permission of the author.

Woodie Guthrie, "Union Maid" (1940). Copyright 1940 by Woody Guthrie. Copyright renewed. Reprinted with the permission of The Richmond Organization. All rights reserved worldwide.

Richard Hofstadter, "The Thesis Disputed" from Ray Billington, *The Frontier Thesis*. Copyright 1949, copyright renewed © 1977. Reprinted with the permission of Robert Krieger Publishing Co., Inc.

Jeanne Wakatsuki Houston, "A Tapestry of Hope," speech given at De Anza College, California (June 1994). Reprinted with the permission of the author.

Langston Hughes, "Let America Be America Again" from *Collected Poems*. Originally published in *Esquire* (July 1936). Copyright 1936 and renewed © 1964 by Langston Hughes. Reprinted with the permission of Alfred A. Knopf, Inc.

Art

No Dumping. Courtesy of Ann Watters.

Hasten the Homecoming by Norman Rockwell. Reprinted by permission of the Norman Rockwell Family Trust. Copyright © 1943 the Norman Rockwell Family Trust. Photo: FDR Library.

Join, or Die. Courtesy of Library of Congress.

The U.S. Hotel Badly Needs a Bouncer by Joseph Keppler. Reprinted by permission of *Puck* magazine.

Victory Liberty Loan poster by Howard Chandler Christy. Reprinted by permission of Culver Pictures.

Liberty Introducing the Arts to America [American Allegory]. Reprinted by permission of Culver Pictures.

California, the Cornucopia of the World. © Collection of the New York Historical Society.

There's No Way like the American Way by Margaret Bourke-White. Life Magazine © Time Inc.

Win a Houseful of Beautiful Furniture! Pledge Furniture Sweepstakes advertisement. Reprinted by permission of S. C. Johnson & Son, Inc.

Keep Within Compass [A Virtuous Woman]. Courtesy of the Winterthur Museum.

Enlist—On Which Side of the Window Are YOU? Courtesy of the Poster Collection, Hoover Institution Archives.

Fame Instead of Shame [Charles Atlas advertisement]. Reprinted courtesy of *Popular Writing in America.*

They'll Know You've Arrived [Edsel advertisement]. Reprinted courtesy of *Popular Writing in America.*

Two Women Sewing by Jacob Riis. Courtesy of the Museum of the City of New York.

Duke Kahanamoku, Mid-Pacific Carnival. Courtesy of the Bishop Museum, The State Museum of Natural and Cultural History, Honolulu.

Physical Culture cover. Courtesy Jay Weaver for Physical Culture Publishing Company.

Motrin Spoken Here. Reprinted by permission of Saatchi & Saatchi and McNeil-PPC, Inc.

Dolls by Eudora Welty. Reprinted by permission of the Eudora Welty Collection, Mississippi Department of Archives and History.

Freedom of Speech by Norman Rockwell. Reprinted by permission of the Norman Rockwell Family Trust. Copyright © 1943 the Norman Rockwell Family Trust. Photo: The Norman Rockwell Museum at Stockbridge.

We Smash 'Em HARD. Reprinted by permission of *Popular Writing in America.*

Deliver Us from Evil. Courtesy of the Poster Collection, Hoover Institution Archives.

Saigon Execution. Reprinted by permission of AP/Wide World Photos.

The Terror of War. Reprinted by permission of AP/Wide World Photos.

Giant Redwood Trees of California by Albert Bierstadt. Courtesy of the Berkshire Museum.

Indian Treachery and Bloodshed. The National Police Gazette, edited by Gene Smith and Jayne Barry Smith. Reprinted by permission of Curtis Brown Ltd.

Index of Authors
and Titles

Index of Rhetorical Terms